Preparing for Certification or Licensure

A Guide

LEARNING ABOUT STATEWIDE TESTING FOR LICENSURE

Many states require prospective teachers to take standardized tests for licensure. The following questions and answers will help you learn more about this important step to becoming a teacher.

What kinds of tests do states require for licensure?

Some tests assess students' competency in basic skills of reading, writing, and mathematics, often prior to admission to a professional teacher education program. Many states also require standardized tests at the end of a teacher education program; these tests assess prospective teachers' competency and knowledge in their subject area, as well as knowledge about teaching and learning. The tests assess the extent to which prospective teachers meet state and national standards for beginning teachers.

Do all states use the same test for licensure?

No. Many states use the Praxis Series™ of tests, published by the Educational Testing Service (ETS).

Other states—including Arizona, California, Florida, Illinois, Massachusetts, Michigan, New York, and Texas—have developed their own tests for licensure. You can learn about each state's testing requirements by checking its Department of Education website or contacting the state Department of Education by mail or telephone.

What is assessed in the state tests for licensure?

The tests for licensure usually address prospective teachers' knowledge of the teaching-and-learning process and the subjects they will teach. For example, the ETS Praxis Series™ includes subtests on Principles of Teaching and Learning and on the content and pedagogy of specific subject areas. Other state tests have similar goals.

How do I know which tests to take?

Contact your advisor or student services center if you are currently a student in a teacher education program. If you are applying for licensure through an alternative licensure program, contact the state Department of Education's licensure office. ETS describes the topics covered in each category on their website (www.ets.org/praxis). States that have their own testing requirements also provide information about the tests and preparation materials through their websites.

What courses in my teacher preparation program might apply to state tests for licensure?

Almost all of your teacher preparation courses relate to licensure tests in some way. This text, *Teaching in America*, addresses many concepts that are assessed in these tests. You have probably studied or will study concepts and knowledge related to the four content categories in courses such as educational foundations, educational psychology or human growth and development, classroom management, curriculum and methods, and evaluation and assessment. You may have had or will have field experiences and seminars that provide you with knowledge about these concepts as well.

What other resources will help me prepare for state tests for licensure?

Several organizations have developed standards for teacher preparation and continued professional development. A consortium of more than thirty states, the Interstate New Teacher Assessment and Support Consortium (INTASC), has developed standards and an assessment process for initial teacher certification. The National Council for the Accreditation of Teacher Education (NCATE) also has developed standards for teacher education programs, and the National Board of Professional Teaching Standards (NBPTS) has developed standards for advanced certification of teachers who possess extensive professional knowledge and the ability to perform at a high level. In addition, most states have developed their own standards for teachers as part of their licensure requirements. As you review these documents, you will find that they contain common expectations of knowledge and skills and can provide a guide for you as you prepare for licensure.

How should I prepare for state tests for licensure?

Tests for licensure are typically integrative tests; you will be asked to apply knowledge learned in several courses and field experiences to realistic situations in case histories and short scenarios. It is important, therefore, that you *understand the concepts* covered in the test, *review the content* from your course work that relates to those concepts, and *apply good test-taking strategies* during the test.

TEST TAKING TIPS FOR LICENSURE TESTS

Test-Taking Tip # 1: Know the Test

- **Review the topics covered in the exam.** The ETS booklet *Test at a Glance* (available online at www.ets.org/praxis or free by mail) includes detailed descriptions of topics covered in the Praxis tests. States that require their own tests also provide descriptions of the tests and the concepts covered in those tests on their websites.
- **Take the sample tests** provided on websites and in print materials. Analyze the kind of questions asked, the correct answers, and the knowledge necessary to answer the question correctly.
- **Analyze the sample questions and the standards used for scoring the responses to open-ended (constructed-response) questions.** Carefully read any scoring guides provided in the testing guides. Write your own responses to sample questions and analyze them, using the test-scoring guide. If your responses do not meet all the criteria, revise them.

Test-Taking Tip # 2: Know the Content

- **Plan ahead.** You can begin preparing for standardized teacher licensure tests early in your teacher education program. Think about how each of your courses relates to the concepts and content of the exam.
- **Review what you learned in each course in relation to the topics covered in the test.** Review course textbooks and class notes for relevant concepts and information. At the end of each course, record reminders of how the course's content and knowledge relates to concepts of the test. (*Teaching in America*, Fifth Edition, provides useful review and application activities at the end of each chapter.)
- **Think across courses.** Many of the test items will draw on knowledge from several courses. Think about how knowledge, skills, and concepts from the courses you have taken relate to one another. For example, you might have learned about aspects of working with parents in a foundations course, an educational psychology course, and a methods course. Be prepared to integrate that knowledge.
- **Review the content with others.** Meet with a study group and together review the test and your course work. Brainstorm about relevant content, using the descriptions of each test's categories and representative topics as a guideline.

Test-Taking Tip # 3: Apply Good Test-Taking Strategies

- **Read the test directions carefully.** Even though you have previewed the test format and directions as part of learning about the test, make sure you understand the directions for this test.

For multiple-choice questions:

- **Read each question carefully.** Pay attention to key words such as *not, all, except, always,* or *never.*
- **Try to anticipate the answer to the question before looking at the possible responses.** If your answer is among the choices, it is likely to be correct. Before automatically choosing it, however, carefully read the alternative answers.
- **Answer questions you are certain of first.** Return to questions you are uncertain of later.
- **If you are unsure of the answer, eliminate obviously incorrect responses first.**

For short-answer open-ended questions:

- **Read the directions carefully.** Look for key words and respond directly to exactly what is asked.
- **Repeat key words from the question to focus your response.** For example, if you are asked to list two advantages to a method, state "Two advantages are (1) . . . and (2) . . . ."
- **Be explicit and concrete.** Short-answer responses should be direct and to the point.

For essay questions:

- **Read the question carefully and pay close attention to key words, especially verbs.** Make sure you understand all parts of the question. For example, if the question asks you to list advantages and disadvantages, be sure to answer both parts.

- **Before you write your response, list key points or make an outline.** The few minutes you take to organize your thoughts will pay off in a better-organized essay.
- **Use the question's words in your response.** For example, if the question asks for three advantages, identify the advantages explicitly: "The first advantage is . . ." "The second advantage is . . ." and "The third advantage is . . . ." Make it easy for the reader to score your response.
- **Stay on topic.** Answer the question fully and in detail, but do not go beyond what the question asks or add irrelevant material.

SAMPLE STATE LICENSURE TEST QUESTIONS

The following sample questions illustrate the kinds of questions that typically appear in state licensure tests. The case study, which focuses on elementary education, contains issues and content related to principles of teaching and learning and professional education. It addresses such issues as organizing the curriculum, creating effective learning environments, effective teaching practices, diversity, and professional practice. These concepts are typical of those found in the Principles of Teaching and Learning test in Praxis and the professional education tests in other state tests.

Following the case study are three related multiple-choice questions, two constructed-response questions, and three additional discrete multiple-choice questions. These sample questions focus on content and issues discussed in *Teaching in America*, Fifth Edition; they are not representative of the entire scope of the actual tests.

Answers with explanations and references to test topics, INTASC standards, and appropriate parts of this text follow the questions.

Sample Case Study and Related Multiple-Choice Questions

Case History: K–6

Columbus, New Mexico, is an agricultural community near the international boundaries separating Mexico and the United States. It's a quiet town, where traditional views of community and territory are being challenged. Just three miles from the border is Columbus Elementary School, a bilingual school for kindergarten through sixth-grade students. Of the some 340 students enrolled at Columbus Elementary, approximately 97% are on free or reduced-price lunches. The school is unique because about 49% of the students live in Mexico and attend Columbus Elementary at U.S. taxpayer expense. Columbus Elementary is a fully bilingual school. In the early grades, basic skills are taught in Spanish, but by the third-grade level, students have begun to make the transition to English. Most of the teachers at Columbus Elementary School are English speakers; some have limited Spanish skills. The school also employs teaching assistants who are fluent in Spanish and can assist the teachers in these bilingual classrooms.

Dennis Armijo, the principal of Columbus Elementary School, describes the unique relationship between Columbus and its neighboring community, Palomas, Mexico. "Most of the people who live in Columbus, New Mexico, have relatives in Palomas, Mexico. At one point or another, many Columbus residents were Mexican residents, and they came over and established a life here. And so they still have ties to Mexico, and a lot of uncles and aunts and grandparents still live in Palomas. They have a kind of family togetherness, where they just go back and forth all the time. The kids who are coming over from Mexico, most of them are American citizens who have been born in the United States. Now, the parents may not be able to cross because of illegal status, but the kids are U.S. citizens; they have been born in U.S. hospitals."

Columbus Elementary School's international enrollment poses special challenges for family and parental involvement. Mr. Armijo notes that parental contact is often not as frequent as he would like it to be. The school occasionally runs into problems reaching parents because many don't have telephones and must be reached through an emergency number in Mexico that might be as far as three blocks away or through a relative on the U.S. side of the border. In many cases, school personnel go into Mexico and talk to the parents or write them a letter so they can cross the border legally to come to the school. Despite these barriers, however, Mr. Armijo says that cooperation from the parents is great. "They'll do anything to help out this school."

The parents who send their children across the border to Columbus Elementary are willing to face the logistical difficulties of getting their children to Columbus each day because they want their children to have the benefits of a bilingual education. Mr. Armijo notes that the only reason that many parents from across the border send their kids to Columbus is to learn English. He describes a potential conflict that sometimes arises from this expectation:

"There's—I wouldn't call it a controversy, but there's some misunderstanding, mainly because parents don't understand what a bilingual program is. Some of them don't want their children to speak Spanish at all; they say they are sending the children to our school just to learn English. A true bilingual program will take kids that are monolingual speakers of any language and combine them together. At Columbus Elementary, for example, if you have a monolingual English speaker and a monolingual Spanish speaker, if they are in a true bilingual program you hope that the Spanish speaker will learn English and the English speaker will learn Spanish. And if they live here for the rest of their lives, they will be able to communicate with anybody. So when the students from Mexico come over, they need to learn the skills and the American way of life that lead to the American dream, if you will, of an education. Because at some point or another, they might want to come over. Remember, these students are U.S. citizens, even though they live with their parents in Mexico. I'm almost sure that most of those kids are going to come over across to the United States and live here, and so they need to have this education.

Perspective of Linda Lebya, Third-Grade Teacher

Linda Lebya is in her third year of teaching third grade at Columbus Elementary School. She lives nearby on a ranch with her husband, who is a deputy sheriff. She speaks conversational Spanish, although she is not a native Spanish speaker. About 95% of her third-grade students are Spanish speaking.

Linda's classroom is small but inviting. Colorful posters and pictures on the wall reflect the students' culture, and many words and phrases are posted in Spanish and English. Desks are grouped in clusters of four so students can sit together facing one another. A list of vocabulary words, written in English and Spanish, is on the blackboard.

Linda describes her teaching approaches and some of the challenges she faces. First, she describes a typical spelling lesson:

On Monday as an introduction for spelling vocabulary we have 10 vocabulary words written in English and Spanish. The intent is for them to learn it in English; I also put up the Spanish words with the intent of helping them to learn what the English word means. We discuss the words in English and Spanish, then use them in sentences in each language.

Columbus Elementary is a poor school, and Linda reports that resources are limited:

> Lack of books is a problem because we're supposed to be teaching in Spanish for part of the day but the only thing we have in Spanish are the readers. All the other materials are in English so that is a problem.

One resource that Ms. Lebya does have is a Spanish-speaking instructional assistant. She describes the assistant's role in her classroom:

> All of the teachers here at Columbus K–3 have an instructional assistant to help out with different things. My assistant this year is really wonderful; she helps out a great deal. She teaches the Spanish reading to the students because I'm not as fluent to teach it. I can speak it and I can understand, but to actually teach it, I wouldn't know how; my Spanish is not strong enough.

Linda describes her understanding of multicultural education:

> Multicultural education here means that most of the students are from a different culture. We have a few Anglos but most of the students are Mexicans or Hispanics, and when you are teaching multicultural education, you want to make sure that the students understand that their culture is just as important as the dominant culture. For example, one of our vocabulary words was fiesta, or party. Some of our students were not in school that day because they were making their First Holy Communion, and their families were having a big celebration. We talked about official fiestas like Cinqo de Mayo and family or traditional fiestas like today, and the students made English and Spanish sentences about fiestas and parties. It all helps them to value their culture while they learn about the culture of the United States.

> And as far as the Spanish sentences, that's just giving them an opportunity to do something well because they already know it in Spanish. They have the vocabulary in Spanish, so they're able to do a good job in making the sentences, and that's something they can feel good about, and it helps their self-esteem.

Directions: Each of the multiple-choice questions below is followed by four choices. Select the one that is best in each case.

1. Which approach best describes the philosophy of the bilingual program at Columbus Elementary School?
   (a) Children should receive instruction in both English and their native language and culture throughout their school years, making a gradual transition to English.
   (b) Students should make the transition to English through ongoing, intensive instruction in English as a Second Language.
   (c) Students should be removed from their regular classes to receive special help in English or in reading in their native language.
   (d) Students should be immersed in English, then placed in English-speaking classes.

2. Which approach to multicultural education (defined by Sleeter and Grant) best characterizes the Columbus Elementary School program, based on the comments of Ms. Lebya?
   (a) Human Relations
   (b) Single-Group Studies
   (c) Teaching the Exceptionally and Culturally Different
   (d) Education that Is Multicultural and Social Reconstructionist

3. Ms. Lebya's instructional approach to teaching vocabulary could best be described as
   (a) individualized Instruction
   (b) cooperative learning
   (c) inquiry learning
   (d) direct instruction

Sample Short-Answer Questions

A well-constructed short-answer response demonstrates an understanding of the aspects of the case that are relevant to the question; responds to all parts of the question; supports explanations with relevant evidence; and demonstrates a strong knowledge of appropriate concepts, theories, or methodologies relevant to the question.

The following sample open-ended questions draw from knowledge and concepts covered in this text only. In an actual state licensure test, respondents should use knowledge and concepts derived from all parts of their teacher education program.

4. Ms. Lebya says that she relies on her instructional assistant to teach reading in Spanish because "I'm not fluent enough to teach it. I can speak it and understand it, but to actually teach it, I wouldn't know how." List at least one positive and one negative possible consequence of this teaching arrangement.

5. Is it possible to teach well without textbooks? If so, when? If not, why not?

Sample Discrete Multiple-Choice Questions

The Praxis Principles of Teaching and Learning tests and other state licensure tests include discrete multiple-choice questions that cover an array of teaching-and-learning topics. In an actual state licensure test, respondents would draw from knowledge and concepts learned in all aspects of an undergraduate teacher preparation program. In this sample test, items are drawn from this text only.

6. The Buckley Amendment
   (a) permits corporal punishment as long as district policies and procedures are in place.
   (b) allows all parents access to their children's academic records.
   (c) establishes that married or pregnant students have the same rights and privileges as other students.
   (d) states that all students with disabilities are entitled to an "appropriate" education.

7. Mr. Williams placed a pitcher of water and several containers of different sizes and shapes on a table. He asked a small group of students, "Which container holds the most water? Which holds the least? How can you figure it out?"

Mr. Williams's philosophical orientation probably is:
   (a) behaviorism
   (b) perennialism
   (c) constructivism
   (d) essentialism

8. Ms. Jackson was planning a unit of study for her 11th grade American History class. She wanted to determine what students already knew and what they wanted to know about the topic prior to beginning the unit. Which forms of preassessment would be most useful?
   (a) a norm-referenced test
   (b) a teacher-made assessment
   (c) a criterion-referenced test
   (d) a summative assessment

ANSWERS

1. **The best answer is (a).** In the Columbus Elementary School's bilingual program, children learn primarily needs and in Spanish during their first few grades, then begin the transition to English in the third grade. They are not experiencing an intensive English instruction or pullout program, nor are they immersed in English.

   Related Praxis and Other State Test Topics: Organizing content knowledge for student learning and needs and characteristics of students from diverse populations; creating an environment for student learning and appropriate teacher responses to individual and cultural diversity

   Related INTASC Standards: Adapting Instruction for Individual Needs.

Related material in this book: Chapter 4, Teaching Diverse Students I: Multiculturalism and Gender in Today's Classrooms.

2. **The best answer is (c).** Both Mr. Armijo and Ms. Lebya emphasize that the purpose of their bilingual program is to help the students assimilate into American culture and acquire language and skills that will help them be successful if they choose to live in the United States.

   Related Praxis and Other State Test Topics: Organizing content knowledge for student learning and characteristics of students from diverse populations; creating an environment for student learning and appropriate teacher responses to individual and cultural diversity

   Related INTASC Standards: Adapting Instruction to Individual Needs

Related material in this book: Chapter 4, Teaching Diverse Students I: Multiculturalism and Gender in Today's Classrooms.

3. **The best answer is (d).** Ms. Lebya uses a teacher-directed approach, in which she asks specific questions of the students and provides praise or corrective feedback.

   Related Praxis and Other State Test Topics: Organizing content for student learning and creating or selecting teaching methods, learning activities, and instructional materials or other resources that are appropriate for the students and are aligned with the goals of the lesson; teaching for student learning and repertoire of flexible teaching and learning strategies

   Related INTASC Standards: Multiple Instructional Strategies; Instructional Planning Skills Related material in this book: Chapter 11, Teaching the Curriculum

4. A strong response to this open-ended question will explicitly state at least one potential positive consequence and one potential negative consequence to the teaching arrangement. The respondent will use or paraphrase the question and answer explicitly in complete sentences.

   Sample Response: One potential positive consequence of having the Spanish-speaking teaching assistant teach reading in Spanish is that the students will acquire better reading skills in Spanish. If they become good readers in Spanish, they may find it easier to become good readers in English later on. One potential negative consequence of having the Spanish-speaking teaching assistant teach reading in Spanish is that she may not have the knowledge or skills to teach reading. (Many teaching assistants have not had the educational preparation that licensed teachers have.) Ms. Lebya's Spanish may not be strong enough to pick up on those problems or correct them. Thus, the children may not become strong readers in Spanish.

   Related Praxis and Other State Test Topics: Teaching for student learning and making content comprehensible to students; teacher professionalism and reflecting on the extent to which learning goals were met.

   Related INTASC Standards: Multiple Instructional Strategies; Instructional Planning Skills

   Related material in this book: Chapter 4, Teaching Diverse Students I: Multiculturalism and Gender in Today's Classrooms.

5. A strong response to this open-ended question explicitly takes a position on the necessity of textbooks and will defend that position. The respondent will use or paraphrase the question and answer explicitly in complete sentences.

   Sample Response: Although it is possible to teach well without textbooks, contemporary textbooks can be an invaluable resource. Most textbooks today include a wealth of teaching aids, both as part of the textbook itself and as accompanying materials for the teacher, and a good textbook can provide a solid foundation for learning. Textbooks, however, should never be the only teaching tool. Teachers might also use a collection of other instructional materials including articles and primary sources, or a variety of multimedia resources including Internet sites, films, DVDs, or CDs. Whatever resources a teacher chooses to use, the teacher must have clear goals and select materials that support those goals.

   Related Praxis and Other State Test Topics: Organizing content knowledge for student learning and creating or selecting teaching methods, learning activities, and instructional materials or other resources that are appropriate for the students and are aligned with the goals of the lesson.

   Related INTASC Standards: Multiple Instructional Strategies Related material in this book: Chapter 11, Teaching the Curriculum.

6. The answer is (b). Under the Buckley amendment of the Family Educational Rights and Privacy Act of 1974, schools must protect the privacy of student records while affording parents and students over eighteen years of age access to this information.

   Related Praxis and Other State Test Topics: Professional responsibilities and communicating with families

   Related INTASC Standards: Professional Commitment and Responsibility

   Related material in this book: Chapter 8, Education and School Law:

7. The answer is (c). Mr. Williams encouraged the students to construct meaning or make sense of information for themselves, one of the characteristics of constructivism.

   Related Praxis Topic: Organizing content knowledge for student learning and major theories of human development and learning; teaching for student learning and stages and patterns of cognitive and cultural development

Related INTASC Standards: Knowledge of Human Development and Learning; Instructional Planning Skills

Related material in this book: Chapter 11, Teaching the Curriculum.

8. The best answer is (b). Ms. Jackson can best find out what students know and want to know by designing her own instrument.

Related Praxis and Other State Test Topics: Organizing content knowledge for student learning and structuring lessons based on the knowledge, experiences, skills, strategies, and interests of the students in relation to the curriculum.

Related INTASC Standards: Assessment of Student Learning

Related material in this book: Chapter 10, Standards and Assessment: Their Impact onTeaching and Learning.

REFERENCES

Educational Testing Service (2002). Tests at a Glance: Praxis II Subject Assessments/Principles of Learning and Teaching. Available online: www.ets.org/praxis/prxtest.html

Kent, T.W., Larsen, V.A., & Becker, F.J. (1998). Educational Border Culture in New Mexico. Boston: Allyn & Bacon.

Coverage of Interstate New Teacher Assessment and Support Consortium (INTASC) Standards for Beginning Teacher Licensing and Development

INTASC Standards	
1. The teacher understands the central concepts, tools of inquiry, and structures of the subject being taught and can create learning experiences that make these aspects of subject matter meaningful for students.	Chapters 1, 3, 8, 9, 11
2. The teacher understands how children learn and develop, and can provide learning opportunities that support their intellectual, social, and personal development.	Chapters 4, 5, 8, 9, 10, 11, 13
3. The teacher understands how students differ in their approaches to learning and creates instructional opportunities that are adapted to diverse learners.	Chapters 1, 2, 3, 4, 5, 8, 9, 10, 11, 12
4. The teacher uses various instructional strategies to encourage students' development of critical thinking, problem solving, and performance skills.	Chapters 4, 5, 9, 11
5. The teacher uses an understanding of individual and group motivation and behavior to create a learning environment that encourages positive social interaction, active engagement in learning, and self-motivation.	Chapters 1, 3, 4, 8, 9, 11
6. The teacher uses knowledge of effective verbal, nonverbal, and media communication techniques to foster active inquiry, collaboration, and supportive interaction in the classroom.	Chapters 3, 12
7. The teacher plans instruction based upon knowledge of subject matter, students, the community, and curriculum goals.	Chapters, 1, 3, 4, 6, 10, 11, 12, 13
8. The teacher understands and uses formal and informal assessment strategies to evaluate and ensure the continuous intellectual, social, and physical development of the learner.	Chapters 1, 4, 9, 10
9. The teacher is a reflective practitioner who continually evaluates the effects of his/her choices and actions on others (students, parents, and other professionals in the learning community) and who actively seeks out opportunities to grow professionally.	Chapters 1, 2, 3, 4, 6, 7, 8, 9, 10, 12, 13
10. The teacher fosters relationships with school colleagues, parents, and agencies in the larger community to support students' learning and well-being.	Chapters 1, 2, 3, 4, 5, 6, 7, 12, 13

FIFTH EDITION

TEACHING IN AMERICA

GEORGE S. MORRISON

University of North Texas

Upper Saddle River, New Jersey
Columbus, Ohio

Library of Congress Cataloging in Publication Data

Morrison, George S.

Teaching in America / George S. Morrison.— 5th ed.

  p. cm.

Includes bibliographical references and index.

ISBN-13: 978-0-205-57070-6

ISBN-10: 0-205-57070-4

1. Teaching—United States. 2. Teaching—Social aspects—United States.
3. Teaching—Vocational guidance—United States. 4. Community and
school—United States. 5. Education—United States. 6.
Education—Philosophy. I. Title.

LB1025.3.M67 2009

371.102—dc22

2008007529

Vice President and Executive Publisher: Jeffrey W. Johnston
Executive Editor and Publisher: Stephen D. Dragin
Series Editorial Assistant: Christina Certo
Director of Marketing: Quinn Perkson
Marketing Manager: Erica DeLuca
Senior Developmental Editor: Maxine Effenson Chuck
Production Editor: Paula Carroll
Editorial Production Service: Marty Tenney, Modern Graphics, Inc.
Composition Buyer: Linda Cox
Manufacturing Buyer: Megan Cochran
Interior Design: Anne Flanagan
Photo Researcher: Kate Cebik
Cover Administrator: Linda Knowles

This book was set in Times Roman by Modern Graphics, Inc. It was printed and bound by
R. R. Donnelley & Sons, Jefferson City. The cover was printed by Phoenix Color Corporation/Hagerstown.

Photo Credits appear on p. 529, which constitutes an extension of the copyright page.

Pearson Education Ltd.
Pearson Education Singapore Pte. Ltd.
Pearson Education Canada, Ltd.
Pearson Education—Japan

Pearson Education Australia Pty. Limited
Pearson Education North Asia Ltd.
Pearson Educación de Mexico, S.A. de C.V.
Pearson Education Malaysia Pte. Ltd.

Merrill
is an imprint of

www.pearsonhighered.com

10 9 8 7 6 5 4
ISBN 13: 978-0-205-57070-6
ISBN 10:   0-205-57070-4

About the Author

George S. Morrison is Professor of Early Childhood Education in the Department of Teacher Education and Administration, College of Education at the University of North Texas. He teaches courses in child development, early childhood, and teacher education to undergraduate and graduate students. He is an experienced public school teacher and principal and has supervised student teachers over the years. In addition to the University of North Texas, Dr. Morrison has been a professor at Edinboro University of Pennsylvania, the University of Tennessee, Martin; and Florida International University.

Professor Morrison's accomplishments include a Distinguished Academic Service Award from the Pennsylvania Department of Education, and Outstanding Service and Teaching Awards from Florida International University. His books include: *Early Childhood Education Today, 11th Edition* (also translated into Spanish)*; Fundamentals of Early Childhood Education, 5th Edition* (also translated into Chinese)*;* and *Teaching in America, 5th Edition.* Professor Morrison has also written books about the education and development of infants, toddlers, and preschoolers; child development; the contemporary curriculum; and, parent/family/community involvement.

Dr. Morrison is a popular author, speaker, and presenter. He is Senior Contributing Editor for the *Public School Montessorian* and also writes for a wide range of publications. His speaking engagements and presentations focus on the future of early childhood education, the changing roles of teachers, the influence of contemporary educational reforms on education, and the application of best practices to faith-based programs.

Dr. Morrison is Co-Director of the Center for Success For Life Thailand (SFLT) at Kasetsart University, Bangkok, Thailand. The Center develops curricula and conducts teacher training designed to reform teacher practices. Professor Morrison also lectures extensively on teacher education in Thailand, Taiwan, and China.

For Betty Jane—who lives
out the true meaning of
love every day

Brief Contents

Contents

II STUDIES, FAMILIES, AND COMMUNITIES 75

3 How Schools Are Organized and Connected to Their Communities 76

Our schools ought to be microcosms of what we hope they will carry on in their workplaces . . .   77

III FOUNDATIONS OF AMERICAN EDUCATION   213

9 Historical and Philosophical Influences on Teaching and Learning in America   302

They are getting what they need in the warmth of this special environment.   303

IV TEACHING AND LEARNING   353

12 Technology, Teaching, and Learning   418

13 Your Teaching Career   448

Preface

Teaching is an active process: teachers think about what they do, research about and reflect on their practice, make decisions, and strive to improve their performance in order to help their students learn. *Teaching in America, Fifth Edition*, embraces this evolving process of professional practice and provides prospective teachers with the professional tools necessary to be high-quality teachers. *Teaching in America* is an active learning text—readable, practical, and based on the most current ideas about teaching. It provides many opportunities for students to participate in their own learning. On almost every page, students will find possibilities for reflecting on and writing about what they are learning and applying the content of the book to the real world of schools and classrooms. This revision was guided by advice from teacher educators, experienced teachers, novice teachers, and my own background as a public school teacher and administrator, a professor of education, and a researcher and writer.

Teaching in America is a core text for courses in Introduction to Teaching, Introduction to Education, and Foundations of Education taught within teacher education programs. This text explores the knowledge, attitudes, behaviors, and skills of effective teachers; it also provides a comprehensive background for the foundations of education, with clear and realistic links to actual classrooms and your role as a teacher. Features—In the Classroom, What's New in Education?, You Decide, What Does This Mean for You?, Observe and Learn, and Your Turn—all bring the content of this book into the real world. Students will hear real voices of real teachers, explore real programs, and be called on to think about real issues. Reflect & Write activities strategically placed throughout the text allow students to stop and think about concepts and practices that will impact them as new teachers. What I hope this book will do for students is help them make the transition from thinking about becoming a teacher to understanding what their decisions mean—so that they can enter the profession of teaching as active, confident participants. By building a firm foundation—of self-knowledge, knowledge of education as an institution and a career, knowledge of teaching competencies, and knowledge of issues in education—students will grow in their professional development as teachers.

WHAT THIS BOOK IS ABOUT

Teaching in America, Fifth Edition, is built on the ideas of active and interactive learning based on personal reflection. It provides a wealth of opportunities for decision making, collaboration, and creative problem solving. It also asks students to draw on their own prior knowledge—what they have learned about the process of education in their years as students—and to integrate that knowledge with what they learn from these pages and from the course they are taking. *Teaching in America* is designed as a "working text"—one in which students reflect and respond on the pages and apply information and ideas in authentic contexts. This working-text format enables students to construct knowledge and ideas about teaching so that they will think, plan, and decide as a professional. There are several themes occurring frequently in this text:

- *Meeting professional standards.* To become a teacher, students will need to pass some kind of certification examination. More and more, they also will be asked to meet additional standards once they have become teachers, as they move through their careers. Marginal icons throughout this text show specific material that aligns to INTASC standards, a very important set of standards for teachers and teacher education. An eight-page insert at the front of the text, "Preparing for Certification or Licensure: A Guide," provides guidelines for preparing for initial certification. In addition, there is a wealth of information in appropriate chapters about the focus on standards and accountability.

- *Understanding classroom realities.* The United States is a nation of diversity with children from a variety of cultures, speaking a variety of languages, and with a variety of abilities populating today's classrooms. In addition to a separate chapter on diversity, In the Classroom and What's New in Education? features throughout reflect the diversity of American education. But other realities also will impact America's teachers. More and more, parents and communities are involved in educational decision making; education is becoming a family-centered, community-based process. Prospective teachers will need to understand and work within that process. Finally, the reality of today's classroom is accountability. Teachers will find themselves held accountable for their students' success. This book provides the tools to help them understand the impact of accountability.

- *Making decisions as a teacher.* Decision making is at the heart of teaching; every minute of every day, teachers make decisions large and small. Every chapter of this book models the professional, ethical, practical, and reality-based decision-making processes that are a critical part of the teaching profession. In addition, much of the first part is devoted to exploring the knowledge base that teachers need to make decisions effectively. You Decide and Ethical Dilemma features highlight some current issues.

- *Understanding and using technology.* More and more, technology is central to teaching just as it is to our lives in general. Technology means both the technologies of teaching and learning and the technologies of course management and assessment. In addition to a separate chapter on technology, teaching, and learning, marginal URLs identify references to useful websites that correlate to in-text information. In addition, marginal icons for MyEducationLab provides references to a wealth of useful video, simulations, activities, case studies and online resources that will enrich your use of this text.

FEATURES THAT HELP STUDENTS LEARN

Teaching in America provides a sound basis for understanding the field of education and what is required to be a teacher today. A number of guideposts support learning throughout the text.

Each of the four parts of the text begins with a brief part introduction that explains the content of the chapters that follow.

New to This Edition

- **Your Turn** placed in the margin near relevant content asks students to imagine themselves in a particular situation and explain how they would resolve related issues.
- **Marginal URLs** are presented throughout the text to drive students to relevant websites that tie to the text. These URLs, as well as URLs listed at the end of some of the box features, are particularly useful for on-line courses, where both you and your professors are already using the Web to interact.

- **Observe & Learn** Observation is a powerful tool that can tell teachers a lot about their students and about how to run their classroom. These short feature boxes recommend ways in which students can use observation to inform their instruction and to use as an assessment tool when teaching.
- **Ethical Dilemmas** are found at the conclusion of each chapter with a situation in which new teachers may find themselves, whether they are put in a position in which they have to challenge authority, or they may disagree with senior members of a committee on which they are a new member, or they may wonder why their students aren't getting their fair share of school supplies. After each scenario is presented, they are asked to determine how they might respond to these real-life dilemmas.
- **End of Chapter Summaries and Key Terms** are new to this edition, allowing students to quickly assess whether they have grasped all of the key issues discussed in the chapter and whether they have integrated the key concepts into their education vocabulary.

In addition to the new features in this edition of *Teaching in America*, this text has been extensively revised to ensure that readers are provided the most current and relevant information available.

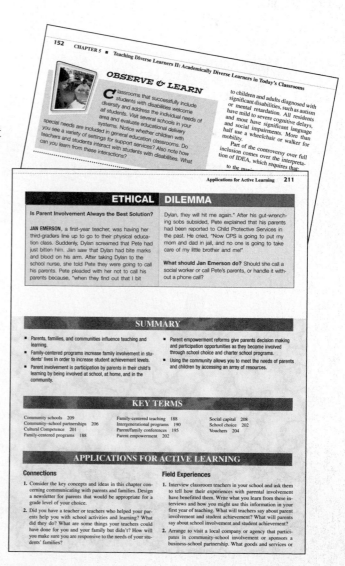

UPDATED IN THIS EDITION

- **All new chapter opening vignettes** are written by classroom teachers or administrators, giving readers a glimpse of life in the classroom and in schools and their communities.

- **Reflect & Write** activities facilitate student interaction throughout the text and encourage active learning while promoting reflective practice to assist with retention and learning. Organized around the key theme of active learning, this feature, in combination with other features throughout the text, provide students with more opportunities than any other text for personal reflection and creative problem solving.

- **You Decide** boxes present discussions of current controversial topics in education and ask students to weigh in on their views using research and what they have learned in the chapter to support their perspective.

AMBERLY WALKER This year we tried a new approach in working with some of our at-risk students. We implemented an intervention program in an attempt to encourage higher attendance rates, boost student achievement, and improve student attitudes. A group of 10 teachers spent 3 hours per week working with the at-risk students who volunteered to participate. All the teachers have different areas of expertise with content areas, including English as a Second Language (ESL). We meet from 2:30 to 5:30 P.M. every Wednesday in the high school library.

We have learned many things from this first year's implementation of the after-school program. Even I was amazed at some of the limitations many of our students have in their background experiences. For example, a student survey shows that only 5 of our 110 student participants have ever been to a museum. Outsiders looking at our beautiful new high school would never dream that we have students who lack this kind of broadening experience. However, many of our students are bussed onto campus from surrounding, low-income neighborhoods. One thing I do know is that we need to continue including the community in our projects!

One particular science project in our plans involves a trip to the Dallas Museum of Nature and Science. Currently, the museum and IMAX theatre are featuring an exhibit on the human body that should prove interesting to this age group. This plan also addresses our students' lack of experiences outside their own neighborhood. However, the cost of admission to the museum plus movie tickets is $27 each. I called the museum director and described our dilemma. I was thrilled when he provided us free admission! This is proof that you never know how your community may help you if you ask!

Our search for financial support has been informative and rewarding. We located two websites that provide aid opportunities for students. *After-School-for-All*[1] and *Donors Choose*[2] are sites that offer teachers needed funds. Our next appeal will be posted on these websites to help our program provide the experiences our students need. The response from our community has been exemplary. Gerardo, a tenth-grader, said, "This program is the best thing that has happened to me in my whole life!" I know many of these opportunities would not have been possible without our community partnerships.

"Students benefit from community participation."

As you read this chapter...

Think about:

- How parents, families, and communities influence teaching and learning
- How you can implement family-centered teaching and learning in your classroom
- How you can foster parent/family involvement both inside and outside your classroom
- What educational reforms are promoting greater parent empowerment
- How you can use the community to teach

Amberly Walker is an intervention specialist at Sachse High School in the Garland, Texas, Independent School District. She and a group of teachers and administrators started an after-school program for at-risk students.

▶▶ Go to MyEducationLab and select "Family and Community" and watch the video "Involving Parents."

183

---

228   CHAPTER 7 ■ The Politics of American Education

REFLECT & WRITE

Is it good public policy for each state to operate its state system of education independent from those of other states? Some school critics say that there should be much more unity between states. What do you think?

Intermediate educational units (IEUs) Educational service organizations that provide school districts human and material services and programs.

Roles of Intermediate Education Agencies

The governance of education involves cooperation among states and localities through the actions of intermediate education agencies. These agencies are called **intermediate educational units (IEUs)**, also known as regional educational units (REUs), regional educational service areas (RESAs), or educational service agencies (ESAs). Intermediate units are designed to provide services that individual districts might not be able to afford on their own, thus maximizing existing resources and promoting interdistrict collaboration. In New York, the intermediate educational unit is the Board of Cooperative Educational Services (BOCES). The Monroe number 1 BOCES develops programs to meet the diverse needs of general, special, talented, and at-risk students. BOCES provides unique and innovative solutions for the complex challenges of its member school districts. These varied programs enable districts to meet the needs of general, adult, special, and emotionally and medically fragile students. As students' needs change, BOCES programs adapt in response to these emerging needs.[12]

Another type of intermediate agency, the **Council of Chief State School Officers (CCSSO)**, is composed of state commissioners or superintendents of education and provides a forum for interstate discussion and information exchange. The chief state school officer is appointed either by the governor of a state or the state board of education. One of the CCSSO sponsors is the National Teacher of the Year Program.

Council of Chief State School Officers (CCSSO) An intermediate agency, composed of state commissioners or superintendents of education, that provides a forum for interstate discussion and information exchange on educational advances and issues.

REFLECT & WRITE

Over the last decade, there has been a growing trend for state governors and legislators to exert more control over education. Do you think this is a good trend? Why or why not?

Roles of Local Government in Education

In educational policy and issues, local government regulates education, which are the governing bodies for schools affecting education at the district and city levels.

What Are Your Legal Responsibilities As a Teacher?   273

Avoiding Sexual Harassment

Title VII of the Civil Rights Act of 1964 (PL 88-352) prohibits discrimination based on gender and defines sexual harassment as unwelcome sexual advances, requests for sexual favors, and other verbal or physical conduct of a sexual nature. Teachers have a responsibility to conduct themselves in such a manner that they do not sexually harass students, staff, colleagues, and parents. As a teacher, it is important that you:

- Be familiar with your school's or district's sexual harassment policy.
- Avoid situations in which you are alone with a student. If you think it is necessary and appropriate, ask another teacher or a parent to be present.
- Act appropriately at all times.
- Don't talk about sex, engage in flirtatious behavior, or tell sexually oriented jokes or stories.
- Ask your teacher-mentor or principal for advice and assistance in dealing with a difficult student or colleague.

In a 1998 case involving sexual harassment of students by teachers, *Gebser v. Lago Vista Independent School District*, the Supreme Court ruled that a school district cannot be held liable under Title IX of the Education Amendments of 1972 unless an official in a position to take corrective action knew of a teacher's harassment of a student and was "deliberately indifferent to it." As you will recall, Title IX prohibits sexual discrimination in educational programs that receive federal money. Remember also that the Supreme Court has ruled that sexual harassment

● Your Turn

You are in your first year of teaching. One of your students, Emily, is the 9-year-old daughter of the town's leading physician, and you found her crying in the girls' restroom today. She would not tell you why she was crying. Emily seems frightened of everyone, and she frequently wears long-sleeved shirts in very hot weather. She seems to have accidents more often than other children in your class. What should you do?

YOU DECIDE

Is It Sexual Harassment or Sex Discrimination?

Marissa, a junior in high school, is an all-around athlete. She is active in sports year round and enjoys being competitive. She also enjoys the companionship she gets from her teammates. Over the years, her soccer, basketball, and lacrosse coaches—some male, some female—have been close with their players, giving them pats of support on the back, and, when necessary, guiding them physically through the motions of the sport to improve their performance.

Recently, Marissa has been feeling uncomfortable with her basketball coach, Coach Bob, as he likes to be called. In the past, some coaches would pat her on the back or squeeze her shoulder to show support; however, Coach Bob pats her on her backside and rubs up to her in a way that makes her feel uncomfortable. Several of her friends have been complaining about Coach Bob's touchy-feely behavior to each other, but only jokingly, because they are afraid he will find out and make them work even harder or kick them off the team. One day after practice, Marissa was called in to Coach Bob's office. He said he wanted to talk to her about her plans for playing basketball in college. As they were talking, he made some sexual comments about her and her friends that made her very uncomfortable. This encounter made her so depressed that she considered quitting the team so she wouldn't have to deal with Coach Bob's sleazy behavior and innuendos.

Title IX prohibits sexual discrimination in educational programs that receive federal money. Additionally, the Supreme Court has ruled that sexual harassment is a form of sex discrimination, but there has been considerable public debate about this decision.

In Marissa's case, is Coach Bob guilty of sex discrimination, and therefore subject to the conditions of Title IX? As Marissa's teacher, if you were to catch wind of Coach Bob's behavior, would you consider it to be sexual harassment, and, if so, how would you respond to the situation?

For more information on sex discrimination and sexual harassment, visit the Equal Rights' Advocates website at www.equalrights.org/publications/kyr/shschool.asp.

- **In the Classroom** feature boxes replace Profiles from the previous editions. These boxes describe the practices of leading teachers and administrators, often in their own words. Many of these features are new or have been updated reflecting classrooms with increasingly diverse learners.

- **What's New in Education?** replaces Education on the Move from previous editions. These features present new approaches, trends, legislation, and innovations that are impacting today's schools.

- **Marginal INTASC** standards are linked to chapter material by marginal icons throughout the text; NCATE standards are listed and correlated to relevant chapters on the inside cover of the text.

- **What Does This Mean for You?** explains how information in the text concerning educational policy, philosophy, finance, laws, and so on, will impact the reader's role as a teacher.

ALSO IN THIS EDITION

REVISED! Every chapter in this text has been meticulously updated to make sure that all information is the most current available. With more in-class examples and its increased focus on accountability, this text is even more applied than past editions. In particular, the chapters on teaching as a profession (Chapter 2), teaching in diverse classrooms (Chapter 4), teaching students with exceptionalities (Chapter 5), parent and community involvement (Chapter 6), standards, assessment and accountability (Chapter 10), curriculum and instruction (Chapter 11), and technology (Chapter 12) have been extensively revised.

EXPANDED! The emphasis on standards and accountability has been enhanced, with new material in almost every chapter, particularly on the federal No Child Left Behind law and its impact on schools and teachers. In addition to the correlation charts and marginal icons that appeared in the last edition, the eight-page insert, "Preparing for Certification or Licensure: A Guide," will help any prospective teacher get ready for the national or state certification examination that is required of almost all prospective teachers.

The pedagogical emphasis of the text continues to be on providing practical information and making clear links to actual classroom teaching. This is supported by many new Reflect & Write activities, Observe and Learn features and Your Turn marginal activities.

SUPPLEMENTS

Supplementary resources accompany this text, include:

- For instructors: A comprehensive Instructor's Manual with Test Bank, a Computerized Test Bank
- For instructors and students: Access to MyEducationLab, an outstanding, comprehensive resource that will benefit students and instructors alike.

> "Teacher educators who are developing pedagogies for the analysis of teaching and learning contend that analyzing teaching artifacts has three advantages: it enables new teachers time for reflection while still using the real materials of practice; it provides new teachers with experience thinking about and approaching the complexity of the classroom; and in some cases, it can help new teachers and teacher educators develop a shared understanding and common language about teaching. . . ."[1]

As Linda Darling-Hammond and her colleagues point out, grounding teacher education in real classrooms—among real teachers and students and among actual examples of students' and teachers' work—is an important, and perhaps even an essential, part of training teachers for the complexities of teaching today's students in today's classrooms. For a number of years, we have heard the same message from many of you as we sat in your offices learning about the goals of your courses and the challenges you face in teaching the next generation of educators. Working with a number of our authors and with many of you, we have created a website that provides you and your students with the context of real classrooms and artifacts that research on teacher education tells us is so important. Through authentic in-class video footage, interactive simulations, rich case studies, exam-

---

1. Darling-Hammond, I., & Bransford, J.,Eds.(2005). *Preparing Teachers for a Changing World.* San Francisco: John Wiley & Sons.

ples of authentic teacher and student work, and more, **MyEducationLab** offers you and your students a uniquely valuable teacher education tool.

MyEducationLab is easy to use! Wherever the MyEducationLab logo appears in the margins or elsewhere in the text, you and your students can follow the simple link instructions to access the MyEducationLab resource that corresponds with the chapter content. These include:

- **Video:** Authentic classroom videos show how real teachers handle actual classroom situations.
- **Homework and Exercises:** These assignable activities give students opportunities to understand content more deeply and to practice applying content.
- **Building Teaching Skills:** These assignments help students practice and strengthen skills that are essential to quality teaching. By analyzing and responding to real student and teacher artifacts and/or authentic classroom videos, students practice important teaching skills they will need when they enter real classrooms.
- **Case Studies:** A diverse set of robust cases drawn from some of our best-selling books further expose students to the realities of teaching and offer valuable perspectives on common issues and challenges in education.
- **Simulations:** Created by the IRIS Center at Vanderbilt University, these interactive simulations give hands-on practice at adapting instruction for a full spectrum of learners.
- **Student and Teacher Artifacts:** Authentic student and teacher classroom artifacts are tied to course topics and offer practice in working with the actual types of materials encountered every day by teachers.
- **Readings:** Specially selected, topically relevant articles from ASCD's renowned *Educational Leadership* journal expand and enrich students' perspectives on key issues and topics.

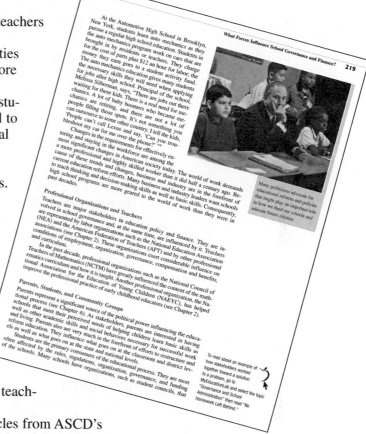

Lesson & Portfolio Builders: With this effective and easy-to-use tool, you can create, update, and share standards-based lesson plans and portfolios.

MyEducationLab is easy to assign, which is essential to providing the greatest benefit to your student. Visit www.myeducationlab.com for a demonstration of this exciting new online teaching resource.

ACKNOWLEDGMENTS

Writing a textbook is not a solitary endeavor! Good writing, like all good things in life requires the cooperation, collaboration, and support of many people. I am blessed beyond belief by the care, concern, and help of many individual who wanted to make *Teaching in America*, *Fifth Edition* a book that really makes a difference in the lives of students and teachers.

Steve Dragin, Executive Editor and Publisher of Allyn & Bacon is a key player in this revision with his many ideas for making *Teaching in America* the best. Steve is always shepherding and guiding writing, design, and production.

Max Effenson Chuck, Senior Development Editor, is a wonderful editor. Max is bright, dedicated, and very focused on making sure the writing and editing are just right. Max is very persistent. A day without a barrage of e-mails got so it didn't seem like a normal day! Thanks Max, for all you do for me!

I work with an outstanding group of research assistants: Whitney Dwyer, Karen Walker, Cheryl Anderson, Su-Chuan He, and Wen-Chuan Chang. These individuals have been faithful and dedicated in meeting deadlines and seeing the book through to publication.

I appreciate and value all of the people who contributed vignettes and other accounts of their professional experiences to this edition. Through my writing I meet and talk with many teachers all across America and I am always touched, heartened, and inspired by their openness, honesty, and unselfish sharing. I am particularly impressed by the many local, state, and national teachers of the year, all of whom went above and beyond to contribute—even when I asked them for help at the last minute.

I thank all the reviewers who suggestions helped redefine this edition. They are:

Susan Anaton, Hostos Community College

Lori Antonelli, Warren County Community College

Beverly Coursey, Central Maine Community College

Dorothy V. Craig, Middle Tennessee State University

Emilie Johnson, Lindenwood University

Kristen Ramirez, California State University, Bakersfield

1

Choosing Teaching as Your Profession

Congratulations! You have chosen teaching as your profession! As a teacher, you will have many opportunities to help your students learn, grow, and become contributing members to society. At the same time, you will also have many opportunities to grow professionally and help change the teaching profession and society.

Teaching today is not what it was like when I started teaching. And, what teaching is like today is not what it will be like 5 years from now. Change is a constant force in society, and teaching and what and how we teach changes as our society changes. For example, when I started teaching I conducted many heated classroom discussions about the Vietnam War and America's role and place in the world. Today, that same discussion is centered on the war in Iraq. Issues of students' rights have been and will continue to be topics of debate. As a high school teacher, part of my responsibilities involved enforcing dress codes about hemlines and belts. Today, teachers are asked to monitor similar dress code guidelines. Much has changed over the past 40 years. However, in today's classroom, you will have an opportunity to engage your students in many interesting topics critical to their futures and our nation's. You will teach curricula about global warming and the Green movement; you will be involved in reform and accountability issues with regard to standards and testing; you will help students develop good nutrition habits in an effort to curb obesity; and you will combat bullying. In addition, you will apply technologies—from text messaging to blogging to handheld computers—to your teaching. What an exciting time to be a teacher!

Part One looks at the choice you are making to become a teacher and provides a context for that choice. We will look first at what teachers need to know and what they do: the knowledge base good teachers must have, the ways in which teachers put that knowledge base to work in the classroom, and how teachers are held accountable. We'll also explore the profession of teaching—the opportunities and challenges, the realities—and the ways in which educational reform is reflected in today's schools. Finally, we will examine the role of schools in the larger society—how they are organized, and how they are changing.

Will you be one of the teachers who shape public education in the decades to come? Part One will help you explore the world of teaching so that you can answer this question confidently and positively.

1 What It Means to Be a Teacher

JOSH ANDERSON In her 1929 essay *A Room of One's Own*, author Virginia Woolf writes about the "essential oil of truth," her metaphor to describe what remains when all the personal, political, and accidental baggage of writing has been stripped away and only that which truly matters remains. To harvest this essential oil, Woolf advocates for a place for women to write—a room that is free from the social distractions of finances, family, and formality. A metaphorical room, she rightly notes, that men have always enjoyed.

As you read this chapter . . .

Think about:

- What makes a good teacher
- Teacher accountability today
- What teachers do
- Why teachers teach
- How teaching is changing

Teachers need a room of their own, too. In this high-stakes, politically charged climate of results and returns, it is exceedingly difficult for our teachers to hear their own voices above the cacophonous din of shifting mandates and measurements that have become moving targets in a political game of tug-of-war. How can teachers possibly extract the essential oil of truth from themselves and their students when our decision makers so rarely agree on what is essential and what is truthful?

The least optimistic among us view our national struggle to define teaching and learning in the twenty-first century with skepticism and disdain. Yet, for so many of us inside the profession, we have hope—great, wonderful, tremendous hope. And we find it in students like Danny.

Danny was a student in my speech and debate program a few years ago who is literally the most compassionate and caring person in the entire world. In the final round of the state speech championship, Danny shared a story from first grade. There was a child in his class with a severe speech impediment. It was so severe that few people could understand a word he said. The other children in the class were such merciless bullies that it became part of their daily routine to tease, punch, hit, kick, and often ignore their classmate. Any attempt by this child to defend himself dissolved into a heartbreaking string of sputters and spurts that always ended in tears. And the teacher? The teacher was the biggest bully of them all. He even had a nickname for this child: Pokey. "C'mon Pokey," he'd say, "you're behind again." "I can't understand you, Pokey." "Stop crying, Pokey." "Get up off the floor, Pokey." "You're embarrassing yourself, Pokey."

> **I am proud to be a teacher.**

As Danny continued his speech, he shared facts and figures about the current status of bullying and teasing afflicting children across the country today. Near the end, though, he rhetorically asked whatever happened to Pokey. In response, he slowly raised his finger to his chest and pointed to himself. Danny was Pokey, and Pokey grew up to be a three-time state speech champion, and later the National College Debate Champion, and now Pokey works as an intern in the United States House of Representatives. Danny's ultimate goal? He wants to be a teacher. Get up off the floor, Pokey? You're embarrassing yourself, Pokey? It took more than years of speech therapy and an inspirational teacher for Danny to overcome as much as he did. It required a vision of a better future, an unwavering belief in his ability to achieve it, and the ability to say "yes I can" when everyone around him said "no, you can't."

It's true that to outsiders, our nation's schools may seem—at times—a little Pokey. But for those of us who work with children every day, we know that our

Josh Anderson was the 2007 Kansas Teacher of the Year.

▶▶ Go to MyEducationLab and select the topic "The Teaching Profession" and then watch the video "Becoming a Teacher."

nation's schools are places of hope where we can say "yes, we can" when the personal, political, and accidental baggage of teaching might make outsiders say "no, you can't."

In conversations and presentations to thousands of educators all across the country, I have discovered one essential truth: We already have a room of our own. It is a single room, defined by an entire institution of caring people who are committed to their charge. The house of education is no longer divided by walls and borders. It is a shared community to which all of us belong. Within its space is all the knowledge discovered and left behind by generations of teachers. It is our responsibility to learn from these experiences, create new ones, and pass them on to the next generation of teachers. We must continue to find new ways to hear our own voices and to create our own spaces in a world that changes fast and for students who change even faster.

We have much work to do to keep our house in order. The safe shadow of the public trust is disappearing, but it is replaced by an illuminating light that opens our eyes to new opportunities and new challenges. I am proud to be among the architects who stand firmly resolved to remodel and redesign the house of education for the twenty-first century. I am proud to be a teacher.

WHAT MAKES A GOOD TEACHER?

As evidenced in the opening vignette, Josh Anderson's dedication to the field shines through in his interaction with his students and his engagement with their achievements; he is driven by the possibility of advancing the lives of many. His innovative teaching style has offered opportunities for academic achievement that his students might not have received elsewhere. How did Josh develop his teaching style? How will you develop yours? And how will you know you have become a good teacher? How is "good teaching" measured?

Most educators agree that good teaching is based on four things: bringing an appropriate core of knowledge into the classroom with you (and being willing to expand that knowledge throughout your career); promoting student achievement through use of your proficiencies and skills (teacher effectiveness); believing in yourself as a teacher and as a person who matters (teacher efficacy); and being accountable for what you and your students achieve (teacher accountability).

As a teacher, you will be the driving force behind your students' success. As you develop effective teaching skills, you will also develop a belief in yourself. The more you believe in your ability to teach your students, the more you can help all students and yourself be accountable for student learning. Your beliefs about education and teaching will also encourage your students to set challenging goals for themselves as well. After all, accountability is a three-way process. Teachers are accountable for their teaching; students are accountable for their learning; and society is accountable for providing the support for high-quality education for all.

Andrea Peterson, 2007 National Teacher of the Year, has this to say about accountability:

> Too often, our society accepts mediocrity as satisfactory. In and out of school, we tell children it is acceptable to do things incorrectly, as long as they feel good about themselves. The intrinsic problem, of course, is that human beings never feel good about themselves unless they are achieving. America's students are frustrated because they know they are being short-changed; they know they are achieving below their true potential. We need to challenge students, not lower our expectations so they can achieve grade level standards lower than they should be. We are doing a further disservice because students are not learning that facing difficulties is an opportunity for learning. We are simply removing difficulties, thereby losing most true learning.[1]

Go to MyEducationLab and select the topic "Teaching Profession," watch the video "Teaching at Different Grade Levels" then complete the activities.

■ **INTASC**

STANDARD 1 The teacher understands the central concepts, tools of inquiry, and structures of the subject being taught and can create learning experiences that make these aspects of subject matter meaningful for students.

An Expanding Knowledge Base

To become a good teacher, you will need to acquire basic knowledge in a number of areas, and perhaps even more important, you will need to be open to learning more throughout your career. Good teachers are good learners: they reflect on what they do and learn from it; they continue to look for answers as long as they teach.

What is the **knowledge base** that you will need to begin teaching? To be an effective teacher for the students in your classroom, you will need to know:

Knowledge base The knowledge needed in the process of effective teaching.

- **What to teach.** You need to be competent in the subject areas you will be teaching—English, science, math, social studies, or any other subject area in which you intend to teach. Many teacher education programs believe that knowledge of the arts and sciences is essential for all teachers, including prekindergarten and primary-grade teachers. For example, in my program at the University of North Texas, undergraduate teacher education students are not education majors but rather take 59 hours in the university's core curriculum, 50 hours in interdisciplinary studies, and only 24 hours of education classes, including student teaching.

- **How to teach.** Teachers must be skilled in teaching a variety of students from differing cultural and socioeconomic backgrounds, as well as in motivating students and guiding their behavior, managing and organizing classrooms, and using educational technology. Chapter 11 explores the issues of what and how to teach.

■ **INTASC**

STANDARD 10 The teacher fosters relationships with school colleagues, parents, and agencies in the larger community to support students' learning and well-being.

- **About students.** How do students learn? How do children develop? What roles do gender, ethnicity, culture, and socioeconomics play in the process of instruction? Today's students represent a more diverse range of backgrounds, languages, and abilities than ever before in this country's history. Good teachers understand all this—and care about individual students within their own classrooms.

Justin Minkel, 2007 Arkansas Teacher of the Year, believes in the value of being attentive to individual students:

> I believe everything we do as teachers should honor that individual light within each child. Schools in every country in the world are notorious for creating mechanisms that seek to mold children to the systems created by adults. I believe that we should be doing the opposite: shaping our systems to each child and each community of children who walk through our doorways each year.[2]

Chapters 4 and 5 focus on who our students are, how they learn, and how you can support their learning.

- **About state and local standards.** In every school district in every state, standards—statements of what students should know and do—are driving discussions about what and how to teach. You will need to know the standards in the state and district in which you plan to teach. Chapter 10 looks more closely at standards and their impact on individual classrooms.

- **About working collaboratively.** Effective teachers work with parents, families, colleagues, administrators, and community members. Good teachers recognize that parents and other family members play a powerful role in students' learning. Good teachers also understand the need for collaboration within their own school settings. Chapter 6 focuses on these various partnerships.

Every day you must ask yourself, "Am I being an effective teacher?" What are some characteristics that all teachers should demonstrate? How do you plan to demonstrate your teaching effectiveness?

Your effectiveness as a teacher will also rest on a wider range of knowledge about the context in which you teach—both the professional world of teaching, and the foundations of public education in the United States. You will be a better teacher if you know:

- **About the profession of teaching.** Participating in professional organizations and activities will provide you with a wealth of resources and support beyond what is available to you in your school or district. Professional standards and ethical practices will help shape your professional career, as will thinking of yourself as a professional. Seeing yourself as a professional increases your confidence in dealing with colleagues, families, and the wider community.
- **About the foundations of education.** Why learn about the history, philosophy, politics, economics, and legal background of public education in the United States? Why understand the sociocultural role of schools in American society? All of these areas have a direct impact on the classroom in which you teach. Chapter 3 and Chapters 7 through 9 will help explain why.

Finally, becoming a teacher means becoming a lifelong learner. How can you accomplish this? Here are two ways:

- **Be a reflective practitioner.** Self-knowledge and self-assessment are hallmarks of reflective practice. Good teachers are constantly evaluating their own behavior and finding better ways of doing things. Think about your teaching, test new ideas, and evaluate the results—and you will improve your teaching practice.
- **Be a teacher/researcher.** Teacher/researchers are active, inquiring producers of knowledge and information who contribute to their own learning and their students' learning by examining how students learn (or don't learn), how to connect curriculum to students' lives and interests, and how to make more and better connections with parents and families. An almost unlimited wealth of research is available. Explore what's already there—or create your own research project to answer a question for yourself.

These lists of what you need to know might appear daunting, but this is what teacher preparation programs are designed to help you learn. Teachers are evaluated on their proficiencies in these areas as well as on their effectiveness with learners. Many states have adopted standards for preparation and certification as guides to preservice preparation, professional development, and teacher appraisal. These standards for teacher preparation provide you with specific information about what you will be expected to know and be able to do. You will want to be familiar with the standards for your state and the state in which you plan to teach. Figures 1.1 and 1.2 identify the teacher preparation standards for Texas and Kentucky.

■ INTASC

STANDARD 9   The teacher is a reflective practitioner who continually evaluates the effects of his/her choices and actions on others (students, parents, and other professionals in the learning community) and who actively seeks out opportunities to grow professionally.

■ INTASC

STANDARD 2   The teacher understands how children learn and develop, and can provide learning opportunities that support their intellectual, social, and personal development.

FIGURE 1.1 Pedagogy and Professional Responsibilities (EC–12) Standards in Texas

Texas, like other states, specifies standards that all teachers must meet for certification and licensing. Standards assure minimum levels of competence necessary for a high quality teaching profession.

Source: State Board for Educator Certification, *Pedagogy and Professional Responsibilities (EC–12) Standards, 2006.* (Online). Available at www.sbec.state.tx.us/SBECOnline/standtest/standards/allppr.pdf and www.sbec.state.tx.us/SBECOnline/standtest/edstancertfieldlevl.asp.

Standard I.	The teacher designs instruction appropriate for all students that reflects an understanding of relevant content and is based on continuous appropriate assessment.
Standard II.	The teacher creates a classroom environment of respect and rapport that fosters a positive climate for learning, equity, and excellence.
Standard III.	The teacher promotes student learning by providing responsive instruction that makes use of effective communication techniques, instructional strategies that actively engage students in the learning process, and timely, high-quality feedback.
Standard IV.	The teacher fulfills professional roles and responsibilities and adheres to legal and ethical requirements of the profession.

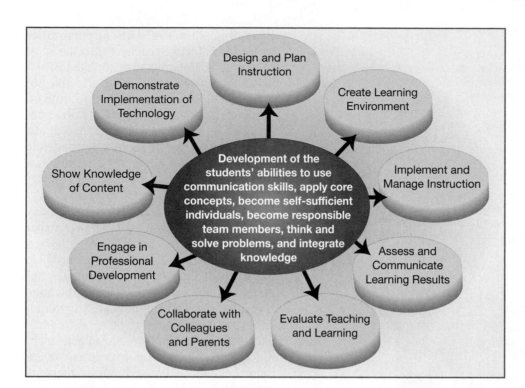

FIGURE 1.2 New Teacher Standards for Preparation and Certification in Kentucky

Source: Kentucky Department of Education, *New Teacher Standards for Preparation and Certification (2006).* (Online). Available at www.kyepsb.net/teacherprep/ newteachstandards.asp.

REFLECT & WRITE

States are restructuring requirements for teacher preparation and certification programs. One reason is to make schools and teachers accountable. What are some other reasons that states are restructuring their requirements?

Effective Practices That Promote Learning

One measure of good teaching is **teacher effectiveness**. Effective teachers use their proficiencies to promote student learning in the following ways:[3]

- **Communicating positive teacher expectations.** Effective teachers have high expectations for learners and believe that all students are capable of learning—and they successfully communicate those expectations to all students. If students do not learn something the first time, effective teachers teach it again or find another way to teach it; if the regular curriculum materials do not do the job, effective teachers find or make other materials.

    Karen Smith of the Institute on Community Integration at the University of Minnesota, Minneapolis, offers the following guidelines to help teachers better communicate their expectations for students:

- Talk directly to the students.
- Be courteous.
- Speak in the first person (for example, "Mario, I want to discuss with you how you can write a more effective paragraph.").
- Give feedback.
- Make positive statements.[4]

Teacher effectiveness How well teachers are able to promote learning in their students.

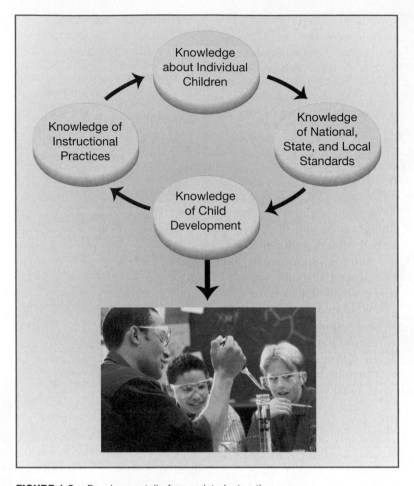

FIGURE 1.3 Developmentally Appropriate Instruction

The essence of developmentally appropriate practice is taking into consideration knowledge about how children grow and develop and matching this knowledge to content and strategies in planning and teaching. All domains of development—physical, social, emotional, linguistic, and cognitive—need to be considered. Although developmentally appropriate practice is widely used with primary and elementary children, the concept applies to all students in all grades.

■ INTASC

STANDARD 3 The teacher understands how students differ in their approaches to learning and creates instructional opportunities that are adapted to diverse learners.

Developmentally appropriate instruction Instruction that is age and individual appropriate for each student in a program. Involves matching teaching practices and curriculum content to the developmental stages of children and adolescents.

■ **Providing students with opportunities to learn.** Effective teachers allocate most of their available time to academic instruction rather than to goals in the affective domain. Their students spend more time on academic tasks than do students of teachers less focused on instructional goals. Such teachers provide a mix of academic tasks designed to allow students to comprehend key ideas and connect and apply those ideas, not simply memorize.

Integrating technology in inner-city schools is not easy, but math teacher Alesia B. Slocumb Bradford of Jefferson Junior High School in Washington, D.C., has dedicated herself to providing her students with the best mathematics education possible. She realized that one way to motivate her students and improve their skills was through technology. Alesia uses technology to help her students learn fundamental math skills and apply them to real-world problems. For example, one student project used technology to analyze traffic problems in Washington, D.C. Using decision-support systems and queuing theory, as well as a study of the effects of the Internet on corporate marketing, students gained perspective on the value of technology.[5]

■ **Providing classroom leadership and organization.** Effective teachers organize their classrooms as supportive learning environments and use individual and group management approaches that maximize the time students spend on learning tasks. These teachers maintain pleasant, friendly classrooms and are perceived as enthusiastic, supportive instructors. Research suggests that effective teachers tend to show charisma, compassion, a sense of fairness, and a sense of humor.[6] For example, Kerry Fretwell, the Chesterfield County, Virginia, 2008 Teacher of the Year, uses a combination of humor, hopeful attitude, and integrity to teach her ninth-grade English students. In her class for struggling readers, every student has advanced their reading level by 2 to 4 years in only one semester. She believes a positive attitude, as well as developing connections between the students and the adults within their school, are important to each student's education.[7]

■ **Pacing curriculum and instruction for individual learners.** Effective teachers move through a curriculum rapidly but in small steps that minimize student frustration and allow continuous progress. They adapt curriculum and pace instruction to meet individual student needs, learning levels, and learning styles. They understand the need for **developmentally appropriate instruction** (see Figure 1.3). Many elementary teachers employ developmentally appropriate practices. At the middle and high school levels, attention to the developmental needs of students is expressed through individual attention to students. For example, in the accompanying *In the Classroom*, let's look at the classroom prac-

In the Classroom

with **Donna Tardif, Jessica Archer, and Susanne MacArthur**

Developmentally Appropriate Practice

D onna Tardif, the 2006 Maine Teacher of the Year, is a kindergarten teacher at Montello Elementary School in Lewiston, Maine. Donna consistently demonstrates a well-developed understanding and successful application of research-based best practices. She has high expectations for herself and for her students. She is an exceptional classroom manager and is able to create a successful experience for very challenging students. She has clear and consistent expectations of her students, establishes well-defined routines in the classroom, and demonstrates an attention to detail. Donna is very skilled at engaging students in the teaching and learning process. She is very good at multitasking and provides students with individual, small group, and whole group learning experiences. She demonstrates empathy for the learners in her classroom and addresses the needs of students with various learning styles. Donna uses assessment as a tool to inform her instruction and to fully understand the learning needs of each child. She challenges her students to do their best while interacting with them with patience and encouragement.

As a 7–8 grade math, science, and reading teacher at Orono Middle School in Orono, Maine, Jessica Archer's first priority is the teaching of her students. Her understanding of the science and math subjects and curriculum make her an outstanding teacher who recognizes the individual needs of her students. Her knowledge of the curriculum allows her not only to teach to the entire classroom, but also to assist students on a one-on-one basis. She is extremely patient, and treats every student with respect and insists on the same standards for all her students. Jessica's connection to students allows her to transcend any barriers and teach students of diverse backgrounds.

If students are the best judges of a teacher's effectiveness in the classroom, then Susanne MacArthur is absolutely exceptional. Susanne teaches 10–12 grade English and "A Struggle for Meaning," an honors-level interdisciplinary course at South Portland High School in South Portland, Maine. It is one of the most rigorous and popular classes at South Portland High School. Students of all academic abilities aspire to take it and many of the students who enroll in the class have not taken honors classes before, but because of Susanne's outstanding teaching practice, all of her students are successful. Their success is directly linked to her unique and extraordinary ability to connect with students; design relevant, meaningful and engaging lessons; and personalize instruction to meet her students' diverse learning needs.

Source: Maine Public Broadcasting Network. (2006). *Teaching with Maine.* (Online). Available at www.mainepublicradio.org/teach /nominees05.html. Accessed May 17, 2007.

tices of the 2006 Maine Teacher of the Year and two finalists, a kindergarten, middle school, and high school teacher.

- **Teaching actively.** Effective teachers demonstrate skills, explain concepts and assignments, conduct participatory activities, and review when necessary. They actively teach rather than expecting students to learn merely by interacting with curriculum materials. Active teachers emphasize concepts and understanding in addition to skills and facts. At Newton South High School in Newton, Massachusetts, Robert Lampol believes that his English classes learn the most when they are actively involved in learning. His students worry less about their grades as the knowledge he teaches them develops a life of its own, as the novels, characters, issues, and events take on meaning for each individual student. He believes that his students are successful at learning because they make the effort to learn the facts beyond what is on the written page.[8]

- **Providing student-centered teaching.** Effective teachers focus on students' needs and interests, engage students in projects and problem-solving activities,

Go to MyEducationLab and select the topic "Teaching Profession," then read the article "The Satisfaction of Teaching" and complete the activities.

and provide cooperative learning opportunities for students to work with other students. At Mountain View Middle School in Moreno Valley, California, students who perform "basic" on the California Standards Test attend a summer academy aimed at improving their math and language skills. Because of the program's student-centered approach, teachers are able to present targeted and focused lessons that facilitate active learning. The teachers believe that creative lessons enable students to be more involved, and, as a result, more serious about learning.[9]

■ **Teaching for mastery.** Effective teachers provide opportunities for students to practice and apply new content. They monitor each student's progress and provide feedback and remedial or accelerated instruction as needed to make sure that all students achieve mastery and receive enrichment as appropriate.

At the De Paul School in Louisville, Kentucky, teachers use a mastery approach that involves teaching one thing at a time and connecting it to what students already know. They teach knowledge and concepts until students can apply and generalize them to new situations before moving on to the next concept. Teachers at the De Paul School believe that students need time to explore, practice, and discuss new concepts before moving on to something new and unfamiliar.[10]

REFLECT & WRITE

Given the need to consider developmental appropriateness in teaching, might there be alternative ways children could be grouped other than by age?

_____

_____

_____

_____

_____

Teacher Efficacy

Teacher efficacy Teachers' beliefs about their ability to teach effectively and about the ability of their students to learn.

A teacher's belief that he or she can reach and help even difficult students to learn is called **teacher efficacy**. Teachers who believe in themselves and their abilities as teachers—and who believe that their students can learn—generally have students who achieve well. Research shows that teachers who have a high sense of efficacy are "more confident and at ease within their classrooms, more positive (praising, smiling) and less negative (criticizing, punishing) in interactions with their students, more successful in managing their classrooms as efficient learning environments, less defensive, more accepting of student disagreement and challenges, and more effective in stimulating achievement gains."[11] Furthermore, research suggests that teachers with a strong belief in their own effectiveness are more committed to teaching[12] and more likely to use effective motivational strategies with exceptional students. One recent study indicates that general and **special education** teachers with a high sense of personal and teaching efficacy are more likely to agree with general class placement of an exceptional student.[13] In addition, high-efficacy teachers use specific instructional processes when teaching students with disabilities, including planning instruction that is based, in part, on state and local standards, explicitly teaching what students are to learn, providing feedback to students about their progress, and individualizing instruction, using methods appropriate for each student.

Special education A teaching specialty for meeting the needs of exceptional learners.

In the Classroom

with **Beverly San Agustin**

The Qualities of a Good Teacher

Beverly San Agustin is the assistant principal of curriculum at Simon Sanchez High School and the 2001 Guam Teacher of the Year.

This list of what makes a good teacher is based on my experiences and my interactions with many great teachers, but also on input from my students, who have continuously reaffirmed my own sense of good teaching. A good teacher is . . .

- *Passionate*—good teachers are always committed to teaching. Their passion is conveyed in every moment in the classroom.
- *Resourceful and innovative*—good teachers constantly improve their teaching strategies by taking classes and workshops and seeking new information. They dare to be risk takers, always willing to try out new ideas.
- *Encouraging and optimistic*—good teachers accept challenges as opportunities to make a difference. They exude confidence that things will get better, not worse.
- *Flexible*—good teachers improvise in the best interest of their students. They find "teachable moments" in every crisis.
- *Entertaining*—the best teachers are hams—willing to make lessons relevant and interesting through drama, comedy, or force of personality.

- *Humorous*—good teachers create a classroom conducive to learning, break up the pace to prevent boredom, and are able to defuse stressful or difficult situations through good humor.
- *Compassionate*—good teachers nurture all their students with empathy and understanding.
- *A leader*—good teachers support positive ideas, seek creative new strategies, and challenge students to try something different. Good teachers also take active leadership roles in school committees and use the opportunities presented to them to participate in school governance.
- *A mentor*—good teachers promote collaboration, share their own knowledge, and support effective practices among colleagues.

Good teachers do what they do because they love what they do and cannot imagine doing anything else; they are committed to making a difference in the lives of their students. Every teacher begins with that commitment and some of the qualities listed above. The best teachers continue to learn, improve, and acquire more of these qualities throughout their careers.

Learn more about the qualities of a good teacher at www.highlandschools-virtualib.org.uk/ltt/inclusive_enjoyable/teacher.htm.

Teacher efficacy stems from teachers' beliefs and attitudes, but it is also influenced by the conditions of the community, school, and classroom. Factors that contribute positively to teachers' sense of efficacy include:

- Moderate and reasonable role demands
- Adequate salaries
- High status
- Recognition for efforts
- Opportunities to interact with other professionals
- Validation from others that what they are doing is right
- Empowerment to make decisions
- The perception that the work they are doing is meaningful
- Good morale within their school and among fellow faculty[14]

OBSERVE & LEARN

Teacher efficacy plays a powerful role in student achievement. You can learn a lot about efficacy by observing effective teachers in action. Based on the dimensions of efficacy discussed in this chapter, develop a checklist that you can use when observing teachers in action. How does the teacher's efficacy benefit students? How does it help students to succeed? How do your observations inform your own teaching?

Collective Teacher Efficacy

Collective teacher efficacy A group's shared belief in its capabilities to organize and execute courses of action required to produce given levels of attainment.

When teachers as a group share the perception that the efforts of the faculty as a whole will have a positive effect on students, the result is **collective teacher efficacy**—a shared sense of efficacy.[15] According to researchers, collective efficacy develops when teachers engage in two key tasks: analysis of the teaching task and assessment of teaching competence.

- **Analyzing the task.** Faculties that see themselves as effective educators analyze—at both the individual and the school levels—what will be required as they engage in the act of teaching. This analysis provides information about the challenges of teaching in that school—including the abilities and motivations of the students, the availability of instructional materials, the presence of community resources and restraints, and the appropriateness of the school's physical facilities—and what it would take for teachers in that school to be successful.

Teachers with high efficacy believe they can teach all students and that all students, regardless of disability, learning style, or socioeconomic status, will learn at high levels.

- **Assessing teaching competence.** Teachers make explicit judgments about the teaching competence of their colleagues in light of the analysis of the teaching task in their specific school. They assess teaching skills, methods, training, and expertise, and they develop strategies for mentoring and correcting perceived weaknesses.

High collective teacher efficacy results, according to research, in the acceptance of challenging goals, strong organizational efforts, and a persistence that leads to better student learning performance.[16]

■ **INTASC**

STANDARD 9 The teacher is a reflective practitioner who continually evaluates the effects of his/her choices and actions on others (students, parents, and other professionals in the learning community) and who actively seeks out opportunities to grow professionally.

HOW ARE TEACHERS HELD ACCOUNTABLE TODAY?

Teachers who bring with them an appropriate knowledge base, who are able to integrate that knowledge into an effective teaching style, and who believe in their own ability to teach and in their students' ability to learn will generally be successful teachers. But how is success as a teacher measured?

One way of defining a "good" teacher is from the **process-product perspective**—that is, a teacher is perceived as effective if students receive high scores on standardized measures of achievement. More and more, teachers are being held to this particular standard of **teacher accountability**. The accountability movement, which began in the late 1970s and continues today, is based on the idea that teachers (and other school personnel) are always accountable to the public—to parents in particular as well as to public agencies such as boards of education, state departments of education, and the federal government.

Although controversial, researchers have developed highly sophisticated data systems to objectively assess teacher performance. Tennessee has implemented a tracking system that helps target teachers for professional development training. The All Students Can Achieve Act was also designed to allow school districts to use the accountability data to provide merit pay for teachers. Although what makes a "good" teacher is still a matter for debate, student progress is the ultimate indicator of an effective teacher.

The teacher accountability movement continues to move forward in the United States as more and more students are determined to be "low performing" based on state education exams.[17] Teachers are impacted by accountability initiatives in several ways. First, teacher professional development is focused on specific topics and methodologies designed to change teaching practice and on the use of those practices to increase student achievement.[18] Second, teachers are expecting more of themselves and their students. For example, 2006 Elementary Science Award winner Ann Marie Wotkyns teaches fourth grade at John B. Monlux Math, Science, and Technology Magnet School in the Los Angeles Unified School District. She says, "I want all students to be more involved in and responsible for their own learning. I want all students to set high goals for themselves and to work hard to reach those goals. I want to inspire all my students to become lifelong learners."[19]

Performance-Based Teaching

Part of the education reform movement of the last 20 years has focused on performance-based education, meaning that teachers are responsible for ensuring that children learn. The teacher's role has shifted from being responsible only for input—teaching students—to being responsible for output—what students have learned and are able to do. **Performance-based teaching** constitutes a dramatic change in both teacher role and teacher responsibility. It has also dramatically changed how teachers are educated.

Historically, legislatures have shied away from imposing regulations on teacher education programs. However, legislators currently are attempting to mandate school and teacher accountability through the implementation of performance-based standards. As of 2007, 24 states were encouraging teacher education institutions to focus more on demonstrations of teaching competence. As a result, many colleges are reforming their education programs, adding fifth years of study, internships, and professional development programs. All states have some sort of approval mechanism for teacher education institutions, usually related to regional or national standards. Forty-six states have partnerships

Process-product perspective The relationship between the teacher's practices and the students' outcomes; usually based on students' academic achievement.

Teacher accountability Teachers' responsibility to parents, boards of education, and the general public for student learning.

Performance-based teaching Teachers' responsibility to students to ensure that they learn.

with the National Council for Accreditation of Teacher Education (NCATE), and 18 states use NCATE professional performance-based standards as the basis for their state program.

The regents at Georgia State have instituted a 10-point plan to improve teacher preparation for all education majors. Education majors are now required to take additional coursework in their subject specialty. The plan also provides additional training for those unable to demonstrate effective teaching skills in their first 2 years of teaching. The Maryland Department of Education requires all institutions of higher education that offer teacher training programs to receive NCATE accreditation. Washington State does not require NCATE accreditation, but has state approval standards that parallel those of the national association. Although requirements vary from state to state, the general consensus is that performance-based teaching is the new measure of a teacher's effectiveness.[20]

Also embedded in the accountability movement is the linking of performance to monetary reward: Student achievement can lead to higher pay for teachers (see *What's New in Education?*); for schools, overall student performance attracts more money to operate programs. Denver Public Schools has one of the nation's most widely publicized merit pay programs. ProComp, the teacher compensation system designed in a partnership between the Denver Classroom Teachers Association and Denver Public Schools, is a new program that offers a comprehensive way to pay teachers that links compensation to the district's mission of student learning. The four major components of this program include: (1) knowledge and skills; (2) professional evaluation; (3) student growth, and (4) market incentives. ProComp enables teachers to build career earnings while fulfilling the goals of the school district for better student achievement.[21] Tying student achievement to monetary incentives is controversial. For example, teachers who choose (or are assigned) to work with students who perform below grade level will not have the same opportunity for enhanced pay as teachers who work with students who perform above grade level and have a history of outstanding achievement. Similarly, schools in higher socioeconomic districts will typically show higher performance results than schools in districts with fewer resources and less parent involvement.

This is exactly what happened in Orlando, Florida. At Palm Lake Elementary, two out of three teachers earned a bonus through Orange County Public Schools' merit pay plan. At Richmond Heights Elementary, the number was zero. Palm Lake is a predominantly white school in the affluent area. Richmond Heights is a predominantly black school in a poverty-stricken pocket of Orlando. The two schools illustrate a marked disparity in the distribution of merit bonuses to 3,911 Orange County teachers and administrators. Teachers at predominantly white and affluent schools were twice as likely to get a bonus as teachers from schools that are predominantly black and poor.[22]

Go to MyEducationLab and select the topic "Standards and Accountability," then select the simulations "Accountability: High Stakes Testing for Students with Disabilities." After watching the video, complete the activities.

REFLECT & WRITE

Not all teachers agree that performance-based teacher pay plans are a good idea. Would you welcome the opportunity to teach in a district with a performance-based pay plan? What do you think are some of the pros and cons?

Assessment and Accountability

Recently local, state, and national testing has emerged as a way to help ensure student learning and to promote accountability. Some educators argue that the emphasis on standardized testing has encouraged many teachers to "teach to the test" to boost student achievement—a move that results in a narrow curriculum focus. Achievement measured only by what is on the test cheats students of the benefits of a full curriculum. The use of achievement test scores to measure and reward teacher effectiveness poses many challenges and ethical questions for teachers and schools both.

Schools are clearly accountable to state departments of education and federal agencies from which they receive funding. Schools and teachers both are accountable to the students they teach and the parents of those students. But finding an appropriate way to measure success—to hold teachers and students accountable—is very difficult. Despite controversies, the accountability movement continues to exert strong influence on educational practice. The demand for teacher accountability and performance-based teaching will no doubt continue to influence how you and your colleagues teach.

REFLECT & WRITE

Accountability for student achievement can create ethical challenges for teachers. What are some of these challenges? How would you respond to them? Why do you think accountability tied to achievement is so popular?

What's *New* in Education?

Special Teachers Are Rewarded (STAR) Program

"**S**tudents that turn around tough situations and make great gains are rewarded in our system through scholarships—why not their teachers?" Florida State Senator Don Gaetz asked. "I think that rewarding high performers builds better results in the long term."

Florida's STAR program rewards the top 25 percent of public school teachers with an annual bonus equivalent to 5 percent of their base pay. The state currently has $147.5 million allocated to the program, which will be divided among the participating school districts. The STAR program rewards elementary, middle, and high school teachers through an instructional evaluation system based on the performance of their students. Student achievement is measured by students' performance on standardized test scores in reading and mathematics tests and by instruments that measure the Sunshine State Standards for grade-level content and critical-thinking skills.

Although controversial, Senator Gaetz believes that teachers will respond proactively to the legislation because it offers them monetary rewards for high-performance students. Some believe merit pay programs create a more positive work environment for teachers because their hard work is rewarded. The Florida State Board of Education believes the STAR program will help keep and attract the best teachers to the state.

To learn more about the STAR program visit www.fldoe.org/STAR.

Source: Florida Department of Education. (2007). *Merit Award Program.* (Online). Available at www.fldoe.org/STAR.

● *Your Turn*

You teach at a large suburban high school where students consistently score well on state tests and attend prestigious colleges. The principal of the inner-city school you attended has offered you the challenging job of establishing a college-bound program. You believe you are the right person to institute some exciting changes. But there is a catch. Teacher salaries are tied to student test scores. Because the school offering you the job has a history of low test scores, you will have to take a 10 percent pay cut if you accept the offer. What will you do? What factors affect your decision-making process?

Requirements for Highly Qualified Teachers

The No Child Left Behind (NCLB) Act allocated $2.8 billion dollars to states to train, recruit, and retain qualified high-quality teachers.[23] NCLB funds can be used in a variety of ways to assist states in preparing teachers, including reforming teacher certification, providing training, developing alternative routes to licensure, developing recruitment and retention strategies, providing high-quality professional development, and supporting activities that improve instructional practices. The NCLB is a reauthorization of the Elementary and Secondary Education Act (ESEA) passed by the U.S. Congress in 1965, and it requires that all kindergarten through twelfth-grade students must be taught by "highly qualified teachers."

Provisions of the NCLB represent the largest and most comprehensive federal investment in preparing, training, and recruiting teachers and administrators in the history of U.S. public education. The act has three goals: (1) to increase student academic achievement through the use of instructional strategies and materials that are proven successful through scientific research; (2) to increase the number of highly qualified teachers and principals; and (3) to hold educational agencies and schools accountable for improvements in teacher quality and student achievement. (We will discuss the NCLB in greater detail in Chapter 7.)

All states are required to meet the provisions of the NCLB. The NCLB defines a highly qualified teacher as one who meets the following requirements:

- Holds at least a bachelor's degree
- Has obtained full state certification or licensure
- Has demonstrated subject area competence in each of the academic subjects in which the teacher teaches

However, each state's specific definition of a "highly qualified" teacher remains unique. And, because licensure requirements based on these definitions vary from state to state, what constitutes a "highly qualified" teacher does, too. The 2006 report on Teacher Quality states that 97 percent of the nation's classroom teachers were fully certified, 95 percent of new teachers completing preparation programs had passed their certification exams, 50 states had initial teacher certification programs, and 44 states have taken steps toward meeting teacher content-knowledge standards.[24]

REFLECT & WRITE

Reflect on these criteria that define a "highly qualified teacher," according to the federal government in the No Child Left Behind Act. Do you think these criteria are sufficient to make a beginning teacher highly qualified? What would you add to this list, if anything?

_____

_____

_____

_____

_____

_____

WHAT DO TEACHERS DO?

If you asked most teachers what they do, they would tell you that they wear many hats and that their jobs are never done. Teachers are decision makers, planners, creators, organizers, actors, managers, collaborators, evaluators, reporters, community partners, professional learners, and sometimes parent substitutes. This may sound overwhelming, but remember: You will have a lot of help and support on your journey to becoming a good teacher. The program that prepares you, your instructors, your participating classroom teachers, and this textbook are all designed to help you learn how to meet the many responsibilities of becoming a teacher.

Teachers Are Decision Makers

Decision making may be the single most important function of teachers. Every day is made up of a myriad of decisions—large ones (what to teach, how to teach it) and small ones (which child to call on, what to display on the walls). Making these decisions becomes almost second nature to experienced teachers; first-time teachers will rely on the kind of knowledge base discussed in the first section of this chapter.

As a first-year teacher and beyond, you will make daily decisions based on your knowledge of:

- Basic subjects and core academic content
- Effective teaching methodologies that meet the needs of all learners, including exceptional children
- Child growth and development
- How to assess learning
- Curriculum planning and design
- Effective methods for integrating technology into classrooms
- National, state, and local standards for what students should know and be able to do
- Professional standards, practices, and ethics
- Culturally appropriate curriculum, including bilingual and gender-fair instruction, and how to accommodate children's culture into teaching
- How to create classroom environments and use management strategies that support learning
- The historical, legal, and philosophical foundations of education

The more experienced you become, the more these various pieces of knowledge will integrate into a coherent whole. But before you begin, your competencies in most of these areas will be measured in some way—through the PRAXIS exam, which is required for the certification of teachers in over 44 states, or through a variety of state-specific certification tests. For example, in Texas teachers must pass the Texas Examinations of Educator Standards (TExES) before being certified to teach. A sample question from that exam, which emphasizes your ability to apply what you have learned, is shown in Figure 1.4.

■ INTASC

STANDARD 9 The teacher is a reflective practitioner who continually evaluates the effects of his/her choices and actions on others (students, parents, and other professionals in the learning community) and who actively seeks out opportunities to grow professionally.

A middle school teacher arranges a meeting with the parents of Kara, a student who consistently fails to complete homework assignments. The teacher discusses the problem with the parents and then describes steps he plans to take to encourage Kara's completion of assigned work. The parents respond by offering to do whatever they can to help resolve their child's problem. In this situation, it would be most appropriate for the teacher to ask the parents to take which of the following actions?

a. Allocate time each evening to sit with Kara as she does her homework, answering questions and providing assistance with challenging assignments, as needed.
b. Use Kara's performance on homework assignments, as reported to the parents by the teacher on a weekly basis, to determine rewards and limits for Kara in the home.
c. Help Kara identify a quiet place to study, and work with her to implement a daily study schedule that the parents can monitor on an ongoing basis.
d. Provide the teacher with a brief written summary once every week or two to keep the teacher informed about any changes occurring in Kara's study habits and attitudes.

FIGURE 1.4 TExES Sample Question: Applying Knowledge and Skills to Teaching

During your teaching career you will experience varying levels of cooperation with the families of your students. How will you apply knowledge and skills to work with families and students in many different situations?

Source: Texas State Board for Educator Certification/Texas Education Agency, *Texas Examinations of Educator Standards Preparation Manual: 110 Pedagogy and Professional Responsibility, 4–8* (2006), p. 40. (Online). Available at http://texes.ets.org/assets/pdf/testprep_manuals/110_pedprofresp4_8_55014_web.pdf.

**REFLECT &
WRITE**

Do you think that the test item shown in Figure 1.4 provides a good evaluation of how effective a teacher might be? Can you think of other ways that states could maintain high standards for educators?

BEFORE TEACHING

How do I engage and teach my students?

- What do I want my students to learn?
- What is the purpose of what I'm going to do?
- What are the student outcomes?
- How do I integrate content areas?
- How do I make the content multicultural, gender, and socioeconomically appropriate?
- What are the needs of my students?

How do I keep my students interested?

- What approach/model/style works best with my students (e.g., cooperative learning, Socratic seminar, lecture)?
- How will I group my students?

What resources will I need?

- How much time do I allocate?
- How much space will I need?
- What concrete materials will I need?

What background knowledge do my students have?

- What background knowledge do my students bring to the learning situation?

AFTER TEACHING

- Have I been self-reflective and thoughtful about my teaching?
- Did I assess the success of my students?
- How will I report students' achievement to parents?
- How will I provide feedback to my students?
- What will I do differently the next time I teach a similar lesson?

DURING TEACHING

Have I used the students' prior knowledge to gain their interest and give them a focus?

Am I presenting the lesson well?

Am I constantly evaluating my students?

- Am I providing feedback to my students?
- Am I asking my students open-ended and analytical questions?

Am I responding to the immediate needs of my students?

- Are my students actively engaged?

Am I introducing new concepts and information?

- Am I motivating and challenging my students?
- Am I providing my students with behaviors and skills to work on on their own?

Am I reviewing and debriefing with my students?

- Am I summarizing information for my students?

FIGURE 1.5 Pathways to Successful Teaching and Learning

Can you think of anything you might add to the lists? These will help you plan most effectively.

Teachers Are Planners

Research points clearly to the importance of planning for student achievement; effective teachers are able to bring about intended learning outcomes.[25] For effective teachers, the planning process is an ongoing one; it involves thinking and making decisions before, during, and after providing instruction. Figure 1.5 illustrates a teacher's planning process during these phases of instruction. Reflect on these processes as you develop lesson plans and unit plans, set instructional goals, and create learning objectives and outcomes for your students.

■ **INTASC**

STANDARD 7 The teacher plans instruction based upon knowledge of subject matter, students, the community, and curriculum goals.

REFLECT & WRITE

Planning for successful teaching involves many dimensions. Consider the process outlined in Figure 1.5. Which part of this process do you think is most important? Which is most often ignored?

Teachers Build Positive Learning Environments

Teachers spend a huge amount of time in classrooms and schools and, as a consequence, invest a lot of themselves in developing **learning environments** where teaching and learning can become meaningful and rewarding. Today there is a great deal of emphasis on the enriched learning environment, and one indicator of an enriched environment is the quality of the **classroom climate**, or classroom atmosphere. Classroom climate is defined by a number of factors:

- Daily routines and practices
- Approach to classroom management
- Strategies for assessment of students' progress
- Quantity and quality of instruction
- Number and kind of student-teacher interactions

The classroom atmosphere also is affected by the extent to which teachers and students share common interests and values and have common goals. For example, in classrooms where both teachers and students believe that learning is important and that everyone is capable of learning and where everyone is valued, the classroom atmosphere will promote learning, achievement, and social cohesion.

A positive learning environment also takes into consideration the variety of student learning styles, including both cognitive and cultural styles. For example, many classrooms are highly organized and designed to promote individual achievement. Some children may come from cultures, however, where cooperative involvement is valued; a teacher who doesn't understand this will find progress slow and frustration levels high. In building effective learning environments, teachers consider a number of factors: physical, organizational, sociological, political, economic, and cultural (see Figure 1.6). Let's look briefly at some of these dimensions. (We will return to these in more depth in later chapters.)

Physical Components

In addition to being a place that facilitates learning, classrooms serve as a home away from home for students. To promote learning and comfort, teachers must pay attention to the physical components of their workplaces—that is, whether the teaching/learning environment is safe, comfortable, well maintained, and well equipped. Safety is a top concern for all schools today, given the horrific events of the past few years, including the shootings at Columbine High School in

Learning environments Environments or settings in which students learn—such as schools, classrooms, community agencies, and homes.

Classroom climate Includes routines and practices, classroom management approach, assessment of student progress, quantity and quality of instruction, and student–teacher interactions.

■ **INTASC**

STANDARD 5 The teacher uses an understanding of individual and group motivation and behavior to create a learning environment that encourages positive social interaction, active engagement in learning, and self-motivation.

FIGURE 1.6 Dimensions of
Effective Teaching and Learning
Environments

Many factors contribute to an
effective learning environment. You
will want to consider all of these
dimensions in making classroom
decisions.

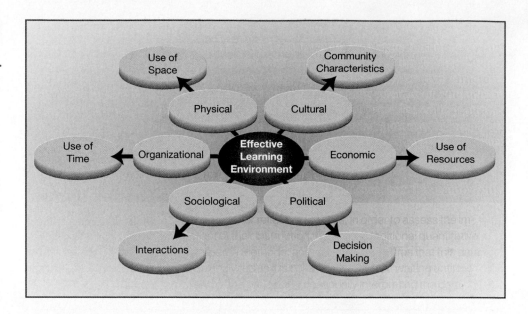

Colorado, the Nickel Mines Amish School shooting, and the Virginia Tech Massacre. We take a close-up look at school safety in Chapter 3.

Organizational Structures

Teachers are constantly assessing and making decisions about how school and classroom activities are organized, teaching loads, schedules, and what is included in the curriculum. Educators generally agree that the amount of time spent on learning tasks has a direct influence on how well students learn, so a major decision you will make as a beginning teacher is how you and your students use time. Teachers who create a positive classroom atmosphere for learning generally try to devote as much time as possible to what is known as **academic learning time**. Academic learning time is the portion of engaged time during which students are not only actively learning, but are learning successfully. Effective instruction maximizes the amount of time a student is focused on learning at an appropriate difficulty level and experiencing a high level of success. For example, Jason Kamras, the 2005 National Teacher of the Year, taught seventh- and eighth-grade math at the John Philip Sousa Middle School in Washington, D.C. Kamras worked diligently to raise math achievement at Sousa, lobbying his principal to double the instructional time allotted for the subject, redesigning the math curriculum to emphasize the increasing use of technology, meeting all learning styles, and putting instruction into a real-world context. The curricular changes, piloted with his own students, helped the percentage of students scoring "below basic" on the Stanford 9 achievement test to fall from approximately 80 percent to just 40 percent in one year. Additionally, his students met the school district's math "adequate yearly progress" target every year since the NCLB was implemented.[26]

As Jason Kamras demonstrated in his class, making good use of classroom time creates an atmosphere in which learning and student achievement are important and valued. We will explore the importance of classroom organization and management in Chapters 11 and 13.

Sociological Factors

In many ways, teaching is about interpersonal and intrapersonal relationships. Interpersonal relationships are relationships (interactions, associations, and communication) between two or more people. Intrapersonal relationships are how individuals relate, reflect, and monitor themselves. Part of building a positive

Academic learning time   The portion of
engaged time during which students are
not only actively learning, but are learning
successfully.

learning environment consists of understanding how you as a teacher relate to and interact with your students, your colleagues, other school staff and administrators, parents, and families—and how students relate to one another. You will want to stress the importance of harmony and cooperation in the classroom, and you will want to understand how to arrange your classroom and instructional processes to encourage positive interactions. For example, you will want to evaluate how your interpersonal relationships influence your students' perception of your commitment to the teaching process. If you are very involved with students, other teachers, and the school, your students will view your dedication as positive and interactive, which, in turn, provides motivation for them. We will examine instructional processes based in sociology in Chapter 11.

Go to MyEducationLab and select the topic "Classroom Management/ Productive Learning Environments." Read the artifact "Mr. Shipley—6th Grade Teacher" then complete the activities.

Political Factors

Schooling is a political process—that is, what happens in schools and classrooms is affected by legislative and administrative processes at national, state, and local levels. Much of what goes on in schools results from political decisions about how schools are governed and operated; the same applies to individual classrooms. In this sense, power and politics are an important aspect of the classroom learning environment. Power frequently becomes an issue in teachers' relationships with students. When teachers share power with students and try to find a balance between teacher-centered and student-centered learning and decision making, they create positive learning environments. Part of building a positive environment depends on how students are included in the social processes of the classroom; by the same token, teachers who are included in political decisions—such as hiring new faculty, collaborating on curriculum reform, choosing textbooks, and so on—tend to view their own work environments more positively. The role of schools in society is discussed in depth in Chapter 3, and the politics and governance of public education in Chapter 7.

Economic Factors

Funding for schools, classrooms, teachers, and students affects the learning environment in a number of ways, including the nature and content of the curriculum, the quality of the physical plant, the teacher-to-pupil ratio, the number of federally subsidized lunches served daily, teachers' salaries, and the number and quality of curricular and extracurricular programs. Teachers help decide how schools spend their money by working with parent and community groups to advocate for adequate school funding and to raise money for school and classroom projects. Chapter 7 focuses on examples of how political and social factors influence schooling.

Cultural Factors

The learning environment is shaped by the culture of the school and of the surrounding local community. Teachers need to be aware of their school's history and the community's cultural heritages and lifestyles. This knowledge can be used to develop meaningful learning activities and make learning appropriate and relevant for all students; it can also lead to effective collaborative programs with students and families. You also need to consider your own interactions with others in relation to culture, gender, and socioeconomic background—that is, how you as a teacher can provide culturally appropriate instruction and curriculum materials for your students.

In today's schools, cultural factors are an ever-growing consideration in the learning environment. Explain what you as a teacher will do to use your school's cultural factors to enhance the overall learning environment.

Building a positive and effective learning environment and collaborating with colleagues, parents, administrators, students, and others to achieve this goal is a critical part of being a teacher. Such efforts will encourage productive home and school relationships, enhance opportunities for personal growth, and make teaching a rewarding experience for you.

Teachers Create Personal Metaphors

Whatever is included in your teacher knowledge base, you will develop a way of thinking about yourself, your students, and what you are doing in your classroom. When you express these thoughts, the words you use will reveal your personal metaphors for teaching.

Every day we use metaphors to describe and compare things and people. The metaphors teachers use to describe themselves and their classrooms reflect their thinking and influence the way they teach. For example, a teacher who sees her classroom as a "workplace" and herself as a "manager" might see students as workers and emphasize on-task behavior and a smoothly functioning, well-managed classroom. In contrast, a teacher who sees his classroom as a "learning environment" and himself as a "guide" might emphasize cooperative learning and design his classroom as an active learning community.

As a teacher, you will be in a constant process of constructing, changing, and reconstructing your personal metaphors of teaching. It is important that you articulate these metaphors in order to analyze how they influence aspects of your teaching.

Experience and reflection help teachers change how they view teaching and students and themselves as teachers. For example, one preservice teacher described how adopting a metaphor for being a "bridge" developed after having contact with students:

> When we first wrote about teaching metaphors . . . All I knew was that I wanted to create a nonthreatening environment where all students could participate and, hopefully, learn something. . . . I want to be able to create a bridge between the content and the lives of the students. I want some aspect of the class to personally touch and engage each student. . . . I want my students to feel good while they are in my class . . . [and] an issue which has emerged for me is that of making connections. . . . I have started thinking about, and have discussed with my cooperating teacher, how to engage different types of students. . . . Most of the students want to make a connection; they wanted to know me . . . [and to have] a personal relationship with me.[27]

Teachers often think of instruction as a product to be delivered. They deliver a lesson on reading, a module on physics, a unit on social studies, or a problem set in math. This "delivery" metaphor is especially common when educators talk about technology; teachers "deliver" instruction on the Internet or via closed circuit television. The metaphor of teaching as product delivery implies efficiency and views teachers as deliverers and students as recipients.

"Community of learners" is another metaphor often mentioned by those who embrace a **constructivist approach** to teaching and learning. When teachers see their classrooms as learning communities, they typically see students and teachers as collaborators, working together to support one another's learning and develop solutions to real-world problems.

The ways that teachers see themselves are many and varied—and almost always have implications for what happens in the classroom. As you read the following metaphors that may be used to describe teachers, reflect on the implications they might have for your teaching, your learning, and student learning.

- **Teacher as student.** Teachers are lifelong learners who grow in their ability to teach as they think actively about their teaching and try out new strategies.

Constructivist approach The belief that students construct a body of knowledge from their own experience and prior knowledge rather than from direct instruction by teachers.

Teachers who see themselves as students are open to change and to expanding their own knowledge through their students.

- **Teacher as facilitator.** Teachers are professionals who set the stage, organize the environment, and make it possible for students to learn. Facilitators view students as active learners who are responsible for their own learning and often capable of learning on their own.
- **Teacher as sage.** Sages are repositories of knowledge, wisdom, and expertise. Like a tribal elder or a Zen master, the sage challenges learners and models the importance of learning how to think.
- **Teacher as coach.** Coaches exhort and encourage students to perform to the limits of their individual capabilities, to train for future performance, and to contribute to the team. Coaches also model behaviors and demonstrate skills.
- **Teacher as leader.** Leaders—ship captains, generals, CEOs, presidents—share a common core of behaviors that includes making decisions, delegating authority, and taking responsibility. Many good leaders share their leadership; similarly, teachers may share leadership with students and colleagues and encourage others to lead, too. Teachers who see themselves as leaders provide opportunities for their students to assume responsibility and often take leadership roles within the school community by participating in action research teams, study groups, and school discussion teams.
- **Teacher as researcher.** Increasingly, teachers see themselves as researchers; they use research to inform and guide their practice.
- **Teacher as nurturer.** Many teachers are nurturers; they are student centered and are interested in their students. They facilitate student work, they listen to their students, and include them in classroom planning. As you read *In the Classroom with Betsy Rogers: Teachers as Nurturers* on page 24, reflect on how this teacher nurtures her students.

REFLECT & WRITE

Pick three of the metaphors above. Do you see teachers in this way? What implications might that have for student learning?

WHY DO TEACHERS TEACH?

Think about your favorite teachers whom you have encountered throughout your academic career. Based on your experience as their student, what do you believe motivated them to teach? Do you believe their motivations were the same as those of your least favorite teachers? Typically, people choose to teach because the profession offers a broad array of intrinsic and extrinsic rewards.

Intrinsic Rewards of Teaching

Intrinsic rewards are those based on feelings of personal satisfaction—feelings that stem from individual needs, beliefs, values, and goals—and vary greatly from

In the Classroom

with **Betsy Rogers**

"Teachers as Nurturers"

Betsy Rogers was 2003 U.S. Teacher of the Year.

Teaching is a way of life in my family. For years, I've heard about how my grandmother started teaching in the Alabama hills when she was 16, with students older than she was. She and her two sisters all had to quit teaching public school when they married—regulations of the time prohibited teachers from being married—but they continued to teach in Sunday school. My mother joined their ranks, teaching 7- and 8-year-old children in Sunday school for over 50 years. As a child, I attended many a lesson planning meeting, and the commitment of these women to provide inspiring lessons in a caring environment greatly influenced the standards I have set for myself as a teacher.

When I returned to public school teaching myself after an 8-year hiatus to raise my sons and teach in private kindergarten, I was unprepared for the situations faced by the children in my first-grade class. The poverty, neglect, and abuse that they experienced every day overwhelmed me. I wanted to change the world for them—and it took me several years to realize that I could only change a small part of it. From my family, I had learned the value of caring for others: I had watched my parents and grandparents serve their community and church by teaching, visiting the sick, gathering clothes and food for those in need, celebrating births, and grieving deaths. Now I realized that this need to serve, this ability to care, could become my greatest contribution to the children I teach.

For many of the children I teach, school is the best part of their world. I committed myself to making my classroom a haven of safety and an environment full of joy. I also made a commitment to build positive relationships with their families. I realized that many of these families loved their children deeply and were doing the very best they could.

My classroom is learner centered, with an environment of security and positive reinforcement. I believe with William Glasser that teachers need to create warm, supportive climates in their classrooms, and with Nel Noddings that "We should want more from our educational efforts than adequate achievement, and we will not

achieve even meager success unless our children believe that they are cared for and learn to care for others." My class is unofficially known as "the nurturing class" in our school; my students are often handpicked, based on their need for extra stability and nurturing. My goal is to make lasting memories for these children. I try to make daily lessons memorable by incorporating art, music, cooking, and literature. For more than a decade, my mother served as our "classroom grannie," coming to class every week with special snacks and sitting in her rocking chair, reading to the children. Her visits were a great highlight; she brought with her the influence of a caring older person that was often lacking in their lives.

Asked to create a school for the workers of Emil Mott's Waldorf-Astoria cigarette factory, Rudolf Steiner tried to build what he called a "third parent" through the cultivation of a long-term teacher–student relationship. I've tried to create this same thing for my students by building strong triangular relationships among students, parents, and myself. I believe strongly that getting to know my students' families is vital: it gives me insight into their backgrounds and the influences in their lives. I send home monthly newsletters and weekly parenting tips, and I provide a parenting backpack with books and brochures. I schedule two conferences each year with all parents (although this is not required in my school) and open my home to students and their families for annual cookouts and swimming parties. As often as possible, I attend students' baptisms, ball games, birthday parties, and graduations. I visit in student homes at times of celebration and sadness. I correspond with many students and their families who have moved away, and when I'm aware of a need, I try to find community or church resources to fill it.

I believe that teachers make a difference—that students' lives can be changed by a classroom that fosters growth and stability. I think the song "Wind Beneath My Wings" must have been written about teachers—I strive to be the wind beneath my students' wings.

To learn more about becoming a nurturing teacher visit http://assist.educ.msu.edu/ASSIST/ArchiveNewsletters/December06final.html.

person to person. Intrinsic rewards for teachers include a love of teaching and learning and of working with children and young people as well as feelings of satisfaction derived from helping others or participating in a public service. Such rewards are powerful motivators for choosing teaching.

Love of Learning

Many teachers are attracted to the teaching profession because it offers the opportunity for continuous learning. Theresa Stapler is a *USA Today* All-USA Teacher; this is how she views teaching:

> As a veteran teacher with 22 years' experience, I sometimes wonder who is learning more in my classroom, my students or me. There is never a day that passes that I don't learn something from my students. . . . Sometimes my newfound knowledge may be something I may not want to know! However, most of the time, the students teach me something great. I always seek opportunities for continual growth through learning and will never consider myself to be educationally complacent. My love of learning is what inspires me to greet each new day with vigor.[28]

Love of Teaching

Perhaps when someone asks you why you chose teaching, you will respond, "Because I love to teach." Research shows that many teachers feel this way. Many say it is the love of teaching that keeps them in the profession. But what, really, do we mean by "love of teaching?" As the following comments reveal, love of teaching means love of their students and of the subjects they teach. For Tom Campbell, associate superintendent for Catholic Schools in Atlanta, the love of teaching is a desirable goal for both administrators and teachers:

> Any good administrator [or teacher] . . . has to have a love for teaching, first and foremost. I think having as your objective what is best for the students, whether you stand before a classroom or sit behind the desk, helps you to keep in mind why you're doing what you're doing . . . Every initiative I take, I want to keep in mind what is best for the students. I also want to serve the teachers, and help them to do their job, as they'll help me to do my job.[29]

Desire to Work with Young People

An overwhelming majority of new teachers cite a desire to work with children as the main reason they choose to teach.[30] Contributing to students' learning and facilitating their achievement and positive behavior are powerful motivating forces for—and one of the major benefits of—teaching. Being around children and youth, developing relationships with them while earning their respect, is a compelling reason to enter the classroom.

A Desire to Help Others

Many people choose to teach because they see teaching as a life of service to others. As Sister Alice Hess, a ninth-through-twelfth-grade teacher, puts it, "I make eminently clear to them that [my] classroom is a room for champions, that I will be content with nothing but their best and that I am ready to go to great lengths to help them learn."[31]

■ **INTASC**

STANDARD 9 The teacher is a reflective practitioner who continually evaluates the effects of his/her choices and actions on others (students, parents, and other professionals in the learning community) and who actively seeks out opportunities to grow professionally.

Go to MyEducationLab and select the topic "Teaching Profession," then watch the video "Teaching Fifth Grade," and complete the activities.

People choose to teach for a number of reasons. What intrinsic reward is this teacher getting from her job?

● **Your Turn**

Teachers are motivated by different things. Visit a school in your district and ask several teachers, first, what expectations motivated them to become teachers, and second, whether those expectations have been fulfilled. Are the rewards they actually experience from teaching different from those they anticipated receiving? How do the rewards they now value compare to your expectations for yourself?

Desire to Provide Public and/or Professional Service

The motivation to make a difference in the world and the lives of others often stems from a commitment to service. The desire to serve and make society and the world a better place is a powerful influence in many people's lives.

The ideal that people should devote part of their lives to helping others has a strong tradition in American culture, and currently a national movement encourages high school students to spend some of their educational time in service activities. For high school students in Delaware, for example, community service is a requirement for graduation.

Teaching offers many lifetime opportunities and rewards to those who seriously dedicate themselves to it. When asked why, after 21 years, he was still so enthusiastic about teaching, Leo Ramirez, a math teacher at McAllen High School in Texas, answered without equivocation, "Because of the difference my students are making in the lives of others because of me!" Mr. Ramirez is influencing generations. What a reason to teach!

REFLECT & WRITE

When did you decide you were interested in teaching as a career? What intrinsic rewards do you expect from this career? What extrinsic rewards?

_____

_____

_____

_____

_____

Extrinsic Rewards of Teaching

Extrinsic rewards of teaching include status and material benefits, which also lead to teacher satisfaction. Some cite a teacher's hours and more opportunities for time with their own families; others enjoy the respect the role brings. These external factors can make teaching attractive.

Lifestyle

Teaching appeals to many people as a way of life. The appealing qualities of a teacher's life include a work year of 180 to 210 days, with summers off and long vacations throughout the year, and the correspondence of a school day and year with children's schedules. Being "off" two or three months each year offers teachers opportunities to travel, take on other work, take graduate courses, devote time to their families, or renew themselves for the next school year. The school calendar benefits teachers who are also parents; they find that working in a profession whose hours correspond to their children's school year is ideal. As more and more schools implement new approaches to the school calendar—including year-round schooling and four-day weeks—teachers are beginning to experience shorter vacations spread over longer periods of time. Many teachers initially demonstrate negative feelings toward these changes, but studies show that the more experience they have with this kind of work calendar, the more they begin to prefer it to the traditional system.[32]

Community Respect

Status and respectability contribute to people's decisions to select teaching as a career. Although public attitudes toward teachers vary widely, teaching typically brings comparatively high status and community respect. The public generally has high expectations of teachers and places trust in teachers to educate their children. In the eyes of the community, teachers are exemplars.

Security

Material advantages for teachers include a reasonable salary (much improved over the last 20 years in most areas) and benefits, steady employment, and opportunities for advancement. Salaries are rising, and the demand for qualified teachers is growing and will continue to do so. (See Chapter 2 for reasons.) Because most teaching positions are tenured, with guaranteed job security after a certain point except in extraordinary conditions, you could, if you wished, remain a teacher for your lifetime.

REFLECT & WRITE

The desire to work with young people far outranks any other reason given for choosing teaching as a profession. What are your top five reasons for considering teaching as a career? Which reason is most important?

HOW IS TEACHING CHANGING?

Rapid change, a characteristic of American society in general, also is reflected in the teaching profession. The changing nature of teaching results from a variety of factors: new knowledge derived from educational research; changes in society; state and national school reform efforts (including legislation); children's health issues, such as obesity and nutrition; immigration; rapidly changing technology; and safety concerns.

Obesity and nutrition are influencing lesson plans, school lunch programs, and school funding as childhood obesity levels continue to rise. As a result, school food programs are on a diet! As schools scramble to comply with federal requirements that every school district develop a wellness plan to provide students with healthier foods, many are banning a wide array of unhealthy food options. California is a case in point; it has banned deep fryers and now serves baked fries and chicken nuggets.[33]

Immigration and the changing composition of American society also is affecting teaching and learning. As students face the obstacles associated with acculturation into U.S. society, teachers are facing the challenge of meeting the needs of their increasingly diverse classrooms.

New technologies are changing the way we think and live. The Internet, cell phones, and social networking are all influencing how students think, learn, and socialize, both inside and outside of the classroom. Cell-phone-accessorized teens may think that is just "GR8," but as the lexicon spawned by a 160-character message limit starts to spill off the cell phone screen into written work, some of their English teachers are not exactly "ROFL." Nor does seeing text-message abbreviations in essays bring a smiley face to college admission officers. Veteran high school English teacher Ruth Maenpaa started noticing how much text messaging was affecting her students, in both subtle and not-so-subtle ways. The first time Maenpaa flagged the use of "4" for "for" in an essay, the student said she was so used to text-messaging that she did not even think about it. "As I watch students texting, I see them routinely using abbreviations to the point that they do not know how to spell the word correctly."[34]

You need to prepare for how such changes, as well as new ones, will affect the teaching profession. Changes in society spur new efforts in educational research, which in turn propel reform movements; new legislation driven by increased youth obesity drives "junk food" out of schools; new technology leads to new educational research and development, which in turn fuels new legislation. All of these factors impact the day-to-day lives of teachers and the way public schools function in the United States. Being a teacher means living with and adapting to change.

Patterns of Educational Reform

Throughout your teaching career, you will need to respond to change resulting from movements for reform within either the educational community or the political community, or both. Educational reform tends to be cyclical; that is, movements rise, fall, and often rise again in slightly different forms 20 or 30 years later. A vocal chorus in the 1980s and early 1990s, for example, decried the traditional use of phonics and decoding and endorsed a **whole language**, or immersion, approach to teaching young children to read. By the mid 1990s, the backlash against whole language propelled phonics once again to the foreground, and the current approach to reading instruction calls for a balanced, or comprehensive, melding of several approaches. Similarly, advocates of **open education** in the late 1960s and 1970s attempted to make learning more student centered and "relevant" by establishing nongraded programs, classrooms without walls, learning stations, multi-age grouping, active learning, individualized instruction, and team teaching. Although some of these practices quickly fell out of favor (classrooms without walls turned out to be noisy and difficult to manage), many of the ideas introduced in this reform movement are now a standard part of the teaching repertory.

We talked earlier about metaphors for teaching. You might picture education reform movements as waves regularly rolling onto the sandy shores of the educational establishment with different effects, depending on the nature and content of the wave itself and the willingness of teachers, administrators, and others to accept what is being proposed. Some reform efforts, like small ripples, leave very little evidence of their existence. Others, like a tsunami, can change the landscape for years to come. Most major reform movements derive, at least initially, from social changes or from reports documenting perceived weaknesses in the current educational system. Figure 1.7 can help you visualize the major educational reform movements since the mid-twentieth century.

Reforms of the 1950s and 1960s: Education for Democracy and Educational Opportunity

The first wave of contemporary school reform movements derived from the launching of the first Russian manned spacecraft, *Sputnik*, in 1957. Public outcry over the Russians being first into space led to reform movements focused on improving learning and instruction in math and science; more emphasis on basic

---

Whole language A "top-down" approach to teaching reading that relies on immersion of the child in language.

Open education A movement toward combining multiage groups in classrooms without walls.

■ INTASC

STANDARD 9 The teacher is a reflective practitioner who continually evaluates the effects of his/her choices and actions on others (students, parents, and other professionals in the learning community) and who actively seeks out opportunities to grow professionally.

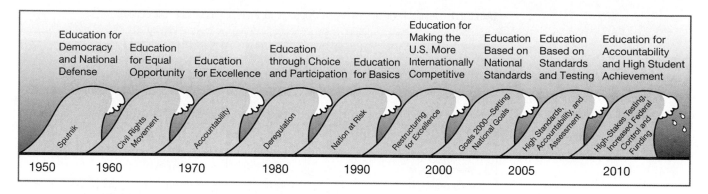

FIGURE 1.7   Waves of Reform in Education, 1950 to 2010

Although reform movements typically last 10 to 20 years, some are short lived while others are longer and more influential.

skills (reading, writing, and mathematics); the development of new curricula (including inquiry-based science); and beginning schooling at an earlier age.

A second wave of reform in the late 1950s and 1960s resulted from the Civil Rights movement and the crises of the Vietnam era and led to major new pieces of national legislation affecting education. The Economic Opportunity Act of 1964 created Head Start, which was designed to provide for the cognitive, social, and health needs of preschool disadvantaged children as a means of helping them succeed in school. The Elementary and Secondary Education Act of 1965 (ESEA) was designed to provide remedial assistance to disadvantaged students who achieved below-grade-level results in math and reading. Legislation with the goal of improving education for children with special needs was also passed. Much of this legislation continues to affect education today. ESEA was substantially amended by the Improving America's Schools Act of 1994 and the No Child Left Behind Act of 2001.

Go to MyEducationLab and select the topic "History of Education." Read the article "The Evaluation of Middle Schools" and then complete the activities.

Reforms of the 1980s and 1990s: Accountability and Deregulation

During the tumultuous decades of the 1960s and 1970s, the new national legislation passed in the mid 1960s informed basic changes in American schooling. Then, in 1983, the U.S. Department of Education issued a report called *A Nation at Risk: The Imperatives for Educational Reform.* Highly critical of the nation's schools, the report linked a decline in U.S. economic competitiveness to a decline in the quality of public schooling. "A rising tide of mediocrity . . . threatens our very future as a nation and a people. We have, in effect, been committing an act of unthinking, unilateral disarmament."[35] The idea that America's economic edge in the world depends on the excellence of its schools continues to influence educational reform and practice today.

Although this report again emphasized the need for a focus on basic skills, the responses to *A Nation at Risk* initially focused almost exclusively on test score accountability. Schools and teachers were, for the first time, evaluated and rewarded based on students' test scores. Some districts instituted teacher bonuses for increases in scores. Schools compared test scores among classrooms and teachers; districts compared scores from school to school; states compared districts; and the federal government compared national results to those of students in other countries like Japan and Germany.

This "accountability" movement continues to gain strength today, and each year more and more states institute standardized testing programs at various grade levels, and more and more lists are published evaluating and comparing student performance across schools, districts, states, and the nation. Table 1.1 shows how

TABLE 1.1   Annual Performance Report, 2005–2006, State of California Public Schools

2005 College Preparatory Test Results		
	CALIFORNIA	NATION
ACT—Average Score	21.6	20.9
ACE—Participation Rate (%)	14.0	40.0
SAT Reasoning Test—Average Score	1026	1028
SAT Reasoning Test—Participation Rate (%)	50.0	49.0

2005 State Proficiency Results		
	CALIFORNIA	NATION
Grade 4		
Reading	21	30
Mathematics	28	35
Grade 8		
Reading	21	29
Mathematics	22	28

Source: Standard and Poor's. (2006). *California Public Schools and Districts.* (Online). Available at www.schoolmatters.com/; Council of Chief State School Officers.

the State of California meets demands for accountability through testing and informing parents of the results.

Accountability and comparison through testing as a process of reforming and improving education represents a strong tradition in American education and has many adherents. At the heart of this approach lies a strong commitment to centralized control, with authority and power vested in a central administration at the school, district, and state levels. At odds with this emphasis on centralization was another reform movement that grew out of the economic turmoil of the 1980s: restructuring through deregulation. School choice and school restructuring called for teachers, administrators, parents, community members, and even students to participate in decision making about how to improve teaching and learning. Underlying the deregulation movement are calls for school-based management teams and shared decision making; classroom-based approaches, such as cooperative learning; and alternative forms of testing based on performance and product.

Contemporary Reform Movements

Goals 2000, part of the Educate America Act of 1994, set standards to be achieved nationwide by the year 2000, including supporting readiness for school and high school completion for all students; setting world-class standards in math and science; establishing adult literacy and lifelong learning opportunities; providing safe, drug-free schools; supporting teacher education and professional development; and providing opportunities for parent participation in education. The Goals 2000 legislation provided a foundation for the NCLB, which sets standards in many of these same areas.

Another focus in current educational reform is on what the U.S. economy needs. *What Work Requires of Schools: A SCANS Report for America 2000,*[36] a report developed by the Secretary's Commission on Achieving Necessary Skills (SCANS) of the U.S. Department of Labor, identifies five competencies that are important for job performance:

- Knowledge of and use of resources
- Interpersonal skills
- Ability to acquire information
- Ability to understand complex interrelationships
- Ability to work with a variety of technologies

The reform movement based on this report emphasizes the needs and conditions of the workplace and supports a seamless transition from school to workplace; worker training in information technologies; and a curricular emphasis on critical

Goals 2000   Part of the Educate America Act (1994), these goals stressed readiness for school, high school completion, student achievement and citizenship, world-class standards in math and science, adult literacy and lifelong learning, safe and drug-free schools, teacher education and professional development, and parental participation.

thinking, problem solving, decision making, and group collaboration—all skills that employers say they need in today's workers.

During the 2008 presidential election, domestic issues such as health care, the environment, and international issues, including the war in Iraq, global warming, and the role of the United States in world affairs, overshadowed educational issues. Nonetheless, the presidential election raised issues related to merit pay, universal prekindergarten, incentives to hire new teachers, and more programs for disadvantaged students. Surpassing all of these issues, however, is the reauthorization of the NCLB, which continues to have many proponents and opponents. What is clear, however, is that many of the core components of NCLB—high standards, standardized testing, teacher and school accountability, high-quality teachers, parent/family involvement, and closing the achievement gaps among all socioeconomic and diverse populations of students—remain powerful trends in American education.

Also, and perhaps most important, is the role that the federal government is playing in pre-K–12 education—a role greater than ever before. In fact, federal control of education, especially through the NCLB, is one of the major issues facing U.S. education today.

What Reform Movements Mean to Teachers

Whatever **education reform movement** might be sweeping the shores when you enter teaching, you will need to be able to respond to it. Let's look at trends that will undoubtedly impact your own career in the years to come.

Education reform movement A comprehensive effort made during the 1980s and 1990s to improve schools and the preparation of teachers.

Teaching in Restructured Schools

The waves of education reform that have rolled onto the beaches of American education over the past 50 years have resulted in a significant restructuring of schools and teaching. **Restructuring**—major changes in the rules, roles, and relationships within an institution—is a common term for changes made in response to reform movements in both business and industry and education. As you might predict, restructuring means that teachers work extra hours planning, communicating with families, teaming, participating in common planning time, and spending what was formerly personal time on school-based activities, helping to ensure that students learn—and will perform well on standardized tests.

Restructuring Reorganizing how schools are controlled at the local level so that teachers, principals, parents, and community members have significant authority.

Specialization of Schools

Specialization is common in secondary education and is becoming more common in middle and elementary schools. Smaller high schools that teach a specialized curriculum are growing in number. Such schools allow students to focus on things that they are really interested in, as well as get a solid foundation in the basics. New York City is a prime example of this. The city offers high schools that specialize in just about anything you can think of: hospitality and tourism, health careers, culinary arts, architecture, and the performing arts. Although the admissions process differs for each school, most are open to all students.

Teaching in Diverse Schools

One reality of teaching today is the increasing racial, ethnic, cultural, and socioeconomic diversity of students, their families, and the communities in which they live. Diversity is greatest in urban school districts. Of the five largest school districts in the United States, the Chicago school district has the highest percentage of minority students (91.2%); followed by Los Angeles (91%); Miami-Dade Florida (89.9%); and Clark County, Nevada (56%). In the 20 largest school districts, the minority student population is 79.7 percent.[37]

■ INTASC

STANDARD 3 The teacher understands how students differ in their approaches to learning and creates instructional opportunities that are adapted to diverse learners.

The U.S. population is approximately 300 million. About one-third of the U.S. population is composed of minorities. California has a minority population of 20.7 million, which is 21 percent of the nation's total. Texas has a minority population of 12.2 million, or 12 percent of the U.S. total.[38]

Schools and teachers must celebrate diversity; they must educate all students to their full potential regardless of socioeconomic status, race, ethnicity, language, religion, gender, national origin, or membership in any other category. This means that you as a teacher will need to know and respect your students—their individual differences and the sources of their diversity. You will also need to make sure that your classroom, curriculum, and teaching methods are appropriate for and responsive to students' needs as both individual learners and members of diverse groups. See *In the Classroom with Caridad Alonso*.

Meeting All Students' Learning Needs

As a new teacher, you will have available to you a greater variety of instructional methods and materials than did teachers in the past. Today, student assessment is based on the ability to demonstrate mastery through state testing programs, as well as higher-level thinking and problem solving through the completion of projects, performances, written self-assessments, and work samples collected in a portfolio.

In the Classroom
with **Caridad Alonso**
Teaching Is Not Just a Job!

Caridad "Charity" Alonso is a Spanish reading specialist for grades 1–5 at William C. Lewis Dual-Language Elementary School in Wilmington, Delaware, and the 2007 Delaware Teacher of the Year.

Charity Alonso helped found El Jardin Espanol/The Spanish Garden, a nonprofit language-immersion preschool in Wilmington, Delaware. The goal of the program is to provide native English speakers ages 2 through 5 with a rich second-language learning experience and to foster a positive attitude toward cultural differences. The program also allows Alonso to work within Immigration and Naturalization Service (INS) guidelines to sponsor degreed teachers from Central and South America. As a result of her work, parents created a separate nonprofit entity called The Friends of the Spanish Garden to help raise funds for El Jardin Espanol/The Spanish Garden. Alonso also is spearheading an after-school tutoring program for former kindergarten and first grade students of the program to help them continue their Spanish literacy skills.

When asked about her philosophy on teaching, Alonso stated, "Teaching is not just a 'job' for me. It is my passion. In fact, I know I was born to do this. Each school year, I am dedicated to providing a positive instructional climate where my students feel encouraged, safe, and excited to learn." Added Alonso, "As an educator, I accept the responsibility of becoming a lifelong learner as new ideas, new technology, and new ways to approach teaching become available. I thrive on opportunities to learn more, reflect upon these, and put them into practice. I also have the challenge as our world becomes more diverse to find ways to meet the educational needs of each student and to make an effort to understand each individual's experiences."

Search for foreign language immersion programs in your area at www.cal.org/resources/immersion/.

Source: R. Gough, *Caridad Alonso Named Delaware Teacher of the Year for 2007.* (2007 September 16). State of Delaware. (Online). Available at www.doe.state.de.us/news/2006/1026.shtml.

Authentic learning tasks and assessments—that is, tasks that address real needs and problems that students will encounter outside the classroom and assessments that measure the ability to complete those tasks—are valued.

Active learning means that students are out of their seats, working with classmates as evaluators, investigators, decision makers, creative problem solvers, and critical thinkers. Students are also more involved in self-teaching and peer teaching and in **cooperative learning**. Typically, today's students work together on academic tasks in small, mixed-ability groups, sharing responsibility for their own learning.

Using Instructional Technologies

Social studies teacher Eric Langhorst is the 2008 Missouri Teacher of the Year. He uses high-tech tools to teach his eighth-grade students about the past. In his American history class, he incorporates twenty-first-century technology to make learning meaningful and exciting for his students. Eric strives to make the classroom experience fresh and exciting and uses cutting-edge technology to actively engage his students. His students participate in live debates, play computer simulations of presidential elections, and invite local elected officials as guest speakers. "Technology has become a tool that I utilize in my classroom to bring the outside world to my students and allow my students to share their experiences with a global community," Eric said. "The focus for today's student has shifted from the art of obtaining information to the art of evaluating and applying the information they receive." For example, when students study the presidential election of 1860, they are assigned the project of creating a 30-second television ad for Abraham Lincoln to help him win the presidency. Students work as Abraham Lincoln's campaign staff and apply the information they are learning through this modern-day problem-solving experience.[39]

As a beginning teacher, you will teach students who grew up with computers, and you will belong to a generation of teachers who are more computer and multimedia literate than teachers of the past. Clearly, **instructional technologies** will play a larger and larger role in every classroom. You will probably use technologies not only as instructional tools but in other ways as well—for example, to communicate with parents, collaborate with other teachers, assist students with disabilities, and monitor and record student progress and achievement. (See *What's New in Education?*)

Authentic learning tasks and assessments Assignments and assessments that reflect real needs and problems that students will encounter outside the classroom.

Active learning Process whereby students are mentally and physically active in learning through activities that involve gathering data, thinking, and problem solving.

Cooperative learning An instructional and learning process in which students work together on academic tasks, help each other, and take responsibility for one another's learning.

■ **INTASC**

STANDARD 10 The teacher fosters relationships with school colleagues, parents, and agencies in the larger community to support students' learning and well-being.

Instructional technologies Any technology—such as computers, video recorders and DVD players, and television—that promotes and supports the teaching-learning process.

What's *New* in Education?

A Computer for Every Student

One way or another, the idea of ubiquitous, low-cost computer access for schoolchildren, both in the United States and abroad, is fast approaching becoming reality. Major technology players, including several large companies and a nonprofit group that is focusing on developing countries, have been working in different ways to advance the cause.

Things are moving along so quickly, in fact, that Stephen Dukker, chairman and CEO of NComputing, predicts that by 2009 many schools will be able to provide their students with portable, online capabilities for as little as $100 each. "Wireless capacity," says Dukker, "should be a relatively inexpensive bonus by then."

NComputing has just broken new ground with an announcement that the Republic of Macedonia will become the first nation in the world to provide computer workstations for every elementary and secondary school student—400,000 in all.

Source: R. L. Jacobson, *Low-cost School Computing Set to Take Off.* (2007, September 17). *eSchool News.* (Online). Available at www.eschoolnews.com/news/pfshowStory.cfm?ArticleID=7365.

OBSERVE & LEARN

Teachers like Eric Langhorst use technology every day in their classrooms. You will want to begin thinking about how you will apply technology in your classroom. Visit classrooms and observe how teachers use technology to promote and stimulate learning. As you observe, make a grid showing the various kinds of technology in use. Provide a specific example of a technology application; rate your impression of students' responses to the particular technology application; and then comment as to whether the technology application you observed would be something that you might use in your classroom teaching.

Chapter 12 will help you learn more about applying technology to your teaching.

Working with Colleagues, Families, and Communities

Teachers have traditionally conceived their role as working with students in a classroom and helping them learn academic material. As a new teacher, however, you will find that there is a growing emphasis on collegiality and on parent and community involvement. Today, teachers might work with entire families to help facilitate student learning; family-based education is becoming the rule rather than the exception. Most teachers recognize the need for family involvement and say they would like to see the level of parental participation increase.[40] Many teachers also work with community leaders to garner support—economic and political—for school projects.

Working with colleagues may involve participating in team teaching (also known as *co-teaching*), collaborating to integrate curriculum, or planning joint learning experiences. Benefits of **professional collaboration** typically include:

Professional collaboration Working cooperatively with teachers, staff, parents, and community members to improve schools and the teaching-learning process.

- Increased sense of professional interaction and support
- More effective use of individual teacher talents and abilities
- Opportunities for peer coaching or mentoring and reflective practice
- Opportunities to meet all students' needs more fully and enrich learning
- Increased student achievement and overall student performance

Teaching in Inclusive Classrooms

Reform movements of the last several decades have resulted in the inclusion of more and more students classified with disabilities in the general classroom. A **disability** is a physical, cognitive, or behavioral impairment that substantially limits one or more major life activities. Disabilities include speech and language impairments; hearing and vision impairments, including deafness and blindness; specific learning disabilities; and orthopedic and health impairments, including traumatic brain injury, mental retardation, serious emotional disturbance, and autism.

Disability A physical or mental impairment that substantially limits one or more major life activities.

Students with disabilities may be taught in special programs but more and more often are part of a **mainstream** or **inclusion** program for all or part of the school day. As a beginning teacher, you can expect to be responsible for one or more students with special needs in your classroom. You will learn more about this in Chapter 5.

Mainstreaming The educational and social integration of children with special needs into the schoolwide instructional process, usually in the general classroom.

We began this chapter with Josh Anderson, 2007 Kansas Teacher of Year, who revealed how one of his students, Danny, inspired him. Danny, a National College Debate Champion, who had been in one of Josh's speech courses, overcame great obstacles in school—at the hands of cruel and insensitive students and teachers—as the result of one inspirational teacher whose belief in him changed his life. Danny's story, in turn, served as a great inspiration to Josh, who believes that all teachers need a room of their own where they can make a difference in their students' lives; where they can learn from their experiences in order to create new

Inclusion The practice of ensuring that all students with disabilities participate with other students in all aspects of school.

Collaborative efforts among teachers provide supportive opportunities that promote creativity and problem solving.

ones; and where they can embrace new opportunities and challenges. He is proud to be a teacher, as are the many teachers and administrators you will meet throughout this text and throughout the course of your study. Regardless of how you get your first teaching position or where you teach, expect a career full of happiness, challenges, opportunities, and possibilities.

ETHICAL DILEMMA

"Should I Report Her to . . . ?"

ELENA MARTINEZ, a seventh-grade math teacher, has just had a conversation with the new seventh-grade math teacher at her school, Kim Mattingly. Because Elena had recently reworked her curriculum to better accommodate the emphasis on standards, she had offered to help Kim do the same. Kim thanks Elena, but explains that she feels the current emphasis on standards is just a lot of hype generated by the NCLB. She also tells Elena that she really doesn't create lesson plans, but instead plans week by week. She prefers to do what comes naturally to her, without a formalized plan.

Elena is very concerned. She fears that Kim's students won't be ready to take the National Assessment of Educational Progress math test in eighth grade. She is considering talking to Marty—the seventh-grade-level team leader; however, she doesn't want to get off to a bad start with Kim.

What do you think Elena should do?

SUMMARY

- An expanding knowledge base, using effective practices that promote learning, and teacher efficacy are all factors that make a good teacher.
- Teacher accountability today maintains that teachers are responsible for their students' achievements or lack of them. The No Child Left Behind Act holds teachers accountable by striving to make sure teachers are highly qualified to teach their subject and grade level.
- Teachers today are decision makers and planners. They are responsible for building positive learning environments and creating personal metaphors.
- Teachers teach due to the many intrinsic and extrinsic rewards that teaching offers.
- Educational reform has changed and continues to change the teaching profession.

KEY TERMS

Academic learning time   20

Active learning   33

Authentic learning tasks and
    assessments   33

Classroom climate   19

Collective teacher efficacy   12

Constructivist approach   22

Cooperative learning   33

Developmentally appropriate
    instruction   8

Disability   34

Education reform movement   31

Goals 2000   30

Inclusion   34

Instructional technologies   33

Knowledge base   5

Learning environments   19

Mainstreaming   34

Open education   28

Performance-based teaching   13

Process-product perspective   13

Professional collaboration   34

Restructuring   31

Special education   10

Teacher accountability   13

Teacher effectiveness   7

Teacher efficacy   10

Whole language   28

APPLICATIONS FOR ACTIVE LEARNING

Connections

1. Create a picture or graphic that shows connections that are meaningful to you from Chapter 1. Here is an example of a graphic representation of some key ideas from this chapter.

2. Being a professional is about making connections with students, colleagues, families, and the community. Create a visual representation that shows the different connections you will make as a professional teacher and why each connection is important to your profession.

Field Experiences

1. Teacher stories are a good way to learn about teaching. Ask some teachers to share stories or anecdotes about significant teaching events that helped make a difference in students' lives. Share teacher stories with classmates.

What patterns do you observe in teachers who make a difference in people's lives?

2. You can learn a lot through observing. One key to observing is to plan for your observation. Your plan should detail *why* you want to observe, *what* you want to observe, and *where* you want to observe. A second key to observing is to use a checklist while you observe. The checklist will guide your observation and help to ensure that you observe what you want to observe. For example, when you observe teachers in a classroom, some things you will want to notice are:

- Evidence of planning
- Classroom organization that supports instruction
- Evidence that teachers engage and involve students
- Classroom management
- Evidence that students are learning

Record the results of your observation in your portfolio.

Personal Research

1. Recall teachers who were positive influences in your education and your life. What were those teachers like? How did they act as teachers? How did you benefit from knowing them and being their student?

2. The No Child Left Behind Act has changed how teachers teach and how students learn—teaching to standards and ongoing testing are two examples. The teacher vignettes in this chapter provide additional examples. Interview teachers and gather information about how their professional lives have been changed by the NCLB. Also find out how they believe the NCLB has impacted their students' learning.

PREPARING TO TEACH

For Your Portfolio

In this section, and others like it at the end of every chapter, you will be asked to collect your own writing as well as information you gather about teaching from other sources. The portfolio you develop will be invaluable to you in articulating your own answers to typical interview questions for your first job and will provide resources for your first year of teaching.

1. Collect your Observe and Learn findings and other pertinent information into your teaching portfolio under the heading "What Teaching Means to Me." Later in the course, check back and reflect on your responses to see whether your views of teaching are changing. Keep in mind that you will probably be asked some version of these questions—What does teaching mean to you? Why did you choose to become a teacher?—at job interviews.

2. Collect your information about teacher proficiencies (knowledge and skills) as they are defined in your state and begin developing a plan and timetable for acquiring these proficiencies.

Idea File

In this section, and others like it at the end of every chapter, you will be encouraged to create a file of teaching ideas, both general ideas and specific lesson plans, for use in your first teaching position.

1. In what ways do you think teaching will change in the future? What are some advantages and disadvantages of these potential changes? Begin an idea file for ways you might prepare yourself for each change you identify.

2. Join a Future Teachers club if your school sponsors one, or start a club for future teachers on your own. What three topics might you include on the agenda of your first meeting?

LEARNING AND KNOWING MORE

In this section and others like it at the end of each chapter, you will find lists of electronic and print resources that you may find valuable in preparing for a career in teaching.

Websites Worth Visiting

Pathways to School Improvement. Created and maintained by the North Central Regional Laboratory
www.ncrel.org/sdrs

Lists of topics to explore further including assessment, preservice education, and professional development.

American Association of Colleges for Teacher Education
www.aacte.org

Information about teacher preparation programs and teacher education.

The Four "Sacred Cows" of American Education
www.riggsinst.org/cows.htm

A discussion of educational reform versus tradition in American education.

Kentucky Education Reform Act
www.education.ky.gov

Information and an up-to-date publications list about Kentucky's ongoing reform programs.

Teachers Using the Internet to Conduct Research
www.brint.com/research.htm

List of links for teachers interested in using the Internet to conduct research.

Books Worth Reading

Kelly, M. (2004). *The Everything New Teacher Book: Increase Your Confidence, Connect with Your Students, and Deal with the Unexpected.* Cincinnati, OH: Adams Media Corporation. Recognizes that during the first couple of years in the classroom, teachers need effective suggestions on how to have a positive and lasting impact on their students. From the rules and tools of a successful learning environment to advice on behavior management.

Thompson, J. G. (2007). *First Year Teacher's Survival Guide: Ready-to-Use Strategies, Tools, and Activities for Meeting the Challenges of Each School Day.* San Francisco, CA: Jossey-Bass.
Gives new teachers a wide variety of tested strategies, activities, and tools for creating a positive and dynamic learning environment while meeting the challenges of each school day. Helps new teachers with everything from becoming effective team players and connecting with students to handling behavior problems and working within diverse classrooms.

Wong, H. K., and Wong, R. T. (2004). *The First Days of School: How to Be an Effective Teacher.* Mountain View, CA: Harry K. Wong Publications.
Walks teachers through the most effective ways to begin a school year and continue to become an effective teacher. This is the most basic book on how to teach.

2 Teaching as a Profession

CATHERINE DUPREE SHIELDS My desire to continually improve my effectiveness as a teacher motivated me to complete my Ph.D. in educational psychology and it pushes me to pursue National Board Certification for Teachers (see Chapter 13). Involvement with others in my field through professional organizations and meetings has given me friendships with people I enjoy and colleagues to whom I refer students for mentoring in specific research areas.

Painful recollections of the steep learning curve during my first year of teaching motivate me to help new teachers. When several educators in my community began teaching AP Biology at different schools, I was reminded how desperately I needed someone with experience to walk with me through my first year. As I observed terror in the eyes of my friends and colleagues, I decided I was the person to introduce these course novices to people who were able to offer experience and encouragement. We began meeting once or twice a month at a local coffee shop to discuss ideas, ask questions, and offer emotional support. Merrill, a first-year teacher, often shared how the support she received from the group helped her survive and provide better instruction during a difficult first year. For those new to other science courses, experienced faculty members produced curriculum guides for our school district containing ideas, pretests, posttests, and suggestions for inquiry activities to promote critical thinking.

Teaching is more than educating it is an opportunity to invest in the lives of children. As a teacher of adolescents, it is important to understand that students are searching for an identity. While my focus is on anatomy and health, it is also on loyalty, fairness, curiosity, and lifelong learning.

When Cristin, a quiet girl in the back of the room, left my class for the last time this year, she shocked me by whispering in my ear, "You have changed my life." I did not change the many difficulties Cristin faced at home, but she said I helped her see she could make choices to help her have a better life. I tried to help Will see the same thing, but he chose to hand in a blank exam paper and leave our school. Another one of my students, Matt, gradually quit coming to school, dropped out, and got a job. The money was good for a teenager living at home. He returned at the end of the year for the senior picnic and told me he had learned the value of an education by watching men work 16-hour days and still be unable to pay their bills. He had earned his GED and was headed to college.

I'll never forget students dancing for joy in the hall late one Friday afternoon because they had figured out the molecular formula for sucrose. Nor will I forget the wonder on the face of a student who had just seen the blood vessels of a retina for the first time or the thrill of a student whose hard work was rewarded with a scholarship or a trip to a national competition.

As you read this chapter . . .

Think about:

- Why teaching is your profession of choice
- The five dimensions of professionalism and why they are important
- The development of your own philosophy of education
- How you will use research in your professional practice
- What opportunities exist for your professional development
- How education reform is changing teacher education
- Characteristics of America's teachers and how they affect the profession
- Teaching jobs available today and whether teaching is a good fit for you

> **I am proud to be a professional!**

▸▸ Go to MyEducationLab and select the topic "Philosophical Foundations" then watch the video "Developing a Philosophy of Education."

Catherine DuPree Shields, Ph.D., RN teaches anatomy and health at Jefferson County International Baccalaureate School at Shades Valley High School in Birmingham, Alabama.

There is no more valuable investment than in educating children. Like most teachers, I get tired, frustrated, and irritable. But if I can provide something positive to give students the chance to find a healthy identity and learn something academic along the way, I count myself fortunate. I am proud to identify with the many professionals whose life's work is cultivating, developing, and educating people. I am a professional.

WHY CHOOSE TEACHING AS YOUR PROFESSION?

Profession   An occupation that requires advanced education and training and that involves intellectual skills.

A **profession** is an occupation that requires advanced education and training and involves intellectual skills. Typically, a profession is self-governed by standards and requires some sort of entry certification, such as the bar exam for lawyers or medical boards for physicians. Professional practice incorporates a common set of knowledge; in turn, professionals learn from those in the profession who are more experienced and through personal study. This is true in the field of education. Beginning teachers engage in personal study by means of college courses, with the goal of meeting the requirements for teacher certification. These beginning teaching professionals also learn from those who are more experienced as they take part in student teaching. The foundation of a strong profession is a shared body of knowledge based on research and public confidence that the professionals are fit to practice.[1]

You are preparing to be a professional. When you have completed a program of teacher education you will be required to pass a certification exam—and then you will join 6.2 million other teachers, all dedicated to educating America's children to the fullest extent of their abilities.[2] You will have many opportunities and responsibilities that will enrich your life and change the lives of others.

The teaching profession has the following standards:

- Teachers spend 4 or more years gaining the specialized knowledge they must have to ensure that all students will learn.
- Teachers pass rigorous state and national examinations to earn the initial certificate to teach.
- Teachers practice under the supervision of mentor teachers and administrators in order to gain a license to teach.
- Teachers continually engage in ongoing study and professional development to renew their licenses to teach and to keep current in their fields.
- Teachers follow codes of ethical conduct established by professional organizations, state departments of education, and local school districts.
- Teachers exercise autonomy by continually making decisions about what and how to teach.
- Teachers belong to professional organizations as one means for ongoing professional development.
- Teachers are held in high regard by the communities in which they teach.

Teaching is a helping profession. Teachers are dedicated to helping students learn and grow. Teachers are also committed to helping parents, families, and communities build strong educational programs. Your decision to become a teacher—to be able to say, "I am a teacher"—is an ennobling one. You might be pursuing a traditional teacher education program, working toward certification and a license to teach, or you might be involved in an alternative, nontraditional program.

The following are some programs whereby you and others can become a teacher:

- A traditional 4-year teacher education program leading to a baccalaureate degree.
- A 5-year program leading to a bachelor's and a master's degree and teacher certification.
- An alternative or a nontraditional teacher education program. These programs can be offered outside a college setting. Many school districts conduct alternative teacher education programs.
- A master's degree in education resulting in teacher certification. These programs are often called *post-bac certification* programs.

Regardless of the path you have chosen, you will change your life and the lives of those you teach. In the final analysis, it is what you do with your talents, abilities, and knowledge that will enable you to be called a professional.

REFLECT & WRITE

Which teacher certification program are you enrolled in? Do you think alternative certification undermines this goal?

Becoming a Teacher: Praxis and Teacher Certification Testing

Most professions have specific requirements for licensure. As a requirement for licensure and entry into teaching, you will more than likely have to pass a standardized test as part of your certification process. Many states require a passing score on a state-developed test or on the **Praxis** series of professional assessment for beginning teachers. The Praxis series is developed and administered by the Educational Testing Service (ETS) and consists of academic skills assessments, subject assessments, and classroom performance assessments.

Praxis, which means "theory into practice," is used by nearly 88 percent of the states that require testing as a component of their teacher licensure process, and the exams are given three times annually.[3] Praxis is explained in greater detail in Chapter 13, as are other topics relating to teacher certification.

Not all states require Praxis for initial certification. However, the chances are good that you will have to pass a state exam for initial certification. For example, whereas Praxis is required in Connecticut, Delaware, Georgia, and New Hampshire, in Alabama a college or university exam is required, as well as meeting requirements of the Alabama Prospective Teacher Testing Program (APTTP), whereas in Texas, a state exam, the Texas Examinations of Educator Standards (TExES), is required of all who seek initial certification.

Professionals also are subject to ongoing or routine evaluation for quality of performance. As a teacher, you will participate in a performance review at least annually and may be required to take tests at various points during your career.

Praxis   A national battery of tests prepared by the Educational Testing Service available for the initial certification of teachers. Consists of assessments in three areas: academic skills, knowledge of subject, and classroom performance.

Up-to-date information about Praxis is available on the ETS website (www.ets.org/praxis).

WHAT ARE THE DIMENSIONS OF PROFESSIONALISM AND WHY ARE THEY IMPORTANT?

Professionalism has five integrated dimensions, all of which are important to your present and future growth as a high-quality teacher. The five dimensions of professionalism are:

1. Content knowledge
2. Pedagogical content knowledge and skills
3. Professional and pedagogical knowledge and skills
4. Student learning
5. Professional dispositions

Each of these dimensions plays a powerful role in determining who and what a professional is and how professionals practice in the classroom. Let's consider each of these dimensions and see how you can apply them to your developing professional practice (see Figure 2.1).

Content Knowledge

Professionals know the content knowledge they plan to teach and can explain important principles and concepts outlined in professional, state, and institutional standards.[4] This means that you will know the content of your discipline, whatever that discipline is (e.g., English, language arts, mathematics, science, social studies, computer science, technology education, health, physical education, foreign languages, English as a second language, or special education). In addition to knowing the content of your discipline, you will be able to pass state content ex-

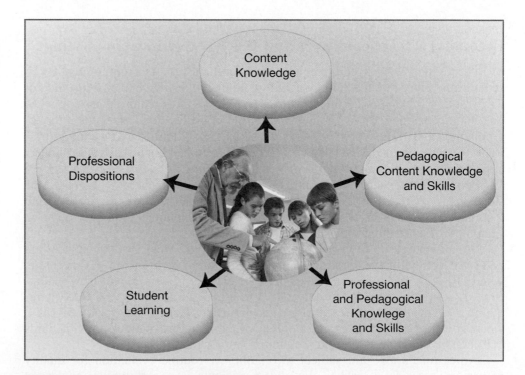

FIGURE 2.1   The Five Dimensions of Professionalism

How can you implement these five dimensions in your teaching practice?

aminations in states that require them for licensure. Ann Stewart is a middle school physical education teacher at Basalt Middle School in Colorado. Ann's colleagues say that "Her knowledge of all topics related to physical education and middle school education is impressive."[5]

Pedagogical Content Knowledge and Skills

The pedagogical content knowledge and skills dimension of professionalism means that you understand the relationship of content and content-specific pedagogy as outlined in professional and state standards. It also means that you have a broad knowledge of instructional strategies and that you can facilitate student learning of content in clear and meaningful ways and through the integration of technology (see Chapter 12).[6]

Professional and Pedagogical Knowledge and Skills

Applying professional and pedagogical knowledge and skills means that you consider the school, family, and community contexts in which you work (see Chapter 6) and use the prior experiences of your students to develop meaningful learning experiences. It also means that you reflect on your practice.[7] In addition, your professional knowledge base includes:

- Applying knowledge related to the social, historical, and philosophical foundations of education (see Chapter 9)
- Professional ethics, law, and policy (see Chapter 8)
- Cultural influences on learning and diversity of student populations (see Chapter 4)
- Exceptionalities (see Chapter 5)
- Integrating technology (see Chapter 12)
- Using research in teaching and other professional roles[8]

Ethical Behavior: Acting on High Morals and Values

Professional teachers practice in ways that are legally and ethically proper. Professionals want to do what is right and honest in their relationships with students, colleagues, and parents.

Many professions, such as medicine and law, have unified and universal codes of ethics that govern practice. Although the teaching profession lacks such a code, professional organizations, such as the **National Education Association (NEA)**, have codes of ethics (see Figure 2.2). The *Ethical Dilemma* at the end of all chapters will help you apply ethical practices and will sharpen your skills in making ethical decisions.

Civility is an important part of ethical behavior and a requirement when working with each and every student; such behavior includes courtesy, patience, tolerance, respect, and acts of kindness and helpfulness in interaction with children, parents and families, colleagues, and others. As a teacher, you should also demonstrate dedication, trustworthiness, enthusiasm, understanding,

National Education Association (NEA) The oldest and largest professional association for teachers and administrators.

OBSERVE & LEARN

Seeing the five dimensions of professionalism in action in everyday classroom practice is a good way for you to familiarize yourself with them. You can start now to develop concrete practices for how you can implement them in your teaching. Observe in a classroom of your choice. Give specific examples of how a teacher demonstrates any or all of the five dimensions.

PREAMBLE

The educator, believing in the worth and dignity of each human being, recognizes the supreme importance of the pursuit of truth, devotion to excellence, and the nurture of democratic principles. Essential to these goals is the protection of freedom to learn and to teach and the guarantee of equal educational opportunity for all. The educator accepts the responsibility to adhere to the highest ethical standards.

The educator recognizes the magnitude of the responsibility inherent in the teaching process. The desire for the respect and confidence of one's colleagues, of students, of parents, and of the members of the community provides the incentive to attain and maintain the highest possible degree of ethical conduct. The *Code of Ethics of the Education Profession* indicates the aspiration of all educators and provides standards by which to judge conduct.

The remedies specified by the NEA and/or its affiliates for the violation of any provision of this *Code* shall be exclusive and no such provision shall be enforceable in any form other than one specifically designated by the NEA or its affiliates.

PRINCIPLE I

Commitment to the Student

The educator strives to help each student realize his or her potential as a worthy and effective member of society. The educator therefore works to stimulate the spirit of inquiry, the acquisition of knowledge and understanding, and the thoughtful formulation of worthy goals. In fulfillment of the obligation to the student, the educator—

1. Shall not unreasonably restrain the student from independent action in the pursuit of learning.
2. Shall not unreasonably deny the student access to varying points of view.
3. Shall not deliberately suppress or distort subject matter relevant to the student's progress.
4. Shall make reasonable effort to protect the student from conditions harmful to learning or to health and safety.
5. Shall not intentionally expose the student to embarrassment or disparagement.
6. Shall not on the basis of race, color, creed, sex, national origin, marital status, political or religious beliefs, family, social or cultural background, or sexual orientation, unfairly—

a. Exclude any student from participation in any program.
b. Deny benefits to any student.
c. Grant any advantage to any student.
7. Shall not use professional relationships with students for private advantage.
8. Shall not disclose information about students obtained in the course of professional service, unless disclosure serves a compelling professional purpose or is required by law.

PRINCIPLE II

Commitment to the Profession

The education profession is vested by the public with a trust and responsibility requiring the highest ideals of professional service.

In the belief that the quality of the services of the education profession directly influences the nation and its citizens, the educator shall exert every effort to raise professional standards, to promote a climate that encourages the exercise of professional judgment, to achieve conditions which attract persons worthy of the trust to careers in education, and to assist in preventing the practice of the profession by unqualified persons.

In fulfillment of the obligation to the profession, the educator—

1. Shall not in an application for a professional position deliberately make a false statement or fail to disclose a material fact related to competency and qualifications.
2. Shall not misrepresent his/her professional qualifications.
3. Shall not assist any entry into the profession of a person known to be unqualified in respect to character, education, or other relevant attribute.
4. Shall not knowingly make a false statement concerning the qualifications of a candidate for a professional position.
5. Shall not assist a noneducator in the unauthorized practice of teaching.
6. Shall not disclose information about colleagues obtained in the course of professional service unless disclosure serves a compelling professional purpose or is required by law.
7. Shall not knowingly make false or malicious statements about a colleague.
8. Shall not accept any gratuity, gift, or favor that might impair or appear to influence professional decisions or action.

—Adopted by 1975 Representative Assembly. © 2002, 2006 nea.org

FIGURE 2.2 NEA Code of Ethics of the Education Profession

Use this code of ethics to help you to behave ethically in your classroom.

Source: National Education Association of the United States, *Code of Ethics.* (Online). Available at www.nea.org/aboutnea/code.html. Reprinted by permission.

intelligence, and motivation. If we want these qualities in our future professionals, we need to promote them now, in our teaching of all students. Home and school experiences are critical for developing these character qualities.

Reflective Practice

Professionals are always thinking about and reflecting on what they have done, what they are doing, and what they will do. The following is a good guideline for thinking and reflecting: Think before you teach, think while you are teaching, and think after you teach. This cycle of **reflective practice** will help you to become a good professional and will help your students learn.

Consider for a moment the importance of reflective practice in Michael Kelly's professional practice. Michael is a physical education teacher at Mountain Ridge Middle School in Mountain Ridge, Colorado, and was named an Outstanding Young Professional by the Colorado Association for Health, Physical Education, Recreation, and Dance:

> Michael is a model of collaboration and professionalism. He continually reflects on his practice and seeks refinement through study, collegial interaction, and feedback. Michael's natural ability to form authentic and purposeful relationships with kids and colleagues makes him a powerful adult role model in the building. He understands that positive classroom and building culture impacts social and academic growth for all students. Through his coaching, he teaches lifelong lessons of compassion, teamwork, and motivation.[9]

Student Learning

Teaching is all about student learning. In fact, as you know from our discussion so far, American education places a high premium on student achievement. Part of being a professional means that you can assess and analyze student learning, make appropriate adjustments to your instruction, and monitor student progress. You also are able to develop and implement meaningful learning experiences for your students based on their developmental levels and prior experiences.[10] Math teacher Luajean Bryan in Cleveland, Tennessee, used hot air balloon rides to generate acceleration and velocity data for her calculus class. Encouraged by her administrators, Bryan has used large projects since moving to Walker Valley High when it opened in 2001. "Before, I didn't think I could teach with the projects without interfering with the curriculum," she says. But she saw that the students responded well to them, and the math concepts stuck better. "The students connect with the material in a way they wouldn't have otherwise," she says. The projects are just one product of Bryan's enthusiasm for math and exhaustive efforts to help students master it. Her students know she is available before and after school to help them, and she has a standing policy allowing students to get before- or after-school tutoring and then retake a bombed test. "She works hard to make sure you grasp the concepts more than anything," says 17-year-old student John Gibson. "She doesn't leave anybody behind."[11]

Developmentally Appropriate Practice

Part of your knowledge base as a professional is knowing child and adolescent development. This knowledge enables you to understand how your students grow and develop across all developmental areas—cognitive, linguistic, social, emotional, and physical. Once armed with knowledge of child growth and development, you will be able to provide care and education that is appropriate for every child. Such knowledge is essential for understanding how to conduct developmentally appropriate instruction, which is the recommended teaching practice of the profession.

Developmentally appropriate practice (DAP), which is based on how children grow and develop and on individual and cultural differences, goes far beyond mere knowledge of how children develop:

> Developmentally appropriate practice requires that teachers integrate the many dimensions of their knowledge base. They must know about child development and the implications of this knowledge for how to teach, the content of the curriculum—what to teach and when—how to assess what children have learned, and how to adapt curriculum and instruction to children's individual strengths, needs, and interests. Further, they must know the particular children they teach and their families and be knowledgeable as well about the social and cultural context.[12]

Reflective Practice The active process of thinking before teaching, during teaching, and after teaching in order to make decisions about how to plan, assess, and teach.

Go to MyEducationLab and select the topic "Learning Readiness to Learn/Children and Adolescents." Read the article "Differentiating for Tweens" and then answer the questions that follow.

Developmentally appropriate practice (DAP) Practice based on how children grow and develop and on individual and cultural differences.

Teachers who use developmentally appropriate practice in their classrooms derive satisfaction when they see that their students are engaged and enthusiastic about learning.

Award-winning teacher Nina Lavlinskaia at High Tech High School in New Jersey puts developmentally appropriate practice into use by supporting students as they make life choices. She recognizes the underachiever who wants to blossom and the exemplary student who is missing a passion for learning. As educators struggle to reverse declining interest in science, Lavlinskaia has contributed to nearly 20 percent of High Tech's graduates choosing science majors in college—a particularly notable achievement for a school where 40 percent of students are considered "at risk" and more than 70 percent are from minority backgrounds. Annie Rose London, a senior at High Tech, said Lavlinskaia—or "Dr. Nina" to her students—"made me fall in love with biology." "Dr. Nina's enthusiasm is utterly contagious," London said. "I am not alone in this belief—she is the only teacher I have ever had who has managed to create a real family that students stay connected to even after they graduate."[13]

Jessie Auger, the 2006–2007 Massachusetts Teacher of the Year, demonstrates developmentally appropriate practice in her classroom at the Rafael Hernandez School in Boston, Massachusetts. Jessie aims to create a learning environment that will help her students to become confident, competent, and successful.[14] She works closely with the five other teachers on the K–1 team to provide high-quality integrated curriculum that meets the needs of a wide range of learners. What gives Jessie the greatest satisfaction is seeing her students develop skills with joy and excitement, filled with pride in their newly created competence.[15] In math class, Jessie routinely asks her students to develop their own problem-solving strategies and to record their ideas in their own ways. Students explain their thinking and questions as they discuss problems and construct mathematical understanding together. During these discussions, Jessie points out connections between students' ideas, maintains high expectations for listening to one another, and models how to ask for clarity. In this way, the students learn that their own ideas are always the starting places for problem solving.[16]

Professional Dispositions

Professional dispositions   The values, commitments, and ethical decisions and practices that influence behavior toward students, families, colleagues, and members of the profession and community.

As a professional, you will be familiar with the professional dispositions described in professional and state standards. **Professional dispositions** are values, commitments, and ethical decisions and practices that influence behavior toward students, families, colleagues, and members of the profession and community. You will demonstrate classroom behaviors that are consistent with the idea of fairness and the belief that all students can learn.[17] The faculty of the College of Education at California State University in San Marcos identifies the following dispositions for all of its preservice teachers:

- Social justice and equity
- Collaboration
- Critical thinking
- Professional ethics
- Reflective teaching and learning
- Lifelong learning[18]

Additional Dispositions

Other dispositions that are crucial for a successful teaching professional are love and respect for children and their families, compassion, empathy, friendliness, sensitivity, warmth, and caring.

For teaching professionals, caring is a very important disposition. Effective teachers care about students; they accept and respect all students and their cultural and socioeconomic backgrounds. As a professional, you will work in classrooms, programs, and other settings where things do not always go smoothly—for example, students will not always learn ably and well, and they will not always be clean and free from illness and hunger. Students' and their parents' backgrounds and ways of life will not always be the same as yours. Caring means that you will lose sleep trying to find a way to help a student learn to read and you will spend long hours planning and gathering materials. Caring also means that you will not leave your intelligence, enthusiasm, and other talents at home but will bring them into the center, the classroom, administration offices, boards of directors' meetings, and wherever else you can make a difference in the lives of students and their families.

If you do not already know the professional dispositions for your teacher education program, now would be a good time for you to ask your professors for them.

Advocacy

Many colleges and universities across the United States include advocacy as one of their professional dispositions. **Advocacy** is the act of pleading the causes of your students and their families to the profession and the public and engaging in strategies designed to improve their circumstances. Advocates move beyond their day-to-day professional responsibilities and work collaboratively to help others. Students and their families need adults who understand their needs and who will work to improve their health, education, and well-being. You and other teaching professionals are in a unique position to know and understand your students and their needs and to make a difference in their lives.

Advocacy The act of engaging in strategies designed to improve the circumstances of children and families. Advocates move beyond their day-to-day professional responsibilities and work collaboratively to help others.

There is no shortage of issues to advocate for in the lives of your students and their families. Some of the issues that are in need of strong advocates involve quality programs, abuse and neglect prevention, poverty, good housing, and health. In order to change policies and procedures that negatively affect your students, you must become actively engaged. The following are some of the ways in which you can practice advocacy for students and their families:

- *Become familiar with organizations that advocate for students and their families,* such as the Children's Defense Fund, Stand for Children, and Voices for America's Children.
- *Participate in community activities that support students and their families.* Help others in your community who work to make a difference. Donate to an organization that supports children and families or volunteer your time at a local event that supports students. For example, at Meadow Lands Elementary School, third-grade teacher Maria Hinajosa organized a walkathon to raise money to buy new multicultural books for the school library and classrooms.
- *Investigate the issues that face students and their families today.* Read the news and become informed about relevant issues. For example, subscribe to an e-mail newsletter from a group that supports students and their families, then share the news with colleagues, family, and friends.
- *Talk to others about the issues that face students and their families.* Identify a specific concern you have for students and their families, and talk to others about that issue. For example, if you are concerned about the number of your students who do not have adequate health care, learn the facts about the issue in your community and then talk to people about ways to solve the problem. Begin with your own circle of influence—your colleagues, friends, family members, and those in other social groups in which you are a member.
- *Seek opportunities to share your knowledge of students.* Inform others about the needs of students by speaking with groups. For example, volunteer to meet with a group of parents at a local school event to help them learn how to help their children with their homework.
- *Identify leaders who can help you make desired changes.* Learn who the leaders are who represent you in local, state, and national government. For

example, identify the members of the local school board, and find out who represents you on the board. When issues arise, contact that person to express your concerns and offer solutions.

- *Enlist the support of others.* Contact others who can help you to disseminate information about an issue. For example, enlist the help of your local PTA in a letter-writing effort to inform town leaders about the need for safety improvements at the local playground.[19]

- *Develop an advocacy relationship with students.* For example, all students benefit from a relationship with a significant adult. Such a relationship fosters increased academic success and supports student needs throughout school. At East Chapel Hill High School in North Carolina, teachers have created an advocacy group in which teachers meet with student advocates. Active student participation in the advocacy group promotes a sense of belonging to the wider school community. Student advocates accomplish the following through the advocacy program:
  - Conduct regular self-assessment of academic progress during the year in all subjects, concentrating specifically on major projects and test performance.
  - Engage in discussion of issues important to the school and community.
  - Receive assistance in monitoring and planning the completion of the service learning requirement.[20]

- *Be persistent.* Identify an issue you are passionate about, and find a way to make a difference. There are many ways to advocate for all students and their families. Change takes time!

In Chapter 1, we went into the classroom of National Teacher of the Year Betsy Rogers, who talked with us about how teaching is a way of life. We now go back into Betsy's classroom where she shares with us the true meaning of being a professional.

In the Classroom
with **Betsy Rogers**
"I have a practice."

To establish a professional climate, as teachers we must first view ourselves as professional educators with a teaching practice. I taught almost 20 years before I really understood that I had a professional practice. This revelation came to me in the wee hours of the night while working on my National Board Certification Portfolio. The questions continually referred to my practice and it finally dawned on me that, "I had a practice!" (in my mind only doctors and lawyers had a practice). I loved this concept and I used the phrase throughout my portfolio, "In my practice . . ." I used it so frequently that my colleague who did much of my proofreading would scratch it out every time. Maybe he did not know he also had a practice! Teachers must have this sense of professionalism.

In my school, I see a need for models of how professionalism looks at various stages. I was blessed to have mentors along my way who demonstrated to me what it is to maintain a professional manner even in difficult circumstances, never start the day without being completely prepared, were actively involved in professional development, constantly strived to improve their teaching, and are not embarrassed about being passionate about their work.

Source: Available at http://blogs.edweek.org/teachers/brogers/archives/2005/04/. Accessed on November 29, 2007.

HOW DO YOU DEVELOP A PHILOSOPHY OF EDUCATION?

Professional practice includes teaching with and from a philosophy of education, which helps you to base your teaching on what you believe about students and their families. A **philosophy of education** is a set of beliefs about how students develop and learn and what and how they should be taught.

Your philosophy of education is based on your philosophy of life. What you believe about yourself, about others, and about life infuses your philosophy of education. Knowing what others believe is important and useful, because it can help you clarify what you believe, but when all is said and done you have to know what *you* believe. Moment by moment, day by day, what you believe influences what you will teach and how you will teach it.

A philosophy of education is more than an opinion. A personal philosophy is based on core values and beliefs. **Core values** relate to your beliefs about the nature of life, the purpose of life, your role and calling in life, and your relationship and responsibilities to others. **Core beliefs** and values about education and teaching include what you believe about the nature of students and the purpose of education and the role of teachers. Your philosophy of education will guide and direct your daily teaching. Your beliefs about how students learn best will determine whether you individualize instruction or try to teach the same thing in the same way to everyone.

As you read this text, start developing your own philosophy of education. Once you have determined your philosophy of education, write it down and have others read it. This will help you to clarify your ideas and redefine your thoughts, because your philosophy should be understandable to others (although they do not necessarily have to agree with you).

Finally, evaluate your philosophy against the following points:

- Does my philosophy accurately reflect my beliefs about teaching? Have I been honest with myself?
- Do other people understand my philosophy?
- Does my philosophy provide practical guidance for teaching?
- Are my ideas consistent?
- Have I been comprehensive, stating my beliefs about (1) how students learn, (2) what students should be taught, (3) how students should be taught, (4) the conditions under which students learn best, and (5) what qualities make up a good teacher?

Philosophy of education Beliefs about children's development and learning and the best ways to teach them.

Core values The values that relate to your beliefs about the nature and purposes of life; your role and calling in life; and your relationship and responsibilities to others.

Core beliefs The beliefs that include what you believe about the nature of students, the purpose of education, and the role of teachers.

Go to MyEducationLab and select the topic "Curriculum and Instruction," then read the article "Having It All." Complete the related activities.

HOW DO YOU USE RESEARCH IN PROFESSIONAL PRACTICE?

Teaching is a research-based profession. Strengthening the teaching profession depends on increasing the knowledge base for teaching through research *and* basing professional practices on research and the results of student assessment. Using research to anchor teaching is extremely important to the profession of teaching.

> A consistent body of data has developed around a few well-researched teacher behaviors which show a strong correlation with gains in academic achievement. Research findings have relevance and potential usefulness as a basis for developing prescriptions for practice, but valid use of the findings requires interpretation by educators who are knowledgeable about classroom functioning and mindful of the limitations and qualifications that must be placed on any guidelines induced from such research.[21]

As a beginning teacher, you will be expected to base your teaching on what research says constitutes good teaching and practices that promote quality learning and schools.

As we have discussed, the No Child Left Behind Act holds states, school districts, and schools accountable for student achievement. The regular assessment of students provides data that inform decisions about how best to increase achievement. **Data-driven instruction** is based on such data. Data from assessment can be useful for focusing major stakeholders in the educational process. We will discuss data-driven instruction in more detail in Chapter 11.

Data-driven instruction   The practice of using assessment data measuring student performance to evaluate and change instructional practice so that all students succeed.

Professional Development Schools

Professional development school (PDS)   A school that has formed a partnership with a college or university for the purposes of improving teacher preparation programs, student achievement, and reforming schools.

A **professional development school (PDS)**, also called a professional practice school (PPS) or partner school, is a collaboration of schools, colleges, or departments of education with four major functions: preparation of new teachers, support of student achievement, teacher induction, and development of school and university faculty practice. According to the American Association of Colleges for Teacher Education, the purpose of professional development schools is to "identify, develop, test, and refine practices that promote student achievement; to support initial preparation and continuing professional development for teachers and other school-based educators; and to support applied inquiry designed to improve pupil and educator development."[21]

The University of South Carolina's College of Education is a pioneer in the development of PDSs as vehicles for creating learning communities. The PDS communities provide guidance to teachers, administrators, counselors, and other support personnel as well as professional development opportunities for inservice educators and research opportunities focused on increasing student achievement. The 17 PDSs that form the University of South Carolina (USC) PDS Network include 2 high schools, 2 middle schools, 1 child development center, 1 magnet school, and 11 elementary schools in 6 school districts in the Greater Columbia area, including the Fort Jackson School District. PDS teachers spend time investigating, developing, and sharing curricular innovations. For example, teachers develop and participate in onsite research projects. They are actively involved in focus and inquiry groups; take courses offered on curriculum, instruction, and assessment (on and offsite); and attend and present at USC PDS Network–sponsored workshops and conferences.[22] More than 1,000 PDSs are currently in

Go to MyEducationLab, select the topic "Theory and Research" then watch the video, "Research: Early Adolescence" and complete the activities.

operation. They facilitate the development of new knowledge and are an important part of the reform of teacher education.[23]

Teacher as Researcher

Individual teachers also conduct classroom research through systematic observation and analysis in decision-making contexts. Chapter 1 introduced the concept of teacher as researcher and pointed out that part of the new teacher's role is to engage in action research. **Action research**, shown in Figure 2.3, is a continuing process whereby teachers identify a problem specific to their own teaching and plan and implement a program to solve the identified problem. Teachers study and reflect on the outcomes of their action research. This reflection produces more questions for teachers to investigate, and the action research cycle begins again. Through action research, teachers seek to solve classroom and school-based problems and apply their solutions to everyday practice. Read now how two teachers used action research in their teaching practice in *In the Classroom with Susan Kraus and Stacia Stribling* on page 52.

Action research   The continuing process whereby teachers identify a problem specific to their own classroom situation and plan and implement a program to solve the problem.

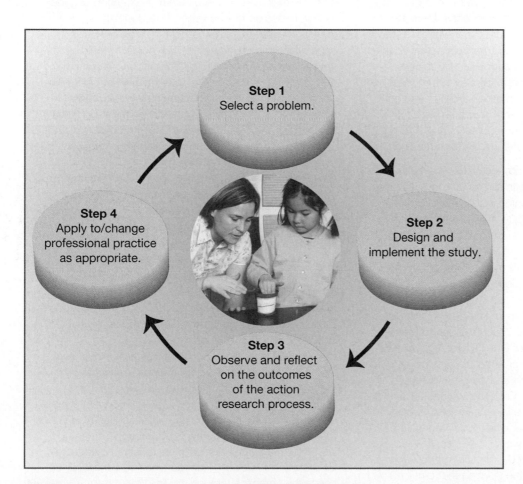

FIGURE 2.3   The Empowerment of Teachers through Action Research

One source of information for decision making is action research. Use these steps when conducting your own action research project.

In the Classroom

with **Susan Kraus and Stacia Stribling**

Action Research

Susan Kraus is a first-grade teacher with 25 years of experience at the elementary school level. Stacia Stribling, a former first-grade teacher, is on the instructional faculty of the Initiatives in Educational Transformation Master's Program at George Mason University.

As veteran teachers, we recognize that in order to meet the various needs of our students and build on the experiences they bring to the classroom, we must continue to be learners ourselves. Our learning never ends; there are always aspects of our classroom practice that warrant further exploration and experimentation, and we believe that action research is an important tool that supports this process. While all teachers might try new approaches in their classrooms, teacher researchers systematically collect data and reflect on classroom practice in order to more deeply understand the teaching and learning process. The following four steps are essential when conducting action research:

■ *Develop a question.* In this step, teachers choose a piece of their curriculum to examine in depth, asking questions not only about *what* is happening in the classroom around this curriculum but *why* it might be happening. In our action research project, we decided to look at first-grade writers and how to help them set their own writing goals and be active participants in the assessment of their writing. Armed with this piece of our curriculum, we formed our initial research question: "What happens when first-graders set their own writing goals?" With action research, we, as teachers, must be open to the research questions evolving over time. Therefore, while we began with this question, the process of implementing strategies, collecting data, and analyzing the data led us to refine the question. One of the goals we had for our students was for them to write more interesting stories, so in the end, our question became: "How can we emphasize story content in our writing instruction?" Teachers must be flexible and allow their inquiry process to be shaped by the students and the learning that emerges throughout the research project.

■ *Collect and analyze data.* In action research, data collection and analysis are intertwined. Teachers collect various types of data, such as student work, student surveys, field notes,

and teacher reflective journals, in order to assess the impact of their instruction. But unlike traditional quantitative research methods, action research requires that this data be analyzed as it is collected rather than waiting until the end of the project. By continually interpreting the data, searching for emerging themes and deeper understandings, teachers can adjust their instruction. For example, in our research study we developed a lesson where students analyzed their own stories to determine elements of good writing. Based on interviews conducted with the students, we assumed that they would focus on the mechanics (i.e., capitalization and punctuation), and our task would be to develop activities that focused students on the content of their compositions. Once we looked at the new data—our observations of the lesson documented in field notes—we realized that students already recognized the importance of content as an element of good writing; this analysis pushed us to rethink our instruction in order to build on what the students already understood.

■ *Draw conclusions.* While each piece of data has the potential to inform a teacher's understanding of the learning process, it is the pattern of understanding across the data sets that lead to powerful conclusions. For example, we encountered information about students' ability to reflect on their writing process in our research project, but a stronger theme that emerged across multiple data samples centered on the tension between content and mechanics in first-grade writing. Therefore, we drew conclusions based on this tension supported by the evidence found within our data.

■ *Develop the next steps.* Action research provides teachers an opportunity to develop a deeper understanding of the teaching and learning process, knowledge that is invaluable to classroom practice. Equally important are the new questions that often emerge within action research projects that can then be explored through further studies. Action research, therefore, becomes a powerful tool for professional development as teachers continually enhance their practice through inquiry.

You can access Susan Kraus' and Stacia Stribling's action research study at www.journal.naeyc.org/btj/vp/VoicesStriblingKraus.pdf.

WHAT OPPORTUNITIES EXIST FOR PROFESSIONAL DEVELOPMENT?

As a beginning teacher and throughout your teaching, you will be involved in an ongoing process of **professional development**, which consists of learning opportunities designed to help you gain new knowledge, skills, and attitudes, resulting in increased effectiveness.

The terms *professional development*, *staff development*, and *teacher inservice education* are often used synonymously. The No Child Left Behind Act suggests that high-quality professional development includes activities that

- Improve and increase teachers' knowledge of academic subjects and enable teachers to become highly qualified.
- Ensure that teachers are an integral part of broad schoolwide and districtwide educational improvement plans.
- Give teachers and principals the knowledge and skills to help students meet challenging state academic standards.
- Improve classroom management skills.
- Are sustained, intensive, and classroom-focused and are not one-day or short-term workshops.
- Advance teacher understanding of effective instruction strategies based on scientific research.
- Are developed with extensive participation of teachers, principals, parents, and administrators.[24]

Part of your professional development may occur in a **professional learning community**, which includes grade-level teaching teams, school and district committees, and middle and high school department groups.

Professional Organizations for Teachers

Teachers are represented by professional and labor organizations such as the National Education Association (NEA) and the **American Federation of Teachers (AFT)**. These organizations exert considerable influence on conditions of employment, organization, governance, compensation and benefits, and curriculum.

The NEA, now with 3.2 million members, was founded in 1857 "to elevate the character and advance the interest of the profession of teaching and to promote the cause of education in the United States."[25] The AFT, founded in 1916, has over 1.3 million members. "The mission of the [AFT AFL-CIO] is to improve the lives of our members and their families, to give voice to their legitimate professional, economic, and social aspirations, to strengthen the institutions in which we work, to improve the quality of the services we provide, to bring together all members to assist and support one another, and to promote democracy, human rights, and freedom in our union, in our nation, and throughout the world."[26] The NEA and AFT have formed the NEAFT partnership, an agreement that leaves both groups free to differ and to conduct work separately but also enables them to collaborate on joint projects and expand their areas of cooperation.[27]

Both organizations influence the nature of the relationship among teachers, principals, and boards of education. Unions help set the conditions of employment and the conditions for school-based management and reform. Unions also are very much involved in the professional development of teachers, informing the public about the nature and needs of public education, and in political activities aimed at influencing the nature and course of education. The NEA and AFT are politically active and support and endorse candidates they believe support their positions on

Professional development The process of growing and becoming a professional.

Professional learning community A defined group of educational stakeholders brought together to enable teachers and others to collaborate in support of reflective practice, action research, and ongoing professional development.

American Federation of Teachers (AFT) A national professional association for teachers, affiliated with the AFL-CIO; the second-largest organization of educators.

■ INTASC

STANDARD 10 The teacher fosters relationships with school colleagues, parents, and agencies in the larger community to support students' learning and well-being.

Membership in professional organizations offers teachers numerous opportunities for taking part in meetings and conferences that promote professional growth and development and peer networking.

education and will help implement their goals. They also confront issues that encourage equity and fairness to teachers. For example, NEA president Reg Weaver has been promoting the message that the teaching profession must not only be well prepared, but also ethnically diverse. This makes sense, because nearly 40 percent of public school students are minorities, but just 11 percent of the teachers are. Over one-third of America's public schools have no person of color on staff. "With public schools redoubling their commitment to closing achievement gaps and ensuring that all teachers are highly qualified," Weaver notes, "recruiting and retaining more teachers of color can be crucial to our success in these areas."[28]

In contrast to their role in social activism, teachers' unions are sometimes seen as preserving the status quo in terms of how schools operate and how teachers are hired and dismissed. Critics of schools frequently cite teachers' unions as a barrier to change. However, noted education historian Diane Ravitch maintains that, "Teacher unions around the country continue to play important roles in protecting the rights of teachers, especially in the current climate of school reform." She also states that teachers' unions are needed "to protect teachers' rights, to sound the alarm against unwise policies, and to advocate on behalf of sound education policies."[29]

As a beginning teacher, you might not have a choice of whether to join the union. In some instances, belonging to a union is part of the contractual process. Nonetheless, you can take your role and responsibilities as a union member seriously and work within the organization for change and for improving the profession.

Independent Teacher Organizations

In addition to NEA and AFT, there are also many large independent teachers' organizations. The largest of these are:

- United Federation of Teachers, 140,000 members.
- Association of Texas Professional Educators, 108,000 members.
- Missouri State Teachers Association, 43,000 members.
- Mississippi Professional Educators, over 7,800 members.
- Professional Educators of North Carolina, 7,500 members.
- Palmetto State Teachers Association (South Carolina), 6,000 members.[30]

Other professional organizations reflect interest in particular content areas or in particular student groups. For instance, in the past decade, professional organizations such as the National Council of Teachers of Mathematics have exerted considerable influence over the content of mathematics and how it is taught. Many organizations that represent professionals in a particular academic area feel that they must take responsibility and initiative for helping determine what should be taught and how the classroom and school should be organized for effective teaching and learning.

Go to MyEducationLab and select "Licensure and Standards" in the Resource Section. Here you will find national standards and links to professional organizations.

The National Association for the Education of Young Children (NAEYC) is the largest professional organization of early childhood professionals, with more than 100,000 members. NAEYC helps improve the professional practice of early childhood educators, sets standards for professional practice, and increases public understanding of high-quality programs for young children and their families.

HOW ARE REFORM MOVEMENTS CHANGING TEACHER EDUCATION?

The reform of schools and the reform of teacher education go hand-in-hand. Colleges and universities are changing how teachers are educated to prepare them for their new roles in schools and to ensure the success of educational reforms.

Just as school reform was and is influenced by reform reports (see Chapter 1), so teacher education reforms are fueled by similar reports. The **Carnegie Task Force on Teaching as a Profession**—which authored *A Nation Prepared: Teachers for the 21st Century*[31]—has been particularly influential. This report was critical of how the nation's colleges and universities prepare teachers and recommended more rigorous education in their preparation. As a result, an increasing number of the 1,300[32] teacher-training programs in the United States are seeking ways to better educate teachers so that they have the knowledge and skills for both effective teaching and effective participation in school restructuring activities. Some colleges of education have formed and joined organized reform groups specifically designed to promote teacher education reform. Some of these are:

- *Holmes Partnership.* The Holmes Partnership (originally the Holmes Group) is named after Henry W. Holmes, former dean of the Harvard Graduate School of Education. One of the major accomplishments of the Holmes Partnership has been the creation of the professional development school (PDS), as discussed in the previous section. The Holmes Partnership, a consortium of research universities, public school districts, and organizations that represent professional educators, has six principal goals:

  Goal 1: High-quality professional preparation. Provide exemplary professional preparation and development programs for public school educators.
  Goal 2: Simultaneous renewal. Engage in the simultaneous renewal of public K–12 schools and teacher education programs.
  Goal 3: Equity, diversity, and cultural competence. Actively work on equity, diversity, and cultural competence in the programs of K–12 schools, higher education, and the education profession.
  Goal 4: Scholarly inquiry and programs of research. Conduct and disseminate educational research and engage in other scholarly activities that advance knowledge, improve teaching and learning for all children and youth, inform the preparation and development of educators, and influence educational policy and practice.
  Goal 5: School and university-based faculty development. Provide high-quality doctoral programs for the future education professoriate and for advanced professional development of school-based educators.
  Goal 6: Policy initiation. Engage in policy analysis and development related to public schools and the preparation of educators.[33]

- *Project 30 Alliance.* This organization endeavors to erase the lines between education and liberal arts courses and to add more liberal arts courses to teacher training. The concept is that teachers should have a thorough knowledge of the subject disciplines they teach.

- *Renaissance Group.* This group believes teacher training programs must have the full support of colleges and universities and that classroom experiences for prospective teachers must begin before their senior year.

Although all teacher education reform efforts differ in their details and the priorities they advocate, they all have reform as the common goal.

Carnegie Task Force on Teaching as a Profession   This group issued the report *A Nation Prepared: Teachers for the 21st Century* criticizing how the nation's colleges and universities prepare teachers and recommending more rigorous teacher education.

A Nation Prepared: Teachers for the 21st Century   A Carnegie Foundation report that criticizes how the nation's colleges and universities prepare teachers and recommends more rigorous teacher preparation.

■ INTASC

STANDARD 9   The teacher is a reflective practitioner who continually evaluates the effects of his/her choices and actions on others (students, parents, and other professionals in the learning community) and who actively seeks out opportunities to grow professionally.

To learn more about Project 30 Alliance visit: http://depts .washington.edu/cedren/nner/ resources/A&STeacherEdStudy.pdf.

More information about the Renaissance Group is available at http://education.csufresno.edu/ rengroup.

Federal legislation, such as NCLB, and state and national standards all influence teacher reform. The intended reform is implemented through several means:

- Colleges of education change and modify their programs, raise standards for admission, and emphasize the teaching of content and pedagogy that students must master to pass university and state teacher tests.
- Federal and state politicians lobby colleges of education to reform their programs.
- Federal agencies and state governments provide grants to entice and encourage colleges of education to reform their programs.

Teacher education reform has resulted in:

- More rigorous teacher education programs
- Teacher education programs based on national and state standards
- Testing programs for licensure and certification
- Higher standards (e.g., higher GPA) for admission to teacher education programs
- Creation of alternative and multiple types of programs for teacher education and certification
- Colleges of education engaging in collaborative programs with public schools, such as professional development schools
- Five-year teacher education programs
- Emphasis on performance-based teaching

REFLECT & WRITE

Identify two ways your teacher education program has been influenced by a reform initiative. Is your education program more challenging as a result? What reform initiatives do you believe benefit beginning teachers the most?

_____

_____

_____

_____

_____

Changing Standards for Teacher Education

One way states are seeking to change and improve teacher education is through new and higher standards. This is reflected through new certification standards that specify what teachers should know and be able to do. Although there is an arbitrary standard for what teachers should know, various organizations also have specific standards for what teachers should know and be able to do.

The Interstate New Teacher Assessment and Support Consortium (INTASC) is a consortium of state education agencies, higher education institutions, and national educational organizations dedicated to the reform of the education, licensing, and ongoing professional development of teachers. Created in 1987, INTASC's primary constituency is state education agencies responsible for teacher licensing and professional development. Its work is guided by one basic premise: an effective teacher must be able to integrate content knowledge with pedagogical understanding to ensure that all students learn and perform at high levels.[34] INTASC has identified 10 core standards that beginning teachers should be able to meet. Review these standards, which are presented in Table 2.1 as a checklist you can use to guide you for how you will become a high-quality teacher.

TABLE 2.1 INTASC Core Standards of What Beginning Teachers Should Know and Be Able to Do: A Developmental Checklist
Review and reflect on each INTASC standard. Then, circle your current level of achievement of each standard. Then, reflect on how you will achieve each standard and a target date for achieving your goals.

Standard	Desired Professional Outcome	Level of Accomplishment (Circle One)	If High Provide Evidence of Accomplishment	If Needs Improvement, Specify Action Plan for Accomplishment	Target Date for Completion of Accomplishment
1. Content Pedagogy	I understand the central concepts, tools of inquiry, and structures of the discipline I teach and can create learning experiences that make these aspects of subject matter meaningful for students.	High Needs Improvement			
2. Student Development	I understand how children learn and develop and can provide learning opportunities that support their intellectual, social, and personal development.	High Needs Improvement			
3. Diverse Learners	I understand how students differ in their approaches to learning and can create instructional opportunities that are adapted to diverse learners.	High Needs Improvement			
4. Multiple Instructional Strategies	I understand and use a variety of instructional strategies to encourage students' development of critical thinking, problem solving, and performance skills.	High Needs Improvement			
5. Motivation and Management	I use an understanding of individual and group motivation and behavior to create a learning environment that encourages positive social interaction, active engagement in learning, and self-motivation.	High Needs Improvement			
6. Communication and Technology	I use knowledge of effective verbal, nonverbal, and media communication techniques to foster active inquiry, collaboration, and supportive interaction in the classroom.	High Needs Improvement			
7. Planning	I plan instruction based upon knowledge of subject matter, students, the community, and curriculum goals.	High Needs Improvement			
8. Assessment	I understand and use formal and informal assessment strategies to evaluate and ensure the continuous intellectual, social, and physical development of the learner.	High Needs Improvement			
9. Reflective Practice: Professional Growth	I am a reflective practitioner who continually evaluates the effects of my choices and actions on others (students, parents, and other professionals in the learning community) and who actively seeks out opportunities to grow professionally.	High Needs Improvement			
10. School and Community Involvement	I foster relationships with school colleagues, parents, and agencies in the larger community to support students' learning and well-being.	High Needs Improvement			

Source: Adapted from Interstate New Teacher Assessment and Support Consortium, *Model Standards for Beginning Teacher Licensing and Development: A Resource for State Dialogue* (Washington, DC: Council of Chief State School Officers, 1992). (Online). Available at www.ccsso.org/content/pdfs/corestrd.pdf. Reprinted by permission.

What Does This Mean for You?

The INTASC standards have implications for you as a teacher education student and as a beginning teacher. For example, you will receive much more extensive and specialized preparation based on theory, research, content area methods, and guided practice than teachers of the past. Furthermore, you will be more accountable for student success, as measured by local, state, and national standards and tests.

More than likely, your teacher preparation program has been and is being influenced by the INTASC standards. As your author, I have integrated the INTASC standards into every chapter and topic. Margin notes alert you to content that addresses INTASC standards. In addition, state and national teacher exams are written to test your and your classmates' knowledge of what standards say you should know and be able to do.

In addition to national organizations setting standards for new teachers, states are also increasing the requirements of teacher education programs. For example, in California, new teachers are required to have a bachelor's degree and to have taken a reading instruction course called Developing English Language Skills, a U.S. Constitution course, a subject matter competency exam, a computer technology course, and a reading-instruction competence assessment. Kansas requires that teacher education graduates have a bachelor's degree and at least a 2.5 GPA for a first-level license. Kansas candidates must also demonstrate recency, meaning graduates must have at least eight credit hours or one year of accredited teaching experience completed within the past six years. These are typical of the ways states and colleges of education are helping ensure that teachers will have sufficient knowledge of the areas in which they will teach.

The American Council of Education (ACE), in its influential report "To Touch the Future: Transforming the Way Teachers are Taught," challenges colleges and universities to reform teacher education. "Colleges and universities have educated virtually every teacher in every classroom in every school in the country; thus, it is colleges and universities that must take responsibility for the way teachers are taught, and ultimately the way children are taught."[35]

What Does This Mean for You?

The reform movement in teacher education will profoundly affect your career as a teacher in a number of ways.

- Both as a preservice teacher and as a beginning teacher, you will have to meet the definition of "highly qualified" that is in place at the national level and in your state and local school district.
- You may have to meet recertification standards at regular intervals. A major trend is for teachers to periodically renew their license to teach through ongoing education. Lifetime licenses to teach are being replaced by periodic demonstrations that teachers meet the "highly qualified" standard.
- As school districts constantly monitor and upgrade their teaching staffs, you will participate in staff development designed to ensure that you and your colleagues are in fact highly qualified, and that you are teaching in ways that will ensure student learning.

A teacher is never finished with her professional education. Current forces of teacher education reform probably will mean that your education is never entirely complete.

Teacher Education Reform: Making Every Teacher Accountable

The school accountability movement has encouraged and promoted reform in teacher education. The public and politicians have demanded more accountability of schools and classroom teachers to increase student achievement and to ensure that all students learn. This school-based accountability movement has, in turn, beamed the spotlight of accountability on colleges of education to educate more highly qualified teachers.

The No Child Left Behind Act also plays a significant role in the reform of teacher education by its call to raise the quality of the nation's teachers. NCLB requires that every student be taught by a highly qualified teacher by 2014. Consequently, colleges of education are under significant pressure to ensure that all of their graduates are "highly qualified." This accounts, in part, for the increased emphasis on testing of teachers to help ensure that they are qualified to teach.

Not only do teachers have to be tested, they must also prepare students who will be tested. As a result, NCLB has caused much controversy. Many teachers feel that they are spending all of their time preparing students for testing. They object to the fact that one test measures teachers' success, students' success, and schools' success. For example, Frank Burger, a high school teacher and NEA member from Grand Blanc, Michigan, stated:

> Each year, I have to give a test that will measure how well our school is doing with respect to NCLB. It does not take into account the other factors that could tell how well a school is achieving. One problem is that high-stakes testing is not the only way to measure a school's success. The other problem is that it feels as if teachers are now teaching to the test so students can pass it. Many factors should be used to help students achieve, not just one test.[36]

In December 2006 the Educator Roundtable organized a petition drive against NCLB. The organization claims that the NCLB Act, among many other things, "misdiagnoses the causes of poor educational development, blaming teachers and students for problems over which they have no control, [and] places control of what is taught in corporate hands many times removed from students, teachers, parents, local school boards, and communities."[37] The petition began with a goal of obtaining 1,000,000 signatures. The petition has gathered about 30,000 signatures since it started in December 2006. Whether you support the No Child Left Behind Act or not, the current emphasis on improving the nation's schools by providing every student with a "highly qualified" teacher will have an impact that should not be underestimated.

Teacher Education Programs in Transition

Reverend Samuel Hall established the first private normal school, or standard teacher-training school, in 1823 in Concord, Vermont. Horace Mann helped establish the first state-supported normal school in 1839 (some sources say 1837) in Lexington, Massachusetts. Formal teacher education began with Henry Bernard in 1867, with the first Department of Education in the federal government and the first normal teaching programs in 1896. Teacher education lasted 2 years and consisted mainly of learning how to teach. Beginning in the 1950s, many normal schools made the transition to state teacher colleges. Gradually, the "teacher" designation was dropped, and today many former normal schools are state universities. So, change in teacher education as in all of education is a natural and evolutionary process. We would expect teacher education to change as society changes and as the public, politicians, and educators develop new visions for what teaching is and what it should be like.

Four-Year Programs

Today, many teacher education programs are 4-year programs. Generally, the first 2 years are devoted to general studies at the "lower division" consisting of arts and sciences courses. Students then meet teacher education admissions requirements—usually grade-point averages and basic skills tests—and are admitted to the teacher education program and "upper-division" courses. The final 2 years are devoted to professional studies and clinical field experiences culminating in a semester-long student teaching experience.

Go to MyEducationLab, select the topic "Professional Development" and watch the video "Types of Professional Knowledge." Answer the questions that follow.

Student teachers gain valuable experience in the classroom through observation and hands-on experiences with children. How might education reforms and the raising of professional standards affect teacher education programs?

Alternative teacher education/certification (AC) programs Programs designed to recruit, prepare, and license individuals who already have at least a bachelor's degree and who often have other careers.

● *Your Turn*

The teaching force is getting older, it is predominantly female, and it lacks diversity. There also is an ongoing teacher shortage. These factors have created a need for more and different kinds of teachers than those educated by traditional colleges of education. One result is the tremendous growth of alternative teacher education programs. Make a list of different kinds of alternative teacher education programs. Begin by logging on to the Troops to Teachers Program at www.proudtoserveagain.com and the National Teacher Recruitment Clearing House at www.rnt.org.

Five-Year Programs

Some professional schools of education, especially those that belong to the Holmes Partnership, have 5-year teacher education programs. These programs are generally of two kinds. The teacher-training program is extended across 5 years, providing for more arts and sciences courses, especially in a content area, and for more field experiences. In these programs, students graduate with a bachelor's degree. In other 5-year programs, students earn a bachelor's degree, which includes only arts and sciences courses, or a combination of arts and sciences classes and education courses as well as field experiences. Students then apply for admission to teacher education and take education courses culminating in a master's degree.

Each type of teacher training program has a number of pros and cons, depending on whose point of view is considered. Four-year programs enable students to enter teaching sooner and cost students less money. They also supply more teachers to meet the rising demand for teachers. Five-year programs provide a more rigorous preparation and a solid grounding in the liberal arts. Not all students agree that entering the teaching field with a master's degree is an advantage. They argue that they have a better chance of getting a job without the master's because they will be hired at a lower level on the salary scale than will a person with a master's degree. Also, they argue that many school districts will reimburse for master's-level courses and provide a salary increment for earning the master's.

Alternative Teacher Education Programs

One of the most influential reforms in teacher education in the past decade has been the emergence and rapid expansion of school-district-based and for-profit programs for providing teacher education and certification. **Alternative teacher education/certification (AC) programs** are designed to:

- Provide quick entry into the teaching profession to those who have a college degree.
- Enable people to easily change careers and enter the teacher workforce without having to complete lengthy and time-consuming teacher preparation programs.
- Enable school districts to train and hire the teachers they need.

In the field of teacher preparation, considerable tension exists as to which of the many pathways to teacher certification is most appropriate and meets schools' needs for high-quality teachers. On the one hand, many believe that traditional 4-year teacher education programs are best at helping students become better teachers. On the other hand, some maintain that alternative certification programs provide teachers a relatively quick and appropriate means for getting much needed teachers into the classroom. Existing college and university teacher preparation programs do not have the capacity to provide the nation with all of the teachers it needs, so there has to be alternative means for people who want to teach to enter the profession. The challenge facing teacher preparation programs is to find a satisfactory means for meeting the nation's insatiable need for teachers.

Preparation for Teaching in Diverse Schools

Students in schools represent the diversity of the population as a whole. They bring varied cultural and ethnic backgrounds and differences in values, learning expectations, and family expectations to the classroom. Some of your students—about one in five—will speak a primary language other than English. Some of your students will be new immigrants who will need your help to make sense of a new language, culture, and behavioral standards.

All students have the same basic needs—for food, clothing, shelter, safety, belonging, and affection. Students also have individual needs based on their individual histories, backgrounds, and how well their basic needs have or have not been met. Your students will also have needs based on their abilities, achievements, and learning styles.

Being aware of the various dimensions of diversity that students have will enable you to better address their educational needs. One of your biggest challenges will be to provide a variety of worthwhile and growth-producing experiences for all your students. The following are some strategies you can use to infuse multicultural content and experiences into your teaching and learning:

- Take multicultural education courses to help you incorporate multicultural education content throughout your curriculum and instruction methods. Multicultural education is very important for helping students develop an awareness of and appreciation of other cultures and beliefs.
- Attend workshops on multicultural education.
- Complete preservice programs on multicultural education that include a field experience in which you are immersed in a culturally diverse community to help prepare you for work in urban schools or for teaching all students in any type of school.
- Team up with teachers who have a thorough knowledge of multicultural education and who focus on multiculturalism in their classrooms.
- Expand your knowledge of multicultural education through as many venues as possible. Readings, preservice experience in multicultural schools, and living in a multicultural community are all ways that you can learn more about diverse cultures and diverse learners. You can also do projects or complete assignments that require you to critically analyze race, class, and gender issues.[38]

■ **INTASC**

STANDARD 3 The teacher understands how students differ in their approaches to learning and creates instructional opportunities that are adapted to diverse learners.

• *Your Turn*

You have just been selected as a student member of a team that will review the college's teacher education program to ensure that it is preparing future teachers to take an active part in multicultural education when they become teaching professionals. What will you want to know about the courses currently being taught in your school's program? What will you suggest that teachers do to prepare themselves for a diverse classroom?

WHO ARE TODAY'S TEACHERS?

When you think about teachers, of whom do you think? Perhaps you think about your favorite teacher from high school or the teacher who helped you learn to read. Perhaps you picture the teacher you want to be. Whatever your vision, the fact is that the nation's 6.2 million teachers are a diverse group. One way of looking at teachers is to examine their characteristics. The following information about teachers and the teaching force will help you understand who teachers are.

Characteristics of the Teaching Force

Table 2.2 reveals two striking characteristics about today's teaching force: It is female and white. Seventy-five percent of all teachers are female, and the overwhelming majority are white or Anglo-European American. Approximately 26 percent of elementary and secondary school teachers are between the ages of 40 and 49, and 42 percent are over 50 years old.[39] The graying of the teaching force means that the demand for teachers will be greater as more teachers approach retirement age. Many people think that the teaching force should be more balanced—that because the student population is more diverse, so too should be the teaching force.

REFLECT & WRITE

What are some implications for having a teaching force that is not as diverse as the student population?

_____

_____

_____

TABLE 2.2 Teachers in Public and Private Elementary and Secondary Schools, 2003–2004

Total	3,500,000
Men	1,104,700
Women	2,395,300
Race/ethnicity	
White	3,104,600
Black	177,100
Hispanic	119,500
Asian or Pacific Islander	35,900
American Indian or Alaskan	41,900
Average Age	
Teachers in public elementary and secondary schools	42.6 years
Teachers in private elementary and secondary schools	42.2 years

Source: National Center for Education Statistics, at _Characteristics of Schools, Districts, Teachers, Principals, and School Libraries in the United States 2003–04. Schools and Staffing Survey, 2006_, tables 18–19, 2. (Online). Available at http://nces.ed.gov/pubs2006/2006313.pdf.

What skills do new professional teachers need to teach diverse students? What reasons are given for seeking to increase racial and ethnic diversity in the teaching force? What reasons are given for seeking to increase the proportion of male teachers in the teaching force?

Teacher Diversity

While the nation's population becomes more multicultural and multiethnic, the teaching force remains nondiverse, much as it was two decades ago. Thirty-eight percent of the student population is multicultural—African American, Latino, Asian American, and Native American—but only 15 percent of the teaching force is multicultural.[40] For the first time in the nation's history, the number of Latino children under age 18 surpasses African American children. Latino children are the largest minority group. The impact of the lack of minority teachers to teach minority students—or indeed students of any culture—stands out in sharper contrast when we look at teacher-to-student ratios. For example, in the Miami-Dade County School System in Florida there is 1 white teacher for every 5 white students, 1 black teacher for every 19 black students, and 1 Latino teacher for every 25 Latino students.[41]

The comparative lack of racial and ethnic diversity among teachers has a number of implications. First, colleges of education and school districts must increase their efforts to recruit and attract minorities into the profession. Second, public and private schools and other agencies must implement programs to attract minority students to teaching as a career.

One effort to provide ethnic diversity in the classrooms is the Call Me MISTER (Men Instructing Students Toward Effective Role Models) teacher recruitment program at Clemson University. This program was created with the intention of increasing the number of black male teachers in states such as South Carolina, where there is an average of just 1 black male teacher for every 4 of the states' 600 elementary schools. The title for the Call Me MISTER recruitment program comes from the movie _In the Heat of the Night_, in which Sydney Poitier tells a southern, white sheriff that, "Up north, they call me Mister Tibbs."[42]

Phi Delta Kappa, the professional fraternity in education, sponsors Future Educators of America (FEA), an organization designed to provide middle and high school students with opportunities to explore teaching as a career option and to help students gain a realistic understanding of the nature of education and the role of the teacher. FEA also helps encourage students from diverse backgrounds to think seriously about the teaching profession. Additionally, FEA offers a chance to influence our nation's future by shaping the future of the education profession and gives teachers opportunities to examine, clarify, and explain their role in students' lives. For colleges, FEA expands the pool of applicants to teacher education programs and provides early identification of potentially excellent future teachers.

Some states, such as South Carolina, have statewide programs to recruit students into teaching, especially minority students. For example, the Teacher Cadet Program for High School Students and the Pro Team Program for Middle School Students actively involve students in opportunities to consider teaching as a career.

More information on the Pro Team Program is available online at www.cerra.org/cadets.asp.

REFLECT & WRITE

Why are there not more men and minorities in teaching? What would you propose to attract minorities and men to the profession?

_____

_____

_____

_____

_____

Teacher Shortage

The U.S. Department of Education estimates than an additional 2.2 million teachers will be needed over the next decade. This number exceeds the annual production of new teachers. More specifically, "hard-to-staff" schools in high-poverty urban and rural districts will require more than 700,000 new teachers over the next 10 years. In light of these daunting figures, low-income districts have enacted new tactics to attract high-quality teachers. Some states provide financial incentives to attract teachers, including scholarships, housing benefits, salary increases, free or discounted training programs, and yearly bonuses.[43] For example, in the Douglas County School District near Denver, Colorado, teachers who demonstrate outstanding performance in boosting school performance are eligible to receive the Outstanding Teacher Award, but instead of just receiving a plaque or certificate, the award comes with a $1,250 bonus. Math teacher Sarah Staebell has won this award several times and states, "My favorite thing I ever got in acknowledgment of my work was a note that my math class wrote to me . . . But the reality is that you need to make more money, and to receive a stipend helps out in more ways than just making you feel good."[44]

The dangers of teacher shortages are far-reaching. Although the growing need for teachers affects all schools, low-income and hard-to-staff schools feel the greatest impact. To counteract these shortages, low-income schools tend to employ greater numbers of teachers who are not highly qualified. It is important that more incentives be offered to experienced, high-quality teachers to improve performance in hard-to-staff schools.[45] See *What's New in Education?* on page 64.

REFLECT & WRITE

Why is it that low-income schools hire teachers who are not highly qualified? Do you want to teach in a low-income school? Why? Why not?

_____

_____

_____

_____

_____

What's *New* in Education?

Investing in Teacher Housing in Chicago

Diana M. Johnson is the director of the CPS Teacher Housing Resource Center in Chicago, Illinois.

Neighborhoods in Chicago feature many diverse housing styles—bungalows, condos, apartments, lofts, single-family homes—but no matter the style, "the Windy City," like most big cities, has big housing costs, which can present a challenge for public school teachers who must reside within the city limits.

To address this problem, the City of Chicago and Chicago Public Schools (CPS) launched a housing program to attract bright, young teachers to the city and to provide incentives to experienced veteran teachers to remain in the system.

In March 2003, the CPS initiated the Teacher Housing Resource Center (THRC), a unit devoted to developing a range of affordable housing options for CPS's 25,000-member teacher workforce and student teachers. Housing options range from short- and long-term rentals to first-time home ownership.

To support teacher intern recruitment, the THRC partners with local community development corporations (CDCs) to provide affordable, furnished rental housing close to Chicago public schools throughout the city. The THRC identifies available apartments, negotiates terms, furnishes the units, and subsidizes the rent. The CDC serves as property manager and community orientation coordinator for the interns who, in addition to their classroom work, learn about the communities in which their students live. The CPS reports that this experience proves extremely grounding for teacher interns; they report better connections with their students by having a broader understanding of the issues their families face every day in the neighborhood.

The CPS offers rental housing discounts from 29 property management partner companies—some with dozens of buildings in their portfolio—located in 28 different Chicago neighborhoods. In exchange for marketing assistance through its website (www.teacherhousing.cps.k12.il.us) and exposure at monthly CPS teacher career fairs, these companies offer full-time Chicago public school teachers up to 2 months in free rent, reduced security deposits, waived application fees, and even free parking at some locations. Through the THRC website, prospective teachers from out of state can learn about Chicago neighborhoods and rental partner companies located close to the Chicago public schools where they will teach; prospective teachers can even take virtual tours of properties and negotiate availability.

As with most other large urban public school districts, retaining highly qualified, experienced teachers remains a major challenge for the CPS. The capstone program of the THRC, home ownership, combats the problem of losing teachers to suburban districts by assisting teachers in purchasing homes in Chicago. The CPS targets teachers in their first 5 years of teaching, when the teacher turnover rate is the highest and their credit rating often underdeveloped. Through several "financial fitness" classes, teachers focus on the goal of home ownership. When they are ready, in exchange for a commitment to continue teaching with the CPS for an additional 5 years, teachers qualify for a grant of up to $7,500, which can be combined with other first-time homebuyer programs, lender discounts, or developer incentives, to purchase their first home in Chicago. By bridging teachers through their fifth year through this program, the CPS reduces attrition, helps teachers build personal wealth, and strengthens Chicago's neighborhoods.

WHAT JOB OPPORTUNITIES DO YOU HAVE AS A TEACHER?

As a prospective teacher, you will analyze job opportunities in terms of a number of key factors: salaries offered, benefits available, and vacancies reflecting teacher demand in different parts of the country and in different subject areas. You will balance these factors with your own feelings about where you want to teach and the students you are most comfortable teaching. The following sections will give you an idea of what to expect.

Salaries and Benefits

Teachers' salaries vary greatly from state to state and region to region. Table 2.3 shows teachers' salaries by state. The lowest-paying states are North Dakota and South Dakota, and the highest-paying states are Connecticut and California, but

TABLE 2.3   What Teachers Earn (estimated teacher salaries by state)

As this table illustrates, where you teach determines, in part, how much you earn. Connecticut is the highest paying state in teacher salaries; South Dakota is the lowest.

State	Average Annual Teacher Salary 2004–2005	State	Average Annual Teacher Salary 2004–2005
United States	47,602	Montana	38,485
Alabama	38,186	Nebraska	30,441
Alaska	52,467	Nevada	43,212
Arizona	39,095	New Hampshire	43,941
Arkansas	41,489	New Jersey	56,635
California	57,604	New Mexico	39,391
Colorado	43,965	New York	55,665
Connecticut	57,760	North Carolina	43,343
Delaware	52,924	North Dakota	36,449
Florida	43,095	Ohio	49,438
Georgia	46,437	Oklahoma	37,879
Hawaii	47,833	Oregon	48,320
Idaho	40,864	Pennsylvania	53,281
Illinois	56,494	Rhode Island	56,432
Indiana	46,591	South Carolina	42,189
Iowa	39,284	South Dakota	34,039
Kansas	39,351	Tennessee	42,076
Kentucky	41,075	Texas	41,009
Louisiana	39,022	Utah	37,006
Maine	40,935	Vermont	44,346
Maryland	52,330	Virginia	45,377
Massachusetts	54,668	Washington	45,722
Michigan	53,959	West Virginia	38,404
Minnesota	47,411	Wisconsin	43,099
Mississippi	38,212	Wyoming	40,487
Missouri	39,064		

Source: American Federation of Teachers, *Survey and Analysis of Teacher Salary Trends 2005.* "Table 11-1: Average Teacher Salary in 2004–05. State Rankings," 2005. [Online]. Available at www.aff.org/salary/2005/download /AFT2005SalarySurvey.pdf.

salaries must be evaluated in relation to differences in the cost of living, which is higher in states such as Connecticut and California. In other words, a teacher in Connecticut earns more but has to pay more for food, clothing, and housing. By region, the southern states are the lowest paying, and the northeastern the highest paying. In general, southern states, on average, provide less support to public education.

The conventional view that public school teachers are woefully underpaid may be wrong according to a report by Michael Podgursky, an expert on teacher pay. Contrary to popular belief, teachers' salaries compare favorably to the salaries of other professions and occupations. When salaries are computed on an hourly basis, teachers generally earn more than registered nurses, accountants, engineers, and other middle-class workers.[46]

Do teachers in some areas make more money than teachers in other areas? Yes. Teachers who teach in big school districts—districts with more than 10,000 students—make less than teachers in smaller districts. Salaries in urban districts are lower for a number of reasons. First, many urban districts are faced with declining tax bases and therefore are trimming budgets. This accounts for why urban teachers' salaries are often below those of their suburban counterparts. Second, urban school districts tend to have younger and less experienced teachers, and their salaries are lower than those of the older and more experienced teachers in suburban districts.

The geographic region in which you teach also determines the salary you will receive as a teacher, as Table 2.3 illustrates. There are a number of reasons why salaries vary based on metropolitan and geographic area. Most school boards operate within budgets that depend on income from property taxes. Most property owners do not like to see their property taxes raised. So, as long as the majority of a school's budget comes from property taxes, there will always be pressure to keep school expenses and expenditures as low as possible, including teachers' salaries. In addition, many inequalities exist when schooling is financed through property taxes. Districts in suburban areas, where incomes and property values are higher, have more dollars to spend on their schools. The opposite is true in less affluent rural and inner-city neighborhoods. In many respects, teaching is a two-tiered profession. Teachers of poor and minority students

FIGURE 2.4 Average Teacher Salaries

As you consider salaries, you also need to think about where you are going to teach! Today, going where the jobs are and where salaries are the highest will mean more money for you over your career.

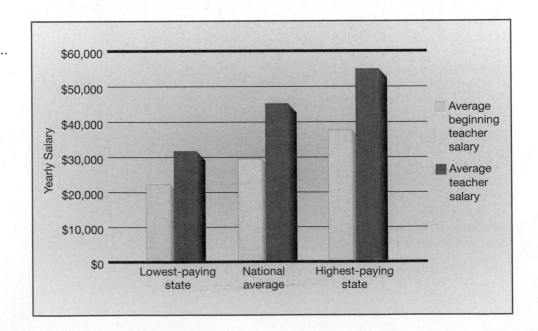

teach in schools with more teacher turnover, more teacher vacancies, less parent involvement, and fewer textbooks and other learning materials. Where you teach does indeed influence not only how much you get paid, but other conditions of teaching as well.[47]

_____

_____

_____

_____

_____

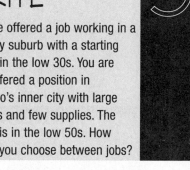

REFLECT & WRITE

You are offered a job working in a wealthy suburb with a starting salary in the low 30s. You are also offered a position in Chicago's inner city with large classes and few supplies. The salary is in the low 50s. How would you choose between jobs?

What salary will you earn as a beginning teacher? Figure 2.4 helps answer this question. As a beginning teacher, you should receive a salary schedule by which you can quickly determine the salary you will receive after 5, 10, and 30 years of teaching. In addition, some school districts are implementing **merit pay**, or **performance pay**—an incentive system that rewards teachers for extra service, an exceptionally well-done job, or increases in student achievement. Increasingly, performance pay plans are gaining in popularity. Iowa became the first state to base teacher pay on classroom performance and student achievement rather than years spent in teaching.

Georgia has put in place a merit pay program based on four goals designed to reward overall school improvement. These goals are:

- Academic achievement
- Resource development
- Educational programming
- Client involvement[48]

Merit pay   Pay based on meritorious service, performance, and/or special assignments.

Performance pay   Salary increases based on student achievement and classroom performance. Gradually replacing the term _merit pay_.

Increasingly, incentive pay plans are based on higher levels of education, different levels of teaching responsibilities, more professional responsibilities, and additional certifications.

Benefits are another part of a salary package, and when you are considering a teaching position, you will want to inquire about them. Major benefits that are part of a salary package include health and life insurance and a retirement plan. For example, the Houston (Texas) ISD provides these benefits: medical plan, dental plan, life and accidental death insurance, income replacement plan, cancer care plan, hospital indemnity plan, group legal services, flexible spending accounts, and a health connection plan.

School districts also are becoming more creative in their benefits to attract and keep quality teachers. The Santa Clara (California) Unified School District, in a first-of-a-kind effort, built lower-cost housing for teachers on school property. A lottery was held to determine which teachers would get one of the 40 slots in the new apartment building in Casa del Maestro. Rents run at about half the price of regular apartments.[49]

Also, California has what is believed to be the first in the country to provide income tax credit for teachers. Public and private school teachers with at least 4 years of service are eligible to receive credits ranging from $250 to $1,500, depending on how long they have taught.[50]

For a description of the benefits, access www.hisdbenefits.org/.

YOU DECIDE

Merit Pay for Teachers

K–12 public education today is experiencing increased pressure to improve school performance nationwide. NCLB, the introduction of demanding national and state standards, as well as numerous assessments continually push school districts to meet this goal. In an attempt to achieve improved school performance, some districts have adopted a system of merit pay for teachers.

Merit pay is based on the assumption that rewarding teachers for excellent performance will provide incentives for improved student achievement scores. Over the past few years, merit pay plans have been adopted in several cities, including Charlotte, North Carolina; Denver, Colorado; and Little Rock. Arkansas. In fact, in Little Rock re-

searchers found that offering bonuses to teachers based on students' math proficiency resulted in significantly improved math scores.

Merit pay programs do have critics. Teacher unions have argued that teacher evaluation is too subjective for merit pay to be distributed fairly. Teachers also have claimed that merit pay programs create competition among fellow teachers for the bonuses, which undermines the teaching process.

What do you think? In an age where schools are pressured to increase school performance, are merit pay programs an effective method to reach this goal?

Sources: B. Kisida and B. Riffel, "Recent Research: The Merit of Merit Pay Programs," *The Heartland Institute*, April 1, 2007. (Online). Available at www.heartland.org/Article.cfm?artId=20844&CFID=1940749&CFTOKEN=58502808. M. S. Littlepage, "Merit Pay for Teachers Improves Student Achievement in Arkansas," *The Heartland Institute*, April 1, 2007. (Online). Available at www.heartland.org/Article.cfm?artId=20838&CFID=1940749&CFTOKEN=58502808. R. Holland, "Merit Pay for Teachers: Can Common Sense Come to Public Education?" *Lexington Institute*, October 2005, p. 2. Oregon School Boards Association, "Performance Pay Primer—Teacher Merit Pay," 2007. (Online). Available at www.osba.org/lrelatns/perfpay/primerc.htm.

REFLECT & WRITE

South Dakota is the lowest-paying state in both average teacher salary and beginning teacher salary. What reasons can you give to explain this? How would a state's average salary motivate you to teach or not teach there?

_____

Teaching in Private, Independent, and Parochial Schools

About 22 percent (781,000) of the nation's teachers choose to teach in private schools.[51] The average salary for private school teachers is $30,707.[52] This is well below the $47,750 average salary for public school teachers.[53] Although salaries in private schools are lower than those in the public sector, some teachers prefer private settings because they feel they have more autonomy and more to say about what should be taught and how it will be taught. This is especially true in parochial schools. The separation of church and state has driven religious teaching out of public schools. Parochial schools engage in religious education in addition to the standard curriculum, giving teachers the opportunity to teach in an environment that is based on a religious ideology. *In the Classroom with Fraser A. Randolph* on page 70 will help you capture the essence of what teaching in independent schools is like and what motivates these teachers as professionals.

Is Teaching for You?

In Chapter 1 and in this chapter, you have read and thought about what teaching means and about teaching as a profession. Now is a good time to pause and reflect more about choosing teaching as a career. The self-analysis in Figure 2.5

The following self-analysis will help you reflect on your choice of teaching as a career. You might want to discuss with friends, classmates, colleagues, and instructors any items that you answer "no" or "undecided."

	Yes	No	Undecided
1. Do I believe that all children can learn?	❑	❑	❑
2. Do I have high expectations for myself and others?	❑	❑	❑
3. Am I dedicated to learning the necessary content knowledge and teaching skills?	❑	❑	❑
4. Do I see myself as a professional?	❑	❑	❑
5. Do I look forward to reading professional journals?	❑	❑	❑
6. Do I look forward to participating in professional organizations for teachers?	❑	❑	❑
7. Am I willing to uphold high ethical and professional standards for myself?	❑	❑	❑
8. Am I willing to learn new things and to change?	❑	❑	❑
9. Am I willing to devote myself to ongoing professional development as a teacher?	❑	❑	❑
10. Do I see myself as a lifelong learner?	❑	❑	❑
11. Am I willing to continue my teacher education to improve my knowledge and skills?	❑	❑	❑
12. Am I committed to basing my classroom practice on education research?	❑	❑	❑
13. Do I want to spend my days in close contact and interaction with children and young people?	❑	❑	❑
14. Are teachers the kind of people with whom I want to work?	❑	❑	❑
15. Am I willing to invest time and energy in professional collaborations?	❑	❑	❑
16. Am I willing to do more than what is "required" of me?	❑	❑	❑
17. Am I willing to give more time to students than a teaching contract may specify?	❑	❑	❑
18. Am I willing to communicate my teaching philosophy and practices to parents and others?	❑	❑	❑
19. Am I willing to work at developing parent-school and community-school partnerships?	❑	❑	❑
20. Am I willing to teach children of all cultures and racial and ethnic backgrounds?	❑	❑	❑
21. Do I have the energy, sense of humor, enthusiasm, and outgoingness teachers need?	❑	❑	❑
22. Am I a flexible person and able to deal with situations in highly active environments?	❑	❑	❑
23. Do I have good organizational, managerial, and leadership skills?	❑	❑	❑
24. Do I have a strong sense of self-efficacy as a teacher?	❑	❑	❑
25. Am I willing to undertake periods of apprenticeship as a preservice and novice teacher?	❑	❑	❑
26. Am I willing to undergo periodic formal evaluations of my teaching performance?	❑	❑	❑
27. Am I willing to explore many alternatives in finding job opportunities as a teacher?	❑	❑	❑
28. Will I be willing to relocate to take advantage of teaching opportunities?	❑	❑	❑
29. Can I initially meet my needs on a teacher's starting salary and benefits?	❑	❑	❑
30. Will I be satisfied with a salary based on educational attainment and years of service?	❑	❑	❑

FIGURE 2.5 Is Teaching for Me?

Have you learned anything new about your motivation for teaching?

provides a basis for further clarifying your motivations for teaching and can assist you in identifying those areas you want to strengthen throughout this course and throughout your teacher education program.

In the Classroom

with **Fraser A. Randolph**

Teaching in an Independent School

Fraser Randolph teaches at New Canaan Country School, an independent school in Connecticut with about 600 students, prekindergarten through ninth grade.

I really did love my eighth-grade English position at an urban Connecticut junior high school. I was challenged; I felt I was making a difference in some kids' lives; I enjoyed the subject matter. On the other hand, in 1989 I was in my mid-thirties, and it was beginning to look as though all I would ever do in my life was teach English to 13-year-olds. Union regulations made it impossible for me to change grade levels or schools, and my school was becoming increasingly "burned out." Discipline loomed larger and larger, and the administration was uninspired and ineffective.

A year's leave of absence during which I taught fifth grade at New Canaan Country School convinced me I was ready for a change. At Country School, I was greeted by teachers who welcomed me as if to their family and offered advice and material to ease my transition. I was immediately given a key that opened virtually every door on the campus, as well as social studies and math classes, in addition to English, to teach. I also was able to coach basketball and baseball during the school day.

Both students and teachers are serious about education at Country School. My students expect to work and are truly curious about everything that goes on in the classroom. They supplement the curriculum with materials from home and shared experiences, and needless to say, parents are eager to know what is going on as well—how their children are faring, how they can facilitate the learning process. In my 15 years at Country School, I have always found parents available and willing to do whatever was needed to help their children succeed.

Country School is a community where everyone shares a common philosophy about children and how they learn. While many instructional methods are practiced here, you will not find busy work, tedious drills, and "teaching to the test." Classes are rigorous and interactive. The walls and lobbies are festooned with the creative and intellectual products of students in all subjects. This is a progressive school, but one with a traditional background. Teachers practice Piagetian methods, offering children concrete experiences with new ideas and skills and gradually leading them into abstract ideas. Teachers often compare our children to flowers, each blossoming in his or her own time.

Country School is "formal" about the job of educating children but informal in its administrative approach. Forms and bureaucracy are kept to a minimum. Nor must teachers wrestle with the stifling demands of discipline, tracking down absent children, and taking attendance each and every class. The small corps of administrators, who all also teach, make teachers' lives easier by identifying tutorial, emotional, and psychological help for students who need it and by keeping abreast of the ever-changing daily schedule.

Is there a downside to this experience? There are certainly challenges: demanding parents, a frenetic pace, and "entitled" children who always expect more. Country School is also challenged by its own mission statement to diversify the student body and faculty. With limited space and great demand, the competition for admission is intense, and we are constantly looking at ourselves to find other avenues to attract students and teachers of more diverse cultures.

Am I glad that I made this decision to leave public education? Perhaps at the end of my career I will return to the public schools and rejoin the fight for quality education there. But I have learned in my 15 years at New Canaan Country School that all children have this need. It's the service that counts.

REFLECT & WRITE

After reading Chapters 1 and 2, and after completing Figure 2.5, you have some pretty good answers to the question: "Is teaching for me?" Write your personal statement about why teaching is or is not for you.

_____

_____

_____

_____

_____

ETHICAL DILEMMA

"Why Don't My Kids Get Their Fair Share?"

COLLEEN GILMORE is a novice seventh-grade teacher in Rocky Springs School District. Her class of 28 students includes 15 Latino students, 9 African American students, and 4 Vietnamese students. Colleen's room is sparsely furnished, many of the tables and chairs need repair, and the classroom library of 37 books is old and worn. Last week at an orientation for seventh- and eighth-grade teachers held across town at the new junior high school, she learned that the students there are 90 percent White and class size averages 19. A tour of the classrooms revealed the latest in furniture and equipment, as well as well-stocked classroom libraries. Colleen is concerned about the unequal distribution of resources in the school district; she feels as though her students are not getting their fair share.

What should Colleen do?

SUMMARY

- Teaching is a multifaceted profession that involves years of study and certification testing.

- The five dimensions of professionalism are content knowledge, pedagogical content knowledge and skills, professional and pedagogical knowledge and skills, student learning, and professional dispositions.

- Teachers use research in their professional practice by means of professional development schools and action research.

- Professional organizations, such as the National Education Association and the American Federation of Teachers, are one way teachers can pursue ongoing professional development.

- Reform movements are changing teacher education by implementing new and higher standards, demanding increased accountability, and encouraging new types of teacher education programs.

- The teaching workforce is predominantly female and white, but there is an increasing demand for more diversity as the student population becomes more multicultural. Although the number of teachers in the United States is growing, a considerable teacher shortage continues to exist.

- With the many job opportunities available for new teachers, several factors should be analyzed, when selecting a position such as geography, salaries and benefits that vary from state to state, and the type of school—public, private, independent, or parochial.

KEY TERMS

A Nation Prepared: Teachers for the 21st Century 55
Action research 51
Advocacy 47
Alternative teacher education/certification (A/C) programs 60
American Federation of Teachers (AFT) 53
Carnegie Task Force on Teaching as a Profession 55

Core beliefs 49
Core values 49
Data-driven instruction 50
Developmentally appropriate practice (DAP) 45
Merit pay 67
National Education Association (NEA) 43
Performance pay 67
Philosophy of education 49

Praxis 41
Profession 40
Professional development 53
Professional development school (PDS) 50
Professional dispositions 46
Professional learning community 53
Reflective practice 45

APPLICATIONS FOR ACTIVE LEARNING

Connections

1. Think about how teacher education is being reformed. Create a graphic that shows these reforms and the resulting changes.

2. With the passage of the No Child Left Behind Act, accountability now must be addressed at all levels of education, from the school board and school system to the individual classroom and teacher. Articles often appear in newspapers, magazines, and online publications that address accountability. Over a 2-week period, review these sources and determine what accountability issues are "in the news." Place these materials in your portfolio or teaching file.

3. The whole "pay-for-performance" issue will continue to be contentious and hotly debated in the years to come. Make a connection to this topic by gathering information about the pros and cons of the issue. You can begin by logging onto www.educationworld.com and searching for "pay for performance."

Field Experiences

1. Observe teachers in various classrooms to determine their core beliefs about teaching. Make a list of these core beliefs, and reflect on them as you continue to consider your philosophy of education.

2. Research the following question: What have been some positive and negative influences of teachers' unions nationally? Begin now by making a few predictions about what you think you will find.

3. Interview various teachers in your area about the different certification programs they completed. Find teachers who have completed both alternative and national certification programs in your state. Make a list of pros and cons of these programs compared to the traditional teacher certification process.

Personal Research

1. Gather information about your state certification exam, including sample outcomes, performance criteria, and test items.

2. Research several strategies that educators use to remain accountable to families. What communication tactics do educators use to communicate effectively with families when reporting assessment results? Make a list of five key guidelines to use when sharing test and assessment data with families.

3. Research projections of teaching opportunities, salaries, and benefits in the state or region in which you plan to teach. What preparation is required or recommended? How will this information influence your decisions about becoming a teacher?

PREPARING TO TEACH

For Your Portfolio

1. Extend the clipping file you started in Chapter 1 by reviewing articles from education and professional journals

in your subject area. Consider, for example, the following publications:

American Educator
American Journal of Education

American School Board Journal

Childhood Education

Educational Leadership

Education Next

Elementary School Journal

Exceptional Children

High School Journal

Instructor

Kappa Delta Phi Record

Phi Delta Kappan

PTA Today

Teacher Magazine

Young Children

2. Keep selected results of your personal research in your portfolio, especially information about teachers' profes-

sional standards, organizations, state requirements, and job opportunities. Also include any personal checklists you develop from the following Idea File activities.

Idea File

1. Develop a list of tips for becoming a professional and share your ideas with classmates.

2. Using your research on the state certification exam, develop a personal checklist of what you will need to know and be able to do before you take the exam.

3. Review the INTASC standards and underline those terms and phrases whose meanings and implications are not clear. Using these underlinings, develop a list of specific questions about becoming a teacher that you would like answered by the time you finish this course.

LEARNING AND KNOWING MORE

Websites Worth Visiting

Following are a list of valuable sources of information. The Federal Government offers a lot of current statistics and policy information. The federal government is also a valuable source of information. For example, the Department of Education maintains a constantly updated website with current news and information regarding federal programs and government decisions on the subject of schools and education. Their website is www.ed.gov/index.jsp.

Teaching as a Profession
  www.library.uiuc.edu/schoolreform/teaching.htm
  A gateway site with links to a series of helpful websites.
The Praxis Home Page
  www.ets.org/praxis
  Detailed information about all aspects of Praxis.
Teach For America
  www.teachforamerica.org/
  A national corps of outstanding recent college graduates of all academic majors who commit to teach in urban and rural public schools for two years, becoming leaders in the effort to expand educational opportunity.

Many professional organizations provide you the opportunity to be involved with colleagues who are interested in particular career and discipline areas. Some of these are:

- Council for Exception Children (CEC)
  www.cec.sped.orgt
- National Science Teachers Association (NSTA)
  www.nsta.org
- National Council for the Social Studies (NCSS)
  www.ncss.org
- National Association for Music Education (MENC)
  www.menc.org
- National Association for the Education of Young Children (NAEYC)
  www.naeyc.org
- International Reading Association (IRA)
  www.reading.org
- National Council of Teachers of Mathematics (NCTM)
  www.nctm.org
- American Alliance for Health, Physical Education, Recreation, and Dance (AAHPERD)
  www.aahperd.org
- National Association for Bilingual Education (NABE)
  www.nabe.org

Books Worth Reading

Brown, Dan. (2007). *The Great Expectations School: A Rookie Year in the New Blackboard Jungle.* New York: Arcade Publishing.

This memoir recounts the author's first year as a fourth-grade teacher in an inner-city school in New York. The reader is introduced to his many challenges, including unruly children, absent parents, and a failing administration. This book takes the reader on a journey of an inner-city class and their teacher revealing the story of a broken educational system and all those struggling within and fighting against it.

Wilke, Rebecca L. (2006). *The First Days of Class: A Practical Guide for the Beginning Teacher.* Thousand Oaks, CA: Corwin Press.

This step-by-step guide reviews important issues and things to consider for beginning, substitute, returning, and emergency credential teachers. The book includes easy-to-reference sections within each chapter, tip boxes, and classroom material samples.

Goldblatt, Patricia F., and Smith, Deirdre. (2005). *Cases for Teacher Development: Preparing for the Classroom.* Thousand Oaks, CA: Sage Publications, Inc.

The cases in this book detail real-life experiences from the field that identify major challenges all educators face.

II Students, Families, and Communities

The role of schools today is to provide education that is fair and equitable to all students. American students today represent greater racial, cultural, and linguistic diversity than at any other time in the past. This diversity is both a source of enrichment and a challenge for teachers and schools and the communities they serve. One of the greatest continuing challenges to public schools is educating children of non-English-speaking immigrants and students with limited English proficiency. At the same time, many immigrant students are ready and eager to learn. They and their families see the American education system as a great source of opportunity and a means for upward mobility.

In addition to the challenges posed to teaching and learning by the increasing presence of different cultures and languages in our society and schools, other factors create special needs for some students. Environmental, social, physical, and emotional factors place students at risk. As a teacher, you likely will be working with at-risk students and other exceptional learners in the inclusive classroom and will need to be familiar with the laws and practices that affect such instruction.

Parents and families and the communities they represent also have an impact on teaching and learning. Families are becoming increasingly empowered to make decisions that affect education.

Community agencies and corporations are partners with schools in the education of children and youth today. These partnerships have many faces: community-based intervention programs for students at risk, school-to-work business-sponsored programs, company-subsidized high-tech magnet schools and private school programs, and public schools run by private corporations. At issue are the implications of privatization for public education.

Part Two introduces you to issues related to how schools today are organized and how they promote teaching and learning in today's diverse, collaborative, and demanding society.

3 How Schools Are Organized and Connected to Their Communities

STEVE CLARK Schools are, in all reality, equipping centers—equipping students for learning, for reaching their potential, for establishing ways to work and develop that benefit them and those around them. Thus, the structures we put in place to make schools work ought to be designed with such equipping in mind. It is not about the organization, it is about the students that are within that organization, and our greatest errors come when we make it more about the system than about the people we serve within that system.

What excites me most about our work as professionals is the fact that we have a chance to help create the kind of people and cultures that we want in our world in the future. Our students' capacity for achieving great things is often traced back to the skills they gained when they were in our schools. They hone their ability to problem-solve, work collaboratively, push through struggles, and gain that necessary knowledge base—most of which is developed over the 12+ years they are with us. Let's not forget that. Our schools ought to be microcosms of what we hope they will carry on in their workplaces and homes in the future. When we say that educating our youth is important work, we are not kidding, and we must take it very seriously.

In our school, we focus on the academic as well as the nonacademic. Both are vital to the success of our students in the future. Our school culture, though not perfect, is one of the most positive environments you will find anywhere in our city. Our students know that this school is about them. It is built on a group of highly trained, committed teachers who are busting their backs everyday to help students find success.

Consider the plight of one of our students, Angel G., a 17-year-old Hispanic boy, transferred to our school 2 years ago after being kicked out of a neighboring school for fighting (six fights in 2 years) and for overall lack of performance. Rather

> **Our schools ought to be microcosms of what we hope they will carry on in their workplaces ...**

than see him as a "problem child," we met with him right away to help him understand that we were about his success, that we were going to expect much from him—and that he would get much in return. After a few weeks with us, he could see that our culture was different—no posturing or disrespect, no reason for him to "step-up" to other kids, and that this place could work for him. He began to raise his head and look people in the eye. He let down his guard and let in those who could help. He has never been in a

fight at our school, and he passed almost all of his classes this year. He was recently named the "Student of the Semester." He is becoming all that we—and he—hoped he could be. At this rate, he will be a contributor in society. That is our greatest link to our community—to help every child succeed.

Our goal, for all our students, is that they will be academically equipped and ready for the greater society—with such skills as commitment, integrity, hard work, and the ability to serve with all their hearts.

Our three Collective Commitments that administrators, teachers, and students established together are:

1. Treat all members of the Bellingham High community with dignity and respect.

Steve Clark is the principal at Bellingham High School in Bellingham, Washington. He was named a finalist for the National Principal of the Year in 2005.

As you read this chapter . . .

Think about:

■ The basic purposes of schools and schooling

■ How schools are organized

■ What it is like to teach in urban, suburban, and rural schools today

▶▶ Go to MyEducationLab and select the topic "Diversity and Multiculturalism" then watch the video "Newcomers High."

2. Take care of this great place.
3. Expect quality work from everyone, all the time.

These commitments are the launching point we use as we connect students to the greater community. They are the glue that holds us together and the oil that keeps our organization moving smoothly and efficiently. Establish what your essential commitments are and pour all that you have into making them become realities—for your school and the greater community.

WHAT IS THE PURPOSE OF SCHOOLING?

Surely you and I agree with Steve Clark that schools play a vital role in our students' success and, in turn, in American society. But just what is that role? And what should it be? Take a minute to reflect on this question. Jot down your answers, and keep them in mind as you read this chapter.

Here are some things that I think American public education should accomplish. Compare your thoughts with mine. I think public schools in the United States should:

- Educate all students to their fullest potential regardless of race, culture, gender, and socioeconomic status
- Instill a love of learning
- Prepare students for responsible democratic living
- Educate students of good moral character
- Ensure that student educations are well rounded

Federal and state laws also mandate certain roles for public education, including:

- Increasing student achievement
- Testing and being accountable for student achievement
- Expanding roles for parents and communities
- Providing more opportunities for students with disabilities
- Ensuring that all students are taught by highly qualified teachers[1]

As you can see, although we might all agree that the role of the school is to teach students, the issues are in the details. Because of differences in our beliefs about the purposes and functions of schooling, the role of education varies from state to state and from school to school.

What schools teach is what teachers, parents, the community, states, and the federal government think students should know and do in order to lead meaningful and productive lives in the twenty-first century. If schools are not successful in achieving this goal, then children, youth, and society are the losers. That makes it doubly important that you, as a teacher, understand how education is organized and connected to American society. How schools are organized and linked to society determines to a large extent what is taught, how teachers teach, and if students learn.

Aims of Education

Aim   A purpose, intention, or goal.

An **aim** is a purpose, intention, or goal. Many schools and school districts have aims that guide their teaching and help determine what students will learn. For example, the aims of one school might be to help students become responsible, encourage habits of organization, and involve them in setting personal and academic goals. Because educational aims reflect the dominant values and beliefs of the society, they change over time as society's goals shift and change. Aims also vary according to the beliefs and values of specific communities.

Aims of schools often are reflected in the form of *mission statements*. These are brief statements that capture a school's purpose, philosophy, and goals and that explain how the school plans to achieve those goals. For example, the mission statement of the Peters Township (Pennsylvania) schools, a rural/suburban district, is as follows:

> . . . to ensure that all students acquire the knowledge base and skills necessary to become contributing members of society and lifelong learners by providing the highest-quality resources and staff within a comprehensive, result-oriented program implemented by caring people.[2]

The mission statement of Klein Oak High School in Spring, Texas, states that:

> Klein Oak is committed to excellence in education and believes that all students possess inherent worth and the ability to learn. Based on this premise, its purpose is designed to help students reach their full potential as individuals and become happy, competent, productive members of society. Pursuing this goal, Klein Oak teaches those skills necessary for success in a competitive world. Students are taught to think for themselves, apply their knowledge, and develop an appreciation of the world around them. To instill these abilities, Klein Oak High School provides a broad spectrum of educational opportunities designed to meet various students' needs. Professional educators present programs in a manner that creates a learning environment in which students can enhance their abilities. In doing so, young people acquire the discipline and sensitivity needed to become responsible citizens.[3]

One of the most influential sets of aims was issued in 1918 by the National Education Association's (NEA) Commission on the Reorganization of Secondary Education. The commission's report, *The Cardinal Principles of Secondary Education*, recommended that the high school curriculum be organized around "seven cardinal principles":

- Health
- Command of fundamental processes
- Worthy home membership
- Citizenship
- Ethical character
- Vocational preparation
- Worthy use of leisure time[4]

Many think these seven cardinal principles remain appropriate for guiding decisions about what to teach. However, what society thinks the aims of education are or should be in one decade is not necessarily appropriate for another.

The seven cardinal principles were influential in the decades from 1920 through the late 1950s, when education emphasized a decidedly utilitarian purpose. In the late 1950s and early 1960s, after the Soviet Union launched the space satellite *Sputnik*, national defense became a top priority. The aims of education consequently shifted toward science and an emphasis on teaching students how to think. In the late 1960s and 1970s, the emphasis moved to promoting equal educational opportunity, making education "relevant," and promoting awareness of ecological issues. In the 1980s, academic excellence was stressed, and schools emphasized basic skills. As society's goals shifted again in the 1990s, educational aims followed suit; excellence was to be achieved through high "standards" in all the content areas in order to make the United States economically competitive.

Although a narrow focus on academics often is justified as a way of reforming schools and increasing excellence, an education that addresses the "full person" is perennially an education the public views as most desirable. The aims of education as outlined in *The Cardinal Principles of Secondary Education* continue to reflect efforts to identify what constitutes the knowledge, skills, and attitudes

Go to MyEducationLab, select the topic "Philosophy of Education" and read the article "Back to Whole." Complete the questions that follow.

• *Your Turn*

You are a second-year fourth-grade teacher in an urban school. Although you are relatively new, you have seen how the constantly changing political and social climate of American society keeps the goals of education in flux. There is always tension between those who advocate a more comprehensive, well-rounded education and those who prefer a more narrow approach to education focused on "the basics"—literacy, math, and science. Because you are new to the school and offer a fresh perspective, your principal asks you what you think is best for American society and its future citizens: Do you advocate a more comprehensive education or one that stresses basic academics? Your response should be supported with examples.

REFLECT & WRITE

If you were a faculty member asked to help draft a mission statement for your school, whom might you want on the committee with you? Why?

_____

_____

_____

_____

_____

that all citizens should possess. For example, the following education goals reflect the research about what society wants for its citizens:

- *Basic academic skills in core subjects:* Reading, writing, math, knowledge of science and history.
- *Critical thinking and problem solving:* Ability to analyze and interpret information, use computers to develop knowledge, apply ideas to new situations.
- *Social skills and work ethic:* Good communication skills, personal responsibility, ability to get along well with others and work with others from different backgrounds.
- *Citizenship and community responsibility:* Knowledge of how government works and of how to participate in civic activities such as voting, volunteering, and becoming active in communities.
- *Preparation for skilled work:* Vocational, career, and technical education that will qualify youths for skilled employment that does not require a college degree.
- *Physical health:* A foundation for lifelong physical health, including good habits of exercise and nutrition.
- *Emotional health:* Tools to develop self-confidence, respect for others, and the ability to resist peer pressure to engage in irresponsible personal behavior.
- *Proficiency in the arts and literature:* Capacity to participate in and appreciate the musical, visual, and performing arts. Development of a love of literature.[5]

The breadth and depth of these educational goals address all of the dimensions that we traditionally think about when we talk about a well-rounded and comprehensive education. Yet, how achievable are these goals? Many critics of the current emphasis in education today contend that the emphasis on standardization and teaching—particularly in the areas of reading and mathematics—is forcing teachers and schools to spend too much time and effort on these areas of education to the detriment of many of the goals just presented. Standards-based education is the center of many political and educational debates.

Standards-Based Education

Today, reforming schools and setting high standards for what students should know and be able to do dominates educational discussion. The standards movement became popular because its advocates believe that having standards for what should be taught in the nation's schools will increase achievement and quality. The case for standards is articulated by Margaret Spellings, Secretary of the U.S. Department of Education: "High standards and accountability raise achievement levels among American students, particularly in the early grades."[6] The assumption is that higher standards will improve the quality of education.

Standards-based education draws, in part, on content standards developed by professional groups for history, geography, the arts, science, math, and other

Standards-based education Instruction aimed at providing students the specific skills and levels of competency necessary to move through the educational system.

subjects. Opponents of standards maintain that they could become what amounts to a national curriculum controlled by federal bureaucrats and could erode the right of states and local schools to set their own curriculum guidelines and standards and make decisions about what our children should learn. Furthermore, critics maintain that standards promote inequality, diminish cultural diversity, and force students into a "one size fits all" curriculum.

Current public sentiment is that citizens are willing to support national and state standards but still want the option to teach at the local level what communities think is important. The public also is interested in ensuring that what students learn in school is applicable to the real world of jobs and careers. For example, *In the Classroom with Kathryn and Roberto: Bringing Relevance to the Classroom* shows how two students apply their classroom experiences to real-world careers.

Americans still value local control of schools and the freedom to make decisions about what is best for children at the local level. At present, current educational reform is focused on the following issues: high standards, testing to ensure standards of achievement and accountability, smaller schools, smaller classes, alternative approaches to education, and national efforts to reform the basic purposes of American education. Chapter 10 discusses in detail standards and assessment.

In the Classroom
with Kathryn and Roberto
Bringing Relevance to the Classroom

Kathryn Marxen crouches behind her tripod, focusing on the next scene. "Can you walk this way again?" she shouts to Adam Grishman, 50 yards down the path. "OK, go ahead!" The apprentice trainer at Guide Dogs for the Blind leads Binny, a 14-month-old yellow Lab, toward the camcorder. Marxen, 17, is making a how-to video for community volunteers interested in providing basic training to guide dogs. Most of the video will feature her demonstrating commands with one of the guide dog puppies she has raised herself. Marxen's video is her career project at Oregon City High School, which is a requirement for graduation.

Under a little-known state mandate, Marxen and some 43,000 other Oregon public high school seniors must complete an extended career-related project that brings relevance to what students have learned in the classroom. Marxen has raised three guide dog puppies herself and knows the training regimen well. She has put 30 hours into her video so far, writing a 25-page script and consulting a videographer to help her learn the basics of filming. It is the biggest project she has done in high school. Her mother, Debra, said Kathryn has tackled her senior project with purpose because it involves something she loves—animals.

High school senior Roberto Gonzales works in a local hardware store on weekends and during vacations. Roberto explains how he uses his knowledge of trigonometry to solve real-world problems: "The other day one of the guys who fixes our rental equipment had to cut a piece of metal to make a support for one of our commercial lawn-mowing machines. He was having trouble figuring out what size to cut and the specific angles. I measured the areas he was talking about and was able to draw him a diagram for exactly what he needed to cut in order to make the support he needed. I try to put my trig skills to good use every day."

Consider how you can help your students apply what they learn to the real world. For tips on how you can bring relevance into the classroom visit www.glencoe.com/ps/teachingtoday/weeklytips.phtml/48.

Sources: S. Carter, "Schoolwork in Oregon Now Includes Class About Real Work," *The Oregonian*, April 30, 2007. (Online). Available at www.oregonlive.com/oregonian/stories/index.ssf?/base/news/1177905703273480.xml&coll=7. Accessed May 31, 2007.

One of the realities of American public education over the last two decades has been the expansion of the federal government's role in holding public schools accountable for:

- Student achievement, as measured by annual tests
- The learning of all students, regardless of race, family income, gender, or disability

This expansion of accountability, in exchange for federal support, represents a significant change in the role of the federal government in public education. It has

In the Classroom

with **Sharon Byrdsong**

Meeting the Challenge of Teaching Adolescents in the Twenty-first Century

When I was assigned to Azalea Gardens Middle School as the principal, I discovered that the igniting of imagination, the sustaining of conviction and hope, and the strengthening of dreams were concepts in educational journals on the school's resource shelf. The instructional practices at that time did not demand academic rigor or differentiation of instruction, and they were not driven by best-practice strategies based on data analyses.

I studied the students, the faculty, the parents, and the school community. I assessed their strengths, and I documented areas needing improvement. Then I met with my department chairs, team leaders, student leaders, parent advisory board, PTA, and area civic leagues so that I would understand their points of view, their core beliefs, and their expectations. I clearly understood that their support was vital; I knew that if I was going to make significant changes, I had to validate their importance and seek their support. We collaborated and created a shared vision. This collaboration was a turning point for us: We became a team, determined to take that pilgrimage that would eventually move us to "good" and then, ultimately, to "great."

Our total program is grounded in rigorous academic standards. My teachers and I study and discuss current educational practices and practitioners such as Reeves, Wiggins, McTighe, Schmoker, Marzano, Tomlinson, and many other educators who are at the forefront of educational reform and success. I often purchase books for the entire faculty that we read and reflect upon during faculty meetings and book talks. We have become experts in the use of data-driven decision making, because we understand its critical power in all educational practices. In addition, all teachers use a great variety of educational "tools" in their instructional practices so that all learning styles and modalities are addressed within a class period.

To further empower my teachers to be the best, I encourage their attendance at conferences and workshops, and I ask them to present their best practices at monthly faculty meetings. However, I do believe that one of the greatest "tools" I have provided for my teachers is a collaborative-planning bell. Each and every day, teachers "rub and polish" their minds against the minds of their colleagues, creating common threads among their lessons. This maximizes the inclusion and utilization of each and every teacher's specific areas of skill and expertise within the lesson for all students, no matter which teacher is standing in front of the class. Students, as well as teachers, benefit from this common planning.

Furthermore, maintaining a safe and secure environment in a middle school is paramount. At Azalea, discipline is proactive. Students understand that behavior is a code of conduct with clear expectations; it is consistent throughout the school; and due process is afforded to all students. Rules and regulations are clearly stated, defined, posted, and enforced consistently and equitably throughout the entire school building.

The transformation of Azalea, however, did take time. Each school year, we built strategy upon strategy, best practice upon best practice, and we saturated and energized our mission with commitment, determination, and just plain hard work. We are meeting the many challenges of educating adolescents in the twenty-first century by successfully preparing our students to exceed benchmarks and by creating conditions for them to become lifelong learners.

greatly influenced how schools operate, what they teach, and what and how students learn. It is likely that this expanded federal role for making schools accountable for student achievement will continue into the future. The theme of being accountable for students and their learning is illustrated in *In the Classroom with Sharon Byrdsong.*

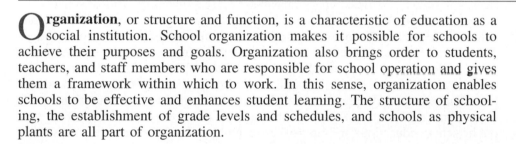

HOW ARE PUBLIC SCHOOLS ORGANIZED?

Organization, or structure and function, is a characteristic of education as a social institution. School organization makes it possible for schools to achieve their purposes and goals. Organization also brings order to students, teachers, and staff members who are responsible for school operation and gives them a framework within which to work. In this sense, organization enables schools to be effective and enhances student learning. The structure of schooling, the establishment of grade levels and schedules, and schools as physical plants are all part of organization.

Organization The structure and administration of education.

The Structure of Schooling in the United States

Schooling is structured in the United States with the progression of education for students at different ages from preschool through kindergarten and the elementary grades through secondary and postsecondary education. Consider how much you have learned about the structure of schooling through your personal experience as a student. As a teacher, you will view education from the broader perspective of an organizational structure that accomplishes specific educational goals. From this view, the organization of schooling is influenced by administrative needs; the nature of the faculty; students' ages, experiences, and cultural backgrounds; time and resources available for teaching; and the size of the student body.

How schools are organized depends in part on where they are located. Factors that contribute to and affect how schools are organized include location and geography (urban, suburban, or rural), number and kind of students in a district, monetary and other resources available, and the goals of the district and communities for their schools. How schools are organized—range of grades included, ratio of students to teachers and administrators, and so on—impacts student learning in a variety of ways.

Organization at the District Level

School district An administrative unit empowered by a state to run a community's school system.

A **school district** is an administrative unit empowered by a state to run a community's school system. Although school districts differ across the United States, most are similarly organized—namely, with top-down administrative structure, grade-level organization, and individual teachers teaching groups of students in self-contained classrooms. However, each school district provides education in a unique way, and each is structured to achieve its particular purposes. The nature of the local community—how big, small, rural, or urban it is—shapes and defines the nature of the educational enterprise. (You will read about district organizations in greater detail in Chapter 7 on governance and finance.)

School districts often are compared on the basis of size, but this can be misleading. Over 20 percent of the school districts in the United States have enrollments of under 300 students.[7] Although megaschools exist—for example, Belmont Senior High School in Los Angeles has 5,336 students in grades 9 to 12[8]—there are 5,437 public schools in the United States that operate pre-K–12 programs as one unit.[9] The size of a district influences the way it is organized and the number and kinds of staff it employs.

Grade-Level Organization

Age-graded approach Assigning children to a grade level according to their age.

Think about the buildings in which you attended school and about the schools of today. To what extent are they the same? Many schools are square or rectangular, with classrooms for each grade level opening onto a main corridor leading to offices, cafeterias, libraries, and gymnasiums. The architecture of most schools reflects an **age-graded approach** to schooling. In this organization, when children enter school in the fall, they are assigned to a grade level according to their age. The graded approach to school organization was introduced by Horace Mann in 1848 at the Quincy Grammar School in Boston. Mann thought the graded approach, which he observed in Prussia, would bring efficiency to American education. The age-graded approach is reflected in the structure of education in the United States. Note from Figure 3.1 that education is now pre-K–12, meaning that public school education for 3- to 4-year-old children has become almost universal.

REFLECT & WRITE

The structure of schooling in the United States provides a progression from the earliest years through graduate education. It also provides for the education of a large number of students. What advantages and disadvantages do you see in that pattern?

Multi-age/multi-ability grouping The mixing or integration of students of different ages in one classroom or learning setting.

Criticisms of the graded approach have led to **multi-age/multi-ability grouping**, the mixing or integration of students of different ages and abilities in one classroom or learning setting. Multi-age/multi-ability grouping is becoming popular in the United States and Canada, especially in grades pre-K–3. British Columbia has mandated multi-age grouping in K–3 for the entire province, and Kentucky recommends it for the whole state. Although Kentucky leaves the choice of multi-age/multi-ability or graded classes to individual schools, the majority of primary

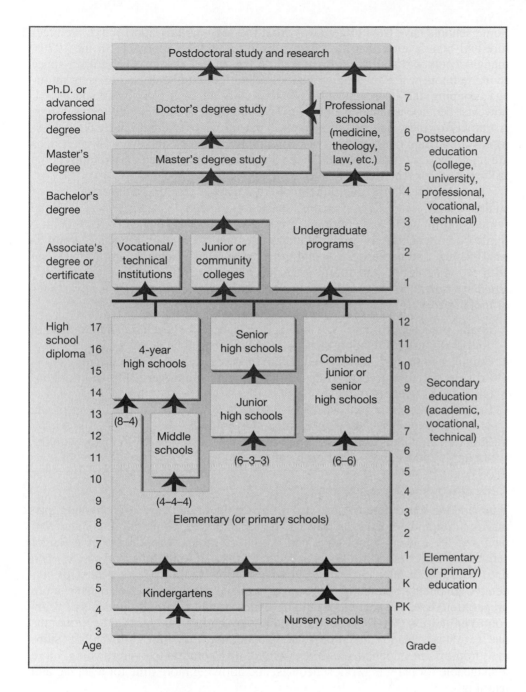

FIGURE 3.1 The Structure of Education in the United States

The structure of education in the United States is based on the age-graded approach and is now pre-K–12, meaning that public school education for 3- to 4-year-old children has become almost universal.

Source: National Center for Education Statistics, *Digest of Education Statistics, 2005* (2005). (Online). Available at http://nces.ed .gov/programs/digest/d05/figures/fig_01 .asp?referer=list. Accessed July 11, 2007.

programs use multi-age/multi-ability classes. Teachers and schools elect to use multi-age/multi-ability classes because they

- Enable teachers to use a wide variety of curricula and materials so that each student's needs are met.
- Enable students to help and learn from each other.
- Promote a positive feeling of success and accomplishment.
- Are designed to prevent grade and school failure. Lisa Gross of the Kentucky Department of Education notes: "Children who experience failure in the early grades of school tend to view education bleakly. The nongraded primary program removes the possibility of early failure and enables children to learn at their own pace."[10]

Go to MyEducationLab, select the topic "School Organization" then read the article "The Modern Multi-Age Classroom," then answer the questions that follow.

Some schools have tried to get away from the "egg carton" approach to architecture and organization that has characterized the graded approach. In the 1970s, many schools were built and organized on the "open" design—large open-space rooms without walls—with the intent of accommodating and encouraging multi-age grouping and open education practices. Not all such plans were successful, however, because teachers were not always comfortable teaching in open settings. A number of these schools subsequently put up walls to create individual classrooms. Education in many ways is a conservative process, and even when changes are made they are often reversed. Even so, many of these open classroom schools still exist across America.

Looping breaks the traditional mold of a teacher teaching a different class of students each year. Looping enables teachers to spend 2 or more years with the same group of same-age children. In other words, a teacher involved in looping might begin teaching a group in kindergarten and then teach the same group as first-graders, and perhaps as second-graders. Another teacher might do the same with second-, third-, and fourth-graders. Other names for looping are *student-teacher progress, multi-year instruction*, and *multi-year grouping*. The advantages of looping are that it

- Enables teachers to develop a family atmosphere for teachers and children to develop long-term relationships
- Provides a sense of stability and security, especially for young children
- Provides freedom to expand and enrich the curriculum vertically and horizontally over a 2-year period
- Enables teachers to gain weeks of instructional time at the beginning of the school year because they already know the children
- Supports individualized instruction because teachers are more familiar with the strengths and weaknesses of each child

Time and School Organization

Time and the scheduling of time also influence the organization of schooling, primarily through the 6-hour day and 180-day school year. Some reformers are campaigning for longer school days and school calendars. Proponents of a longer school day believe that if schools opened at 7:00 A.M. (or before) and stayed open until 6:00 P.M. or later, they could provide before- and after-school care for students and other community services as well. Teachers would also have more preparation time, and students would have more time to learn. Proponents of **year-round education** (**YRE**) say that extending the school year calendar to 12 months has several advantages, including making better use of facilities, preventing "summer drop-off" in student achievement, providing a solution to overcrowding, more manageable for parents' work schedules, and allowing more time for teaching and learning.

Many argue that the traditional school calendar, based on the needs of an agrarian society, no longer meets the needs of today's technological society. To respond to today's schedules, many school systems have instituted a number of changes:

1. *After-school programs.* **After-school programs** also are referred to as *after-school time* and *out-of-school time*. Such programs are becoming increasingly common and important. More than 14 million students between kindergarten and twelfth grade take care of themselves after school. That includes 40,000 kindergartners and almost 4 million middle school students in grades 6 to 8.[11] After-school programs provide a safe place for students while parents are at work. After-school programs not only extend the day, they meet other legitimate educational and social needs as well. They help maintain, extend, and enrich

Looping A nontraditional approach to learning in which the teacher moves from grade to grade with the students.

■ INTASC

STANDARD 3 The teacher understands how students differ in their approaches to learning and creates instructional opportunities that are adapted to diverse learners.

Year-round education (YRE) An approach to promoting continuous learning that allows schools to reorganize the school year by breaking up the long summer vacation into shorter, more frequent vacations throughout the year.

After-school programs Programs provided by schools that extend the school day and provide programs and activities to support student social and educational needs.

skills learned in the classroom, and offer extracurricular opportunities and participation. According to Joyce Shortt, codirector of the National Institute of Out-of-School Time, "Having a safe place with constructive activities and nurturing adults can be a very positive experience for kids."[12]

2. *21st Century Community Learning Centers (21st CCLC).* This program is a key component of the No Child Left Behind Act. It is an opportunity for students and their families to continue to learn new skills and discover new abilities after the school day has ended. **21st Century Community Learning Centers** provide expanded academic enrichment opportunities for children attending low-performing schools. Tutorial services and academic enrichment activities help students meet local and state academic standards in subjects such as reading and math. In addition, the 21st CCLC program provides youth development activities; drug and violence prevention programs; technology education programs, art, music, and recreation programs; and counseling and character education to enhance the academic component of the program. About 8,498 public schools participate as 21st Century CCLCs.[13]

21st Century Community Learning Centers (21st CCLC)   A component of the No Child Left Behind Act, this program provides opportunities for students and their families to learn new skills and abilities after the school day has ended.

3. *Summer school.* Summer school is becoming commonplace for more students. Approximately 10 percent of all students in elementary through high school enroll in summer school programs. Studies show that students lose about 1 month of instruction over their summer vacation. This loss of instruction is not equal for all students. Children from lower-income families experience a greater achievement drop, particularly in reading, than their more-advantaged peers. For these and other struggling students, the summer represents an opportune time to prevent this decline in learning.[14]

4. *Flex high school graduation programs.* The Rochester (New York) and the Chicago School Districts graduate students in 3, 4, or 5 years. The districts design curriculum and programs that enable incoming freshmen to meet their individual graduation target.

5. *Year-round education.* Also called *extended year programs* and *year-round schooling*, these arrangements work in several ways. Year-round education centers on reorganizing the school year to provide more continuous learning by breaking up the long summer vacation into shorter, more frequent vacations throughout the year. The National Association for Year-Round Education promotes year-round education by providing leadership and service to individuals and organizations on all aspects of time and learning. Teachers at Roosevelt-Perry Elementary School in Kentucky praise the year-round calendar for its potential to help students retain what they learn. Roosevelt-Perry principal Pam Howell says that the year-round calendar has the biggest effect among at-risk and low-income students who make up a large portion of the school population. Nearly 99 percent of the school's students qualify for free or reduced-price lunch. Howell says that these students, in particular, are negatively affected by long summer vacations, because they "don't do much reading or learning at home during the summer, making the summer learning loss significant."[15] Nationally, 3,045 year-round schools enrolled about 2.2 million students in the 2005–2006 school year.[16]

For more information about year-round education, log on to www.nayre.org.

6. *Eliminating the senior year.* Some question the usefulness and importance of the senior year. The National Commission on the High School Senior Year calls for a transformation that will result in a more productive senior year. As an alternative, Florida has a fast-track graduation law that allows students to graduate with six fewer credits. Six of the required credits must be in specified rigorous-level courses, and students must maintain a cumulative weighted grade point average of a 3.5 on a 4.0 scale. In all other classes, students must earn at least a 3.0 grade point average. This law requires higher-level mathematics

courses than the traditional program, and because it focuses so heavily on academics, students are allowed to take fewer elective courses.[17] The purpose of this program is twofold: to give students the option of graduating earlier and to reduce class size by moving students out of the school more quickly.

Regardless of whether such changes are implemented, school organization is affected by how time is used throughout the school day and the school year. High schools, for example, typically use the **Carnegie Unit** of instructional time. Under this system, one unit of high school credit is earned by meeting for the class four or five times a week for 40 to 60 minutes for 36 to 40 weeks each year—a total of 120 hours in the subject.[18] Recognizing that 40- to 60-minute classes effectively prevent many kinds of learning enterprises, educators are now devising alternative ways of scheduling the school day, such as **block scheduling**. In block scheduling, students attend four 90-minute classes each day, changing classes in the middle of the year. Block scheduling frees students from "seat time" defined in Carnegie Units, allows students to complete eight classes a year, rather than seven, and enables students to investigate subjects in more depth.[19]

Other scheduling variations, such as the trimester system, are being tried by many school districts. By dividing the school year into three 12-week terms (trimesters), students can take three or four classes a term, earning nine or more credits a year. At Angola High School in Indiana, there are four 90-minute periods in the school day. More efforts likely will be made to organize the school day into longer periods.

Carnegie Unit A credit awarded for successfully completing a high school course and used in determining graduation requirements and college admissions.

Block scheduling School class schedules that provide students longer periods of time, for example, four ninety-minute classes each day.

REFLECT & WRITE

What are your thoughts about year-round education? Would you want to teach in a year-round school? Why? Why not?

_____

_____

_____

_____

_____

School Size and School Organization

The size of schools is another factor that influences organization. There are 376 one-teacher schools in the United States.[20] The average size of enrollment in elementary schools is 476. Although the average size of secondary school enrollments is 727, there are nearly 300 high schools with more than 3,000 students.[21] Large schools enable educators to provide more varied curriculum offerings than would be possible in smaller schools. However, research indicates that small schools have higher graduation rates, promote greater student involvement in co-curricular activities, and experience better student behavior than their counterparts attending larger schools.[22] One response to the advantages of small schools has been to organize large schools into smaller units called *learning communities* or *schools within schools*, with their own principals and teachers. This organization provides for a feeling of community and caring.

Go to MyEducationLab and select the topic "School Organization," and read the article "Welcome to the House System." Answer the questions that follow.

Is Smaller Better?

Approximately 27 percent of secondary schools enroll over 1,000 students.[23] However, the public and many parents and educators believe that smaller is better.

America's high schools are in transition. Pressure to reform high schools is coming from all sectors of society. Across the country, there is a general consensus that the comprehensive high school that has served America over the last 50 years is in need of restructuring and reform.

School reformers want to ensure that all students are prepared to enter college and/or the workforce. The National Governors Association has initiated a $20 million grant program underwritten by the Bill and Melinda Gates Foundation to be dispersed among 10 deserving states to ensure that students are prepared for college and the workforce. The states, which include Arkansas, Delaware, Indiana, Louisiana, Maine, Massachusetts, Minnesota, Michigan, Rhode Island, and Virginia, are required to follow a blueprint requiring the implementation of 10-year performance goals to improve high school graduation rates and rates of college readiness.

In addition to federal initiatives, individual states also have enacted reform movements of their own. The Texas High School Project (THSP) is a $261 million public–private initiative committed to increasing graduation and college enrollment rates in every Texas community. THSP partners have invested more than $30 million to redesign existing high schools and to help schools break up into small, rigorous, and personalized learning communities.

Other sectors of society, for example, the Association for Career and Technical Education (ACTE), believes that American high schools should reform to engage students in specific career-related learning experiences and prepare students who may choose to enter the workforce directly after high school.

Some reformers believe high schools should prepare all students for college. What do you think?

Where Do You Stand on High Schools' Shifting Mission?

Sources: Jessica Tonn, "High School Redesign Moves Ahead in States," *Education Week*, February 21, 2007, p. 23; Texas Education Agency, "*Texas High School Project*," February 2, 2007. (Online). Available at www.tea.state.tx.us/ed_init/sec/thsp/. Accessed July 11, 2007; Association for Career and Technical Education, *Reinventing the American High School for the Twenty-first Century*, January 2006, p. 1.

In a Rural School and Community Trust policy brief entitled *The Hobbit Effect*, Dr. Lorna Jimerson cites 10 reasons why small public schools are more effective than larger schools:

- There is greater participation in extracurricular activities, which is linked to academic success.
- Small schools are safer.
- Kids feel they belong.
- Small class size allows for more individualized instruction.
- Good teaching methods are easier to implement.
- Teachers feel better about their work.
- Mixed-ability classes avoid condemning some students to low expectations.
- Multi-age classes promote personalized learning and encourage positive social interactions.
- Smaller districts mean less bureaucracy.
- More grades in one school alleviate many problems of transitions to new schools.[24]

Small schools have also been found to be more cost-effective than their larger counterparts. A 2005 study by the Knowledge Works Foundation analyzed the budgets, educational programs, and academic achievement of 25 small schools across the nation with diverse populations and approaches. The study found that, on average, these small schools spent 17 percent less per student than comparable schools in their districts while achieving equivalent or better educational results.[25]

Graduation rates have also proven to be higher at smaller schools than their larger counterparts. In New York City, graduation rates at 47 new small public high schools that have opened since 2002 are substantially higher than the city-wide average. This may be due to the administration's decision to break up many large failing high schools into smaller learning communities. Most of the new schools have performed better than the large schools they replaced. Eight schools out of the 47 small schools graduated more than 90 percent of their students. One campus of small schools at the old Erasmus Hall High School in Brooklyn, for example, reported a 92 percent 4-year graduation rate in June 2007, a significant increase from the 40 percent that graduated in 2002.[26]

In another small school in Atlanta, one student, Crishanna Jones, is a shining example of a student who has benefited from being at a small school. See *In the Classroom with Ninth-Grader Crishanna Jones.*

Some of the issues small schools hope to address are student achievement, safety, anonymity, and social alienation. In a study of high schools, researchers found that poor students do better in smaller schools and worse in larger schools. However, students in affluent communities do better in larger schools.[27]

The U.S. Department of Education's Smaller Learning Communities Program is a $94 million competitive grant program that enables school districts to develop and implement smaller learning communities in large high schools of over 1,000 students.

One way large high schools are implementing smaller learning communities is through creating separate wings within the school. In Minnesota, Farmington School District's new high school, to be completed in 2009, is designed around four 500-student wings, in which students could stay together for much of their high school years, helping teachers to know them better and helping students feel more at home.[28]

For more information, go to www.ed.gov/programs/slcp/index.html.

In the Classroom
with **Ninth-Grader Crishanna Jones**

A Case for Smaller Schools

Ninth-grader Crishanna Jones exudes confidence as she shares with her classmates and Atlanta School District administrators how Atlanta's Carver High School has changed her life.

"My dream for my future has blossomed," Crishanna tells her audience. She also reveals her plans of traveling to Panama and Costa Rica during the summer and of attending Harvard University. Crishanna concludes by saying, "Years after I leave this program, I want to come back."

Crishanna is only one example of many that illustrates how students' lives have been changed as a result of the remaking of Carver High School. The change was made possible because of a $10.5 million grant from the Bill and Melinda Gates Foundation. This grant, according to Atlanta superintendent Beverly L. Hall, also is being used to convert all of Atlanta's high schools to smaller, 400-pupil schools that will provide opportunities for all students.

Learn about other ways schools can create small learning environments at www.ed.gov/programs/slcp/strategies.html.

Source: Bridget Gutierrez, "Gates Fund Gift Helps Transform Atlanta Schools," *The Atlanta Journal-Constitution*, April 19, 2007, p. B1.

Creekland Middle School in Georgia is another school that has implemented the program. With 2,745 students, Creekland still tries to feel small. Creekland is divided into five "communities" (also called "houses" or "schools within a school"), each of which has its own administration. Creekland's teachers work in teams of two, with each teacher responsible for two subjects. Teachers believe the two-team approach enables them to get to know their students better than if they were in teams of four. The communities are integrated for elective classes, thus enabling students to meet other students outside their communities.

Just making schools smaller, however, is not necessarily sufficient in and of itself, because simply reducing class size does not necessarily result in increased learning and achievement. In the case of smaller schools, the following are necessary to support student learning:

- *Relationships between students and adults are strong and ongoing.* These relationships develop most often through extensive advisory systems.
- *Relationships with parents are strong and ongoing.* In most small schools, advisors and parents communicate regularly, not simply when a student experiences problems.
- *The school's organization is flat, with broadly distributed leadership.* Small schools have a leaner administrative structure, without specialized academic departments.
- *The school does not attempt to be comprehensive.* Most small schools concentrate on a few goals and insist that all students meet them, finding ways to honor student choice through the development of projects or other learning activities within a course rather than through an extensive course catalog.
- *The school develops its own culture.* The culture of small schools typically revolves around the expectations of hard work, high aspirations, respect for others, and success for all students.[29]

For a closer look at Creekland Middle School, log on to www.creeklandms.org.

Your Turn

As a beginning teacher, you have been asked to participate in discussions and decisions about transforming your district's high schools into small schools or expanding them into larger high schools. What considerations will you take into account to help you weigh in on behalf of either small or large high schools?

■ INTASC

STANDARD 10   The teacher fosters relationships with school colleagues, parents, and agencies in the larger community to support students' learning and well-being

REFLECT & WRITE

Schools are organized to support effective teaching and learning. Would you prefer to work in a large school, a mid-sized school, a small school, or a large school organized into learning communities? Why?

Pre-K Programs

Today, it is common for many children to be in a school of some kind beginning as early as age 2 or 3, and child care beginning at 6 weeks is commonplace for many children of working parents. Forty states currently invest in preschool, or pre-kindergarten education, whether as public preschools or as support for Head Start. **Preschool** or **pre-kindergarten (pre-K)** is for children ages 3 to 5, before they enter kindergarten. Preschool education continues to grow, with greater numbers of 4-year-olds entering preschools.

In 2006, the 40 states enrolled 20 percent of the nation's 4-year-olds, with over 942,766 children participating in state pre-kindergarten programs.[30] State-funded

Preschool and prekindergarten (pre-K)   Programs that serve children ages 3 to 5.

preschools represent an important and increasing component of the nation's support of early childhood programs.

A number of reasons help explain the current popularity of preschool programs:

- More parents are in the workforce than ever before. This places a great demand on the public schools and the early childhood profession to provide more programs and services, including programs for 3- and 4-year-olds.
- Parents, politicians, and researchers believe early intervention programs designed to prevent social problems such as substance abuse, school dropout, and delinquency work best in the early years. Research supports the effectiveness of this early intervention approach.
- Brain research makes it clear that the foundation for learning is laid in the early years and that 3- and 4-year-old children are ready and able to learn.

As preschool programs continue to grow in number and popularity they also have undergone significant changes in purpose. Previously, the predominant purposes of preschools were to help socialize children, enhance their social-emotional development, and get them ready for kindergarten or first grade. Although there is a decided move away from socialization as the primary function of preschool, early childhood professionals recognize that socialization matters, and there are renewed efforts to provide for the whole child. Nonetheless, preschools are now promoted as places that accomplish the following:

- *Support and develop children's innate capacity for learning.* The responsibility for "getting ready for school" has shifted from being primarily children's and parents' responsibilities to being a cooperative venture between the child, family, home, schools, and communities.
- *Provide academic, social, and behavioral skills necessary for entry into kindergarten.* Today, a major focus is on developing children's literacy and math skills.
- *Solve or find solutions for pressing social problems.* The early years are viewed as a time when interventions are most likely to have long-term positive influences. Preschool programs are seen as a way of lowering the number of dropouts, improving children's health, and preventing serious social problems, such as substance abuse and violence.

The goals of the "new" preschool are dramatically changing how preschool programs operate and teachers teach. Given the changing nature of preschool, the preschool years are playing a larger role in early childhood education.

Pre-K programs come in many different formats, depending on their purposes, the children served, and the funding agencies. Preschools can be either public or private and are operated by many different agencies. Although a common goal of all programs is to provide quality education and services for all children, how they achieve this goal depends on the children served, the parents, and the philosophies of the programs.

Head Start

Head Start has had more influence on early childhood programs than any other single program or agency. **Head Start** began in 1965 as a program to help children from low-income families who would enter first grade. Now it is a year-round program for children ages 3 to 5. Head Start has a federal budget of $6.9 billion and enrolls 909,201 children in 18,875 centers. Early Head Start, initiated in 1994, serves children 6 weeks to 2 years in age. Currently, low-income families are served in more than 650 Early Head Start Programs, with an annual enrollment of nearly 62,000 children.[31] Head Start components include:

- Education
- Parent involvement

Go to MyEducationLab, select the topic "Assessment" and then watch the video "Observing Children in Authentic Contexts." Notice how the teacher integrates assessment into her teaching. Answer the questions that follow the video.

Head Start   Started in 1965, the first major early childhood program subsidized by the federal government provides comprehensive services to low-income children and their families.

■ INTASC

STANDARD 10   The teacher fosters relationships with school colleagues, parents, and agencies in the larger community to support students' learning and well-being.

- Health services (including psychological services, nutrition, and mental health)
- Social services
- Staff development to provide the knowledge and skills needed for administration and management of programs

REFLECT & WRITE

How do current changes in early childhood education reflect the link between society and education? Why is pre-K of growing importance in education? Does pre-K teaching appeal to you? Why? Why not?

_____

_____

_____

_____

_____

Kindergartens

Perhaps you have heard the saying, "Everything I need to know in life I learned in kindergarten." This pretty well sums up the view that kindergarten plays an important role in many children's lives. Kindergartens are sponsored by private and public schools and enroll 5- and 6-year-old children, although the ages of kindergarten children vary from state to state, depending on entrance age cutoff dates. Many school districts require children to be 5 years old by September 1 of the school year in order to be eligible to enter kindergarten. Most kindergartens provide for the academic, intellectual, social, emotional, and physical development of children.

Just as there is growing support for universally available public preschools, there is wide public support for compulsory and tax-supported public kindergarten. In keeping with this national sentiment, most children attend kindergarten, though it is mandatory in only 14 states.[32] In many ways, kindergarten is now considered the first grade of school.

The kindergarten of today is not the same as the kindergarten of 5 years ago. Kindergarten is now a program that focuses primarily on academics, especially early literacy, math, and science, and activities that prepare children to think and problem solve. These changes represent a transformation of great magnitude and will have a lasting impact on kindergarten curriculum and teaching in the future.

Kindergarten is either a half- or whole-day program. Texas, for example, leaves the decision to districts to provide full- or half-day programs. However, Florida has compulsory full-day kindergarten for all children.

A concern in early childhood education is that programs, materials, and instructional methods be appropriate to children's levels of physical, cognitive, and social development. This is especially important today with the increased academic demands on children in early childhood education—especially kindergarten students.

Full-day kindergartens are becoming more common because they better meet the needs of children and working parents than do half-day programs.[33]

The National Education Association (NEA) believes that kindergarten attendance should be mandatory and supports full-day—as opposed to half-day—kindergarten and prekindergarten. In addition, the NEA supports the establishment in every state of 2 years of universal (available to all) prekindergarten for all 3- and 4-year-olds.[34]

Public support for compulsory and tax-supported public kindergartens and preschool programs is widespread. For example, in Arizona over 75 percent of parents have expressed support for publicly funded, full-day kindergarten, with an even higher level of support among Hispanic parents.[35] Indiana residents support publicly funded kindergarten as well. According to the 2006 Public Opinion Survey on Education in Indiana, 74 percent of residents indicated support for state-funded full-day kindergarten, and 61 percent supported full-day kindergarten even if a tax increase was necessary to fund it.[36]

Primary and Elementary Schools

Grades K through 3 are known as the *primary grades*, whereas grades 4 through 6 are referred to as the *elementary grades*, although it is common to refer to grades 1 through 6 as the *elementary school years*. This structure is somewhat fluid, however, with many middle schools enrolling sixth-graders and many elementary schools enrolling children in grades K through 5. Within a school, the typical organization reflects the graded approach, with 20 to 25 students and a teacher in a self-contained classroom. Some states have maximum class sizes. For example, in Texas the maximum class size for grades K–4 is 22.

Elementary schools come in all sizes and have different missions and purposes. For example, William Land Elementary school in Sacramento, California, might be the most diverse elementary school in the United States. Its 322 students speak 189 languages other than English. Ernest R. Graham Elementary school in Hialeah, Florida, is one of the nation's largest elementary schools, with 2,257 students in grades pre-K–6.

The definition of what elementary schools are for and how they should operate is changing. Schooling in the primary and elementary grades has become a serious enterprise, for both political and social reasons. It is in the primary grades, especially grades 3 and 4, where state and national testing begins. There is therefore an emphasis on ensuring that children know what will be tested and that they will do well on the tests. For example, the federal government and many states (including Texas and California) have a goal that all children will read on grade level by grade 3. This goal makes the teaching of reading a high priority. The National Assessment of Educational Progress (NAEP), known as the "nation's report card," is given in grades 4, 8, and 12. The NAEP project is carried out by the Commissioner of Educational Statistics in the Department of Education. The No Child Left Behind Act requires states to participate in NAEP in order to validate student progress. The pressure for high performance on state and national tests begins early in children's school careers.

Changes also are occurring in classroom organization and in teachers' roles. Changes in curriculum and instructional methods have affected how classrooms are organized. Instead of sitting in seats in straight rows and engaging in solitary learning activities, students are now out of their seats, discussing projects with classmates and collaborating on completing them. While the elementary teacher's roles of facilitator, learning collaborator, and coach are still popular teachers also are focusing on their role as instructional leaders, teaching students the skills they need for school and life success.

The reforms taking place in elementary schools reflect a nationwide movement toward a new vision of the elementary school: one that centers on giving

To learn more about these schools, visit http://schools.scusd.edu/williamland/william%20land%20home.htm and www.dade.k12.fl.us/graham/.

■ **INTASC**

STANDARD 3   The teacher understands how students differ in their approaches to learning and creates instructional opportunities that are adapted to diverse learners.

For more information, visit the NAEP website at http://nces.ed.gov/nationsreportcard/sitemap.asp.

What's *New* in Education?

K–8 Schools—Back to the Future

Cincinnati, Baltimore, Milwaukee, New York, Philadelphia, and Pittsburgh are just some of the cities that are restructuring to include K–8 schools—an idea that went out of fashion years ago. Cleveland has converted 80 schools and Pittsburgh 20. The change is being driven by research and a rising pile of anecdotes that suggest that K–8 configurations increase academic performance, decrease discipline problems, enhance parent involvement, and save money. Research in both the Baltimore and Philadelphia school districts indicates that students in the K–8 grade configuration have higher achievement test scores.

The wave of K–8 reorganization comes as educators, pressured by new federal mandates, are seeking ways to boost student achievement. Most district leaders who favor the K–8 model see it as one part of an overhaul that includes smaller, more personalized schools able to meet the needs of varying age groups with the improved curricula and better staff training. Long heralded as the solution to many preadolescent social and learning problems, middle schools in many districts are being reexamined. Two solutions, both with supporters, are the K–8 and the 7–12 grade configurations. Both are gaining momentum across the United States.

Source: F. Schouten, "Kids Like Get-out-of-Junior-High Card," *USA Today*, October 16, 2002. (Online). Available at www.usatoday.com/news/health/2002-10-16-middle-school-usat_x.htm. Accessed July 17, 2007.

children of all abilities many opportunities and ways to achieve state standards and be successful socially and academically. Such schools shun practices that march every child of the same age through the same drill at the same time. Instead, these schools group pupils in ways that allow them to move at their own rates while working cooperatively with peers of different ages and abilities. Some also keep children with the same teacher for more than 1 year, promoting a view of teachers as children's guides and coinvestigators. The tools of the teaching trade have also changed—from textbooks to technology, which we discuss in Chapter 12.

REFLECT & WRITE

In the short time since you attended elementary, middle, and high school, a lot of changes have occurred. Based on your observations, reading, and research, what would you characterize as the most notable changes?

Middle and Junior High Schools

Junior high schools enroll students in grades 7 and 8 or 7 through 9. In 1909, the first junior high schools opened in Columbus, Ohio, and Berkeley, California, and this organizational structure has been an important feature of American education ever since. Beginning in the 1960s, middle schools have been gradually replacing junior high schools as the organizing model for educating young adolescents.

Middle schools typically serve children in grades 6 through 8 (ages 10 through 14) and provide an earlier transition from the elementary school. Other grade configurations for middle schools include grades 5 through 7 and 7 through 9. Some

Middle schools are designed to address the unique developmental needs of emerging adolescents.

junior high schools have changed their names to "middle schools." The organization, operation, and effectiveness of middle schools receive a lot of attention. The following issues are some that confront middle schools:

- Finding a balance between providing for academics and students' social-emotional development.
- Ensuring that middle school teachers are entitled specifically to teach middle school students. Many middle school teachers hold elementary and senior high school certification; however, many colleges of education offer middle-grade certification for teachers who are entering teaching in middle schools.
- Following curriculum that fails to meet the academic needs of students. Some call the curricula of many schools "shallow, fragmented, and unchallenging."[37]

Middle schools are designed to address the unique developmental needs (cognitive, psychosocial, and physical) of emerging adolescents. Many adolescents change schools during these formative years, moving from the comforting confines of a neighborhood elementary school to a large middle school, junior high school, or high school. These changes disrupt familiar peer group structures, introduce youth to different standards and achievement expectations, and provide opportunities for new extracurricular activities as part of both the planned curriculum and the hidden curriculum (what students learn simply because they attend school).

Recently, junior high schools have come under increased criticism. Many middle schools have exhibited low school performance and student achievement. Factors such as parental dissatisfaction, high absenteeism, discipline problems, and dropout rates have plagued middle schools as well. To address these issues, more and more school districts have begun to implement the K–8 configuration, doing away with junior high schools altogether. Available data show that students in K–8 schools score higher on standardized tests than their middle school counterparts. However, these studies do not account for other factors that could affect student performance; consequently, more research is needed on the success of K–8 grade configurations.[38] For now, middle schools remain the predominant form of school organization for early adolescents. (See *What's New in Education?* K-8 Schools—Back to the Future.)

Three essential features characterize quality middle schools: guidance programs; transition programs; and instructional organization that includes team teaching, career exploration, and athletics.

1. Effective guidance systems provide adult mentors, teachers, and guidance counselors who give advice on academic, personal, social, and vocational matters.

Transition programs Programs designed to help children and parents make the passage from one program or educational setting to another, for example, from the elementary grades to the middle school and from the middle school to the senior high school.

2. **Transition programs** help children (and often their parents) make the passage from one educational setting to another—from the elementary grades to the middle school, and from the middle school to the senior high school. Transition programs are designed to help minimize confusion or distress. Activities include orienting students before their arrival at the new school, informing parents of the philosophy of the school and providing them with opportunities to visit classes, and inviting students already enrolled at the new school to talk to arriving students. *In the Classroom with Therese Samperi* illustrates how one such transition program works. The former principal of a ninth-grade school discusses how her school helps students transition to the high school years.

In the Classroom
with **Therese Samperi**

A Transition Program for High School Freshmen

Therese Samperi is the former Principal of MacArthur Ninth-Grade School in Houston, Texas.

In our school of 930+ students, we put a total and complete focus on the students during their freshman year of high school. This focus has resulted in higher academic performance, fewer dropouts, fewer pregnancies, and a higher graduation rate.

- Prior to the opening of the ninth-grade campus, we had 350 to 400 repeat ninth graders a year. Since the ninth-grade campus opened, that number has dropped dramatically to 125 this year.
- We have maintained a dropout rate that has been less than 1 percent over the past 8 years.
- Prior to opening the ninth-grade campus, we had more than 35 freshman pregnancies a year. On average, we will have five to six pregnancies a year.
- Our graduation rate has grown from approximately 440 graduates before we opened the ninth-grade campus to more than 530 students this year.

It is so easy to see that taking the freshman out of the large environment and giving them the individual attention that they deserve will allow them to be successful throughout their high school career. The only real drawback to having the ninth-graders on a separate campus is that by the time you get to know the students, they move on to the big high school campus. In our district, students can only stay on the ninth-grade campus for 1 year.

All students go to the big high school even if they have not successfully completed the ninth grade. Of course, this has its good points and its bad points, but the good points definitely outweigh the bad ones.

The main thing to keep in mind is that focusing on the student as an individual is key to student success. Bottom line, having a ninth-grade campus is what is *best* for *students*!

3. Instructional trends in middle-level schooling include teaching strategies that emphasize inquiry teaching and learning, cooperative learning, independent study, and exploratory opportunities. Courses that provide exploratory opportunities include computer education, industrial arts, music, home economics, technology education, typing, fine arts, career education, and community service.

> You can take a virtual tour of these schools at www.schoolstowatch.org/visit.htm

The National Forum to Accelerate Middle Grades Reform sponsors a "Schools-to-Watch" program to call attention to high-performing schools, such as Thurgood Marshall Middle School in Chicago, Illinois; Jefferson Middle School in Champaign, Illinois; Barren County Middle School in Glasgow, Kentucky; and Freeport Intermediate School in Freeport, Texas.

REFLECT & WRITE

Do you think middle schools are good for students and teachers? Why or why not? On a scale of 1 (low) to 10 (high), rank your desire to teach in a middle school.

High Schools

Each weekday morning, more than 13 million teenagers report to public high school classrooms across the United States.[39]

High schools serve students in grades 9 or 10 through 12 and vary in size from a few hundred students to almost 5,000. Today's **comprehensive high schools** serve a large and diverse student body and provide a range of services and curricula to students.

Richard Schafer, principal at Ft. Myers High School in Florida, says that running a high school today is a lot different from the way it was 20 years ago when he entered the profession. He identifies the following ways that things have changed:

- *Politics.* There is much more politics involved in providing education to students. As a consequence, a principal has to spend a lot of time being a politician and being involved in political affairs.
- *Business affairs.* More and more, schools are being run like businesses, and principals are more responsible for the financial affairs of the school than ever before.
- *Activities.* Schools today provide a wider range of activities and services for their students. Some schools have staff members whose sole job is to coordinate, supervise, and facilitate student activities.
- *Collaboration and cooperation.* Schools are no longer run by the principal. Today, teachers, students, staff, parents, community members, and others are included in decisions about what is taught and how it is taught.
- *Community issues and concerns.* Community needs, educational needs, and professional needs have to be balanced and evaluated so that community needs alone do not run the school. Certain community advocacy groups can be very powerful and exert tremendous influence. Some special interest groups are designed to protect the rights of children—for example, children with disabilities. Others are designed to promote the teaching of certain topics in the public schools, for example, school prayer. Advocacy groups are intent on making their positions known and on advancing their particular agendas.
- *Public relations.* Today, many school personnel are public relations experts. They are involved in speaking to groups and community agencies about community and school issues. How well the schools get along with stakeholders and how well they articulate their programs to them determines to some degree how successful schools are as educational agencies.
- *Delivering a quality education program.* The primary goal of schools is to provide their students with a quality educational program that will serve them well in the world after grade 12, whatever that world might immediately be. Because of the constant criticisms of the schools, more and more professionals are concentrating their efforts on basic skills training. They are intent on ensuring that they are capable of delivering a quality product, in this case, students who can read, write, compute, and think; who are technologically literate; and who can take their place in the nation's work force.[40]

Comprehensive high schools High schools that serve a large and diverse student body and provide a wide range of services and curricula to students.

■ **INTASC**

STANDARD 1 The teacher understands the central concepts, tools of inquiry, and structures of the subject being taught and can create learning experiences that make these aspects of subject matter meaningful for students.

■ **INTASC**

STANDARD 10 The teacher fosters relationships with school colleagues, parents, and agencies in the larger community to support students' learning and well-being.

Schools today offer students a wide range of services and programs. Such opportunities promote curiosity and allow students to explore various interests and to broaden their awareness and knowledge.

_____

_____

_____

_____

_____

Alternative Learning Programs and Schools

Social and educational change is reflected in the creation of alternative learning programs or **alternative schools**. Alternative schools are designed to provide alternatives to the regular or typical school program. Alternative schools come in many configurations.

> **Alternative schools**   Schools formed by public schools and private groups as alternatives to existing public schools.

At-Risk Students

One type of alternative school is specifically designed to meet the needs of students who are at risk for some reason, such as constant truancy, drug use, and having been expelled from the regular school program. This school can be in a separate building from the regular school or a school within a school. In this type of alternative school, teachers provide remedial programs as well as individualized and specialized counseling services, and the class size is generally small. The goal of the alternative approach is to keep students in school (in most states students have to stay in school until they are 18), help students address and overcome their problems, and assist students to graduate.

> To learn about yet another type of alternative school, go to MyEducationLab, select the topic "Family and Community," then read the article "A Community School." Answer the questions that follow.

Parental Choice

A second kind of alternative school is designed to provide parents with choices relating to their expectations of curriculum and schooling. For example, the Poudre School District in Ft. Collins, Colorado, has elementary alternative schools open to any student in the district, depending on space. These schools include:

1. **The Traut Core Knowledge School,** a school of choice, uses the cultural literacy curriculum developed by E. D. Hirsch (this approach is discussed in Chapter 10). This back-to-basics elementary school stresses character education, parent partnerships, and literacy instruction.
2. **The Lab School for Creative Learning** is at the opposite end of the educational continuum. It offers a nontraditional school setting that emphasizes a small pupil-teacher ratio and a child-centered, developmental curriculum.
3. **The Harris Bilingual Immersion School** offers strong bilingual language skills and cross-cultural knowledge to a balanced mix of predominantly Spanish-speaking and predominantly English-speaking elementary students.

> **■ INTASC**
>
> **STANDARD 3**   The teacher understands how students differ in their approaches to learning and creates instructional opportunities that are adapted to diverse learners.

Magnet Schools

Magnet schools are public schools that are a part of the nation's efforts to achieve voluntary desegregation. Magnet schools offer a special curriculum and program capable of attracting students of different racial backgrounds.[41]

> **Magnet schools**   Designed to attract diverse students from all over a district or attendance area and to address issues of equity in course and program offerings. Many magnet schools have a particular curriculum or program emphasis.

For example, Houston now supports 54 magnet elementary schools, 28 magnet middle schools, and 27 magnet high schools. These magnets are tasked with meeting two objectives: to provide academic programs whose quality and special focus will attract students from across the district and to increase the percentage of students attending integrated schools.

The DeBakey High School for Health Professions, located in the Texas Medical Center, is an example of a magnet with a unique theme strong enough to attract excellent students from all over this huge district. The school provides a rigorous and comprehensive precollege program for students pursuing careers in medicine, health care, and the sciences.[42]

Magnet schools are fairly ineffective at integrating schools and reducing segregation. Adding magnet schools to a voluntary desegregation plan does not seem to produce any more interracial exposure than does a voluntary desegregation plan without magnets.[43] Recent research has also shown that magnet schools are not more effective in improving student learning than their public school counterparts. In fact, a 2003 study by the American Institutes of Research found that academic progress in magnet schools was no greater than in a comparison set of regular public schools.[44]

Private For-Profit Schools

A fast-growing segment of the educational enterprise is private for-profit schools. Many of these schools serve an increasing number of students who have been expelled for violating drug and weapons policies and for other disciplinary reasons. During the 2004–2005 school year, students ages 12 to 18 were victims of 1.4 million nonfatal crimes at school, including 863,000 thefts and 583,000 violent crimes. Students ages 5 to 18 were victims of 28 school-associated violent deaths during the same period. In response, about 46 percent of public schools took at least one serious disciplinary action against students—including suspensions lasting 5 days or more, removals with no services (i.e., expulsions), and transfers to specialized schools.[45]

Some states require school districts to provide alternative schools and programs for expelled students. For example, in 1995 the Texas Legislature enacted the Safe Schools Act requiring each of its 27 counties with populations of 125,000 or more to provide alternative schools. Many districts find it easier and more cost-effective to let for-profit companies provide the services. These privately operated alternative schools are both day and residential schools. Additionally, more affluent parents are turning to private alternative schools to help their children overcome addiction and other problems. Although some alternative schools receive support from tax revenue, tuition for private alternative schools can be quite expensive.

Charter Schools

One of the most talked-about innovations in public education, **charter schools**, or "contract" schools, are custom designed by individuals or groups and are a major aid in reforming public education. Charter schools have a great deal of public and political support. Funding for charter schools comes from the district that granted the charter and from states, foundations, and individuals. Although they are considered independent, these schools are not exempt from state laws governing education. Charter schools:

- Seek to realize an alternative vision of schooling
- Provide local, autonomous control of education
- Free teachers and schools from cumbersome, bureaucratic state and local board of education red tape (though they remain subject to all state laws applying to public education)

Charter schools have their supporters and detractors. Here are two news stories—pro and con—about the success or lack of success of charter schools. Read these accounts and then you decide—Have charter schools lived up to their promise?

"CHARTER SCHOOL TEST SCORES HIGHEST IN NY"

Long Island's first charter school, which only a year ago appeared in administrative disarray, has bounced back under new leadership this year with the highest elementary test scores for any charter school in the state.

Latest results show that 87 percent of fourth-graders at Roosevelt Children's Academy scored at the proficient level or higher on state-administered English tests. That's the highest rate among more than thirty charter schools operating statewide and is competitive with scores in many of [Long] Island's more affluent school districts.

YOU DECIDE

Have Charter Schools Lived Up to Their Promise?

"CHARTER SCHOOLS NOT AS INTEGRATED AS MANY WOULD LIKE"

When the Reverends Michael Nickleson and Vernon Graham set out to start a local charter school, they wanted to offer a choice to families in the southwest part of East Allen County Schools.

But now, after years of fighting with local school districts to make sure schools are integrated, the two men find themselves on the board of directors for the Timothy L. Johnson Academy, a charter school on South Anthony Boulevard with a student body experts call "hypersegregated"—95 percent of the students are black.

Need help making up your mind? Here are some links to help you.

- USCS: United Charter Schools homepage— www.uscharterschools.org
- National Education Association—www.nea.org/charter/
- Charter Schools USA—www.charterschoolsusa.com/
- National Charter School Institute— www.nationalcharterschools.org/

Sources: Adapted from selected information from J. Hildebrande, "Charter School Test Scores Highest in NY," *NY Newsday*, June 8, 2004. (Online). Available at www.nynewsday.com/; K. Stockman, "Charter Schools Not as Integrated as Many Would Like," *The Journal Gazette*, May 16, 2004. (Online). Available at http://nl.newsbank.com/nl-search/we/Archives?p_action=list&p_topdoc=41.

- Provide parents and students with alternative choices to public education
- Strive to be innovative in curriculum, teaching, and delivery of services

Minnesota was the first state to approve charter schools in 1991. There are many kinds of charter schools, designed to meet many different purposes.

For example, the Vivian Banks Charter School of the Bonsall Union School District in Bonsall, California, is a K–5 school on the Pala Indian reservation north of San Diego. The main goal of Vivian Banks is to achieve literacy for all children in reading, writing, speaking, and listening. Computers are used for instruction, and there is an emphasis on small class size and parent participation.

Alianza School (*alianza* means "alliance") is a two-way bilingual immersion elementary charter school in Watsonville, California. Alianza's mission is to teach understanding and respect for racial, cultural, and linguistic diversity. Alianza has implemented a schoolwide two-way immersion in Spanish program. Two-way immersion programs integrate language-minority and language-majority students, providing instruction in both English and the native language of the language minority students. They promote bilingualism and biliteracy, grade-level academic achievement, and positive cross-cultural attitudes and behaviors in all students.

Nationwide, more than 3,602 charter schools operate in 41 states and the District of Columbia. Table 3.1 shows the top 10 states for charter schools. Charter schools have an average enrollment of 268. Nationwide, 963,724 students attend charter schools.

TABLE 3.1 Top 10 States for Charter Schools, 2005

State	Number of Charter Schools
California	574
Arizona	499
Florida	338
Ohio	268
Texas	241
Michigan	216
Wisconsin	188
Minnesota	131
Pennsylvania	114
Colorado	113

Source: U.S. Charter Schools. (2005). (Online). Available at www.uscharterschools.org/cs/sp/query/q/1595. Accessed September 7, 2007.

REFLECT & WRITE

Increasingly, schools are called on to address and solve many of society's problems relating to violence, substance abuse, crime, and teenage pregnancy. Do you think the schools are being asked to do too much for too many students?

WHAT IS IT LIKE TO TEACH IN URBAN, RURAL, AND SUBURBAN SCHOOLS?

■ INTASC

STANDARD 3   The teacher understands how students differ in their approaches to learning and creates instructional opportunities that are adapted to diverse learners.

You have read about how schools are organized. Another way to look at public schools is according to population densities and other characteristics (such as cultural diversity, socioeconomic status, and funding available for education) of the communities in which they are located. Geography provides another lens through which we can look at schools. Where schools are located frequently determines their nature, curriculum, and purpose. In this kind of classification, there are three types of schools: urban (also called inner-city or metropolitan), suburban, and rural. Each type has its unique student populations, features, and cultures. Even within each type, individual schools differ. For example, the Laredo (Texas) Independent School District is 13.83 square miles. It has 24,745 students and 3,736 full-time employees on 30 campuses. This district has all categories of schools—urban, suburban, and rural. The unique differences of individual schools arise not only from the American tradition of local control of schools, but also from each school's responsiveness to the nature and character of the local community. Figure 3.2 shows some of the sources of differences among urban, rural, and suburban schools.

REFLECT & WRITE

Which type(s) of schools have you attended? Consider the sources of differences displayed in Figure 3.2, and then answer this question: How did the characteristics of the schools you attended affect your learning and school life?

Urban School Districts and Schools

An urban school district is one in which 75 percent or more of the households served are in the central city of a metropolitan area. Urban schools take their character from the cities of which they are a part. Urban schools tend to be large, and student bodies tend to reflect the diversity of urban communities. Miami, for ex-

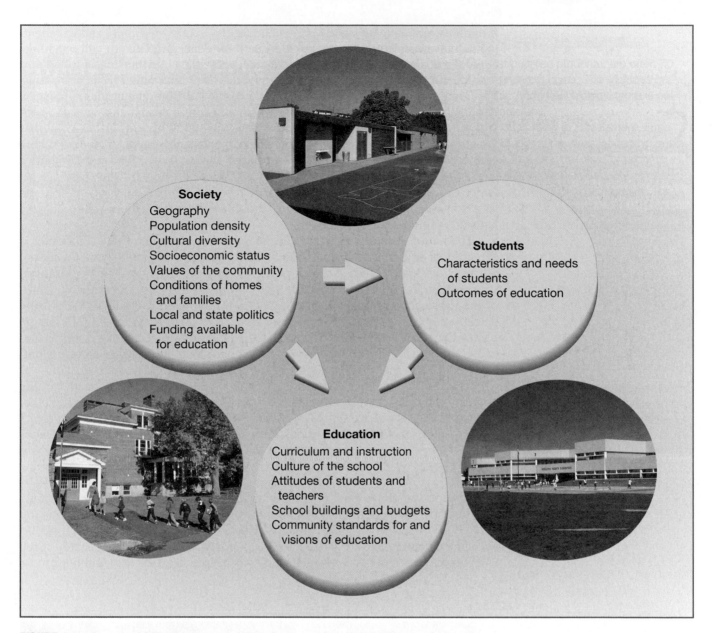

FIGURE 3.2   Sources of Differences among Urban, Rural, and Suburban Schools

For each of the characteristics in the figure, think about how they differ based on whether a school is urban, suburban, or rural.

ample, has large populations of Cubans, Haitians, and Central Americans. Los Angeles has large populations of Hispanics and Asian Americans. Approximately 73.3 percent of the Los Angeles school district is Hispanic American. Belmont High School in downtown Los Angeles is a year-round school with an enrollment of 4,045 students. Fifty percent of the students are classified as English learners.[46]

The social problems of urban areas and the educational needs of students exert great influence on the curriculum, the learning environment, and the day-to-day operation of schools. Despite the pressures and challenges of urban districts, many urban schools are excellent, with vibrant school cultures, outstanding curricula, and highly dedicated teaching professionals. For example, Reading, Pennsylvania, a city of over 81,000, has only one high school with a population of 4,399 in grades 9 through 12, making it Pennsylvania's largest. It provides a full range of

■ **INTASC**

STANDARD 10   The teacher fosters relationships with school colleagues, parents, and agencies in the larger community to support students' learning and well-being.

programs, including advanced placement classes, a jazz ensemble, and a student-to-student peer mediation program designed to reduce violence by allowing specially trained students to help other students solve their conflicts peacefully.[47]

A central issue for urban schools is how to ensure the safety of their students. Providing a safe learning environment is a key to fulfilling the academic mission of all schools. Some districts are employing prevention design and devices to ensure safer schools. For example, Town View Magnet School in Dallas combines the latest in safe-school design (barriers to keep intruders out) with modern school security technology. Thirty-seven surveillance cameras are monitored 24 hours a day, and each student wears a photo identification card. Five full-time campus security officers monitor the school. Many schools use metal detectors to help ensure that weapons are not brought to school, and security officers patrolling the halls are almost commonplace.

The national School Security Technologies and Resource (SSTAR) Center, a Department of Energy (DOE) research and development laboratory based at Sandia, Albuquerque, advises schools about security technologies. This advisement stresses low-tech approaches that are both cost-effective and safety effective. Some of the low-tech approaches include radios and communication devices, intrusion detection systems, handheld metal detectors, ID badging systems, and visitors' passes that expire after 1 day. Sandia also advises on nontechnology approaches that contribute to safe schools, including campus cleanliness, crime-reporting hotlines, crisis intervention programs, drug dogs, fences, and school design.

In addition to using zero-tolerance, expulsions, metal detectors, and security guards to ensure safety, some schools are turning to other means. There are other methods that work. Safe schools depend on safe communities. For one teacher's view about teaching in urban schools, see *In the Classroom with Marty Walker*.

Rural Schools

Rural schools reflect a sense of community and are often the center of community life. Just how much of a sense of community is conveyed in rural schools was impressed upon new high school principal Hasse K. Halley of Cabot, Vermont. "At the annual Fourth of July parade, she was introduced to the village atop a red Chevy pickup. . . . They want the school to be the heart of the community . . .

■ **INTASC**

STANDARD 6   The teacher uses knowledge of effective verbal, nonverbal, and media communication techniques to foster active inquiry, collaboration, and supportive interaction in the classroom.

For more information about Sandia's security work, visit www.sandia .gov/media/Newsrel/NR2002/ skoolsecwkshop.htm.

Rural communities have a culture very different from urban and suburban communities, and the schools reflect this culture. What considerations might a teacher in a rural community have to make that would be unique to the setting?

In the Classroom

with Marty Walker

Teaching in an Urban School

Marty Walker teaches at H. Grady Spruce High School in the Dallas Independent School District and was the Dallas Golden Apple Teacher of the Year and is a Texas Outstanding Teacher of Humanities. Spruce is located in a changing neighborhood in which middle-income families are moving out, and low-income families are moving in. These new families are less educated, and many are single parents. Many of the students receive free breakfasts and lunches.

Marty teaches regular English IV (seniors), English IV AP, and is chairman of the English department; trains new teachers for the Dallas School System; and serves on the Campus Leadership Instructional team.

I choose to be in an urban school. I've been asked to change jobs and go to other schools, but I feel a calling to my school. I have a lot to offer my students, and there is a need for role models in my school. I grew up disadvantaged and lived on the "other side of the tracks." I am what I am because of my teachers, and I want to return the opportunity to my students to have good teaching. Perhaps some of them will be inspired to select teaching as a career and teach in the inner city.

It's different teaching in an urban school. Every morning every student must go through a metal detector—they are located at every entrance. Also, the assistant principals and aides are at tables, and they go through all book bags and purses in order to keep guns out of schools. We have a "youth action officer," a plainclothes police officer who is in the school all the time. We also have a female uniformed police officer in the school all the time. She patrols the halls and lunchroom to help maintain order. If there is a rumor of any impending school disturbance, then we have more police officers. We do all we can to have a safe and violence-free school for our students.

I really and truly love the kids. That's why I choose to be here at Spruce. You need to have a calling to help students, and you have to look beyond the poverty and look beyond the surface and have a great desire to help students become all that they can become.

As you work with inner-city students, you are always looking for a hook to get them interested in learning. I do a lot of praising in my teaching. The students need to hear words of praise. They do not get many words of encouragement in their homes, so I have to provide it in school. I also do a lot of correcting; it is one way of letting students know I care. You must care about students. You have to have a vision for the kids. If you don't, you shouldn't be teaching. If you are a person who doesn't care for kids who don't look right and act right all the time, then chances are you wouldn't be happy teaching in an inner-city school. You have to see persons, not color, and look at character, not just the surface.

Teaching in an urban school is stressful. You have to give 150 percent. Every day, I come home from school wiped out. I am a high-energy person, and I put a lot into my teaching. I tell new teachers that some things they can do to handle stress are to take vitamins, to go to bed as early as possible, and to be good to themselves.

Learn more about urban schools at www.urbanschools .org/.

that's the old way, and that's the way they are going to keep it."[48] While by no means free of social problems, rural communities and families tend to have close ties, and children often attend the same school their parents and grandparents attended.

Many rural school districts cover hundreds of square miles. Outside of small community centers, people often live far from each other, and students travel long distances to and from school. Rural schools are found primarily in the Midwest, West, and South. *Rural* is defined by the Census Bureau as communities with fewer than 2,500 people. Texas has 532,378 rural students, the greatest absolute number found in any state. Rural students make up more than 30 percent of the enrollment in 17 other states.[49] Pennsylvania's smallest school is in Austin and has an entire student population of 280 students, with prekindergarten to twelfth grade all housed in one building. Students participate in a wide range of activities, including five varsity sports and a variety of clubs and organizations. In such a school, strong relationships are possible.

The nature and character of rural life affects teachers, who are expected to support community values, adhere to community standards, and participate in community affairs and activities. For one teacher's view on teaching in rural schools, see *In the Classroom with Juanita Wilkerson*.

Suburban Schools

Suburban areas, and therefore suburban schools, are adjacent to large cities. Although people move to suburbia to escape some of the problems frequently associated with city life, the problems of city life have frequently followed people to suburbia. Today, violence, substance abuse, teenage pregnancy, and other "urban" problems are as prevalent in suburbia as they are in the inner city.

In the Classroom
with **Juanita Wilkerson**

*Teaching in a
Rural School*

Juanita Wilkerson taught preschool (4-year program) and kindergarten at the Paris, Kentucky, Elementary School, which has an enrollment of 500 students.

I designed the 4-year program, wrote the goals and objectives and the curriculum. I even painted the furniture! My husband helped me prepare my room before school started. In a rural school we are expected to do more. Because of a limited budget, I spend a lot of my own money. I supplemented my classroom supplies by going to yard sales and buying toys and other materials to put into my learning centers. As a rural teacher, I also save everything, because sooner or later I will find a use for it.

Teaching in a rural school is very challenging. Teachers are very important in the rural community, and parents expect us to teach the basics and we do. Many of the new teaching ideas are unfamiliar to parents, and some do not approve of them. We have to try to preserve the best of the old while educating parents to new ideas and practices that will help their children to learn better. Things happen slower in a rural school and evolve in a slower way. For example, we have site-based management. This means the teacher

and parents are involved in discussions about how the school operates. It took the faculty and administration a lot of time and effort to get parents involved.

One of the best things about teaching in a rural school is parent support. When I teach, I always tell parents it is their classroom, too. My students' parents help with everything—arts and crafts activities, musical programs, physical activities, cooking, parties, and field trips.

The kids are great in rural schools. They love to learn, and I try to provide experiences that they might not otherwise have had. Some of the children have limited opportunities, so I try to provide a variety of classroom experiences.

New teachers need to get to know the parents and the children, so parent conferences are very important. In past years, about three-quarters of the parents came in for conferences, and if they didn't, I made home visits. In this regard, teachers can expect to spend more time with parents than they might otherwise anticipate. Also, teachers should not expect to change everything during their first year of teaching. Change is much slower in rural schools.

Learn more about rural schools at www.ruraledu.org.

As more people live in less space in older suburbs, these areas become more city-like. Many suburbs are served by local and regional shopping malls, where youth can spend their money and time, socialize, and be free of parental supervision.

Suburban curricula tend to be geared toward college preparation. Many schools measure success by average SAT scores and the number of students accepted to colleges. One other measure of school quality is the number of students taking Advanced Placement courses. Teachers are expected to help parents achieve academic success for their children. For one teacher's view on teaching in suburban schools, see *In the Classroom with Don Bott*.

What Makes a Good School?

Regardless of where a school is located, everybody wants children to go to "good" schools, and every teacher wants to teach in one. But what are the characteristics of a good school? Over the past decade, researchers have conducted many studies on what makes good or effective schools.

Effective schools are those that have been successful in teaching the adopted curriculum to all students. These schools have adopted both quality and equity standards. The quality standard expects the highest levels of performance of every

> **■ INTASC**
>
> **STANDARD 5** The teacher uses an understanding of individual and group motivation and behavior to create a learning environment that encourages positive social interaction, active engagement in learning, and self-motivation.

> **■ INTASC**
>
> **STANDARD 9** The teacher is a reflective practitioner who continually evaluates the effects of his/her choices and actions on others (students, parents, and other professionals in the learning community) and who actively seeks out opportunities to grow professionally.

In the Classroom
with **Don Bott**

*Teaching in
Suburban Schools*

Don Bott teaches different levels of English at Amos Alonzo Stagg High School in Stockton, California. He is also the advisor to the school newspaper, the *Amos Alonzo Stagg Linc*. Stagg High has an enrollment of 3,001 students, most of whom are Anglo-European American, African American, and Hispanic.

I feel there are so many discrepancies between what you hear about schools and what schools are really like. I don't feel unsafe nor have I encountered students who feel unsafe at school. For some students, the climate of the school is the safest they have.

Students are the one thing that makes me love teaching. The kids do not automatically respect you because you are a teacher. They want a reason to respect you and to come to school to learn. Students today have a "show me" attitude, and you have to prove to them that they have a reason to be at school. I would prefer it if students had a little more giving attitude, but teachers have to deal with reality. Some teachers are working hard and trying to make it worthwhile for students. They really want to be good teachers.

A basic problem with suburban schools—and perhaps inner-city schools as well—is that it is very hard to get consistency in instruction and to get professionals to agree on what students should be learning.

When deciding where to teach, new teachers need to consider the kind of school they attended. Teachers have to build on what they know. Going from a rural school to an inner-city school can be very different. I'm not saying that you have to teach in the kind of school you went to, but you do need to consider the contrast between your school and another school where you might want to teach. I've seen young teachers, who have a vision of what school should be like, get discouraged because the students were not like the ones they went to high school with or the ones they encountered in their field experiences. We have to teach the students who come to us. Being nostalgic or wishing students would change to fit a stereotype doesn't get the job done.

Read stories from several suburban school districts at www.centerforpubliceducation.org/site/c.kjJXJ5MPIwE/b .1696217/k.1811/Stories_from_suburban_school_districts .htm.

student, and the equity standard ensures that student achievement is not a function of gender, economic status, or ethnicity.[50] Effective schools have to:

- Prioritize student achievement and have high expectations for their students.
- Implement a coherent, standards-based curriculum and instructional program.
- Use assessment data to improve student achievement and instruction.
- Ensure availability of instructional resources.[51]

How these characteristics are translated into practice depends on the staff and the setting of each school. A study of highly effective urban high schools in four states identified the following common characteristics:

- Teachers described the schools as pleasant environments where goals and rules were well articulated.
- Teacher turnover rates were low.
- Principals were instructional leaders.
- Teachers felt they had a meaningful role in school decision making.
- Teachers felt the support of administrators, parents, and community.
- Students were positive about the learning and social atmosphere.
- Parents were proud of the school and praised teachers and principals.
- The community provided support in the form of college scholarships and sponsorship of school activities.[52]

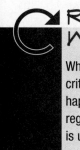

REFLECT & WRITE

What factors do you think are critical for your success and happiness as a teacher, regardless of whether the school is urban, suburban, or rural?

_____

_____

_____

_____

_____

How Schools Are Changing

This chapter has identified many changes and trends in the organization of schooling in the United States. These include:

- Larger schools (for the sake of economy)
- Smaller schools, including merged school districts and schools within schools (for improved student performance)
- Different approaches to the use of time in the school year and school day, such as implementing block scheduling
- Multi-age grouping
- Integrated or interdisciplinary curricula
- More academically oriented elementary and early childhood education
- Middle-level schooling and transition programs designed to meet students' unique needs
- Alternative public schools, magnet schools, and charter schools
- Instructional technologies and distance learning
- National and state standards that specify what students should know and be able to do
- Testing and comparisons of student achievement

- Privatization of education (for-profit public and private education)
- Schools as marketplace (increased choice regarding school purposes and curricula)

Some dimensions of schooling, such as the age-graded approach and the self-contained classroom, have changed little over the years. But other aspects have changed dramatically and will continue to do so in response to changing expectations, social issues, and needs of students. One thing is certain: Change is the driving force that reforms and transforms schools to fit and respond to society's needs.

REFLECT & WRITE

Effective schools pay attention to academics and are places that care about students and try to meet their needs. What qualities would make a school attractive to you as a teacher?

_____

_____

_____

_____

_____

ETHICAL DILEMMA

"I Don't Care What They Say, Smaller Doesn't Work for Me!"

AGNES BOULDIN teaches in an urban high school with an enrollment of over 3,200 students in grades 9 through 12. At a recent faculty meeting, the principal announced plans to form a series of study groups to consider creating a ninth-grade campus and restructuring the high school into four smaller "schools-within-schools." Agnes' friend and colleague, Yumi Ho, is excited about the prospects that restructuring has for teachers and students. Agnes, however, has never believed that smaller is better, and wants nothing to do with the proposed restructuring. In fact, she is determined to do her

best to talk Yumi and her other colleagues out of supporting the proposed plan. Agnes asks Yumi to help her form a group to oppose the restructuring: "Yumi, I don't like the sound of this. It is just going to make a lot more work for us. I like things the way they are. Let's see how many teachers we can get to support us. Why don't you create a blog to generate some grassroots opposition?"

WHAT SHOULD YUMI DO? Tell her friend Agnes how she really feels and risk losing a good friend and colleague? Keep quiet and say nothing? Should she try to persuade Agnes to change her mind? Or, should she pursue some other course of action? What would you do if you were in Yumi's position?

SUMMARY

- The foremost purpose of schooling in the United States is to educate all students, regardless of race, culture, gender, and socioeconomic status, and to teach them to lead meaningful and productive lives. Today, national, state, and local aims of education are expressed through state and federal standards, which dictate what students should know and be able to do.

- Schools are organized in order to fulfill their mission, including establishing order and enabling effective teaching and learning. A number of factors affect the structure of schools in the United States, including the instructional approach, schedule, hours, and school size. Pre-kindergarten programs, primary and elementary schools, middle and junior high schools, and high schools differ greatly across the nation in terms of organization. Social and educational change also is reflected in the creation of alternative learning programs and schools.

■ Schools are organized based on population demographics and other characteristics of the communities in which they are located. Based on these criteria, schools are grouped into urban, rural, and suburban schools. As schools continue to strive to be high quality and serve ever-increasing diverse populations, change will be a constant and dominant theme in American education.

KEY TERMS

After-school programs 86
Age-graded approach 84
Aim 78
Alternative schools 99
Block scheduling 88
Carnegie Unit 88
Charter schools 100

Comprehensive high schools 98
Head Start 92
Looping 86
Magnet schools 99
Multi-age/multi-ability grouping 84
Organization 83
Preschool and prekindergarten (pre-K) 91

School district 84
Standards-based education 80
21st Century Community Learning
   Centers (21st CCLC) 87
Transition programs 96
Year-round education (YRE) 86

APPLICATIONS FOR ACTIVE LEARNING

Connections

1. This chapter has identified several changes and trends in the organization of schooling in the United States. Do any of these changes or trends surprise you? If so, which ones and why? Review how your own beliefs about how schools should be organized compare to current school organization trends in your community.

2. Although each school is a unique entity, schools share some characteristics based on the kinds of communities they represent—urban, suburban, and rural. Teachers do not necessarily have to teach in the same type of community in which they grew up, but they must be realistic about their role as teacher in that community. Considering your own background and skills, would your best match be an urban, suburban, or rural school? Create a profile of your characteristics in relation to the three types of schools.

3. Many urban schools have begun to implement the schools-within-schools organization technique. What are your thoughts on this issue? Compare a list of advantages and disadvantages of both large urban schools as one unit and large urban schools that have divided themselves into multiple small schools.

Field Experiences

1. Collect data on the structure of schooling in a district in your area. How many students are served? What is the size of the teaching force and the pupil-to-teacher ratio? How are grade levels organized? What alternative schools are offered? How are the uses of time and space in schools organized? Analyze your data in light of the information in this chapter.

2. Visit social services agencies in your community and list the services they offer. Describe how you can work with these agencies to meet the needs of your students and their families. Invite agency directors to meet with your classes to discuss how they and education professionals can work cooperatively to help students.

3. Over the next 3 or 4 months, keep a journal about changes you notice in school organization. Include these topics:

   a. What changes intrigue you the most?

   b. You may agree with some of the changes, but not all of them. Make a list of changes that you think have a positive effect on students and a list of those you feel will have a negative effect.

Personal Research

1. Bookmark online articles from the "Education" or "Learning" sections of online newspapers that describe schools in which you think you would enjoy teaching. What patterns do you observe in the qualities you will be looking for in a school?

2. Research alternative schools and charter schools in your state or region. Who attends them? On what basis were they founded? Would you ever be interested in teaching in an alternative school? In a charter school? Why or why not? Note your current opinions here.

PREPARING TO TEACH

For Your Portfolio

Develop position statements explaining your beliefs about the aims of education and your reasons for choosing the type of school, size of school, and grade level in which you plan to teach. Add these documents to your teaching portfolio.

Idea File

1. The following are some ways that teaching may be different in rural schools. How might you address these differences as a teacher?

   ■ Students may lack experiences often associated with urban and suburban living. They may have few opportunities to visit zoos, museums, or other educational attractions.

   ■ Student populations may be comparatively homogeneous and lack experience with cultural and ethnic diversity.

   ■ Many districts transport students long distances. Students spend long periods of time on school buses coming to school.

   ■ Many districts have a small or shrinking tax base and therefore have less money to provide materials.

2. The following are some ways that teaching may be different in inner-city schools. How might you address these differences as a teacher?

   ■ Students may not have had the opportunity, resources, or encouragement to have the cultural and educational experiences often associated with urban living.

   ■ Students may come from comparatively homogeneous neighborhoods and lack experience with cultural and socioeconomic diversity.

   ■ Students may bring concerns about personal safety in getting to and from school, being on school grounds, or moving from place to place within the school.

   ■ Many districts have low socioeconomic populations and therefore have less money to provide a quality learning environment.

LEARNING AND KNOWING MORE

Websites Worth Visiting

National Center for Family and Community Connections with Schools
www.sedl.org/connections/welcome.html

The National Center for Family and Community Connections bridges research and practice, linking people with research-based information and resources that they can use to effectively connect schools, families, and communities.

National Center for Restructuring Education, Schools, and Teaching (NCREST)
www.tc.edu/ncrest/home.htm

NCREST works to develop understandings that help schools become learner centered, by focusing on the needs of learners in school organization, governance, and pedagogy; knowledge based, by restructuring teacher learning and professional development; and responsible and responsive, by restructuring accountability and assessment practices.

Distance Learning on the Net
www.hoyle.com/distance/portals.html

Numerous links to other sites and searchable online repositories of information about distance education.

Books Worth Reading

Cuban, Larry. (2007). *The Blackboard and the Bottom Line: Why Schools Can't Be Businesses.* Cambridge: Harvard University Press.

In this text, Cuban argues against the influential view that American schools should be organized to meet the needs of American businesses and run according to principles of cost-efficiency, bottom-line thinking, and customer satisfaction. He believes that an attempt to run schools like businesses leads to dangerous overstandardization—of tests, and of goals for students.

Juvonen, Jaana. (2007). *Focus on the Wonder Years: Challenges Facing the American Middle School.* Santa Monica, CA: RAND Corporation.

Juvonen explores the world of young teens in middle school and the changes they undergo that set them apart from other students. The author describes some of the challenges and offers ways to tackle them, such as reassessing the organization of grades K–12, assisting the students most in need, finding ways to prevent disciplinary problems, and helping parents understand how they can help their children learn at home.

Newell, Ron. (2005). *The Coolest School in America: How Small Learning Communities Are Changing Everything.* Lanham, MD: Scarecrow Education.

Newell discusses the development of the Minnesota New Country School (MNCS), a small charter school that has no formal classes, but rather supports student-directed projects. The book offers a series of essays about learning communities, experiential learning, and place-based learning and examines how these initiatives are producing positive outcomes.

4 Teaching Diverse Learners I: Multiculturalism and Gender in Today's Classrooms

KATHLEEN PONZE The Young Women's Leadership School (TYWLS) was founded in 1996 by Ann and Andrew Tisch in collaboration with the New York City public schools in order to bring a dynamic and effective educational alternative to inner-city girls. The vision for the school was to make a college education an undeniable reality for inner-city girls who were losing their way. Girls from across New York City were shutting down their human potential at an alarming pace by dropping out, getting pregnant, and being faced with a variety of other social, economic, and cultural circumstances. TYWLS has been very successful and has gained national attention as a model for school choice in the public school system and as a model of success for inner-city minority girls. We now draw on over 10 years of high-quality public single-sex educational practice with a focus on results. We set the bar high and provide the students the necessary supports to be successful.

As you read this chapter . . .

Think about:

- How America is a nation of diverse learners
- How racial and ethnic diversity affect teaching and learning
- What multicultural education is and what it involves
- How language influences teaching and learning
- How gender affects teaching and learning

Located in East Harlem, TYWLS is a Title I school with 85 percent of its students—66 percent Latina, 32 percent African American, and 1 percent Southeast Asian—eligible for free and reduced-price lunches. TYWLS serves grades 7 through 12, with none of our schools growing to more than 550 students. All students wear uniforms and follow a rigorous college prep curriculum.

Undeniably, the most essential component of our college acceptance success rates is TYWLS' vision of working in partnership with the school to embed the CollegeBound Program into the life of every student. The graduation rate in New York City has hovered at around 58 percent, and despite recent progress on that front, only about half (53%) of the graduates go on to 4-year colleges. Furthermore, an extremely low percentage of African American and Latino students graduate with Regents diplomas, which have more stringent requirements than local diplomas, especially in the passing grade required on high school exit exams. At TYWLS, we consistently beat all of these odds. Since the program's inception in 2001, 79 percent of these students are still enrolled, graduated, or are in graduate school. Due to increasing demand and with the support of the Gates Foundation, TYWLS has now been replicated in the South Bronx, South Jamaica, Queens, Astoria, and Brooklyn which will open in September 2008.

> **Every teacher promotes inquiry and dynamic participatory learning . . .**

Our core initiatives are rigorous. The college prep curriculum focuses on math, science, and technology—areas of traditional underrepresentation for girls; leadership development; health and wellness of "female adolescent development" in its broadest sense; and college preparation for all. Every teacher, in addition to being a competent content specialist, is also an advisory teacher. Additionally, every teacher promotes inquiry and dynamic participatory learning and models leadership both in and out of the classroom.

Here is what one parent has to say about TYWLS:

> We all agree that it takes a village to raise a child. As a single parent, I know that raising my daughter was going to take a village and then some. I genuinely believe that The

Kathleen Ponze is the director of education for The Young Women's Leadership Foundation in New York City.

▶▶ Go to MyEducationLab and select the topic "Diversity and Multiculturalism" then watch the video, "Self-esteem in a Multicultural Classroom."

Young Women's Leadership School saved my daughter. She enrolled in TYWLS in the seventh grade as a resistant girl from the South Bronx who did not like school. She is now completing her senior year at Gettysburg College on a full scholarship!

It is very gratifying to be able to offer this life-changing opportunity to girls in the inner city. Our challenge is to make sure our teachers are well prepared and well trained to work with adolescent girls of average ability and to combat the toxic culture of low expectations that has stymied the development of so many of them. Another ongoing challenge is to ensure that our partners and those who are funding our program help us to provide opportunities to expose our students to the wider world and to let them experience and conquer new challenges so that they build their competencies and their courage to try new things. Once they see it, they know they can be it!

For more of what people say about TYWLS, visit www.ywlfoundation.org/about_people.htm. Also visit The Foundation for the Education of Young Women, which is based in Texas, to read about what TYWLS affiliates there are doing at www.feyw.org/feyw/.

AMERICA—A NATION OF DIVERSE LEARNERS

The opening vignette about TYWLS is a vivid example of how schools across America are helping today's diverse learners succeed in school and in life. It is also illustrative of the need for programs that can help diverse learners, whatever the nature of their diversity.

As Figures 4.1 and 4.2 aptly illustrate, America is a diverse country and is becoming more so all the time. In fact, in 2007 the nation's minority population reached 100.7 million. There are more minorities in this country today than there were people in the United States in 1910.[1] We can count on the fact that an increase in **diversity** will be the demographic norm rather than the exception. When we talk about diversity, we often think of race and ethnicity, but these are only part of what diversity is. More and more students come to school speaking a language other than English. You will be confronted with a wide, rich variety of native lan-

Diversity   The range of race, ethnicity, sexual orientation, socioeconomic status, cultural heritage, gender, and ability or disability represented in society.

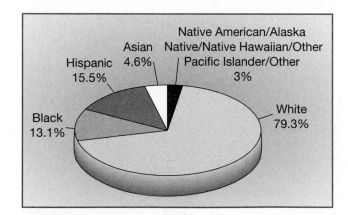

FIGURE 4.1   Diversity in the United States

The United States is becoming increasingly diverse. How will you modify your teaching to accommodate growing diversity in your classroom?

Source: U.S. Census Bureau. (2004, March 18). *U.S. interim projections by age, sex, race, and Hispanic origin.* (Online). Available at: www.census.gov/ipc/www/usinterimproj/. Accessed: July 13, 2007.

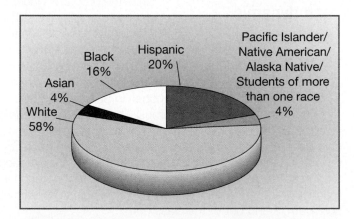

FIGURE 4.2   Diversity in U.S. Schools

As the United States becomes more diverse, the nation's schools will also see an increase in diversity. Much of your time as a teacher will be spent finding ways to meet the diverse needs of your students.

Source: National Center for Education Statistics. (2007). *The Condition of Education, 2007.* (Online). Available at http://nces.ed.gov/pubs2007/2007064.pdf.

guages and will need to consider what programs will help your students learn what they need to know to succeed in school and life. Your students will represent a spectrum of socioeconomic backgrounds. **Socioeconomic status (SES)** is a reflection of family income, maternal education level, and family occupation. It greatly affects and influences students' achievement. This chapter explores what schools, and teachers, can do to help students overcome the debilitating effects low SES has on their achievement.

It seems obvious that students also are male and female. Yet we often overlook the impact of this fact on our teaching. Despite best efforts, boys and girls often are reared and educated differently. These differences in child rearing and education have a profound influence on school achievement and on career and life outcomes. You will also teach gay and lesbian students and will have opportunities to interact with their parents, who also might be gay or lesbian. Gay, lesbian, bisexual, and transgender students bring diverse needs to the classroom. One of your responsibilities as a high-quality teacher is to provide a nonthreatening and safe learning environment and to protect all your students from harassment. (Legal issues relating to gay, lesbian, bisexual, and transgender students are covered in Chapter 8.)

Socioeconomic status (SES) The social and economic background of an individual or individuals.

■ **INTASC**

STANDARD 3 The teacher understands how students differ in their approaches to learning and creates instructional opportunities that are adapted to diverse learners.

REFLECT & WRITE

If you were to identify three things that you needed to do now to prepare yourself to be a culturally aware teacher, what would they be? Based on the geographic area where you plan to teach, what culture do you need to learn most about?

Students bring particular needs to the classroom, in part as a result of their different racial, ethnic, cultural, and socioeconomic backgrounds and in part because of their gender and sexual orientation. They bring different approaches to learning as well as a variety of aspirations for achievement. This academic diversity is a given in today's classroom. You likely will spend many hours planning for how to best provide academic and extracurricular programs that will meet your students' particular needs, learning styles, and abilities. (Issues of academic diversity are addressed further in Chapters 5 and 11.)

The socioeconomic backgrounds of students have a significant effect on the type and quality of teaching they receive as well as on their ultimate academic achievement. Socioeconomic level affects the funding of school districts and, because students are typically assigned to schools based on where they live, the kind of school they attend. Students who live in upper-income neighborhoods generally have access to better schools and more highly educated teachers, whereas students from lower-income neighborhoods are much more likely to be in schools that lack the material infrastructure necessary for quality education. The United States still has a long way to go in establishing equity within public schools.

Maternal education level is a powerful predictor of how well students do in school. As a mother's education increases, so does student achievement (see Figure 4.3). This helps explain why, from a social and educational policy perspective, a U.S. priority is to prevent teenage mothers from dropping out of school.

● *Your Turn*

Reflect on your own experience as an elementary and secondary school student. Did the socioeconomic status of your fellow students affect their treatment or opportunity in school? If so, how?

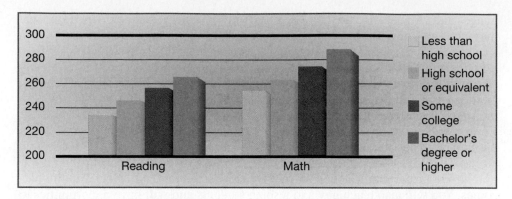

FIGURE 4.3   Mean Reading and Math Scores of Students Age 13, Based on Mother's Education Level

How well students do in school is due in part on their mothers' education level. The higher the maternal education level, the greater the student achievement.

Source: Colorado Literacy Research Initiative. (2005, July 15). *Parents' Education Levels Consistently Predict Students' Reading & Math Scores, 1980–2004. Lit Scan, 9*(5). (Online). Available at www.literacyresearch.org/download/litscan95_trends_NAEP.pdf. Accessed July 13, 2007.

Family income also correlates with how well students do in school, whether they drop out, the kind and type of schools they attend, and the quality of their teachers. Students' socioeconomic status is used to determine eligibility for many state and federal programs such as Head Start and Title I programs. (Refer to Chapter 9 for further discussion of Title I.) One Head Start eligibility criterion, for example, is that the child's family meets federal poverty income criteria for enrollment, and many schools provide free or reduced school lunches based on family income. Table 4.1 shows the 2007 Department of Health and Human Services (HHS) poverty guidelines.

In addition, the Supreme Court recently ruled in *Meredith v. Jefferson County Board of Education* that schools cannot rely on race to segregate schools—even if done voluntarily to achieve a racial balance in public schools. Many schools are now turning to socioeconomic status as a means of desegregating schools (see Chapter 8).

TABLE 4.1   2007 U.S. Health and Human Services Poverty Guidelines

Size of Family Unit	48 Contiguous States and Washington DC	Alaska	Hawaii
1	$10,210	$12,770	$11,750
2	13,690	17,120	15,750
3	17,170	21,470	19,750
4	20,650	25,820	23,750
5	24,130	30,170	27,750
6	27,610	34,520	31,750
7	31,090	38,870	35,750
8	34,570	43,220	39,750
For each additional person, add	3,480	4,350	4,000

Source: U.S. Department of Health and Human Services, *The 2007 HHS Poverty Guidelines—One Version of the* [*U.S.*] *Federal Poverty Measure* (2007). (Online). Available at http://aspe.hhs.gov/poverty/07poverty.shtml.

How does socioeconomic status affect the kind of school a student attends? First, it can affect the quality of teaching. Schools in low-income neighborhoods often have a high percentage of teachers teaching "out of field"—that is, teaching subjects they are not academically prepared for or certified to teach. (See Figure 4.4.)

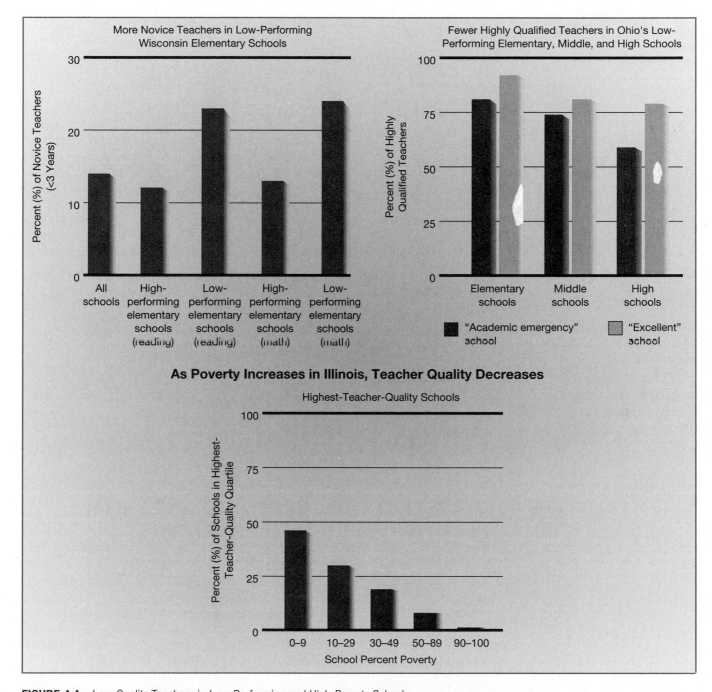

FIGURE 4.4   Low-Quality Teachers in Low-Performing and High-Poverty Schools

In Wisconsin, Ohio, Illinois, and several other states, teacher quality decreases in low-performing and high-poverty schools.

Source: Adapted from H. G. Peske, and K. Haycock (2006, June). *Teaching Inequality.* The Education Trust, pp. 5–7.

**REFLECT &
WRITE**

Why do you think the poorest
schools get poorest teachers?
Do you think that the student
achievement gap can be
explained by the teacher gap?
How?

_____

_____

_____

_____

_____

Socioeconomic status has a profound effect on students' educational opportunities. Given this fact, the American public education system has a daunting task: All students must be provided with high-quality teachers and the resources that they need to learn. As schools become more ethnically, culturally, and socioeconomically diverse, all educators—teachers and administrators—are faced with the challenge of ensuring that they are able to meet the needs of all of the diverse learners in their schools and classrooms. How will you make sure that you are prepared?

**REFLECT &
WRITE**

Consider a classroom of students
who are of mixed genders and
sexual orientation and of different
racial, ethnic, and socioeconomic
backgrounds. How would
teaching such diverse students
affect the way you teach?

_____

_____

_____

_____

_____

HOW DO RACIAL AND ETHNIC DIVERSITY AFFECT TEACHING AND LEARNING?

Research in the area of student achievement has consistently shown that students of different races and ethnicities achieve at different levels in school, causing an achievement gap. Standardized test results continue to place African Americans and Latino students behind their non-Latino white peers. Research has shown that higher standards can help to close this achievement gap, but some believe that teachers expect more from white students than from their minority peers—especially African American and Latino students.[2]

Cultural Impacts on Teaching and Learning

In today's classrooms, an array of cultural frames of reference exist. Despite this fact, however, schools operate based on a cultural context involving Anglo-European American values. Students from this background typically experience the greatest familiarity with the way schools operate and with school norms.

Students who come from cultural and language backgrounds that vary significantly from traditional school culture often are less familiar with the school environment and school norms. In a sense, these students have a double task: (1) to learn the norms of a school environment that are already familiar to others and (2) to learn the same academic content that all students are expected to master. These tasks have become increasingly difficult for minority students to master with the strong presence of standardized testing, which does not accommodate different cultures.

Teachers who recognize that the complexity of learning tasks increases for students who are less familiar with traditional school culture provide a variety of teaching approaches as well as ample time for instruction. The goal for these teachers is not *equal* treatment but *equitable* treatment—that is, providing students with teaching approaches and attention that are proportional to their academic needs.

Issues of diversity greatly influence the direction of education, as cultural needs and traditions of diverse populations offer wonderful learning opportunities for students and teachers alike.

The proportion of minority students in this nation's schools in 2000 was 42 percent.[3] Table 4.2 shows the racial or ethnic composition of students in the nation's 10 largest school districts for the school year 2003–2004. As you can see from the table, these school districts have a majority of students who are classified as minorities. In these cases, minorities are actually majorities. Two realities of changing demographics of school populations are that (1) you and other beginning teachers will, in all likelihood, teach minority students, and (2) school districts and colleges of education will have to increase their efforts to recruit minority teachers (see Chapter 2). Teachers who have the skills to succeed in culturally and linguistically diverse classrooms will be in ever-greater demand. Teacher education programs that prepare teachers for the multicultural classroom will be producing graduates with the right backgrounds for teaching in the twenty-first century.

The cultural backgrounds of students play a major role in the learning process. Culture frequently influences how students respond to various teaching approaches.

TABLE 4.2 Proportion of Minority Students in the 10 Largest Public School Districts in the United States, 2003–2004

Name of Reporting District	State	Percentage of Minority Students
New York City Public School District	NY	85.2
Los Angeles Unified School District	CA	90.9
City of Chicago School District	IL	90.9
Dade County School District	FL	89.6
Broward County School District	FL	63.7
Clark County School District	NV	56.0
Houston Independent School District	TX	90.9
Philadelphia City School District	PA	85.4
Hawaii Department of Education	HI	79.8
Hillsborough County School District	FL	51.3

Source: National Center for Education Statistics, *Digest of Education Statistics* (Washington, DC: Office of Educational Research and Improvement, 2005). Available online at http://nces.ed.gov/programs/digest/d05/tables/dt05_088.asp.

Students from Native American cultures will often not respond to questions posed openly before the entire class. What might be viewed as disinterest is actually a cultural norm that one should not venture answers in public before one is certain. For another example, a classroom that is highly teacher centered and structured might be effective with Asian immigrant students who were accustomed to this model in their countries of origin. However, the same approach might be ineffective with Mexican American students, who prefer cooperative learning environments.

Although no single teaching approach is uniformly effective with all students, teachers often rely heavily on one method. This is increasingly true as grade levels get higher. What is most beneficial is to use a variety of instructional approaches that are reflective of the different learning modalities present in every classroom (see Chapter 11).

Helping English Language Learners

English language learner (ELL) Student whose primary language is not English.

The No Child Left Behind (NCLB) Act requires that all children, including English language learners (ELLs), reach high standards by demonstrating proficiency in English language arts and mathematics by 2014. **English language learners (ELLs)** are students whose primary language is not English. Schools and districts must help ELL students, among other subgroups, make continuous progress toward this goal, as measured by performance on state tests, or risk serious consequences. Through these mandates, NCLB establishes high expectations for all students and seeks to reduce the achievement gap between advantaged and disadvantaged students.

A goal of all schools and teachers is to help ensure that all children learn. Here are some things you can do to make the goal a reality:

■ **INTASC**

STANDARD 10 The teacher fosters relationships with school colleagues, parents, and agencies in the larger community to support students' learning and well-being.

- **Reduce the cognitive load.** One very important step teachers can take is to make every effort to reduce the cognitive load of the lessons they teach. The key is to choose activities and assignments that allow students to draw on their prior knowledge and life experiences. It is crucial during the process of lesson planning that teachers take into account the capacities of the students involved.

- **Evaluate teaching strategies and approaches.** Teachers also need to pay attention to how they run their classrooms. Some students may have difficulty coping with the style of classroom management that the teacher has chosen. For example, in many countries, students are not to speak unless the teacher asks them a question directly. To volunteer answers might be considered boastful or conceited. Many students will not question what the teacher says even if they know it to be wrong.

Go to MyEducationLab and select the topic "Diversity and Multiculturalism" and watch the video "Teaching Bilingual Learners." Complete the activities that follow.

- **Reduce the cultural load.** Showing respect for the immigrant child's life begins by building personal relationships with the students and their families and by making an effort to include aspects of each child's culture in the classroom on a regular basis. Some simple actions each teacher can take include learning to pronounce each student's name correctly, finding out where each student is from, and gathering a little background information about each one.

- **Reduce the language load.** Teacher talk is often filled with words that are unfamiliar to English language learners, which can put a great deal of pressure on students as they try to process what the teacher says or what they have to read. To lighten this heavy language load for the student, teachers can employ a number of strategies. They can rewrite difficult texts using simpler terms or at least explain the original language simply. They can also break up complex sentences into smaller sentences. They can point out new and particularly difficult words, define them, and explain how they are used.[4] Read about how ELL teacher Miriam Cohen uses creative and innovative methods to teach English language learners in *In the Classroom with Miriam Cohen.*

In the Classroom

with **Miriam Cohen**
Teaching ELL Students

Although my certification was in English, I was faced with the daunting task of instructing a brother and sister from Vietnam who could speak no English. As a new teacher, common sense told me to use TPR and BICS (total physical response and basic interpersonal communication skills, respectively), the meat and potatoes of ELL instruction. I am now ELL certified and have taught all levels and ages, from high school to the university to the corporate sector.

Teaching ELL high school students is challenging. Moving, family hardships, the need to work, or just personal reasons have interrupted many students' education. Some ELL high school students are functioning academically on an elementary school level. I might have a student who is illiterate in his own language or who comes to school half asleep after a night of work. There are health issues, emotional concerns, and fears of deportation.

Despite the challenges, there is nothing more rewarding than to see the smile of comprehension, the sparkle in the eyes that comes with the excitement of a competitive game, or the hug that signals gratitude for kindness and sensitivity when someone is in crisis. As I work with English teachers to plan units that will engage students, it is important to consider different learning styles as well as individual strengths and weaknesses. Students relish a variety of activities when they practice reading, writing, speaking, and listening. I was grateful to receive a grant for purchasing Spanish-English translators with a voice synthesizer. Students prefer the translator to a bilingual dictionary. Another technique that helps students with their writing skills is peer correction. Flashing a piece of student writing on a screen promotes interest, because students are naturally curious about what their classmates think. This activity draws more attention than using examples from a textbook. I am a fan of *Scope Magazine* in part because it contains plays based on literature or current movies. Students who are ordinarily reluctant to speak in class actively take part in role-playing. Graphic organizers allow students to prove their understanding of ideas without having to write at great length. Students take ownership of the vocabulary words or idioms by recording them in a journal. They enjoy researching a topic of their choice on the Internet and then presenting their findings to their peers.

Many of our ELL students represent a milestone to their families as the first to obtain a high school diploma and have the promise of a bright future.

Learn additional strategies for teaching ELL students at www.celt.sunysb.edu/ell/tips.php.

Academic Achievement and Race

One of the great hopes of proponents of school integration, as well NCLB, is that as African American and Latino students receive more opportunities, gaps in academic achievement among racial and ethnic groups will diminish and eventually disappear. This goal has been only partly fulfilled, as the following data indicate:

- 83 percent of all students in public high schools graduate.
- 85.5 percent of white students graduate, whereas only 74.4 percent of all African American students and 73.7 percent of all Latino students graduate.[5]
- Graduation rates in the Northeast and Midwest are higher than graduation rates in the South and West.[6]
- The state with the highest graduation rate in the nation is New Jersey; the state with the lowest graduation rate in the nation is Nevada.[7]

At the beginning of this century, students who failed to succeed in school were not regarded as a problem. They were defined as "school leavers," not "high school dropouts." Today, however, in this technological age, literacy is key to survival, and educators must recognize that no student is "disposable."

■ INTASC

STANDARD 10 The teacher fosters relationships with school colleagues, parents, and agencies in the larger community to support students' learning and well-being.

Diversity Issues in School Life

Schools tend to be microcosms of the communities in which they are situated. If a community exhibits diversity and is open and receptive to it, schools in that community tend to emulate that pattern. For example, in the Puyallup School District in Washington State, the school district's director of the Office of Diversity Affairs encourages the community to embrace diversity. As a result of this encouragement, the elementary and junior high schools in the district have added a multicultural curriculum to their classrooms. This curriculum uses books and accompanying artifact kits that are designed as a multicultural read-aloud series to support and enhance existing curriculum in kindergarten through grade six and to give students a glimpse of what it is like to live in other cultures. At the junior high schools, the curriculum is designed to tell a story or share a piece of history through the eyes of a particular ethnic group. The curriculum also helps teachers educate students about prejudice and stereotypes. The Puyallup School District has received statewide recognition for its efforts to promote and value diversity and **multicultural education** in its schools and community.[8]

Multicultural education   Education designed to ensure that all students receive equal opportunities regardless of socio-economic status, gender, sexual orientation, and racial and cultural backgrounds.

In communities where diversity is not found, or where it is present but not valued, schools frequently play down or ignore diversity issues. For example, at Endeavor Alternative School in Kansas City, Kansas, attempts have been made to erase diversity issues altogether. During the 2005 school year, two students were sent to the principal and later suspended from school for speaking Spanish to one another within the school but outside of class time. The principal maintains that the students have been asked many times before not to speak Spanish at school.[9]

A common issue involving diversity is social acceptance. To what extent do the racial, ethnic, or socioeconomic groups to which students belong affect their acceptance among peers, faculty, and staff in our schools? Consider the case of a 15-year-old freshman who tested the limits of tolerance when she donned a burqa in school as part of a Middle Eastern Studies course.[10] The reactions of other students were both alarming and illuminating. Read about this controversy in *In the Classroom with Caitlin Dean.*

Other diversity issues can have an impact on classroom procedures. For example, parents and students often ask teachers and schools to provide accommodations for their religious practices. Consider how the Seattle school district provides accommodations based on students' religious practices.

Go to MyEducationLab and select the topic "Diversity and Multiculturalism" and read the article "The Difference a Global Educator Can Make." Answer questions that follow.

> On Friday afternoons, Nathan Hale High School senior Abdisiyad Adan asks his fifth-period teacher what he'll miss in class, writes down the homework for the weekend, and leaves school.
>
> Other Muslim students at Nathan Hale pile into Adan's car, and they set off for the Idriss Mosque, a little more than a mile away. By the time they return from their mandatory Friday prayers, the school day is nearly over. . . .
>
> . . . Seattle School District guidelines give school administrators the responsibility of deciding how to handle Muslim prayer. At Garfield High School, an empty classroom is provided for Muslims to pray during lunch periods, Principal Ted Howard said. Students who don't want to miss lunch can have an extra 10 minutes to pray after the lunch period provided their teachers sign off on it. On Fridays, Muslims are allowed to go to a nearby mosque. . . .
>
> In Shoreline, Muslim students are provided with an empty classroom for prayers and are usually allowed to miss class for their prayers. Shorewood High School senior Omar Sarhan said teachers sometimes suggest that students remain in class for particularly important assignments.[11]

School culture   The collective "way of life" characteristic of a school; a set of beliefs, values, traditions, and ways of thinking and behaving that distinguishes one school from another.

School Culture

School culture is composed of the values and norms of a school as well as a school's operating procedures. Students enter schools in the United States with different levels of familiarity with school culture. Students discover whether beliefs

In the Classroom
with Caitlin Dean
A Test of Tolerance

Caitlin Dean, a 15-year-old freshman, volunteered with a few other students to wear traditional Muslim clothing to school for an entire day in February 2007 after a Middle Eastern Studies teacher at Bacon Academy in Connecticut announced that she was looking for students to promote her class by wearing the garb. Caitlin was raised not to discriminate against others because of their race or religion. But being a white suburban teen of Italian and Irish descent, she often wondered what it would be like to be the target of such abuse. She found out "behind the burqa." Caitlin covered her slender frame and short brown hair with a periwinkle burqa, which concealed her face. The hateful and abusive comments she endured that day horrified teachers, the teen, and many of her classmates.

A partial list of the comments to Caitlin—some were not printable—appeared in the student newspaper, *The Bacon Courier*, along with a front-page story headline, "Some at Bacon Fail the Test of Tolerance." Caitlin called it "The Girl Behind the Burqa."

In the days that followed, teachers and students at Bacon Academy discussed the need for tolerance of other cultures. The school has a Gay-Straight Alliance with some openly gay members, a save Darfur group, and a diversity committee. Chris Anderson, a senior at Bacon who also wore some of the traditional Muslim clothing to school and who was also a target of ethnic slurs, said educators are not trying hard enough to expose students to other cultures. He criticizes school leaders for replacing world studies in middle school with more American history. "The prejudice displayed at Bacon Academy is proof enough that education about world cultures cannot be ignored," he said. "The misunderstood are feared and hated."

At Bacon Academy, Caitlin's experience has made a difference. Teacher Angie Parkinson, who once had only 12 students enrolled in her Middle Eastern Studies class, now has 48.

Source: Adapted from T. G. Fox, Behind burqa, student gets an education in bigotry. *The Hartford Courant*, March 12, 2007. (Online). Available at www.campus-watch.org/article/id/3118.

and values that are important in their home cultures are reflected in the overall school culture. When both the school's culture and student population are multicultural, students of diverse backgrounds feel vital and included in school life. Even when the school's student population is not diverse, a multicultural school culture prepares students as citizens of a culturally diverse nation. When the student population is diverse but the school's culture reflects only one cultural perspective, some students feel like outsiders in their own school. Schools like these may be desegregated, but they are not integrated. Even if the faces at a school assembly reflect a rainbow of colors, certain groups of students may not feel like an integral or valued portion of that school's community. **Culturally responsive teachers** are culturally and socially aware and are both responsible for and capable of bringing about

Culturally responsive teacher   A teacher who is culturally and socially aware and who is both responsible for and capable of bringing about educational change that will make schools more responsive to all students of all cultures.

REFLECT & WRITE

Diversity has many dimensions, as discussed. How do you plan to respond to the dimensions discussed so far? What other kinds of diversity do you think you might encounter in the classroom?

educational change that will make schools more responsive to all students of all cultures. This includes looking for new ways to promote a sense of community and inclusion in their classrooms.

Students with diverse backgrounds sometimes do not do well in school because the teachers might not be highly qualified or because the facilities and materials might not support their learning. Consequently, NCLB allows for families in schools that are not meeting their children's needs to transfer their children to other schools. Charter schools are established specifically to meet parents' school choice needs. (See *You Decide: Parents, Vouchers, and School Choice*). However, in other schools, teachers are culturally responsive to students, and consequently students do quite well academically.

Diversity Issues in the Curriculum

Eurocentric Focusing on European and European-American history and culture.

Four decades ago, the public school curriculum was almost entirely **Eurocentric**, reflecting the European roots of the majority culture in the United States. Today, the school curriculum reflects the more diverse society of the United

---

One of the provisions of the No Child Left Behind Act is that parents whose children attend "failing" schools, defined as failing to meet adequate yearly progress for 5 or more years, have the option to transfer their children to better-performing schools in the district. In his 2007 State of the Union Address, President Bush said,

> We can lift student achievement even higher by giving local leaders flexibility to turn around failing schools, and by giving families with children stuck in failing schools the right to choose someplace better. We must increase funds for students who struggle—and make sure these children get the special help they need.

YOU DECIDE

Parents, Vouchers, and School Choice

One of the programs that the Bush administration has developed to help parents exercise their choice to select better schools for their children is the America's Opportunity Scholarships for Kids initiative. The program would provide school vouchers (in the form of a $4,000 scholarship) to parents of children in failing schools. Parents could use the voucher to send their children to public or private schools.

Washington, D.C., has an America's Opportunity Scholarships for Kids program that has been in operation for 5 years. The program offers low-income parents up to $7,500 in scholarship funds for children to attend private elementary or high schools. This is the first time that federal monies have been used to send children to private schools.

Proponents of school choice and vouchers argue that programs such as the America's Opportunity Scholarships for Kids provide parents the options that are promised to them under the No Child Left Behind Act. Opponents of school vouchers, such as the National Education Association, argue that student achievement ought to be the driving force behind any education reform initiative, and that direct efforts should be made to upgrade failing schools. The American Federation of Teachers supports parents' rights to send their children to private or religious schools, but opposes the use of public funds to do so.

What do you think? Should federal dollars be used to provide parents with vouchers or scholarships so that they can choose to send their children to other schools?

Sources: President Bush delivers state of the union address. *The White House*. 2007. (Online). Available at www.whitehouse.gov/news/releases/2007/01/print/20070123-2.html; A. R. Paley, and T. Labbe, Voucher students show few gains in first year, June 22, 2007, *Washington Post*. (Online). Available at www.washingtonpost.com; D. Lips, *White House proposes national opportunity scholarship initiative*. July 2006, The Heartland Institute. (Online). Available at www.heartland.org; National Education Association, *Vouchers*. (Online). Available at www.nea.org/vouchers/index.html?mode=print; American Federation of Teachers. *The many names of school vouchers*. (Online). Available at www.aft.org/topics/vouchers/index.htm.

States. Beginning in the 1960s, monoethnic units such as Black History or Hispanic Literature were added to the high school curriculum, mainly to benefit students from these groups. During the same time period, in elementary schools heroes and holidays representing minority groups were added to the curriculum and school calendar. Although monoethnic materials added diversity to the school curriculum, they reached relatively few students and teachers. Multicultural education, by contrast, attempts to broaden the perspectives of all students at all grade levels. We will discuss multicultural education further in the following section.

Global education (or international education) is an effort to ensure that information and perspectives emanating from outside the United States are brought to bear in the classroom. This is particularly true for non-Western content, which historically has been underemphasized. Multicultural education is linked with global education, because students must understand cultural diversity in a national context before they can understand diversity in a more complex global setting.

> **Global education** An effort to ensure that information and perspectives emanating from outside the United States are brought to bear in the classroom.

WHAT IS MULTICULTURAL EDUCATION?

Multicultural education is designed to ensure that all students receive equal opportunities regardless of socioeconomic status, gender, sexual orientation, and racial and cultural backgrounds.

Multicultural education looks at academically relevant knowledge and events from the perspectives of all ethnic or cultural groups. Although not everything taught in our schools has a multicultural dimension, most topics do. Even subjects that are perceived to have little cultural content, such as mathematics and science, have multicultural dimensions. For example, the multicultural and global history of mathematics is seldom presented when that subject is taught strictly from a problem-solving perspective. But mathematics has a cultural aspect, too. *Algebra* is an Arabic word meaning "restitution." Al-Khwarizmi, an early mathematician, acknowledged that in an equation one adds and subtracts identical quantities on both sides. One tries to keep an equation like a scale—in perfect balance. Similarly, when studying science, students can learn about scientific contributions made by peoples of other cultures. Topics such as Native American knowledge of the medicinal qualities of plants or the contributions of the physician Ar-Razi to the field of medicine can be included in the science curriculum.

In teaching language or literature, teachers using a multicultural approach explore the richness of African, Latino, Asian, and Native American literature. Multicultural and global teachers of history present events from diverse perspectives. For example, the American Revolution would be examined from the perspectives of the loyalists, African Americans, and Native Americans, along with the traditional focus on the revolutionaries. Likewise, in a social studies class, the concept of western expansion would be traced and analyzed from the views of European settlers and Native American groups.

In order for multicultural education to really work and be effective, it must become an integral part of the curriculum and school life. Figure 4.5 shows guidelines for embedding multicultural education in the fabric of school life and for making it explicit to students, teachers, administrators, and the public. This figure can help you understand what you can do to be a culturally responsive teacher and to ensure that multicultural education is integrated into your curriculum and teaching.

> ■ **INTASC**
>
> **STANDARD 2** The teacher understands how children learn and develop, and can provide learning opportunities that support their intellectual, social, and personal development.

> ■ **INTASC**
>
> **STANDARD 3** The teacher understands how students differ in their approaches to learning and creates instructional opportunities that are adapted to diverse learners.

To read about issues related to equity and access in multicultural schools, go to MyEducationLab, select the topic "Diversity and Multiculturalism" then read the article "Profoundly Multicultural Questions." Answer the questions that follow.

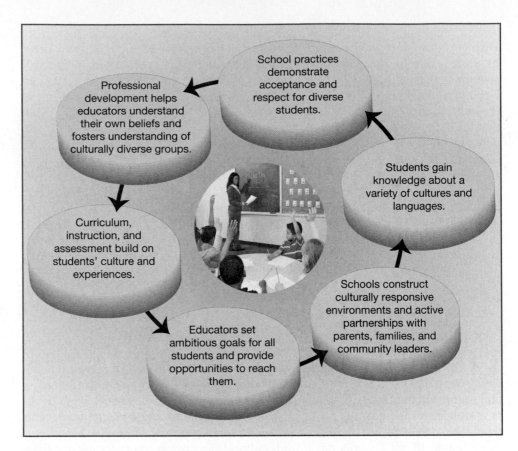

FIGURE 4.5 Guidelines for Developing Authentic Multicultural Education

Using these six guidelines will help you develop your own authentic, multicultural education curriculum.

Source: Figure created by author based on information drawn from "Promising Program and Practices in Multicultural Education" (1995), North Central Regional Educational Library. (Online). Available at www.ncrel.org.

REFLECT & WRITE

Which of these six guidelines can you begin to implement on the first day of your teaching?

_____

_____

_____

_____

_____

_____

■ INTASC

STANDARD 2 The teacher understands how children learn and develop, and can provide learning opportunities that support their intellectual, social, and personal development.

What Are Models of Multicultural Education?

One important dimension of multicultural education is how it broadens the academic achievement of all students. There are five basic approaches to multicultural education:

1. *Teaching exceptional and culturally different students.* This approach targets students who are behind academically (see Chapter 5). The curriculum is made

relevant to the students' background, and instruction often focuses on student learning styles. Examples of this approach include a dropout prevention program, a transitional bilingual program, and classes for students with particular learning disabilities.

2. *Enhancing student self-concept, reducing prejudice, and promoting positive feelings among students.* This approach targets human relations. Common activities used in this model to help promote positive feelings are cooperative learning, role reversal, and simulation. This approach is more frequently found in elementary classrooms.

3. *Single-group studies.* In this approach, the curriculum focuses on the background of one group. Examples of this are African American or Native American studies. Implicit in single-group studies is that students not only learn about a group, but also work toward social change that benefits the identified group.

4. *Multicultural education.* This approach targets all students and organizes curriculum to provide culturally relevant activities in all subjects. Critical thinking and instruction tailored to student learning styles are key elements of multicultural education. In addition, this approach stresses that evaluation procedures should assess a variety of abilities and that the community be included as an integral part of the school.

5. *Promoting education that is multicultural and devoted to the rebuilding or reform of society.* This approach shares many curricular principles with multicultural education. The major difference is the high degree of emphasis placed on social action and on having students work toward promoting equal opportunity and equality.

How can students' multicultural needs be met through the learning environment and through curricula that enhance students' individual and academic self-concepts? What other schoolwide approaches enhance teaching and learning in multicultural schools?

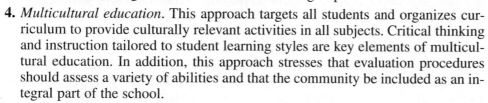

REFLECT & WRITE

Did you experience any of these five models as a student? If so, how effective was it? Which of the five approaches fits in best with your professional preparation?

The Politics of Multiculturalism

School curriculum has always been influenced by political and economic factors in the society at large. Curricular change may be perceived as political in nature whenever it introduces new paradigms or ways of thinking to students.

It is not surprising that multiculturalism has generated some controversy. Multicultural education increases the visibility of issues that the traditional curriculum might not cover. Some critics argue that a focus on cultural differences will disunite our society. Other educators argue that we need not ignore the *pluribus* to achieve the *unum*.

REFLECT & WRITE

Do you agree or disagree with the idea that discussing culturally diverse themes in the United States generates division? Explain your view.

_____

_____

_____

_____

_____

Transformative Knowledge

Two elements of multicultural education are its emphasis on critical thinking and the presentation of **transformative knowledge**. Transformative knowledge includes "the facts, concepts and themes which challenge mainstream academic knowledge and revise established theories and explanations."[12]

Transformative knowledge can be presented in a variety of ways but should always be age appropriate. For example, an elementary teacher could point out that Squanto spoke to the Pilgrims in English. How did Squanto learn English? He had been captured earlier by English fishermen and lived for a period of time in England before returning to Massachusetts and joining the Wampanoag. This information can help transform the way students think about American history.

When middle and high school teachers discuss the Mexican War, they can look at the conflict from the perspective of Mexico as well as that of the United States. What did each nation have to gain or lose from this conflict? How did Mexico respond to efforts by the United States to purchase the northern territories? What was the U.S. administration's response when Congressman Abraham Lincoln challenged President Polk to point out where on American soil American blood had been spilled? The answers to these questions provide students with transformative knowledge. Such knowledge helps engage students in the subject and encourages them to be participants in learning.

Transformative knowledge The facts, concepts, and themes that challenge mainstream academic knowledge and revise established theories and explanations.

The Culturally Responsive Teacher

How can you become a culturally responsive teacher? **Cultural responsiveness** is a characteristic of educators who perceive and acknowledge differences among their students without making value judgments about these differences. Teachers must resist the tendency to see themselves, their values, and their way of life as the standard against which all others are to be judged. Teacher-training programs recognize the importance of culturally responsive teachers. The National Council for Accreditation of Teacher Education (NCATE) defines a "multicultural perspective" as an understanding of the social, political, economic, academic, and historical constructs of ethnicity, race, socioeconomic status, gender, exceptionalities, language, religion, sexual orientation, and the geographical area.[13]

The culturally responsive teacher actively seeks out experiences that lead to increased understanding and appreciation of other cultures. The more you can learn about the backgrounds and cultures of the students you will teach, the more

● *Your Turn*

Examine some books for students on African American and Latino themes. Would you feel comfortable teaching this content in your class? If so, why? If not, what would you need to do to become comfortable with this content?

Cultural responsiveness Ability to perceive and acknowledge cultural differences among people without making value judgments about those differences.

culturally aware you will be. Learning about the student's home environment also helps teachers see through their students' eyes.

Culturally responsive teachers

- Take the time to learn about students' backgrounds and the cultural characteristics of their families and community
- Respect and accommodate students' individual and culture-based learning styles
- Provide accurate and age-appropriate multicultural information and instructional materials
- Challenge and avoid using stereotypes
- Use culture-fair and gender-fair language and examples
- Integrate multicultural perspectives throughout the curriculum

Your attitude regarding diversity will have a strong influence on your ability to address diversity issues, reach all your students, and deliver a multicultural curriculum.

■ INTASC

STANDARD 9 The teacher is a reflective practitioner who continually evaluates the effects of his/her choices and actions on others (students, parents, and other professionals in the learning community) and who actively seeks out opportunities to grow professionally.

REFLECT & WRITE

What qualities and experiences do you possess that will affect your ability to be a culturally responsive teacher? Are there any qualities you lack that might affect your ability to be culturally responsive? If so, what can you do to address them?

HOW DOES LANGUAGE INFLUENCE TEACHING AND LEARNING?

Nothing is more fundamental to instruction than full communication and comprehension between teacher and student. When understandable instruction is a problem, academic achievement declines.

America is a land of diverse culture. With cultural diversity comes diversity of language. In the United States, 10.6 million students ages 5 to 17 speak a language other than English at home, and approximately 3 million students speak English with difficulty.[14] In Florida's Miami-Dade County School District, a total of 94 different languages are spoken, with Spanish being the most prominent. Other widely spoken languages are Haitian, Creole, French, Portuguese, Chinese, and Arabic.[15] The Los Angeles Unified School District has 293,566 students enrolled who are classified as English language learners.[16]

Few issues in education today are as controversial as the use of any language other than English as the main language of instruction. As you can see from Table 4.3,

TABLE 4.3 Number and Proportion of English Language Learners Receiving Services

State	Number of Students Receiving ELL Services	Percentage of Students Receiving ELL Services
California	1,585,647	25.2
Texas	684,583	15.7
Florida	214,562	8.1
Arizona	194,171	20.2
Colorado	90,372	12.0
Washington	75,103	7.6
Nevada	71,557	18.0
North Carolina	68,381	5.0
Virginia	66,970	5.7
Oregon	64,676	12.5

Sources: J. Sable and J. Hill, *Overview of Public Elementary and Secondary Students, Staff, Schools, School Districts, Revenues, and Expenditures: School Year 2004–05 and Fiscal Year 2004* (NCES 2007-309). (Washington, DC: U.S. Department of Education, National Center for Education Statistics, 2006).

In families where English may be a second language, homework has additional challenges. What types of programs are available for students with limited English proficiency?

Bilingual Education Act Enacted in 1968 to provide funds to assist local school districts in carrying out elementary and secondary programs for students whose first language is not English.

Lau v. Nichols Landmark U.S. Supreme Court decision stating that equal educational opportunities are denied when non–English-speaking students receive the same English language instruction as that given to all students.

Bilingual education Education in two languages.

English as a second language (ESL) Instruction in which students with limited-English-proficiency attend a special English class.

Proposition 227 (California) Passed in 1998, this proposition outlawed bilingual education in California schools, but did provide for a waiver process if a school district wished to retain some form of bilingual education.

ten states have many ELLs who are receiving services from the public schools. These numbers will continue to grow and, more than likely, you will have ELL students in your classroom. Although there is little disagreement that all students in the United States should try to reach the goal of full fluency and literacy in English, for students whose native language is not English, a vital issue is whether learning a second language means losing proficiency in their native language. Language is an integral part of culture and identity. As non–English-speaking students are immersed in the English language, over time their native language may be lost, hampering the individual from participating in vital cultural activities such as social gatherings, religious observations, and family exchanges that occur within the ethnic community.

Bilingual Education Legislation and Court Cases

The **Bilingual Education Act** (Public Law 90-247) was enacted in 1968 to provide funds to assist local school districts in carrying out elementary and secondary programs for students whose first language is not English.

In 1974, a landmark U.S. Supreme Court decision in *Lau v. Nichols* stated that equal educational opportunities are denied when non–English-speaking students receive the same English language instruction as that given to all students. The Court did not mandate **bilingual education**, but required that special programs providing understandable instruction be made available to limited or non–English speakers.

In 1979, the Supreme Court ruled in *Dyrcia S. et al. v. Board of Education of New York City* that students with disabilities who have limited English proficiency have the same rights as their English-proficient peers to receive special educational services. Schools could meet this requirement using a bilingual or **English as a second language (ESL)** approach to special education services.

In 1998, the voters of California passed **Proposition 227**, which outlawed bilingual education in California schools. The proposition did provide for a waiver process if enough citizens in a school district wished to retain some form of bilingual education.

The legislation concerning bilingual education illustrates that efforts to address the educational needs of limited-English-proficiency (LEP) students have brought many gains.

NCLB and English Language Learning

The No Child Left Behind Act has significantly transformed the ways in which language-minority students are educated. NCLB replaced the Bilingual Education Act with the English Language Acquisition, Language Enhancement, and Academic Achievement Act. "The purpose of this act is (1) to help ensure that children who are limited English proficient, including immigrant children and youth, attain English proficiency, develop high levels of academic attainment in English, and meet the same challenging State academic content and student academic achievement standards as all children are expected to meet."[17]

Under NCLB, the term *bilingual* is seldom used. In its place, the term *English language learner (ELL)* is used instead. The new terminology reflects NCLB's intent to teach students English as rapidly as possible.

As you can see, NCLB brings ELL students into the same context of standards and accountability as their native English-speaking peers. NCLB has major implications for mainstream teachers. As Kathleen Leos of the Office of English Language Acquisition states:

> The role of every teacher in every classroom in the nation has never been more important than today. The teacher, who is the key component within the standards reform model, must link core academic instruction to the content standards set by the state. In classrooms with language diverse populations, teachers must also ensure that the curriculum and teaching strategies reflect an alignment with English Language Proficiency Standards.[18]

Methods for Promoting English Language Learning

A number of different programs have been proposed and implemented for teaching ELLs. Some of these programs, which are presented in the following list, include English as a second language (ESL) programs, transitional ELL programs, developmental ELL programs, and dual-language programs:

- **English as a second language (ESL) programs.** ESL programs emphasize learning and using English in the classroom and preparing ELLs to function in "mainstream" English-language classrooms. The ultimate goal of these programs is English proficiency.
- **Transitional ELL programs.** Also called *early exit ELL education*, **transitional ELL programs** use students' native language in the classroom to help students learn academic content while they are learning English. These programs are designed to transition students to English as quickly as possible.
- **Developmental ELL programs.** Also called *maintenance ELL education* or *late exit ELL education*, **developmental ELL programs** develop and maintain proficiency in students' native language as well as English.
- **Dual-language education programs.** These programs serve a mix of ELLs and native English-speaking students, teaching language and content in both English and in a target language (e.g., Spanish, Japanese, etc.).[19]

Research on English Language Learning

Research in the area of English language acquisition over the past two decades has shown some encouraging results. Among the major findings:

- There is steady growth in the number of immigrant children in the nation's schools and therefore a growth in the ELL population. In 2005, 27 percent of children ages 5 to 17 spoke a language other than English at home. About 6 percent of children ages 5 to 17 had difficulty speaking English.[20]

Transitional ELL programs English as a second language programs that use the second language to teach English while using the first language to teach other subjects.

Developmental ELL programs Transitional ELL programs that also infuse English into content area instruction with the goal of biliteracy.

REFLECT & WRITE

What steps might you take to help students in your class who have not yet achieved cognitive academic language proficiency in English?

■ **INTASC**

STANDARD 4 The teacher uses various instructional strategies to encourage students' development of critical thinking, problem solving, and performance skills.

- Spanish speakers are increasingly predominant in the U.S. population. Among school-age children, about 69 percent of Latino children speak a language other than English at home.[21]
- Students in California, Texas, New York, Florida, and Illinois account for about 68 percent of all ELLs in elementary schools.[22]
- ELL students constitute a larger share of students in kindergarten than in other grades.[23]
- The majority of ELL elementary school students are concentrated in a small number of schools: Nearly 70 percent of the nation's ELLs are enrolled in only 10 percent of the nation's elementary schools.[24]
- Nearly half of all elementary schools in the United States enroll no ELL students.[25]
- Schools serving high concentrations of ELL and minority students tend to be large and urban, whereas schools serving low concentrations of ELL and minority students tend to be smaller, serve a predominantly white student population, and are mostly suburban or rural.[26]
- The incidence of poverty and health problems is significantly higher in schools serving high concentrations of ELL students than in other schools.[27]

The question of how to best teach students whose first language is something other than English can be expected to remain a front burner topic for some time to come, especially when this country's role in the wider world is hotly debated.

In our discussion of ELL, it is evident that most everyone agrees that ELL students should become fully literate in English. Differences exist over how to accomplish this goal.

REFLECT & WRITE

Bilingual education is a "hot button" topic in education and society. What makes bilingual education such a flash point? Where do you stand on this topic?

_____

_____

_____

_____

_____

HOW DOES GENDER AFFECT TEACHING AND LEARNING?

In an ideal gender-fair school, teachers would have the same expectations of all students in all subjects. Male and female students would participate equally in classroom discourse. Students of both genders would receive a similar amount and quality of attention from teachers. Counselors would advise on career choices based on student interest, aptitude, and academic achievement. Administrators would have similar leadership expectations of male and female students.

Academic Achievement and Gender

When we examine how gender and achievement interact, we discover that it is a complex issue, with very few apparent differences. A decade ago, educators were concerned about girls' academic underachievement. Thanks to heightened public awareness of the problem, special school programs and teachers' dedicated focus have helped to bolster girls' success rates. As a result, the large academic achievement gaps that once existed between males and females have been eliminated in most cases and have significantly decreased in others. For example:

- Females are less likely to repeat a grade and to drop out of high school.
- Differences in enrollment in math and science courses based on gender appear to be shrinking.
- Female high school seniors tend to have higher educational aspirations than their male peers.
- Females have made substantial progress at the graduate level overall, but they still earn fewer than half of the degrees in many fields.[28]

Women have made substantial gains educationally, although they are still underrepresented in some fields of study, such as computer science, engineering, and the physical sciences.[29] However, white girls are now almost equal with boys in mathematics and science achievement. Boys now considerably underachieve in reading and writing, especially boys of color. The typical boy lags one and a half years behind the typical girl.[30]

The Boys Project at the University of Alaska Fairbanks has identified five of the most promising interventions for increasing the success of boys in reading and writing. These include:

- Educating teachers on gender differences in development and learning
- Delaying school enrollment for slower developing boys
- Creating "focus schools" that offer nurturing and personalized education
- Connecting boys in groups with caring adults
- Respecting boys[31]

Go to MyEducationLab and select the topic "Diversity and Multiculturalism" then watch the video "Gender as a Multicultural Education Concept." Answer the questions that follow.

REFLECT & WRITE

Do you recall any incidents of gender bias toward you or your classmates in school? If you do, please explain. If you do not, what made your school gender fair?

_____
_____
_____
_____
_____

Gender Issues in School Life

School provides an academic and social milieu in which male and female students interact with each other and with teachers and administrators. A gender-fair school environment provides equitable educational opportunities to students of both genders. In addition, **gender-fair schools** provide social climates in which students may interact without encountering sexism or sexual harassment in nonacademic activities or in interpersonal interactions.

One of the most influential forces in establishing a more gender-fair school environment was the passage of **Title IX** of the Education Amendments of 1972, which banned discrimination on the basis of gender. This legislation states:

> No person in the United States shall, on the basis of sex, be excluded from participation in, be denied the benefits of, or be subjected to discrimination under any educational program or activity receiving Federal financial assistance.[32]

However, when we consider that it has been over 50 years since the *Brown v. Board of Education* Supreme Court decision and over 30 years since the passage

Gender-fair schools Learning environments in which male and female students participate equally and respond to similar high expectations in all subjects.

Title IX Part of the Education Amendments of 1972 that prohibits exclusion on the basis of sex from participation in or benefits of any education program or activity receiving federal funding.

What gender issues affect student achievement and school life? How can teachers and schools provide education that is gender fair?

of Title IX barring discrimination by gender, a glance at the gender equity report card indicates that we still have a long way to go to provide equal opportunity and education for all students. Consider the following facts:

■ Sexual harassment remains pervasive in public schools—81 percent of students surveyed have experienced it.
■ Sex segregation persists in career education, with more than 90 percent of girls clustered in training programs for the traditionally female fields of health, teaching, graphic arts, and office technology.
■ Female students typically receive less attention, praise, criticism, and encouragement from teachers than male students.
■ The lower test scores of African American females, Native American females, and Latinas compared to their white and Asian peers remains a serious and deep educational divide.
■ Pregnant students are steered toward separate and less academically rigorous schools.[33]

Gender remains a salient factor in school life. You must take care to ensure that female and male students are given equitable academic and extracurricular opportunities in schools. One issue that is in the forefront currently is the question of gender equity for boys. After years of focusing on the needs of girls, many now contend that it's boys who are being shortchanged. (See *What's New in Education? The New Gender Gap: Boys Lagging.*)

REFLECT & WRITE

What are some suggestions that you have for how public education could increase the rate at which it brings gender equitable education to all students?

_____

_____

_____

_____

_____

Providing a Gender-Fair Education

Providing a gender-fair curriculum is far more than injecting a vignette about Madame Curie into a science class or giving students a glimpse of the life of Harriet Tubman or Sojourner Truth during Women's History Month. Gender-fair treatment involves a reconceptualization of subjects, gender issues, and how to best meet the needs of boys and girls. Providing a gender-fair education can take many forms:

■ INTASC

STANDARD 2 The teacher understands how children learn and develop, and can provide learning opportunities that support their intellectual, social, and personal development.

1. Being aware of your patterns of discussion in the classroom. As a beginning teacher, some questions to ask yourself are:
   ■ Do I pay more attention to boys than girls, or vice versa?
   ■ When selecting students for participation in events and activities, do I favor one sex over the other?
   ■ Do I give more constructive feedback to boys than girls, or vice versa?
2. Making classroom arrangements gender fair so that both genders are represented fairly in books, displays, and study materials.

What's  in Education?

The New Gender Gap: Boys Lagging

Women today are filling roles that were once held only by men. More women are becoming doctors, CEOs, and principals than ever before. Thirty years after the passage of equal opportunity laws, girls are graduating from high school and college and going into professions and businesses in record numbers.

Now, it's the boys who could use a little help in school, where they're falling behind their female counterparts.

And if you think it's just boys from the inner cities, think again. It's happening in all segments of society, in all 50 states. As shown in the figure, during the 2003–2004 school year 66 percent of all male students earned a standard high school diploma, compared to almost 74 percent of female students. This is why more and more educators are calling for new efforts to put boys on equal footing with girls.

One of these efforts that has provoked considerable controversy is the idea of single-sex classes or schools. In 2006, the U.S. Department of Education introduced new regulations allowing public schools to group students by gender provided that both gender groups receive an education that is "substantially equal." In the June 2006 report "The Truth about Boys and Girls," author Sara Mead notes that some educators have found that classrooms are too rigid for boys, who tend to have more trouble sitting still than their female counterparts. Others say that reading materials and class assignments are not geared to the interests of males. Some educators have made efforts to alter curriculum and instruction to accommodate male learning in order to shrink the gender gap between boys and girls.

Despite efforts to close the gender gap, in many schools girls prevail over the boys. For example, at Hanover High School in Massachusetts, girls take home nearly all honors, including the science prize.

According to Hanover High principal Peter Badalament, "[Girls] tend to dominate the landscape academically right now," even in math and science.

The school's advanced placement classes, which admit only the most qualified students, are often 70 to 80 percent girls. This includes calculus. And in AP biology, there is not a single boy.

According to Badalament, three out of four of the class leadership positions, including the class presidents, are girls. In the National Honor Society, almost all of the officers are girls. The yearbook editor is a girl.

Although girls are achieving in school more rapidly than boys in many areas, experts continue to debate whether there is a "boy crisis." Some believe that this debate is distracting attention from more serious issues, such as large racial and economic achievement gaps, and practical ways to help both boys and girls of all races and socioeconomic backgrounds succeed in school.

Sources: "The Gender Gap: Boys Lagging," *CBS News*, May 25, 2003 (2004). (Online). Available at www.cbsnews.com; L. Sterling, "Gender Gap in Graduation," *Education Week*, 2007. (Online). Available at www.edweek.org/rc/articles/2007/07/05/sow0705.h26.html?levelId=1000&; S. Mead, "The Truth About Boys and Girls," *Education Sector*, June 27, 2006. (Online). Available at www.educationsector.org/analysis/analysis_show.htm?doc_id=378705; M. R. Davis, "New U.S. Rules Boost Single-Sex Schooling," *Education Week*, November 1, 2006. (Online). Available at www.edweek.org/ew/articles/2006/11/01/10gender.h26.html.

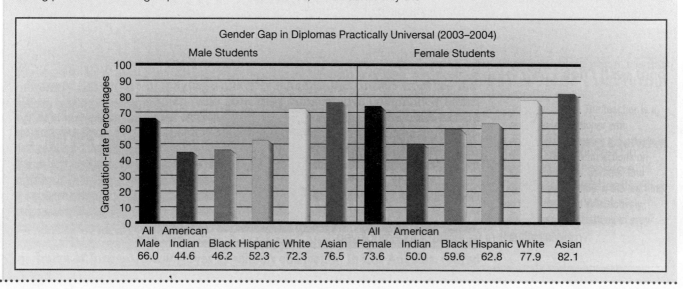

Gender Gap in Diplomas Practically Universal (2003–2004)

	Male Students						Female Students				
	All Male	American Indian	Black	Hispanic	White	Asian	All Female	American Indian	Black	Hispanic	White	Asian
	66.0	44.6	46.2	52.3	72.3	76.5	73.6	50.0	59.6	62.8	77.9	82.1

Graduation-rate Percentages

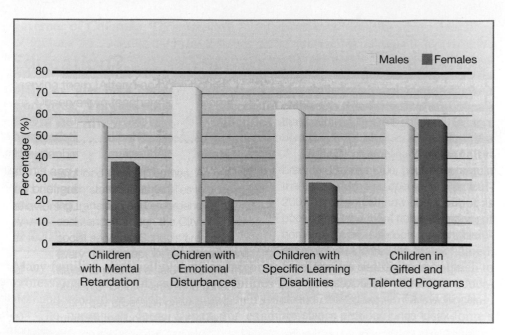

FIGURE 4.6   Enrollment of Boys and Girls in Special Education

Males tend to have higher enrollment in special education than females. How will you put forth gender-fair practices to ensure that neither boys nor girls are over- or underrepresented in special education programs?

Source: U.S. Department of Education, "State and National Projections for Enrollment and Selected Items by Race/Ethnicity/Sex," *Civil Rights Data Collection 2004*, 2005. (Online). Available at http://vistademo.beyond2020.com/ocr2004rv30/VistaView/dispview.aspx.

---

3. Putting into practice gender-fair special education and gifted programs so that neither boys nor girls are over- or underrepresented in special education programs. Figure 4.6 shows the enrollment of boys and girls in special education.

4. Conducting high-quality programs that help to ensure that all students graduate from high school. High school graduation rates for males are lower than for females. In addition, the high school graduation rate for all students is much lower than it should be.

REFLECT & WRITE

Based on what you have read about gender equity and on your educational experiences, what are some strategies you will use to ensure gender equity in your classroom?

Single-Sex Schools and Classes

Educators, politicians, and the public are constantly seeking new ways to provide opportunities for boys and girls to excel. Single-sex schools, although not new, are now being tested as one way to ensure that boys and girls get the most of their educational opportunities.

On March 3, 2004, the U.S. Department of Education published new regulations governing single-sex education in public schools. The new regulations allow coeducational public schools (elementary and secondary schools) to offer single-sex classrooms, provided that the schools

1. Provide a rationale for offering a single-gender class in that subject. A variety of rationales are acceptable (e.g., if very few girls have taken computer science in the past, the school could offer a girls-only computer science class).
2. Provide a coeducational class in the same subject at the same school.
3. Conduct periodic reviews to determine whether single-sex classes are still necessary to remedy whatever inequity prompted the school to offer the classes in the first place.

Just as important, the new regulations clear the way for single-sex schools—schools that are all girls or all boys. In fact, the new regulations provide some incentive for school districts to offer single-sex schools rather than single-sex classrooms within coed schools. Single-sex schools are specifically exempted from two of the three requirements above. They do not have to provide any rationale for their single-sex format, and they do not have to conduct any periodic review to determine whether single-sex education is "necessary" to remedy some inequity. They will have to offer "substantially equal" courses, services, and facilities at other schools within the same school district, but those other schools can be single-sex or coed. In other words, a school district may offer a single-sex high school for girls without having to offer a single-sex high school for boys. A school district can offer an all-boys elementary school without having to offer an all-girls elementary school.[34]

In 2006, the Bush administration gave public school districts the green light to expand the number of single-sex classes and schools created under the 2004 regulations. The 2006 regulations allow districts to create single-sex schools and classes as long as enrollment is voluntary. School districts that implement single-sex programs must also make coeducational schools and classes of substantially equal quality available for members of the excluded sex.[35]

The number of public schools experimenting with single-sex education is increasing. At least 33 states have public schools or classes that are gender exclusive. Ohio and New York are in the lead with 10 single-sex public schools each. Indiana has at least seven schools, and Pennsylvania follows with six.[36] In Philadelphia, Chief of Schools, Paul Vallas, believes that many more public schools will implement single-sex education and states that "there's a lot of support for this type of school model in Philadelphia."[37]

Although single-sex education has many proponents, some oppose the gender-separation approach to education, citing that the research does not support single-sex education and that this style of teaching conflicts with Title IX—the 1972 law that banned sex discrimination in educational institutions that receive federal funds.[38] For example, the American Association of University Women strongly supports Title IX and opposes any efforts that would weaken its effectiveness. The association maintains that factors such as small class size, qualified teachers, and parental involvement, as opposed to gender separation, are much more important in improving the education of both boys and girls.[39]

Research on single-sex education has generally been inconclusive; however, in 2005 a comprehensive study from the Department of Education found the following trends:

- Achievement test scores in all subjects tend to be higher in single-sex schools than in coeducational schools.
- Single-sex schooling usually results in higher academic aspirations, as evidenced by students showing more interest in and taking more difficult courses; however, there is no noticeable difference in long-term academic achievement among students in single-sex schools and those in coeducational schools.
- Single-sex schools do not appear to be more effective than coeducational schools in terms of addressing procedural issues (e.g., classroom treatment) and outcome measures of gender inequity.
- A majority of students in single-sex schools tend to put more focus on academics and leadership than their coeducational counterparts and less emphasis on social status.[40]

ETHICAL DILEMMA

We Shouldn't Cater to Them!

BETH has just been hired to teach seventh grade in River Bend School District, which has had an influx of minority students during the past few years. The minority students are almost the majority. Not everyone thinks that the rapid increase in the minority student population has been beneficial to the school district or the town. Some of Beth's colleagues think that the school district is bending over (too far) backward to

meet minority students' needs. At Beth's first meeting with Harry Fortune, her new mentor teacher, he remarked, "Respecting minorities and catering to them are two different things. I'm going to stress with my parents that this is America and American culture comes first, and that includes speaking English!" Beth does not agree with his sentiment or his approach.

What should Beth do?

SUMMARY

- America is a nation of diverse learners. Diversity refers to the range of race, ethnicity, gender, sexual orientation, socioeconomic status, cultural heritage, and ability and disability.

- Racial and ethnic diversity affect teaching and learning. One goal of American education is to promote equal treatment for all children. The No Child Left Behind Act was enacted to foster equality, though some educators question whether the standardized testing that has resulted from the act is fair to ELL students or those from ethnic backgrounds.

- Multicultural education is designed to ensure that all students receive equal opportunities regardless of socioeconomic sta-

tus, gender, sexual orientation, and racial and cultural backgrounds. It also requires culturally responsive teachers to use multicultural education models in the classroom.

- The number of students in U.S. schools with limited English proficiency is increasing. Students who have not mastered English face numerous challenges. To help address these challenges, a number of programs have been developed to accommodate ELL students.

- Gender affects teaching and learning. Boys and girls learn differently. Teachers must find ways to minimize as well as accommodate these differences.

KEY TERMS

Bilingual education   130
Bilingual Education Act   130
Cultural responsiveness   128
Culturally responsive teacher   123
Developmental ELL programs   131
Diversity   114
English as a second language (ESL)   130

English language learner (ELL)   120
Eurocentric   124
Gender-fair schools   133
Global education   125
Lau v. Nichols   130
Multicultural education   122
Proposition 227 (California)   130

School culture   123
Socioeconomic status (SES)   115
Title IX   133
Transformative knowledge   128
Transitional ELL programs   131

APPLICATIONS FOR ACTIVE LEARNING

Connections

1. In the chapter opener, you read about The Young Women's Leadership School, which serves inner-city girls of different ethnicities, many of whom face a variety of social and economic hardships. As a beginning teacher, you will be presented with students with diverse backgrounds, cultures, socioeconomic statuses, and beliefs. How will you modify your teaching style and lesson plans to accommodate all children in your classroom?

2. How does the information in this chapter relate to the discussion of urban, rural, and suburban schools in Chapter 3? Write a paragraph using the concepts in this chapter to describe the differences among schools presented in the previous chapter.

Field Experiences

1. Interview teachers about their views on multicultural education and their experiences with multicultural curricula. How do you account for the range of views you find? Which views do you think are most constructive in promoting both quality and equity in the education of culturally diverse learners? Relate the teachers' views and experiences to the five models of multicultural education presented in this chapter. From a practical standpoint, what seem to be the requirements, benefits, and challenges of each approach?

2. Observe students in a culturally diverse school. How, if at all, do race, ethnicity, language, gender, and culture seem to influence students' interactions and social relations? On the basis of your observations, what recommendations might you make for improving learning environments for diverse learners?

Personal Research

1. In response to increasing illegal immigration to the United States, the federal government has begun to crack down on the problem. Oftentimes this includes deporting illegal immigrants to their country of origin, regardless of their having children, legal or illegal, in the public school systems. Research national immigration laws and read articles about the deportation of immigrants with schoolchildren online and in the news. How is this affecting the children of illegal immigrants? Find out how this issue is being handled within the school system.

2. Research the literature, both pro and con, on single-sex schools and classrooms. Do the data support the implementation of these programs?

PREPARING TO TEACH

For Your Portfolio

1. Getting to know—I mean really know—English-language learners is one way to enhance your professional growth. You can achieve this goal by developing a "portrait" of an ELL student. Here are some things to include in your ELL portrait:

   - A word picture of the student
   - A brief description of culture and language

   - A description of family and home background
   - A description and analysis of how and in what way the student's home language is influencing—positively or negatively—school performance
   - Your recommendations for how to enhance the student's language and school achievement

   Place your ELL portrait in your portfolio.

2. In the midst of the "boy crisis" and gender-gap debate, it is important that you understand the learning styles, similarities, and differences among the boys and girls in your classroom. Include a gender portrait for a boy and a girl to include in your portfolio. Your gender portrait might include:

- A description of the student
- Basic pattern of behavior, temperament, and social interactions with other boys and girls
- Work samples from the student
- The level of participation in and the type of extracurricular activities for the student

Idea File

1. Think of two or three creative and effective strategies you could use in each of the following situations to achieve multicultural education goals. In each situation, the students are in the process of entering or leaving your classroom.

- Students of different races use racial epithets in talking with one another.
- Students of the same race use racial epithets in talking with one another.
- A male student makes unwanted, aggressive, or inappropriate physical contact with a student of the opposite sex.
- A male student makes unwanted, aggressive, or inappropriate physical contact with a student of the same sex.
- A teacher reprimands a student for disturbing the class. The student challenges the teacher by saying his cultural background is the only reason he is being singled out.

2. A new student who does not speak English is transferred to your class from another state with very little notice. What are the first five things you will do to set the stage for this student's social integration and academic success? What are the next five things you will do?

LEARNING AND KNOWING MORE

Websites Worth Visiting

As we have discussed in this chapter, many of your students will benefit from a number of different kinds of programs. Fortunately, many programs exist to help students who need special help and support. One of these is the School Development Program: The Comer Process. A primary goal of this program is to promote the overall development of students, including significant gains in academic and social behavior skills, by providing enriched school experiences. Comer is at the Yale Child Study Center, which you can visit online at http://info.med.yale.edu/comer. Also, you can learn more about multicultural education online at the Pathways to School Improvement project at www.ncrel.org/sdrs/

Electronic Magazine of Multicultural Education
www.eastern.edu/publications/emme

This electronic journal provides articles, instructional ideas, reviews, and literature for young readers in the area of multicultural education.

Multicultural Awareness in the Classroom
www.edchange.org/multicultural/activityarch.html

This site contains excellent sources for increasing multicultural and diversity awareness in the classroom.

Multicultural Perspectives in Mathematics Education
http://math.coe.uga.edu/Multicultural/MathEd.html

Explores multicultural dimensions of mathematics, a field often regarded as difficult to teach multiculturally.

National Association for Multicultural Education
www.nameorg.org

The website of this national organization provides a free sample of its journal, *Multicultural Perspectives*.

National Multicultural Institute
www.nmci.org

This site is operated by the Washington-based National Multicultural Institute and explores many facets of diversity.

North Central Regional Education Laboratory
www.ncrel.org

This website contains links to multicultural school initiatives, professional development programs, organizations, and curricula.

National Women's History Project
www.nwhp.org

This site contains excellent resources for faculty or students wishing to research women's history or gender issues.

Multicultural Book Reviews
www.isomedia.com/homes/jmele/homepage.html

This is a useful site for educators to preview existing and new titles in multicultural education.

Books Worth Reading

Banks, J. A., and Banks, C. A. (Eds.). (2004). *Multicultural Education: Issues and Perspectives* (5th ed.). New York: Wiley.

Articles treat characteristics, goals, content, and methods in multicultural and multilingual education, including gender equity. This book offers research-based perspectives on issues and controversies in the field of multicultural education.

Faltis, C. J. (2007). *Teaching English Learners and Immigrant Students in Secondary Schools.* Upper Saddle River, NJ: Prentice Hall.

Written for traditional, non-ESL classroom teachers, this text is filled with practical, research-based approaches and strategies based in recent sociocultural theories on teaching and learning. It helps teachers address the needs of immigrant English learners who are 2 or more years below grade level when they enter secondary school.

Gurian, M., Stevens, K., and King, K. (2008). *Strategies for Teaching Boys and Girls—Secondary Level.* San Francisco: Jossey-Bass.

Offers many strategies for teaching styles for teaching to boys and girls based on learning differences. Strategies are geared for students in grades 6 through 12.

Manning, M. Lee (Ed.). (2004). *Multicultural Education of Children and Adolescents* (4th ed.). New York: Allyn & Bacon.

This text expands the definition of multicultural to include gender, disability, and sexual orientation. It is an invaluable resource, providing suggestions for working with families of culturally diverse backgrounds as well as with school administration and special school personnel.

Salomone, R. C. (2005). *Same, Different, Equal: Rethinking Single-Sex Schooling.* New Haven, CT: Yale University Press.

This text provides an examination of the history and politics of gender and education. The author makes the argument that voluntary single-sex education is a legally acceptable option that ought to be widely available in the United States, especially to disadvantaged children, by examining single-sex schools and discussing the *Brown v. Board of Education* decision and Title IX.

Schrag, P. (Ed.). (2004). *Final Test: The Battle for Adequacy in America's Schools.* New York: New Press.

This book is designed to help present and future educators acquire the concepts, paradigms, and explanations needed to become effective practitioners in culturally, racially, and language diverse settings for the education of students from both genders and from different cultural, racial, ethnic, and language groups.

5 Teaching Diverse Learners II: Academically Diverse Learners in Today's Classrooms

SUSAN HENTZ Congratulations! You are about to embark on a career that has a direct impact on every facet of our society. Yes, teaching is the only career in the world that touches every individual's life. Children who will ultimately become nurses, teachers, lawyers, sanitation workers, builders, cosmetologists, and firefighters will walk through your door as students. Regardless of ability or disability, these students come to school highly receptive to the learning process.

As a special educator for the past 21 years, my experience has afforded me the opportunity to work with students ranging from birth through adult. I believe my greatest contribution to the field of education is my personal dedication and enthusiasm in working to positively influence the life of each and every student that walks through my classroom door. My experience has taught me that fostering positive self-esteem within my students ultimately results in future academic successes and sustained motivation to learn. By setting standards of behavior and high academic expectations, I give my students the opportunity to succeed, which in turn helps to develop and maintain positive self-worth. My teaching environment for students from birth through adulthood has been consistent: high expectations in a safe environment with teacher and parent collaboration focusing on student achievement.

As you read this chapter . . .

Think about:

- What you must do to comply with federal and state mandates to ensure a free, appropriate education for all children

- Your role in meeting the special needs of students in your classroom through mainstreaming and inclusion

- Actions you can take to promote communication and collaboration with families and other professionals to meet the needs of exceptional learners

- How you can teach the exceptional learners in your classroom

- How you can implement assistive technology and differentiated instruction to assist students in your classroom

- How you can identify and support children with a range of education needs or who are at risk for school failure

> By setting standards of behavior and high academic expectations, I give my students the opportunity to succeed.

As a beginning teacher, it is your responsibility to have an awareness of the diverse learning styles and influences that will affect the learning process of each student. It is imperative that you respect and value your students while having a clear vision and high expectations for all. Additionally, you must be prepared to utilize a variety of teaching strategies to address the physical, behavioral, intellectual, and cultural differences of each individual student. Three questions you can use to guide your teaching are these: What do I expect my students to learn? How will I assess my students to determine if learning occurred? What will I do when students do not learn the material? If you can consistently provide answers to these three questions, you will be well on your way to helping your students reach their full potential. Needless to say, the challenges you will face are extreme. However, the positive educational outcomes are equally extreme and professionally rewarding. The adventure of teaching will enable you to touch your students, both mentally and emotionally, so they achieve and become contributing members of our society.

▶▶ Go to MyEducationLab and select the topic "Inclusion and Special Needs" and watch the video "Smartboards for Students with Hearing Impairments."

Susan Hentz is the Florida Council for Exceptional Children's 2003 Teacher of the Year.

DO FEDERAL AND STATE LAWS PROVIDE FOR THE EDUCATION OF EXCEPTIONAL LEARNERS?

Imagine being told that your child was not welcome at your neighborhood public school because he had a speech impairment, required medication for a chronic disease, or displayed behaviors not considered to be "normal." Prior to the passage of Public Law 94-142 in 1975, children with disabilities could be segregated or denied basic educational opportunities. In fact, before Congress realized the importance of special education, approximately 1 million children with disabilities were excluded from the public school system.

Exceptional learners, or students with special needs, are in every school and in every classroom in the United States. As a beginning teacher, you will teach students who have special needs for a variety of reasons. They may come from low-income families or different racial and ethnic groups; they may have exceptional abilities and disabilities. Students with special needs often are discriminated against because of their disability, socioeconomic background, language, race, or gender. Your challenge will be to provide for all students an education that is appropriate to their physical, mental, social, and emotional abilities and to help them achieve their best. In addition, you must also learn as much as you can about the special needs of your students and collaborate with other professionals to identify and develop teaching strategies, programs, and curricula for them. Most of all, you need to be a strong advocate for meeting all students' individual needs.

⟳ REFLECT & WRITE

Why do you think laws are necessary to ensure that all students receive an appropriate education?

_____

_____

_____

_____

_____

Students with Disabilities and the Individuals with Disabilities Education Act (IDEA)

Students with special needs require modifications or accommodations to the regular school curriculum to help them succeed. Historically, students with disabilities did not receive appropriate services and failed to reach their full potential. This is one reason laws are required to ensure that schools and teachers will have high expectations for these students and that they will have special education and related services. The federal government has passed many laws protecting and promoting the rights and needs of children with disabilities. One of the most important federal laws is the **Individuals with Disabilities Education Act (IDEA)**, originally passed in 1975 as the Education for All Handicapped Children Act. The law was renamed IDEA in 1990. Congress has periodically updated IDEA, with the latest revision in 2004.

Individuals with Disabilities Education Act (IDEA) A federal act providing a free and appropriate education to disabled youth between ages 3 and 21.

The purpose of IDEA is to ensure that all children with disabilities have access to a free appropriate public education that emphasizes special education and related services designed to meet their unique needs, to ensure that the rights of children with disabilities and their parents or guardians are protected, to assist states and localities to provide for the education of all children with disabilities, and to assess and ensure the effectiveness of efforts to educate children with disabilities."[1]

What's *New* in Education?

Winkelman v. Parma City School District

On May 21, 2007, the Supreme Court ruled that parents do not need to hire an attorney to represent their children's interests in special education disputes. IDEA provides parents the procedural right to represent their child in an administrative hearing. The Parma City School District claimed the parents of a boy with autism, Jacob Winkelman, could not act as legal counsel for their son in a court of law because the right to a free, appropriate public education belonged to their child. The decision in *Winkelman v. Parma City School District* concluded that parents have a vested interest in their child's education and have the legal right to challenge a public school district's individualized plan for their child with disabilities, even if they are not licensed attorneys. Administrators believe this change will increase the substantial cost of special education litigation as inexperienced and emotionally involved parents, unable to find or afford a lawyer, go to court to dispute the school district's proposed plan for their child.

Source: M. Walsh, "High Court Backs Parents' Rights to Argue Cases Under IDEA" *Education Week*, May 22, 2007. (Online). Available at www.edweek.org/ew/articles/2007/05/21/38scotus_web.h26.html?. Accessed May 24, 2007.

IDEA defines **students with disabilities** as "those with mental retardation, hearing impairments (including deafness), speech or language impairments (including blindness), serious emotional disturbance, orthopedic impairments, autism, traumatic brain injury, other health impairments, or specific learning disabilities; and who, by reason thereof, need special education and related services." IDEA also allows states the option of classifying students between the ages of 3 through 9 who have disabilities as developmentally delayed. Developmental delays may be in one or more of the following areas: physical development, cognitive development, communication development, social or emotional development, or adaptive development. About 10 to 12 percent of the nation's students have some type of disability and need special education services. Table 5.1 lists the

Students with disabilities   Children with physical impairments (hearing, speech or language, visual, orthopedic) or mental/emotional impairments (mental retardation, autism, emotional disturbance, traumatic brain injury) or specific learning disabilities and who, by reason thereof, need special education and related services.

TABLE 5.1   Children Ages 3 to 21 with Disabilities Served under IDEA

Go to MyEducationLab, select the topic "Ethical and Legal Issues" and watch the video "PL94-142". Complete the activities below.

	Numbers Served	Percentage Served
All disabilities	6,606,702	100.00%
Learning disabilities	2,892,694	43.78
Speech or language impairments	1,428,568	21.62
Mental retardation	613,888	9.29
Emotional disturbance	487,037	7.37
Multiple disabilities	140,209	2.12
Hearing impairments	79,197	1.20
Orthopedic impairments	83,701	1.27
Other health impairments	405,969	6.14
Visual impairments	29,240	0.44
Autism	137,708	2.08
Deaf-blindness	1,846	0.03
Traumatic brain injury	22,476	0.34
Developmental delay	284,169	4.30

Source: U.S. Department of Education, Office of Special Education and Rehabilitative Services, Office of Special Education Programs, *26th Annual (2004) Report to Congress on the Implementation of the Individuals with Disabilities Education Act*, vol. 1, Washington, DC, 2005.

number of persons from birth to age 21 with disabilities in the various categories covered under IDEA.

IDEA establishes seven basic principles with regard to providing educational and other services to children with special needs:

1. *Zero reject.* IDEA calls for educating all children and rejecting none from an education. Whereas before IDEA many children were excluded from educational programs or were denied an education, this is not the case today.

2. *Nondiscriminatory evaluation.* A fair evaluation is needed to determine whether a student has a disability, and, if so, what the student's education should consist of. IDEA specifies the use of nondiscretionary testing procedures in labeling and placement of students for special education services. These include:
   - Testing of students in their native or primary language, whenever possible
   - Use of evaluation procedures selected and administered in such a way as to prevent cultural or racial discrimination

3. *Multidisciplinary assessment.* This is a team approach in which a group of people use various methods in a child's evaluation. Having a **multidisciplinary assessment (MDA)** helps ensure that a child's needs and program will not be determined by one test or one person. The evaluation team might include an educational diagnostician, a school psychologist, a speech-language pathologist, an occupational or physical therapist, an adaptive physical education therapist, and other professionals.

4. *Appropriate education.* Instruction and related services need to be individually designed to provide educational benefits to students in making progress toward meeting their unique needs. Basically, IDEA provides for a **free and appropriate education (FAPE)** for all students between the ages of 3 and 21. *Appropriate* means that children must receive an education suited to their age, maturity level, condition of disability, past achievements, and parental expectations.

5. *Least restrictive placement/environment.* All students with disabilities have the right to learn in the **least restrictive environment (LRE)**—an environment consistent with their academic, social, and physical needs. Such a setting may or may not be the general classroom, but 95 percent of children with disabilities spend at least part of their school day in general classrooms.

6. *Procedural due process.* IDEA provides schools and parents with ways of resolving their differences by mediation and/or hearings before impartial hearing officers or judges.

7. *Parental and student participation.* IDEA specifies a process of shared decision making whereby educators, parents, and students collaborate in deciding a student's educational plan.

Referral Process

Under the provisions of IDEA and other guidelines that specify the fair treatment of students with disabilities and their families, educators must follow certain procedures in developing a special plan for each student. These procedures occur through the school referral planning and placement process (see Figure 5.1). Referral of the student for special services can be made by a teacher, parent, doctor, or some other professional. The referral is usually followed by a comprehensive individual assessment in order to determine if the student possesses a disability and is eligible for services. In order for testing to occur, parents or guardians must give their consent.

Multidisciplinary assessment (MDA) A team approach using various methods to conduct a child's evaluation.

Free and appropriate education (FAPE) Children must receive education suited to their age, maturity, condition of disability, past achievements, and parental expectations.

Least restrictive environment (LRE) The principle that, to the maximum extent appropriate, students with disabilities are to be educated with their peers who are not disabled.

■ **INTASC**

STANDARD 10 The teacher fosters relationships with school colleagues, parents, and agencies in the larger community to support students' learning and well-being.

Phase 1	Phase 2	Phase 3	Phase 4
Initiating the Referral	**Assessing student eligibility and educational needs**	**Developing the Individualized Education Program (IEP)**	**Determining the Least Restrictive Environment (LRE)**
Any concerned person, including parents, doctors, school, or agency personnel can request an evaluation of a child suspected of having a disability affecting their educational progress. The school must receive parents' informed written permission to evaluate eligibility to receive special education services.	A comprehensive and accurate initial evaluation using multidisciplinary and nondiscriminatory assessment tools provides information to identify the child's strengths and special education needs. The results of the evaluation provide the basis for developing a written statement of goals, objectives, and related services if the child meets eligibility requirements.	Parents, and students when appropriate, collaborate with school personnel and related service providers to determine how to address educational needs. The IEP includes level of present performance, annual goals, and necessary support services.	Based on the student's individual needs, the educational placement decision must provide the most opportunities to participate with nondisabled peers to the maximum extent appropriate, justifying any removal of the student from the general education classroom.

FIGURE 5.1   The Four-Phase Special Education, Referral Planning, and Placement Process

This four-phase process will help you understand the seriousness and responsibilities you have in ensuring children with special needs receive a free and appropriate education.

Source: Adapted from M. Hardman C. Drew, and M. Egan, *Human Exceptionality: School, Community, and Family*, 8th ed. (Boston: Allyn & Bacon, 2005), fig 2.2, p. 37. Copyright 2005 by Pearson Education. Reprinted by permission of the publisher.

REFLECT & WRITE

After reviewing the four-phase process, did you have any "surprises"? What were they? Which of these phases is the most critical? In what way?

_____

_____

_____

_____

_____

If the student is determined to be eligible for special education services, a committee is formed consisting of:

- A parent or parent representative
- At least one regular education teacher
- At least one special education teacher
- A school administrator
- A professional qualified to interpret evaluation results

Individualized education program (IEP) A plan for meeting an exceptional learner's educational needs that specifies goals, objectives, services, and procedures for evaluating progress.

• *Your Turn*

Consider Michelle Pham, a child in your fourth-grade class. Michelle is of above-average intelligence, but 2 years ago she suffered a spinal cord injury that left her with no movement or sensation from the waist down. Who should you consult, and what sources of information can help clarify your role in supporting Michelle in your general education classroom?

Individualized family service plan (IFSP) A plan designed to help families reach their goals, for themselves and for their children, with the following support services: special education, speech and language pathology and audiology, occupational therapy, physical therapy, psychological services, parent and family training, and counseling.

- Other individuals, invited by the parent or school, including related service providers
- The student, when appropriate

This committee meets at least once each year to develop, review, or revise an **individualized education program (IEP)**. The IEP is a written plan describing the terms of the student's special education and related services that adheres to the federal regulations outlined in IDEA. The modifications, accommodations, and services listed in the IEP constitute a binding legal document that must be followed by all committee members and school personnel.

A complete reevaluation, conducted every 3 years, establishes the need for continued services or determines that the child no longer meets the definition of a child with a disability. When it is determined that the child no longer needs support services to succeed in general education, the committee will dismiss the student from special education.

Individualized Education Programs and Individualized Family Service Plans

As stated earlier, schools must provide services to meet the unique educational needs of students with disabilities and their parents. The IEP specifies what will be done for the child, how and when it will be done, and by whom it will be done. Figure 5.2 shows a sample IEP form. Each school district develops its own form, which must include the items shown in the sample form in Figure 5.2.

In 1986, Congress passed PL 99-457, the Education of the Handicapped Act Amendments, which was landmark legislation relating to infants, toddlers, and preschoolers with disabilities. This law extends to children with disabilities between the ages of 3 and 5 the same rights that are extended to children with disabilities under IDEA and establishes a state grant program for infants and toddlers with disabilities. Most states participate in the infant and toddler grant program.

The process of helping infants and toddlers through age 2 with disabilities begins with referral and assessment and results in the development of an **individualized family service plan (IFSP)**, which is designed to help families reach the goals they have for themselves and their children. Planned services must meet the developmental needs of infants and toddlers. These services can be provided by a variety of educators, agencies, and service centers. Although the focus of the IFSP is on the child, parents and caregivers also receive training and counseling so they can help meet their infant's or toddler's special needs on a daily basis.

A written IFSP must contain a statement of the child's present levels of development; a statement of the family's strengths and needs in regard to enhancing the child's development; a statement of major expected outcomes for the child and family; the criteria, procedures, and timelines for determining progress; the specific early intervention services necessary to meet the unique needs of the child and family; the projected dates for initiation of services; the name of the case manager; and transition procedures from the early intervention program into a preschool program.

REFLECT & WRITE

Are there any items that you feel would be valuable to add to the sample IEP shown in Figure 5.2? If so, please describe.

_____

_____

_____

_____

SAMPLE FORM   Individualized Education Program

The Individualized Education Program (IEP) is a written document developed for each eligible child with a disability in accordance with IDEA Part B regulations.

Present levels of educational performance

How the child's disability affects involvement and progress in general education. For preschoolers, how the disability affects participation in appropriate activities.

Measurable annual goals

Clearly stated goals (benchmarks or short-term objectives) describing the plan to enable progress and involvement in general education, including a statement of measurement and reporting procedures.

All services, aids, and modifications needed

	Frequency	Location	Beginning Date	Duration
Special Education & Related Services				
Supplementary Aids & Services				
Program Modifications or Supports for School Personnel				

Administration of state and districtwide assessments

Any individual modifications needed for the child to participate in assessments of student achievement. If determined that the child will take an alternative assessment, include a statement of why the child cannot participate in the regular assessment and a description of the alternative assessment.

Transition services

Beginning at age 16, or younger, the IEP must include transition goals related to training, education, employment, and, where appropriate, independent living skills.

Rights that transfer at age of majority

Beginning at least one year before the child reaches the age of majority under State law, the IEP must include a statement that the child has been informed of their rights under Part B of IDEA, if any will transfer to the child on reaching the age of majority.

FIGURE 5.2   Sample IEP Form

The IEP is literally the heart and soul of providing special education services for children with disabilities. It is a document that will guide your teaching providing other services.

Source: Adapted from U.S. Office of Special Education Programs, "Building the Legacy: IDEA 2004." (2005). (Online). Available at http://idea.ed.gov/static/modelForms.

WHAT ARE MAINSTREAMING AND INCLUSION?

What if you broke your wrist falling down some stairs and your professor told you that you could no longer attend class because you could not complete the assignments or take the exams without modifications? Fortunately, a variety of laws prevent discrimination against people with disabilities. The federal laws you just read about support the practice of providing a child with disabilities an education in the general education classroom, with the services and accommodations needed by that student.

Adaptive education An educational approach aimed at providing learning experiences that help each student achieve desired educational goals.

Mainstreaming Also known as *inclusion*, the educational practice of educating students with disabilities with nondisabled peers.

Natural environments Educational settings where students would be if they did not have a disability.

Inclusion An interpretation of the least restrictive environment concept whereby students with disabilities receive instruction in general education classrooms.

■ **INTASC**

STANDARD 3 The teacher understands how students differ in their approaches to learning and creates instructional opportunities that are adapted to diverse learners.

A variety of adaptations are used to ensure that all students, regardless of abilities, have equal access to a quality education. **Adaptive education** is an educational approach aimed at providing learning experiences that help each student achieve the desired educational goals. Education is adaptive when school learning environments are modified to respond effectively to student differences and to enhance the individual's ability to succeed in learning in such environments.

Mainstreaming implies the placement of students with disabilities in general classrooms, called **natural environments**.

The Full-Inclusion Debate

Inclusion supports the right of all students to participate in natural environments. *Full inclusion* means that students with disabilities receive the services and supports appropriate to their individual needs entirely in the general classroom. *Partial inclusion* means that students receive some of their instruction in the general classroom and some in pull-out classrooms or resource rooms, where they work individually or in small groups with special education teachers.

Studies indicate that students educated in natural environments have higher academic achievement, greater self-esteem, and better physical health. They are more likely to graduate from high school, attend college, and find employment.[2] IDEA does not require inclusion, but states that considerable effort must be made to find an appropriate placement for students with disabilities to learn and to participate effectively within mainstream school settings.

The concept of full inclusion is not unanimously accepted and is the subject of debate among parents and educators. Table 5.2 provides arguments for and against full inclusion. According to an analysis of a U.S. Department of Education survey by Richard Ingersoll, a professor of education and sociology at the University of Pennsylvania, about one-third of teachers who leave the profession or transfer to another

TABLE 5.2 The Full-Inclusion Debate

Support for Full Inclusion	Opposition to Full Inclusion
■ **Every student has a basic civil right to education based on equal opportunity.** For example, in the 1993 case of *Oberti v. Board of Education of the Borough of Clementon School District* the Court ruled that Rafael, an 8-year-old child with Down syndrome, should not have to earn his way into an integrated classroom; it was his right to be there from the beginning. ■ **Many view separate programs as a form of segregation.** Students learn to communicate and interact from each other. ■ **Individual differences provide rich diversity and promote acceptance.** Inclusive education motivates students with special needs to improve and allows their nondisabled peers to assume leadership roles.	■ **Education cost is higher per student.** The cost of educating a student with disabilities ranges from $10,558 to $20,095; the cost of educating a student without disabilities is $6,556. Expenditures for students with special needs are 1.5 to 3 times higher than those for their nondisabled peers. ■ **Some teachers do not feel they have the training or time to accommodate students with special needs.** Oftentimes, students with special needs require more attention due to behavioral needs or complicated modifications. Without sufficient training, teachers cannot attend to a wide range of abilities and might lower standards for general or higher-level students. ■ **Many parents believe their children are best served in special settings.** For instance, in the 1997 case of *Mark Hartmann v. Loudon County* the Court determined that the social benefits of mainstreaming were less important than ensuring that a child with a disability receive educational benefit.

Source: Jay G. Chambers, Thomas B. Parrish, Jamie L. Shkolnik, Roger Levine, and Freya E. Makris. *The Special Education Expenditure Project*, 2005. Available at www.csef-air.org. Accessed March 11, 2007.

school cite difficulties with mainstreaming as a primary reason for their dissatisfaction. Many teachers claim a lack of training and support. Tom Horne, Arizona's state superintendent of schools, agrees that mainstreaming is "a big factor in teachers' leaving." He states that special education students with behavior problems can be "extremely destructive" to teachers' morale.[3] Unpredictable and unsettling behavior disrupts learning in the general education classroom. Teachers need adequate preparation and assistance from administrators and the special education team to provide for students with special needs in the general classroom.

Many educators and special education advocates support providing special needs children a continuum of services. A **continuum of services** means that a full range of services is available for individuals, from the most restrictive to the least restrictive placements. This continuum implies a graduated range of services, with one level of services leading directly to the next. For example, the least restrictive setting is the general education classroom. The most restrictive setting for a child with a disability would be a publicly or privately owned residential school or facility (see Figure 5.3). The Center for Discovery in Harris, New York, offers residential programs

Continuum of services   A full range of educational services available for individuals from the most restrictive to the least restrictive placements.

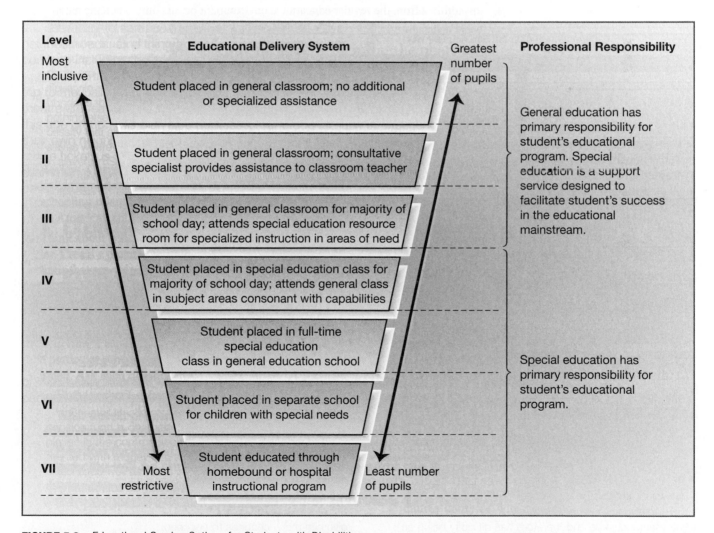

FIGURE 5.3   Educational Service Options for Students with Disabilities

The continuum of service options range from the most physically integrated at the top to the more restrictive at the bottom. Schools have an obligation to see that the full range of service needs are met.

Source: Extracted from M. L. Hardman, C. Drew & M. Egan, *Human Exceptionality: School, Community, and Family*, 8th ed. (Boston: Allyn & Bacon, 2005). Copyright 2005 by Allyn & Bacon. Reprinted by permission of Pearson Learning, Inc.

OBSERVE & LEARN

Classrooms that successfully include students with disabilities welcome diversity and address the individual needs of *all* students. Visit several schools in your area and evaluate educational delivery systems. Notice whether children with special needs are included in general education classrooms. Do you see a variety of settings for support services? Also note how teachers and students interact with students with disabilities. What can you learn from these interactions?

to children and adults diagnosed with significant disabilities, such as autism or mental retardation. All residents have mild to severe cognitive delays, and most have significant language and social impairments. More than half use a wheelchair or walker for mobility.

Part of the controversy over full inclusion comes over the interpretation of IDEA, which requires that:

> to the maximum extent appropriate, children with disabilities . . . are educated with nondisabled children, and that special classes, separate schooling, and the removal of children with

disabilities from the regular educational environment occurs only when the nature or severity of the disability is such that education in regular classrooms with the use of supplemental aids and services cannot be achieved satisfactorily.[4]

As a teacher, you will be expected to provide for all of the students assigned to you. Figure 5.3 gives you an idea of the options available to you for achieving this goal. The *In the Classroom with Chris* feature gives you an example of the benefits of accommodating to students' special needs.

Given the amount of interest in and controversy surrounding full inclusion, discussions regarding its appropriateness and how best to implement it will con-

In the Classroom
with Chris
A Chance to Succeed

Teaching exceptional students involves constantly finding ways to open new doors to new programs and new accommodations.

Chris is a student with an emotional disability and has required a self-contained special education classroom since the third grade. He has a great smile but otherwise is disheveled and has poor personal hygiene. He is a large student and tends to be verbally impulsive. Chris has poor interpersonal skills and therefore has difficulty being accepted by his peers. He often exhibits angry, inappropriate behavior and annoys his peers and teachers; Chris seems to thrive on the negative and positive attention.

In the tenth grade, Chris was given a variety of accommodations, including one-on-one intervention strategies coupled with positive reinforcement and the opportunity to participate in a vocational program half-day. This experience has been pivotal in Chris's school success. Chris has excelled in the "hands-on" active learning environment of the half-day vocational program. Chris feels valued as a member of the program, and he is valued by his teachers, who give him many chances to succeed.

tinue. As a beginning teacher, you will have many opportunities to participate fully in this discussion and to help shape the policies of implementation and classroom practice. Participating in discussions about children with disabilities will include how to provide appropriate accommodations so they can learn and thrive.

Teaching Students with Learning and Other Disabilities in an Inclusive Classroom

As Table 5.1 on pg. 145 showed, students with learning disabilities represent the largest category of students in need of special education services. You will most likely have one or more students with learning disabilities in your classroom. The federal government defines a learning disability this way:

> The term "specific learning disability" means a disorder in one or more of the basic psychological process involved in understanding or in using language, spoken or written, which disorder may manifest itself in an imperfect ability to listen, think, speak, read, write, or spell, or do mathematical calculations.[5]

Unexpected underachievement is a practical definition of learning disability. A child with a learning disability shows a noticeable difference between learning to read, write, listen, or do math and how well they could do as indicated by their intelligence or ability. Learning disabilities tend to be diagnosed in early elementary school when the curriculum focuses on the learning tasks that prove difficult for the child. Young children diagnosed with developmental delays often are later diagnosed with a specific learning disability. Most schools identify learning disabilities by comparing a student's scores on standardized intelligence and achievement tests. The 2004 reauthorization of IDEA allows for other options of identification so that a child might receive services before falling significantly behind.

Attention Deficit/Hyperactivity Disorder (ADHD)

Learning disabilities and **attention deficit/hyperactivity disorder (ADHD)** often occur simultaneously. Some studies indicate that as many as 70 percent of children with ADHD also have an identified learning disability.[6] Children with ADHD alone can qualify for special education services in the "other health impairments" category, if the condition significantly interferes with their educational performance.

Doctors do not have a clear idea about the causes of ADHD, but generally children with ADHD do not have enough of or the right kind of certain chemicals in their brains that help control behavior and sustain focus. As a result, children with ADHD have difficulties in three main areas: attention, impulse control, and hyperactivity. The *Diagnostic and Statistical Manual of Mental Disorders-IV* defines ADHD as "a persistent pattern of inattention and/or hyperactivity-impulsivity that is more frequent and severe than is typically observed in individuals at a comparable level of development."[7] The DSM-IV establishes diagnostic criteria for determining whether a child has ADHD. At least eight of the characteristics must have continued for more than 6 months before age 7 and must occur in more than one setting. ADHD is diagnosed more often in boys than in girls. It is estimated to affect between 10 and 20 percent of the school-age population in the United States.

Behavior-control drugs, such as Ritalin, Dexedrine, or Concerta, help some children with ADHD focus and attend to assigned tasks. These types of drugs stimulate the production of chemicals, called *neurotransmitters*, in the brain to alter the core symptoms of ADHD. Controversy surrounds the use of these drugs, and some parents choose not to medicate their children. Nevertheless, students with ADHD must have access to strategies for managing their behavior.

Go to MyEducationLab and select the topic "Inclusion and Special Needs" and watch the video "The Inclusive Classroom." Complete the activities that follow.

Attention deficit/hyperactivity disorder (ADHD)   Children with ADHD have an unusual degree of difficulty with attention and self-control, which leads to problems with learning, social functioning, and behavior that occur in more than one situation and that have been present for a significant length of time.

Go to MyEducationLab and select the topic "Inclusion and Special Needs" and then watch the video "Students with Autism: Social Skills Instruction." Complete the activities that follow.

Autism

Students with *autism* require support with social interaction and behavior issues. For decades, it was thought that autism affected only 4 to 5 of every 10,000 children. Using current diagnostic criteria, the Centers for Disease Control (CDC) now estimates that approximately 1 in 166 children have some form of autism.[8] Prior to 1990, public schools labeled children with autism as having mental retardation or an emotional disorder. Public awareness and the addition of the disorder as a special education category under IDEA '90 (PL 101-476) led to improved diagnostics and reporting.

Asperger's Syndrome

The above statistics come from a broader definition of autism, which includes *Asperger's Syndrome (AS)* added to the DSM-IV in 1994.[9] AS is more common in boys, and affects a child's ability to socialize and communicate. Children with AS typically have normal intelligence, but have problems with social interaction and abstract concepts. They often obsess about peculiar topics, such as the weather or vacuum cleaners, so they may appear quirky or odd. Most have extreme difficulty reading facial expressions or body language, and do not understand the give-and-take of conversation. To help your students with AS,

- *Use clear, concrete language.* While students with AS may have an impressive vocabulary about specific topics, they rarely understand jokes or sarcasm.
- *Help develop social skills.* Encourage partner or group work with assigned tasks. You will need to model appropriate behaviors or provide a written script for your students with AS.
- *Monitor peer relationships.* Many children with AS are bullied on a daily basis. If you sense students with AS are being intimidated or mistreated, step in and let those who are bothering the student know that teasing or harassing is not allowed in your classroom or in the school.

Effectively teaching and supporting students with learning and other disabilities in the inclusive classroom requires a little extra effort and some separate planning. But you have the opportunity to make an enormous difference in a student's life. You will need

- **Knowledge of students and their needs.** Learn all you can about the characteristics of your students' disabilities and identify their individual strengths and needs. This will help you foster social acceptance of students with special needs.

    Never assume that students with a certain disability behave or learn the same way. The signs of ADHD in girls look very different from those exhibited by boys. Some studies estimate that 50 to 75 percent of girls go undiagnosed and are diagnosed, on average, 5 years later than boys. Most children with ADHD have trouble staying organized and paying attention, but boys tend to act impulsively and have trouble sitting still. Girls with ADHD may talk excessively and seem emotionally sensitive, behaviors misunderstood as immaturity. All students with ADHD need help to refocus and stay engaged in lessons.[10]

- **Knowledge and skills in curriculum and instruction.** Develop and modify instruction to meet individual needs using a variety of instructional methods to reach a range of learning styles. To be effective, you will need to determine techniques to assess what students know.

    Just as you need to adapt the ways you teach children with disabilities, testing what students know is not a one-size-fits-all system. No Child Left Behind (NCLB) requires that the majority of students with mild to moderate disabili-

■ **INTASC**

STANDARD 3   The teacher understands how students differ in their approaches to learning and creates instructional opportunities that are adapted to diverse learners.

ties participate in high-stakes testing. Accommodations such as extra time and extra breaks can be written into a student's IEP. Even so, for children with learning disabilities or ADHD, standardized tests can result in agony that can be damaging to their self-esteem and motivation. In California, researchers believe tests are too long and too difficult. Struggling students are overwhelmed, and many give up and mark answers at random. Some experts recommend partial testing. For example, slow readers could complete half of the required reading selections. This option decreases the duration of the test while still providing data about a student's abilities.[11]

- **Classroom leadership and classroom management skills.** Plan and manage the learning environment to accommodate students with special needs. Always provide clear rules and set high expectations. To help your students achieve these expectations, however, you will need to teach learning strategies as well as organizational and study skills that will help *all* students.

  Karen Sauer, a special education teacher at Empire Garden School in San Jose, California, helps her second graders by studying each student to find individual needs and situations that set off misbehavior. She provides structure and consistency by establishing consequences, but she also rewards students who behave well. She is serious about teaching, but connects with her students by singing, dancing, and laughing. Sauer keeps her class focused by wearing goofy glasses and asking questions like a reporter and making up songs about classroom rules.[12]

- **Professional collaboration skills.** Participate in planning and implementing the student's IEP. Consult with special educators and related service providers and involve parents to enlist their support. The skills you need to effectively consult and collaborate with professionals and parents are discussed in the next section.

HOW CAN PROFESSIONAL COLLABORATION ENHANCE EDUCATION IN INCLUSIVE CLASSROOMS?

> *"I not only use all of the brains I have, but all I can borrow."*
>
> Woodrow Wilson (1856–1924)

This quote from President Woodrow Wilson describes the purpose of professional collaboration among educators. Teachers must make decisions about how to present curriculum to students with diverse backgrounds and learning needs. An effective teacher knows when and who to ask for help with a first-grader

Students with special needs, their teachers, and their peers all benefit from collaboration among teachers, parents, and professionals to provide needed assistance.

who has difficulty waiting for a turn or attending to a story, a third-grader who always has the correct answer during group lessons but cannot pass a written test, or an adolescent who has suddenly lost motivation and has not turned in assignments for the past 3 weeks. Consulting with parents or other professionals will help you respond to students' individual needs.

As a beginning teacher in an inclusive classroom, you will want to participate in **consultation**, seeking advice and information from colleagues. You will also engage in **collaboration**, working cooperatively with a range of professionals, special educators, parents, and administrators to provide services to students with disabilities and students at risk. Some of your collaboration will involve working with

- **Itinerant teachers**, who travel from school to school and provide assistance and teach students
- **Resource teachers**, who provide assistance with materials and planning
- Diagnosticians, who are trained to test and analyze students' strengths and weaknesses
- Physical therapists, who treat physical disabilities through nonmedical means
- Occupational therapists, who direct activities that develop muscular control and self-help skills
- Special educators, who are trained to instruct students with special needs
- Speech and language pathologists, who diagnose and treat problems in the areas of speech and language development

Consultation Seeking advice and information from colleagues.

Collaboration To work jointly and cooperatively with other professionals, parents, and community members.

Itinerant teachers Professionals who travel from school to school or district to district and provide assistance and teach students.

Resource teachers Professionals who provide assistance with materials and planning for teachers of exceptional students and teachers in mainstreamed classrooms.

Roles of Key Collaborators

A key member of the special education team is the *paraprofessional*, or *classroom aide*. IDEA allows for appropriately trained and supervised educational assistants to help in the delivery of services to students with disabilities. Another important team member, the *paraeducator*, also contributes by accommodating a wide variety of student needs. For example, a paraeducator may be a job coach who trains older students to function in a workplace, tutors students with learning disabilities in a resource room, or works one-on-one with a student who benefits from inclusion in a regular education classroom. Aides are present in almost every educational setting, under the supervision of a teacher. Teachers rarely receive preparation in training or supervising paraprofessionals. The following principles will help you as you work with these valuable members of the school staff:

- Create a "job description," listing responsibilities and expectations.
- Observe paraprofessionals as they interact with students.
- Provide written feedback of your observations, communicating the paraprofessional's strengths and needs.

For example, say that in the resource room a supervising teacher observes a paraprofessional working with a student completing an assignment with multiple-choice questions. The aide appears unable to provide useful prompts, and ultimately answers the questions for the student. Following an observation, the supervising teacher should describe techniques to the paraprofessional, such as allowing appropriate wait time, using context clues, or eliminating choices, that will help students discover the correct answers for themselves.

Consultations among Teachers and Key Players

Consultation enables you to understand the goals of inclusion, gain important insights, and consider teaching strategies you might not have thought of on your own. As a classroom teacher, you will provide knowledge of grade-level or course-curriculum objectives, sequence, and measures of evaluation. Special education teachers contribute information about the characteristics of exceptional learners, techniques to support appropriate behavior, and ideas about how to modify assignments and tests to meet their students' learning needs. Related service providers, such as occupational or physical therapists, can help you create the physical environment that best meets the needs of the exceptional learners in your classroom. Your school principal or campus administrator understands the legal and procedural matters surrounding special education services. You may want to appeal to your supervisor for additional planning time to provide opportunities to collaborate and consult about students with special needs.

Go to MyEducationLab and select the topic "Inclusion and Special Needs" and watch the video, "The Collaborative Process." Complete the activities that follow.

Consultation and collaboration also include working with and involving parents, families, and members of community agencies. The development of an IEP requires that you work closely with parents in developing learning and evaluation goals for students with disabilities. Also, some parents may want to spend time in your classroom to help you meet the needs of their children. All parents have information about their children's needs, growth, and development that will be helpful to you as you plan and teach. Here are some things you will want to consider when you collaborate in developing an IEP or IFSP:

- *Involve parents.* Involving parents and working with them is an absolute must for every classroom professional. You should learn all you can about parent conferences and communication, parent involvement, and parents as volunteers and aides. IDEA emphasizes parent participation as well as that of children.
- *Collaborate and cooperate.* Working with all levels of professionals offers a unique opportunity for you to individualize instruction. All professionals need help in individualizing instruction; therefore it makes sense to involve all professionals in this process.
- *Assess needs.* As individual education becomes a reality for all children and families, you will want to develop skills in assessing student behavior and family background and settings.
- *Consider students' learning styles.* Taking into account the visual, auditory, and tactile/kinesthetic learning styles of all students helps to provide for special needs. Some students may learn best through one mode; other students, through another.

REFLECT & WRITE

Why is collaboration important for successful inclusion? What are some barriers to collaboration?

_____

_____

_____

_____

_____

How Cooperative Teaching Works in the Inclusive Classroom

Cooperative teaching The process by which a regular classroom teacher and a special educator or a person trained in exceptional student education team teach, in the same classroom, a group of regular and mainstreamed students.

Cooperative teaching, also known as _co-teaching_, describes an inclusive educational setting where a general classroom teacher and a special education teacher work together to differentiate instruction to meet the unique needs of all students.[13] Both teachers contribute to planning, presentation, evaluation, and classroom management. Most important, both accept responsibility for all students in the classroom. Sharing expertise requires organization, commitment, and flexibility. Co-teachers authentically model effective communication skills as they develop an appreciation for each other's talents and challenges. Lower student/teacher ratio and greater pedagogical resources benefit students in this inclusive environment with more individual interaction and teaching strategies that address a wide range of learning styles.

REFLECT & WRITE

As a new teacher, will you be comfortable having another person in your classroom helping teach a subject or assisting students? How do students benefit from having two teachers collaborate?

_____

_____

_____

_____

_____

HOW CAN YOU TEACH EXCEPTIONAL LEARNERS IN YOUR CLASSROOM?

As you have learned in previous sections, to accommodate exceptional learners you will need to make adjustments in your classroom arrangement, curriculum, and teaching plan to provide for _all_ your students. You have read that a variety of strategies are necessary, but knowing how and when to use these strategies is key.

Karen Elledge, who teaches exceptional learners, has found a strategy that has worked well for her students:

I feel that my college education was very thorough, but nothing could quite prepare me for the planning and preparation it requires to teach my students at so

■ INTASC

STANDARD 3 The teacher understands how students differ in their approaches to learning and creates instructional opportunities that are adapted to diverse learners.

many different levels. Once I got to know my students a little better, things they were interested in, what they were good at ... it became much easier. Even though no two students are alike, I learned how to group them. Sometimes, I put groups together to work on specific skills, but my best groups were when the students got together because of the topic or the activity. For example, during our unit on the human brain one group created a Public Service Announcement about brain food and safety, another made a clay model and very scientifically taught us about the five parts of the brain, the last group researched how the brain is involved with laughter.

As Karen explains, finding ways to accommodate all students does not happen overnight. The following are some steps you can take to accommodate all of the students in your classroom:

- *Get to know students' individual learning needs.* The process of consultation and collaboration will give you a great deal of information about which students' needs require special attention and accommodation, but you will determine how to meet those needs in your classroom and monitor the effectiveness of your interventions throughout the year.
- *Communicate with your administrator or special education staff about additional training, assistance, or support.* An important part of learning how to help students with special learning needs is getting the appropriate training and education. You might need to attend workshops on classroom management strategies and behavior management techniques for inclusive settings. School districts often have itinerant teachers who provide ongoing help. For example, District 24 in Queens, New York, employs full-time facilitators who visit classrooms each week to mentor and to address teacher concerns about inclusion. At Dorsey Middle School in Pittsburgh, Pennsylvania, staff development has been key to successful inclusion. Teacher training was provided through Gateways: Pennsylvania Statewide System Project, whose staff provided on-site technical assistance to support inclusion efforts.[14]
- *Educate students about accepting and helping students with special needs.* Find out if your campus participates in a disability awareness program that provides information about disabling conditions and offers support and opportunities for discussion to promote understanding and respect of individual differences.

Using Assistive Technology

Public Law 100-407, the Technology-Related Assistance for Individuals with Disabilities Act (Tech Act), defines an **assistive technology device** as "any item, device or piece of equipment, or product system, whether acquired commercially off the shelf, modified, or customized, that is used to increase, maintain, or improve functional abilities of individuals with disabilities."[15]

Assistive technology covers a range of products and applications, from simple devices, such as adaptive spoons and switch-adapted battery-operated toys, and recordings for the blind, to complex devices, such as computerized environmental control systems. You will have opportunities to use many forms of assistive technology and modified educational software with all ages of students with special needs.

Assistive technology is particularly important for students with disabilities who depend on technology to assist them to communicate, learn, and be mobile. For example, closed-circuit television can be used to enlarge print, a Braille printer can convert words to Braille, and audiotaped instructional materials can be provided for students with vision impairments. Closed-captioned television and FM amplification systems can assist students who are deaf or hard of hearing. Classroom amplification systems are becoming more common in classrooms to assist

Assistive technology device Any item, device, piece of equipment, or product system—whether acquired commercially off the shelf, modified, or customized—used to increase, maintain, or improve the functional abilities of individuals with disabilities.

■ **INTASC**

STANDARD 6 The teacher uses knowledge of effective verbal, nonverbal, and media communication techniques to foster active inquiry, collaboration, and supportive interaction in the classroom.

all students in hearing and listening. Touch-screen computers, augmentative communication boards, and voice synthesizers can assist students with limited mobility or with disabilities that make communication difficult. In addition, computer-assisted instruction provides software tools for teaching students at all ability levels, including programmed instruction for students with specific learning disabilities. See *In the Classroom with Lana*.

In the Classroom
with Lana
Using Assistive Technologies

Lana is a happy, curious 9-year-old with cerebral palsy who has been diagnosed with mental retardation. She enjoys school and is in a special education class for students with moderate to severe disabilities. She also participates in a third-grade inclusion class. Lana is nonverbal with a severe speech impairment. She also has an orthopedic impairment and uses a wheelchair for mobility.

Lana and her family moved from a small rural district to a larger metropolitan district at the beginning of the school year. Her current district uses a team approach to determine the best supports for Lana. The team includes Lana's parents, special and regular education teachers, a speech-language pathologist, an occupational therapist, a physical therapist, and an adapted physical educator. The team assessed Lana to determine how to best help her to be as successful as possible. The team developed goals, which are continually reassessed to minimize barriers to Lana's communication and participation in the classroom. The team also makes instructional adjustments to increase Lana's opportunities for success.

During the school day, Lana uses a notebook with a daily schedule that uses pictures. The schedule lists different activities and helps Lana stay organized to know what is happening throughout day. The picture symbols are affixed to small jar lids so that Lana can independently manipulate them. Lana also uses picture symbols on a choice board that enables her to choose activities for leisure time. Opportunities for choice-making are incorporated into Lana's day as much as possible, allowing her to have more opportunities for communication and increased independence.

Throughout the school day, Lana uses many different types of assistive technology devices. During calendar time, she uses her own calendar notebook with picture symbols

for the days of the week, months, and the weather. Lana also utilizes a BIGmack® communicator by Ablenet, which is a one-message voice-output device. She uses this to answer questions and/or make comments during group activities. She also uses the Step-by-Step® communicator by Ablenet, a sequencing voice-output device. She loves using this to give instructions to her peers, to tell jokes or stories, and to cheer during physical education class.

Lana actively participates with her peers in a variety of settings. She uses the All-Turn-It® spinner by Ablenet, which is a switch-activated spinner. Overlays can be changed for the specific game or activity. She has a Big Talk Triple Play by Enabling Devices, which has a combination of single, sequential, and random message capabilities. The ability to use different types of messages is great for bingo and games that use dice and cards.

For environmental control, Lana uses the PowerLink® 3 control unit by Ablenet, which has the ability to control most electric appliances and toys with a switch. This allows her to turn on a lamp or her radio. Lana loves to use the PowerLink to turn the music on and off for musical chairs.

Lana also utilizes the computer for educational and leisure activities. Because Lana is unable to use a mouse, she uses the IntelliSwitch®, a wireless switch interface engineered by Madentec. This allows Lana to search for software and programs on the computer or search for information on the Internet from her wheelchair.

Lana's access to a range of supports has enriched her school experience. She has taught her teachers and peers about problem solving and self-determination. Lana is well on her way to discovering more about the world and her own potential.

Teaching Gifted Learners

As a beginning teacher, you will want to be aware of the characteristics of gifted learners. Students who are gifted tend to get their work done quickly, often seek additional work, ask probing questions, prefer to select their own learning activities, have a greater depth of understanding of topics, and have interests in areas that are more like the interests of older students. Some gifted learners may have difficulty with social adjustment or may be underachievers, but research shows that students who are gifted and talented tend to be successful in a range of contexts.

The Jacob K. Javits Gifted and Talented Students Education Act of 2001 (originally passed in 1988) defines gifted and talented children as those who "give evidence of high performance capability in areas such as intellectual, creative, artistic, or leadership capacity, or in specific academic fields, and who require services or activities not ordinarily provided by the school in order to fully develop such capabilities."[16] The definition distinguishes between **gifted,** referring to above-average intellectual ability, and **talented**, referring to excellence in drama, art, music, athletics, or leadership. Students can have these abilities separately or in combination. About 10 to 20 percent of students are gifted. State and local school districts have varying definitions of gifted and talented. They also have different criteria for determining how gifted and talented is evaluated. It seems clear that districts tend to be very inclusive in identifying students as gifted and talented. Florida and Wisconsin led the way to renewed focus on gifted education by implementing new admission requirements that provide services to students who work hard, but who may not have a genius IQ. When we fail to challenge our brightest students, they get bored and dislike school. Many drop out. Those who go to college where they must exert effort often cannot cope because learning has always come quickly and easily.[17]

More likely than not, you will have to provide for students who are gifted and talented in your classroom. Here are some of the things you can do to help meet their needs:

- Avoid treating their probing questions as challenges to your authority or expertise.
- Provide alternative projects and activities that introduce greater novelty and complexity.
- Help students achieve a level of sophistication on advanced material.
- Arrange independent studies based on, but extending, the curriculum.
- Arrange for students to self-select and self-monitor alternative assignments.
- Arrange for students to contract for specific projects and grades.
- Allow students the extra time they may need to explore a topic to a satisfying depth.
- Connect students with opportunities to participate in science fairs and similar programs that give them opportunities to use their talents and abilities.
- Connect students with opportunities to contribute to others or to the community through their talents and abilities, such as arranging for them to be peer or cross-age tutors or creative contributors to community service initiatives.
- Encourage and reward creativity and critical thinking in all your students.

Students with disabilities are among the gifted and talented. A talented 5-year-old may have a learning disability, for example, and a student with physical disabilities may be gifted. Like low-income and minority students, students with disabilities are disproportionately underrepresented in the ranks of students identified as gifted and talented. For more information about the changing rules for gifted programs, see *What's New in Education?* on page 162.

Gifted   Students with the potential for high performance because of strengths in one or more of the following areas: general intellectual ability, specific academic aptitude, creative or productive thinking, leadership ability, ability in the visual or performing arts, and psychomotor ability.

Talented   Exceptional students who demonstrate excellence in drama, art, music, athletics, or leadership.

Go to MyEducationLab and select the topic "Multiculturalism and Diversity" then read the article "Raising Expectations for the Gifted." Answer the questions that follow.

REFLECT &
WRITE

Which do you think would be
more challenging—teaching
gifted and talented students, or
teaching students with learning
disabilities? Does your answer
give you any insight into your
strengths as a teacher?

_____

_____

_____

_____

_____

Acceleration

Acceleration   Involves moving students through the curriculum as rapidly as they are able and to the extent that acceleration is in their best interests.

Curriculum compacting   Students who are gifted and talented study the same themes and topics as their classmates but in greater depth or detail than their classmates and with greater opportunities for real-world applications.

Acceleration and enrichment are two traditional ways of providing for the needs of students who are gifted and talented. **Acceleration** involves moving students through the curriculum as rapidly as they are able and to the extent that acceleration is in their best interests. Some approaches to acceleration include early entrance into programs—for example, early entrance to kindergarten and first grade, middle school, high school, and college. Other acceleration methods include skipping grades, taking extra courses or honors courses, participating in advanced placement programs, and completing high school in 2 or 3 years.

In inclusive schools, acceleration is provided in the general education classroom through special instructional programs such as **curriculum compacting** and

What's *New* in Education?

Increasing Minorities in Gifted Programs

TiShanna Smith is an 11-year-old African American from a single-parent family who was identified as gifted by a special test intended to boost minority enrollment. Under South Carolina's old rules, TiShanna wouldn't be considered gifted. Under its new rules, she is. Every Tuesday, the fifth-grader at Greenview Elementary, in Greenville, South Carolina, attends a 3-hour advanced class in which she studies algebra and researches topics such as the history of hot air balloons.

Around the country and especially in the South, new tests are propelling more minority students into predominantly white gifted education programs. Proponents applaud what they say is an overdue easing of racial disparities in gifted education, stressing that special classes can open greater opportunities for African Americans, Latinos, and Native Americans.

But it's not that simple. By changing the standards for gifted education, traditionalists say, school districts seeking classroom equity are undermining academic excellence.

Aided by the new test, Greenville has nearly doubled the numbers of African American gifted students to 606, or 7.6 percent of gifted students, up from 320 in 1999–2000. Gifted white students have increased 43.4 percent, to 7,027, from 4,904 in 1999–2000.

Greenville has also tailored its gifted curriculum to students who have difficulty reading by emphasizing hands-on lessons. In math, third-through fifth-graders simplify algebraic equations by removing number cubes and chess pawns, which stand for the unknown X, from either side of a scale. Once they have mastered this approach, it is easier for them to make the leap to abstract equations and working on paper.

Source: D. Golden, "Boosting Minorities in Gifted Programs Poses Dilemmas," *Wall Street Journal*, April 7, 2004, pp. A1–A14. Reprinted by permission.

Gifted and talented students provide many challenges for teachers. High-ability and accelerated learners have the potential for an extraordinary level of achievement and need well-constructed programs designed to meet their special needs.

accelerated integrated learning. In these programs, students who are gifted and talented study the same themes and topics as their classmates, but in greater depth or detail and with greater opportunities for real-world applications. Also, in inclusive schools all students may have access to activities for gifted and talented learners through schoolwide enrichment programs.

Enrichment

Enrichment is the process of offering students additional activities and experiences not usually found in the curriculum. Enrichment activities occur through many arrangements in addition to enrichment within the classroom. A group of gifted students might work a few hours each week with a resource teacher outside of the regular classroom on intellectually stimulating activities and important ideas, giving students the opportunity to practice their problem-solving abilities. Students can participate in special classes outside the school setting or with members of the community in apprenticeship and mentoring programs. Other programs encourage individual study so students can pursue personal interests at their own pace.

Apprenticeship programs pair students with people in the community for periods of time; students acquire knowledge and skills through direct observation and practice.

Mentoring programs provide gifted students with a positive role model, support, and encouragement. Gifted students often are good at and want to explore many areas of interest. Although this is an asset, it can pose college and career-planning problems if

Enrichment   The process of offering students additional activities and experiences not usually found in the curriculum.

Apprenticeship programs   Programs that pair students with people in the community for periods of time during which students acquire knowledge and skills through direct observation and practice.

Mentoring programs   Support systems aimed at enhancing academic success and self-esteem of at-risk students; also programs to help new teachers.

OBSERVE & LEARN

How might a school identify gifted and talented students? To find out, observe a class or program for gifted and talented students. Start by recording characteristics of student communication and performance that may have contributed to their being identified as exceptional learners. Then talk with the teacher of that class and ask how that school identified those students.

students cannot focus on long-term goals. Mentors can help students find their sense of direction by sharing in stimulating conversation about values, attitudes, and passions. The purpose of the relationship can focus on career goals, community service, cultural enrichment, common heritage, social skills, or talents, such as art or sports. A mentorship often creates a lifelong connection as the adult and young person continue to learn from one another, growing both personally and professionally.[18] For example, Joyce Stoneham, director of the MentorWorks program in Fairfax County Public Schools in Virginia, pairs student council members with corporate executives to enhance the students' leadership skills.[19]

REFLECT & WRITE

You can use mentoring programs to help all children with disabilities extend and enrich their learning. What are some ideas you have for how you will provide mentoring experiences for your students with disabilities?

_____

_____

_____

_____

_____

Using Differentiated Instruction

Differentiated instruction (DI) Using a variety of methods, materials, and activities to meet the learning needs of all students.

Differentiated instruction (DI) is another means of providing for the needs of all students. In differentiated instruction, teachers use a variety of methods, materials, and activities to meet the needs of all students. In addition, teachers offer students a number of learning options that enable students to meet learning goals. Carol A. Tomlinson, a 20-year classroom veteran, states that teachers need to envision their classroom as an "escalator" going higher and higher, not as a "stairwell" that takes students to a certain grade-level landing where they stop. Tasks have to be "respectful of kids, hands-on, engaging, and thought provoking."[20] The following guidelines will help you prepare for using differentiated instruction in your classroom:

1. Differentiated instruction is _proactive_. The teacher assumes that different learners have differing needs and proactively plans a variety of ways to "get at" and express learning.

2. Differentiated instruction is more _qualitative_ than quantitative. Differentiated instruction focuses more on understanding concepts than on producing work. However, it does not necessarily mean giving some students less work to do. Rather, the emphasis is on adjusting the nature of an assignment to match students' learning characteristics as opposed to merely increasing the quantity of the assignment.

3. Differentiated instruction provides _multiple_ approaches to assessment, process, and product. Teachers offer different practices and approaches based on how individual students learn and how they demonstrate what they have learned. What these different practices and approaches must have in common, however, is that they are crafted to encourage substantial growth in all students and are based on high standards for all students.

4. Differentiated instruction is _student centered_. Learning experiences are most effective when they are engaging, relevant, and interesting. All students will not

always find the same avenues to learning equally engaging, relevant, and interesting. Understandings must be built on previous understandings, and not all students possess the same background knowledge at the outset of a given investigation.

5. Differentiated instruction is a *blend of instruction*, including whole-class, group, and individual instruction. There are times in all classrooms when it is more effective or efficient to share information or use the same activity with the whole class. Such whole-group instruction establishes common understandings and a sense of community for students by sharing discussion and review.

Kari Sue Wehrmann teaches English at Hopkins West Junior High School in Minnetonka, Minnesota. She relates one way that she differentiates instruction for some of the gifted students in her class. In differentiating content for a small group, her objective is to create an individualized, alternative learning experience for talented writers during a formula essay unit so that gifted students might show growth and retain an interest in writing.

> Four of my English 9 students had demonstrated their mastery of the formula essay, so I gave them the option to demonstrate their growth in writing in an independent study format or to do a series of formula essays with the general class. All four students chose the independent study option.
>
> Each student developed a different project. One student penned an essay and entered it in a creative writing contest. Another student wanted to work on using colorful details in her narrative writing. Her incredible first draft was ten single-spaced pages. The third student read *A Prayer for Owen Meany* and wrote a comparison/contrast paper of the book and the movie *Simon Birch*. The fourth student researched influential figures from the Civil Rights movement and wrote a historical fiction piece.
>
> This learning opportunity allowed four students to work on the same concept that the rest of the class was working on but allowed for individual differentiation of curriculum in content and process. The product, a paper, was the same for all students.[21]

Clearly, no two students are alike, nor do two students learn in identical ways. As a beginning teacher, you must create several ways for students of different abilities to have equally engaging learning tasks. This means that you should provide three or four different options so that students with specific needs have opportunities for developing individual skills and more advanced students can work on activities of greater complexity that encourage higher-level thinking. This process allows your students to take greater responsibility and ownership for learning so that all are challenged and none are frustrated.

■ INTASC

STANDARD 4   The teacher uses various instructional strategies to encourage students' development of critical thinking, problem solving, and performance skills.

Some websites that can help and inform you about differentiated instruction are web.uvic.ca/~jdurkin/edd40isu/Differentiated.html and www.ascd.org/pdi/demoe/diffinstr/differentiated1.html.

REFLECT & WRITE

What other steps could you take to meet the needs of gifted and talented students while teaching all students in your class?

WHAT FACTORS PLACE STUDENTS AT RISK AND AFFECT TEACHING AND LEARNING?

> "... I would tell him like, I haven't finished high school. I don't have a diploma. I don't have a job. I am broke. ... You can't make it without that. You can't go anywhere, for real, on the legal side. ... If you go to school, get your diploma, you can do more things the right way. You might succeed."
>
> —Male focus group participant discussing regrets about dropping out of school, from *The Silent Epidemic: Perspectives of High School Dropouts*, March 2006.

Students with disabilities are at risk of school failure because of their special learning needs. Likewise, gifted and talented students might not reach their full potential if they do not receive the support they need to develop their special abilities and interests. Many other factors also place **students at risk** for failing or dropping out of school. Regardless of their abilities or disabilities, any child or adolescent can experience problems in their home, school, and community environment that can negatively impact their development and maturation. Risk factors affect students' academic performance, emotional well-being, and physical health.

Children and youth are placed at risk by economic and political forces and social problems in their families and communities. The effects of risks on children's health, safety, growth, and development and on their learning and academic success depend mainly on their age, the number of risk factors in their environment and degree of exposure to them, and family and community resources for reducing or eliminating the sources and effects of those risk factors. Supportive families, good schools, caring teachers, and responsive communities can make all the difference in the world to students when they are at risk.

The risks that American children and youth face today are a national concern. According to the CDC the youth of today face risk factors that include tobacco use; unhealthy dietary behaviors; inadequate physical activity; alcohol and other drug use; and sexual behaviors that may result in HIV infection, other sexually transmitted diseases, and unintended pregnancies. The National Middle School Association has developed the program Safe Passage: Voices from the Middle School in order to help young people navigate through their adolescent years safely and securely. Safe Passage calls for schools that are safe, adults who are caring and involved, safety nets that are in place when things get difficult, elimination of the power of the bully, and reaching high academic goals.

Many students, individually and as groups, face barriers to learning and developing to their full potential. Review the risk factors and characteristics of students at risk in Figure 5.4. Students can come to school tired, hungry, abused, neglected, and from homes where adults are not supportive of children or their learning. Other students live in poverty, suffer from substance abuse, or live in fear of neighborhood violence. Teenage students can have children before they graduate from high school. These and other factors place students at risk for failure and affect their development toward a mature and productive adulthood if their problems are not identified and addressed by caring, responsive adults to help them overcome harmful attitudes and to foster **resiliency**. During times of trauma and stress, resilient children bounce back more quickly and more easily than children who lack the ability to cope with difficult experiences.

Poverty

Almost 18 percent (nearly 13 million) of all children in the United States under age 18 live in poverty. About 35 percent of African American children live in poverty. Poverty rates for Latino children are 28 percent overall. Despite indica-

---

Students at risk   Students whose living conditions and backgrounds place them at risk for dropping out of school.

• *Your Turn*

You have noticed that 7-year-old Raymond has been coming to school with two different shoes, neither of which fit, and he has been falling asleep in class. Some of his classmates have begun pointing and snickering. How should you handle this situation?

You can read more about the Safe Passage program at www.courttv.com/safepassage/index.html.

Resiliency   The ability to adapt and recover quickly from obstacles and adversity.

■ **INTASC**

STANDARD 7   The teacher plans instruction based upon knowledge of subject matter, students, the community, and curriculum goals.

RISK FACTORS

- Alienation from school (feelings of not belonging)
- Low SES—lives below the poverty level
- Minority status
- Non-English or limited-English speaking
- Dysfunctional family (abuser, drug use, etc.)
- Lives in community/neighborhood with gang activity, high crime, drug use, etc.
- Transient (moves a lot, unstable home life)
- Families have low education levels
- Poor health and nutrition
- Teenage pregnancy
- Single-parent family

CHARACTERISTICS

- Truancy/poor school attendance
- Suspension/expulsion from school
- Delinquency
- Grade failure
- Poor school achievement/low test scores
- Low or no involvement in school activities
- Drug use
- School behavior problems
- Not interested in school
- Not cooperative in class

FIGURE 5.4   Risk Factors and Characteristics of Students at Risk
. . . .
Certain risk factors characterize at-risk students. Although the lists in this figure are not exhaustive, they illustrate some of the leading risk factors.

tions of economic improvement and growth, the number of children living in poverty increased 11 percent between 2000 and 2005.[22]

Living in poverty means families do not have the income to purchase adequate health care, housing, food, clothing, and education services. In 2007, poverty for a nonfarm family of four meant an income of less than $20,000.[23] The federal government annually revises its poverty guidelines, which are the basis for distribution of federal aid to schools and student eligibility for services such as Head Start, and free and reduced school breakfasts and lunches.

Homelessness can be a consequence of poverty. The Stewart B. McKinney Homeless Assistance Act protects the right of homeless children to attend public school. The act also established the Education of Homeless Children and Youth (EHCY) program. This program provides grants to school districts to provide additional services for homeless children. The Thomas J. Pappas School in Tempe, Arizona, is the largest school for homeless children in the United States. *What's New in Education?* on page 168 discusses one community's efforts to make sure homeless children maintain their right to an education.

Children and youth have no control over the social, economic, and family conditions that contribute to the conditions of poverty. Living in a rural community and in a rural southern state increases the likelihood that families will live in poverty. Cities with the highest number of school-age children living in poverty are in the South and East. Also, living in the inner city means that the chances of being poor are higher. With increases in rural and urban poverty go

■ **INTASC**

STANDARD 2   The teacher understands how children learn and develop, and can provide learning opportunities that support their intellectual, social, and personal development.

OBSERVE & LEARN

Resiliency is the ability to adapt and succeed in the face of risk and adversity. As you observe exceptional student learners, identify the skills and behaviors they use to cope with adversity. What teaching strategies can you use to support the development of resiliency in the classroom?

What's *New* in Education?

Educating Children of Homeless Families

The Thomas J. Pappas Regional Schools are nationally recognized public schools that provide a safe educational environment for elementary and middle school children of homeless families in central Arizona. Presently, Maricopa County Regional School District (MCRSD) serves over 1,100 children who lack permanent housing each day and approximately 3,000 students each school year. Many of these amazing children become "Pappas Kids," participating in a comprehensive educational program with teachers and staff trained to understand and support needs that go far beyond those found in the regular school setting.

Pappas Schools provide its students with clothing, routine medical and dental care, counseling services, and food for their families. An outreach staff assists families in accessing transition and emergency assistance through the City of Phoenix social services. Schools are open every day, except weekends and holidays, to provide a safe haven for their students. Before, after, and school-every-day programs provide structured recreational and social-skill activities during noninstructional time and allow students to interact with other children who have similar life stories and experiences. A very special service is the Birthday Closet, which provides a traditional birthday party to students whose parents are unable to do so.

The outreach department is responsible for tracking the children who travel to and home from school on one of the 12 buses that travel more than 1,200 miles each day. Home may have changed by the end of the day. A dedicated staff ensures that each child returns safely to his or her family.

The OfficeMax/Nina Wildman Library for Pappas Kids, housing more than 15,000 books, opened in March 2007. Children can now check out books and take them home, wherever home might be. Although the schools are mainly funded by the State of Arizona, Pappas also depends on the generous support of volunteers, donors, and sponsors. The additional assistance provides funds for extended day programs, extensive transportation costs, a food bank, library books and computers, health care, and outreach services in what is today the most successful national model in addressing the specific and unique needs of children from homeless families.

To learn more about the Thomas J. Pappas Regional Schools, visit www.pappaskids.org.

---

decreases in wealth and support for education. This, in turn, means that as a whole, children living in poverty will attend schools that have fewer resources and poorer facilities.

The effects of poverty and homelessness are detrimental to students' academic achievement and future success. Children from low-income families start kindergarten with fewer reading and math skills and finish third grade with smaller academic gains. Statistics indicate that high school students living in low-income families drop out of school at six times the rate of their peers from high-income families.[24]

REFLECT & WRITE

The growing number of students defined as at risk presents challenges to all educators. Do you think society asks too much of teachers and schools in the prevention and controlling of student risk factors? State your reasons, pro and con.

_____

_____

_____

_____

_____

Substance Abuse

Substance abuse includes the use of illicit drugs, alcohol, and tobacco. Some students abuse multiple substances. Drug use among teenagers has fluctuated since the U.S. Department of Health and Human Services first began monitoring drug use among high school seniors in 1975 with the Monitoring the Future (MTF) survey. The 32nd annual study was conducted in 2006. Drug use has decreased since its peak in the mid 1990s; 48.2 percent of high school seniors reported using some form of illicit drug at least once, and 31.5 percent have used marijuana in the past year.[25] Al-

Risk factors increase the likelihood of substance abuse problems. Protective factors, such as strong and positive family support and success in school, decrease the probability of drug abuse.

though overall drug use is down nationwide, according to the Partnership for a Drug-Free America, kids as young as 12 are using prescription pain relievers, stimulants, sedatives, tranquilizers, and over-the-counter cough medicine to get high.[26] This growing trend is the biggest change in the landscape of substance abuse in the last 25 years. Many teenagers think these drugs are safe because they are made in a lab. Because many of these drugs can be taken from a medicine cabinet at home, they are more readily available than illicit drugs.

The MTF indicates that 66.5 percent of seniors engaged in drinking and 21.6 percent smoked cigarettes during the past month.[27] Young people who start drinking before age 15 are four times more likely to become alcoholics than those who begin drinking at age 21.

Smoking is a serious health hazard for many students. Although the use of tobacco is down for the population as a whole, its use by teenagers, especially female teenagers, is on the rise. Each year more than a million young people start smoking. Cigarette smoking is seen as a "gateway function" to the use of other drugs, and programs designed to inhibit, prevent, or stop smoking are seen as critical in helping students lead healthy lifestyles.[28]

Effective prevention programs address all forms of substance abuse, including the underage use of legal drugs (e.g., alcohol or tobacco); the use of illegal drugs (e.g., marijuana or cocaine); and the inappropriate use of legally obtained substances (e.g., inhalants), prescription medications, and over-the-counter drugs. Drug education provides information about the immediate harmful effects and the potential for long-term addiction.

Society looks to schools and teachers to play a major role in the delivery of programs to prevent substance abuse. As a result, schools are a major factor in the delivery of programs to prevent the use of drugs, alcohol, and tobacco. These programs help students be informed and empowered to decide not to use harmful substances. In Richardson, Texas, administrators, teachers, and students have established a Student Assistance Program designed to prevent substance abuse and assist students and their families, through teacher referral, to an intervention team of teachers, administrators, and counselors. Teachers use a Referral Concern Form to identify students who exhibit "signs of concern," which include low grades and achievement, absenteeism, tardiness, increased visits to the school nurse, erratic behavior, and sleeping in class.

Go to MyEducationLab and select the topic "Inclusion and Special Needs" then watch "Motivating At-Risk Students." Complete the activities that follow.

? *What Does This Mean for You?*

Why should you, a beginning teacher, be concerned about teenage pregnancy? Although the teenage birthrate has been declining, teenage pregnancies are still a major concern from a public school and public health standpoint. Many public schools provide special services for teenage parents and their children. Teenage parents need to receive the highest level of education possible so that they can provide their children with high-quality parenting. If students in your classroom become parents, you will probably need to help identify services for them.

Teen Pregnancy

Each year, about 750,000 women under the age of 20 become pregnant. About 80 percent of these pregnancies are unintended, and 81 percent are to unmarried teens. Although the rate of pregnancy for 15- to 19-year-olds has declined 35 percent since 1991, the United States still has the highest rate of teen pregnancy and births among industrialized nations.[29]

In many regards, teen mothers are children themselves, still in the process of maturing and developing. An unintended pregnancy places them and their child at risk for school failure. Teenage mothers are less likely to finish high school—only one-third receive a high school diploma. They are more likely to need public assistance—nearly 80 percent of unmarried teenage mothers receive welfare. Children of teens have lower birth weights, a higher rate of premature births, lower cognitive functioning, and overall poor health and development. These factors place children at risk for school failure. Boys of teenage mothers are 13 percent more likely to be imprisoned, and 22 percent of girls become teenage mothers themselves.[30]

YOU DECIDE

Abstinence-Only Sex Education

Few curriculum topics set off debate like sex education. Parents and community members tend to get very upset over what amounts to a small portion of health instruction. The focus of the dispute is on what information about sex should be included. When you factor in the vast differences among religious, cultural, and moral values present in our nation today, it is no wonder. Abortion, birth control, and homosexuality top the list of the most explosive topics.

Since the late 1980s, federal funding for abstinence-only programs has risen steadily. This type of sex education promotes sexual abstinence until marriage, and generally teaches that abstaining is the only effective method of birth control or protection against sexually transmitted diseases (STDs). Proponents link the significant decline over the past decade in teen sexual activity to abstinence programs.

Critics of the programs feel that students need more comprehensive information on human sexuality, including information on pregnancy, contraception, STDs, and sexual orientation. Since the increase in abstinence-only programs, more teens are engaging in other risky behaviors, such as oral sex.

According to reports from the Guttmacher Institute, the number of teens reporting having had sex has declined. Still, nearly half of all ninth-through-twelfth-graders have engaged in sexual intercourse (46 percent) at least once. Each year, approximately 4 million sexually active teens contract an STD and about 820,000 young women become pregnant.

How can public school districts develop programs to meet the needs of all students, including students who are homosexual, from conservative religions, or who are sexually active or not?

Source: Guttmacher Institute. (2006, May 3). *National day to prevent teen pregnancy*. Available at http://www.guttmacher.org/media/inthenews/2006/05/03/index.html. Accessed December 1, 2007.

Many school districts offer parenting classes for all students in order to raise awareness about parental roles and responsibilities and to provide practical information about child development. These classes are especially important for teenage mothers and fathers as they interact with peers experiencing similar challenges.

Public schools have many programs designed to prevent teenage pregnancy. These include sex education programs and programs designed to enhance the overall health and wellness of all students. Child abuse and prevention programs are another way to reduce teenage pregnancy. The Center on Adolescent Sexuality, Pregnancy, and Prevention reports that roughly half of teenage mothers report they had been sexually abused as children.[31] In addition, schools provide parent education classes for teenage mothers and child care for their children.

REFLECT & WRITE

Many high school teachers will at some time have students in their classrooms who are pregnant or are parents. These adolescents are at risk for educational and financial difficulties. How can beginning teachers help meet the needs of teenage parents?

Child Abuse

Violence in children's lives occurs in many forms. Child abuse and neglect have become serious problems in the United States. The Child Abuse Prevention and Treatment Act of 1974 (PL 100-294) defines abuse and neglect as the "physical or mental injury, sexual abuse or exploitation, negligent treatment, or maltreatment of a child by a person who is responsible for the child's welfare, under circumstances which indicate the child's health or welfare is harmed or threatened."[32] There were an estimated 3.3 million reported cases of child abuse in 2005. About

900,000 children were confirmed victims of abuse or neglect in 2005.[33] The law requires that teachers report any signs or symptoms of child abuse or neglect in their students.

School Violence

Schools remain among the safest places for children and adolescents. Yet, the fact remains that violence of one sort or another exists in most schools today. The rate of serious violent crime—aggravated assault, sexual assault, robbery—has decreased in recent years. Unfortunately, other behaviors, such as bullying and gang activity, have not shown improvement.

Twenty-eight percent of the 12- to 18-years-olds surveyed by the U.S. Bureau of Justice Statistics in 2005 reported being bullied at school within the last 6 months. Of those, 24 percent were injured as a result of the incident. Students experience direct bullying through physical and verbal attacks. Teasing, taunting, racial slurs, threatening language, and sexual harassment also are forms of **bullying**. Indirect bullying through body language, facial gestures, and intentional exclusion might not be as obvious to teachers. Bullying has even gone high tech, as cyber bullies attack their targets with cruel email or instant messages or insults posted on websites.[34]

Students who are bullied lose self-esteem, and many develop health problems, such as stomach problems and headaches, due to stress and anxiety. Long-term victims develop depression and report having suicidal thoughts. In schools where bullying is a problem, all students feel less safe and are less satisfied with the campus climate.[35] Bullying is bad for bullies, too. Students who bully, especially boys, are more likely to be involved in other **delinquent behaviors**, such as vandalism, shoplifting, and drug use, as adults. In fact, bullies are four times more likely than nonbullies to be convicted of crimes by age 24.[36]

Delinquent gangs are a major concern in many cities and towns across the United States. Once confined primarily to the inner city, gangs are now also active in suburban and rural areas. Reports of gang vandalism, crime, and warfare, and the resulting violence, are common on nightly television and in the daily newspapers. Schools have responded to gangs by banning gang attire in the schools, offering programs to take the place of gang participation, and educating parents and the public about the necessity for expanded school-based programs for at-risk students.

Schools across the country are responding to school violence. Some schools are turning to **peer mediation** to prevent at-risk students from dropping out of school. Mediation is a process for resolving disputes and conflicts in which a neutral third party (or parties) acts as a moderator for the process. In mediation, the goal is to work out differences constructively. Trained students help their classmates identify the problems behind the conflicts and find solutions. Peer mediation is not about finding out who is right or wrong. Instead, students are encouraged to move beyond the immediate conflict and learn how to get along with each other—an important skill in today's world. Peer mediators ask the disputing students to tell their stories and ask questions for clarification. The mediators help the students identify ways to solve the conflict. Common situations involving name calling, spreading rumors, bumping into students in the hallways, and bullying have been successfully resolved though peer mediation.

Clearly, there is much the schools and the public must do to help all students, but particularly minority students, graduate from high school. Money for such efforts is well spent when such programs are successful, because 80 percent of prison inmates are school dropouts and 75 percent of teenage parents become dropouts.[37]

Bullying   Intimidating or mistreating someone in a vulnerable situation repeatedly and over time.

Delinquent behavior   Behavior that violates the rules and regulations of society.

Peer mediation   Programs in which students interact, work with, and counsel other students in solving social and behavioral problems.

The websites of Challenge Day (www.challengeday.org) and Life Trax (www.csmp.org) will help you learn more about peer mediation and other violence prevention programs.

_____

_____

_____

_____

_____

WHAT CAN SCHOOLS DO TO HELP STUDENTS AT RISK?

B rad grew up facing multiple risk factors. Born into poverty to a teenage mother, he usually lived with his maternal grandmother in a rough neighborhood. His father, a drug user, showed up occasionally, but visits were short and often ended when the police were called to respond to a domestic violence call. Knowing this much of the story, most people would expect Brad to be in danger of serious academic and emotional trouble. Fortunately, caring, responsive adults, including his grandmother, teachers, and school counselor, supported and encouraged Brad, who overcame the odds and graduated from high school.

Schools can help educate students at risk by providing a school environment and climate that make it possible for students to learn. Table 5.3 identifies some school characteristics that support learning and staying in school, namely, safety, community feeling, positive attitude, respectful treatment, focus on academics, high standards, and parental involvement.

In reducing the risks and enhancing the opportunities for at-risk students, there is often a tendency to focus on a particular problem (such as preventing violence) in isolation from other risk factors. However, according to the Carnegie Council on Adolescent Development:

> One of the important insights to emerge from scientific inquiry into adolescence in the past two decades is that problem behaviors tend to cluster in the same individual and reinforce one another. Crime, school dropout, teenage childbearing, and drug abuse typically are considered separately, but in the real world they

TABLE 5.3   Some Characteristics of Schools That Support Learning and Staying in School

Schools can do the following to help at-risk students
- Provide a safe, violence-free, orderly school environment
- Provide a caring, familylike school and classroom and a source of community
- Develop positive teacher, administrator, and staff attitudes toward all students
- Treat all students with respect
- Focus on academic and school achievement
- Set high standards and expecting all students to meet them
- Conduct and provide a comprehensive program of parent involvement
- Acknowledge your students' self-worth and their value in all classrooms

occur together. Those who drink and smoke in early adolescence are thus more likely to initiate sex earlier than their peers; those who engage in these behavior patterns often have a history of difficulties in school. When young people have a low commitment to school and education, and when teachers or parents have low expectations for the children's performance, trouble lurks. Once educational failure occurs, then other adverse events begin to take hold.[38]

Generic interventions address some reasons for the underlying or predisposing factors that increase the likelihood that an adolescent will engage in high-risk or problem behaviors. These factors include low self-esteem, underdeveloped interpersonal and decision-making skills, lack of interest in education, inadequate information regarding health matters, low perception of opportunities, the absence of dependable and close human relationships, and meager incentives in delaying short-term gratification.

Given the tremendous risk factors facing children and youths today, schools are challenged to provide curricula and services that go beyond the traditional. Whether generic or targeted to specific risk factors, a number of models exist that schools and social service agencies use to help at-risk students in some way. Five basic approaches to educating students at risk are compensatory, prevention, intervention, and transition programs, and providing separate schools and other facilities for at-risk students. Keep in mind that these approaches represent alternatives that are often applied sequentially or in combination (see Figure 5.5).

Go to MyEducationLab and select the topic "Inclusion and Special Needs" then read "The Violence You Don't See." Answer the questions that follow.

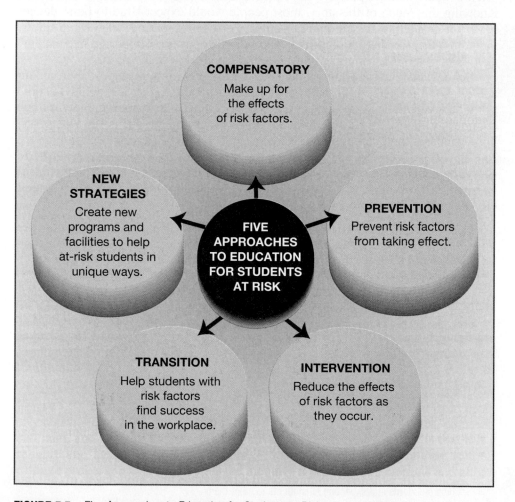

FIGURE 5.5   Five Approaches to Education for Students at Risk

These approaches for educating students at risk allow teachers to respond to the needs of their at-risk students.

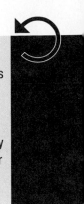

_____

_____

_____

_____

_____

**REFLECT &
WRITE**

Dropping out is not an event, it is a process. How will you encourage at-risk students to become more involved in school activities and let them know they are respected and valued in your classroom?

Compensatory Education

Compensatory programs are designed to compensate or make up for existing or past risk factors and their effects in students' lives. The federal government provides funds through Title 1 grants and programs for family literacy, migrant students, and the education of homeless children and youth. Services and resources include tutorials for remediation, additional staff to reduce class size, or extended day or summer sessions to support disadvantaged students by supplementing reading and mathematics instruction. For example, the majority (84%) of the Amistad Academy's students come from poverty, and almost all (98%) are African American or Latino. Students enter the school in fifth grade generally scoring two years below grade level. This New Haven, Connecticut, public charter school uses Title 1 money to dedicate a three-hour morning block to reading instruction, extend the school day from 7:30 A.M. to 5:00 P.M., and hold a mandatory three-week summer program. They ask parents to sign a daily log showing that students read at least 20 minutes at home and offer tutoring by Yale graduate students to those in need of additional assistance. By eighth grade, students' scores are at the same level as students from some of Connecticut's wealthiest neighborhoods.

Compensatory programs Programs that provide students from low-income families with additional education opportunities beyond those offered in the school's standard program in order to compensate or make up for the effects of risk factors.

Prevention Programs

Prevention programs, as the name implies, are intended to prevent or inhibit certain behaviors. Drug prevention programs, sex education programs, and other education programs are examples of programs designed to prevent student behavior from being affected adversely by such risk factors. In addition, curriculum and instruction in values clarification or character training, self-esteem, decision making, interpersonal problem solving, social skills, communication skills, conflict mediation, and life skills are all part of a preventive approach.

Prevention programs Programs intended to prevent or inhibit certain behaviors, for example, drug prevention programs, sex education programs, and AIDS education programs.

For example, life skills training usually aims to provide students with the awareness and skills necessary for resisting social pressures to smoke cigarettes, consume alcohol, or use marijuana. Training provides accurate information about the negative consequences of high-risk behaviors and about hidden pressures, such as the influence of advertising. Providing experiences that allow students to build self-confidence and self-esteem, to reduce anxiety and stress, and to develop greater autonomy and social competency decreases students' susceptibility to social pressures to engage in high-risk behaviors. Proponents of prevention programs argue that it is easier and less costly to prevent problems than it is to make up for their negative effects.

In preventive health programs, there increasingly is an emphasis on preventing some risk factors even before children are born. Many major childhood risk factors that affect learning ability, such as poor prenatal nutrition and lead poisoning, can be prevented. Many school- and community-based health clinics conduct outreach and education programs to promote maternal, infant, and family health as a way of ensuring healthy children who are ready for school.

Intervention Programs

Intervention programs Programs provided by schools and social service agencies designed to provide support and services to students and their families to help eliminate risk factors and/or reduce their influence.

Schools and social service agencies provide **intervention programs**, which are designed to provide support and services to students and their families to help eliminate risk factors and/or reduce their influence. The goal of intervention programs is enhanced student and family functioning. For example, teenage parenting programs are designed to intervene in the lives of teenagers by teaching them the parenting skills they will need to be good parents and providing them with other information that will enable them to be better-functioning adults.

Early intervention Providing care and support from the prenatal period through the first years of life to enable children to enter school ready to learn.

Intervention programs are frequently found in early childhood programs. **Early intervention** programs are implemented on two basic assumptions. One is that the effects of risk factors can be more easily overcome in the early years than in the teenage or adult years, because young children are thought to be more resilient to negative environmental influences than are youth or adults. The second assumption is that it is more cost-effective to intervene in the early years.

Research supports both assumptions in the education of young children. Children who attend quality preschool programs outperform their peers who did not attend preschool in terms of both educational and life success. Furthermore, over participants' lifetimes, quality preschool programs are estimated to return $7.00 for every dollar invested per participant, in the form of savings in schooling, welfare, and legal costs.[39] Head Start is an excellent example of a national early intervention program.

 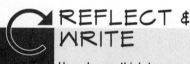

REFLECT & WRITE

How do you think taxpayer dollars are more effective, spent on prevention programs or on intervention programs? Why?

_____

_____

_____

_____

_____

Transition Programs

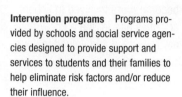

Approximately three-quarters of all high school graduates do not go on to a 4-year college program. One of the problems many of these students face is how to make the transition from school to work. An educational trend is to help students see the relevance between what they are learning in the classroom and the world of work. The linking of work-based learning and classroom-based learning is also seen as one way to keep students in high school and help them move into meaningful employment opportunities. For example, in a school-based morning program, students might learn academic skills such as mathematics used in building construction, and in a job-related afternoon program, students might apply that learning in helping to build a homeless shelter.

New Strategies

One of the problems educators and public policy developers encounter in their efforts to help at-risk students is the "same-old-thing" phenomenon. Doing the same thing over and over can be self-defeating and not provide children and youth the desired outcomes. In other words, programs don't deliver the benefits promised. As a result, community and educational leaders try to engage in "out-of-the-box" thinking that leads to new approaches and programs. Some of these approaches are evident in **alternative schools**, often called second-chance schools, designed to provide the school climate, services, and support that at-risk students need. Many alternative schools target students who are habitually truant, at risk for dropping out, low achievers, and juvenile offenders. More school districts are building separate facilities specifically designed as alternative schools.

In addition to the instructional and curriculum modifications discussed in this chapter, there are a number of other actions you can take as a teacher to help students with special needs and students at risk.

As a teacher of at-risk students, you will need to

- Get the specialized training you may need to respond appropriately to students' needs and problems
- Be willing to work cooperatively and collaboratively with others to address the instructional needs of all students
- Actively seek assistance from others in your school, district, and community to fully serve students and their families
- Report signs of abuse or neglect promptly and refer students to special programs or for evaluation for special education or related services
- Be an advocate for students and their families by encouraging other individuals and agencies to act on these students' behalf
- Help educate parents and others about how to prevent risk factors from developing or from adversely affecting their children and their children's life chances and success in school
- Keep parents informed on a regular basis about their children's progress and needs
- Work with parents to help them connect with their children's development and lives and help their children with school work and life problems
- Engage students so that they trust you and believe you are doing your best for them
- Communicate to students that you have respect and high expectations for them and that you believe they are capable of learning
- Provide instruction designed to help all students learn to the best of their ability, develop positive self-concepts, and build resilience against negative life experiences

Meeting the needs of students with special needs and students at risk makes teaching a challenging and rewarding profession. As more laws are passed protecting the rights of students with disabilities and more initiatives are taken to reduce risk factors for students, the role of the schools and teachers will be expanded and reconceptualized in new and rewarding ways. As society, families, children, and youth change, so will schools and teaching have to change. In a sense, schools and teachers are constantly catching up with the demands

Alternative schools   Programs designed to give students special services, programs, and support necessary for them to be successful in school.

• *Your Turn*

You have been asked to design a smoking prevention program for middle school students. List the key prevention strategies you would include.

of society for meeting societal problems as they affect students and their success in school and in later life.

Part of the challenge for schools and teachers is how to constantly improve their responses to students' problems and improve the condition and quality of education. As more students come to school with special needs, schools will have to continually seek creative responses, including new and different curricula and restructured educational settings, that give teachers more decision-making power and more support to do their jobs.

As a prospective teacher, you are entering a prime time to be in the teaching profession. The opportunities for service and creativity have never been greater. Your students are waiting for you to make a difference in their lives and to help them fulfill their highest potential.

ETHICAL DILEMMA

"He Won't Learn All That Anyway."

REBEKAH LOPEZ teaches ninth-grade history at a large suburban high school and welcomes students with disabilities in her class. Last May, she attended an IEP meeting for an incoming freshman diagnosed with mild autism and mental retardation. "Adam," a friendly, talkative kid, needed support in social situations and had difficulty grasping abstract ideas. He would not be able to master all the general curriculum objectives for her course, but according to his middle school special education teachers he was a wiz with dates and remembered many things from class discussions. When classes began in the fall, Rebekah

was disappointed when Adam didn't come to class. After school, she went to see Mr. Harris, Adam's special education teacher, who told her it was too much trouble to get Adam across the large campus to spend 1 hour in her class. Mr. Harris said, "He won't be able to learn all that history anyway."

What should Rebekah do?

The IEP team decided that Adam would be included in her history class to interact with his nondisabled peers and learn what he can about history. Should she demand that Adam attend her class? Should she contact the parents and risk getting the special education teacher in trouble for not following the IEP?

SUMMARY

- Students with disabilities are guaranteed a free, appropriate education, as mandated by the Individuals with Disabilities Education Act (IDEA).

- Students with special needs receive instruction in the least restrictive environment, which is determined by their individual needs. These settings range from full inclusion to a self-contained classroom to specialized institutional placement.

- Communication and collaboration with families and other professionals provide teachers with valuable in-

sight and innovative approaches to meet the needs of all students.

- Strategies used to support students in the classroom include assistive technology and differentiated instruction.

- Economic and environmental problems place students at risk for failing school; however, prevention programs, intervention programs, and other strategies can help students counter some of these obstacles.

KEY TERMS

APPLICATIONS FOR ACTIVE LEARNING

Connections

1. Think about the concepts and topics introduced in this chapter. What key ideas did you connect with that will help you identify and support children with a range of education needs or who are at risk for school failure?

2. A major theme that runs through Susan Hentz's opening chapter vignette is high expectations. Why do you think Susan places so much emphasis on high expectations? Why is it so important to have high expectations for exceptional learners? Do you think it would be "easier" if teachers had lower expectations for exceptional learners? What can you do to help ensure that you have high expectations for all the students you will teach?

3. Think about a student in your school experiences who was an exceptional learner. How did teachers accommodate that student's needs?

Field Experiences

1. Contact local schools in your area and ask them what activities and services they provide for students before and after school. How are these designed to meet students' special needs?

2. What steps should you take to prepare for teaching students with disabilities? Interview teachers to find out their views about how you can prepare for teaching students with disabilities.

3. What steps should you take to prepare yourself for teaching students at risk? As part of developing answers to these questions, interview a school psychologist or social worker, a special education teacher, and others, such as a juvenile officer, who might be involved with this student population. As you develop your list of steps, identify your goal in each step and any specific resource, such as courses you could take, that seem to match that goal.

Personal Research

1. How can a teacher modify the classroom environment, classroom routines, learning activities, student groupings, teaching strategies, instructional materials, assessments, and homework assignments to meet all students' needs? What human and material resources for successful inclusion are available to teachers and to students with special needs? How do students show social acceptance for their classmates with special needs? Visit an inclusive classroom and take notes on what you observe. Compare and discuss your observations with classmates who have visited different settings across all grade levels.

2. Visit the teacher resource center of a local school district or in the district where you plan to teach. Develop a list of resources that would be available to you in teaching students with special needs in your class.

PREPARING TO TEACH

For Your Portfolio

1. Place in your portfolio the teaching applications you have developed on the basis of your field observations and the plan you have outlined for your professional development as a teacher of students with disabilities, exceptional learners, and students at risk.

2. Write to the Council for Exceptional Children (1920 Association Drive, Reston, VA 22091) and ask for information that will be helpful for beginning teachers in inclusion settings, such as resources for teachers who must supervise paraeducators.

Idea File

Develop an instructional plan for students whose learning is affected by one of the disabilities or risk factors described in this chapter. Include specific instructional activities and ideas for working with resource people and agencies as well as with the students' parents. Extend your idea file by repeating this procedure for other categories of disabilities or risk factors, and then amend your plans according to feedback you get from classmates, teachers, and professors.

LEARNING AND KNOWING MORE

Websites Worth Visiting

The Council for Exceptional Children (CEC) is the largest international professional organization dedicated to improving educational outcomes for individuals with exceptionalities, students with disabilities, and/or the gifted.

www.cec.sped.org

The Office of Special Education and Rehabilitative Services (OSERS) provides a wide array of supports to parents and individuals, school districts, and states in three main areas: special education, vocational rehabilitation, and research.

www.ed.gov/about/offices/list/osers/index.html

The National Dissemination Center for Children with Disabilities (NICHCY) serves the nation as a central source of information on:

- Disabilities in infants, toddlers, children, and youth
- IDEA, which is the law authorizing special education
- No Child Left Behind (as it relates to children with disabilities)
- Research-based information on effective educational practices.

www.nichcy.org

The Regional Resource and Federal Centers (RRFC) Network assists state education agencies in the systemic improvement of education programs, practices, and policies that affect children and youth with disabilities through consultation, information services, technical assistance, training, and product development.

www.rrfcnetwork.org

Wrightslaw is a website about special education law and advocacy.

www.wrightslaw.com

Since 1972, Prevent Child Abuse America has led the way in building awareness, providing education, and inspiring hope to everyone involved in the effort to prevent the abuse and neglect of our nation's children.

www.preventchildabuse.org/index.shtml

The National Center for Children in Poverty (NCCP) is a public policy center dedicated to promoting the economic security, health, and well-being of America's low-income families and children.

www.nccp.org

The Center for Research on the Education of Students Placed At Risk (CRESPAR) was established in 1994 as a collaboration between Johns Hopkins University and Howard University. CRESPAR's mission is to conduct research, development, evaluation, and dissemination of replicable strategies designed to transform schooling for students at risk of failing to meet their potential due to inadequate institutional responses to such factors as poverty, ethnic minority status, and non–English-speaking home background.

www.csos.jhu.edu/crespar/

Books Worth Reading

Devine, J., and Cohen, J. (2007). *Making Your School Safe: Strategies to Protect Children and Promote Learning.* New York: Teachers College Press.

In this practical manual, the authors demonstrate the important relationship between social, emotional, and ethical education and school safety. They combine traditional crisis management and emergency planning with the principles that have become the cornerstones of the field of evidence-based social-emotional learning and character education. Featuring real-life examples and best practices, they cover widespread concerns, ranging from student behavioral issues, such as bullying and social exclusion, to gang-related violence and other tragic events. This essential resource will help schools to be proactive in preventing tragedies, as well as effectively reactive when they occur.

Giangreco, M. F., and Doyle, M. B. (2007). *Quick Guides to Inclusion: Ideas for Educating Students with Disabilities.* Baltimore, MD: Brookes Publishing Company.

Perfect for busy educators, this user-friendly guidebook offers essential information and brief to-the-point advice for improving inclusion skills. The spiral-bound handbook consists of five "Quick-Guides," each one devoted to a relevant topic—from building partnerships with parents to getting the most out of support services. Each section offers easy to follow ideas, tips, examples, and suggestions that teachers, administrators, related services personnel, and parents can put to use immediately in their schools. Equally suitable as an entry-level guide or as a concise summary of practices for seasoned professionals, this inexpensive classroom tool helps administrators and school professionals make inclusion work in any school—and any budget!

Osborne, A. G., and Russo, C. J. (2007). *Special Education and the Law: A Guide for Practitioners* (2nd ed.). Thousand Oaks, CA: Corwin Press.

Comprehensive coverage of IDEA and the most recent regulations designed for preservice and in-service teacher training. It is a valuable resource for special education teachers and administrators needing practical understanding of special education law.

Payne, R. (2005). *A Framework for Understanding Poverty* (4th ed.). Highlands, TX: aha! Process, Inc.

Written as a guide and exercise book for middle-grade teachers, this is the fourth edition of Payne's model for educators working with impoverished students and families. Poverty is about survival. People living in poverty face challenges virtually unknown to those in middle class or wealth—challenges from both obvious and hidden sources. She discusses the hidden rules that govern how each of us behaves in our social class and provides practical, yet compassionate, strategies for addressing the impact of poverty on people's lives.

6 Partners in Learning: Parents, Families, and the Community

AMBERLY WALKER This year we tried a new approach in working with some of our at-risk students. We implemented an intervention program in an attempt to encourage higher attendance rates, boost student achievement, and improve student attitudes. A group of 10 teachers spent 3 hours per week working with the at-risk students who volunteered to participate. All the teachers have different areas of expertise with content areas, including English as a Second Language (ESL). We meet from 2:30 to 5:30 P.M. every Wednesday in the high school library.

We have learned many things from this first year's implementation of the after-school program. Even I was amazed at some of the limitations many of our students have in their background experiences. For example, a student survey shows that only 5 of our 110 student participants have ever been to a museum. Outsiders looking at our beautiful new high school would never dream that we have students who lack this kind of broadening experience. However, many of our students are bussed onto campus from surrounding, low-income neighborhoods. One thing I do know is that we need to continue including the community in our projects!

One particular science project in our plans involves a trip to the Dallas Museum of Nature and Science. Currently, the museum and IMAX theatre are featuring an exhibit on the human body that should prove interesting to this age group. This plan also addresses our students' lack of experiences outside their own neighborhood. However, the cost of admission to the museum plus movie tickets is $27 each. I called the museum director and described our dilemma. I was thrilled when he provided us free admission! This is proof that you never know how your community may help you if you ask!

As you read this chapter . . .

Think about:

- How parents, families, and communities influence teaching and learning

- How you can implement family-centered teaching and learning in your classroom

- How you can foster parent/family involvement both inside and outside your classroom

- What educational reforms are promoting greater parent empowerment

- How you can use the community to teach

> ## Students benefit from community participation.

Our search for financial support has been informative and rewarding. We located two websites that provide aid opportunities for students. *After-School-for-All*[1] and *Donors Choose*[2] are sites that offer teachers needed funds. Our next appeal will be posted on these websites to help our program provide the experiences our students need. The response from our community has been exemplary. Gerardo, a tenth-grader, said, "This program is the best thing that has happened to me in my whole life!" I know many of these opportunities would not have been possible without our community partnerships.

▶▶ Go to MyEducationLab and select the topic "Family and Community" and watch the video "Involving Parents."

Amberly Walker is an intervention specialist at Sachse High School in the Garland, Texas, Independent School District. She and a group of teachers and administrators started an after-school program for at-risk students.

HOW DO PARENTS, FAMILIES, AND COMMUNITIES INFLUENCE TEACHING AND LEARNING?

One thing we can say with certainty about the educational landscape today is that efforts to involve families and communities in the process of educating the nation's youth are at an all-time high. One reason for these efforts to involve parents is the overwhelming evidence that the effect of involving parents, families, and communities in the schools increases student achievement and promotes positive educational outcomes. A summary of research studies regarding parent involvement confirms the benefits of parent/community support:

> The research found that there is a positive and convincing relationship between family involvement and benefits for students, including improved academic achievement. This relationship holds across families of all economic, racial/ethnic, and educational background and for students at all ages: students with involved parents, no matter their background, are more likely to earn higher grades and test scores, enroll in higher-level programs, be promoted and earn credits, adapt well to school and attend regularly, have better social skills and behavior, and graduate and go on to higher education. Family involvement also has a protective effect; the more families can support their children's progress, the better their children do in school and the longer they stay in school.[3]

In fact, the Harvard Family Research Project links family involvement in a child's education with success in school.[4] It is vitally important that schools make efforts to ensure that parents and families are involved in their children's education.

Changing Families Affect Parent Involvement

The family of today is not the family of yesterday, nor will the family of today be the family of tomorrow. For example, households with children, which comprised 45 percent of total U.S. households in the 1970s, comprised only 35 percent in 2005. Table 6.1 shows some of the other ways families have changed over the years. In addition, more mothers are entering the workforce than ever before. This means that at an early age, often as young as 6 weeks, many children are spending 8 hours a day or more in the care of others.

The need for early childhood care has meant a blossoming of opportunities for child-serving agencies—child-care centers and preschools, for example. As a result, more educational agencies, including public schools, provide more parents and families with child development and child-rearing resources and information.

Grandparents as Parents

Grandparents who take on primary parenting roles for their grandchildren are a growing reality in the United States. Since the millennium, more grandparents have stepped into parenting roles than ever before: Over 3.7 million children, or 5.1 percent of all children under 18, are living in homes maintained by 2.5 million grandparents. These numbers should come as no surprise when we realize that one of every four adults is a grandparent.[5]

Many of the children in homes headed by grandparents are "skipped-generation" children—neither parent

---

■ INTASC

STANDARD 10   The teacher fosters relationships with school colleagues, parents, and agencies in the larger community to support students' learning and well-being.

TABLE 6.1   How Families Have Changed

Types of Families	1970 (%)	2006 (%)
Households with own children	45	47
Married-couple families	87	67
Single-mother families with children	12	23
Single-father families with children	1	5
Children living with relative	2	3
Children living with nonrelative	1	1

Source: U.S. Census Bureau (2007). *American Community Survey.* (Online). Available at www.census.gov/acs/www/Products/users_guide/.

An increasing number of grandparents, by default and by choice, now find themselves in the parenting role. Grandparents oftentimes assume the parenting role to provide an improved home atmosphere, to prevent foster care placement, and to protect children from the effects of fragmented homes or abuse and neglect. Schools need to work with grandparents just as they do with parents.

is living with them, perhaps because of drug abuse, divorce, mental and physical illness, abandonment, teenage pregnancy, or child abuse and neglect, incarceration, or even the death of the parents. Grandparent-parents in these skipped-generation households must provide for their grandchildren's basic needs and care as well as make sure that they do well in school. Grandparents who are rearing a new generation, often unexpectedly, need the support of their grandchildren's schools and teachers. Because they are nurturing their grandchildren in a world very different from the one in which they reared their own children, they might not know current thinking about children's learning and development. Your assistance to grandparents can involve linking them with support groups, such as the American Association of Retired Persons (AARP) Grandparent Information Center.

You can learn more about this topic at www.aarp.org/families/grandparents/.

REFLECT & WRITE

How do you plan to inform and assist grandparents who are raising their children's children?

How Does the Federal Government Influence Parent Involvement?

Given the key role that parents play in student education, it should come as no surprise that federal and state governments are taking a leading role in ensuring that parents are involved in schools. The No Child Left Behind Act (NCLB) has changed the way schools need to interact with parents. Prior to NCLB, parental involvement was largely determined by school district policies and administrator and teacher discretion. This is no longer the case: NCLB mandates a wide range of required procedures and activities relating to parental involvement.

The School–Parent Compact

One way in which parents and schools focus their interaction is through the use of a school–parent compact. This type of agreement meets the requirements of NCLB for school districts, parents, schools, and students to enter into a shared responsibility for ensuring high student achievement. The compact describes the school's responsibilities to provide high-quality curriculum and instruction and an effective learning environment, enabling children to meet the state's student academic achievement standards. It serves as a means to inform parents of the ways they will be responsible for supporting their children's learning. Some parental supports include monitoring student attendance, helping with homework completion, monitoring television viewing, volunteering in their children's classrooms, and participating in decisions related to their children's education.

The compact also addresses the importance of communication between teachers and parents on an ongoing basis through:

■ Parent–teacher conferences in elementary schools at least annually, during which the compact is discussed as it relates to children's achievement
■ Frequent reports to parents on their children's progress
■ Reasonable access to staff and opportunities to volunteer in their children's classes and to observe classroom activities

Go to MyEducationLab and select the topic "Family and Community" then read the article "Why Some Parents Don't Come to School." Answer the questions that follow.

Building Capacity for Involvement

Schools receiving Title I funds through NCLB are required to increase the amount of parental and community involvement and to build partnerships with parents to increase student achievement. Schools must provide opportunities to all parents, including those with disabilities or with limited English proficiency. NCLB requires that school personnel:

■ Distribute information to parents and help them understand state academic standards and assessments.
■ Inform parents of dates for distribution of materials and training for parental support.
■ Offer training to staff members as they work in partnerships with parents. Parents will be encouraged to provide input and assist in such training.
■ Coordinate programs within the building that require parent involvement, including early childhood programs.
■ Provide information to parents in a form that will be understood.[6]

As part of their efforts to increase school achievement, schools must also:

■ Help parents understand state and local assessments of their children's progress and know how to monitor progress and work with educators.
■ Provide parents with materials and training to improve their children's achievement, such as literacy training and use of technology.
■ Educate teachers, administrators, and other school staff about the value of and methods of reaching out to parents as equal partners.
■ Integrate parent involvement efforts with other school and community programs, including Head Start, Reading First, Early Reading First, Even Start, Home Instruction Programs for Preschool Youngsters, and Parents as Teachers Programs.
■ Ensure that information about school and parent programs is in a format and language parents can understand.[7]

REFLECT AND WRITE

What specific concerns do you have about partnering with parents? How do you plan to address your concerns?

_____

_____

_____

_____

_____

Other Legislation and Laws

Numerous other federal and state laws recognize the importance of meaningful parental involvement and require that parents take responsibility for helping ensure that their children learn. For example, the National Head Start Program (NHSP), created in 1965, assists children from low-income families. The NHSP requires that all local Head Start agencies have procedures in place to ensure that parents are involved and that health care, nutrition services, and preschool education are provided. By 2007, more than 24 million preschoolers had participated in Head Start.[8]

From our discussions in Chapter 5, recall that IDEA gives parents many rights and responsibilities related to their involvement in their children's education. Parental involvement occurs in other ways, some that you might not have thought about. For example, 38 states and the District of Columbia require school districts to permit parental involvement in sexuality and STD/HIV education. Three of these states require parental consent for students to participate in the programs, whereas 35 states allow parents to remove their children from the programs.

Florida law requires that each parent of a child within a compulsory attendance age shall be responsible for such child's school attendance. The absence of a child from school is evidence of a violation of this law. Furthermore, the law states that parents who refuse or fail to have a child under their control attend school regularly shall be guilty of a misdemeanor of the second degree, punishable by law.[9]

School districts implement attendance policies, and each school district has written attendance guidelines. If students are absent for a certain number of days, as set by the local district, they might be suspended/retained. For example, in Boston Public Schools, when students have more than 3 (middle or high school) or 4 (elementary school) unexcused absences in a term, or 12 absences for the year, they receive a grade of No Credit (NC).[10]

REFLECT & WRITE

What are your thoughts regarding making parents responsible for their children's learning and attendance? How would you address attendance policies and requirements with your students' parents?

_____

_____

_____

_____

WHAT ARE FAMILY-CENTERED PROGRAMS?

Education starts in the home, and what happens there profoundly affects the trajectory of children's development and learning. According to the U.S. Department of Education, education is a family affair: The greater the family's involvement in children's learning, the more likely it is that students will receive a high-quality education.

Schools must address the role that families play in their children's education as they strive to increase student achievement. Consequently, developing family-school partnerships is of crucial importance. To foster such partnerships, **family-centered programs** focus on meeting the needs of students through the family unit. In turn, education professionals recognize that to most effectively meet the needs of students, they must also meet the needs of their families.

Family-centered programs   Programs that focus on meeting the needs of students and their families.

TEACHERS, Pre-K–12

- Parent/family education
- Literacy programs
- Counseling programs
- Referrals to community agencies
- Assistance with problems of daily living
- Programs designed for specific purposes (e.g., how to help with homework)

OUTCOMES/BENEFITS

- Increase knowledge, skills, and understanding of education process
- Help families and children address and solve problems
- Provide greater range of resources and more experts than schools alone can provide
- Relieve families and children/youth of stress to make learning more possible
- Increase student achievement
- Promote school retention and prevent dropout

FIGURE 6.1   Family-Centered Teaching

Both generations are strengthened when parents and children learn together.

Family-Centered Education

Family-centered teaching   Instruction that focuses on the needs of students through the family unit, whatever that unit may be, and is designed to help both generations while strengthening the family unit.

Family-centered teaching is instruction that is designed to help both generations—students and their families (see Figure 6.1). Strengthening the family unit benefits children and promotes their success in school. For example, by addressing multiple family issues, such as health care, teachers can provide a more stable foundation for students by focusing on their cognitive, mental, and emotional needs.

REFLECT & WRITE

Many educational services are delivered to children and families. For example, many literacy programs work with children and parents to improve literacy within the entire family. What else can be taught to children and family members at the same time?

_____

_____

_____

_____

_____

Children's development begins with their family. In some situations, family circumstances can hinder children's growth and development. Therefore, to enhance successful development, family-centered teaching can:

- Help individuals in the family become better parents and family members.
- Help parents gain access to affordable health care and child-care services (such as after-school programs or preschools for younger children).
- Adopt a family approach to literacy that helps parents learn to read so that they can, in turn, read aloud to their children, thereby promoting children's literacy.

An example of family-centered education is the William F. Goodling Even Start Family Literacy Program, a federally funded family literacy program that combines adult literacy and parenting training with early childhood education to break cycles of illiteracy that are often passed on from one generation to another. Even Start is funded under Title I of the No Child Left Behind Act of 2001 and operates through the public school system and provides family-centered education. In particular, Even Start helps parents become full partners in the education of their children, assists children in reaching their full potential, and provides literacy training for their parents. Even Start projects are designed to work cooperatively with existing community resources to provide a full range of services and to integrate early childhood education and adult education.

Go to MyEducationLab, select the topic "Family and Community" and watch the video "Family Literacy Program." Complete the activities that follow.

Family-Centered Approaches to Support Student Learning

In addition to collaborating with parents and families regarding students' at-school learning and achievement, educators also work with parents and families to provide support for learning in the home. This family-centered approach of helping parents help their children to learn at home is an important part of supporting students' ongoing achievement. Here are some ways you can implement this family-centered approach:

- Provide parents with ideas that enable them to work with their children on math homework at home. Suggest to parents that they:
  - Talk about how they use math at work and in the home.
  - Involve children in tasks that require computing, measuring, estimating, building, following directions, problem solving, and reasoning.
  - Look for activities that require children to use their math skills, such as building scale models, cooking, planning trips, and playing logic games.[11]
- Provide books for parents to read and supply aids for homework that link school and home learning. For example, the book *How to Help Your Child With Homework: The Complete Guide to Encouraging Good Study Habits and Ending the Homework Wars*[12] by Jeanne Shay Schumm provides tips for parents to help their children with their homework as well as informing parents on what is new in education.
- Offer in-person and online tutorials for helping children with reading and math through daily activities.
- Provide information about child rearing and how to guide and manage behavior.
- Inform parents about programs and students' progress on a weekly basis through newsletters, e-mail, and websites. For example, visit the website of sixth-grade math teacher Jonathon Damon from West Northfield School District 31 in Northbrook, Illinois.
- Provide specific suggestions for how parents can assist with homework of any kind. Advise parents to:
  - Set a regular time and place to do homework.
  - Remove distractions, such as televisions and cell phones.
  - Provide supplies and resources, such as pens, pencils, paper, and a dictionary.
  - Set a good example.

You can visit Jonathon Damon's website at http://homepage .scholastic.com/CHBuilderWeb/start .action?userAction=USER_LOGIN.

- Be interested and interesting by finding ways to talk to their children about school.
- Attend school events such as plays, sports events, and parent-teacher conferences.[13]
- Provide parents information about the school curriculum, such as the state and local standards for each of the content areas (i.e., reading, math, science, etc.). For example, visit the website of Meriwether Lewis Elementary School in Portland, Oregon (http://lewiselementary.org) and review the curriculum information provided to parents.

As an example of a successful and innovative program involving students, parents, and schools, see *What's New in Education? Math and Parent Partnerships*.

Intergenerational programs are those that promote cooperation, interaction, and exchange between two or more generations. Intergenerational programming is becoming a popular way of bringing younger and older generations together. There are a number of reasons for efforts to join generations. First, Americans tend to become segregated by age and life stages. The young are in child care and

Intergenerational programs Programs promoting cooperation, interaction, and exchange between two or more generations.

What's *New* in Education?

Math and Parent Partnerships

Math and Parent Partnerships (MAPPS) programs were designed by the National Science Foundation in order to involve parents in their children's mathematical success. The program involves parents of K–12 children by empowering them with new mathematical knowledge and with new self-confidence about learning mathematics, creating families that learn mathematics together, improving children's competencies in mathematics, and encouraging the broader community to embrace mathematics as something everybody can do and enjoy.

The program was piloted in four working-class, heavily Latino districts in the Southwest United States—Tucson and Chandler in Arizona; Las Vegas, Nevada; and San Jose, California. Currently, MAPPS programs are in place in 12 districts in 9 states around the country. Typically, over 23,000 parent hours are documented in MAPPS activities at a single site.

A MAPPS program revolves around the following three activities for parents:

1. Workshops that last for 2 hours
2. Mini-courses involving eight 20-hour sessions
3. Leadership development in which parents work with other parents in a cooperative-learning setting. Parents also talk to students about how they use mathematics in real-life situations.

Parents who participate in this program state that they:

- Feel good about "going back to school"
- Experience new, liberating styles of learning mathematics
- Acquire new ways to help their children with math
- Change the dynamic for learning math in their families
- Look forward to getting together with other parents to do mathematics

An overarching philosophy of the MAPPS program is that mathematics is a social activity. In order for students to become competent and confident in doing mathematics, MAPPS emphasizes the importance of peer, school, and family support. If families are to provide support, educators must make them partners in efforts to improve the learning and teaching of mathematics in the school. Parents must experience mathematics with their children, believe that their children can be successful at learning mathematics, and form partnerships with teachers and schools in order to support good mathematical learning and teaching for their children. By knowing what is happening in their children's mathematics classroom, understanding the connection between school mathematics and access to future careers, and being aware of ethnic and gender biases as they relate to expectations and success in mathematics, parents can better support their children.

Learn more about Math and Parent Partnerships (MAPPS) program at http://math.arizona.edu/~mapps/.

Source: Math and Parent Partnerships (MAPPS). Available at http://mapps.math.arizona.edu/

school, adults are in workplaces, and the elderly often are in age-segregated housing, such as assisted-living communities and nursing homes. Second, with cutbacks in federal support for health and social programs, the young and the old especially are in competition for funds and services. One way to reduce this competition and to use existing funds effectively is to provide intergenerational programs for the mutual benefit of all. Most often, intergenerational programming focuses on young people below age 25 and adults over age 60.[14]

Intergenerational programming also includes programs in which young people provide services to older persons, in which older persons provide services to youths, and in which two generations work cooperatively on a project. Providing community services such as these is increasingly a part of school-based curricula and is even a requirement of graduation in some schools. Such community service involvements often team youngsters with the elderly. As a beginning teacher, you might want to explore the many learning opportunities that community service projects offer as a way of promoting active learning and problem solving with your students.

• *Your Turn*

You are determined to implement family-centered curriculum and instruction in your classroom. You have just discovered that the father of a student in your second-grade class was recently laid off from his minimum-wage job. The mother is pregnant, and the other children are ages 2 and 4. What could you do to help this family? Where would you start?

REFLECT & WRITE

Using MAPPS as a model for involving parents in their children's education, can you think of other subject areas, such as science, in which schools can engage parents to foster similar types of cooperation? How would you accomplish this?

WHAT IS PARENT/FAMILY INVOLVEMENT?

In our discussion of parent and family involvement, it is important for us to have a clear understanding of what we mean when we say parent/family involvement. Title I of NCLB defines parent involvement as

the participation of parents in regular, two-way, and meaningful communication involving student academic learning and other school activities, including ensuring that parents:

- play an integral role in assisting their child's learning;
- are encouraged to be actively involved in their child's education at school;
- are full partners in their child's education and are included, as appropriate, in decision making and on advisory committees to assist in the education of their child.[15]

OBSERVE & LEARN

One way to involve parents in their children's education is through observation. Parents have the right to visit and observe in their children's classrooms. Unfortunately, many parents do not know how or what to observe. Some ideas would be helpful for them. Observe in a classroom of your choice as though you were a parent with a child in that classroom. Based on your observations, develop a list of the topics you think parents should pay special attention to when observing.

Three things are significant about this definition. First is the definition itself. This marks the first time that the federal government has defined parent involvement in public education. Second, the definition gives parents "full partnership" in the education of their children. And third, the definition provides the context by which schools and school districts will implement programs, activities, and procedures by which parents will be involved.

Four major approaches toward parent involvement have been identified in the last decade. Each illustrates the kinds of attitudes, knowledge, and skills teachers can acquire to increase their effectiveness with families.[16]

1. *Parent empowerment approach.* This approach was developed by Moncrief Cochran, a professor of human development and family studies. It focuses on strengthening families by promoting the characteristics and traits of robust families. Cochran emphasizes the need to move away from a family-deficit model—one that focuses on troubles or problems—and toward a family-strengths model, which focuses on prevention rather than treatment (equipping rather than repairing).[17]

2. *Cultural competence approach.* Professor of education Luis Moll developed this approach based on the premise that minority and low-socioeconomic status (SES) students benefit academically from family involvement. Although minority and low-SES families share the same desire for academic excellence, they often lack resources to take special situations into consideration. Family structures, biculturalism, lack of parent education, and economic stress often influence parent involvement in these families.[18] Moll promotes educator training so teachers are skilled in using culturally appropriate themes in the curriculum.

3. *Social capital approach.* Sociologist James Coleman developed this approach toward parent involvement. Coleman's definition of *social capital* includes two parts: (1) an entity that has an aspect of social structure and (2) the relationships among people within the entity that create individual or collective action. According to Coleman, social capital in families is extremely important for children's intellectual development, and for developing positive relationships between parents and children.[19] Social capital outside the family is important as well; accordingly, parents' involvement in the community, their social relationships within the community, and their relationship with community institutions will benefit their children. Coleman explored how social capital in tightly bonded communities helps support family expectations for their children's education and consequently reduces high school dropout rates. Coleman believes that social systems promote a sense of inclusion and help students find a place to fit in. Working together, parents and teachers help students find a place where they can be most successful.

4. *Functional approach.* Joyce Epstein, a notable researcher in parent involvement, based her approach on the six National Parent Teacher Association (PTA) standards. This approach emphasizes the importance of ensuring that educators have knowledge about the goals and benefits of family involvement as well as the barriers to it. Epstein believes students are best served when educators are skilled at involving parents of all backgrounds in school and when they also are knowledgeable about the barriers to family involvement.[20]

As you think more about your role in involving parents, consider the six types of family/parent involvement discussed in the following section and presented in Figure 6.2.

Go to MyEducationLab and select the topic "Family and Community" then watch the video "Involving Parents in the Educational Process." Complete the activities that follow.

REFLECT &
WRITE

At this stage of your understanding of parent and family involvement in the schools, which of the four major approaches appeals to you the most? Why?

_____

_____

_____

_____

_____

Six Types of Family/Community Involvement

The six types of family and community involvement can be implemented when determined and dedicated teachers and administrators resolve to make meaningful involvement a reality. In the following sections, you will see authentic examples that illustrate what can result from each type of involvement.

Parenting

Assist families with parenting skills, family support, and understanding child and adolescent development and home conditions to support learning at each age and grade level. Obtain information from families to help schools understand children's strengths, talents, and needs, and families' backgrounds, cultures, and goals for their children.

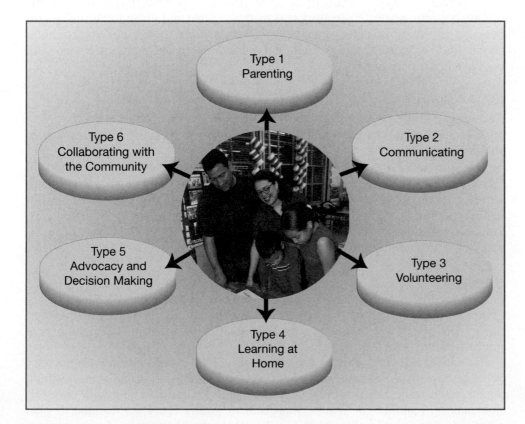

FIGURE 6.2 Six Types of Parent/Family Involvement

Six types of Parent/Family Involvement represent the National PTA Standards and are suggested as guidelines in NCLB.

Learn more about parent involvement at www.tcet.unt.edu/pteconnect/.

Members of the Action Team for Partnerships at Woodbury Elementary School in Shaker Heights, Ohio, provided immunization shots for sixth-graders as a way to assist families and include the community in their plans. The city health department authorized Woodbury Elementary to offer measles, mumps, and rubella (MMR) immunizations to rising seventh-graders for the low cost of $5.00 per shot. During an open house at Woodbury, the school nurse assisted the Shaker Heights director of nursing in giving 33 shots in a 2-hour period. Parents stayed with their children during the procedure; volunteers assisted in organizing the crowd and providing refreshments.[21]

Communicating

Communicate with families about school programs and student progress using school-to-home and home-to-school communications. This creates two-way channels that families can use to easily contact teachers and administrators.

The site-based team at Fayetteville Elementary School in Fayetteville, New York, sought a way to promote more effective two-communication between parents and teachers. The team decided to create eye-catching notepads including the school logo at the top of each page. Using the new communication tool, teachers and parents could quickly glance through papers to see if a note was coming to or from school or home. Teachers and parents report pleasing results.[22]

Volunteering

Enlist parent involvement by improving recruitment and training and by creating activities and schedules to involve families as volunteers. Families should be encouraged to support students and the school's programs.

Educators in Williamston, Michigan, were faced with the challenge of recruiting parent volunteers in the middle and high school. Principals at each campus devised parent surveys to learn of specific resources parents might provide the school. A parent resource directory was then compiled and given to all staff members. An explosion of parent involvement has occurred at the secondary school; parents now chaperone parties, help with cook-outs, make phone calls, and help with teacher paperwork.[23]

Learning at Home

Encourage families to work with their children in academic learning activities at home, including homework, goal setting, and other curriculum-related activities and decisions.

Families were invited to storytelling time at Woodridge Primary School in Cuyahoga Falls, Ohio. Teachers and professional storytellers demonstrated techniques parents could use to share stories with their children at home. Families learned the felt-board storytelling technique as well as the use of manipulatives. Students came in their pajamas, armed with blankets and teddy bears, to participate in the storytelling time with their family members.[24]

Decision Making

Include families as participants in school decisions, governance, and advocacy activities through the PTA/PTO, committees, councils, and other parent organizations. Assist family representatives to obtain information from and give information to those they represent.

There is a saying, "Serve food, and they will come." Aniwa Elementary School in Aniwa, Wisconsin, was faced with the challenge of establishing a school effectiveness team, and it needed large numbers of parents to help with the decision making required for school improvement goals. The PTO decided to plan a potluck dinner and invite entire families to come. During the dinner, parents

To read about another example of positive parental involvement, go to MyEducationLab and select the topic "Family and Community" then read the article "The Rewards of Parent Participation."

met in small groups to discuss school plans, student academic needs, and age-appropriate activities for learning at home.[25]

Collaborating with the Community

Coordinate the work and resources of community businesses, agencies, and cultural, civic, and other organizations to strengthen school programs, family practices, and student learning and development. Enable students, staff, and families to contribute service to the community.

The Action Team for Partnerships at Highlands Elementary School in Naperville, Illinois, sought a way to encourage intergenerational understanding between elementary students and senior citizens. They began by scheduling a staff meeting at Sunrise Assisted Living so teachers could meet the staff and residents. Partnerships were formed between classes and residents at Sunrise, and those partnerships resulted in several meaningful activities. For example, a fifth grade class met one month at Sunrise for their history lesson where they interviewed Sunrise residents about their experiences during World War II. Residents of Sunrise attended school assemblies at Highlands, and they displayed student art work on the bulletin board at the assisted living facility.[26]

> ■ **INTASC**
>
> **STANDARD 10**   The teacher fosters relationships with school colleagues, parents, and agencies in the larger community to support students' learning and well-being.

REFLECT & WRITE

Which of the six types of involvement have you seen in action in schools? Describe at least one of those events.

_____

_____

_____

_____

_____

Parent/Family Conferences

Parents can be involved in a variety of ways, depending on their needs and their willingness and inclination to be involved and the motivation and resources of teachers and schools. Parents and families can be involved by attending school functions, supervising homework, assisting with home-based learning activities, participating in school events and programs, attending school-based parenting classes and other adult education programs, volunteering time and expertise, serving as classroom aides, being an advocate for children and schools, and serving on advisory boards and decision-making committees.

Parent/family conferences are an effective way to communicate with parents and other family members about their children's achievement and behavior and to assess parents' needs as they relate to supporting their children's learning. Significant parent involvement can be facilitated through well-planned and well-conducted parent-teacher conferences. Such conferences are often the first contact many families have with schools. Conferences are critical from a public relations point of view and as a vehicle for helping families, teachers, and other school personnel accomplish their goals. The following guidelines will assist you as you prepare for and conduct parent/family conferences:

Parent/family conferences Meetings between parents/families and teachers to inform parents of students' progress and enable them to actively participate in the educational process.

1. **Plan ahead.** Be sure of the reason for the conference. What are your objectives? What do you want to accomplish? List the points you want to cover and think about what you are going to say.

2. **Invite the child to the conference.** In this way, students will feel you are working together. When appropriate, involve the child in the conversation.

3. **Get to know the parents.** The more effectively you establish rapport with parents, the more you will accomplish in the long run.

4. **Avoid an authoritative atmosphere.** Treat parents and others like the adults they are and sit next to them or in an arrangement that is comfortable for everyone.

Go to MyEducationLab and select the topic "Family and Community" then watch the video "Parent-Teacher Conference." Complete the activities that follow.

5. **Communicate at parents' levels.** Use words, phrases, and explanations that parents understand and that are familiar to them. Avoid jargon or complicated explanations and speak in your natural style.

6. **Accentuate the positive.** Make every effort to show and tell parents what their children are doing well. When you deal with problems, put them in the proper perspective. Relate what a student is able to do, what the goals and purposes of the learning program are, what specific skill or concept you are trying to get a student to learn, and what problems the student is having in achieving. Most important, explain what you plan to do to help a student achieve in school and what specific role the parents can have in meeting these achievement goals.

7. **Learn to listen.** Make eye contact and use body language such as head nodding and hand gestures. Avoid interrupting and arguing with parents. Paraphrase to clarify ideas. As you listen and give parents a chance to talk, you will likely learn more about them and achieve your goals.

8. **Follow up.** Ask parents for a definite time for the next conference as you are concluding the current one. Another conference is the best method of solidifying gains and extending support, but other acceptable means of following up are telephone calls, written reports, mailed letters, e-mails, notes sent home with students, or brief visits to the home. Although these types of contacts might appear casual, they should be planned for and conducted as seriously as any regular parent-teacher conference. No matter which approach you choose, the advantages of a parent-teacher conference follow-up are as follows:
   - Families see that you genuinely care about their children.
   - Everyone can clarify problems, issues, advice, and directions.
   - Parents, family members, and children are encouraged to continue to do their best.

As their children's first teachers, parents play a primary role in promoting student academic success.

- You can offer further opportunities to extend classroom learning to the home.
- You can extend programs initiated for helping families and formulate new plans.

9. **Develop an action plan.** Every communication with families should end on a positive note, so that everyone knows what can be done and how to do it.

REFLECT & WRITE

Which form of follow-up are you most comfortable with—a phone call, a letter sent home with a student, e-mail communication, or a home visit? What might your choice reveal about your communication style as a teacher?

Home Visits

Home visits are becoming more commonplace for early childhood professionals. In fact, California has a $15 million initiative to pay teachers overtime for visiting students' homes (see *In the Classroom with Carol Sharp*). Teachers who do home visiting are trained prior to going on the visits.

A home visiting program can show that the teachers, principal, and school staff are willing to "go more than halfway" to involve all parents in their children's education. Home visits help teachers demonstrate their interest in students' families and understand their students better by seeing them in their home environment. Home visits might be necessary when other communication methods have been ineffective.

These visits should not replace parent-teacher conferences or be used to discuss children's progress. When done early, before any school problems can arise, they avoid putting parents on the defensive and signal that teachers are eager to work with all parents. Teachers who have made home visits say they build stronger relationships with parents and their children and improve attendance and achievement.

Involving Single-Parent Families

Many of the students you teach will be from single-parent families. Based on where you teach, as many as 50 percent of your children could be from single-parent families. The following are some things you can do to ensure that single-parent families are involved:

1. **You must be willing to accommodate family schedules.** Arrange conferences at other times, perhaps early morning (breakfast), midmorning, noon (lunch), early afternoon, late afternoon, or early evening. Some employers, sensitive to these needs, give release time to participate in school functions, but others do not. Teachers and principals need to think seriously about going to families rather than having families always come to them. Some schools have set up parent conferences to accommodate families' work schedules, while some teachers find that home visits work best.

In the Classroom

with **Carol Sharp**

The Home Visit Project

Some called it a throw-away school. Others considered it a school in peril. As far as first-year Principal Carol Sharp was concerned, the Susan B. Anthony Elementary School in Sacramento, California, had lost touch with the community. The overwhelming majority of students were performing below grade level, suspensions had peaked at 140 the previous year, and parents—perhaps the single most important factor in a student's success—had become spectators in their child's education.

That was 1998. Today, the K–6 school has been transformed. Student achievement has skyrocketed; suspensions have been all but eliminated; and parents are respected partners, not outsiders. "It's like a dream," says Sharp of the incredible changes that have taken place at the school and in the surrounding community.

But it wasn't a dream. The changes, as Sharp and others are quick to note, have come about as the result of hours and hours of hard work on the part of students, educators, and parents. They're the result, says Sharp, of a commitment to building relationships between home and school so that everyone—parents, teachers, and students—work together toward common goals.

Barriers to relationship building are present at Susan B. Anthony. Of the school's roughly 450 students, 69 percent are immigrants from countries in Southeast Asia. Roughly 20 percent are African American, and 12 percent are Hispanic. All live in poverty, with 100 percent of the students receiving free or reduced-priced lunches. The average parent has a sixth-grade education. "A lot of assumptions were made about why parents didn't come to school," says Sharp. "But in many cases parents just needed to be asked. They needed to feel welcome."

As parents, educators, and Area Congregations Together (ACT), a faith-based community organization, staff members began meeting, all recognized the considerable disconnect between home and school. Using a model developed by ACT parent leaders and staff, the teachers at Susan B. Anthony took a simple but radical step. Together with teachers at eight other low-performing schools in the Sacramento City Unified School District, the Susan B. Anthony staff began visiting the homes of students. They went in pairs and brought an interpreter or the school nurse, when necessary. They spent time getting to know parents and seeing their students in their home environment. They heard, often for the first time, of the hopes, dreams, and struggles of their families.

Teachers also used the initial home visit as an opportunity to share information with parents about a schoolwide restructuring effort designed to increase student achievement. "We told the community, 'This is a whole new ball game,'" recalls Sharp. "We let them know what we were doing to support their child and asked what we could do for them to support their family."

Each home visit ended with an invitation to come to school to a celebration where Sharp and her staff would talk about a comprehensive plan for school improvement. The impact of those first house calls was immediate and profound. Two months into the home visit program, 600 people came to school for a potluck dinner and to hear about the school improvement plan. It was the first of what would be many celebrations of the school's successes.

Throughout the district, schools were transformed by home visits. The pilot program proved so successful that the state enacted legislation to provide $15 million in annual funding for schools throughout California to conduct them. Parents and educators from as far away as Boston and the South Bronx have traveled to Sacramento to learn about the model program.

As dramatic as they were, the outcomes at Susan B. Anthony Elementary School and its counterparts throughout Sacramento should not have been a surprise. Parents have a profound effect not only on the life of an individual student, but also on the entire school community.

Read an online interview with Carol Sharp at www.edutopia.org/node/1008.

Source: R. Furger, *Secret Weapon Discovered*, 2005. (Online). Available at www.edutopia.org/secret-weapon-discovered. Retrieved June 26, 2007.

2. **When you talk with single-parent families be aware of time constraints.** Ensure that the meeting starts on time, that you have a list of items (skills, behaviors, achievements) to discuss, that you have sample materials available to illustrate all points, that you make specific suggestions relative to the one-parent environment, and that the meeting ends on time.

3. **Suggest some ways that single parents can make their time with their children meaningful.** If a child has trouble following directions, show parents how to use home situations to help in this area. Children can learn to follow directions while helping with errands, meal preparations, or housework.

4. **Get to know families' lifestyles and living conditions.** For example, you can recommend that every child have a quiet place to study, but this may be an impossible demand for some households. Before you set meeting times, you might inquire about some of the homes in your community, decide what family involvement activities to implement, and what you will ask of families during the year.

5. **Help develop support groups for one-parent families within your school, such as discussion groups and classes on parenting for singles.** Include the needs and abilities of one-parent families in your family involvement activities and programs. After all, single-parent families may be the majority of families represented in the program.

Go to MyEducationLab and select the topic "Family and Community" then watch the video "Parents as Child Advocates." Complete the questions that follow.

_____
_____
_____
_____
_____

REFLECT & WRITE

What do you think your greatest challenge will be in meeting the needs of single parents? What are you willing to do to ensure that you accommodate those needs?

Involving Language-Minority Parents and Families

Language-minority parents are individuals whose English proficiency is minimal and who lack a comprehensive knowledge of the norms and social systems in the United States. Language-minority families often face language and cultural barriers that greatly hamper their ability to become actively involved, although many have a great desire and willingness to participate in their children's education.

Because the culture of language-minority families often differs from the majority in a community, teachers who seek truly collaborative community, home, and school involvement must take into account the cultural features that can inhibit collaboration. Traditional styles of child rearing and family organization, attitudes toward schooling, organizations around which families center their lives, life goals and values, political influences, and methods of communication within the cultural group all have implications for parent participation.

Language-minority families often lack information about the U.S. educational system, including basic school philosophy, practice, and structure, which can result in misconceptions, fear, and a general reluctance to respond to invitations for involvement. Furthermore, the U.S. educational system may be quite different from

■ INTASC

STANDARD 9 The teacher is a reflective practitioner who continually evaluates the effects of his/her choices and actions on others (students, parents, and other professionals in the learning community) and who actively seeks out opportunities to grow professionally.

OBSERVE & LEARN

Y ou can learn a lot about parents by observing them. Attend an open house for parents. Observe two teachers' classrooms. The purpose of your observation is to identify parent characteristics and behaviors as they talk with the teachers, examine their children's work, and interact with other parents and students. After you have gathered your data, develop brief guidelines for how you will accommodate such parental behaviors during your own open houses.

what some families are used to. They may have been taught to avoid active involvement in the educational process, with the result that they prefer to leave all decisions concerning their children's education to professionals and administrators.

The U.S. ideal of a community-controlled and community-supported educational system must be explained to families from cultures in which this concept is not as highly valued. Traditional roles of children, professionals, and administrators also have to be explained. Many families, especially language-minority families, are willing to relinquish to professionals any rights and responsibilities they have for their children's education and need to be taught to assume their roles and obligations toward schooling.

The parents of Jorge Lopez, for example, were reluctant to visit Jorge's school. They were new to the United States and had limited ability to speak English. Jorge's English language learning (ELL) teacher, Ms. Lavaca, asked the Lopez family to meet with her at a neighborhood restaurant where she told them she could better teach Jorge if she knew more about him. This opened up the communication between the school and home and helped the Lopez family feel welcome.

Initiating Culturally Appropriate Family Involvement

For language-minority parents there are many unknowns. As a result, these parents might feel some initial discomfort with regard to the school's expectations of them and their children. Some parents of diverse cultural backgrounds report feelings of intimidation regarding the power of schools. Teachers can help alleviate much of this discomfort by interacting with parents in the following ways.

- **Know what parents want for their children.** Find out families' goals for education, careers, and accomplishments. The more you talk to parents, the more you will be able to help them and their children.
- **Be clear about your own educational values and goals.** Share with parents what you believe are the purposes of schooling. At the same time, help parents see how their goals for their children fit with your goals and the school's goals.
- **Help parents learn to participate in the system of schooling.** The process of schooling is complex and confusing for parents. Provide specific examples of how you and the school are working to help them and their children.
- **Build relationships with parents.** Building relationships takes time, but it is worth the effort, because good relationships enhance communication and understandings. You communicate better when you have a relationship, and learning to communicate builds relationships.
- **Learn to be an effective cross-cultural communicator.** Learn about communication styles that are different from your own. What you think a person of another culture means may not be what he or she *really* means. Listen carefully and ask for clarification. When you are clear about what parents mean, then you can be more confident about helping them and their children.
- **Clarify with parents what they think their roles are in educating children.** These roles vary by culture. Once you learn what parents believe about appro-

priate roles, you will be better able to help meet parents' expectations for schooling.

- **When interacting with parents, use a *problem-solving* rather than a *power* approach.** Working together is the key. Be willing to include parents in setting goals, developing plans, and solving problems. Sharing power with parents is the foundation for working collaboratively for the common purpose of helping all students achieve.
- **Commit yourself to education—both your own and that of the families.** Sometimes lack of information or understanding of each other's perspective is what keeps the conflict going.

Cultural Competence

Cultural competence is the ability to interact effectively with students, families, and colleagues of different cultures, as well as an awareness of cultural differences and cultural values. You can practice cultural competence by treating everyone with respect, learning about cultures different from your own through research or asking questions in a sensitive manner, and incorporating cultural considerations into all aspects of your teaching. In addition, you become culturally competent by creating strong home-school relationships, by keeping in touch with parents and families, encouraging them to volunteer in your classroom and to attend school activities, trying to understand their hopes and goals for their children, and by involving them in school activities.

Cultural competence The ability to interact effectively with students, families, and colleagues of different cultures.

REFLECT & WRITE

What is the first thing you will need to do in order to become a culturally competent teacher?

Teachers can also help parents support, extend, and enrich their children's learning in the home.

Communicating about Homework

Teachers should discuss homework with parents during the first parent-teacher conference or sooner. Homework time may impose burdens on parents in a number of ways. First, it takes time; second, parents may not know how to help; and third, parents may have to deal with their children's frustration over forgotten or difficult assignments or a reluctance to complete assignments. Because of these factors, homework can lead to family tensions.

Van Voorhis suggests that the following topics should be addressed with parents before homework issues unfold:[27]

- The amount of student's time that should be spent on homework
- School and the teacher's expectations regarding homework
- The broader purposes of homework beyond instruction
- Ways parents can provide homework feedback

• *Your Turn*

You are asking the parents of your class of middle-class, suburban seventh-graders to take a more active role in helping their children learn at home. Construct a two-page letter offering tips and advice to parents about ways they can help their children with homework assignments. Your letter should use simple and familiar language and short sentences; be direct, while avoiding educational jargon; and use attention grabbers, such as bold headings and borders or boxes.

Some students dread the amount of time required to complete homework. The National PTA and National Education Association suggest the following time-related guidelines:[28]

- Homework in grades K–2 should not exceed 20–30 minutes per night.
- Students in grades 3–6 should spend 30–60 minutes per day on homework, and for older students, the amount varies by subject.
- Homework for junior high students should range between 1 and 10 hours per week.
- Homework for senior high students can range from 1 to more than 15 hours per week.

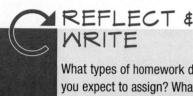

REFLECT & WRITE

What types of homework do you expect to assign? What can you do to help families feel comfortable becoming involved in their children's at-home learning?

_____

_____

_____

_____

_____

WHAT EDUCATIONAL REFORMS PROMOTE GREATER PARENT EMPOWERMENT?

Parent empowerment   Provides parents with decision making and participation opportunities; represents the collaborative achievements of parents and school personnel.

Empowering parents is both a process and a product. As a process, **parent empowerment** provides parents with decision making and participation opportunities as they become involved with the school as partners in their children's education. As a product, parent empowerment represents the concrete achievements of parents and school personnel as they cooperatively and collaboratively work together.

Parent involvement in schools and school-related activities is accelerating and will likely continue in the future. It is also likely that as society continues to expect schools to solve more social problems, teachers and other school leaders will expend increasing efforts to reach out to parents, the community, and the public to assist them in their efforts to address social issues. At the same time, schools will be continually under pressure to improve their services and performance.

School Choice

School choice   Various proposals that allow parents to choose the schools their children will attend.

School choice programs are designed to enable parents to choose the school their children will attend, with certain limitations and within certain constraints. **School choice** is defined in a number of ways. At its most controversial level, it means giving families public funds to send their children to private schools. It also means giving parents the choice to send their children to other public schools in the district and across district lines or school attendance patterns. This process of giving parents the opportunity to choose schools for their children—and providing the means to do so through tax dollars—is a major political issue in education today. In addition to creating much discussion, the school choice controversy has also reinforced and emphasized parents' roles and responsibilities for the education of their children. Furthermore, the debate has placed parents at the center of decision making about where children will attend school and what they will study and learn.

School Choice and NCLB

Under the No Child Left Behind Act (NCLB), students are eligible for public school choice when the Title I school they attend has not made adequate yearly progress (AYP) for 2 consecutive years or longer and is therefore identified as needing improvement, corrective action, or restructuring. Any child attending such a school in a district must be offered the option of transferring to a public school in the district—including a public charter school—not identified as needing improvement. NCLB requires that priority in providing school choice be given to the lowest-achieving children from low-income families. This school choice option really means that parents have the responsibility for making the choice for their children.

One goal of the choice option is that as academically deficient schools lose students, they will be motivated to improve in order to retain students and even attract other students. In addition to the choice option of NCLB, more than one-half of the states have laws supporting school choice. However, merely having laws that permit choice does not necessarily mean that school choice will work. For example, a problem with many choice plans is that some schools will not accept students because their schools are already full, because of a negative effect on racial balances, or because many local boards have policies of not accepting students from outside the district. Results from the 2006 Phi Delta Kappa Gallup Poll show that a large majority of parents want their children to attend a neighborhood school, even when it is noted as not meeting AYP and may be labeled as low performing.[29]

■ **INTASC**

STANDARD 10 The teacher fosters relationships with school colleagues, parents, and agencies in the larger community to support students' learning and well-being.

Parents and community members across the country have become involved in the school reform movement. What options for educational empowerment are available to parents today?

Vouchers

Vouchers Funds allocated to parents to be used to purchase education for their children at public or private schools in the area.

Another expression of school choice is the voucher system. **Vouchers** are certificates good for certain amounts of money that parents can use to pay for some or all of their children's tuition at a private or public school. Milwaukee has had a voucher system since 1990, and, currently, almost 15,000 students are attending a variety of public, private, and parochial schools at state expense.

Vouchers are designed to support efforts at providing parents with choice. Proponents of vouchers say that vouchers are a means of school reform and that they return decision making to parents. Opponents counter that the goal should be to make public schools better rather than going outside the public school system. Critics also maintain that vouchers erode public school support and drain needed tax dollars from schools. Some opponents also claim that vouchers lead to resegregation of the schools.

Public opinion about school choice is mixed. Generally, the public is supportive of the concept of allowing parents to choose the school their children will attend. However, many people do not support allowing parents to send their children to private or church-related schools at public expense. Additional controversy surrounds the issue of accountability. Historically, private and church-affiliated schools have had more flexibility than publicly funded schools with regard to the rules and requirements they establish. Publicly funded schools must abide by the strict constructs of state and federal law or face the threat of losing funding. Many argue that private schools receiving any public monies should be accountable to the same laws.

In a landmark Supreme Court case, *Zelman v. Simmons-Harris*, the Court held, in a 5–4 decision, that a state-enacted voucher program in Cleveland does not violate the U.S. Constitution's prohibition on government establishment of religion. The Court found that the program "is entirely neutral with respect to religion" because it permits the "participation of all schools within the district,

---

YOU DECIDE

School Vouchers

The issues of using vouchers to enable parents to send their children to private schools and public charter schools are many and contentious. As a beginning teacher, you will be asked questions about and be involved in discussions relating to school choice. Reformers see school choice as one way of encouraging low-performing schools to bring their programs up to a higher level. Opponents of school choice believe that allowing parents to send their children, at public expense, to any school they desire erodes or detracts from the role of public education and lets tax dollars flow from the public to the private sector. The table shows how the public responded to a recent opinion poll on the question of school vouchers.

Do you favor or oppose allowing students and parents to choose a private school to attend at public expense?

	2006 (%)	2005 (%)	2004 (%)	2003 (%)	2002 (%)	2001 (%)
Favor	36	38	42	38	46	34
Oppose	60	57	54	60	52	64
Don't know	4	5	4	2	2	2

Source: L. C. Rose and A. M. Gallup, Phi Delta Kappa/Gallup Poll of the Public's Attitude Toward Public Schools, 2006. (Online). Available at www.pdkmembers.org/e-GALLUP/kpoll-pdfs. Accessed June 26, 2007.

Now, it's your turn! How do you decide? Answer the same question. Write a short paragraph expressing your views pro or con regarding vouchers and their use.

For more information about vouchers and choice, visit www.schoolchoices.org.

religious or nonreligious." The Court also ruled that the government provision of funds to religious schools through voucher programs does not violate stands on church-state separation.[30]

The voucher movement is very much a part of the educational landscape and is a "hot" topic politically and educationally. As a beginning teacher, you will be involved in discussions about school choice and vouchers with administrators, colleagues, parents, and the public. Parental choice and voucher systems will continue to be topics of debate in the years to come.

REFLECT & WRITE

Do you think that school choice promotes equity for all students? If not, do you think it is fair to keep children in low-performing school districts without any options? Can you propose any alternatives?

_____
_____
_____
_____
_____

Charter Schools

In Chapter 3 charter schools were discussed as independent public schools designed to enhance efforts at improving and reforming public schools. St. Paul City Academy in Minnesota was the nation's first charter school. It opened its doors in 1992. One of the purposes of charter schools is to provide parents and pupils with more alternatives to public schools, both within and outside of existing school districts. Advocates of charter schools say that these schools encourage innovative teaching, promote performance-based accountability, expand choices of type of public school, create new professional opportunities for teachers, improve student learning, and promote community involvement.[31]

Many states have approved charter school legislation, and more are doing so each year.[32] Charter schools may be new schools or conversions of existing schools. The legal basis for the authority of charter schools varies from state to state. In Arizona, Massachusetts, Michigan, and Minnesota, for example, charter schools are legally independent of school districts. In contrast, in Colorado, Georgia, Kansas, and New Mexico, charter schools are legally part of the traditional school district.

• *Your Turn*

You have been offered a position at a charter school. A friend tells you that there is also an opening for someone with your background in the suburban public school in which he teaches. Which option is most attractive to you? Why? Write a paragraph explaining your decision.

REFLECT & WRITE

If you knew that the families of students in your classroom could remove their children and send them to another school, how do you think this knowledge might affect your teaching and relationships with your students and their families?

_____
_____
_____
_____
_____

HOW CAN YOU USE THE COMMUNITY TO TEACH?

■ **INTASC**

STANDARD 10 The teacher fosters relationships with school colleagues, parents, and agencies in the larger community to support students' learning and well-being.

The community offers an array of resources that can help you to teach better and to better meet the needs of parents and their children. Schools and teachers cannot address the many issues facing children and youth without the partnership and collaboration of powerful sectors of society, including community agencies, businesses, and industry. The following are some actions you can take to reach out to and make use of resources in the community:

■ **Know your students and their needs.** By knowing your students through observation, conferences with parents, and discussions with students, you can identify any barriers to their learning. In this way, you know what kind of help to seek.

■ **Know your community.** You can learn about your community by walking or driving its neighborhoods. Ask parents to introduce you to community members and agencies. Other good ways of learning about a community include reading the local newspaper and attending events in the community.

■ **Ask for help and support from parents and the community.** Keep in mind that many parents will not become involved unless you ask them to do so. The only encouragement many need is your personal invitation.

■ **Develop a directory of community agencies.** You can make such a directory by consulting the yellow pages of the local phone book, contacting the local chamber of commerce, and asking parents what agencies are helpful to them.

■ **Compile a list of people willing to speak to or work with your students.** You can start by asking parents to volunteer and for their suggestions and recommendations of others who might help.

■ **Join and/or network with community-based social and civic organizations.** Many of these service agencies, such as the Kiwanas and Rotary International, actively seek out collaborative opportunities to serve children and youth.

Communities have much to offer teachers who are willing to seek out and build relationships that support collaborative and cooperative ventures. You and your students will be richly rewarded by your efforts in using the community to help support teaching and learning.

Developing Community–School Partnerships

Many of the pressures that influence a community have implications for schools and teaching. Community pressures stem from such issues as how best to pay for schools, what curriculum best fits student and community needs, what kinds of schools are worth supporting, and how to educate students who are able to be productive as citizens and in the workforce. As you work in and through the community, you will have many opportunities to take the pulse of parents and community leaders on these and other issues. It is important for you to be in touch with your school's community so that you can be fully informed and make wise teaching decisions.

Working arrangements and exchanges between school districts and schools and community agencies and businesses are termed **community–school partnerships**. Increasingly, community-based groups are forging relationships that support schools, make the community a better place, and prepare students for work and life. In developing connections with the community, consider all agencies that are potential sources of partnership. Groups to consider include professional associations of doctors, lawyers, architects, nurses, and accountants. For example, an architect might work with your students on issues of public housing and neighborhoods. Also, museums, colleges and universities, ethnic and cultural groups, sen-

Community-school partnerships
Working arrangements or exchanges between school districts and/or schools and community agencies and/or businesses.

ior citizens' centers, religious groups, health organizations, and social and civic groups are all potential collaborators.

REFLECT & WRITE

As a new teacher, how will you build a relationship with the community in which you teach? How do you plan to collaborate with community members to achieve your classroom goals?

Linking Schools, Communities, and Businesses

■ INTASC

STANDARD 10 The teacher fosters relationships with school colleagues, parents, and agencies in the larger community to support students' learning and well-being.

Partnerships between public schools, communities, and businesses are effective in improving the quality of education for students and are found all across the country in grades K–12. These partnerships range from small to large. For example, in Elgin, Illinois, Books at Sunset, a small, locally owned bookstore, sponsored a special "Kids Love a Mystery Night" for every student at Harriet Gifford Elementary School who read a mystery during Kids Love a Mystery Month.[33]

Captain A. J. Tolbert spoke with Air Force ROTC students at Hialeah High School in Hialeah, Florida. All of these students hope to become future aviators. Tolbert is director of the Pilots in Schools Program. The organization's goal is to make students aware of the different careers available to them and to help in their career exploration process. The Pilots in Schools Program had plans to visit 75,000 students in 2007.[34]

More than likely your school and school district will have one or many school/community/business partnerships. You will want to look for ways to participate. In addition, be on the look-out for community/business partnerships that will benefit you and your students. In particular, in today's fast-paced technological environment, many businesses are looking for ways to improve math and science education.

The Pilots in Schools Program is one of the Organization of Black Pilots' outreach programs. It is a minority-targeted program.

REFLECT & WRITE

Think for a minute about some topics you would want to include in your classroom that could be supported by a community/business partnership.

Developing Social Capital

We can further appreciate the value of school-community partnerships by emphasizing a banking metaphor and introducing a concept from macroeconomics.

Social capital is a concept from economics meaning socially valued goods and services that are exchanged in the social transactions within a family or community. *In the Classroom with Geoffrey Canada* describes a program of building social capital to improve the lives of children, youth, and families. For example,

Social capital Concept from economics meaning socially valued goods and services that are exchanged in the social transactions within a family or community.

In the Classroom
with **Geoffrey Canada**

It Takes a Hood:
The Harlem Children's Zone

Geoffrey Canada is a man with a vision—a vision as big as New York City. His vision is that if you really want to change the lives of inner-city children, you change everything—their schools, their families, their neighborhood—all at once. No piecemeal approaches, no one program at a time. You do it all—all at once. Canada was profiled in a *New York Times Magazine* article by P. Tough on June 20, 2004.

Geoffrey Canada's new program, the Harlem Children's Zone, combines educational, social, and medical services. It starts at birth and follows children to college. It meshes those services into an interlocking web, and then it drops that web over an entire neighborhood. It operates on the principle that each child will do better if all the children around him are doing better. So instead of waiting for residents to find out about the services on their own, the organization's recruiters go door-to-door to find participants, sometimes offering prizes and raffles and free groceries to parents who enroll their children in the group's programs. What results is a remarkable level of "market penetration," as the organization describes it. Eighty-eight percent of the roughly 3,400 children under 18 in the 24-block core neighborhood are already served by at least one program, and this year Canada began to extend his programs to the larger 60-block zone. The objective is to create a safety net woven so tightly that children in the neighborhood can't slip through. At a moment when each new attempt to solve the problem of poverty seems to fall apart, what is going on in Harlem is one of the biggest social experiments of our time.

The programs that the Harlem Children's Zone offers are all carefully planned and well run, but none of them, on their own, are particularly revolutionary. It is only when they are considered as a network that they seem so new. The organization employs more than 650 people in more than 20 programs.

At Harlem Gems, a program for forty prekindergarten students at a public school on 118th Street, 5-year-old Keith sits at a computer working away at "Hooked on Phonics," while Luis, a 19-year-old tutor, gives him one-on-one instruction. A few blocks up Lenox Avenue, at the Employment and Technology Center, 30 teenagers who are part of the organization's new investment club are gathered around a conference table, listening to an executive from Lehman Brothers explain the difference between the Dow Jones and the NASDAQ. At P.S. 76 on West 121st Street, fifth-grade students in an after-school program stand in front of their peers, reading aloud the autobiographies they wrote this afternoon. And over at Truce, the after-school center for teenagers, a tutor named Carl helps Trevis, a student in the eighth grade, with a research project for his social studies class, an eight-page paper on the life of Frederick Douglass.

In a nearby housing project, a counselor from the Family Support Center pays a home visit to a woman who has just been granted legal custody of her two grandchildren; in other apartments in the neighborhood, outreach workers from Baby College, a class for new parents, are making home visits of their own, helping teach better parenting techniques. A few blocks away, at the corner of Madison Avenue and 125th Street, construction is under way on the organization's new headquarters, a six-story, $44-million building that will also house the Promise Academy, a new charter school opening in the fall.

Learn more about the Harlem Children's Zone at www.hcz.org.

Source: P. Tough, "It Takes a 'Hood: The Harlem Children's Zone," *New York Times*, June 20, 2004. Reprinted by permission.

in a family social capital can consist of the attention, nurturance, support, and help family members can provide children in their learning and development. When family members provide these things to children, social capital is strong. Low socioeconomic status and family problems—such as substance abuse, unemployment, spousal abuse, divorce, employment stress, lack of education, and the like—weaken social capital. The same concept can be applied to the community. A community with strong social capital has systems in place for children and families, such as parks and playgrounds, senior citizen and community centers, violence- and drug-free environments, and a caring attitude.

When families and communities are weak, the school lacks resources central to its role of effectively educating children. When social capital of the family and the community are weak, it is necessary to rebuild that capital. Such rebuilding can be done by agencies other than the school, but it is in the school's interest to generate activities and programs to accomplish this task. If children are to learn and not merely be taught, the school must help in rebuilding family and community social capital.

Social capital can be built through family-centered programs that acknowledge parents as the first teachers of their children; help them develop skills, knowledge, and abilities; and link them to community agencies. The social capital of the school's neighborhood can be enhanced through community-centered programs linking school programs with community agencies. You and your school can work with families and communities to help develop social capital and the means to use it in the education and development of children and families.

Working with Community Agencies

The range of community groups that you can work with in partnerships includes community agencies; professional associations; and local, state, and federal organizations. For example, the National Coalition for Parent Involvement in Education consists of more than 100 groups, including parent organizations, schools, community and religious groups, and businesses. Community alliances can tackle almost any problem impacting school effectiveness and student learning, often with spectacular results.

Community Schools

Many school districts provide services for students and families. These services can be provided either at the school building, near the school site, or at another agency. A key factor is that they be coordinated between the school and the agencies providing the services. Funding for these linked services generally comes from federal funds, local government agency funds, private donations, fundraisers, and grants.

In a **community school**, youth, families, and community residents work as equal partners with schools and other community institutions to develop programs and services in five areas:

1. **Quality education.** High-caliber curriculum and instruction enable all children to meet challenging academic standards. The school uses all of the community's assets as resources for learning and involves students in solving community problems.

2. **Youth development.** Young people develop their assets and talents, form positive relationships with peers and adults, and serve as resources for their communities.

3. **Family support.** Family resource centers; early childhood development programs; coordinated health care, mental health, and social services; counseling; and other supports enhance family life by building upon individuals' strengths and skills.

■ **INTASC**

STANDARD 10 The teacher fosters relationships with school colleagues, parents, and agencies in the larger community to support students' learning and well-being.

Go to MyEducationLab and select the topic "Family and Community" and watch the video "Incorporating the Home Experiences of Culturally Diverse Students." Answer the questions that follow.

Community schools Coordinate services between schools and agencies providing, for example, health, psychological, family welfare, housing, and other services.

4. **Family and community engagement.** Family members and other residents actively participate in designing, supporting, monitoring, and advocating quality programs and activities in the school and community.

5. **Community development.** All participants focus on strengthening the local leadership, social networks, economic viability, and physical infrastructure of the surrounding community.[35]

Working with Parent Organizations

Many parents and families become involved at the local level through parent-teacher organizations. Many of these are represented at the national level by the National Parent-Teacher Association (PTA), which has 6 million members in 23,000 local units.

REFLECT & WRITE

Think for a minute about students whom you will have in your classroom and the kinds of needs they might have. What community agencies could help you meet your students' needs?

_____

_____

_____

_____

_____

What Parents Can Do

As a beginning teacher, you will have many opportunities to advise parents as to how they can help their children learn and succeed. However, you must be aware that not all parents will be able to follow all your suggestions. Some parents will have more time to spend with their children than other parents, and some parents will be more adept in some areas than others. What is important is that you encourage and support all parents to be involved in their children's lives and education in the best ways they can. You can share the following tips with families about the role of successful parenting in student achievement:

- Set daily and weekly routines for most activities, including going to bed, eating, and completing homework.
- Manage after-school activities.
- Know your children's friends.
- Monitor television and reading habits.
- Become interested in school affairs, what is going on at school, what is being learned, and successes and difficulties.
- Attend school events and activities.
- Communicate with teachers.

REFLECT & WRITE

Parents have many responsibilities for helping their children be successful in school and life. What are two specific things you can do to help parents assume the above roles?

_____

_____

_____

_____

_____

ETHICAL DILEMMA

Is Parent Involvement Always the Best Solution?

JAN EMERSON, a first-year teacher, was having her third-graders line up to go to their physical education class. Suddenly, Dylan screamed that Pete had just bitten him. Jan saw that Dylan had bite marks and blood on his arm. After taking Dylan to the school nurse, she told Pete they were going to call his parents. Pete pleaded with her not to call his parents because, "when they find out that I bit

Dylan, they will hit me again." After his gut-wrenching sobs subsided, Pete explained that his parents had been reported to Child Protective Services in the past. He cried, "Now CPS is going to put my mom and dad in jail, and no one is going to take care of my little brother and me!"

What should Jan Emerson do? Should she call a social worker or call Pete's parents, or handle it without a phone call?

SUMMARY

- Parents, families, and communities influence teaching and learning.
- Family-centered programs increase family involvement in students' lives in order to increase student achievement levels.
- Parent involvement is participation by parents in their child's learning by being involved at school, at home, and in the community.

- Parent empowerment reforms give parents decision making and participation opportunities as they become involved through school choice and charter school programs.
- Using the community allows you to meet the needs of parents and children by accessing an array of resources.

KEY TERMS

Community schools   209
Community-school partnerships   206
Cultural competence   201
Family-centered programs   188

Family-centered teaching   188
Intergenerational programs   190
Parent/family conferences   195
Parent empowerment   202

Social capital   208
School choice   202
Vouchers   204

APPLICATIONS FOR ACTIVE LEARNING

Connections

1. Consider the key concepts and ideas in this chapter concerning communicating with parents and families. Design a newsletter for parents that would be appropriate for a grade level of your choice.

2. Did you have a teacher or teachers who helped your parents help you with school activities and learning? What did they do? What are some things your teachers could have done for you and your family but didn't? How will you make sure you are responsive to the needs of your students' families?

Field Experiences

1. Interview classroom teachers in your school and ask them to tell how their experiences with parental involvement have benefitted them. Write what you learn from these interviews and how you might use this information in your first year of teaching. What will teachers say about parent involvement and student achievement? What will parents say about school involvement and student achievement?

2. Arrange to visit a local company or agency that participates in community-school involvement or sponsors a business-school partnership. What goods and services or

capital investment does the company provide? How do spokespersons define the company's role, the goals for the partner, and the benefits to the company and its employees? How do they collaborate with the school to operate and evaluate the program? Compare your findings with your classmates' observations of other companies.

Personal Research

1. Find out about the School for the Talented and Gifted Student at Yvonne A. Ewell Townview Magnet Center in Dal-

las, Texas. After reading about it, describe why you think it was chosen by *Newsweek* as the best public high school in the United States in 2007.

2. Selectively compile an education-oriented list of local, state, and national agencies and organizations, including phone numbers and the services provided. How could you use each agency's services to help you teach and meet the needs of students and their families? Add this information to your Teaching Resource file in your portfolio.

PREPARING TO TEACH

For Your Portfolio

On the basis of your interviews, reading, and reflection, develop and write a specific plan to help parents incorporate learning at home. Include this plan and any support materials you develop, such as letters to parents, homework guidelines and suggestions, schedules, lesson suggestions, and so on.

Idea File

Brainstorm "Ten Best" ideas for involving parents of students at the grade level you plan to teach. You might develop this idea file on an ongoing basis by brainstorming ideas for involving parents in each unit of the content area(s) you plan to teach.

LEARNING AND KNOWING MORE

Websites Worth Visiting

When schools and community agencies collaborate to address the pressing needs of children and their families, the results are beneficial for everyone involved. Families, schools, churches, and other community institutions play a critical role in shaping children's academic success. One way to keep abreast of what's happening with school-community partnerships is through the work of the Appalachia Education Laboratory. You can visit their website at www.ael.org.

The National Coalition for Parent Involvement in Education (NCPIE)

www.ncpie.org

NCPIE is dedicated to developing effective family-school partnerships in schools throughout America.

The National PTA Home Page

www.pta.org

Provides information as well as other links for PTA organizations.

The Center for Education Reform

www.edreform.com

Provides information pertaining to charter schools. Includes demographics, statistics, and other relevant information.

Books Worth Reading

Barbour, C., and Barbour, N. H. (2005). *Families, schools, and communities: Building partnerships for educating children*, 3rd ed. Upper Saddle River, NJ: Prentice Hall.

The authors seek to combine the knowledge and experiences that emerge from the three social settings of each child's life—home, community, and school—into educational strategies that will create nurturing learning environments.

Lawrence-Lightfoot, S. (2003). *The essential conversation: What parents and teachers can learn from each other.* New York: Ballantine.

Through vivid portraits and parables, the author captures the dynamics of complex, intense relationships from the perspective of both parents and teachers. She also identifies new principles and practices for improving family–school relationships.

Patrikakou, E. N., Weissberg, R. P., Redding, S., & Walberg, H. J. (Eds.). (2005). *School-family partnerships for children's success.* New York: Teachers College Press.

The most influential experts in the field of school–family partnerships provide essential information to better understand and improve the nature and quality of these relationships for the benefit of all children. Each chapter includes recommendations to help educators, parents, and policymakers create and sustain successful partnerships to support children's development.

Sornson, B. (2005). *Creating classrooms where teachers love to teach and students love to learn.* Golden, CO: Love and Logic Institute.

Among the 15 chapters in this book, Sornson has devoted one chapter to connecting with parents. His narrative style is easy to read, and he provides interesting, authentic experiences from the classroom in this text.

III

Foundations of American Education

E vents and ideas that shape teaching and
learning are influenced by local, state, national, and international politics and economic conditions. These influences are reflected in school budgets, in efforts of education lobbies, and in legislation and court rulings on matters such as school finance reform, home schooling, and charter schools.

One of the most remarkable educational changes of the twenty-first century is how teachers' status and roles have changed. In previous generations, teachers were passive responders to events shaping education. Today's teachers are remarkably political. More than ever, they are involved in educational decision making, especially at the school and community levels. Teachers' unions and associations represent teachers at the state and national levels. Teachers are expected to be leaders and decision makers and are held accountable for their students' learning. You are joining a profession that is engaged, proactive, and dynamic.

Time and place also link the events and ideas that shape teaching and learning. Today's schools reflect historical developments in education, from the Socratic method of classical Greece to the school desegregation movement of the 1950s to NCLB in 2001. In the classroom you will see educational philosophy in action, translated into classroom arrangements, expectations for teaching and learning, instructional methods, and curriculum materials and activities.

The chapters in Part Three explore how the historical and philosophical roots of the Western world influence education in America today. You, as a teacher, will experience the impact of these historical, philosophical, and legal influences as you work with students, parents, colleagues, administrators, and other professionals.

7 The Politics of American Education

JEFFREY R. RYAN There are those who say that teachers, as public servants, have no place in the realm of politics. While this belief may arise from a desire to avoid controversy, I submit that we owe it to our students to show them that all citizens must exercise their rights all the time, not just when it is convenient, not when they have the time, or when they are sure they won't offend anyone. Our most important task is to lead our pupils to the recognition that democracy only works when the people participate in it. They must help to lead their own country and make it even better than it already is. We need to be active in the public arena ourselves in order to show our children how to do it.

In November of 2005, I was asked to speak before the Joint Committee on Public Service at the Massachusetts State House. Here is what I said:

> I should like to thank Senator Nuciforo and all the supporters of the current bill that calls for divestment of state pension funds from companies that do business with Sudan. As a history teacher at Reading Memorial High School, I am constantly trying to show my students the connection between the study of the past and the pursuit of justice in our own day. Currently my Honors United States History students are learning about the conflict over the expansion of slavery in nineteenth century America and the struggle for the abolition of human bondage that was waged at the same time. I stress to my students that if they remember nothing else at the end of the year, they must forever keep in their minds the absolute necessity that all citizens of this republic remain dedicated to the continued emancipation of slaves wherever they be held in chains. There are hundreds of thousands of people held in slavery in Sudan right now, and we must do all we can to set them free.

> Later in the year when I teach the story of the Second World War, there is much emphasis on the extermination of the millions of racial minorities at the hands of the barbarous Nazi regime. I implore my pupils to dedicate themselves to taking a stand against any genocide that may occur at anytime or in any place in our world.

> A year ago I learned that some of the money that is taken out of my paycheck each week is given to companies that are investing in Sudan, arguably the most vicious and sanguinary regime in the world today. I was appalled that, while I did my best to teach my children the importance of fighting against slavery and genocide, my own money was being utilized to support the government of Omar Bassan al-Bashir and his rampaging Janjaweed militias. When I informed my students of this screaming paradox I was saddened to see no expressions of outrage and betrayal on their idealistic faces.

> Senator Nuciforo's bill will do much to set this problem right. Certainly the state pension fund is charged with fiduciary responsibility. Yet I know not a single public employee in the commonwealth who would want her or his retirement fund to be augmented with money accrued from a country that practices the enslavement of its citizens, as well as mass murder, deportation, arson, gang rape, and forced starvation as state policy. As the 2003 Massachusetts Teacher of the Year, as a resident of this Commonwealth, as a citizen of the United States, and as a member of the human race,

As you read this chapter . . .

Think about:

- The forces that influence school governance and finance
- Factors that contribute to how education is governed
- How schools are held accountable
- Who is responsible for how schools are governed and administered
- The different sources of funding for education
- The many issues of governance and finance that affect education today

> ## Students must help lead their country and make it better...

▶▶ Go to MyEducationLab and select the topic "Governance and School Administration" then watch the video "The Principal as Leader."

Jeffrey R. Ryan is a history teacher at Reading Memorial High School in Reading, Massachusetts. In 2003, he was recognized as the Massachusetts Teacher of the Year.

I ask that the legislature support Bill #2166. I thank you, and so do my colleagues and so, in the end, do my beloved students.

I am overjoyed to report that both chambers of the Massachusetts legislature voted to divest from companies that invest in Sudan, and on November 2, 2007, Governor Deval Patrick signed this bill into law. It is a small step, but a vital one, in the struggle to save the Darfuri people from the horrors of their own government. It is also a lesson for my students that a teacher's voice can have a profound impact. If we show the power of political activism, they will realize that they themselves have power and that they can, in the words of President Kennedy, "truly light the world."

WHAT FORCES INFLUENCE SCHOOL GOVERNANCE AND FINANCE?

Governance   Decision making about the overseeing, monitoring, and implementing of educational functions.

As Jeffrey Ryan's opening vignette illustrates, politics can play a powerful role in classroom teaching and in the process of schooling. **Governance** refers to the process of making financial and other decisions; these decisions inform school boards, administrators, and teachers. Every day, politicians, administrators, and teachers make decisions about what to teach, how to teach, and what programs should and should not be funded. All of these decisions are based on the politics and finance of schooling. For example, some school districts might decide to implement sex education and teenage pregnancy prevention programs or random drug-testing programs, whereas other districts may feel such programs are politically disadvantageous. In this chapter, you will learn about the reasons for how and why schools are governed and financed.

Public Opinion and Social Issues

The public is always interested in and concerned about how schools spend their taxes; taxpayers want to make sure they are getting the biggest bang for their tax bucks. They also want the schools to educate all students so they achieve the high standards prescribed by the federal government and the states.

With the escalation of school violence over the past decade, steady rates of substance abuse and teen pregnancy, and the rise in self-mutilation among teens, the need for resources and money persists. In 2007, board members at King Middle School in Maine voted to allow children as young as 11 to obtain birth-control pills at a middle-school health center in an attempt to address the social issue of teen pregnancy. Board members said that this new policy is aimed at a tiny number of sexually active students. King Middle School will become the first middle school in Maine, and one of only a few in the nation, to make a full range of contraception available. Students need parental permission to use the city-run health center in the school, but they do not have to tell their parents they are seeking birth control.[1]

Addressing social problems such as school violence, teen pregnancy, and contraception costs money. The public believes that of all the problems facing schools today, the biggest is lack of money (see Table 7.1). How to get the money they need is a constant challenge for schools. There are never enough resources to achieve all the goals. School governance and finance is a constant balancing act of how to allocate limited resources in the face of voracious demand.

Public opinion plays a powerful role in what schools teach and how they operate. For example, as Table 7.1 shows, the public believes that lack of discipline is a major problem. This concern is reflected in the emphasis on providing gun-

TABLE 7.1 Biggest Problems Facing Local Public Schools

Problem	National Total %	Respondents with No Children in School %	Public School Parents %
Lack of financial support/funding/money	22	21	26
Lack of discipline, control	10	11	5
Overcrowded schools	7	6	9
Fighting/violence/gangs	5	5	8
Difficulty getting good teachers/quality teachers	5	5	4
Concern about standards/quality	4	4	4
Use of drugs/dope	4	5	3

Source: L. C. Rose and A. M. Gallup, "The 39th Annual Phi Delta Kappan/Gallup Poll of the Public's Attitudes toward the Public Schools," *Phi Delta Kappan,* 2007, Table 43.

free schools and reducing school violence. The public believes that until and unless schools are safe and orderly, they will not be able to provide a high-quality education for the nation's students. In addition, issues of how to finance and support education are reflected in increased federal funding, more state control of education, and higher local taxes.

Social issues also affect how schools operate and what schools teach. This is evident in schools' efforts to address such social concerns as violence, substance abuse, teenage pregnancy, single parenting, and even global warming.

A primary example of how schools and teachers are involved in social issues is reflected in "the greening of schools." Schools and faculty are teaching curricula about global warming, energy conservation, and the protection of natural resources. California's San Jose Unified School District has joined the green movement by unveiling what it says might be the largest solar power and energy-efficient program in U.S. K–12 education. The program started in 2007 at four of the system's six high schools and will incorporate the construction of solar arrays on school roofs and parking canopies that will generate 5 megawatts of power. Over the 25-year lifespan of the project, the district expects to save $25 million in energy costs and reduce its power demand by 25 percent. Overall, the district estimates it will cut the equivalent of 37,000 tons of carbon dioxide emissions. The San Jose School District, working with corporate partners Chevron Energy Solutions and Bank of America, plans to make additional energy-saving upgrades to its lighting system and other infrastructure. Like many districts that have gone green, San Jose will take advantage of the schools' new solar energy panels by adding an environmental component to its curriculum. "There's community learning, which to me is symbolic; then there's the educational component for kids," says Superintendent Don Iglesias. "For the community's public institutions, we can't just preach it, we have to live it. This is a step in the

YOU DECIDE

Should Middle Schools Provide Birth Conrol?

Should middle schools and high schools dispense birth control pills to their students? Sarah L., the mother of a boy and a girl who graduated from middle school in 2006, said she was "elated" at the committee's vote to allow 11-year-olds to obtain birth control. She said critics, shocked that 11-year-olds have sex, should "get over it." But parent Jay S. disagrees. He says, "They should not be handing out condoms or birth control pills without parental consent."

What do you think?

right direction. Kids are watching what we do and what we say." Students will study and analyze the effect of solar energy's cost efficiencies.[2]

Stakeholders in Education

Stakeholders are people and agencies with a particular interest in the schools. Stakeholders are interested in and concerned about the process of schooling and want to help ensure that the schools do a good job. The public is interested in education for five basic reasons:

- Most people have gone to school, and therefore feel that their school attendance has given them a certain knowledge and authority on school matters.
- Education in America is essentially viewed as being controlled and influenced by citizens who believe that one role of the public schools is to educate future citizens for democratic living.
- Many citizens are parents, and thus are concerned about what happens to their children in school and how this affects their children's future.
- People, who pay taxes, feel they deserve a say in how schools operate and educate students.
- The business community has a stake in the public schools, because they believe it is the responsibility of the public schools to prepare citizens for the workforce.

As you can see, a great variety of individuals and groups are stakeholders in education.

Political Interest Groups

Politicians are interested in schools because they educate future citizens. Politicians use schools as a way of implementing policies they believe are good for the states and the nation. For example, many gubernatorial candidates run on platforms that advocate literacy, high standards, reductions in class size, and fiscal accountability.

Political interest groups play a significant role in exerting political influence on how schools are organized and governed and on what they teach. For example, **lobbyists** represent particular groups such as teachers, boards of education, state departments of education, and manufacturers of school products. Lobbyists are groups and individuals often paid to lobby for a particular cause and help influence legislation and policy. The Quality Education for Minorities (QEM) Network, for example, is dedicated to improving opportunities for the education of African Americans, Alaska Natives, Native Americans, Mexican Americans, and Puerto Ricans.

Business and Industry

Businesses, both large and small, have a considerable vested interest in the public schools. They want future workers who can perform well in the labor force. In particular, they want students who can think, work well with others, and make decisions. For example, at Kern County High School in California, students learn technical skills every day that will help them move into a career. At the town's Regional Occupational Center, students learn how to run a business, fight crime, fight fires, repair engines, weld, care for animals, and design and model clothes. "We want a good workforce in Kern County, and we're preparing that workforce," says Principal Sandy Banducci. Jordan Serna, a student at Kern High School, is the president of the computer repair class's IT club and wants to work in technology as a career. He says, "The best part [about the program] is I can learn what I want to do for my career . . . so for the future, I know how to work on technology."[3]

At the Automotive High School in Brooklyn, New York, students learn auto mechanics as they pursue a regular high school education. Students in the auto mechanics program work on cars that are brought in by residents or teachers. They charge for the cost of parts plus $12 an hour for labor; the money they earn goes to a student activity fund. The auto mechanics education gives many students the necessary skills they will need when applying for jobs after high school. Principal of the school, Melissa Silberman, says, "There are jobs out there waiting for these kids. There is a real need for mechanics. A lot of baby boomers who became mechanics are retiring, and there are not a lot of people filling those spots. It's not something you can outsource to some other country. I tell the kids, 'People can't call Lexus and say, 'Can you troubleshoot my car for me over the phone?' "[4]

Changes in the requirements for effectively entering and staying in the workforce are among the most significant changes in American society today. The world of work demands a more professional and highly skilled worker than it did half a century ago. Because of these trends and changes, business and industry are in the forefront of current education reform efforts. Many business and industry leaders want schools to teach thinking and decision-making skills as well as basic skills. Consequently, high school programs are more geared to the world of work than they were in past decades.

Many politicians advocate for educational reforms and policies that might play an important role in how we fund our schools and educate future citizens.

Professional Organizations and Teachers

Teachers are major stakeholders in education policy and finance. They are involved in school governance and, at the same time, are influenced by it. Teachers are represented by labor organizations such as the National Education Association (NEA) and the American Federation of Teachers (AFT) and by other professional associations (see Chapter 2). These organizations exert considerable influence on conditions of employment, organization, governance, compensation and benefits, and curriculum.

In the past decade, professional organizations such as the National Council of Teachers of Mathematics (NCTM) have greatly influenced the content of the mathematics curriculum and how it is taught. Another professional organization, the National Association for the Education of Young Children (NAEYC), has helped improve the professional practice of early childhood educators (see Chapter 2).

Parents, Students, and Community Groups

Parents represent a significant source of the political power influencing the educational process (see Chapter 6). As stakeholders, parents are interested in having schools that meet their perceived needs of helping children learn basic skills as well as other academic skills and social behaviors necessary for successful work and living. Parents also are very much in the forefront of efforts to restructure and reform education. They influence what goes on at the classroom and district levels as well as what goes on at the state and national levels.

Students are the primary consumers of the educational process. They are most often affected by the rules, regulations, organization, governance, and funding of the schools. Many schools have organizations, such as student councils, that

To read about an example of how stakeholders worked together toward a solution to a problem, go to MyEducationLab and select the topic "Governance and School Administration" then read "No Homework Left Behind."

provide students opportunities for a voice in school decisions and policies. Students are often interested in governance issues that directly affect them, such as rules for behavior, dress codes, and curriculum.

Students also are getting involved in social activism. Social activism can take many forms: they might fight for a cause that is meaningful to them or they might advocate for their rights as consumers. Some even take on the lunch lady, as second-graders did when they raised their voices over reheated frozen green beans. The menu at William V. Wright Elementary School is getting a makeover after Constantine Christopulos' class went on a polite letter-writing campaign to see less of that particular vegetable in the cafeteria. "A little boy said, 'Anything, anything, I'll even eat broccoli,' " said Connie Duits, the lunch lady. "So that one touched my heart."[5]

Many community groups are focused on particular, or single, school-related issues. Groups organize to change attendance boundaries, teaching practices, curriculum content, school policies, and school-funding issues. As stakeholders in education, community groups reflect and influence local issues and priorities.

REFLECT & WRITE

In your experience, what stakeholder groups most influenced your education? How? What are some of the most influential stakeholder groups today? What are they advocating? Why?

_____

_____

_____

_____

_____

HOW IS EDUCATION GOVERNED?

The three branches of government—executive, legislative, and judicial—influence the governance and finance of education at both the state and federal levels. The executive branch of the national government and the federal court system exert considerable influence on education. State legislatures make the laws that govern education in each state. The judicial branches of government influence education policy, practice, and curriculum through court decisions and interpretations of laws. State and federal courts and the U.S. Supreme Court have ruled on many issues important to educators, parents, students, and the public. In Chapter 8, you will learn more about how federal and state laws and court decisions help determine the character of American education.

Although it might seem that all governance of education occurs at the local level—in the school district and school—this is not the case. The control of education really resides with state government; however, the federal government also plays a major role. Much of the politics of education involves balancing the role of the federal and state governments with the wishes and desires of local communities.

Roles of the Federal Government in Education

The federal government has a long history of involvement in education. The original Department of Education (DOE) was created in 1867 to collect information on schools and teaching that would help the states establish effective school systems. Although the agency's name and location within the executive branch have changed over the past 130 years, this early emphasis on getting information to teachers and policymakers about what works in education continues to the present day.

In 1965, the Elementary and Secondary Education Act launched a comprehensive set of programs, including the Title I program of federal aid to disadvantaged children, to address the problems of poor urban and rural areas. In that same year, the Higher Education Act authorized assistance for postsecondary education, including financial aid programs for needy college students.

In 1980, Congress established the DOE as a cabinet-level agency. Today, the DOE operates programs that touch on every area and level of education. Its elementary and secondary programs annually serve more than 14,000 school districts and some 56 million students attending more than 97,000 public schools and 28,000 private schools.[6] In addition, the federal government operates the Department of Defense Dependent Schools (DODDS system), which educate the children of armed services personnel and other Department of Defense employees. The armed services also operate an extensive system of child care for soldier-parents.

The U.S. Constitution

The word *education* does not appear in the U.S. Constitution. When the Constitution was written, responsibilities and functions not specifically given to the federal government were reserved for the states. Because education is not mentioned in the Constitution, the Tenth Amendment expressly makes education a state function and responsibility. The majority of states delegate day-to-day responsibility for operating schools to local districts.

Justifications for the involvement of the federal government in education come from the general welfare clause of the preamble to the Constitution and key amendments. The preamble makes it the business of the federal government to promote the general welfare of its citizens. As Figure 7.1 suggests, promoting the general welfare includes making sure that states uphold the First and Fourteenth Amendments.

■ INTASC

STANDARD 10 The teacher fosters relationships with school colleagues, parents, and agencies in the larger community to support students' learning and well-being.

THE FIRST AMENDMENT

Congress shall make no law respecting an establishment of religion, or prohibiting the free exercise thereof; or abridging the freedom of speech, or of the press; or the right of the people peaceably to assemble, and to petition the Government for redress of grievances.

THE TENTH AMENDMENT

The powers not delegated to the United States by the Constitution, nor prohibited by it to the States, are reserved to the States respectively, or to the people.

THE FOURTEENTH AMENDMENT

No state shall make or enforce any law which shall abridge the privileges or immunities of citizens of the United States; nor shall any State deprive any person of life, liberty, or property without due process of law; nor deny to any person within its jurisdiction the equal protection of the laws.

FIGURE 7.1 Constitutional Amendments Relating to Education

How will these constitutional amendments affect your teaching style?

REFLECT & WRITE

Courts usually cite one of the amendments in Figure 7.1 to justify their decision. Have these three amendments affected your educational life in any way? How might they affect you as a beginning teacher?

Federal Legislation

In addition to appropriating funds for education, the national government influences education through legislation, program initiatives, and the dissemination of information. As one example, the **No Child Left Behind Act** signed by President Bush in January 2002, reauthorizes the Elementary and Secondary Education Act originally passed in 1965. Currently, both houses of Congress are locked in heated debates over the reauthorization of the No Child Left Behind Act. Opponents of the act want to either eliminate it entirely or reduce the provisions of the law that provide for mandatory student testing. Time will tell how the reauthorization of NCLB plays out. Whatever happens, you will find that as a beginning teacher, the chances are good that you will teach a program supported in some way with federal dollars.

The DOE collects and disseminates education statistics, gives awards and grants, and promotes the cause of education. During the first decade of the twenty-first century, the DOE has played a more influential role in reforming and restructuring American education than at any time since its creation as a cabinet-level office.

Influence of the Executive Branch

National leaders advocate programs and practices they think are good for the nation's children and families. For example, President George W. Bush advocated for school choice, defined in Chapter 6 as the practice of letting parents choose the school(s) they want their children to attend. Today, many school dis-

No Child Left Behind Act   Signed by President Bush in 2002, this act reauthorized the Elementary and Secondary Education Act, originally passed in 1965.

What's *New* in Education?

Pay to Play

Greg Brynaert, athletic director at Romeo High School in Michigan, was sitting in his office a few days after the start of football practice in August when a ninth-grader showed up to turn in his uniform. He asked the boy why, and the answer tugged at his heart: "Because my family can't afford the $160 fee." That ninth-grader, a *Detroit News* study has found, is one of more than 88,000 southeastern Michigan students who pay a cumulative $10 million in fees to play sports during the school year—activities that once were considered vital to public school education and that were provided for free.

As school districts started to see expenses climb and revenues ebb, a *pay-to-play* system was adopted, wherein school districts charged fees for sports and other extracurricular activities. The other option was to not offer these activities at all. As a result of the pay-to-play system, thousands of middle- and high-school students simply walk away, victims of a system that shifts costs from schools to families.

In the majority of Michigan school districts, pay-to-play fees have risen steeply the past few years. In West Bloomfield, for exam-ple, a $50 fee begun in 2004 has risen $50 each September since, to $200 this year. Plymouth-Canton schools charged $125 two years ago, $150 last year and $160 this year. Bedford schools started its fee at $40 in the 2004–2005 school year; today it is $125.

According to Diane L. Hoff, associate professor of education at the University of Maine, who has studied pay-to-play, "Nationwide, there's about a 35 percent drop in participation when students are asked to pay for extracurricular activities." That, across the board, affects students of lower incomes and students who tend to be minority."

Source: F. Girard, "Pay-to-play saps parents' wallets, sidelines students," *The Detroit News*, October 5, 2007. (Online). Available at www.detnews.com/apps/pbcs.dll/article?AID=/20071005/SCHOOLS/710050413.

tricts have implemented choice programs that enable parents to send their children to schools within or outside a district. In addition, President Bush advocated for high and vigorous standards, testing, and accountability. As governor of Arkansas, former President Clinton presided over a governor's conference that initiated Goals 2000. In this program, the federal government established eight goals for America's schools, which laid the foundation for the current emphasis on such initiatives as school readiness, math and science skills, and parent/community participation.

_____

_____

_____

_____

_____

Roles of State Governments in Education

States play a powerful role in how schools are governed, what is taught, and how it is taught. Many governors are in the forefront of shaping education policy and initiatives in their state. For example, as governor of Arizona, Janet Napolitano was one of the nation's most innovative and influential educational leaders. Among the initiatives she championed were quality schools and voluntary full-day kindergarten for all Arizona children. She also provided record financial support for Arizona's universities and community colleges, recognizing the need for a well-educated workforce to ensure the success of Arizona's future.[7]

The Tenth Amendment gives responsibility for education to each of the 50 states. How the states use this power depends on each state and on the political and social climate of the times. For example, in the 1980s and 1990s, in response to the public's demand for school reform, many states became more directive and prescriptive in what they wanted students to achieve and in holding teachers and administrators accountable for students' achievement. This was a time of strong, top-down direction in an effort to "fix" the education system. The decade of 2000–2009 is known as the decade of standards, tests, and accountability. All three of these areas have had strong state backing and are discussed in Chapter 11.

The control and governance of education at the state and local levels are shown in Figure 7.2. Figure 7.3 shows four basic models for the structure of governance at the state level. The following sections describe the governing bodies involved.

State Boards of Education

The **National Association of State Boards of Education (NASBE)** is an association that represents state boards of education. The principal objectives of NASBE are to strengthen state leadership in educational policy making, to promote excellence in the education of all students, to advocate equality of access to educational opportunity, and to ensure continued citizen support for public education.[8]

■ **INTASC**

STANDARD 10   The teacher fosters relationships with school colleagues, parents, and agencies in the larger community to support students' learning and well-being.

National Association of State Boards of Education (NASBE)   An association that represents state boards of education.

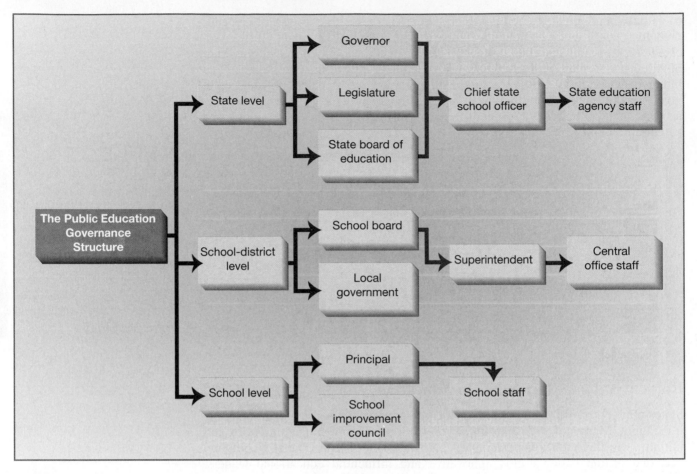

FIGURE 7.2 The Control and Governance of Education at the State and Local Levels

To the outsider, the governance and organization of education at the state level seems overwhelming—and it is! When you consider the number of schools that each state operates, the number of students and teachers, and the size of its budget; it is little wonder that states must have a considerable bureaucracy dedicated to educating the state's children.

Source: Center for Educational Networking, *Leading Change*, Winter 2004, Accessed November 5th, 2007, from http://cenmi.org/downloads/LC/W04/gov_structure_chart.pdf.

State boards of education exist in all states and generally have responsibility for education, including vocational education and in some cases postsecondary learning. Some states have two boards: one responsible for pre-K–12 and another responsible for higher education. Although the scope of the boards' responsibilities is defined differently in each state, common areas of jurisdiction include:

- Setting statewide curriculum standards
- Determining qualifications for professional education personnel, including teacher certification
- Making recommendations on state education statutes
- Adopting standards to ensure equal access and due process
- Undertaking quasi-legislative and judicial functions
- Administering federal assistance programs
- Formulating standards on school facilities

State boards of education also are involved in accrediting schools, disseminating information about education, and supporting and conducting research. State

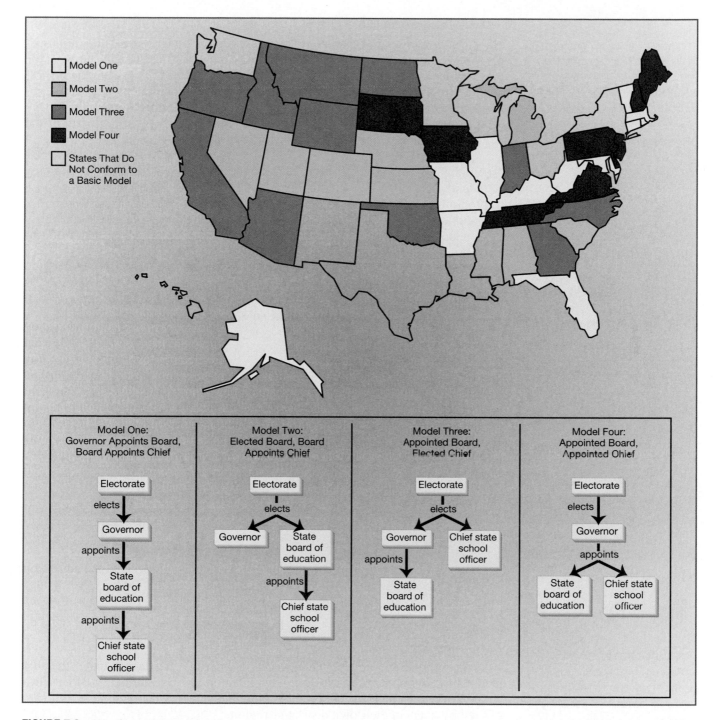

FIGURE 7.3   How States Govern Education

How does your state govern education?

Source: Indiana Education Policy Center, *State Education Governance Structures* (Denver, CO: Education Commission of the States, 2000). Copyright 2000 by Education Commission of the States. Reprinted by permission.

boards of education are very involved in creating "seamless" systems of education for pre-K–12 and pre-K–16. Florida reorganized its system to K–20 (kindergarten to graduate school), the first in the nation to do so. The Florida state board seeks to be the unified voice for education in the state.

State Standards Boards

All states except South Dakota have **state standards boards**, which are responsible for the governance and regulation of professional practice. These boards set the criteria for teacher certification and for entry into and dismissal from the profession. Membership on standards boards is usually by appointment by the state superintendent or state board of education. Teachers are included in the membership of state standards boards. For example, the Texas State Standards Board, of the Texas Education Agency, has the following functions:

- Administer and monitor compliance with education programs required by federal or state law, including federal funding and state funding for those programs
- Conduct research, analysis, and reporting to improve teaching and learning
- Conduct hearings involving state school law at the direction and under the supervision of the commissioner
- Establish and implement pilot programs
- Develop and implement a teacher recruitment program
- Carry out powers and duties related to adult and community education
- Review school district budgets, audit reports, and other fiscal reports[9]

State Departments of Education

When legislators and boards of education establish policies affecting education in each state, state departments of education help implement those policies. Major responsibilities of state departments of education include approving local districts' applications for federal funding and administering and monitoring the use of federal monies. For example, federal monies for specific programs and entitlements flow to local districts through the state departments of education. State departments have a stake in acquiring more responsibility and authority over federal revenues and how they are spent at the local level.

In addition to managing, monitoring, and distributing federal funding as it affects education, state departments of education have the following responsibilities:

- Overseeing public and private elementary, secondary, and vocational education
- Working cooperatively with the state legislature
- Providing for and promoting staff development
- Conducting public relations
- Monitoring school compliance with state regulations

For example, in Vermont, local standards boards were formed under the auspices of the Vermont Standards Board for Professional Educators (VSBPE). Educators in Vermont public schools are accountable to a board of their peers, who are elected by peers in their own district or region.

Each educator in the public schools must have a recommendation from the appropriate local or regional board to be relicensed. Within guidelines established by the VSBPE, each board sets local standards for high-quality professional development and relicensure. Each educator is accountable to the local or regional board for the development of an acceptable Individual Professional Development Plan, professional development necessary for relicensure, and a professional portfolio.[10]

In most states, the state department of education is headed by a person with overall responsibility for implementing educational policy in that state. This person is known as the State Secretary (or Director) of Education or the State Super-

In the Classroom
with Jack O'Connell

California's Superintendent of Public Instruction Sets Priorities

Jack O'Connell is California's State Superintendent of Public Instruction. He serves as Secretary and Executive Officer for the State Board of Education and is the chief executive officer of the Department of Education. Superintendent O'Connell's agenda for education in California is as follows:

- **Accountability:** Hold local education agencies accountable for student achievement in all programs and for all groups of students.
- **Building capacity:** Build local capacity to enable all students to achieve to state standards.
- **Professional development:** Expand and improve a system of recruiting, developing, and supporting teachers that instills excellence in every classroom, preschool through adult.
- **Technology:** Provide statewide leadership that promotes effective use of technology to improve teaching and learning; increase efficiency and effectiveness in administration of kindergarten through grade 12 education, including student record keeping and good financial

management practices; and provide broader and more effective communication among the home, school, district, county, and state.

- **Learning support systems:** Establish and foster systems of school, home, and community resources that provide the physical, emotional, and intellectual support that each student needs to succeed.
- **Adequate flexible funding:** Advocate for additional resources and additional flexibility, and provide statewide leadership that promotes good business practices, so that California schools can target their resources to ensure success for all students.
- **Department management:** Improve the effectiveness and efficiency of the department.

Learn more about California's Superintendent Jack O'Connell at www.cde.ca.gov/eo/index.asp.

Source: California Department of Education. (2006). *Mission and vision.* (Online). Available at www.cde.ca.gov/eo/mn/mv. Accessed November 5, 2007.

intendent of Education (or of Public Instruction). The *In the Classroom with Jack O'Connell* illustrates the complexities of a state superintendent's job.

Influence of State Governors

The **National Governors' Association (NGA)** is an organization of state governors devoted to addressing problems common to all states. State governors play a leading role in ongoing reform in education. For example, one of the NGA's initiatives is to support expanded learning opportunities (ELOs). ELOs, including after-school, summer learning, and extended-day programs, provide students opportunities to learn outside the traditional school day. "Governors recognize the potential of ELOs to improve overall student success," says John Thomasian, director of the NGA Center. "These summits support governors' efforts to make explicit connections between ELOs and related policy priorities, such as high school reform, adolescent literacy, and early childhood education efforts."[11]

National Governors' Association (NGA) An organization of state governors devoted to addressing problems common to all the states; reflects governors' increasing leadership role in ongoing education reform and change efforts.

REFLECT & WRITE

Is it good public policy for each state to operate its state system of education independent from those of other states? Some school critics say that there should be much more unity between states. What do you think?

_____

_____

_____

_____

_____

Roles of Intermediate Education Agencies

The governance of education involves cooperation among states and localities through the actions of intermediate agencies. These agencies are called **intermediate educational units (IEUs)**, also known as regional educational units (REUs), regional educational service areas (RESAs), or educational service agencies (ESAs). Intermediate units are designed to provide services that individual districts might not be able to afford on their own, thus maximizing existing resources and promoting interdistrict collaboration. In New York, the intermediate educational unit is the Board of Cooperative Educational Services (BOCES). The Monroe number 1 BOCES develops programs to meet the diverse needs of general, special, talented, and at-risk students. BOCES provides unique and innovative solutions for the complex challenges of its member school districts. These varied programs enable districts to meet the needs of general, adult, special, and emotionally and medically fragile students. As students' needs change, BOCES programs adapt in response to these emerging needs.[12]

Another type of intermediate agency, the **Council of Chief State School Officers (CCSSO)**, is composed of state commissioners or superintendents of education and provides a forum for interstate discussion and information exchange on educational advances and issues. The chief state school officer is appointed by either the governor of a state or the state board of education. One of the programs CCSSO sponsors is the National Teacher of the Year Program.

Intermediate educational units (IEUs)   Educational service organizations that provide school districts human and material services and programs.

Council of Chief State School Officers (CCSSO)   An intermediate agency, composed of state commissioners or superintendents of education, that provides a forum for interstate discussion and information exchange on educational advances and issues.

REFLECT & WRITE

Over the last decade, there has been a growing trend for state governors and legislators to exert more control over education. Do you think this is a good trend? Why or why not?

_____

_____

_____

_____

_____

Roles of Local Government in Education

In educational policy and issues, local government refers to local boards of education, which are the governing bodies for schools that make decisions affecting education at the district and city levels. Boards of education implement state regulations and policies, make and implement local policies, tax residents to raise funds, incur debt, build facilities, hire and pay school personnel, create the curriculum, and respond to community needs through special programs and initiatives. The structure of governance at the local district level is shown in Figure 7.4.

■ INTASC

STANDARD 7   The teacher plans instruction based upon knowledge of subject matter, students, the community, and curriculum goals.

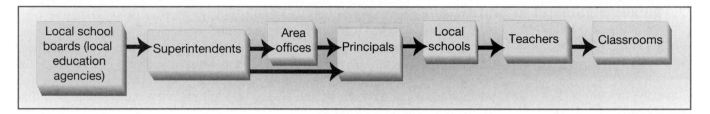

FIGURE 7.4   Control and Governance of Education at the Local Level

The organization of schooling at the local level follows a top-down model as depicted above. However, at the schoolhouse level, there is more shared responsibility and decision making.

REFLECT & WRITE

A major trend is for more decision making to occur at the local school and classroom levels, but federal and state governments are stressing standards and accountability. How do you think these two trends will affect you as a beginning teacher?

Local Education Agencies

School districts, often referred to as the **local education agency (LEA)**, come in all sizes and shapes. The largest school district is New York City schools.

Local education agency (LEA)   Local school districts.

The geographic area encompassed by a school district takes many forms. The state of Hawaii has one school district, although it is divided into seven administrative areas. Some states—such as Florida, Georgia, Kentucky, Maryland, Virginia, and Utah—are organized along county lines. Some cities, such as Baltimore, exist as a school district within a county system. Many big cities—such as New York, Los Angeles, Chicago, Philadelphia, Memphis, Milwaukee, Houston, Dallas, and Albuquerque—operate their own school districts.

In many states, such as Pennsylvania, the township is a common local political and administrative unit. School district boundaries often are the same as townships, with the townships operating the school districts. Sometimes the townships operate only elementary schools; junior, middle, and high school students attend schools in merged or consolidated school districts.

Since the mid 1970s, the trend has been for small school districts to merge into larger school districts that cut across township and county lines. The merging of school districts and the creation of regional schools combine resources and may serve students better. There are currently 14,205 school districts, down from 14,859 in 2001.[13]

● **Your Turn**

Your state has recently rewrote its guidelines for local school boards. You have been asked to write the procedure for selecting the one nonvoting student who will sit on the board. What selection criteria will you recommend?

■ **INTASC**

STANDARD 10 The teacher fosters relationships with school colleagues, parents, and agencies in the larger community to support students' learning and well-being.

Independent school districts cross city and county boundaries and are often the result of legislative action. Independent school districts often are regional school districts serving large numbers of students. Texas, for example, has independent school districts that cut across town and county boundaries.

Local Boards of Education

Authority for education in the states resides in state departments of education, but the responsibility for education at the local level is delegated to local boards of education. Local boards are composed of five to nine members who are directly elected by voters or who are appointed by mayors or other public officials. Board politics can be highly entwined with local municipal politics. Although the goal is to provide the best possible education for everyone, how to achieve this goal, how much to spend, and what to spend it on are issues of perennial contention at the local level. In reality, school boards have only the powers delegated to them by the states. In addition, they must function within local, state, and federal laws.

Individual school board members cannot act independently; rather, the board must act as a whole. This principle of the board acting as a whole applies in several ways. The board makes decisions as a body at legally called public meetings. Board members cannot make decisions for the board on their own.

Superintendents of Schools

Administration of the local school district is vested in superintendents, who are appointed or elected by the local board of education. Generally, superintendents are hired for a contracted period of time—for example, 4 or 5 years. However, superintendents serve at the pleasure of the board, so when the political makeup of a board changes or if the board is not satisfied with the job done, then their contract is terminated or bought out. Big-city superintendents in particular have demanding jobs and often have short and tempestuous tenures. (See *In the Classroom with Superintendent Beverly Hall.*)

Superintendents' responsibilities include working in close consultation with the local board of education as they plan, organize, direct, control, and coordinate the activities of the school district. Superintendents also have to work collaboratively and collegially with school district personnel, labor leaders, community leaders, and appointed and elected officials on local, regional, and national fronts.

What are the powers and responsibilities of a local school board? How are the powers of local school boards limited? How do local education agencies influence education at the district and school level?

In the Classroom

with Superintendent
Beverly Hall

*Top Administrator Focuses on
Standards and the
Achievement Gap*

Dr. Beverly Hall is the superintendent of Atlanta Public Schools in Georgia. In 2006, she was honored with the Council of the Great City Schools National Urban School Superintendent of the Year Award.

Under the leadership of Dr. Beverly L. Hall, the Atlanta, Georgia, Public Schools have seen achievement rise and the achievement gap shrink. In the following interview she had with *Education World* (EW), she discusses her thoughts on how to improve education in urban schools.

EW: What are your goals as superintendent of the Atlanta Public Schools?

Dr. Hall: Our overarching goal is to make the Atlanta Public Schools a high-performing urban school system. In order to do this, we must increase the number of students meeting and exceeding state standards while closing the achievement gap.

EW: Which accomplishments while in office have been the most satisfying for you?

Dr. Hall: The achievement level of our elementary schools has been the most satisfying so far. I am also pleased that we have been able to renovate or reconstruct the majority of our school facilities. Finally, we have seen improvements in our graduation rates.

EW: What do you think are the biggest challenges facing urban schools today?

Dr. Hall: We still have a lot of work to do to get our middle and high school students to perform at high levels and

to get more of them graduating prepared for postsecondary options. We need teachers who are better prepared to teach in urban school systems, and who have a good grasp of their content areas. We also need professional development of high quality for current staff so they can teach all students to the standards. We need more time, that is, longer school days and longer school hours, along with the necessary resources to provide a quality education for our students.

EW: What do you want people to know about urban schools?

Dr. Hall: Urban schools continue to improve, and more students are learning to higher standards. In spite of all the challenges that they face, when given the support and the resources, urban educators are producing good results, especially in our elementary schools. Urban schools are not afraid to be measured against higher standards and they are confronting the achievement gap. There are many examples of fine urban schools all across this country that should be highlighted so that the general population understands that indeed all children can learn—including children in urban schools.

To learn more about improving urban schools go to www.cgcs.org/.

Source: E. Delisio, "Top administrator focuses on standards, achievement gap." *Education World*, December 6, 2006. Available at www.education-world.com/a_issues/chat/chat197.shtml. Accessed October 31, 2007.

More and more big urban school districts are turning to noneducators to help them address the multitude of complex problems involved in ensuring a high-quality education for all children. These new leaders come with backgrounds in law, politics, the military, and business. Don Gaetz was once the CEO of a health care company. Now he is superintendent of Okaloosa County, Florida, schools, which has an enrollment of 30,000 students in 40 schools. Says Gaetz, "I became interested in what we could do to bring in business practices, not just to improve [school] finances but also academic achievement." In New York City, Joel Klein, former chairman and CEO of Bertelsmann (and one-time antitrust czar at the U.S. Department of Justice), today serves as schools chancellor. In Los Angeles, retired U.S. Navy Vice Admiral David L. Brewer III replaced Roy Romer, the former governor of Colorado. These executives-turned-education-leaders have a number of reasons for making the switch. Some believe that only an overhaul of public schools can close the growing gap between the wealthy and the poor in the United States—a threat, they believe, to the fabric of American democracy. Others cite a desire to "give back," a repayment to society for their own good fortune in their work lives. "I always attributed [a successful career] to the strength of my education in the early years, and many minorities just don't get that start," says Gasper Mir, cofounder of a Houston public accounting firm who took a top post in the Houston school system.[14]

REFLECT & WRITE

Do you feel that noneducators offer a useful perspective to school districts? Can you think of other occupations than those mentioned that might lend themselves to offering new insights on how to improve education?

HOW ARE SCHOOLS HELD ACCOUNTABLE?

Accountability is the watchword of the public schools today. From boards of education, superintendents, and principals to teachers and students, everyone is being held accountable. The current emphasis on accountability is the result of the No Child Left Behind Act (NCLB).

NCLB and School Accountability

The No Child Left Behind Act, which you have read about in different chapters throughout this book, was created to mandate accountability. The provisions of the NCLB hold that all schools and districts must meet state standards by 2014. The overriding goal of the NCLB is to improve student achievement and to close the achievement gap between white and minority students.

The NCLB requires states to administer standards-based assessments in reading, math, and science with the goal of having all students proficient in those subjects by 2014.[15] Many school districts and schools across the country issue school accountability report cards. For example, the report card for Chavez Elementary School in the San Diego Independent School District reports that 26.7 percent of its students scored at or above the 50th percentile in reading achievement.[16] In the Florida report cards, the Gadsden County public schools earned a D, and the Brevard County public schools earned an A.[17] These report cards are readily available to parents and the public.

Teacher Accountability

Teachers are also being held accountable for student learning. In fact, teacher accountability and student learning go hand in hand. According to the National Education Association, accountability is achieved in a number of ways:

> NEA supports strong accountability of teachers, students, and schools. A good accountability system uses multiple measures of progress, instead of relying

Go to MyEducationLab and select the topic "Standards and Accountability" and read the article "The Purpose of No Child Left Behind." How will this affect the way you teach?

What's  in Education?

Bloomberg Unveils Performance Pay for Teachers

After months of negotiations, the Bloomberg administration and the New York City teachers' union arrived at an agreement on a performance-pay plan. Under the agreement, bonuses for teachers are based on the test scores of students at high poverty schools. The merit pay plan is a major breakthrough for the New York school administration, who wanted a merit pay system for high-performing teachers.

Teachers' unions are traditionally opposed to merit pay programs, which break from salary schedules based on seniority and degrees. However, across the country, merit pay plans are gaining in popularity.

Source: E. Gootman, "Bloomberg unveils performance pay for teachers," *New York Times*, October 12, 2007. Available at www.nytimes.com/2007/10/17/nyregion/17cndteachers.html?ex=1350273600&en=a859e327c12555af&ei=5118&partner=rssaol&emc=rss. Accessed November 7, 2007.

solely on standardized test scores. Schools, teachers, and students should all be held to high standards, and NEA believes that accountability should be shared by schools, education employees, policymakers, and parents—with the ultimate goal of helping every student succeed.[18]

Teachers are being held accountable for student learning, and they are increasingly being rewarded for it in the form of **performance pay**, which is awarded in the form of bonuses or raises that are based on student achievement. As the accompanying *What's New in Education?* describes, more school districts, including the New York City school district, the nation's largest, are installing performance pay systems.

Performance pay The policy of awarding teachers bonuses or raises based on student achievement or other criteria.

REFLECT & WRITE

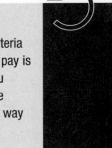

Do you believe that the criteria for receiving performance pay is fair to all teachers? Do you believe that it will motivate teachers to reevaluate the way they teach? Explain.

HOW ARE SCHOOLS GOVERNED AND ADMINISTERED?

Governance and administration at the school level are complex processes that involve principals, teachers, students, parents, and community leaders. **Administration** is the management of the affairs of the school and involves putting into everyday practice the policies established by the state legislature, state board of education, and the local board of education. The administration of a school involves, for example, scheduling classes, teacher assignments, use of facilities, and evaluation of teachers and staff. Although there is always a need for administration, there is less of a tendency today to invest the sole responsibility for

Administration The management of the affairs of a school or education agency based on the policies established by the state legislature, state board of education, and local board of education.

administration with one person. The preferred approach to administration is one that involves as many of the school's stakeholders as possible.

Principals and Assistant Principals

At the school level, the principal is responsible for the management of human and material resources to effectively support teachers' teaching and children's learning. Some principals manage more than one school.

How the school is organized also depends on its size and the personnel employed. Although much of education is organized on a top-down, or hierarchical, model, there is currently more emphasis on cooperation and collaboration among principals, teachers, and parents in all matters related to how schools function. The principal's role thus goes beyond management and administration.

Effective principals emphasize programs; set overall school direction; are concerned about building staff morale; and, even more important, provide a rationale for their priorities. Also, they employ deliberative models for problem solving and skillfully empower their staffs to develop a sense of ownership in the arrangement and direction of the school.

Today, there is less talk about managing schools and more talk about leadership. As a beginning teacher, you will be called on and looked to for leadership. When you think of a leader and leadership, what do you think of? Perhaps you think of leaders as people who take charge and get things done their way or the way "things should be done." Or, perhaps you think of a leader as a person who empowers others and shares decision making to achieve mutually agreed-on goals. This latter conception of leaders as enablers is more in keeping with how school leadership is envisioned today, with teachers as leaders in participatory school-based management.

For example, in characterizing the principal of an award-winning elementary school, the faculty said, "She is totally nonthreatening—she gives us a sense of our own importance. We are free to make mistakes, and we are not afraid to voice our opinion about the curriculum, the students, and school policies." Embedded in what the teachers said about their principal are attributes that Thomas Sergiovanni characterizes as moral leadership. Sergiovanni believes that moral leadership occurs when teachers and administrators are guided by professionalism and the guiding principle is not "what is rewarded gets done," but "what is good gets done."[19]

Go to MyEducationLab and select the topic "Governance and School Administration" then watch the video "Peer Observation and Evaluation." Answer the questions that follow.

■ INTASC

STANDARD 9   The teacher is a reflective practitioner who continually evaluates the effects of his/her choices and actions on others (students, parents, and other professionals in the learning community) and who actively seeks out opportunities to grow professionally.

⟳ REFLECT & WRITE

What do you consider to be good criteria for effective leadership? As a first-year teacher, how will you know good leadership when you see it?

_____

_____

_____

_____

_____

School-based management (SBM)   A governance process based on the premise that people who are affected by decisions should be involved in making them; also called site-based management.

School-Based Management

In many schools across the country, a new form of governance is changing how decisions are made and how things get done. This new form of governance is **school-based management (SBM)**, and shared decision making. School-based management is designed to empower those affected by decisions by involving them in the decision-making process. The rationale behind school-based management is that if people are involved in the decision making, they will be more likely to carry out the decisions. In schools where school-based management has had a major impact, teachers report they use innovative practices.

As a beginning teacher, you probably will have opportunities to participate in school-based decision making. For example, at the Jefferson County Public Schools in Golden, Colorado, groups use school-based decision making to facilitate the following:

- A common student-centered vision
- A climate of trust
- Respect for diverse ideas and interests
- Open dialogue and debate
- A shared leadership, accountability, authority, and responsibility
- An actively involved, broad-based representation of employees, parents, students, and the community

The goal of school-based decision making is to ensure the staff, parent, and community involvement needed will accomplish the district's mission through its strategic plan. The district's mission is "To provide a quality education that prepares all children for a successful future." All Jefferson County schools are evaluating how they use the school-based decision-making process to ensure they are achieving accreditation expectations.[20]

School-based decision making depends on teachers being leaders. As the definition and role of being a professional in education continues to expand, teachers are challenged to lead—in the classroom, the school, the district, and beyond.

Who is involved in school-based management? What conditions and resources are needed for school-based management to succeed?

REFLECT & WRITE

Would you like to find a position in a school that uses school-based management? Why or why not?

School Advisory Councils

A major factor in school improvement efforts is the **school advisory council (SAC)**. SAC membership generally consists of school and community stakeholders—students, teachers, parents, community leaders, administrators, and other school staff. As you enter the profession, there is a good possibility you will be involved in some way with SAC responsibilities. The primary purpose of advisory councils depends on the state and school district. For example, in Florida each school must have an SAC. Each Florida SAC includes the principal and an "appropriately balanced" number of "stakeholders." These stakeholders are individuals who represent the ethnic, racial, and economic makeup of a given school's community. Each SAC is responsible for strategic planning for the school improvement plan. The organization

School advisory council (SAC) SAC membership consists of school and community stakeholders—students, teachers, parents, community leaders, administrators, and other school staff—who make decisions and recommendations regarding school operation.

works jointly with the principal and staff after analyzing relevant data.[21] Also, schools establish SACs for special purposes. For example, Lakeville Area Public Schools in Lakewood, Minnesota, has a district Chemical Health Advisory Committee. The purpose of the committee is to unite students, parents, staff, and community members who are interested in increasing youth participation in healthy, constructive activities and decrease participation in high-risk activities. The Chemical Health Advisory Council builds awareness of adolescent chemical use/abuse problems within the community.[22]

REFLECT & WRITE

Not everyone agrees with the practice of involving parents/families in decisions about school policies and programs. What do you see as the pros and cons of involving parents in school decision making?

_____

_____

_____

_____

_____

HOW IS EDUCATION FUNDED?

■ **INTASC**

STANDARD 10 The teacher fosters relationships with school colleagues, parents, and agencies in the larger community to support students' learning and well-being.

The funding of American education is a major and costly enterprise. In the United States, schooling is big business. The public school education enterprise is enormous, involving children and youth from birth to age 21. More than 3.2 million teachers and 2.3 million administrative and support staff in 97,000 school districts are involved in the process of educating the 49.6 million students in the nation's public elementary and secondary schools. Total expenditures for elementary and secondary schools are more than $489.4 billion annually.[23] The cost of educating American children and youth is put into better perspective when you consider that the per-pupil expenditure to educate each student in the public schools is about $9,969 per year.[24]

The majority of financial support for public elementary and secondary schools comes from three sources: the federal government, state governments, and local communities. Other sources include businesses, industry, and foundations. Figure 7.5 shows the proportion of funding from the principal sources.

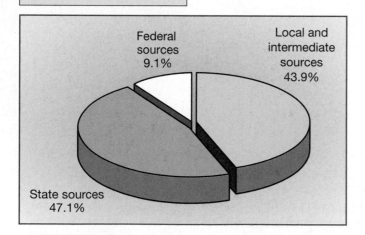

FIGURE 7.5 Sources of Public Revenue for Public Elementary and Secondary Schools

Local and state sources are the primary sources of revenue for public elementary and secondary schools while the federal government offers the least amount of funds.

Source: National Center for Education Statistics, _Digest of Education Statistics, 2006_ (Washington, DC: U.S. Government Printing Office, 2006).

Federal Support and Mandates

Although education is a state responsibility, the federal government in 2006 spent an estimated $70.7 billion on elementary and secondary programs.[25] Total federal funding for education is more than $558 billion from a variety of federal departments and agencies. In 2004, public elementary and secondary schools received 9.1 percent of their revenue from the federal government, which amounted to about $41.9 billion.[26] Federal expenditures have increased from $202 billion in 1990 to $333 billion in 2006.

Part of the federal government's support of public schools comes through specific legislation. **Categorical grants**, also called block grants, are designed to help particular groups of students. For example, in 1964 Congress passed the Economic Opportunity Act, which authorized the formation of Head Start in 1965 (see Chapter 3). Head Start serves about 30 percent of the nation's economically disadvantaged preschool children and greatly affects the curriculum of kindergarten and first-grade students. In 2007, Head Start had a budget of $6.8 billion.[27]

Regardless of how a state or school district receives federal funds, it has to comply with the federal spending guidelines attached to the funds. Recipients of federal funding also have to agree to comply with all other existing federal rules and regulations. In this way, the federal government exerts considerable influence over educational practice. When and if school districts and states do not comply with conditions of federal funding, they can lose that funding, be fined for noncompliance, or lose the right to future federal funding.

? *What Does This Mean for You?*

If you have not thought much about school funding at the state level, consider this scenario.

In a small river town in southern Illinois, Sarah Delaney prepares to start the day in her fourth-grade classroom. Hundreds of miles away in a northern suburb of Chicago, Albert Thorpe is getting ready to greet his fourth-graders. Today, both classes will take the Illinois Standards Achievement Test. The students and teachers in both classrooms will be held accountable for the state educational performance and content standards. Both teachers worked hard to prepare their students, and both classes studied diligently. Both teachers have taught for 30 years, both graduated from a state-accredited teacher education program, and both went on to earn a master's degree.

Despite these similar backgrounds and accountabilities, when Sarah retires in another 10 years, she will receive a pension of $37,000 a year; Albert's annual pension will be closer to $60,000. Over the course of their careers, Sarah will have earned about $250,000 less than Albert. This discrepancy exists because the state funding formula relies heavily on local property taxes. Almost every aspect of the education program is similarly affected in the two schools—not only salaries, but also instructional resources and physical plant. So funding really does matter.

Categorical (block) grants   Federal government support of the public schools that comes through specific legislation designed to help particular groups of students; sometimes called block grants.

REFLECT & WRITE

School districts embrace federal funding for special programs, but they don't always want to embrace the strings that are attached! Why do you think this is so? What solutions would you propose for this dilemma?

_____

_____

_____

_____

_____

Funding at the State Level

Historically, local property taxes were the major source of state funding for education. However, in 2004, 47.1 percent of funding came from the state level, whereas funding from local sources was 43.9 percent.[28]

All states have a variety of ways of collecting money to support education, including sales taxes, income taxes, inheritance taxes, various license and occupation fees, and state lotteries. One of the reasons sales taxes are popular is that they are relatively painless, because people pay in small amounts as they spend and because the state collects the revenue from businesses rather than from each individual taxpayer.

State Funding Formulas

Flat grants Provide equal funding based on a district's average daily attendance, which is established during "count weeks," generally during October and February; some states give variable amounts of funding based on particular needs.

States employ a variety of ways to distribute money to local districts. **Flat grants** provide equal funding based on a district's average daily attendance and calculated on enrollments in "count weeks," generally during October and February. As a beginning teacher you will be asked to help provide accurate attendance data, since student average daily attendance helps determine state funding. In addition, school districts now aggressively enforce mandatory attendance laws in an effort to improve attendance, which determines state reimbursements. Some districts threaten truants with jail time in their efforts to improve attendance. For example, Illinois State Attorney Charles Garnati held a press conference reminding parents of the strict truancy laws governing Williamson County. He said that parents who allowed their children to remain truant from school would be prosecuted. Furthermore, he warned that older children who were truant from school could face consequences as well. "I want to remind everybody in the county that we do take truancy very seriously in Williamson County," Garnati said. "I think it's important to point that out early in the school year."[29]

Foundation grants Grants based on the property values in a school district. Funding is usually in inverse relation to community wealth; school districts in poorer communities with low property values receive more grant funding than do school districts in more affluent communities.

Some states use variable flat grants and give variable amounts of funding based on particular needs. A district with a bilingual program, for example, would receive a larger grant than would a district without such services, because such programs are more expensive to operate. **Foundation grants** guarantee each district a certain amount of funding, which varies inversely with community wealth. Poor communities with low revenues from property taxes receive more money than wealthy communities. States constantly seek funding formulas that will be effective and fair.

REFLECT & WRITE

Both local and state governments constantly look for ways to equitably fund schools at the level needed to provide a quality education for all students. What two recommendations would you make to state legislators about this?

_____

_____

_____

_____

_____

• *Your Turn*

Your school district just received a $1 million grant to "improve education at the local level." You chair the committee that will recommend to the school board how this money should be allocated. What steps would you take first in determining the schools' needs?

Funding at the Local Level

About 44 percent of the funding for schools comes from the local level (see Figure 7.5). The majority of local funding support for schools is raised from property taxes, which are based on the assessed value of real estate—homes, commercial land, and buildings.[30] The primary advantage of the property tax is that it is a reliable and steady source of revenue. A major problem with funding schools through property taxes, however, is the inequity it produces. In districts and neighborhoods where property values are high, property taxes provide greater funding for schools than in districts and neighborhoods where property values are low.

This means that some school districts, because of low property values, cannot support their schools at the same level as other higher-value districts, even if they tax their property owners heavily. This inability of local school districts to ade-

If professional sports teams can sell the naming rights for their stadiums and other facilities, why can't cash-starved public schools? Why not indeed! Chances are that a school stadium, gymnasium, or building near you is—or will soon be—"branded" with a corporate name. This strategy can bring in dollars.

quately support education is especially evident in rural and urban areas. Rural southern states tend to be poorer in terms of income and property values; therefore, the South spends less on education than does the North. Also, in inner cities, where property values are low, the ability to support schools is less than it is in wealthier suburban neighborhoods.

Another problem with raising money through property taxes is that the tax falls mainly on homeowners, who are increasingly less willing to have their taxes raised to support schools. Funding of schools at the local level can be a problem when taxpayers set limits on what school boards can spend on education. Given these limitations, the amount of money to operate schools may be insufficient, and students and teachers may not have the materials and resources needed for adequate teaching and learning. Some schools find alternative ways to cut costs, as the *What's New in Education?* illustrates.

■ **INTASC**

STANDARD 10 The teacher fosters relationships with school colleagues, parents, and agencies in the larger community to support students' learning and well-being.

What's *New* in Education?

Schools Find Corporate Sponsors

A growing number of cash-strapped schools are selling naming rights to gyms, locker rooms, and even the principal's office. Kitchens at two Sheboygan, Wisconsin, high schools will soon be called the Kohler Credit Union kitchens, thanks to a $45,000 donation. The cafeterias are up for grabs for $300,000. Ben Salzmann, CEO of Acuity in Sheboygan, eagerly paid $650,000 to put the name of his insurance company on two new high school field houses forever.

Naming rights for school facilities are handled by the Sheboygan Public Education Foundation, a nonprofit foundation that came up with the idea to help pay for programs and facilities that the Sheboygan Area School District cannot afford, foundation president David Sachse says.

Without the money, schools superintendent Joe Sheehan says, ". . . we'd still be surviving, offering our kids a strong base, but nowhere near where we are with the help of this program."

Source: J. Keen, "Wisconsin schools find corporate sponsors," *USA Today*, July 26, 2007. (Online). Available at www.usatoday.com/news/nation/2006-07-27-naming-rights_x.htm. Accessed November 7, 2007.

⟲ REFLECT &
  WRITE

As more school districts become
starved for cash, what strategies
can you think of to raise money?

_____

_____

_____

_____

_____

Private Funding

Foundations provide support for many kinds of educational programs. Grants and other private funding illustrate that foundations and businesses are willing to donate money to schools, but only if the funding is targeted to reforming education, with particular emphasis on urban, minority, and special education. Donors want their financial efforts to have significant and measurable outcomes.

Two notable examples of private funding include the Bill and Melinda Gates Foundation and the Annenberg Foundation. The Bill and Melinda Gates foundation made a $122 million investment to fund Washington, D.C., schools in order to create high school and college scholars from among some of the city's poorest and lowest-achieving students. It is one of the foundation's largest investments for education to date. As a result of this grant, more than 2,000 students will become D.C. Achievers over the next 15 years and receive college scholarships of up to $10,000 each year for a maximum of 5 years. The money is meant to jumpstart low high school and college graduation rates among students living in parts of northeast and southeast Washington, where statistics show that within a span of 5 years, 66 percent of high school students fail to complete high school and just one in 20 high school graduates earns a college degree.[31]

The Annenberg Foundation donated $20 million to a nonprofit group working to bolster New York City's small middle and high schools, which are a hallmark of Mayor Michael R. Bloomberg's effort to turn around the troubled system. The group, New Visions for Public Schools, has helped create 112 of the more than 200 small schools that have opened throughout New York City since 1993. "I think that there's both anecdotal as well as hard evidence now that small schools are producing some very good results for students and teachers and school staff alike," said Dr. Gail Levin, executive director of the foundation. "These small schools are here to stay. We want them to be part of the story that allows them to stay."[32]

These are just two examples of private donations made to enhance educational opportunities for children. Many foundations throughout the country are offering students opportunities that they would not have had otherwise.

Go to MyEducationLab and
select the topic "Financing
Schools" and read the
article "The Battle Over
Commercialized Schools." Answer
the questions that follow.

⟲ REFLECT &
  WRITE

Where do you stand on the
liberal-conservative continuum?
How do your political views affect
how you believe schools should
be governed and financed?

_____

_____

_____

_____

WHAT ISSUES OF GOVERNANCE AND FINANCE AFFECT EDUCATION TODAY?

Issues of governance and finance constantly face the public. Furthermore, these issues are intertwined: Issues of governance almost always raise accompanying issues of finance; solutions to a particular finance issue almost always raise issues of governance. These issues reflect basic contradictions in the politics and economics of American education, as Figure 7.6 suggests.

Federal versus State Control

According to a 2007 public opinion survey, 49 percent of the American public believes the local school board should have the greatest influence in deciding what is taught in the public schools.[33] This is an 11 percent decrease from a decade ago, when 60 percent of the public felt that local boards of education should make such decisions. It is fair to say that the public is showing an increasing willingness to shift decision-making authority over local public schools to other levels of government.

The issues involved in national versus state control of education have to do primarily with who will decide what is best for students and what they will learn. On the one hand, some believe it is in the national interest for the federal government to set standards and specify what students should know and be able to do.

■ **INTASC**

STANDARD 9   The teacher is a reflective practitioner who continually evaluates the effects of his/her choices and actions on others (students, parents, and other professionals in the learning community) and who actively seeks out opportunities to grow professionally.

■ **INTASC**

STANDARD 10   The teacher fosters relationships with school colleagues, parents, and agencies in the larger community to support students' learning and well-being.

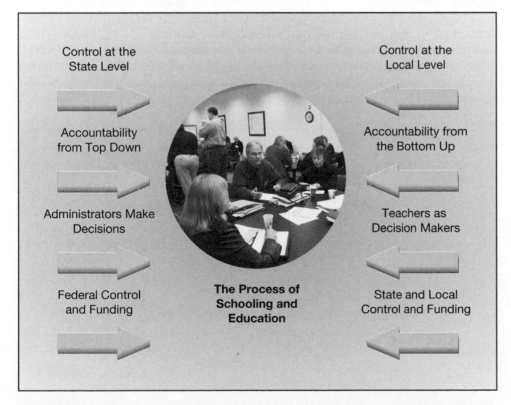

Control at the State Level

Accountability from Top Down

Administrators Make Decisions

Federal Control and Funding

The Process of Schooling and Education

Control at the Local Level

Accountability from the Bottom Up

Teachers as Decision Makers

State and Local Control and Funding

FIGURE 7.6   Contradictions in the Organization and Governance of American Education

In the debate over how to best fund schools, there is a constant and inevitable tension between state governments, who maintain constitutional oversight of public education, and local districts, who feel they understand their own needs better than state legislators do.

On the other hand, some believe that states are most qualified and constitutionally mandated to make all decisions about learning and teaching.

State versus Local Control

States differ in the ways they concentrate power at the state level. In particular, states such as California, Florida, and Texas, more than other states, tend to concentrate authority and power at the state level. In fact, over the last several decades, a significant trend in American education is the continuing concentration of power and control of education at the state level.

Local control over implementing and achieving state mandates and rules leads inevitably to conflicts. For example, although states delegate responsibility for operating schools to local districts, states remain responsible for the quality and effectiveness of the educational process. If local school districts fail to do their job, then cities and states, under provisions of the NCLB, can take over the school district. This is what happened in Philadelphia. Since 2002, Philadelphia has been the site of the nation's largest experiment in the state takeover and private management of public schools. Fed up with years of low achievement and budget crises in the Philadelphia schools, the Pennsylvania state government seized control of the district in 2002 and replaced its school board with an appointed School Reform Commission. The commission hired Paul Vallas, former chief executive officer of the Chicago public schools, to take the helm in Philadelphia. Vallas instituted sweeping changes. He modernized efforts in hiring and retraining qualified teachers, launched an ambitious program of school construction and renovation, pushed vigorously for an upgraded curriculum, and balanced the budget. He mandated frequent assessments, a zero-tolerance discipline policy, assistance for low-performing schools, extended day and summer school for poorly performing students, and the dismantling of middle schools in favor of K–8 schools. These district-wide initiatives applied equally to all schools, including those operated by private providers. The most controversial change of all was the diverse provider model: turning over management of 45 of the district's elementary and middle schools to seven private managers.[34] Under the accountability provisions of NCLB, it is likely that state takeovers of school districts will accelerate.

Go to MyEducationLab and select the topic "Governance and School Administration" and read the article "The Trouble with Takeovers." Answer the questions that follow.

REFLECT & WRITE

More and more, teachers are becoming political activists. They see themselves as key players in decisions about how schools are controlled and funded. Identify two ways you will be involved in educational activities related to governance and finance.

_____

_____

_____

_____

_____

Funding Equity

One of the problems in funding education is that great disparity can exist both between and within states for the support of education. Figure 7.7 shows per-pupil expenditures on education for each state. Of all states, Alaska spends the most per

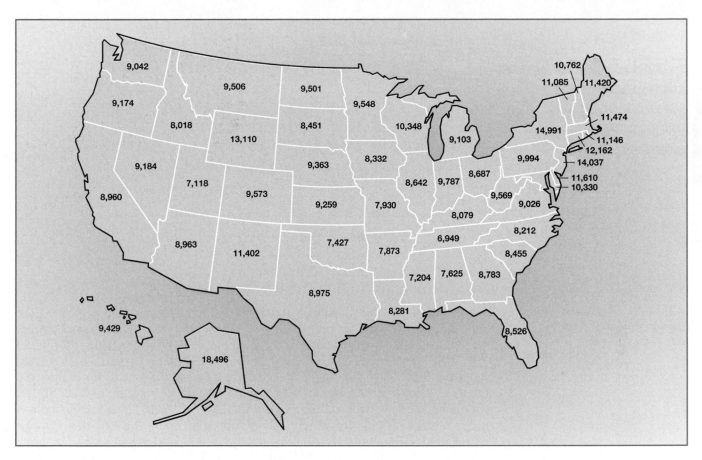

FIGURE 7.7   Per-Pupil Expenditure, 2005

Per-pupil expenditure varies from state to state. Expenditure is greatest in Alaska and lowest in Tennessee.

Source: National Center for Education Statistics, *Common Core of Data, National Public Financial Survey, 2005.* (Online). Available at nces.ed.gov/ccd/.

pupil, at $18,496. In the lower 48 states, New York spends the most at $14,991 per pupil, and Tennessee spends the least with $6,949.[35] These figures reflect comparative wealth and costs of living in the two states.

Funding equity issues relate to the unequal ability of school districts to pay for quality education. Districts where the property values and wages are low have a harder time raising the tax dollars they need to adequately support their schools. Similarly, rural districts have a lower tax base because agricultural land is taxed at a lower level than residential or commercial property. A recurring challenge for educators and citizens is to find ways of equalizing the support for education in all school districts.

The issue of tax equity is related to funding equity. According to a public opinion survey, a minority of respondents (21 percent) said they think using property taxes to finance schools is fair.[36] This attitude helps explain why citizen tax revolts have increased in frequency. The taxpayers' revolt began in California and has spread to other states. These tax reform efforts seek to limit the amount of revenue that can be raised through property taxes, with state aid replacing lost local revenues. There has been a consequent increase of state funding to local districts over the past decade. State aid can mitigate the inequities that result from primary reliance on property taxes, especially in districts with a property tax base that is

Funding equity   Involves issues of equable funding; relates to the unequal ability of school districts to pay for quality education. Some states provide additional funding to compensate for school districts' inability to adequately fund education.

eroding due to demographic changes, declining property values, and business and industry closings or downsizing.

REFLECT & WRITE

How do differences in per-pupil expenditures affect students and teachers?

_____

_____

_____

_____

_____

Privatization of Public Schools

Privatization   The operation of public schools by business and industry; a public-private partnership.

The operation of public schools by business and industry is called **privatization**. Some agencies operate for profit, whereas others are nonprofit. Tesseract Group, Inc., for example, opened South Pointe Elementary School in Miami, Florida, in 1991. This was the first public school in the United States operated by a private company. Tesseract is no longer in operation. Edison Schools, Inc. is now the country's largest private manager of public schools, overseeing a total of 150 schools in 24 states with a combined enrollment of 84,000.[37] Imagine Schools is an operator of charter and private schools for students in kindergarten through twelfth grade. The company educates nearly 20,000 students at some 70 public charter schools in nine states and Washington, D.C.[38]

Local control is very much at the heart of privatization in communities that want to find innovative ways to improve education. Local control supporters say citizens, not teachers' organizations, should set the agenda for schooling.

Opponents of privatization see it as a system for businesses and other groups to profit at the public's expense. They feel that school boards are surrendering their responsibilities to others and that privatization represents an attempt to destroy public education by tapping into public discontent. In addition, teacher organizations oppose privatization because it often leads to loss of teacher jobs and erosion of support for the teaching profession.

Regardless of this debate, it is likely that privatization efforts will accelerate and that you will have many opportunities to engage in discussions about what you think make appropriate ways to use your talents and those of others in reforming public education.

REFLECT & WRITE

What are your feelings about privatization? Does it threaten public education or does it offer an innovative way to improve education?

_____

_____

_____

_____

_____

How Are School Governance and Finance Important to Classroom Teachers?

Issues related to governance and finance are relevant to all teachers because they directly impact instructional potential, cooperative effort, teacher empowerment, and professionalism.

Informed Professional Participation

Knowledge and understanding of how state departments of education, school districts, and schools are organized help teachers comprehend the process of schooling. Knowledge of school governance and funding will help you understand how political and economic issues affect what you teach, how you teach, and in what conditions and environments you work. This understanding will help you become a fully functioning professional. Today's professionals are more than "just teachers." They are involved in the governance of schools through school-based management and shared decision making. Increasingly, the national government, state departments of education, and school boards are giving professionals at the local level responsibility and authority for how schools are organized and operated.

Accountability

Governance brings accountability to the educational enterprise. School board members are accountable to the public and the state for how well they provide for a district's students. Superintendents are responsible for how well school board policies are implemented, and administrators and teachers are responsible for providing evidence of what children know and are able to do. Accountability is much more of an issue now than it was several decades ago, and the public is demanding much more of schools than ever before, as is evident from the preceding discussions. Almost every dimension of education has an accountability component.

Teacher Empowerment

Knowledge of governance and finance also can empower you to participate effectively in the political process. Those who know, understand, and participate in the political process are better able to influence and change the teaching and learning process. Change is needed to achieve such educational goals as providing quality education for all students. Today, new forms of governance, such as site-based management and creative funding formulas, give stakeholders more power, authority, and responsibility for decision making. Empowerment gives you a voice in how your classroom, school, and education agencies operate.

Education is a political process. The idea of having people who are affected by decisions participate in decision making was not always and is still not a universally accepted approach to governance. However, empowerment is now a politically popular concept. Those who know, understand, and participate in the political process are much more likely to influence and change the teaching and learning process.

? *What Does This Mean for You?*

The average school in the United States is 42 years old. You may be lucky—your school may be "younger." Or it may be even older.

It takes money—a lot of it—to build and maintain schools. The price tag for maintaining and building new school facilities in this country in 2007 was $25 billion.

Even in the best-funded district, you can count on being affected by school finance. Community members may object to rising taxes—and you may find yourself playing an advocate's role in helping your district gain the funding necessary to help you do the job you were educated to do. Identify two ways you think you will be affected by school finance as you enter the teaching profession.

Organization and governance should be changed if they interfere with or prevent the provision of quality education for all. It is most important that we not use excuses such as "We have always done it this way" to keep us from making the organizational and governance changes necessary for effective teaching and learning.

REFLECT & WRITE

In this chapter, I have stated that "education is a political process." Can you think of any educational topic that is not influenced by politics? How will you be involved politically in decisions that will affect you and your students?

_____

_____

_____

_____

_____

ETHICAL DILEMMA

SECOND-YEAR TEACHER PASQUALI ESTABARO is upset that he and his fellow teachers will not be getting a raise during the coming year. The school board has said that it is out of money, and that no new money is coming from the state. Pasquali thinks it is time to take action. He goes to Reston Ferris, the teacher's union representative, and suggests that the teachers go on strike. Pasquali said that he is willing to picket to get "a fair wage for fair work."

Are Pasquali's actions unethical? What would you advise Pasquali to do?

SUMMARY

- The forces that influence school governance and finance include public opinion and social issues; stakeholders, such as political interest groups, business and industry, and professional organizations; and teachers, parents, students, and community groups.

- Education is governed by the federal government, state government, intermediate education agencies involving a collaboration of state and local governments, and the local government. The balance of the executive, legislative, and judicial branches of government is vital to the governance and finance of U.S. education.

- Accountability is very important in education today. As a result of the No Child Left Behind Act, schools and teachers are held accountable for student learning. The NCLB requires states to administer standards-based assessments in reading, math, and science. Using these tests as a gauge of teacher accountability has been a controversial issue.

- Schools are governed and administered through a combined effort of principals, assistant principals, school-based management teams, and advisory councils. These individuals and groups put into daily practice the policies established by the state legislature, state board of education, and local board of education.

- Education is funded from many sources, including federal support and mandates, state-level funding, local-level funding, and contributions from the private sector.

- Many issues of governance and finance affect education today. For example, how much influence the federal government should have over state government in making public school decisions; how much influence should be given to state governments over local governments; funding equity; and the privatization of public schools. Because of its direct impact, the governance and financing of schools are very important to classroom teachers.

KEY TERMS

Administration 233
Categorical (block) grants 237
Council of Chief State School Officers (CCSSO) 228
Flat grants 238
Foundation grants 238
Funding equity 243
Governance 216

Intermediate educational units (IEUs) 228
Lobbyists 218
Local education agency (LEA) 229
National Association of State Boards of Education (NASBE) 223
National Governors' Association (NGA) 227

No Child Left Behind Act 222
Performance pay 233
Privatization 244
School advisory council (SAC) 235
School-based management (SBM) 234
Stakeholders 218
State standards boards 226

APPLICATIONS FOR ACTIVE LEARNING

Connections

1. Review Chapter 3 on how schools are organized and linked to society. How do aims of education and trends in schooling relate to the political and economic influences on American education described in this chapter?

2. Think about concepts and topics introduced in this chapter. Create a picture, graphic, or figure that shows connections that are meaningful to you among this chapter's key ideas and information.

Field Experiences

1. Interview a superintendent or school principal about how a particular school district or school is organized and governed. Ask such questions as:

   - How is school governance changing?

   - What current problems or issues relate to governance and finance?

   - How does the national government influence education in the district?

   - What advice do you have for beginning teachers about their participation in school governance?

   - What successes and failures have you observed in schools using school-based management?

2. How much schools are funded makes a difference in everything from facilities to classroom materials to teacher quality. Observe two schools in your district or one in your district and another in a neighboring district and write about your experiences at each school. What inequities do you observe? Do you think these inequities are a result of differences in funding or do you attribute them to something else? Support your conclusion with at least three examples.

Personal Research

1. Attend a meeting of the local board of education or school board. Record your observations on these points:

   - What issues seem to be most important? Why?

   - What diverse viewpoints are expressed by various board members on particular topics?

   - Is there evidence of stakeholder influence on the board's decisions?

2. Investigate the tax and other monetary support for schools in your district.

   - Where does the money come from? How do the percentages of support compare with those discussed in this chapter?

   - How does the national average for per-student expenditures compare with the amount distributed in your state?

3. Some education finance reformers believe that there should be a federal formula for equalizing funding for education among the states. Write a paragraph illustrating whether you support such a proposal and why.

PREPARING TO TEACH

For Your Portfolio

1. Many school districts publish annual reports. Sometimes these are called parent/community report cards. Obtain two of these reports from school districts and answer the following questions: What are the similarities and differences in how the schools are governed? Financed? How do the schools compare in teacher salaries? Student achievement? Expenditure per pupil? Total budget? What conclusions can you draw from your comparison of the two reports?

Idea File

Write to state agencies requesting information about their services for classroom teachers. You can place some of the information in your portfolio and other information in your idea file for use when you begin teaching.

LEARNING AND KNOWING MORE

Websites Worth Visiting

As you know from reading this chapter, the federal government plays a major role in funding education and determining what is taught. It is a good idea for you to keep abreast of what the federal government is doing. You can do this through their website at www.ed.gov. Additionally, you can reach the individual governing bodies by accessing the following websites: House of Representatives at www.house.gov, the Senate at www.senate.gov, and the White House at www.whitehouse.gov.

Quality Education for Minorities (QEM) Network
http://qemnetwork.qem.org

The QEM network was established in 1990 and is dedicated to improving education for minorities throughout the nation. The site provides information related to current legal issues, current statistics and facts, and other pertinent information.

National Governors Association (NGA)
www.nga.org

The NGA is the only bipartisan national organization of, by, and for the nations' governors. Through the NGA, governors identify priority issues and deal collectively with issues of public policy and governance at both the national and state levels. The site contains publications and provides an in-depth look at the structure and levels of the NGA as well as current information related to relevant educational and policy issues.

Board of Cooperative Educational Services (BOCES)
www.wswheboces.org

BOCES provides cost-effective, shared educational programs and support services that complement component school districts in strengthening the quality of living and learning in their communities. The site provides additional links to other organizations as well as current information related to educational issues.

National Association of State Boards of Education (NASBE)
www.nasbe.org

The NASBE is an organization representing state and territorial boards of education. NASBE principal objectives include strengthening state leadership in educational policy making; promoting excellence in the education of all students; advocating equality of access to educational opportunity; and ensuring continued citizen support for public education.

Congressional Budget Office
www.cbo.gov

CBO provides Congress with the objective, timely, nonpartisan analyses needed for economic and budget decisions and with the information and estimates required for the Congressional budget process.

Committee for Education Funding
www.cef.org

The Committee for Education Funding, a nonpartisan, nonprofit coalition of over one hundred education organizations, provides updates on federal education funding.

National Center for Education Statistics
www.nces.ed.gov

The National Center for Education Statistics (NCES) is the primary federal entity for collecting and analyzing data related to education in the United States and other nations.

Books Worth Reading

McCluskey, N. P. (2007). *Feds in the Classroom: How Big Government Corrupts, Cripples, and Compromises American Education.* Lanham, MD: Rowman & Littlefield Publishers, Inc.
The federal government is deeply entrenched in American public education and virtually dictates what can be taught to students. Why? At what cost? And what are the benefits to public school students? To public schools?

Manna, P. (2006). *School's In: Federalism and the National Education Agenda.* Washington, DC: Georgetown University Press.
A look at the evolution of the complicated politics surrounding national education policymaking. A must-read whether you study or work on education policy.

8 Education and School Law

In the affluent Boston suburb of Sudbury, Massachusetts, students at Lincoln-Sudbury Regional High School did not fear for their safety. However, that all changed when on the morning of January 19, 2007, a high school sophomore stabbed a freshman with a carving knife in the boys' restroom. Teachers and administrators rushed toward the screams they heard in the hall, finding one boy severely wounded and the other covered in blood. Shortly after, James Alenson, a freshman at Lincoln-Sudbury, died of two knife wounds in the abdomen. Sixteen-year-old John Odgren, who was new to the school, was led away in handcuffs. The events left the school and the community of Sudbury in shock. Continuing to believe "it couldn't happen here" was simply naïve.

John Odgren had a history of psychological problems, which put him in special classes in school for part of the day and kept him separated from his peers. Diagnosed with Asperger's syndrome, a form of autism that is not usually linked with violent behavior, and attention-deficit hyperactivity disorder (ADHD), John's learning ability and social interaction were affected, but not his intelligence. He was reported to have shown a keen interest in violence and antisocial behavior around his classmates and the school psychologist. He did not previously have any connection to James Alenson, and according to the prosecution, he "randomly chose a victim."

On two occasions, John Odgren had brought a pocketknife and a toy handgun to school, which were confiscated by the school psychologist. Several students claimed they had seen him using the school computers to research a "homemade bomb" and frequently heard him talking about violent subjects in class. He claimed to have a handgun at home.

The prosecution claims that John's behavior was calculated. Odgren pleaded not guilty, and his defense lawyer claims that the students' reports are false. Whatever the outcome of this case, it raises many questions and invokes many deep-seated fears about the safety of our schools and school law.

The interpretation of laws, student rights, and education law are changing, and these changes are impacting teachers and students. For example, in Odgren's case, was it the fault of the school psychologist for not recognizing the potential warning signs? What actions can legally be taken to prevent something like this from happening again? What actions would not infringe on students' rights? Knowing your rights and responsibilities and those of students, parents, and administrators will help you prepare for teaching and give you a more complete view of the legal backdrop of your classroom.[1]

As you read this chapter . . .

Think about:

- Federal and state laws and court cases that form the basis for school law
- The legal responsibilities of states and school districts
- Your legal responsibilities and rights as a teacher
- How you can practice legal and ethical behavior
- Students' legal rights
- Parents' legal rights and responsibilities

Knowing your students' rights and responsibilities will help you prepare for teaching.

▶▶ Go to MyEducationLab and select the topic "Ethical and Legal Issues" then watch the video "Brown vs. Board of Education."

WHAT IS THE BASIS OF SCHOOL LAW?

At the beginning of the school year, Principal Gorin sent a note home to all parents stating that under no circumstances were children allowed to bring any peanut products to school. This was a problem for Aaron Koppel, who would eat only peanut butter on whole-wheat bread or nothing at all. Aaron's parents protested that last year there were separate tables for children with food allergies, but Principal Gorin said he made this new rule because those children felt stigmatized. Aaron's mother protested that now her son was being penalized because a few children were stigmatized. She expressed a desire to pursue legal action, if necessary.

As a beginning teacher, you will be involved in issues relating to freedom of religion, freedom of speech, desegregation, students' rights, teachers' rights, and discriminatory practices as they affect teaching, hiring, and dismissal. You need to know what your legal rights are, as well as those of your students and their parents so that you can be an informed teacher.

Laws The principles and regulations established by governing authorities.

There are four sources of **law** in the United States. The first is the U.S. Constitution, which provides the law for the nation and forms the legal basis for all individual rights. Other sources of law are federal laws, state constitutions and laws, and court decisions (see Figure 8.1). All those who vote participate in the creation and enactment of laws.

FIGURE 8.1 Sources of School Law and Their Influences

This shows the sources of school law and their influences.

REFLECT & WRITE

Four sources of school law affect school districts, teachers, students, and parents. Which of these four sources do you think has the greatest influence? How will your rights and responsibilities be affected by each of these sources?

The U.S. Constitution, Basic Rights, and Education

Although the Constitution does not mention education and contains no explicit provisions for it, basic rights guaranteed to individuals do affect, influence, and determine what happens in education. Individual constitutional rights are enforceable in parochial, private, and public schools. The Supreme Court and other courts frequently refer to and use provisions of the Constitution when rendering their decisions. For example, the Preamble of the Constitution contains a general welfare clause, which states:

> We, the people of the United States, in order to form a more perfect Union, establish justice, insure domestic tranquility, provide for the common defense, promote the general welfare, and secure the blessings of liberty to ourselves and our posterity do ordain and establish this Constitution for the United States of America.

Using the premise that it is promoting the general welfare, the federal government spends money and provides support for education and, at the same time, establishes certain conditions for their use. By accepting federal financial assistance and grants, state agencies and local school districts agree to comply with federal laws.

Three amendments to the Constitution have a great influence on educational practice.

The First Amendment

The First Amendment of the Constitution states that:

> Congress shall make no law respecting an establishment of religion, or prohibiting the free exercise thereof; or abridging the freedom of speech, or the press; or the right of the people to peaceably assemble, and to petition the government for redress of grievances.

Many issues relating to freedom of religion and speech affect what happens in schools. For example, in Cobb County, Georgia, the school board voted in 2002 to put "evolution disclaimer" stickers on the inside cover of the school's science textbooks. The controversial stickers read:

> This textbook contains material on evolution. Evolution is a theory, not a fact, regarding the origin of living things. This material should be approached with an open mind, studied carefully and critically considered.

Concerned parents, along with the American Civil Liberties Union (ACLU), took the Cobb County School Board to court to have the stickers removed. In early 2005, U.S. District Judge Clarence Cooper agreed that the stickers singled out evolution as a theory that could significantly encourage political and religious discrimination. The stickers clearly segregated students' and teachers' political and religious beliefs, the judge said, and could cause conflict. The ACLU and the Cobb County School Board came to an agreement and removed the stickers from 35,000 science textbooks.[2]

The Fourth Amendment

The Fourth Amendment provides citizens with basic privacy and security rights. It states:

> The right of the people to be secure in their persons, houses, papers, and effects, against unreasonable searches and seizures, shall not be violated, and no warrants shall issue, but upon probable cause, supported by oath or affirmation, and particularly describing the place to be searched, and the person or things to be seized.

The Fourth Amendment has particular educational implications for everyone, and sometimes in ways that we might not always consider. For example, urine tests for participation in athletic programs are required in many school districts. However, according to *The Deskbook Encyclopedia of American School Law*:

> Drug testing by urine sample constitutes a search under the Constitution. Courts have frequently found drug testing of general student populations in conflict with constitutional requirements of individualized suspicion. . . . Testing limited to potential interscholastic sports participants has met with court approval where the tests are limited in scope, provide for student privacy, and clearly state the consequences of positive tests.[3]

In Williamsburg, Virginia, the Williamsburg-James City Council School Board voted unanimously to employ random student drug testing for students in grades 6–12, starting in 2006. The decision came after a mandatory random drug-testing program was strongly opposed by the ACLU of Virginia as well as by many parents and students. The superintendent's proposed mandatory random drug testing program would have been the most expansive in the state of Virginia and would have required all high school students involved in extracurricular activities or who use the school parking lot to be subjected to random drug testing.

However, the ACLU and concerned parents urged the school board to reject this measure because it violates the privacy rights of students. Also, there is no research that shows such programs to be effective deterrents to drug use. However, the school board's vote to make the program voluntary "allows families, not the government, to decide when drug testing is appropriate," according to Kent Willis, the executive director of the ACLU of Virginia.[4]

Students' rights issues have tremendous implications for teaching and learning. Some say restricting the rights of students makes them less independent and responsible and casts schools and teachers in even greater paternalistic roles. Others believe, as the Supreme Court does, that students should not leave their rights at the schoolhouse door. So, students' rights are restricted in certain regards, but not in others.

In 1998, students in Tecumseh, Oklahoma, schools became subject to a new rule: All students who participated in extracurricular activities were subject to random drug testing. An honor student and active member of the school's band and choir decided to challenge the constitutionality of this rule. Lindsay Earls argued that the new rule violated students' Fourth Amendment rights. The Fourth Amendment guarantees the right to be free of all unreasonable searches and seizures.

Fellow student Daniel James decided to join Earls in court, along with their parents.

The Supreme Court held in 2002 in *Pottawatomie v.* *Earls* that random drug testing served the best interest of the school and that it did not violate students' Fourth Amendment rights.

What do you think? Do you think that random drug testing infringes on students' constitutional rights? Will random drug testing help students and schools be more successful? You can read a transcript of the case online at www.law.cornell.edu/supct/html/01-332.ZS.html.

Random Drug Testing

Pros of Random Drug Testing	Cons of Random Drug Testing
■ Results from urine testing are accurate and reliable; results are almost instant and do not require a lab technician.	■ Results can be easily faked. There is also a three-day window of detection, which means that students can "cheat" and that results may not be totally accurate.
■ Students might be more encouraged to abstain from drug use if they knew they were going to be tested when participating in certain activities.	■ Students might abstain from activities where negative drug tests are required for participation.
■ Intercession for students who test positive may be more readily available; clinical rehabilitation or counseling may be administered and possible addiction or future health problems avoided.	■ Students may feel like they have no right to privacy.
■ Results are private and confidential, although they will be shared with administrators who need to know and the students' parents.	■ Additional rules or laws regarding unsolicited searches and seizures may follow, limiting students' privacy and possibly infringing on constitutional rights.

Source: Office of National Drug Control Policy. (2002). What you need to know about drug testing in schools. Available at www.doe.state.in.us/sdfsc/pdf/DrugTestingONDCP.pdf. Accessed December 3, 2007.

The Fourteenth Amendment

The Fourteenth Amendment contains the due process provision and, of all the constitutional amendments, is the most frequently referred to in deciding education-related cases. This amendment states, in part:

> No state shall make or enforce any law which shall abridge the privileges or immunities of the citizens of the United States; nor shall any state deprive any person of life, liberty, or property, without due process of law; or deny to any person within its jurisdiction the equal protection of the law.

Simply stated, **due process** means that the federal, state, and local governments can deprive a person of life, liberty, or property only after following a fair decision-making process. The due process clause helps ensure that teachers and students are not deprived of life, liberty, and property without the safeguards of fair procedures and protects them from unreasonable, vague, and capricious rules. Many laws and court decisions define and spell out the rules, regulations, and procedures that must be followed in due process proceedings.

Due process The legal process that the government—or any other party—must go through before denying a person his or her rights to life, liberty, or property.

The meanings of life, liberty, and property are often interpreted by courts in ways different from what you might normally think. The courts have generally held that there is a property interest in teachers' reemployment as tenured teachers, a liberty interest in being free to enter into contracts for employment, a liberty interest as it relates to privacy (for example, personal property), and liberty interests in free speech and the exercise of religious beliefs.

REFLECT & WRITE

One of the missions of the education process is to promote the "general welfare" of the children. For example, schools must ensure that all students become literate. Give three examples of a school's responsibility to its students.

_____

_____

_____

_____

Federal Laws

The federal government passes laws related to education in order to promote the general welfare and to uphold and promote the principles inherent in the Constitution. As you have read, the Supreme Court rules on cases that affect students' and teachers' constitutional rights, privileges, and educational actions. Three laws in particular affect teachers and students greatly: Title VI, the Civil Rights Act; Title IX of the Education Amendments of 1972 (also known as the Patsy T. Mink Equal Opportunity in Education Act); and the Education for all Handicapped Children Act.

The Civil Rights Act of 1964 states that any agency receiving federal money cannot exclude from participation or deny any benefits to an employee based on race, color, or national origin. This law came at a tumultuous time in America, and because it is a federal law its reach extended to all states' hiring practices. Although many Americans are still affected by discrimination, this law made discrimination illegal in federally funded workplaces, including public schools.

The Education Amendment, Title IX of 1972, states that no person in the United States can be discriminated against or denied the benefits of any federally funded activity or program based on their sex. This opened educational opportunities to all, male or female. It also affected hiring practices, requiring that they be fair and balanced, and not discriminatory because of a prospective employee's sex.

In 1975, Congress passed the Education for All Handicapped Children Act, which requires that all federally funded educational institutions make accommodations for and ensure the equal treatment and education of children with all disabilities. In short, this means that teachers and schools must have adequate training and educational facilities to meet the needs of students who may have mental, physical, or emotional disabilities. In 1997, the act was changed to Individuals with Disabilities Education Act (IDEA), putting a "person-first" perspective on the act and providing specific guidelines to educators, administrators, parents of children with disabilities, and the children themselves to ensure that their educational needs are met.

TABLE 8.1   Three Major Federal Laws that Impact Educational Practices

Title VI: Civil Rights Act (1964)	Title IX: The Education Act (1972)	Education for All Handicapped Children Act (1975)
This law ensures that no person in the United States will be excluded from participation or be denied any benefits of any federally funded program or activity based on race, color, or national origin.	Ensures that no person in the United States shall be discriminated against or denied benefits of any federally funded activity or program on the basis of their sex.	Ensures the protection of the rights of students with disabilities and extends to them and their parents due process in matters relating to their education.

As a teacher, familiarizing yourself with these laws will help you understand your position as a fair educator. With regard to IDEA, because you will probably have students who meet the requirements for federal involvement in this program, you must familiarize yourself with its guidelines in order to ensure compliance and provide the best education to your students. You might be asked to sit in on meetings with students, parents, and counselors to recommend, change, or discontinue a student's specific curriculum needs (see Chapter 5). Therefore, understanding federal laws and how they apply to your classroom can make a difference in your effectiveness as a teacher.

Table 8.1 summarizes how these federal laws have affected the states. These three laws are by no means the only laws currently affecting education; however, they are significant in that to a great extent they changed the face of education as we know it today. Before the passage of civil rights laws, minority ethnic groups were discriminated against, not only by individuals, but also by institutions. The Civil Rights Act leveled the playing field and institutionalized the notion of nondiscrimination.

Title IX changed education by ensuring that women and girls have full and equal access to all extracurricular activities that men and boys have access to. Balanced hiring and admissions practices have led to more women graduating from high school and continuing on to secondary education, as well as taking on more positions of power in the workplace.

Finally, IDEA ensured that all educational facilities are accessible to children with special needs. Previously, children with special needs were pushed into private institutions for instruction, and sometimes even hospitalized if their parents could not provide for them.

These laws have created a more inclusive school environment where, ideally, everyone is treated equal. Although the goal of equality is not always achieved, these laws have been responsible for considerable changes in education. As a new teacher, you will have the opportunity and responsibility to see that schools continue to change to better meet the needs of our increasingly diverse society.

Federal laws are not the only laws that affect education. In fact, most laws affecting education are state laws. Therefore, depending on the state in which you obtain your teacher certification and in which you choose to teach, a number of factors may influence your teaching and classroom responsibilities.

REFLECT & WRITE

As we have discussed, many federal laws provide for equal and fair treatment of students. Can you think of any instances in which education is not fair and equal for all students? What can you do about these situations?

_____

_____

_____

_____

_____

Go to the Resources section of MyEducationLab to learn more about your state standards.

State Laws

The Tenth Amendment to the U.S. Constitution protects the power of the states to provide education for its citizens. Therefore, states can decide how to conduct most of their education process in a way that is unique to that state. Education is not a nationally guaranteed right, and it can be greatly influenced by the political process. Because states have the responsibility for controlling education, most laws affecting education are state laws.

For example, as an aspiring teacher, you must look to your state laws to find out what is required for you to get your teacher certification. Does your state require courses in state history and multicultural education? What is the minimum requirement for basic certification? Is there an alternative certification process, and, if so, who qualifies? What are the rules regarding ethical practices for teachers in your state? And, finally, what are the public schools' state-mandated procedures for hiring and dismissal?

If you are reading this book for a college course, you have had to comply with the state's laws for high school graduation. Think back on your high school experience. You might not have attended public school, but instead attended a private or parochial school or pursued home schooling—state law impacts these curricula. Did the state you live in have a minimum number of hours you had to take to graduate? Did you have to pass a state standardized test or some other equivalent in order to graduate? In Texas, in 2007 alone, 16 percent of all high school seniors, approximately 40,000 students, failed the state's exit-level standardized achievement test, TAKS. According to state law these students were unable to receive a high school diploma. States also determine laws concerning attendance, dismissal, residency, and due process of law relating to students' freedom of religion, freedom of speech, school searches, and drug testing.

Your state sets many regulations concerning the content, curriculum, and course requirements for the individual public schools and school districts. Schools have a relative amount of freedom in the way of extra activities and certain courses, but there are laws that govern the way a school operates and what information is taught. For example, in many instances textbooks must be approved by the state. If you are teaching certain courses, such as history, regulations might require you to teach the Holocaust, African American history, and state history. School and student activities, such as having girls' sports teams available with equal funding, or requiring a certain number or type of liberal arts programs, and, finally, requiring mandatory achievement testing in certain grades, are all functions of state legislatures.

The residents of each state vote on the laws and regulations for their state's education policy, and state educational laws generally reflect what the residents want. State laws and local school board policies determine what is taught, the nature of the educational process, and how schools operate. Within each state, local school districts work to create educational policies in accordance with that state's laws. In doing this, policymakers hope to serve the people's interest and, at the same time, address social problems. Ensuring integration and equal rights, dealing with drug use and gang membership, and addressing teen sexuality and pregnancy are all impacted by these policies. In the process of addressing these issues, policymakers also hope to teach usable and marketable skills to the future workforce and ensure a literate and responsible society.

Laws reflect the views and values held by society at a particular time. For example, the law once specified that African Americans, Native Americans, immigrants, and women were not entitled to the same educational opportunities as white males. However, the laws were changed to reflect a new set of values. The court system, which includes a jury of regular citizens, decides when and how educational laws may be interpreted in a new way. Educational law creates a reflection of what the citizens want, instead of being a function solely of the state. This is a core value of the American democratic process.

REFLECT & WRITE

All states have requirements for high school graduation. Do you think these requirements are necessary? What requirements would you add to your state's list for high school graduation?

The Courts

Federal and state courts have ruled on many topics of substantial interest to educators. Figure 8.2 lists Supreme Court cases affecting the rights of teachers and school districts. Many decisions will influence how you practice your profession. Almost daily, issues relating to students', teachers', and parents' rights are in the news. Many cases involve issues of the separation of church and state.

Religion in the Schools

States frequently pass laws that directly support or encourage such practices as public prayer and Bible reading. For example, a Georgia law mandates a minute of silent reflection for all students before school begins. Although this moment of silence is not directly encouraging a certain religion, denomination, or even prayer, do you think it is appropriate for schools to facilitate a moment of silence, considering the separation of church and state? The federal courts have ruled that yes, it is appropriate, given that "a period of quiet reflection" does not violate the Constitution's ban on government establishment of religion. The Georgia law was part of a legislative package designed to minimize crime among juveniles. More recently, the Supreme Court refused to hear an appeal to a Virginia state law that requires a minute of silence from all students, allowing it to remain in effect.[5]

Brown v. Board of Education of Topeka (1954). The Court ruled that state-sanctioned segregation in public schools violated the equal protection of the Fourteenth Amendment.

Engle v. Vitale (1962). The Court ruled that public school officials could not require pupils to recite a state-composed prayer at the start of each school day, even if the prayer was nondenominational and pupils who so desired could be excused from reciting it.

Abbington School District v. Schempp (1963). The Court ruled unconstitutional a Pennsylvania law requiring daily recitations of Bible verses and the Lord's Prayer in public school classrooms. The Court said any practice that advances or inhibits a religion is unconstitutional.

Green v. County School Board of New Kent County (1967). The Court identified six areas in which progress toward desegregation is tested.

Epperson v. Arkansas (1968). The Court held that to forbid the teaching of evolution as a theory violates the First Amendment.

Pickering v. Board of Education (1968). The Court ruled that a teacher could not be dismissed for speaking as a citizen on matters of public concern.

Alexander v. Holmes County Board of Education (1969). The Court ordered the end to all dual systems of education.

Swann v. Charlotte-Mecklenburg Board of Education (1971). The Court ruled that involuntary busing was a legitimate means of achieving school integration.

Lemon v. Kurtzman (1971). The Court devised a three-part test that is used in considering whether government violates the establishment clause. This is referred to as the *Lemon test.*

Keyes v. School District No. 1 (1973). The Court ruled that gerrymandering results in de jure segregation.

Cleveland Board of Education v. LaFleur (1974). The Court said it was discriminatory to make pregnant teachers take mandatory pregnancy leaves at fixed periods before and after giving birth.

Ambach v. Norwick (1979). The Court held that a New York statute forbidding permanent certification as a public school teacher of any person who is not a United States citizen, unless that person has manifested an intention to apply for citizenship, does not violate the equal protection clause of the Fourteenth Amendment.

North Haven Board of Education v. Bell (1982). The Court ruled that Title IX provides protection from discrimination for teachers and students. Under Title IX, the Department of Education can investigate complaints of sexual discrimination and can curtail federal funding to programs and agencies that do so.

School District of the City of Grand Rapids v. Ball (1985). The Court held that even the praiseworthy, secular purpose of providing for the education of schoolchildren cannot validate government aid to parochial schools when the aid has the effect of promoting religion.

Wallace v. Jaffree (1985). The Court ruled unconstitutional an Alabama law authorizing a daily moment of silence in public schools for "meditation or voluntary prayer."

Edwards v. Aquillard (1987). The Court said that a state cannot require that schools teach the biblical version of creation.

Board of Education of the Westside Community Schools v. Mergens (1990). The Court ruled that a Bible study group was denied equal access to the use of school property. The Court said the students could "form a Christian club that would have the same privileges and meet on the same terms and conditions as other Westside student groups, except it would have no faculty sponsor."

Lee v. Weisman (1992). The Court ruled that prayers by a clergyman at a Providence, Rhode Island, middle school graduation violated the establishment clause.

United States v. Fordice (1992). The Court ruled that states that perpetuate policies and practices traceable to its prior de jure dual system that continue to have segregative effects violate the equal protection clause.

Lamb's Chapel et al. v. Center Moriches Union Free School District et al. (1993). The Court ruled that denying a church access to school premises to speak violates the freedom of speech clause.

Missouri v. Jenkins (1995). The Court ruled that a federal judge exceeded his powers by requiring a plan designed to attract white suburban students into the Kansas City School District.

Gebser v. Lago Vista Independent School District (1998). The Court ruled that a district cannot be held liable for a teacher's sexual harassment of a student under Title IX unless a district official with the authority to take corrective action had actual knowledge of teacher misconduct and was deliberately indifferent to it.

Santa Fe Independent School District v. Doe (2000). The Court ruled that student-led prayer at public high school football games is an unconstitutional establishment of religion.

Mitchell v. Helms (2000). The Court ruled that federal programs that put instructional equipment into religious schools is not a violation of the separation of church and state.

Goodnews Club v. Milford Central Schools (2001). The Court ruled that elementary schools must allow religious student organizations to meet on campus.

Zelman v. Simmons-Harris (2002). The Court ruled in June 2002 that vouchers for religious schools in Cleveland, Ohio, are constitutional and do not violate the separation of church and state.

Locke v. Davey (2003). The Court ruled that a state does not violate the First Amendment's free exercise clause when it funds secular college majors but excludes devotional theology majors. A student who forfeited his Promise Scholarship money (given by Washington State) in order to major in pastoral ministries at a private Christian college brought the case to court.

Elk Grove Unified School District v. Newdow (2004). The Court unanimously overturned a lower-court decision that teacher-led recitation of the Pledge of Allegiance in public schools is unconstitutional. The Court did not rule on whether the Pledge was violating the separation of church and state because of the inclusion of the phrase, "under God," but instead ruled that Newdow, the father of the third-grade girl required to recite the pledge, did not have the right to sue because he was not being required to recite the pledge.

FIGURE 8.2 Supreme Court Cases Affecting the Rights of Students, Teachers, and School Districts

The Supreme Court cases have affected the rights of students, teachers, and school districts throughout the nineteenth, twentieth, and into the twenty-first centuries.

REFLECT &
WRITE

Which court decisions will have
the most relevance to you, your
school, and your students when
you begin teaching?

From the beginning of schooling in America, many schools have included some form of religious activity in their curriculum. Before 1962, Bible reading and prayer were an accepted part of many school-opening exercises. The reading was generally without comment, and students who objected to the reading were excused from listening. However, in 1961, the State Board of Regents of New York wrote the following 22-word prayer: "Almighty God, we acknowledge our dependence upon Thee, and we beg Thy blessings upon us, our parents, our teachers and our country."

The Board of Regents believed the prayer was nondenominational and was based on "our spiritual heritage." They considered the prayer to be denominationally neutral and encouraged school districts to use it. Parents of 10 pupils brought action in a New York state court and challenged the constitutionality of the use of the prayer and the school district's right to order its recitation. The case eventually went to the Supreme Court. In *Engle v. Vitale*, the Court ruled that public school officials could not require pupils to recite a state-composed prayer at the start of each school day, even if the prayer was nondenominational and pupils who so desired could be excused from reciting it. Official state sanction of religious utterances, the Court declared, is an unconstitutional attempt to establish religion. The Court declared, "It is neither sacrilegious nor antireligious to say that each separate government in this country should stay out of the business of writing and sanctioning official prayers and leave that purely religious function to the people themselves and to those the people choose to look to for religious guidance."[6]

Establishment clause   The clause of the First Amendment that states: "Congress shall make no law respecting an establishment of religion." This clause creates a "wall of separation" between church and state.

Almost one year later, in *Abbington School District v. Schempp*, the Court ruled unconstitutional a Pennsylvania law requiring daily recitations of Bible verses and the Lord's Prayer in public school classrooms. The Court said any practice that advances or inhibits a religion is unconstitutional.

Does allowing students to hold prayer services on school grounds violate the establishment clause? Are private schools held to the same standards regarding prayer?

The Establishment Clause

Freedom of religion is basically an issue of separation of church and state. The **establishment clause** of the First Amendment of the Constitution states: "Congress shall make no law respecting an establishment of religion." The establishment clause most often applies when schools try to initiate practices that have religious content or when state or federal aid benefits religious organizations.

■ **INTASC**

STANDARD 3   The teacher understands how students differ in their approaches to learning and creates instructional opportunities that are adapted to diverse learners.

Schools can teach the Bible as history and literature, and religion can be part of the curriculum. Generally, schools can teach about religions but cannot promote a particular religious view or support a particular religion or denomination. In *Abbington*, the Court pronounced the following test for examining establishment clause cases:

> The test may be stated as follows: what are the purposes and the primary effect of the enactment? If either is the advancement or inhibition of religion then the enactment exceeds the scope of legislative power as circumscribed by the Constitution. That is to say that to withstand the strictures of the establishment clause there must be a secular legislative purpose and a primary effect that neither advances nor inhibits religion.[7]

The Court further stated its position as not being hostile to religion or the Bible:

> It might well be said that one's education is not complete without a study of comparative religions or the history of religion and its relationship to the advancement of civilization. It certainly may be said that the Bible is worthy of study for its literary and historic qualities. Nothing we have said here indicates that such study of the Bible or religion, when presented objectively as part of a secular program of education, may not be effected consistent with the First Amendment. But the exercises here do not fall into those categories. They are religious exercises, required by the States in violation of the command of the First Amendment that the government maintain strict neutrality, neither aiding nor opposing religion.[8]

Go to MyEducationLab and select the topic "Ethical and Legal Issues" then read the article "Decisions That Have Shaped U.S. Education." Answer the questions that follow.

The offering of public school courses in religion is gaining in approval. Although such courses are few and far between, more are being added to the public school curriculum. In New Braunfels High School in New Braunfels, Texas, students can take a Bible literacy course. In 2006, Georgia became the first state in recent years to fund high school elective classes on the Old and New Testaments, using the Bible as the main text.

Two Bible curriculum courses, developed by private institutions to pass the separation of church and state guidelines, are now used in 460 districts and in at least 37 states. Polls report that over 60 percent of Americans favor teaching the Bible in public schools. Although there is continuing debate over the constitutionality of these courses, the courts have upheld that the Bible can be taught without teaching or endorsing a religion. Given the growing need to address religion in an increasingly multicultural society, the issue of religion in schools is one that cannot be quietly ignored.[9]

In June of 2001, the Supreme Court literally unlocked the schoolhouse door for religious clubs by ruling that public elementary schools must open their doors to after-school religious activities just as they do for other clubs. (High school students were already allowed to hold non-school-sponsored religious activities.) In *Goodnews Club v. Milford Central Schools*, the Court ruled that allowing the Goodnews Club to meet in rooms of a school would "ensure neutrality, not threaten it." Furthermore, the Court ruled, "We cannot see the danger that children would misperceive the endorsement of religion is any greater than the danger that they would perceive a hostility toward the religious viewpoint if the club were excluded from the public forum." The Goodnews Clubs are sponsored by the Child Evangelism Fellowship, Inc., which operates in 155 countries with 4,964 clubs in the United States.

The Lemon Test

● ***Your Turn***

A group of students has approached you to sponsor a club they will call Students for Understanding the Religions of the World. They propose that each year members will paint a mural in the cafeteria showing some aspect of a major religion and that this year's mural will focus on Islam. How will you advise them, using the Lemon test as your guide?

Since 1963, many conservative organizations, such as the Christian Coalition, have sought to restore prayer and Bible reading to the public schools. In 1971 in *Lemon v. Kurtzman*, the Supreme Court devised a three-part test that is used in considering whether government practices violate the establishment clause. These

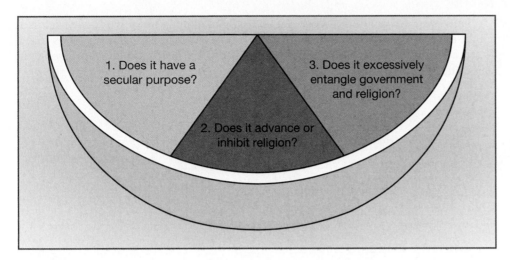

FIGURE 8.3 The Lemon Test Determines a State's Practices in Relation to the Establishment Clause

The Supreme Court justices often apply the three part "Lemon test" when deciding whether specific practices or policies constitute an establishment of religion.

are referred to as the Lemon test (see Figure 8.3). "The Lemon test requires (1) a government practice or enactment must have a secular purpose, (2) its principal or primary effect must be one that neither advances or inhibits religion, and (3) it must not foster an excessive government entanglement with religion."[10]

REFLECT & WRITE

Which parts of the Lemon test do you think are most important? Why? Do you think the Lemon test is fair? Why or why not?

Efforts to provide for prayers in schools persist. In 1985 in *Wallace v. Jaffree*, the Court ruled unconstitutional an Alabama law authorizing a daily moment of silence in public schools for "meditation or voluntary prayer." In 1992, the Court in *Lee v. Weisman* ruled that prayers by a clergyman at a Providence, Rhode Island, middle school graduation violated the establishment clause.

In one of the biggest school prayer cases in a decade, the Supreme Court, in June of 2000, ruled in *Santa Fe Independent School District v. Doe* that prayer is a private matter and ruled that student-led prayer at public high school football games is an unconstitutional establishment of religion. At issue was whether or not it was constitutional for students in the Santa Fe (Texas) School District to have a student deliver a prayer over the public address system before every varsity home football game. The Court ruled that the establishment clause of the Constitution prohibits a school from forcing a student to endure a "personally offensive religious ritual" and that "the delivery of a pregame prayer has the improper effect of coercing those present to participate in an act of religious worship."

■ INTASC

STANDARD 3 The teacher understands how students differ in their approaches to learning and creates instructional opportunities that are adapted to diverse learners.

However, the separation between church and state is not always as strict as it might appear to be. In 2000, the Supreme Court ruled in *Mitchell v. Helms* that a federal program that placed computers and other "instructional equipment" in parochial school classrooms did not violate the separation of church and state.

REFLECT & WRITE

Do you think that teaching Bible literacy classes is constitutional? Why or why not? As a teacher, would you feel comfortable teaching or participating in these classes?

_____

_____

_____

_____

_____

WHAT ARE THE LEGAL RESPONSIBILITIES OF STATES AND SCHOOL DISTRICTS?

States have the right and obligation to educate all students. As states seek to fulfill this role, they must balance the rights of students, teachers, and parents and endeavor to determine what will work best for all. As they do, laws, roles, and desires intersect and clash, resulting in efforts to find appropriate solutions. Some of these persistent issues address equality and funding.

School Desegregation

There has been a long history of discrimination in public schooling in the United States. Before 1955, many southern and some western states—21 in all—had laws requiring or permitting segregated schools. This is known as **de jure** (according to the law) **segregation**. In addition to traditions of discrimination, the doctrine of "separate but equal" prevailed in American education. The basis for this doctrine was *Plessy v. Ferguson*. In this 1896 case, the Supreme Court ruled that a state law requiring federal railroad trains to provide separate-but-equal railroad cars for African American and Anglo-European American passengers who were traveling within one state did not infringe on federal authority to regulate interstate commerce.

This separate-but-equal doctrine remained in effect for the schools until the decision of *Brown v. Board of Education of Topeka*. In *Brown*, the Supreme Court ruled nine to zero that state-sanctioned segregation in public schools violates the equal protection of the Fourteenth Amendment. In 1954, the Supreme Court ordered school districts to **desegregate** with all deliberate speed. To desegregate a school, workplace, or other public area means to open the institution to members of all races and ethnic groups. Although *Brown* brought an end—at least legally—to de jure segregation, it did not affect **de facto segregation**—that is, "natural" segregation resulting from individual choices of neighborhoods. This is Linda Brown Thompson's reflection on the case her father brought to the courts: "It's disheartening that we are still fighting," said Mrs. Thompson. "But we are dealing with human beings. As long as we are, there will always be those who feel the races should be separate."[11] Linda was just 11 years old when her father, the Reverend Oliver L. Brown, became the lead plaintiff in *Brown*.

De jure segregation Segregation according to the law—that is, segregation that exists because of laws requiring or permitting it.

Desegregate To open all public places to members of all races and ethnic groups by the force of law.

De facto segregation Segregation resulting from individual choices of neighborhoods; also known as "natural" segregation.

The issue of segregation was further addressed in 1969 in *Alexander v. Holmes County Board of Education*, when the Supreme Court put an end to "separate but equal" policies by outlawing dual systems of education. From this ruling, a major implementation principle resulted in *Swann v. Charlotte-Mecklenburg Board of Education* when the Court ruled in 1971 that **involuntary busing** was a legitimate means of achieving school **integration**. Many school districts across the United States have been ordered to bus students as a means of integrating schools. However, busing has been and remains a controversial issue. Proponents of busing see it as a way to achieve equality and equity in education. Furthermore, proponents say that the schools are the basis for an integrated society in which people live and work in peace and harmony. However, opponents see busing as a waste of valuable school resources that could be better spent on other school resources and services. They believe that busing disrupts neighborhood patterns and that it is unfair to bus children of one race to another school to achieve integration. In 2001, the Supreme Court ruled that the Charlotte-Mecklenburg School System was desegregated.[12]

As school districts integrate, busing is not always necessary to achieve desegregation goals. For example, Prince George's County, Maryland, a predominantly white area in 1972, now has one of the area's largest African American populations, thus busing is no long necessary. In 2001 a federal judge approved the phasing out of busing in Prince George's County School District of Maryland. Local school boundaries were restored; the court also approved plans to build three neighborhood schools, to maintain magnet schools, and to provide extra resources for schools whose students were predominantly African American.[13]

Busing is no longer seen as a solution to segregation. Both white and African American leaders say that busing is not the answer to current problems. The NAACP and other leaders stress that emphasis instead should be placed on improving schools in the black community. By doing so, they contend, there will be overall improvement in quality and equity.

When busing programs began in 1971, they were effective. However, a number of legislative, political, and social initiatives also have instigated a great deal of change. Recently, in Boston, Massachusetts, the fight over school assignment by race came before the court. In 2003, families sued over the district's student-assignment policy. Boston City Schools have, for 3 years, reserved half of the seats

Involuntary busing The practice of integration that used buses to transport members of a predominantly African American or other ethnic minority school to a school with a low minority population.

Integration A mix of students of different races and cultures in schools and other educational programs.

■ **INTASC**

STANDARD 3 The teacher understands how students differ in their approaches to learning and creates instructional opportunities that are adapted to diverse learners.

Brown v. Board of Education of Topeka ended in a landmark decision against racial desegregation in the nation's schools.

in the district's elementary and middle schools for children who live in the schools' "walk zones," and half for children from other neighborhoods. The plaintiffs believe that the district bars neighborhood students from going to nearby schools, while it admits students who live in neighborhoods farther away, which are composed mostly of minority students. Although the policy is not overtly centered around race, at issue is the role of race in school desegregation.[14]

REFLECT & WRITE

Earlier, I stated "There has been a long history of discrimination in public schooling in the United States." Can you think of any instances today in which education still discriminates against certain classes of students?

_____

_____

_____

_____

_____

Tests of Progress toward Desegregation

In 1967 in *Green v. County School Board of New Kent County*, the Court ruled that the tests of whether school districts are making progress toward integration consist of activities in six areas:

1. Racial balance in assigning students to attendance centers.
2. Transportation parity (for example, most students of one race should not be bused when another race is not being bused).
3. Equity in physical facilities.
4. Equal access to extracurricular activities.
5. Equitable allocation of resources.
6. Personnel placement that puts majority and minority teachers and principals in each building in proportion to their overall numbers in the system. In legal writings, these six factors are referred to as the *Green* categories or factors.

Although efforts to desegregate the nation's schools continue over half a century after *Brown*, some school districts may be even more segregated than ever because of increasing minority enrollments. For example, as we have discussed, Hispanic populations continue to grow, primarily in four states: Texas, California, Florida, and New York. By 2009–2010, over 9 million Latinos will be enrolled in the nation's public schools. Because of the continuing gains in Latino enrollments, white students will represent a minority of graduates from western high schools in 2013–2014.[15] As America becomes an even more diverse country, school integration will continue to be a major topic of discussion and legal battles.

Brown v. Board of Education is still one of the most influential rulings the Supreme Court has made concerning public education and equal opportunity. Undoubtedly, it opened the door of opportunity for millions of disenfranchised Americans. However, problems with segregation, equality, and education remain. Many schools are becoming segregated simply due to widespread suburban sprawl, with families moving away from the inner city and into rapidly growing suburban communities away from the central metropolis. Faced with issues such as immigration and integration of non-English speakers, it is still difficult to create inclusive environments for many students.

The Impact of Desegregation

One goal of desegregation has been to achieve integration, a mix of students of different races and cultures in schools and other educational programs. Integration provides many educational benefits. In a review of the long-term effects of school desegregation, researchers found that:

- Desegregated African American students set their occupational aspirations higher than do segregated African American students.
- The racial composition of schools African American students attend largely determines whether the colleges attended by students are predominantly white or African American.
- Desegregated African American students choose predominantly white institutions.
- Students attending desegregated elementary and high schools show higher college attainment than those attending segregated schools.[16]

School desegregation has proven to be beneficial over the years, yet it is no longer the only desired goal. Equal educational access and educational integration are goals as well. Educational integration strives for a balance of white and African American students in classes. However, balance is not sufficient. All students must have equal access to curriculum programs as well. (See Chapter 12 for a discussion of access issues in relation to technology.) Many minority leaders are now concentrating on improving schools internally rather than externally through busing and other means of desegregation. For example, Nashville spent $206.8 million to eliminate most cross-county busing and has built 11 new schools, thus allowing students to attend schools in their own neighborhoods.[17]

■ **INTASC**

STANDARD 3 The teacher understands how students differ in their approaches to learning and creates instructional opportunities that are adapted to diverse learners.

School Accountability

Administrators and teachers are held accountable for their programs and practices. States have passed accountability laws to help ensure that students who graduate with a diploma can read, write, and perform basic math skills. These laws are also in response to educational malpractice suits in which students and their parents have sued teachers and school districts because students were graduated without basic skills. Accountability laws or requirements make it mandatory that achievement tests be administered at various points in a student's career, for example, in grades 3, 5, 8, and 11. These tests are designed to assess individual progress, measure school and teacher effectiveness, and determine if students should be promoted and if they should be awarded a diploma. Accountability in relation to standards and testing is discussed in Chapter 10.

OBSERVE & LEARN

Observe a classroom and note how the teacher incorporates assessment methods into his or her teaching. How do the students respond to these methods? Do you think there is anything else the teacher can do to enhance learning? Do you think accountability laws and the push for accountability have influenced this classroom and the teacher-student relationship?

With the passage of the 2001 No Child Left Behind Act, states and schools are now held more accountable than ever. NCLB requires standardized tests that determine the level of achievement made by each school and district. This has had a huge impact on teachers and students, particularly ELL students. With more than 3 million ELL students in 2007 alone, the act requires that "states and school districts will be held accountable for making annual increases in English proficiency from the previous year. Moreover, they will be required to teach children in English after three consecutive years of being in school."[18] NCLB also includes incentives for improving math and science curriculum and instruction and redistributes funding for schools that have shown improvement in test scores.

The Law and School Finance

One of the fastest-growing and publicly popular areas of litigation and law involves states, schools, and finances. Many states, including Arizona, Kentucky, New Jersey, Ohio, and Texas, have had their K–12 funding systems ruled unconstitutional by state supreme courts. One of the most celebrated cases is *Edgewood Independent School District v. Kirby*. In this case, the Texas Supreme Court ruled that Texas's school financing system violated the state constitutional requirement and that an efficient system of public education be created to provide for the "general diffusion of knowledge."[19]

At the heart of school finance problems are three issues. One is the equitable distribution of money among affluent districts (usually suburban districts) and less affluent districts (usually inner-city districts). As you will recall from Chapter 7, school funding is largely based on property taxes. Thus, suburban districts where property values are high have more money available for schools. The opposite is true in many inner-city and poor districts. It is clear that reliance on property taxes hurts poor districts. What state courts are deciding is that although school districts have local control for schooling, states are nevertheless responsible for providing for uniform education throughout the state. As a result, many states are implementing funding strategies designed to equalize funding for all students.

A second issue is the ability of wealthy districts to tax low and spend high. This is due to the fact that large suburban school districts often have more property owners. The homes are more expensive, and the taxes on larger homes are higher, resulting in higher tax revenues and more funding for schools. School districts with fewer property owners, which are often urban school districts where most families live in apartments or housing projects, have a lower tax base. Therefore, the property taxes must be raised in order to fund the district's schools. Urban schools often face additional burdens, such as overcrowding, that limit how much the district can spend to improve schools. The funding of schools via property taxes is highly disputed, and, although there is no basis for this practice in the U.S. Constitution, a lawsuit has gone to court in nearly every state regarding the school-funding issue.

Because education funding is set by states and not by the federal government, voters have a significant influence over these laws. California, for example, has a policy of fiscal neutrality, mandating that per-pupil spending shall be decided not by the wealth of the student's school district, but by the wealth of the state as a whole.[20]

A third issue is the responsibility of the states to provide adequate educational opportunities for all the children of the states, not just those in affluent districts.

The cost of funding public education has always been a controversial issue due to its impact on equality. As more poor school districts seek to equalize funding, more states will voluntarily or through court order reexamine the way they fund schools. In all discussions of funding for education, the relationship between funding and the quality of education must be addressed. As a beginning teacher, you will have the opportunity to witness firsthand the effect of funding on the quality of education.

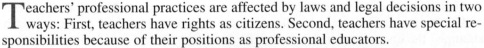

REFLECT & WRITE

In what ways did different levels of funding for education affect your education?

WHAT ARE YOUR LEGAL RESPONSIBILITIES AS A TEACHER?

Teachers' professional practices are affected by laws and legal decisions in two ways: First, teachers have rights as citizens. Second, teachers have special responsibilities because of their positions as professional educators.

Teachers and schools are **in loco parentis**, the theory that the state, in the school context, acts "in the place of parents" in relationship to the care and education of children. Teachers act in the place of parents in many ways—for example, when they provide children with supervision and guidance as would a parent. This principle is often used to justify teachers' intervention in students' behaviors and their right to discipline them in a reasonable and appropriate manner as would a parent. How far teachers and schools should go in carrying out this parental function is a continuing matter of controversy.

Although teachers sometimes act as mentors for their students, providing a safe place for them to discuss issues they may be addressing in their lives, schools are public institutions and teachers must respect the ideas and rights of both parents and students. Many states have switched their health curriculum textbooks to those that only give a limited explanation of sexuality and that promote abstinence as the primary method of birth control and prevention of STDs. Although teachers are guaranteed freedom of speech, these issues are often subject to heated debate, both in the classroom and in the legislature.

In loco parentis The theory that the state, in the school context, acts "in the place of parents."

■ **INTASC**

STANDARD 9 The teacher is a reflective practitioner who continually evaluates the effects of his/her choices and actions on others (students, parents, and other professionals in the learning community) and who actively seeks out opportunities to grow professionally.

Preventing Liability

Businesses and industry are not the only agencies liable for their products, services, and actions. Schools and their employees are liable as well. This liability takes the form of **tort liability**, which is a civil wrong against the rights of others. According

Tort liability Civil wrong against the rights of others.

Teachers must do everything they can to create a teaching and learning environment that will provide for the safety needs of all children. Field trips can pose particular challenges, but teachers must always exercise reasonable care to ensure everyone's safety. Teachers should be aware of school law, their rights, and the rights of students and parents.

Torts Wrongful acts.

Negligence Failure to exercise reasonable care resulting in harm to another person.

Intentional torts Include assault, battery, intent to do harm, and defamation.

Strict liability Injury resulting from unusual hazards, such as when hazardous materials are not kept out of the reach of children and they are injured.

to tort law, a person who causes another person injury is answerable to that party for damages. There are three kinds of **torts**: negligence, intentional, and strict.

Negligence is unacceptable conduct or care that results in the injury of another person. For example, a teacher witnessed a suspicious-looking exchange of some sort of medication between two students in his class, but did nothing to investigate the matter. One of the students took that medication and overdosed. The teacher was found guilty of negligence for not attempting to intercede.[21]

Intentional torts are conduct such as assault, battery, the intent to do harm, and defamation. For example, during a championship football game, a coach slammed the quarterback into a locker for fumbling the ball and losing the game. The quarterback broke his collarbone and charged the coach with intentional tort.[22]

Strict liability applies to injury resulting from unusual hazards, such as when hazardous materials are not kept out of reach of children and they are injured. During a lab, a high school chemistry teacher told students to bring protective eye coverings to prevent exposure to certain chemicals. One of the students did not have adequate eye protection, and the teacher failed to notice this—the student was exposed and grew ill. The teacher was charged with strict liability for not taking extra precautions to ensure the safety of her students.[23]

Although teachers are responsible for protecting students from injury, they are not liable for every accidental injury. In determining the basis for liability,

> Courts have generally held schools or their agents liable for injuries received during the course of regular school events, which resulted from the failure to provide a reasonably safe environment, failure to warn participants of known hazards (or to remove known dangers where possible), failure to properly instruct participants in the activity, or failure to provide supervision adequate for the type of activity and the ages of the participants involved.[24]

Negligence

Teachers are negligent when they fail to use proper standards and care to protect students or fail to foresee and correct potential harm in a situation. Tort law is based on reasonableness. In determining liability, teachers are held responsible for doing "what a reasonable, prudent person, one of ordinary intelligence would do or should have done, in the same circumstances." The standards for judging negligence are typically based on the following points:

- **Duty and standard of care.** This refers to the expectation that teachers supervise students, maintain a safe environment, and give proper instruction.
- **Breach of duty.** This refers to whether or not teachers are derelict in their duties to supervise, maintain a safe environment, and give proper instruction.
- **Proximate cause.** This means that teachers' failure to do their duty resulted in loss or injury.
- **Injury and damages.** This means that a student suffered some loss or injury.[25]

Avoiding Negligence

You should always keep the best interests of students in the forefront of your thinking and planning. These are some things you can do as a first-year teacher to avoid and prevent negligence:

- **Always act in such a manner that you can pass the reasonable, prudent person test.** Be a cautious teacher. Always look for hazards, provide for your students' safety, and do not let your students participate in activities that will put them at risk for injury.
- **Plan for what you are going to do.** During your daily lesson planning, review and reflect on the activities students will participate in and what you need to do to ensure their safety and well-being.
- **Make sure you know your duties and responsibilities.** It is always better to know ahead of time what you are responsible for so you can make appropriate plans and take proper action.
- **Be safety conscious.** Part of being safety conscious is being aware of dangers and hazards in the classroom and other settings. If you are teaching chemistry and there is not enough and/or the right kind of safety equipment to protect your students from harm, then you should discuss this with your principal and make arrangements for providing a safe environment for teaching science.
- **Know the ages and developmental levels of your students.** Third-graders will need a different kind and level of supervision than will sixth-graders.
- **Do your job.** Doing your job requires that you plan for what students will do and supervise their learning and behavior in a professional manner.
- **Teach your students proper behavior and what is expected of them.** When students know what to do and are encouraged to do it, you are providing appropriate guidance.
- **Explore liability insurance provisions.** The National Education Association (NEA) and the American Federation of Teachers (AFT) can provide information on liability insurance provisions.

REFLECT & WRITE

Think about your high school experience. Were there any instances in which teachers did or did not act as a reasonable and prudent person?

_____

_____

_____

_____

_____

Visit http://nccanch.acf.hhs.gov for more information.

■ **INTASC**

STANDARD 9   The teacher is a reflective practitioner who continually evaluates the effects of his/her choices and actions on others (students, parents, and other professionals in the learning community) and who actively seeks out opportunities to grow professionally.

For more information on child abuse, see the Child Welfare website at www.childwelfare.gov/pubs/factsheets/signs.cfm.

Qualified immunity   Official immunity from damages for acts that violate another's civil rights.

TABLE 8.2   Physical and Behavioral Signs of Child Abuse

Types of Abuse	Physical and Behavioral Signs
Physical	■ Unexplained burns, cuts, bruises, or welts in the shape of an object ■ Bite marks ■ Antisocial behavior ■ Problems in school ■ Fear of adults
Emotional	■ Apathy ■ Depression ■ Hostility or stress ■ Lack of concentration ■ Eating disorders
Sexual	■ Inappropriate interest or knowledge of sexual acts ■ Nightmares and bed wetting ■ Drastic changes in appetite ■ Overcompliance or excessive aggression ■ Fear of a particular person or family member
Neglect	■ Unsuitable clothing for weather ■ Dirty or unbathed ■ Extreme hunger ■ Apparent lack of supervision

Source: Recognizing Child Abuse and Neglect: Signs and Symptoms Fact Sheet. (2006). Child Welfare Information Gateway. (Online). www.childwelfare.gov/pubs/factsheet/signs.cfm.

Reporting Child Abuse

Child abuse and neglect are serious problems in contemporary society. A survey by the National Clearinghouse on Child Abuse and Neglect estimates more than 906,000 children are abused or neglected.[26] The Child Abuse Prevention and Treatment Act of 1996 was amended and reauthorized in 2003 by the Keeping Children and Families Safe Act of 2003 (PL 108-36). The act defines abuse and neglect as the "physical or mental injury, sexual abuse, or exploitation, negligent treatment, or maltreatment of a child by a person who is responsible for the child's welfare, under circumstances which indicate that the child's health or welfare is harmed or threatened."

Whenever and wherever adults provide services to children and youth, issues of sexual and physical abuse inevitably arise. In today's litigious climate, more students are charging teachers with abuse. Teachers and principals must seriously consider and weigh students' complaints regarding sexual abuse. To ignore such complaints invites risk. Take, for example, the following 1996 case from Texas:

> The U.S. Supreme Court . . . refused to disturb a federal appeals court ruling that held a high school principal potentially liable for a teacher's sexual abuse of a student. . . . In *Lankford v. Doe* (Case No. 93-1918), the Court turned down the appeal of Eddy Lankford, who has since retired as the principal of Taylor (Texas) High School. Lankford, in a lawsuit filed by a former Taylor High student, was accused of ignoring evidence that she was being sexually abused by one of her teachers.[27]

The *Lankford* ruling is particularly significant for school administrators. By allowing the federal appeals court ruling to stand, this marked the first time in legal history that a principal has been denied qualified immunity. **Qualified immunity** is "official immunity from damages for acts that violate another's civil rights that is granted if it can be shown that the acts do not violate clearly established statutory or constitutional rights of which a reasonable person would be aware."[28] Under the principle of qualified immunity, principals are immune from the consequences of their decisions except in cases of negligence. The *Lankford* ruling is significant in that for the first time, principals are no longer immune from suits and are liable for all their decisions in fulfilling their duties.

Teachers are required by federal law to report all suspected cases of child abuse. In many cases, teachers are the frontline defense in protecting children from abuse by parents and others. Teachers see children every day and are in a special caring relationship with them. Generally, schools and school districts have procedures for how and through what channels teachers are to report suspected cases of abuse. As a first-year teacher, you will want to acquaint yourself with the procedures used in your district for reporting abuse. Furthermore, you should familiarize yourself with some key signs of physical abuse and neglect, sexual abuse, and emotional maltreatment of children (see Table 8.2).

You and other teachers are on the line for reporting abuse. Educational personnel report more cases of abuse than any other group.[29] Although teachers are required to report cases of abuse, they are also protected from being sued for reporting suspected cases.

Avoiding Sexual Harassment

Title VII of the Civil Rights Act of 1964 (PL 88-352) prohibits discrimination based on gender and defines sexual harassment as unwelcome sexual advances, requests for sexual favors, and other verbal or physical conduct of a sexual nature. Teachers have a responsibility to conduct themselves in such a manner that they do not sexually harass students, staff, colleagues, and parents. As a teacher, it is important that you:

- Be familiar with your school's or district's sexual harassment policy.
- Avoid situations in which you are alone with a student. If you think it is necessary and appropriate, ask another teacher or a parent to be present.
- Act appropriately at all times.
- Don't talk about sex, engage in flirtatious behavior, or tell sexually oriented jokes or stories.
- Ask your teacher-mentor or principal for advice and assistance in dealing with a difficult student or colleague.

In a 1998 case involving sexual harassment of students by teachers, *Gebser v. Lago Vista Independent School District*, the Supreme Court ruled that a school district cannot be held liable under Title IX of the Education Amendments of 1972 unless an official in a position to take corrective action knew of a teacher's harassment of a student and was "deliberately indifferent to it." As you will recall, Title IX prohibits sexual discrimination in educational programs that receive federal money. Remember also that the Supreme Court has ruled that sexual harassment

• *Your Turn*

You are in your first year of teaching. One of your students, Emily, is the 9-year-old daughter of the town's leading physician, and you found her crying in the girls' restroom today. She would not tell you why she was crying. Emily seems frightened of everyone, and she frequently wears long-sleeved shirts in very hot weather. She seems to have accidents more often than other children in your class. What should you do?

YOU DECIDE

Is It Sexual Harassment or Sex Discrimination?

Marissa, a junior in high school, is an all-around athlete. She is active in sports year round and enjoys being competitive. She also enjoys the companionship she gets from her teammates. Over the years, her soccer, basketball, and lacrosse coaches—some male, some female—have been close with their players, giving them pats of support on the back, and, when necessary, guiding them physically through the motions of the sport to improve their performance.

Recently, Marissa has been feeling uncomfortable with her basketball coach, Coach Bob, as he likes to be called. In the past, some coaches would pat her on the back or squeeze her shoulder to show support; however, Coach Bob pats her on her backside and rubs up to her in a way that makes her feel uncomfortable. Several of her friends have been complaining about Coach Bob's touchy-feely behavior to each other, but only jokingly, because they are afraid he will find out and make them work even harder or kick them off the team. One day after practice, Marissa was called in to Coach Bob's office. He said he wanted to talk to her about her plans for playing basketball in college. As they were talking, he made some sexual comments about her and her friends that made her very uncomfortable. This encounter made her so depressed that she considered quitting the team so she wouldn't have to deal with Coach Bob's sleazy behavior and innuendos.

Title IX prohibits sexual discrimination in educational programs that receive federal money. Additionally, the Supreme Court has ruled that sexual harassment is a form of sex discrimination, but there has been considerable public debate about this decision.

In Marissa's case, is Coach Bob guilty of sex discrimination, and therefore subject to the conditions of Title IX? As Marissa's teacher, if you were to catch wind of Coach Bob's behavior, would you consider it to be sexual harassment, and, if so, how would you respond to the situation?

For more information on sex discrimination and sexual harassment, visit the Equal Rights' Advocates website at www.equalrights.org/publications/kyr/shschool.asp.

is a form of sex discrimination. There has been considerable public debate about this decision.

The Department of Education and the National Association of Attorneys General have released a guidebook, *Revised Sexual Harassment Guidance: Harassment of Students by School Employees, Other Students, or Third Parties*,[30] recommending procedures school districts can adopt to prevent sexual, physical, and emotional abuse. The guidebook also provides guidelines for disciplining students and teachers who violate the guidelines.

REFLECT & WRITE

The coach of the girls soccer team at the local high school has a habit of "getting in the face of" players who "mess up." Is this sexual harassment?

_____

_____

_____

_____

_____

Observing Copyright Law

Teachers use various types of supplemental materials to support their teaching and to involve students in learning activities. The use of copy machines, DVD players, and computers is routine for the majority of teachers. As a beginning teacher, you need to know what your legal responsibilities are regarding copying and using materials.

The Copyright Law of 1978 (PL 94-553) and its revisions govern what teachers and others can and cannot do regarding the copying of material. Teachers may make single copies of material for their own use and research. They may make multiple copies if each copy carries a notice of copyright, is used only for one course in the school, and meets conditions of spontaneity and brevity. Photocopying is not permitted when it replaces anthologies, is from a consumable product such as a workbook, is intended to replace books, or when students are charged for the copies they make beyond what it costs to copy the materials.

Go to MyEducationLab and select the topic "Ethical and Legal Issues" then read the article "Copyright 101." Answer the questions that follow.

Copying software is governed by license agreements. Software designed for a single user cannot be copied without a license. School districts purchase licenses that enable them to make copies of software programs for use by staff, students, and faculty. New copyright laws relating to electronic documents, such as material pulled from the Internet, both print and video, are discussed in Chapter 12.

Teachers must receive permission in advance to copy television broadcasts. These copies can be kept for only 45 days and must be shown to students within the first 10 days of the 45-day period.

Practicing Ethical Behavior

Professional teachers conduct their practices in ways that are legally and ethically proper. Professionals want to do what is right in their relationship with students, colleagues, and parents. They base their behavior on a code of professional ethics. Many professions, such as medicine and law, have unified and universal codes of ethics that govern practice. The teaching profession does not have a unified code of ethics that governs the practice of all education professionals. However, professional organizations that represent educators, such as the NEA, have developed codes of ethics that help inform and guide professional practice.

Some states have legislated their own codes of ethics for teachers that by law are supposed to guide professional behavior. These state codes of ethics serve three purposes. First, they help establish a uniformity in ethical practice throughout the state. Second, they inform all teachers of the expectations of ethical professional practice. Third, they serve as the basis for guiding decisions of hiring and dismissal.

In your teaching, you will be involved in ethical dilemmas, such as those at the end of each chapter, that will require you to think about what course of action is in the best interests of students, parents, and families. For example, how would you deal with the possible abuse of a student? Would you report a faculty member you had observed harassing another faculty member or a student? Would you put your personal ethics before a job or a threat? Many programs of teacher preparation provide opportunities for prospective teachers to engage in analysis of ethical dilemmas through case studies.

By devoting serious consideration to ethical behavior and how ethics relates to you as a professional you will accomplish three outcomes. First, you will be a better person and a better professional. Second, your students will benefit from your behavior. Third, the teaching profession will grow in public respect and admiration.

WHAT ARE YOUR LEGAL RIGHTS AS A TEACHER?

Just as it is important to know your legal responsibilities as a teacher, it is also important to understand your legal rights. Some relate to your rights as a citizen, others relate to your role as a teacher. Knowing your rights empowers you as a professional and allows you to exercise your informed judgment and take action on the issues you will face in your professional responsibilities.

Nondiscrimination

Teachers have rights relating to nondiscrimination. School districts and school officials cannot discriminate in the hiring, dismissal, promotion, and demotion of teachers. Many cases of discrimination against teachers involve discrimination on the basis of sex, race, or disability; pay equity issues; and unequal treatment.

- **Pregnancy leave.** In *Cleveland Board of Education v. LaFleur* (1977), the Supreme Court said it was discriminatory to make pregnant teachers take mandatory pregnancy leaves at fixed periods before and after giving birth. The Court said that while boards of education could set policy standards about teachers' pregnancy leaves, they could not set arbitrary leave and return dates.
- **Sex discrimination.** Title IX of the Education Amendments of 1972 prohibits discrimination on the basis of sex in education programs or activities that receive federal financial assistance. The Supreme Court, in *North Haven Board of Education v. Bell* (1982), ruled that Title IX provides protection from discrimination for teachers and students. Under Title IX, the Department of Education can investigate complaints of sexual discrimination and can curtail federal funding to programs and agencies that discriminate.
- **Protection of lesbians' and gay men's rights.** More states and school districts are passing laws and drafting policies designed to promote and protect the rights of lesbians, gay men, and bisexual women and men. Massachusetts was the first state in the country to pass a law protecting homosexual youth from discrimination. Teachers are protected as well.

There has been much debate over the legal rights of gay and lesbian teachers. In 1990, the Gay, Lesbian and Straight Teachers Network (GLSTN) was founded. Its mission is to ensure that each member of the school community is valued and respected, regardless of sexual orientation. Even with the support of such a network, no federal legislation has been passed to protect against employment discrimination based on sexual orientation. Whereas Title VII of the Civil Rights Act of 1964 prohibits employment discrimination based on race, color, religion, sex, and national origin, courts have held that Title VII does not prohibit discrimination based on sexual orientation.

Although no federal law prohibits a school district from discriminating against a teacher based on her or his sexual preference, nine states, the District of Columbia, and many cities have passed legislation preventing this type of discrimination. However, many of these laws contain addendums stating that the legislation does not condone or promote homosexuality or bisexuality. The Connecticut law, for example, which prohibits discrimination based on sexual orientation, also states that the law shall not be read:

> to authorize the promotion of homosexuality or bisexuality in educational institutions or require the teaching in educational institutions of homosexuality or bisexuality as an acceptable lifestyle . . .[31]

This issue will continue to develop as the twenty-first-century workforce becomes more diverse, and the civil rights of all employees will need to be clarified. However, case law suggests that unless sexual orientation negatively impacts students or the employee's ability to perform the job, no adverse action should be taken against gays and lesbians.[32]

REFLECT & WRITE

Do you think sexual preference should play a role in determining whether or not any person is granted a contract to teach?

_____

_____

_____

_____

_____

Contracts and Tenure

Once you have earned certification, you must find a job and enter into a contract. When you enter into a contract with a school district, you commit yourself to certain legal obligations. You should read your contract before you sign it in order to know your obligations, your responsibilities, what you need to do to earn or qualify for **tenure** or a continuing contract, and the grounds for dismissal.

Tenure The right to permanent employment after serving a probationary period of successful teaching, ranging in length from 3 to 5 years.

It is surprising how many teachers don't read their contracts until there is a question about their continuing employment. For example, beginning teacher Marlene Mendez, who teaches high school television production, received notice from her principal that she was responsible for developing a student-produced program commemorating Dr. Martin Luther King, Jr., to be shown on district closed-circuit television. When Marlene questioned the additional assignment, her principal showed her the contract she signed, which stated that such additional assignments relating to curriculum development were permitted. Her principal further explained that it was a reasonable assignment, because it was a project she and her students could work on during class time. Generally, the reasonableness test is one often applied in determining what is appropriate in terms of teachers' duties.

Teachers are granted tenure, the right to permanent employment, after serving a probationary period of successful teaching ranging in length from 3 to 5 years. During this time, teachers must demonstrate satisfactory teaching as measured by a district's teacher-evaluation process. The purpose of tenure laws is to prevent the firing of teachers for political or arbitrary reasons and protect teachers' academic freedom. Most states have tenure and dismissal laws that apply to all teachers. Tenure laws provide for dismissal based on certain reasons, such as negligence, and due process must be followed in dismissal proceedings. Tenure provides teachers with two important guarantees: protection from dismissal except for certain causes and the right to dismissal procedures as specified by state law.

Although tenure does provide teachers with security and protection, not everyone thinks it is a good idea. Those who object to tenure maintain it protects incompetent teachers and makes it too difficult to dismiss those who should not be teaching. Proponents of tenure argue that tenure protects competent teachers and frees teachers from the uncertainty about knowing if they will have a job from one year to the next. More important, tenure laws make it easier for teachers to practice their profession. With tenure, they are more confident about trying new methods and techniques, introducing new curricula, and taking risks in their efforts to provide the best possible education for their students.

Alternatives to career-long tenure are **renewable contracts** that are valid for certain periods of time, generally 5 years. Advocates of renewable contracts believe they can act as a safeguard for districts from hiring and then being stuck with a poor teacher forever and can also be an incentive to teachers to constantly do their best.

Renewable contracts A school can renew a teacher's contract after a certain period of time, usually 3 to 5 years. The school evaluates the teacher's performance at that time and decides whether to renew the contract.

REFLECT & WRITE

What questions will you ask about your first-year contract before you sign it?

_____

_____

_____

_____

_____

Evaluations and Grounds for Dismissal

As a beginning teacher, you will be evaluated from two to four times in your first year of teaching. The purpose of these evaluations is to determine your ability to teach, assess your professional strengths and weaknesses, and provide a basis for improvement. Teachers' contracts usually specify the manner and conditions of evaluation. The collective bargaining agreement (contract) between a school district and its bargaining agent (usually a professional organization) outlines in detail the manner, content, and procedure for teacher evaluation. Due process procedures also apply to teacher evaluations.

Most states and school districts have specific causes and procedures for dismissal, which vary from state to state. Grounds for dismissal that have been upheld by various courts include contract abandonment (refusal to do the job or refusal to report to work), failing to meet continuing education and certification requirements, declining enrollments, budgetary reasons, excessive absence and tardiness,

■ INTASC

STANDARD 9 The teacher is a reflective practitioner who continually evaluates the effects of his/her choices and actions on others (students, parents, and other professionals in the learning community) and who actively seeks out opportunities to grow professionally.

immorality, criminal conduct, falsehood, neglect of duty, incompetence, and insubordination.[33]

In addition, most states have specified the procedures to be followed in initiating and conducting dismissal proceedings against teachers. Again, these procedures are designed to protect the due process rights of teachers and to spell out what administrators and boards of education must do.

Collective Bargaining and the Right to Strike

Collective bargaining   The process by which terms and conditions of employment are negotiated by a bargaining agent (usually a professional organization) with the school district on behalf of all teachers.

Collective bargaining is the process by which terms and conditions of employment are negotiated by a bargaining agent (usually a professional organization) with the school district on behalf of all teachers. Many states have collective bargaining laws and agreements that provide public employees the right to organize, bargain collectively, and determine the bargaining agent that will represent them. Bargaining agreements also specify the things that can be bargained (for example, salary, benefits, working conditions, and a range of policy issues) and what happens when the parties bargaining are not able to agree. The AFT or the NEA is the collective bargaining agent for many teachers. About 75 percent of the nation's teachers are covered by a bargaining agreement.

Teachers have the right to organize and to join professional organizations. One of the first decisions you will have to make as a new teacher is whether or not to join a professional organization or labor union. Many school districts have a local teachers' organization that is affiliated with either the NEA or the AFT. Some organizations, such as the Milwaukee Teachers' Association, are not affiliated with national organizations and represent their members as a local agency. Also, Georgia, Texas, and Missouri have three of the largest independent professional organizations in the country. Membership in independent teacher organizations totals over 300,000 in over 21 states.

Some states have laws allowing teachers to strike; other states set limitations on strikes. Some states do not allow teachers the right to strike. What rights to strike or to other work stoppages do teachers have in your state? Would you participate in a strike? Would you walk a picket line as these teachers are doing?

Joining and paying dues to a professional organization offers a number of benefits. One is that the organization represents—through member-elected representatives—teachers in dismissal proceedings and in disputes with the school district. When teachers believe they have been aggrieved by the board of education or administration, they can file a grievance or complaint. The bargaining agreement specifies the procedures for settling such grievances. Another benefit is that teachers may be provided with free legal advice and/or counsel and can purchase liability insurance. Participation in professional organization activities is also another way for teachers to influence local and national education policy.

At any particular time across the United States, but especially at the beginning of the school year, you will read about strikes by teachers. From Detroit to Buffalo, Washington State to Hawaii, teachers strike about pay, terms of employment, and working conditions.

In June 2006, the Detroit teacher's union sought a 15.6 percent pay increase for its top-tier teachers. When this request was rejected, teachers went on strike for 2 weeks. In this high-risk school district, where teachers often have to battle gang violence and drug abuse in the classroom, teachers asked for a 3-year contract, a 5 percent annual raise, and a provision that stated that any student who threatened a teacher would be moved to another class. After a 5-day strike, the teachers, school board, and local and state government reached a compromise. The parties agreed to a 3-year tentative agreement, with a 1 percent raise the second year and a 2.5 percent raise the third year.

Thirty-seven states have laws that prohibit strikes by public employees. One purpose of such legislation is to protect the public interest and to help ensure that settlements occur through collective bargaining agreements. Laws in other states, such as the Pennsylvania Public Employees Relations Act, give teachers the right to strike. However, the state law requires 180 days of instruction by June 30, so the number of days teachers can strike is limited.

_____

_____

_____

_____

_____

REFLECT & WRITE

Teachers' strikes are controversial. Some think teachers should have the right to strike; others think it is unprofessional. Give two reasons, pro or con, about where you stand on the issue of teachers and strikes.

Academic Freedom

In Ms. Garcia's eight-grade health class, students tense a bit as she describes the different types of contraceptives and shows photos of sexually transmitted diseases. In Mr. Prothero's eight-grade health class, he is not allowed to discuss anything other than abstinence-only alternatives to conception and sexually transmitted diseases. Not all teachers and schools are given the same amount of control over what they teach.

Academic freedom is the freedom of teachers to teach subjects in the manner they want and the freedom to express views regarding these subjects. However, teachers cannot do or say anything in the name of academic freedom. Religion is one area that causes a lot of curriculum contention.

Academic freedom The right of teachers to teach what and how they want without constraint from others.

Creationism versus Evolution

In particular, teaching about the origins of the world and humans has caused and causes much debate and legal action. The creationism point of view adheres to the account found in Genesis in the Bible. The evolutionary view supports the theory of evolution as articulated by Charles Darwin. A major legal conflict occurred in Tennessee in 1925. Under the state's Butler Act, it was illegal to teach in the public schools "any theory which denies the story of the Divine Creation of man as taught in the Bible, and to teach instead that man is descended from a lower order of animals." The Scopes trial, also called the "monkey trial," involved the right of John Scopes, a biology teacher who challenged the law, to teach the evolution theory. This trial pitted two legal giants of the day against each other. Clarence Darrow represented Scopes, and William Jennings Bryan, the "silver-tongued orator," represented the state as prosecutor. Scopes was found guilty of breaking Tennessee law and fined $100, but the precedent was nevertheless set for the teaching of evolution.[34]

In 1982, the Louisiana legislature passed a Balanced Treatment for Creation-Science and Evolution Science Act. The Balanced Treatment Act, as it was called, required the teaching of creation science whenever evolution was taught. After a number of court challenges, the Supreme Court in *Edwards v. Aquillard* ruled against the Balanced Treatment Act. The Court held that the purpose of the act was to promote religion and was a violation of the First Amendment.

More recently, the focus has turned from teaching creation science to presenting intelligent design. Intelligent design is the theory that certain features of the universe and of living things are best explained by an intelligent cause, not an undirected process, such as natural selection. The intelligent design curriculum has been scrutinized in numerous court cases. In Pennsylvania in 2005, a U.S. District Judge ruled that teaching intelligent design in biology class was teaching "creationism in disguise," and that it therefore violated the constitutional separation of church and state.[35]

What's *New* in Education?

Knowledge Is Power

From your high school days, recall that you learned about sexual health and responsibility in a health class or similar course. Sex education has been, and remains, a hotly debated issue, with abstinence-only programs becoming increasingly popular. This approach to sex education has both pros and cons. Supporters of abstinence-only programs contend that these programs teach responsibility and help youth attain more "meaningful" relationships. Opponents quote the statistics that over half of teens who take abstinence-until-marriage pledges break those pledges within the first year.

In 2004, the Texas State Board of Education approved four different sex education textbooks. Of the four, three didn't mention condoms or other contraceptives, and one mentioned latex condoms only briefly. All the books considered for adoption presented abstinence as the only 100 percent effective way to prevent pregnancy or STDs.

Many concerned parents, teachers, and students protested the Texas State Board of Education decision. Not only does the board's decision affect what students learn, but it also affects schools across the nation. Texas is the largest buyer of textbooks in the United States. Because of this, publishers' choices are likely to reflect the choices of the market. Textbooks are more likely to be designed according to Texas standards and then distributed across the nation.

Publishers deny that they're censoring information for students, saying that they are providing the books that teachers and administrators want. However, it does raise issues about what is and what is not taught in school textbooks. Many supporters of abstinence-only sex education programs are religious groups, which raises the question: Is the adoption of textbooks that include or exclude certain content censorship? Or, should textbooks reflect the views held by a state board of education, which are a reflection of the views of the majority of its citizens?

Sources: ABC News, Texas Debates Sex Ed Textbooks (2004, October 9). Available at http://abcnews.go.com/WNT/story?id=147827&page=1. Harper, J. (2006, January 22). Youths support abstinence as sex education. *The Washington Times.* Baltimore: The Washington Times.

Freedom of Expression

The First Amendment constitutes a teacher's basic guarantee of **freedom of expression**. The extent to which teachers may exercise their freedom of speech depends on the type of speech involved and its actual or potential effect on the school environment. Generally, challenges to teachers' freedom of expression are not an issue unless such expression is disruptive of or detrimental to the educational process.

In 1968 in *Pickering v. Board of Education*, the Supreme Court ruled that a teacher could not be dismissed for speaking as a citizen on matters of public concern. Pickering, an Illinois teacher, published a letter to the editor of the local newspaper that was critical of the board of education for the way it handled school funding. The board said that Pickering's letter was defamatory and fired him. The case reached the Supreme Court, which ruled that teachers, as experts on the inner workings of the educational system, should not be punished for speaking out against the allocation of funds or any other part of the educational system. This protects teachers who exercise their First Amendment rights if they voice their opinion in a public forum, such as a newspaper.[36]

Academic freedom, as the foregoing examples indicate, continues to be a hotly debated issue. In a closely watched case, the Fourth U.S. Circuit Court of Appeals ruled that teachers have no right of academic freedom in selecting curriculum content. The 1998 case of *Boring v. Buncombe County Board of Education* involved a high school drama teacher, Margaret Boring, who was transferred in response to controversy over a play she chose for students in her acting class. Boring cleared the play with her principal. Later, when a parent objected to the contents of the play, the principal edited several scenes before the play was presented in a state competition at the end of the year. The principal gave Boring "superior" and "well above standard" ratings in all categories on her annual performance review. Nonetheless, the principal recommended that Boring be transferred to another school because of "personal conflicts resulting from actions she initiated during the course of the school year." The superintendent and the school board approved the transfer. Boring sued the principal, superintendent, and school board, claiming they violated her rights under the First Amendment. The court ruled that a high school teacher has no academic freedom to control the curriculum; therefore, "Boring's dispute was nothing more than an ordinary employment dispute."[37]

Freedom of expression   The right of teachers to express their personal beliefs so long as it does not interfere with the teacher's obligations to teach or that it does not substantially jeopardize the maintenance of order and discipline in the school.

YOU DECIDE

Presenting Points of View

Think for a moment about the many topics presented in this chapter that have many different sides. For example, should students be taught that abstinence before marriage is the only means of contraception, or should they hear other viewpoints, too? Given the reality that many topics have many different points of view, would you withhold the information from students? Give a specific example. The NEA Code of Ethics says that professionals "shall not unreasonably deny the student access to varying points of view," meaning that teachers cannot deny students exposure to ideas that might not be mainstream or that are contrary to the views held by the teacher. How would you decide issues based on this guideline? What are some points of view that students might question you about?

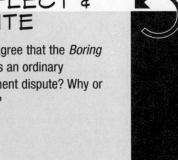

REFLECT & WRITE

Do you agree that the *Boring* case was an ordinary employment dispute? Why or why not?

WHAT ARE STUDENTS' LEGAL RIGHTS?

In many schools, students must walk through metal detectors to get to class. Many schools do not permit students to bring backpacks or purses to class because they could cause disruptions, harbor weapons, or hide cell phones and food. Students have been suspended for wearing clothing that is considered to be subversive or that might cause conflict with other students because it expresses gang allegiance, alternative beliefs, or political and religious views. So what exactly are students' rights? In the past few decades, many students and parents have challenged the legal system to ensure students' rights. Figure 8.4 lists a number of Supreme Court decisions that affect students and parents.

Zucht v. King (1922). The Court upheld the requirement that a child must be vaccinated before attending school.

Pierce v. Society of Sisters of the Holy Names of Jesus and Mary (1925). The Court ruled unconstitutional an Oregon law requiring parents to send their children to public school. The Court said that such a law denied parents the right to control the education of their children.

Tinker v. Des Moines Independent School District (1969). The Court ruled that "it can hardly be argued that either students or teachers shed their constitutional rights to freedom of expression at the schoolhouse gate." Students have a right to freedom of expression. Generally, restrictions on students' and teachers' dress must have a legitimate educational value.

Wisconsin v. Yoder (1972). The Court ruled that Old Order Amish, because of their well-established beliefs, must be given some relief from compulsory attendance.

Lau v. Nichols (1974). The Court struck down a school district practice of requiring Chinese students to attend classes taught in English. This case effectively set the stage for bilingual education.

Ingraham v. Wright (1977). The Court ruled that disciplinary paddling of public school students does not constitute cruel and unusual punishment.

Goss v. Lopez (1975). The Court said that students cannot be suspended without a hearing.

Board of Education of Hendrick Hudson Central School District v. Rowley (1982). The Court defined "free and appropriate" education.

Plyer v. Doe (1982). The Court ruled that Texas could not withhold free public education from undocumented alien children in part because "education provides the basic tools by which individuals might lead economically productive lives to the benefit of us all."

Board of Education v. Rowley (1982). The court ruled that the Individuals with Disabilities Education Act's statutory entitlement to a "free and appropriate public education" for all students, including those with disabilities, means that school authorities must comply with the act's procedural requirements, which include developing individualized education programs for students with disabilities.

New Jersey v. T.L.O. (1985). The Court determined that school officials are not necessarily bound by the Fourth Amendment but by reasonable cause when engaged in searches.

Bethel School District No. 403 v. Fraser (1986). The Court ruled that school officials can restrain student speech.

Hazelwood School District v. Kuhlmeier (1988). The Court ruled that administrators have the right to censor school newspapers, and they can block "speech that is ungrammatical, poorly written, inadequately researched, biased or prejudiced, vulgar or profane, or unsuitable for immature audiences."

Franklin v. Gwinnett County Public Schools (1992). The Court ruled that Title IX authorized students who have been sexually harassed by teachers to recover damages from the school district.

Zorbrest et al. v. Catalina Foothills School District (1993). The Court ruled that the establishment clause does not prevent a school from furnishing a disabled child enrolled in a sectarian school with assistance to facilitate his/her education.

Lankford v. Doe (1994). The Court upheld a ruling that holds a principal potentially liable for a teacher's sexual abuse of a student.

Veronia School District v. Acton (1995). The Court upheld the right of the Veronia, Oregon, School District to conduct a program of random urinalysis testing of middle and high school athletes.

U.S. v. Lopez (1995). The Court said that Congress exceeded its powers in passing the Gun-Free School Zones Act, which mandated compulsory expulsion for one year for students who bring guns to school.

United States v. Virginia (1996). The Court stated that "parties who seek to defend gender-based government action must demonstrate 'exceedingly persuasive justification' for that action." To meet the burden of justification a state must show at least that the classification serves "important governmental objectives and that the discriminatory means employed" are "substantially related to the achievement of those objectives."

Agostini v. Felton (1997). The Court held that a federally funded program providing supplemental, remedial instruction to disadvantaged children on a neutral basis is not invalid under the establishment clause when such instruction is given on the premises of sectarian schools by government employees under a program containing safeguards.

Bragdon v. Abbott (1998). School districts are subject to both the Americans with Disabilities Act (ADA) and the Rehabilitation Act of 1973 if they receive federal funds. The Court ruled that "HIV infection satisfies the statutory and regulatory definition of a physical impairment during every stage of the disease," thus people who carry the HIV virus are entitled to the broad rights given to disabled people through the ADA.

Davis v. Monroe County Board of Education (1999). The Court ruled that schools are held liable if they ignore excessive sexual harassment of one student by another student.

Santa Fe Independent School District v. Doe (2000). The Court held that a district's policy permitting student-led, student-initiated prayer at football games is in violation of freedom of religion.

Troxel v. Granville (2000). The Court affirmed the fundamental right of parents to control the upbringing of their children, including their education.

Owasso Independent School District v. Falvo (2002). Students can grade each other's academic work and announce the results in class without violating a federal privacy law.

Board of Education of Independent School District No. 92 [OK], et al., v. Lindsay Earls, et al. (2002). The Court approved an Oklahoma school district's mandating drug testing for all students who wished to participate in extracurricular activities, including the chess club, the Honor Society, and the marching band.

United States v. American Library Association (2003). The Court ruled that Congress can require public libraries to install computer filters that block access to Internet pornography.

Ashcroft v. American Civil Liberties Union (2004). The Court put on hold the Child Online Protection Act, which would impose criminal penalties on commercial Web publishers who fail to restrict access by minors to sexually explicit material.

Elk Grove Unified School District v. Newdow (2004). On technical grounds, the Court preserved the phrase "one nation under God" in the Pledge of Allegiance. The Court said Michael Newdow could not sue to ban the pledge from his daughter's school because he did not have legal authority to speak for her.

Morse v. Frederick (2007). An 18-year-old student, Joseph Frederick, held up a banner that read "Bong Hits 4 Jesus" in front of television cameras across the street from Juneau-Douglas High School. Principal Morse confiscated the banner and suspended Frederick for 10 days. The Court held that school officials did not violate the First Amendment by confiscating the pro-drug banner and suspending the student.

FIGURE 8.4 Supreme Court Cases Affecting the Rights of Students and Parents

These Supreme Court cases from this and the last century affect students' Freedom of Speech rights and restrictions.

REFLECT & WRITE

Based on the summaries above, which, if any, of these decisions do you think might have implications for you as a teacher? Why?

Freedom of Expression

One result of the increased concern for students' rights is that many laws have been passed and court decisions issued that define, extend, and defend students' rights. In particular, students' rights to free expression in terms of speech and dress have been, and remain, a central legal issue.

Free Speech

When you think about freedom of speech, what comes to mind? Perhaps you think only about speaking and writing, but true freedom of speech encompasses much more than that. It includes all forms of expression—speaking, writing, and even clothing. Political buttons, T-shirts, piercings, tattoos, and hair color all express something about a person. Displaying items such as a sign or symbol on your personal belongings or home also is part of speech. Students express themselves in a variety of ways, some of which are limited by the school, state, and federal government, whereas others are protected.

The Supreme Court ruled in 1969 in the landmark case *Tinker v. Des Moines Independent School District* that the First Amendment protected students who wore a black armband to school in protest of the Vietnam War from suspension or other disciplinary action. Times have certainly changed, and freedom of expression continues to be at the center of many First Amendment cases.

Go to MyEducationLab and select the topic "Ethical and Legal Issues" and read the article "A New Vision for the First Amendment in Schools." Answer the questions that follow.

Many freedom of speech cases now involve the Internet. MySpace (myspace.com) is a site where people can create their own personalized Web pages that include their profile, friends, interests, and music. The site has come under scrutiny in relation to students' rights of freedom of expression. In 2006, a case came before the Indiana Court of Appeals involving a MySpace page reportedly created by the principle of Greencastle Middle School. However, it was not Greencastle's principal, Shawn Gobert, who created the page. A student had posted a spoof profile of Gobert on MySpace, and other students could comment on the page. The case was brought to court when a student who did not create the page posted derogatory comments on it concerning the school's policy on body piercings. The state filed a delinquency petition against the student who left the comments, saying that his acts constituted harassment, identity deception, and identity theft if committed by an adult. The school later dropped most of these charges but found the student to be a delinquent child and placed her on 9 months probation. A juvenile judge also ruled the student's comments were obscene.

When the case was appealed, a Court of Appeals ruled that the student's comments were protected under the First Amendment, and that the juvenile court had unconstitutionally restricted her right of free expression.[38]

REFLECT & WRITE

Do you think students should have any restrictions at all on their freedom of expression in your classroom? Where would you draw the line, if any, on what students could or could not say in your classroom?

_____

_____

_____

_____

_____

■ INTASC

STANDARD 5   The teacher uses an understanding of individual and group motivation and behavior to create a learning environment that encourages positive social interaction, active engagement in learning, and self-motivation.

Sometimes what constitutes freedom of speech is not clearcut. For example, at Newman High School in Carrollton, Texas, students were set to publish an article in the *Odyssey*, the school newspaper, about the efforts of some students to start a gay and lesbian support club. But Principal Lee Alvoia pulled the article. Alvoia defended her decision based on the conservative values of the school district. "Because of the nature of the topic and because of the conservative nature of the community I didn't want a negative reaction before we even had a club. This is not one of your normal teenage clubs. I didn't want undue controversy."[39]

Principal Alvoia does have the right to pull the article from the *Odyssey* based on a 1998 Supreme Court case involving the school newspaper at Westwood High School in Hazelwood, Missouri. At Westwood, students were about to publish two articles in the *Spectrum*, the school-sponsored newspaper. One article dealt with teenage pregnancy and the other with the effects of divorce on children. Principal Robert Reynolds ordered the pages containing the two articles (and four other articles) removed from the paper. The students sued, and the case ended up in the Supreme Court. The Court found in favor of the school district. In *Hazelwood School District v. Kuhlmeier* the Court ruled that administrators have the right to censor school newspapers, and they can block "speech that is ungrammatical, poorly written, inadequately researched, biased or prejudiced, vulgar or profane, or unsuitable for immature audiences."[40] The Court also held that "educators do not offend the First Amendment by exercising editorial control over the style and content of student speech in school-sponsored expressive activities so long as their actions are reasonably related to legitimate pedagogical concerns."[41] Although administrators have this right, some exercise this option, others do not.

In another incident involving censorship, student Matthew Fraser of Bethel, Washington, at a school assembly, nominated a student for a class office. In so doing, he used extended sexual metaphors. Fraser was suspended for 3 days and removed from the list of graduation speakers. In *Bethel School District No. 403 v. Fraser*, the Supreme Court ruled that "the pervasive sexual innuendo in Fraser's speech was plainly offensive to both teachers and students—indeed to any mature person."[42]

In the case of *Morse v. Frederick*, student Joseph Frederick brought charges against Principal Morse of Juneau-Douglas High School in Juneau, Alaska, for suspending him from school. The suspension was in response to a provocative sign that Frederick and his friends held up across the street from the high school (off school grounds) as television cameras filming the passing of the Olympic torch swept the sidelines. The sign read "Bong Hits 4 Jesus." Principal Morse rushed across the street and confiscated the sign and suspended Frederick for 10 days after he refused to divulge the names of the other students who held the sign up with him.

Frederick sued, stating that the principal had violated his First Amendment rights with the suspension. Principal Morse defended the action by stating that the banner offended the public school's antidrug policy and to let Frederick's action go unpunished would send a mixed signal to the rest of the students. The Supreme Court held that schools may take steps to safeguard those entrusted to their care from speech that can reasonably be regarded as encouraging illegal drug use. They concluded that the school officials in this case did not violate the First Amendment by confiscating the pro-drug banner and suspending the student responsible for it.[43]

Dress Codes

Generally, courts have upheld the right of school districts to set "reasonable" standards of dress and appearance for both students and teachers. However, a problem arises with the interpretation of what is reasonable. Also, as noted in *Tinker*, students have a right to freedom of expression. Generally, restrictions on students' and teachers' dress must have a legitimate educational value. What school districts must be able to show is that the regulation of student appearance is necessary for students' proper functioning and related to district and school goals. An example of a high school dress code is shown in Figure 8.5.

Gang attire is a problem in many school districts and is seen by some as one of the factors related to increasing school violence and decreasing school achievement. Although some districts have drafted dress codes directed toward restricting the wearing of gang attire, other school districts are turning to school uniforms to address issues of clothing and accessories. In 1994, the Long Beach (California) School District became the first in the nation to require all elementary and middle school students to wear uniforms. School officials credit uniform wearing with a sharp reduction in school crime, but there is no research to support this connection. Philadelphia requires all students in its 264 schools to wear uniforms. Each school may select its own style of uniform, but all students must wear them every day. Most large school districts—such as New York, Los Angeles, Chicago, Miami, and Houston—have uniform policies. It is likely that in issues of required uniforms, there will be court cases filed by students and their parents who believe their constitutional rights are being infringed. Issues of the abridgment of First Amendment rights and freedom of student expression will be the basis of these suits.

AISD's new Student Dress Code will be implemented in Fall 2004 to maintain a safe, respectful, and positive learning environment and to model good citizenship. All clothing should be appropriate to the student's age, the school setting, and weather conditions. Both students and parents share the responsibility for the student's attire because clothing often sets the pattern for behavior. Students are required to use good judgment, to respect themselves and others, and to demonstrate modesty in selecting attire.

Clothing may not advertise, condone, depict, or promote the use of alcohol, tobacco, or drugs; also prohibited is clothing with vulgar or obscene language, or with images or writings that promote disruption of the educational setting. Consult your school handbook for any additional clothing guidelines.

	Elementary School	Middle & High School
Clothing		
Athletic Shorts Outside of PE		X
Backless Tops	X	X
Baggy Pants	X	X
Bare Midriffs	X	X
Elongated Armholes	X	
Fake Nails and Makeup	X	
Gang-Associated Clothing or Colors	X	X
Halter Tops	X	X
Low Cut Necklines	X	X
Oversize Shirts	X	
Pajamas		X
See-Through Clothing		X
Shorts that Distract	X	X
Skirts that Distract	X	X
Spaghetti Straps	X	X
Strapless Tops	X	X
Tank Tops		X
Visible Undergarments		X
Footwear		
Slippers	X	X
Headwear		
Hats or caps inside (except for religious headwear)	X	X

*Individual campuses may adopt additional requirements.

FIGURE 8.5 Austin, Texas, Independent School District Dress Code

As a teacher, would you strictly enforce dress codes?

Source: Austin Independent School District Dress Code. Available at www.austin.isd.tenet.edu/academics/parentsinfo/dress_code/index.phtml. Accessed November 12, 2006.

REFLECT & WRITE

Do you think the Austin ISD dress code is reasonable? What would you add to the code? What would you delete?

Due Process

The due process provisions of the Fifth and Fourteenth Amendments and the **equal protection clause** of the Fourteenth Amendment are important parts of student discipline policies and codes. Both provisions require that no person shall "be deprived of life, liberty, or property by the government without due process of law." The due process provisions are designed to ensure that everyone is treated fairly.

The definitions of life, liberty, and property are much broader than you might think. For example, free public education is considered a form of property. So, if for some reason a student is denied a free public education, the due process clause applies. Likewise, a student's good name, reputation, honor, and integrity are considered forms of liberty.

Equal protection clause   The clause of the Fourteenth Amendment that prohibits a state from denying any person within its jurisdiction equal protection of its law.

Discipline

Managing student discipline is always an issue in the schools. Conflicts of what is and is not appropriate behavior, issues of power and control, and what is and isn't proper discipline are at the heart of guiding and managing student behavior.

A number of factors relate to school discipline:

- Students must be given notice of the standards of conduct the school wishes to uphold and enforce.
- It is reasonable that students be given an opportunity to regulate their behavior based on standards provided by the school.
- Teachers should discuss with their students the rules of conduct that prevail in the classroom.

> ■ **INTASC**
>
> **STANDARD 2**   The teacher understands how children learn and develop, and can provide learning opportunities that support their intellectual, social, and personal development.

In *Ingraham v. Wright* (1977), the Supreme Court ruled that disciplinary paddling of public school students does not constitute cruel and unusual punishment. However, not everyone agrees that students should be subjected to corporal punishment. In states that do permit **corporal punishment**, local districts have guidelines for administering it. Corporal punishment is the intentional infliction of physical pain as a means of changing an individual's behavior. If you teach in a district that permits corporal punishment, you should familiarize yourself with the guidelines and should do all you can to avoid using any kind of physical punishment. Many states (24 of them) prohibit corporal punishment. In addition, the NEA has an official position statement against corporal punishment.

Corporal punishment   The intentional infliction of physical pain as a means of changing an individual's behavior.

Suspension and Expulsion

As with all affairs relating to student rights, due process also has to be provided in all proceedings relating to suspension and expulsion. In *Goss v. Lopez*, the Supreme Court said that students cannot be suspended without a hearing. Commenting on the propriety of such a process, the Court said, "It would be a strange disciplinary system in an educational institution if no communication was sought by the disciplinarian with the student in an effort to inform him of his dereliction and to let him tell his side of the story."[44]

Suspensions are used to discipline students when the infractions are not of sufficient magnitude to warrant **expulsion**. Suspension may include the short-term denial of school attendance as well as the denial of participation in regular courses and activities. The suspension can be in-school, meaning that students are at school but not attending a class or classes. Or the suspension can be out-of-school, meaning that the student does not come to school for a period of time. Expulsion is the removal of a student from the supervision and control of the school, usually a period in excess of 10 days. Generally, a student may be expelled only by action of the board of education. Likewise, only the board of education can readmit a student after expulsion.

Suspension   The short-term denial of school attendance as well as limiting participation in regular courses and school activities.

Expulsion   The removal of the student from the supervision and control of the school.

What are students' rights to privacy? How is reasonable search and seizure defined? What are students' and parents' rights with regard to the privacy of students' school records?

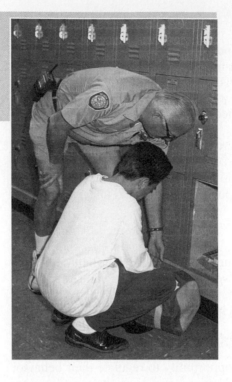

Consider the following situation in which the principal communicated with a student prior to suspension. Mark is a high school senior at a suburban high school. He is very bright, but rebellious and attention-seeking, and teachers consider him to be "difficult." One day between classes, Mark shouted down the front hall that one day he would hold up a school bus and that everyone would see him on TV. His comment was overheard by teachers and administrators, as well as by many students. An assistant principal escorted Mark to the principal's office. Mark's previous school record revealed this was not the first time he had made some sort of violent proclamation on school grounds. Mark claimed that he was joking; it was not meant as a serious threat. The principal suspended Mark and warned him that if he were to challenge or break any of the school's rules one more time, he would risk expulsion. Mark's parents decided to withdraw him from high school and enroll him in an alternative school where he would be in a more supportive environment and could earn his GED and go on to community college.

REFLECT & WRITE

Some psychologists, teachers, and parents believe that spanking children teaches them that violence is an acceptable solution to conflict. What is your opinion on corporal punishment in public schools?

_____
_____
_____
_____
_____

Right to Privacy

The Fourth Amendment is clear about the right of the people to be secure in their persons, houses, papers, and effects. All of these rights also relate to a student's right to privacy at school.

Search and Seizure

The Supreme Court in *New Jersey v. T.L.O.* ruled that the Fourth Amendment applies to searches of students by school officials. It also provides that all persons have the right to be protected from bodily searches or searches of other places in which they expect privacy unless there is a search warrant or unless there are exceptional cases involved. However, the Court ruled that searches were legal as long as they are reasonable under all circumstances. This means that schools, teachers, and administrators do not need probable cause to believe that the student being searched is violating the law.[45]

The Court said that a reasonable search is one justified at its inception and reasonably related in scope to the circumstances that justified the initial interference. The Supreme Court has continued to let stand its decision made in *New Jersey v. T.L.O.* In 1992, the Supreme Court refused to hear the appeal of two Alabama elementary school girls who allege they were strip-searched by a teacher and a counselor.[46] In this case, two 8-year-old second-graders were accused by a classmate of stealing $7 and hiding it in one of their backpacks. No money was found on the girls. However, a teacher took the girls to a restroom and strip-searched them. The case was thrown out by lower federal courts. An appeals court upheld the dismissed case, stating that the school was justified in the search because it was reasonably related to the circumstances. The school board acknowledged that the teacher had committed a "gross error" in judgment, but rejected the superintendent's recommendation that the teacher be fired.[47] Federal Judge Robert G. Doumar offers the following guidelines for school officials to follow in searches for stolen property:

- When school employees want to find property (property of relatively minor value, at least, such as tennis shoes), it is possible to search more than one student so long as employees have enough suspicion to justify each search.
- Teachers and administrators should ask students for voluntary consent to be searched. The Fourth Amendment does not regulate consensual searches—so long as they truly are consensual. If the search is not consensual, it violates the students' constitutional rights.
- Before forcing any searches, employees should investigate to determine whether individualized suspicion exists for the students who did not consent to the search.[48]

Crime and Violence

Many states and local districts have laws designed to curb violence and crime in schools. Given the growth of violence in society and schools and the public's concern with reducing violence, the federal government has entered the fray. In 1990, Congress passed the Gun-Free School Zones Act, which prohibited possession of guns within 1,000 feet of a school. The act mandated that schools must expel for a year any student found carrying a firearm to school. If a state did not adopt such a mandatory 1-year expulsion policy, it lost federal funding. The Supreme Court in *U.S. v. Lopez* struck down this law and ruled that Congress had exceeded its powers.

Congress passed the Gun-Free School Zones Act under its power to regulate interstate commerce on the grounds that violence near schools makes a difference in America's economic well-being and national productivity. It is common for Congress to use its power to regulate interstate commerce as a basis for federal legislation. The Court, however, said Congress did not have such authority under the commerce clause and "that authority, while broad, does not include the authority to regulate each and every aspect of local schools."[49]

Violent crime is a contemporary problem faced by all schools. It is no longer a concern solely of urban schools, as evidenced by the events at Lincoln-Sudbury High School, which we discussed at the beginning of the chapter. According to the National Center for Education Statistics, the percentage of public schools experiencing one or more violent incidents increased from 71 percent in 2002–2003 to 81 percent in 2003–2004. During the 2003–2004 school year, 1,437 homicides occurred in public and private schools.[50] To reduce violence in schools, officials are using metal detectors, surveillance cameras, specially trained dogs to sniff out guns, locker sweeps, identification tags, and a prohibition against bringing book bags to school. Many schools now conduct emergency management drills. These

■ INTASC

STANDARD 2 The teacher understands how children learn and develop, and can provide learning opportunities that support their intellectual, social and personal development.

Go to MyEducationLab and select the topic "Ethical and Legal Issues" then read the article "The Right to Search Students." Answer the questions that follow.

drills include locking down the school and ensuring that all students and teachers lock their doors and are adequately protected in case of a violent intruder or attack. These types of drills have taken place for years in the inner city, but now they are also taking place in the suburbs and rural areas. How schools' efforts to reduce violence play out in practice and in the courts remains to be seen.

A guidebook of strategies to help schools prevent violence by the Department of Education, outlines prevention strategies, including ways to build positive relationships among students, parents, and teachers. The guidebook is available to all schools nationwide.

Student Records

Access to what is contained in student records and their privacy are matters of great concern for teachers and other school personnel. Under the **Buckley Amendment** of the Family Educational Rights and Privacy Act of 1974, schools must protect the privacy of student records while affording parents and students over 18 years of age access to this information. If parents and age-eligible students believe student records are misleading, inaccurate, or contain information that is a violation of their rights, they can ask the school to amend the information. If school personnel refuse, parents and students have the right to a hearing.

Beyond students and their parents, access to student records is limited. Only school officials or teachers who have legitimate educational interests may examine student records. Furthermore, access to students' records is not permitted without parents' written approval. However, a little-known provision of the No Child Left Behind Act requires high schools receiving federal dollars to give military recruiters the names, addresses, and telephone numbers of students.[51]

Maintenance of student records calls for particular care and attention in determining what information should go into students' records and how the records are maintained and safeguarded. For example, policies on how secure student records are and procedures for determining where and how records can be reviewed must be specified and administered by school personnel. Teachers have to be judicious about what they include in student records, who they give access to the records, and what they say to others about the content of the records.

Right to Nondiscrimination

Students are protected, as are teachers, in their right to nondiscrimination. Title IX of the Education Amendments of 1972 prohibits discrimination on the basis of sex. Many girls' school sports programs are the beneficiary of this law. Nondiscrimination means that girls' sport programs receive equal funding and girls participate in more sports programs. See the feature *What's New in Education? Holding Schools Accountable for Equal Opportunities.*

Gender and Sexual Identity

Nondiscrimination of students is apparent in other areas as well. In years past, female high school students who were married or pregnant were routinely expelled. Public policy today is such that schools recognize that married and pregnant students have all the rights and privileges of other students and that marriage and pregnancy are not criteria for the exclusion of students from school or participation in extracurricular activities. However, in a much publicized 1998 case two female students—one an unwed mother, the other 8 months pregnant—sued the school district because the faculty council at Grant County High School in Williamson, Kentucky, rejected their applications to the National Honor Society. The young women charged discrimination for being disqualified for membership in the honor society.[52] In an out of court settlement, the women were admitted to the Honor Society.

The guidebook is available at www.ed.gov/about/offices/list/oser/osep/gtss.html.

Buckley Amendment Part of the Family Educational Rights and Privacy Act, this amendment ensures that schools protect the privacy of student records while affording parents and students over 18 years of age access to them.

■ INTASC

STANDARD 9 The teacher is a reflective practitioner who continually evaluates the effects of his/her choices and actions on others (students, parents, and other professionals in the learning community) and who actively seeks out opportunities to grow professionally.

■ INTASC

STANDARD 3 The teacher understands how students differ in their approaches to learning and creates instructional opportunities that are adapted to diverse learners.

What's  in Education?

Holding Schools Accountable for Equal Opportunities

In 2006, the cheerleaders at Solon High School in Cleveland, Ohio, cheered for the Lady Comets girls' basketball team. Before the Lady Comets went to the state tournament, they rarely had cheerleaders or any type of hype to get the fans psyched for their games. In general, girls' sports do not receive the same amount of attention, pep rallies, and band support as boys' sports. But this lack of support is now coming under national and state attention due to a lawsuit against the Southern New York Tier High Schools.

According to Title IX, the federal rule that prohibits gender discrimination in sports and other educational programs, schools can be sued and held accountable for not providing equal opportunities for girls' sports teams. Title IX entitles girls' teams not only to the same standards of coaching, equipment, locker room facilities, recruitment, medical services, and tutoring, but also to equal publicity—and this means cheerleaders, pep bands, promotions, and prime scheduling. All schools are held accountable to these standards, but only some schools comply.

Band directors want their bands to play to crowds, as do cheerleading coaches. Unfortunately, girls' sports teams still draw fewer crowds than do boys' teams. Some schools are experimenting with scheduling to increase attendance, and in some cases it is working. However, many female athletes are discouraged by the lack of attendance at their events and the considerable discrimination that still exists in many areas related to gender, sports, and school. For example, many schools offer fan days, when students dress up in the school colors or wear buttons supporting the boys' teams, but rarely are those days held for the girls. School administrators, teachers, and coaches must be informed about the lack of gender equality in the area of school sports, and work to creatively and effectively combat discrimination.

Kleinerman, E. J. (2007, March 13). Girls teams prefer fans not fanfare but suit may change way schools respond. *The Plain Dealer*. p. B.1, Available at http://pqasb .pqarchiver.com/plaindealer/access/ 1232058321.html?dids=1232058321: 1232058321&FMT=ABS&FMTS=ABS:FT& type=current&date=Mar+13%2C+2007& author=Ellen+Jan+Kleinerman%3BPlain+ Dealer+Reporter&pub=The+Plain+Dealer& edition=&startpage=B.1&desc=Girls+ teams+prefer+fans+not+fanfare+But+suit+ may+change+way+schools+respond. Accessed December 4, 2007.

In 2005, Poway High School in Poway, California, was found guilty of denying an equal opportunity education to two homosexual students who faced discrimination and bullying that went unpunished by the school.

Massachusetts was the first state in the country to pass a law protecting homosexual youth from discrimination. However, legal protection is not enough. Schools must be proactive in their efforts to provide safety and acceptance for gays, lesbians, bisexuals, and transgender students. The Gay-Strait Alliance Network (GSA) is an organization that works to empower youth in fighting homophobia in schools. It is a youth-led organization that enables gay and straight students to support each other and to work toward creating a safe environment for students to learn about homophobia and other oppressions. Other GSA goals include educating the education community about homophobia, gender identity, and sexual orientation in order to fight discrimination, harassment, and violence.[53]

English Language Learners (ELLs)

The U.S. population is more diverse than ever before. Many students entering public schools do not speak English, or have limited English proficiency (LEP). As you read in Chapter 4, students' home languages are many and diverse.

For most people, *bilingual education* means that children (or adults, or both) will be taught a second language. Some people interpret this to mean that a child's native language (often referred to as the *home language*)—whether English, Spanish, French, Italian, Chinese, Tagalog, or any of the other 125 languages in which

■ **INTASC**

STANDARD 4 The teacher uses various instructional strategies to encourage students' development of critical thinking, problem solving, and performance skills.

bilingual programs are conducted—will tend to be suppressed. For other people, bilingual education means that children will be taught in both the home language and in English. The Bilingual Education Act, Title VII of the Elementary and Secondary Education Act (ESEA), sets forth the federal government's policy toward bilingual education:

> The Congress declares it to be the policy of the United States, in order to establish equal educational opportunity for all children and to promote educational excellence (A) to encourage the establishment and operation, where appropriate, of educational programs using bilingual educational practices, techniques, and methods, (B) to encourage the establishment of special alternative instructional programs for students of limited English proficiency in school districts where the establishment of bilingual education programs is not practicable or for other ap-

In the Classroom
with **Agnes Winslow**

Teaching English Language Learners

My attempts to learn French in college gave me a lot of empathy for English language learners—the frustration, the anxiety that formed in my stomach over every sentence I tried to speak, the fear that I would say something totally inappropriate simply because I thought one word was a verb when it really was a noun. English language learners face these problems and more every day. Many English language learners are from low socioeconomic backgrounds and don't have the privilege of taking a college course in the language they desire to learn—they must learn it in order to survive in our country. Others come to this country lacking many basic literacy skills that we take for granted every day.

The chances are high that you will have English language learners in your classroom. When I got my first teaching job, my class was a very diverse one. Three students had just arrived in this country, and throughout the year I got two more students in who spoke very little English. To help them, I had to strategize. How do you learn if you are unfamiliar with a language or culture? How do you keep information exciting and relevant, instead of scaring your students away from learning with overwhelming amounts of information? Here are some strategies I've found to be very valuable:

■ **Build content around a theme.** Vocabulary words don't sink in when they are simply repeated over and over. There has to be some context for you to remember the difference between a "chair" that you sit in and a "chair-

person," who is clearly not a person made from chairs. English language learners develop vocabulary based on what they can identify with, not what they've had drilled into them over and over. So, plan activities around the vocabulary you're trying to teach in order to tie in everyday experiences for your students to relate to.

■ **Use lots of visual aids and hands-on activities.** Many children are visual or kinesthetic learners. This means that if they only read about something, they're not going to truly understand it until they can see and touch it. This may be difficult with more abstract ideas, but students will pick up more if you use visual cues while you're talking. Making flashcards, using computer programs, and creating games and other activities will help your students trigger meaning from the activity.

■ **Find a routine, and stick with it.** Don't be afraid to think outside the box, but your students who are learning English simply can't handle tons of information presented to them in a different way each day. If you use one set of activities to introduce one set of skills, and it works, stick with that routine. Day by day, find a way to plan out your lessons so that the students know what to expect next, what you're expecting from them, and when you expect them to have completed their assignments.

Teaching in diverse classrooms has taught me so much about how to be an effective teacher. It has taught me how to be an effective communicator and listener, responsive to the needs of my students.

propriate reasons, and (C) for those purposes, to provide financial assistance to local educational agencies.[54]

Ethnic pride and identity have caused renewed interest in languages and have spurred a more conscious effort to preserve children's native languages. In the nineteenth and twentieth centuries, foreign-born individuals and their children wanted to camouflage their ethnicity and unlearn their language, because not speaking English was viewed as being unpatriotic or un-American.

An increasing number of people in the United States speak a language other than English. According to the Census Bureau, about one in five U.S. residents speaks a language other than English, with Spanish being the second most commonly spoken language.[55] Three states—Texas, New Mexico, and California—are now classified as majority-minority states, meaning that more than 50 percent of the population is composed of a traditionally non-white ethnic background.[56] Many of these residents do not use English as their primary language. (See *In the Classroom with Agnes Winslow*.)

Another reason for interest in bilingual education is an increasing emphasis on civil rights. Indeed, much of the concept of providing children with an opportunity to know, value, and use their heritage and language stems from people's recognition that they have a right to them. Just as extending rights to students with disabilities is very much evident today, so it is with students and their languages.

NCLB has had a profound influence on how schools conduct bilingual programs and how they teach English language learners. NCLB changed the focus of bilingual education programs from teaching limited-English-proficient children primarily in their native language to helping LEP children learn English. NCLB requires the following of schools:

- LEP students must be tested for reading and language arts in English after they have attended school in the United States for 3 consecutive years.
- All teachers in a language instruction class for LEP children must be fluent in English.
- Parents must be notified when their LEP child needs English language instruction.[57]

Twenty-six states have official English laws that make English the official language of the state.

Special Education

Approximately 6.1 million children (ages birth to 21) with disabilities are served by federally supported programs.[58] Section 504 of the Rehabilitation Act of 1973 was the first piece of legislation protecting the rights of persons with disabilities. Section 504 prohibited exclusion of individuals with disabilities from participating in, being denied the benefits of, or being discriminated against in any program or activity receiving federal assistance.

The **Individuals with Disabilities Education Act of 1975 (IDEA)** protects the rights of special-needs children in the public schools. This act includes the following standards:

- A free and appropriate education (FAPE) for all persons between the ages of 3 and 21.
- Education in the least restrictive environment (the environment in which a student can learn best).
- Individualization of instruction for each student, taking into consideration his or her needs, disabling conditions, and preferences as well as the preferences of the student's parents. This individualization of instruction is expressed through an individualized education program (IEP). The IEP and its preparation have had tremendous influence on curriculum for special-needs children and how that curriculum is delivered.

Individuals with Disabilities Education Act of 1975 (IDEA)   Protects the rights of special-needs children in the public schools.

■ **INTASC**

STANDARD 2   The teacher understands how children learn and develop, and can provide learning opportunities that support their intellectual, social, and personal development.

The curriculum of most middle and high schools provides students with information about wellness and healthy living. Do you think all students have a right to information about sexually transmitted diseases? Do you feel schools have a responsibility to include sex education in their curricula? At what age do you think it is appropriate to provide this information to students?

- Participation of the parent, and when appropriate the student, in diagnosis, placement, and the development of the IEP.
- Extending to the parents a broad range of rights regarding their children's education.

IDEA added two additional categories of disability—"autism" and "traumatic brain injury."

Some of the provisions of IDEA were and are open to interpretation. The Supreme Court in *Board of Education of Hendrick Hudson Central School District v. Rowley* (1980) ruled on the meaning of "free and appropriate." The Court said it constitutes "personalized instruction with sufficient support services to permit the child to benefit from that instruction."[59]

Another federal law protects and defines the rights of children with disabilities. The Americans with Disabilities Act (ADA) (PL 101-336) uses language similar to that of Section 504 and prohibits discrimination against persons with disabilities. In addition, the Handicapped Children's Protection Act of 1986 (PL 99-372) allows parents to collect attorney's fees when they prevail in suits brought for violations of IDEA.

AIDS

As the number of students with acquired immunodeficiency syndrome (AIDS) has risen, the number of conflicts about AIDS-related issues between school districts and parents has increased. AIDS is caused by the human immunodeficiency virus (HIV), which weakens or destroys the immune system, thus allowing diseases and infections to develop. Children and adults with HIV may not get AIDS. Some may develop symptoms not normally associated with AIDS that are referred to as AIDS-related complex (ARC), whereas others may develop AIDS symptoms. The manifestation of AIDS in children is different than in adults. For example, Kaposi's sarcoma, a form of cancer, is found in about 25 percent of adult AIDS cases but seldom in children. More commonly, children with AIDS develop infections such as pneumonia and central nervous system disorders. Also, some children born with HIV may have some physical problems at birth.

Although some parents have fought to enact policies limiting the school attendance of HIV-positive students, school officials must comply with federal laws and accommodate students who test positive for HIV. Any person who is HIV positive is protected from discrimination by the Rehabilitation Act of 1973. Under this act, "no individual may be excluded from a program or activity receiving federal financial assistance if the individual is 'otherwise qualified' to participate."[60] Although school districts have tried to bar students with HIV/AIDS, their efforts have been unsuccessful. The Supreme Court ruled in *Bragdon v. Abbott et al.* that people who carry the HIV virus are disabled and are entitled to the rights established by the Americans with Disabilities Act. Justice Kennedy said, "HIV infection satisfies the statutory and regulatory definition of a physical impairment during every stage of the disease."[61]

REFLECT & WRITE

What are your beliefs about spending additional taxpayer dollars in order to ensure that all children, regardless of disability, receive a free and appropriate education?

Legal Issues after September 11

The tragic events of September 11, 2001, have raised a number of legal issues regarding education. Before 9/11, schools discouraged students from bringing cell phones to school; however, since the events of that day more students and parents want to have access to a cell phone, in the event of an emergency situation. However, more public and municipal agencies and cities are seeking once again to limit or ban the use of cell phones in schools and public places.

The war in Iraq has also spawned legal issues in schools. Seattle's Garfield High School, for example, is grappling with the issue of military recruiting in public schools. One requirement of NCLB is that public schools that receive federal funding must release the names of its students to military recruiters. Some feel that this is an invasion of privacy prompted by the war effort and an increasing need for new military recruits. In 2005, Garfield High School's Parent Teacher Student Association voted 25 to 5 to adopt a resolution that "public schools are not a place for military recruiters." Other schools might seek to endorse or restrict the amount of access that the military has to potential recruits in the nation's public high schools.[62]

REFLECT & WRITE

Where do you stand on the issue of military recruiters having access to the public schools?

WHAT ARE PARENTS' RIGHTS AND RESPONSIBILITIES?

Within the home and school settings, it is sometimes easy to forget that parents have rights, too. With the current emphasis on parent involvement and parents as partners in the education process (see Chapter 6), it is more important than ever for you, as a beginning teacher, to know and understand the basic educational rights and responsibilities of parents in the education arena.

● *Your Turn*

Your class is arranging a field trip for which you need both parents' consent, as well as $7.50 per student. You recognize that some families might not be able to contribute $7.50, yet the trip is important to your curriculum. You don't want those who can't afford the fee to be left behind. What are your options?

Parental Information and Consent

Parents have rights relating to being informed of their children's school progress and behavior. For example, parents should be informed when their children have been honored for an accomplishment or when they are partaking in a project that requires parents' financial support. Parents also have rights that require their informed consent before their children can engage in certain school activities, such as field trips, or be subjected to discipline procedures.

In addition, many laws, such as IDEA, provide parents with specific rights such as the following:

- The parent must give consent for evaluation of the child.
- The parent has the right to "examine all relevant records with respect to the identification, evaluation, and educational placement of the child."
- The parent must be given written prior notice whenever a change in "the identification, evaluation, or educational placement of the child" occurs.
- This written notice must be in the parent's native tongue.
- The parent has an "opportunity to present complaints with respect to any matter relating to the identification, evaluation, or educational placement of the child."
- The parent has the right to a due process hearing in relation to any complaint.
- The parent has the right to participate in development of the IEP for the child.
- Meetings to develop the IEP must be conducted in the parent's native tongue.
- Meetings to develop the IEP must be held at a time and place agreeable to the parent.

Compulsory School Attendance

Parents have broad powers for control of and responsibility for their children. Parents are responsible for feeding, clothing, and controlling the education of their

YOU DECIDE

No School, No Car Keys

Maryland recently approved a bill that would deny driver's licenses to students with 10 or more unexcused absences the previous year. This bill requires students to show a reasonable attendance record to the Motor Vehicle Administration in order to obtain a driver's license.

Truancy in schools is a growing problem, and educators are not happy when students miss school for any reason. First, students don't learn when they are not in school. Second, state funding is based on average daily attendance. The more absences, the fewer state dollars allotted to the school. More than 6,000 of 133,000 students in Prince George County, Maryland, public schools were absent for more than 20 days in 2005, and educators agree that number is a low estimate. Although the state punishes parents who let their children skip school—criminal penalties can include as many as 10 days in jail or a fine of $50 a day—there are no laws to punish the students. Lawmakers hope that this resolution will inspire students to attend school so that they won't lose their privilege to drive.

Do you think students should lose their licenses for 10 or more unexcused absences? If not, what do you think is a reasonable response to truancy?

Source: Rein, L. (2007, March 16). Md. moves to tie teens' truancy to licenses. *Washington Post*, p. A01, Available at www.washingtonpost.com/wp-dyn/content/article/2007/03/15/AR2007031502112.html. Accessed December 5, 2007.

children. A landmark case involving the rights of parents in relation to the education of their children was the 1925 Supreme Court case of *Pierce v. Society of Sisters of the Holy Names of Jesus and Mary*. The Court ruled unconstitutional an Oregon law requiring parents to send their children to public school. The Court said that such a law denied parents the right to control the education of their children. However, the Court made clear the role of the state in education:

> No question is raised concerning the power of the state to regulate all schools, to inspect, supervise, and examine them, their teachers, and pupils; to require that all children of proper age attend some school, that teachers shall be of good moral character and patriotic disposition, that certain studies plainly essential to good citizenship must be taught, and that nothing be taught which is manifestly inimical to the public welfare.[63]

The Court's ruling in *Pierce* did one other thing: It established the right of private schools to exist and thus enforced the tradition of public and private education in the United States.

The Supreme Court has also protected certain groups from compulsory attendance at state-sponsored schools. In 1972, in *Wisconsin v. Yoder*, the Court ruled that Old Order Amish, because of their well-established beliefs, must be given some relief from compulsory attendance. In this particular case, the defendants, Jonas Yoder and others, declined to send their children ages 14 and 16 to public school after they had graduated from the eighth grade. This was in violation of Wisconsin state law requiring school attendance through age 16. The Court said that the Old Order Amish practice was rooted in tradition and showed strong evidence of sustained faith and regulated the students' way of life. Therefore, the enforcement of the state's attendance law would endanger the free exercise of the student's religious beliefs.[64]

Home Schooling

Growing numbers of parents are opting for home schooling—teaching their children at home. According to the National Center for Education Statistics, roughly 1,096,000 children in the United States were home schooled.[65] Reasons for the growth in home schooling are several. First, some parents are generally dissatisfied with the public schools. They object to standards-based education, lack of individual attention to their children, school violence, and the lack of high achievement standards. Second, some parents believe home schooling is an appropriate way to inculcate the religious values of their choice into their children's value systems. In fact, the exclusion of religious advocacy from the public school curriculum and parents' perceptions that the schools completely ignore or pay little attention to the direct teaching of basic moral values are strong motivators for them to consider home schooling. Third, proponents of family strengthening see home schooling as a contributor to family stability. Finally, some parents believe children learn best when they decide for themselves what, when, and how they will learn. Conditioned by television and newspaper stories of the "hurried child," wary of some educators' efforts to "push" children, and the emphasis in the primary grades on basic education, some parents think home schooling is a natural alternative to these pressures of public schooling.

Before the advent of compulsory public schooling in 1836, home schooling was somewhat widespread. But as education became public, home schooling declined. Since the early 1990s, however, there has been a steady increase in the number of parents who are taking their children out of school to teach them at home. Although most states permit home schooling, the conditions and restrictions for doing so vary from state to state. Some states require parents who home school to be certified. Other states do not require certification.

Critics of home schooling question whether people who are not certified teachers can do a good job of teaching their children at home. Critics also argue that home schooling denies children many social opportunities that are a part of becoming a good citizen. Home schoolers counter that their children's social needs are more than fulfilled through church groups, sports teams, community clubs and organizations, and involvement in service activities.

Tension exists among parents who believe they have the right to provide an alternative equivalent education for their children, those who believe strongly in compulsory public school attendance, and those who believe that home-schooled students should be tested to ensure that they are receiving an equivalent education. Critics think the home school movement undermines the traditional role of the public schools.

REFLECT & WRITE

Do you think parents who home school their children limit their children's opportunities later in life? Why or why not?

_____

_____

_____

_____

_____

ETHICAL DILEMMA

To Tell or Not to Tell

IT'S THE MIDDLE OF THE FIRST SEMESTER of your first year of teaching. One of your students has approached you about a problem she is having with one of the other teachers in your school. She makes you promise not to tell anyone what she is going to say. She tells you that she is failing this teacher's class, and he has asked her to come to tutoring sessions in the morning. She is usually the only student in the room, and when they are alone he makes sexual comments and touches her lower back and shoulders. She feels the tutoring is necessary to pass the course, but says she dreads coming to school early because she has to be alone with him. She tells you that if the teacher finds out that she is upset, he might fail her for embarrassing him.

On the one hand, this student is an active member of the drill team and is involved in student council. On the other hand, you have witnessed her blatantly lie to other students. You do not know her well enough to know whether she is telling the truth about the harassment, but you also do not know the accused teacher well and do not feel you can make a character judgment about him.

You do not want to risk the student's safety or comfort because of sexual harassment. You also do not know whether she is telling the truth, and falsely accusing a co-worker of harassing a student could be detrimental to your working environment. You have promised the student that you would keep her secret, but you do not want to be negligent in your job of promoting a safe and healthy learning environment.

What do you do? Do you go to the principal and report the situation, despite your promise of confidentiality and the risk of unjustly accusing another teacher? Or do you stay quiet and wait for the situation to become visibly noticeable, possibly putting the student at risk?

SUMMARY

- Together, the U.S. Constitution, federal laws, state constitutions and laws, and federal and state judicial decisions form the basis for school law.

- States and school districts have many legal obligations and responsibilities to ensure equal educational opportunities for all. *Brown v. Board of Education of Topeka* was a landmark case that set out to end segregation. Other efforts to ensure equality in education involve an added emphasis on school accountability and efforts to provide equitable school financing to affluent and less affluent school districts alike.

- Teachers' responsibilities include preventing liability, reporting child abuse, avoiding sexual harassment, observing copyright laws, and practicing ethical behaviors.

- Being a teacher gives you a number of legal rights, including the right to be treated without discrimination, the right to work according to terms established in a contract, the right to periodic evaluations, the right to strike, and the right to academic freedom.

- Students have the right to freedom of expression, due process, rights to privacy, and the right to nondiscrimination.

- Parents' rights and responsibilities include the right to be informed about their child's progress and behavior. They are responsible for their childrens' compulsory school attendance.

KEY TERMS

Academic freedom   279
Buckley Amendment   290
Collective bargaining   278
Corporal punishment   287
De facto segregation   264
De jure segregation   264
Desegregate   264
Due process   255
Equal protection clause   287

Establishment clause   261
Expulsion   287
Freedom of expression   281
In loco parentis   269
Individuals with Disabilities Education Act of 1975 (IDEA)   292
Integration   265
Intentional torts   270
Involuntary busing   265

Laws   252
Negligence   270
Qualified immunity   272
Renewable contracts   277
Strict liability   270
Suspension   287
Tenure   276
Tort liability   269
Torts   270

APPLICATIONS FOR ACTIVE LEARNING

Connections

1. In the opening case about the student with Asperger's syndrome, what could school administrators have done to avoid being sued for negligence?

2. Think about the legal concepts and topics in this chapter. Create a picture, graphic, or figure that shows connections that are meaningful to you from this chapter's key ideas and information.

Field Experiences

1. Interview a principal in a school near you to find out what steps have been taken to ensure safety in the school for students and teachers. Has security been increased in response to recent stories about student violence? What role do school board members play in determining these measures?

2. Interview teachers, parents, and students on their views about teaching religion as a content area subject.

Personal Research

1. Identify three teacher behaviors you have encountered during your academic career that you think constituted unethical practice.

2. Perform a Web search on the *Morse v. Frederick* case. Did you find any additional information that you found interesting? Reflect on the other facts about the case that would make it relevant to your classroom.

PREPARING TO TEACH

For your Portfolio

1. Add to your portfolio the materials you collected on school policies regarding ethical practice, sexual harassment, child abuse, discipline codes, and safety codes. For each document, include your assessment of the points you regard as the most important for you to know.

2. Using one of the cases discussed in this chapter, write about a lesson you could construct around the legal issues addressed. What would you do to encourage your students to think about their rights? Identify some websites that explore these issues and that you could use to introduce students to the material and generate discussion.

Idea File

Gather articles from daily newspapers, *Education Week*, and journals such as the *School Law Journal, School Bulletin,* and *School Law Reporter* relating to the legal rights of students, teachers, and parents. Place these in your idea file for future reference.

LEARNING AND KNOWING MORE

Websites Worth Visiting

The United States Supreme Court has a powerful influence on education. You can access all the Supreme Court decisions from 1937 to the present through the following website: www.fedworld.gov/supcourt/index.htm. Another source of United States Supreme Court cases is Oyez Oyez Oyez at http://oyez.at.nwu.edu/oyez.html.

Select one of the cases that you have read about in this chapter and research it in more detail. What are some cases that you have read about in your local newspaper? Are there any cases that directly affect your district or state?

National Committee to Prevent Child Abuse
www.childabuse.org

> The National Committee to Prevent Child Abuse (NCPCA) was established in 1972 to build a nationwide commitment to preventing all forms of child abuse. The NCPCA plays a vital role in spreading the message of child abuse prevention to the public and encouraging the public to get involved. The site contains information and links to various Web pages, which give more information relating to child abuse.

National Association for Bilingual Education
www.nabe.org

> The National Association for Bilingual Education was founded in 1975 to address the educational needs of language-minority students in the United States and to advance the language competencies and multicultural understanding of all Americans. The site contains current information, including information regarding California's Proposition 227.

United States Supreme Court Research
www.usscplus.com

> "USSC+" data base is a searchable data base of Supreme Court decisions. The website contains information on the history of the Supreme Court as well as on books and CD-ROM resources for use in researching the Supreme Court.

FindLaw Internet Legal Resources
www.findlaw.com

> FindLaw is a searchable database of Supreme Court opinions. The database is easy to use and includes Supreme Court decisions since 1893. The site also contains information regarding the U.S. Constitution.

The Legal Information Institute
www.law.cornell.edu/

> The Legal Information Institute website offers Supreme Court opinions under the auspices of Project Hermes, the Court's electronic dissemination project. This archive contains opinions of the Court since 1990.

National Home Educators Research Institute
www.nheri.org

> The NHERI website contains various amounts of information regarding home schooling. NHERI stands by its mission to produce high-quality statistics, research, and technical reports on home schooling.

American Homeschool Association
www.americanhomeschoolassociation.org/aha.html

> The American Homeschool Association (AHA) was created in 1995 to network homeschoolers on a national level. Current AHA services include an online news and discussion list which provides news, information, and resources for homeschoolers, media contacts, and education officials.

Cornell Law School
www.lawschool.cornell.edu

> The Cornell Law School website is easy to use and provides access to court decisions, news related to court cases, directories, and current awareness items.

CNN
www.cnn.com/law

> CNN operates a number of useful websites, including Law Center, which reports on state, national, and international court proceedings.

Library of Congress
http://catalog.loc.gov

The Library of Congress Catalog provides a quick way to access the texts of government bills, including those related to education.

The American Bar Association
www.abanet.org

The American Bar Association's website provides access to its journal, analyses of court decisions, and a large data base of court decisions.

National Education Association
www.nea.org

The National Education Association's website offers legal information and a number of teaching supports for beginning teachers.

The Emory University School of Law
www.law.emory.edu

This website provides easy access to both Supreme Court and state court rulings on current and past school-related cases.

The National Clearinghouse on Child Abuse and Neglect Information
www.childwelfare.gov

The National Clearinghouse on Child Abuse and Neglect Information contains valuable information about these issues.

Books Worth Reading

Bosher, W. C., Kaminski, K. R., and Vacca, R. S. (2004). *The School Law Handbook: What Every Leader Needs to Know.* Alexandria, VA: Association for Supervision & Curriculum Development.

How do you handle a parent's demand that teaching Greek mythology is a violation of the separation of church and state? What do you do if you think one of your students is in an abusive situation? This book lays out the U.S. legal guidelines to help you stay informed about and protect you and your students' legal rights.

Alexander, K., and Alexander, M. A. (2003). *The Law of Schools, Students and Teachers in a Nutshell (Nutshell Series)* (3rd ed.). St. Paul, MN: Thomson West Group.
This book provides useful information on students' and teachers' legal rights and responsibilities under law.

Essex, N. L. (2005). *A Teacher's Pocket Guide to School Law.* Boston: Allyn & Bacon.
This book is an affordable, portable read that can quickly be used to cite and readily understand the basics of school law as they pertain to teachers, students, administrators, and state and federal government.

Yssldyke, J. E., and Algozzine, R. F. (2006). *The Legal Foundations of Special Education: A Practical Guide for Every Teacher.* Thousand Oaks, CA: Corwin Press.
This book examines the relationship between laws that have been passed regarding students with special needs and the impact of IDEA on education.

Yell, M. L., and Drasgow, E. (2004). *No Child Left Behind (Merril Professional Development Series).* Upper Saddle River, NJ: Prentice Hall.
This book examines the 2001 NCLB Act and its effect on education in a way that increases the reader's knowledge about the rules, regulations, and practices as they are instated in public schools.

Chapman, R. (2005). *The Everyday Guide to Special Education Law.* Denver, CO: The Legal Center for People with Disabilities and Older People.
In everyday language, Chapman's book explains the workings of special education law and relates up-to-date information on IDEA to teachers, administrators, and parents in a way that is easy to understand.

9 Historical and Philosophical Influences on Teaching and Learning in America

AMY C. BRAUN I am a teacher. I teach in a unique setting—an intimate setting, which is rapidly vanishing in America. The building where I am privileged to educate young minds is the oldest operating two-room schoolhouse in the United States. It is located in Hancock, Vermont, and was built in 1801 as a schoolhouse when Thomas Jefferson was president. In my classroom, there are the original wooden floors, scuffed with the shoes of parents and grandparents, and even the great-great-great grandparents, of my students.

The building has tall ceilings, antique light fixtures, and many windows looking out to an isolated valley along scenic route 100. It is not a little red schoolhouse, however; it is white. There is even a bell on the top of the building. I feel privileged to pull the rope to call the students inside from recess, as many others have done before me. Sometimes I think about all the students who have played in that lovely field for the last 206 years. Now that they have passed on, do they come back to visit just to hear that bell?

In my old schoolhouse, I can feel the presence of the schoolmarms. I draw on the strength of their legacy and know that they had it harder in many ways than I can ever imagine. For one thing, they were paid in cords of wood!

The Village School has changed over time. The wood stove is gone. To replace it, we have a kitchen and two hot meals served daily for the students who want it. Our cook is "famous" for her shepherd's pie she makes with real mashed potatoes. Our cook is also the administrative assistant. (She can answer the phone while she is serving meals.) The students sit in the classroom to eat, just as they always have. I am "on duty" all day, eating more meals with my students than I eat with my family.

> **They are getting what they need in the warmth of this special environment.**

We are like a family. Everyone in town knows each other; I have been able to get to know my students outside of school as well. I have been invited to birthday parties and baseball games and have been welcomed into people's homes for dinner. Some students have also been to my home and played with my children. I never go to the grocery store anonymously—I always see someone who is a student or a grandparent of a student. That's just life in a small town.

As an educator, I can confidently say that I am aware of the academic level of each of my students and where they need remediation or enrichment. They are getting what they need in the warmth of this special environment. Our adult-to-student ratio is one to four, so it is difficult for children to "fall through the cracks"—someone will notice. A father of one of my students is also a schoolboard member. He feels blessed to be able to walk into the school in the morning to drop off his sons, making eye contact with both of their teachers.

Although there are far more advantages to education in the two-room schoolhouse than not, there are a few things that have an adverse effect on learning. The phone rings all day as it does in the larger schools, but I can hear it ring in my

Amy C. Braun has been teaching elementary school for 12 years. Before coming to The Village School in Hancock, Vermont, where she has taught since 2002, she taught in the Mesa School District in Arizona for 7 years. She is married and has two sons.

As you read this chapter . . .

Think about:

- What schooling was like in the American colonies
- How American education changed after nationhood
- How American education changed after the Civil War
- How education changed after World War II
- How philosophy is relevant for teachers
- How the branches of philosophy relate to education
- The major philosophies of education
- The implications of philosophies of education for you and your students

Maria Montessori

▶▶ Go to MyEducationLab and select the topic "Philosophy of Education" then watch the video "A Montessori Classroom."

classroom, which means the kids can hear it, too. On occasion, the outside stimuli can be disruptive as well. The floorplan of the space causes people to walk through my classroom as if it is a hallway. Because the old floors creak in certain spots, it is impossible to ignore someone walking through the room. If a person in the kitchen wants to use the bathroom, they have to go through one of the classrooms. If someone wants to go upstairs for one-on-one special attention or to the library, they have to use the staircase in my room. My students learn to ignore interruptions, but I work very hard to keep the environment as quiet as possible for their sake.

There is no staff lounge or gymnasium. On days of adverse weather, the children have physical education class right in my room. They have all other specials in the classroom as well, so I am unable to use my "prep time" to prepare. I usually leave the building to take a walk so I can be refreshed. I do not want to disrupt the students in my classroom by walking in and out on the creaky floor.

Enrollment is declining. This past year at the town meeting, the vote almost closed us down. After the original vote, there was a petition circulated by the parents and a revote which kept the school thriving this year.

History is valuable and important. The difference between The Village School and the larger consolidated version is like the difference between the local hardware store and the aisle dedicated to hardware supplies in Wal-Mart. Quality is important, too. Things bought in bulk were made in a hurry. Slow down and savor the goodness of our forefathers.

■ INTASC

STANDARD 9 The teacher is a reflective practitioner who continually evaluates the effects of his/her choices and actions on others (students, parents, and other professionals in the learning community) and who actively seeks out opportunities to grow professionally.

Think about what it would be like to teach in a two-room school in rural Vermont. How do you think educational philosophy has changed since colonial times, even in a situation where students are educated under similar conditions? Do you think teachers today have more or less control over what they teach? How has the transition from small schools in small communities to large schools in growing communities impacted the quality, philosophy, and type of education? The author and historian David C. McCullough once said, "History is a guide to navigation in perilous times. History is who we are and why we are the way we are."[1] The same can be said for the history of education. What schools are like today is a result of what schools were like in years past, just as what schools will be like in the future will be based on what schools are like today. Knowing the history of education helps us have a better appreciation of what is happening in education today. This knowledge helps us understand why schools function as they do and to see where those ideas originated. The following themes in contemporary education were shaped by the early days of education in the United States:

- Universal education for all children is a powerful theme in American educational history. In the colonial period, education was limited to a wealthy, privileged few. However, through the centuries, the promise of universal education for all has influenced who and what we teach. This theme shapes contemporary educational thought and practice.

- Local control of schools is a hallowed principle that has developed throughout the growth of American education. A tension exists between those who advocate local control of schools and those who feel the state and the federal governments need to have more authority over local education.

- Disagreement over what should be taught (the basic curriculum) and how it should be taught (appropriate methods of instruction) has existed for centuries, with changes in curriculum often reflecting the changing needs of society. Such debate continues as educational leaders search for the best ways to help all students learn to their fullest capacities.

Understanding the history of the profession you are about to enter enables you to put what is happening today into a context. It also allows you to understand the forces and issues that help shape American public education today.

WHAT WAS SCHOOLING LIKE IN THE AMERICAN COLONIES?

Education in colonial America was influenced by the earliest settlers who came from Europe. All European roots influenced American education, with the result that education in the American colonies varied greatly. This variety in educational styles continues to influence contemporary curriculum and practice.

In the early colonies, schools were casual arrangements with no formal structure and very little regularity in their curriculum. The location of many schools made them inaccessible to many students. Additionally, attendance differed based on individual family situations. Many parents could not send their children to school during important planting and harvesting seasons. Teachers were not formally trained, which led to a considerable difference in teaching styles, curriculum, and philosophy.[2]

Religion played a very powerful role in the development of colonial schools, both in how they were organized and in what they taught. Bible reading and prayer were a major part of the school curriculum well into the twentieth century. As you read in Chapter 8, issues surrounding religion continue to impact many schools today. During colonial times, as now, religious groups wanted to rear and educate children their way and established schools to do so. The desire for religious freedom contributed to the doctrine of separation of church and state.[3] As you read about the development of education in the United States, keep in mind that the educational thoughts and ideas of sixteenth- and seventeenth-century Europe are the foundations of American education.

■ INTASC

STANDARD 2 The teacher understands how children learn and develop, and can provide learning opportunities that support their intellectual, social and personal development.

The New England Colonies

The Massachusetts Law of 1642 was the first school law relating to education in America that required parents and masters of apprentices to see that children learned to read:

> "In every towne ye chosen men" shall see that parents and masters not only train their children in learning and labor, but also "to read & understand the principles of religion & the capital lawes of this country," with power to impose fines on such as refuse to render accounts concerning their children.[4]

In 1647, Massachusetts passed the Massachusetts Act, often referred to as the **Old Deluder Satan Act,** which set the pattern for compulsory education in New England. This law explicitly stated that it was Satan's foremost goal to keep people from knowing the scriptures of the Bible. Therefore, the law ordered every township with a population greater than 50 to employ a teacher for the town's children. Each community's schoolteacher had to teach reading and writing, as well as a considerable amount of religious doctrine.

These two laws made it possible for the people to have the kind of schools they needed to achieve the religious and social goals on which the colonies were founded. They also became models for laws of other states seeking to provide education.

Old Deluder Satan Act The Massachusetts Act (1647), which set the pattern for compulsory education in New England.

REFLECT & WRITE

What are some ways that religion continues to influence the development of education in America today? Has religion influenced your education in any way?

_____

_____

_____

_____

_____

Dame schools   A common school education open to girls and boys and taught by women.

Hornbook   An instructional device used in the dame school that was shaped like a mirror and had attached to its frame a sheet of paper containing the alphabet, Lord's Prayer, and numbers.

Primer   A small introductory book on a subject; generally, a book intended to teach children to read.

Latin grammar schools   Colonial schools established to provide male students a precollege education; comparable to today's high school.

Dame Schools and Hornbooks

Common schools were typical in early eighteenth and nineteenth century America. Often reflecting the community's agricultural roots, these schools offered a basic education for white children between the ages of 6 and 14. Common schools were funded by local taxes instead of tuition. The small one- and two-room schoolhouses that were discussed at the beginning of the chapter are, however, far removed by history, they are now modern remnants of common school education.[5] Typical of common school education were the **dame schools**. These were open to girls and boys and were operated by women who, for a modest fee, gave children lessons in spelling and reading. In order to learn to write and read, children went to an elementary school of some kind—a neighborhood school, private school, or church-supported parochial school.

The **hornbook** was one of the instructional devices used in the dame school. It was a frame of wood with a handle, similar in shape to a mirror. Attached to the frame was a sheet of paper containing the alphabet, Lord's Prayer, and numbers.

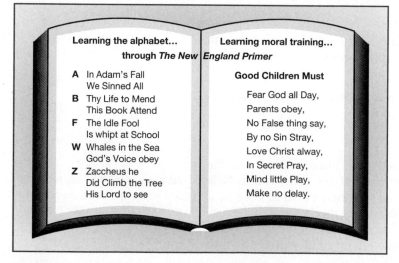

FIGURE 9.1   ABC's and Moral Training in _The New England Primer_

As the great beginning schoolbook, _The New England Primer_ was both a source of educational and moral enrichment.

Source: P. L. Ford, _The New England Primer: A History of Its Origin and Development_ (New York: Teachers College Press, 1962). Reprinted by permission.

The New England Primer

Three books that influenced the curriculum of schooling in America were _The New England Primer_, Noah Webster's _Spelling Book_, and William McGuffey's _Eclectic Reader_. A **primer** is a first book, generally one intended to teach children to read. _The New England Primer_, called "the great beginning school book," served the purposes of educating children and youth in religious belief and the authority of God, family, and government and promoting morality. Students did not merely read _The New England Primer_, they memorized it. Through memorization and recitation, children learned the alphabet as they learned moral truths (see Figure 9.1).[6]

Latin Grammar Schools

The Boston Latin School, founded in 1635, was the first public grammar school in America. Typically, boys between the ages of 8 and 16 attended these schools. The purpose of the **Latin grammar schools** was college preparation.

Since the purpose of the Latin grammar schools was college preparatory, the curriculum was traditional and classical in nature. The number of students who attended these schools was small, and no women attended.

However, college preparation course work was not suitable for life on the frontier. By the end of the colonial period, a new institution took its place that offered more flexibility and that was adapted to the changing face of the country. The **academies** offered instruction geared toward specific careers, such as the military or the fine arts.[7]

Academies Institutions that geared instruction toward specific careers, such as the military or the fine arts.

_____
_____
_____
_____
_____
_____

REFLECT & WRITE

The New England Primer played an important role in developing childrens' character. Every generation grapples with how to rear "good" children. Are you familiar with any books that teach children good character traits? What are they?

The Middle Colonies

In the middle colonies—Pennsylvania, New York, New Jersey, and Maryland—people were more culturally and religiously diverse than they were in the New England colonies. Because of this diversity, schools were also more diverse. Separation of church and government was more common, and differences in religious beliefs were more accepted. All of these conditions affected school development.

Quaker Schools

In the middle colonies, education was more often the responsibility of churches rather than government. For this reason, parochial or denominational education flourished in the middle colonies. In particular, the Quakers were the most active group in education. George Fox, founder of the Society of Friends, believed that schools should be open to all classes and races, and he placed emphasis upon moral and religious instruction.[8]

Additionally, Quakers were strong proponents of equal education for women. The opening of educational opportunities for women came slowly and gradually. The primary focus of women's education was providing roles for women as wives and mothers. Benjamin Rush, a tireless promoter of education, proposed a broad curriculum for women that included reading, writing, grammar, arithmetic, bookkeeping, geography, history, vocal music, dancing, and religion.[9]

REFLECT & WRITE

Identify several educational themes from the colonial period (for example, literacy for all) that are influencing educational practice today.

_____
_____
_____
_____
_____

What did students learn in the eighteenth-century school? How and why did educational aims and institutions vary so widely from one American colony to the next?

Franklin's Academy

The middle colonies were involved in commerce and trade. Consequently, schools provided instruction—such as navigation, surveying, and bookkeeping—that would prepare students for work. Benjamin Franklin's Academy, opened in Philadelphia in 1751, taught these as well as traditional subjects.

Franklin's Academy taught writing as well as art, mathematics, accounting, and some geometry and astronomy. English grammar was taught along with classic authors considered to be integral to education at the time—Tillotson, Addison, Pope, Algernon Sidney, Cato, and others. The general philosophy of the school was to cultivate a well-read individual with some sense of personal style and creativity. Franklin stressed the importance of students writing letters to one another, making connections with what they read, writing the classics in their own words, and talking about the stories they read from their own perspectives. A tutor was there to guide them, revise their work, and offer students a meaningful critique of their work as well as to impress upon them the importance of words and writing.[10]

The Southern Colonies

As with the other colonies, the nature and character of the southern colonies determined the region's system of schooling. Education in the southern colonies was characterized by three tiers, or levels. At the top were wealthy landowners who hired tutors for their children and sent them abroad for higher education. Free, poor, small farmers constituted the vast majority of the population. This group had very limited access to education.

For slaves, educational opportunities were almost nonexistent. In fact, educating slaves was a felony in some states before the Civil War. Wealthy landowners were not interested in educating slaves, because they thought learning and literacy would lead to rebellion. Education consisted of training for field and housework, with some provisions for apprenticeship to learn trades. Missionaries' efforts to educate slaves were largely ineffectual. By 1863 and the Emancipation Proclamation, the literacy rate among slaves was about 5 percent.[11]

REFLECT & WRITE

It is easy to look back on American education and second guess leaders who helped develop early schools. Take yourself back in time to Colonial America. What two things would you do differently?

_____

_____

_____

_____

_____

Education and Native Americans

In the Spanish-settled lands of the Southwest, such as Texas, California, Arizona, and New Mexico, education was provided by Catholic missionaries. Instruction was conducted in Spanish and was designed to spread the Catholic faith and Spanish culture. In addition, education was designed to help keep territories held by Spain under Spanish control and to enculturate people into a way of life. For example:

> The missions were far more than religious outposts: They were social institutions, designed to transform the Indians from scattered hunting and gathering peoples into disciplined farmers, ranchers, and cloth weavers clustered around, and faithful to the church.[12]

The Spanish conquest was very influential on the formal education of Native Americans. Whereas some policies sought to educate the Native Americans and assimilate them into Spanish culture, in reality, most educational practices consistently neglected and abused this power.[13] The history of Native American education consists of basically two phases. From the sixteenth century to the twentieth century, its aims were the neglect, full assimilation, or eradication of Indian cultures. Many people thought that Indians were not capable of being educated and civilized, so there was no need to do anything. Others thought the best policy was to use education to eradicate Native American culture and substitute European cultures and values. The second phase, self-determination, became a feature of the twentieth century.

HOW DID NATIONHOOD CHANGE AMERICAN EDUCATION?

Thomas Jefferson strongly believed that the new states could not and would not long endure if people were ignorant of the laws of government and their roles in the new social order. Furthermore, Jefferson and others believed a democratic government would be only as strong as the ability of its citizenry to make intelligent choices. Jefferson remarked that "if a nation expects to be ignorant and free, in a state of civilization, it expects what never was and never will be."[14] Jefferson and others who were influenced by Enlightenment ideas believed that education was a natural right of people, just as were life, liberty, and the pursuit of happiness.

Nationhood brought a demand for education that would provide citizens who could uphold a democracy. Nationhood also brought demand for more practical and modern education. The Latin grammar schools of New England were gradually replaced by common schools devoted to universal free public education.

Two events hastened the growth and expansion of schools. The first was the **Northwest Ordinance Acts of 1785 and 1787**. These acts provided for the disposing of the Northwest Territories. As states were formed, they were required to set aside the sixteenth section in each township for the support of public schools. The ordinance said in part, "Religion, morality, and knowledge being necessary to good government and the happiness of mankind, schools and the means of education shall forever be encouraged."[15]

The second event was the **Kalamazoo case**, decided by the Michigan Supreme Court in 1873, which upheld the use of tax money to support common schools. This gave the schools, through their boards of education, the power to levy taxes to support schooling.

Northwest Ordinance Acts of 1785 and 1787 These acts disposed of the Northwest Territories and created states in place of the territories. Revenue created by the selling of each township in the new states went to fund public education.

Kalamazoo case In 1873, the Michigan Supreme Court upheld the use of tax money to support common schools.

REFLECT & WRITE

Do you agree with Jefferson that education is essential for a free society? How does this ideal apply to society today?

Common schools Schools designed to teach a common body of knowledge to all students.

The Development of Common Schools

Common schools were designed to educate all children equally using the same kind of curriculum. The growth and popularity of the common schools were based on two basic assumptions: Schools for all could cure the major social, economic, and political problems of society, and schools for all were necessary for the survival of democratic society. Horace Mann was a champion of public education and teacher education and a strong advocate for and supporter of the common school. He believed that common schools were the best way to educate Americans. Although it is difficult to assign a specific date to the beginning of common schools, it was most likely in 1837, when Horace Mann became secretary of the Massachusetts State Board of Education.

The common school movement coincided with rapid industrialization and urbanization in the United States, along with high rates of immigration. One purpose of these schools was to "Americanize" immigrants. Another purpose was to provide skilled and semiskilled laborers for the factories. Common schools admitted young children, were free, and were open to all children.

■ **INTASC**

STANDARD 3 The teacher understands how students differ in their approaches to learning and creates instructional opportunities that are adapted to diverse learners.

The Spread of Education for Women

The spread of education for women is related in many ways to the growth and popularity of the common school. In rural schools, classes were mixed. In large urban areas, especially in the East, "single-sex schools were numerous, if not the norm." However, "the principles of common schooling argued against separation of the sexes."[16]

By the end of the nineteenth century, public schools were mostly open to young men and women in the nation's cities. In conservative areas, such as the South and older eastern cities, separate schooling was still the norm. In general, however, coeducation became the rule. Much of this was due to the predominance of women as classroom teachers. Feminization of the nation's teaching force solidified women as learners and helped to bring coeducation firmly into urban schools.[17]

Emma Willard was one of the pioneers of women's education. In 1814, Willard opened a boarding school for girls in Middlebury, Vermont, and the success of her school encouraged her to become an advocate for education for girls comparable to that of boys. Willard was named superintendent of the Kensington, Connecticut, schools in 1840, the first woman to hold such an office.

Figure 9.2 highlights events in the education of women. To read about teaching in a same-sex school today, read *In the Classroom with Adele Martinez* on page 312.

Go to MyEducationLab and select the topic "Classroom Management/Productive Learning Environments" and read the article "How Tweens View Single Sex Classes." Answer questions that follow.

REFLECT & WRITE

Women have been making strides toward equality for years. In the late 1990s women's educational levels began to outpace men's. What differences do you think this might make to public education in the twenty-first century?

MAJOR EVENTS IN WOMEN'S EDUCATION

1850	Harvard Medical School admits its first woman, Harriot Kezia Hunt, age 44. Hunt withdraws from Harvard after riots by male students protesting her admission.
1875	The Wellesley College for Women opens on September 8 in Wellesley, Massachusetts; the college began the first rowing program for women. One day later, Smith College, also exclusively for women, opens in Northhampton, Massachusetts.
1925	Florence Sabin, one of the era's foremost scientists, becomes the first woman elected to the National Academy of Sciences and the first woman elected to full membership in the Rockefeller Institute.
1975	Title IX goes into effect on June 21. Title IX mandates that all schools allocate equal resources to male and female athletic programs, opening more athletic opportunities to girls and young women.
1975	Women are admitted to the U.S. military academies under a new law signed by President Gerald Ford.
1998	The educational attainment levels of women ages 25 to 29 exceed those of men in the same age group. Ninety percent of women have at least a high school diploma and 29 percent have a bachelor's degree or higher; for men, the respective percentages are 87 percent and 26 percent.
2000	More than 2.5 million girls take part in high school athletic programs during the 1997–1998 school year—triple the number that participated in 1972–1973.
2005	Women now make up the majority—54 percent—of the 10.8 million young adults enrolled in college.

FIGURE 9.2 Major Events in Women's Education

Major events in women's education with college enrollment for women surpassing that of men in 2005.

Source: Mather, M., & Adams, D. The crossover in female-male college enrollment rates. Population Reference Bureau, February 2007. (Online). Available at www.prb.org/Articles/2007/CrossoverinFemaleMaleCollegeEnrollmentRates.aspx. Accessed December 3, 2007.

The Expansion of High School Education

The first high school in the United States was the English Classical School of Boston. Its name was later changed to English High School. This first high school was quite different from the contemporary high school you attended. It was not co-educational and served students we would now consider middle school or junior high school age—from 12 to 15. As in elementary schools, students stayed in the same room with the same teacher all day, and they studied a fixed curriculum: composition, declamation, math, history, civics, logic, navigation, surveying, and moral and political philosophy.[18]

Secondary education remained small scale until the early twentieth century; as late as 1910, only about 10 percent of American youth attended high school. Until the twentieth century, most Americans' formal education ended with elementary school, where they learned to read (especially the Bible), write, and do simple arithmetic. This was sufficient for their agrarian lifestyles. Books, magazines, and newspapers were scarce, and teenage labor was needed in the fields.

In the Classroom

with **Adele Martinez**

Teaching in a Single-Sex School

When I first began teaching ninth-grade English at an all-girl's Catholic school in San Antonio, I expected to meet shy, demure girls who would present a challenge to me to creatively bring them out of their shells. In my experience as a coed teacher, sometimes even the most formidable intelligence just refuses to stand up for itself in a crowd, and I've noticed that girls tend to do this in high school. So the first day, I'd planned a quick ice-breaker, followed by some simple group work to get the class warmed up. Instead of the quiet, silent nods that I expected as I gave my introduction to the course and our reading list, hands shot up—asking questions about me, what I liked to do, was I married, did I have a boyfriend, how long had I been teaching, and did I like teaching in an all-girl's school? Most teachers can relate to the experience. I answered them calmly one by one, but the answers were followed by more questions.

Each day, our lessons continued like this; with questions. Not as many were personal, but as we read the questions led to some very interesting discussions. I was shocked at this impulsive class. In high school, it seems, something happens to young women. They begin to feel as though they must be shy to be liked, to be accepted for their looks rather than what they think. Blame society, blame culture, but any environment of growing adolescents creates pressure on individuals to be more like their peers. I found these girls to be different in a lot of ways.

They spoke their minds. They laughed when we got to the "gross" stuff in Greek mythology, and we could talk candidly about issues facing women in the literature we read. I loved my year with them, and every year since has been an opportunity to expose the minds of young women to literature that made an impression on me when I was a girl—literature that often sparked ideas that I never dared to share in class.

Do I think separate-sex education is the answer to all of our nation's problems? Certainly not. In fact, separate-sex education is definitely not suitable for everyone, and in the past it has not been so "equal" in terms of quality. However, there needs to be a dialogue about how women are socialized in coed education—do they get the same responses from teachers? From boys and girls in the class? How and why are intellectual questions not asked as often by young women as they are by young men? Are classrooms organized so that young women do not feel left out? And of course, the all-important question on many young women's minds—what do you do about boys? At our school, we have social clubs and dances that correspond to the nearby all-boys school, and of course the girls have freedoms outside school determined by their parents. In reality, girls educated this way may not be as socially adapted as girls educated in a coed situation. And in all fairness, I enjoy teaching in both situations, as both offer new challenges and require creative thinking to accommodate my students.

Textbooks for Americans

Nationhood increased demand for American textbooks to replace European educational materials. Noah Webster, the "school master of the Republic," was a champion of public education and advocated the teaching of American language as a means of helping to unify the country. In 1783, Webster published *The American Spelling Book*, one of three in a series devoted to spelling, grammar, and reading. *The American Spelling Book*, or *Blue-Back Speller* as it is commonly referred to, was designed to teach children the "rudiments" of the English language—pronunciation, spelling, grammar, and reading. In the process, it also taught them useful truths and practical information.

William Holmes McGuffey, president of Cincinnati College, published his first *Eclectic Reader* in 1836. It provided illustrated moral stories for reading instruction. The popularity of the **McGuffey readers** increased with the growth and expansion of common schools, thus making it one of the foundations of modern textbooks.

_____
_____
_____
_____
_____

McGuffey readers A popular series of reading books for students in grades 1 through 6, produced in 1836 by William Holmes McGuffey.

REFLECT & WRITE

There is a great deal of difference between the first textbooks and textbooks used today. What do you anticipate will be the next big change to contemporary textbooks?

The Spread of Higher Education

The first colleges in the United States were modeled after Cambridge and Oxford in England. Students were mainly children of the wealthy, and the curriculum was the liberal arts. The first college was Harvard, founded in 1636, followed by William and Mary in 1693 and Yale in 1701.

In 1862, the **Morrill Land Grant University Act** granted each state 30,000 acres of public land for each of its congressional representatives to establish colleges of agriculture and mechanical education. These colleges were known as **land grant colleges**. They emphasized applied studies, helped popularize higher education, and made such education available and accessible to a large part of the population.

Formal teacher education also developed during the nineteenth century. At the urging of Horace Mann, in 1839 the Massachusetts legislature founded the first state-supported **normal school** in the United States for training women as teachers.

Following the establishment of the first normal school in Massachusetts, other states followed suit. The first normal schools (*normal* means "common" or "natural") were year programs and admitted students right out of elementary school. It was not until the early 1900s that a high school diploma was necessary for entering a normal school. The normal school curriculum was similar to a high school program of studies, with additional courses in pedagogy and student teaching that often were provided in a laboratory school connected with the normal school.

In the 1930s, many normal schools started offering 4-year programs and became state teacher colleges. In the 1950s, another evolutionary change occurred, and state teacher colleges became state colleges and offered master's degrees as part of the curriculum. Today, many institutions that began as normal schools and state teachers' colleges are state universities and offer doctoral degrees. All of these changes occurred in response to the need for more teachers, the need for highly trained teachers, and the professionalization of teaching.

Morrill Land Grant University Act This 1862 act ensured that each state received 30,000 acres of public land to establish colleges of agriculture and mechanics.

Land grant colleges Public colleges of agriculture and mechanical or industrial arts established by federal funds guaranteed through the Morrill Act of 1862.

Normal schools A 2- or 4-year teacher education institution in the 1800s and early 1900s.

HOW DID AMERICAN EDUCATION CHANGE AFTER THE CIVIL WAR?

Reconstruction, the period following the Civil War, was a time of upheaval and efforts to help the South and the nation recover. Economic and social conditions in the South were much different than those in the industrialized North. The land and people were suffering from the effects of the war. The economy was in

In the Classroom

with **A Nineteenth-Century Rural Elementary School and High School**

A RURAL ELEMENTARY SCHOOL

According to Nita Thurman of the Denton (Texas) Historical Commission, elementary schools in 1876 were traditional one-room schoolhouses, usually with one teacher for all grades, although schools in larger areas sometimes had more rooms and several teachers. Restrooms were out back—one for boys and one for girls. The classroom had about five rows of double wooden desks with attached seats that were screwed into the floor, and the teacher sat on a raised platform with a desk at one end of the room. There was a blackboard, and each school had one world globe, a map of the United States, and an unabridged dictionary.

The school was heated by an iron wood-burning stove that—like all other wood-burning stoves—nearly cooked the students sitting nearby while leaving those farther away out in the cold. For dark, cloudy days, there was an oil lamp hanging from the ceiling. A pail of water and a communal dipper to drink from were also available.

A standard school day began early. The teacher arrived by 7 A.M. to prepare for the day, which included starting a fire in the iron stove if it was cold weather. Students arrived at about 8 A.M. As they entered the classroom, each boy had to bow from the waist, and each girl had to curtsey to the teacher.

The first lesson was reading, so everyone took out his or her *McGuffey Reader*. Students read aloud and sometimes dramatized the *McGuffey* "pieces."

Arithmetic came next, including the popular exercise called "mental arithmetic." This was problem solving without using pen or paper. Problems from *The Common School Arithmetic* usually were practical, asking, for example: If a farmer erects 72 feet of fencing each day, how much fencing will he complete in a fortnight?

Recess was next. Children went outside to use the toilets and to play games, including hide and go seek, marbles, catch the can, and pitching horseshoes. After recess, the students settled down for a writing lesson. They may have had pens and pencils, or they may have still used slates—rectangular pieces of real slate in a wooden frame. Pupils wrote on slates with the point of a thin rod of compressed slate powder. Slates were handy because anything could be wiped off the slate with a cloth or a shirtsleeve.

Children usually brought their lunches and ate in the classroom. Sometimes the teacher had a pot of soup simmering on the wood stove.

Afternoon lessons were in history and geography. A spelling bee would end the day, and the children left for home between 4 and 5 P.M., but not the teacher—he or she still had to clean up the classroom and sweep the floor. The teacher's contract included custodial work as well as teaching all children for a munificent sum ranging from $4 to $12 a month.

A HIGH SCHOOL

A typical nineteenth-century high school might be a three-story brick building, small by modern standards, with white ceilings, cement floors, and utilitarian furnishings. The classes were big, with at least 30 students each, and discipline might be in the form of a paddle. Half the teachers didn't have college degrees; all were poorly paid. In New York State, the average teacher's salary in 1899 was $700 (the equivalent of about $15,000 today); in 1846 in Niles, Ohio, male teachers were paid $10 a month plus a hundred pounds of iron, produced by local furnaces; female teachers earned $6 a month. (Even then, however, teachers had to pass a certification exam administered by the county to teach in Niles.)

Many teachers were responsible for more than one subject and also had other tasks to do—training the choir or cutting firewood. Lessons were prescribed by textbooks like *McGuffey's New High School Reader* or *The Normal Mental Arithmetic*. The school was open about 135 days a year, but students actually attended an average of only 86 days. For all but America's most affluent families, secondary education was irrelevant: most trades didn't require it, and colleges admitted any man who passed their exams, regardless of where or how he was educated.

Source: N. Thurman, personal communication, September 2004; C. Crossen, "In 1860, America Had Forty Public High Schools; Teachers Chopped Wood," *Wall Street Journal*, September 3, 2003, p. D2. Reprinted by permission.

disarray, people were displaced, and civil authority was limited. Schooling was not a high priority. (See *In the Classroom: A Nineteenth-Century Rural Elementary School and High School.*)

Education for African Americans

The education of African Americans after the Civil War was enhanced and promoted through many agencies and by the heroic efforts of many dedicated individuals. Government census records indicate that before the emancipation of Southern blacks, only a small number of blacks attended school, primarily in the North. After the Civil War, African American school enrollment increased; however, graduation rates between white and black students differed greatly. In 1950, before the Civil Rights Act, only 13.7 percent of African American students graduated from high school. According to the Census Bureau, 80 percent of African Americans graduate from high school.[19]

Individuals such as Booker T. Washington played an important role in the development of education for African Americans. Washington taught himself to read, attended normal school, and became a teacher and then a principal at the state normal school for African Americans in Tuskegee, Alabama.[20] The Tuskegee Institute, now Tuskegee University, became a leading center for the education of African Americans, especially in vocational education. Tuskegee is one of eighty-nine 4-year historically black colleges and universities in the United States. Washington advocated practical education in the trades for African Americans, in contrast to another pioneer in education, W. E. B. Du Bois. (See *In the Classroom with Booker T. Washington and W.E.B. DuBois* on page 316.)

Mary McLeod Bethune (1875–1955), the daughter of former slaves, also advocated development of educational opportunities and civil rights for African Americans. In 1904 she founded the Daytona Normal and Industrial School for Training Negro Girls in Daytona Beach, Florida. Bethune later merged her school with an all-boys school in Jacksonville, and it was named Bethune-Cookman College.

As strong advocates for civil rights, Bethune, Du Bois, and others were instrumental in establishing the National Association for the Advancement of Colored People (NAACP), which has a long history of fighting for civil rights, promoting education, and helping African Americans and others secure their rights under the Constitution.

The Development of Indian Schools

Following the Civil War, the prime goal of educational programs for Native Americans was to assimilate them into American life by having them give up their culture and accept middle-class American culture.[21] Three types of schools were developed to undertake the task of Americanizing Native Americans. Mission schools were run by Catholic and Protestant denominations, many under contract with the federal

---

■ **INTASC**

STANDARD 1 The teacher understands the central concepts, tools of inquiry, and structures of the subject being taught and can create learning experiences that make these aspects of subject matter meaningful for students.

■ **INTASC**

STANDARD 2 The teacher understands how children learn and develop, and can provide learning opportunities that support their intellectual, social, and personal development.

■ **INTASC**

STANDARD 5 The teacher uses an understanding of individual and group motivation and behavior to create a learning environment that encourages positive social interaction, active engagement in learning, and self-motivation.

REFLECT & WRITE

Can you identify ways in which the views of education of Booker T. Washington and W. E. B. Du Bois are reflected in American education today? In what ways can education be reformed to further provide for the education of African American students?

In the Classroom

with **Booker T. Washington and W. E. B. Du Bois**

Approaches to African American Education

At the beginning of the twentieth century, two figures stood out as preeminent leaders in the African American community: Booker T. Washington and W. E. B. Du Bois.

Washington emphasized the need for a practical education in the trades to give African Americans who were unskilled workers a higher economic base. This emphasis on practical education led him to begin Tuskegee Institute, which later became Tuskegee University in Alabama. Washington's approach to the education and social standing of African Americans was to be accommodating to the social norms of the time.

In a speech to a largely non–African American audience at the Atlanta Exposition of 1895, Washington stated the following view about the relationship between African Americans and whites: "In all things that are purely social we can be as separate as the fingers, yet one as the hand in all things essential to mutual progress." (p. 84).

This view was criticized by W. E. B. Du Bois, among others, who felt that accepting social separation carried with it an acceptance of social inferiority. Du Bois, who was the first African American to earn a Ph.D. from Harvard University, felt

Booker T. Washington

African Americans should not wait for full social and political equality. His educational views focused on teaching the "talented tenth" of the African American population to the fullest of their potential. Du Bois felt that if this segment of the African American community could complete university degrees, they could take their place among the business, professional, and intellectual elite of the nation. The "talented tenth" would then provide opportunities for other segments of the African American population.

Du Bois expressed some of his views on education in a speech delivered in 1906 to the second annual meeting of the Niagara Movement:

W. E. B. Du Bois

> And when we call for education we mean real education. We are believers in work. We ourselves are workers, but work is not necessarily education. Education is the development of power and ideal. We want our children to be trained as intelligent human beings should be, and we will fight for all time against any proposal to educate black boys and girls simply as servants and underlings, or simply for the use of other people. They have the right to know, to think, to aspire (p. 172).

When comparing the educational views of these two men, their philosophies must be examined within the social and political climate of the time. Both men wanted to improve the educational and economic circumstances of African Americans. They differed in the degree to which they were willing to accept racial segregation in education and other areas in order to bring about social, economic, and educational progress to African Americans.

Sources: J. A. Banks and C. A. Banks (1978). *March Toward Freedom*, 2nd ed., Belmont, CA: Fearon Pitman; P. S. Foner (ed.), (1970), *W. E. B. DuBois Speaks*. New York: Pathfinder.

How has education for Native Americans changed between the colonial and the modern eras?

government. The focus of the curriculum was the three Rs, vocational and agricultural education, and religion. Although the number of Native American children educated in mission schools was never great, such schools nonetheless did provide education before there were enough schools for these children.

Another type of school was the day boarding school operated by the **Bureau of Indian Affairs (BIA)** on reservations. In addition to these schools, a number of off-reservation boarding schools were established by the BIA. This was in keeping with the belief that the best way to "Americanize" Native American children was to remove them from their tribal setting and provide them with a strict program of cultural transformation. Off-reservation boarding schools, such as the Carlisle (Pennsylvania) Indian School, founded by Richard Henry Pratt in 1879, reflected a harsh approach to assimilation. Pratt's goal, for example, was to "Kill the Indian, and save the Man."[22] Education bore no relationship to reservation life and forced Native American children and youth to reject their families and traditional ways of life.

Today, Native American education is conducted through the Office of Indian Education Programs (OIEP) located within the BIA in the Department of the Interior. The BIA is responsible for all of the management and education functions. OIEP seeks to provide quality education opportunities from early childhood throughout life in accordance with Native Americans' needs for cultural and economic well-being. The education of Native Americans takes into account the spiritual, mental, physical, and cultural aspects of the person within a family and tribal or Alaskan native village contexts.[23] See *What's New in Education?* for more information about progress in Native American schools.

Bureau of Indian Affairs (BIA)   Responsible for all of the management and education functions for Native American education, which is conducted through the Office of Indian Education Programs (OIEP).

To learn more about the plight of Native American children in the early years of American Education go to MyEducationLab and select the topic "History of Education" then watch "Genocide Impact." Complete activities that follow.

REFLECT & WRITE

America does not seem to have a good track record of providing high quality education for Native American children. Why do you think this is so?

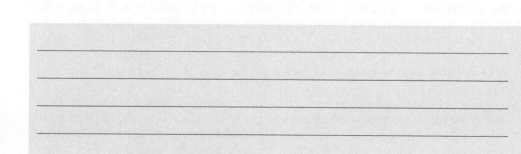

What's *New* in Education?

Does NCLB Leave Native American Culture Behind?

Native Americans have faced tremendous difficulties in retaining their culture, languages, and customs as a result of European colonization and anti–Native American federal policies. Thousands of traditions and languages have been lost and will never be regained. Recently, however, there has been a resurgence of interest in the preservation of Native American languages and customs. Reservation and state and local programs are now teaching traditional languages and providing multicultural training to better prepare teachers for Native American schools. However, the cultural gap has never closed, and educational policies and practices continue to reflect this.

From June 2004 to July 2005, the National Indian Education Association (NIEA) held 11 hearings nationwide on Native American educational issues. Highlighted in these hearings was how NCLB and other federal policies affect Native American education. Teachers, counselors, students, and parents told the NIEA about the impact that NCLB has had on their communities, cultural standards, and traditions. Despite the broad scale of these hearings, representing many diverse populations of Native Americans, the overall results were very similar.

Although witnesses agreed that schools and districts should be held accountable for student success, many stated that the NCLB has significantly affected the teaching of Native languages and culture. The lack of awareness of tribal customs and teaching methods, the cultural structure of the school day, the workload, and the overtly Western idea of standardized testing has caused considerable frustration in Native American communities. NCLB's narrow focus on testing and accountability, witnesses noted, makes it difficult to incorporate a full range of curriculum activities, especially in liberal arts, music, and literature.

Native Americans are concerned that this shift in focus will hurt Native American students who already struggle with connecting what they learn in school to daily life events. They fear that many students internalize the lack of success of their school as an indication that they have failed their community. Although these reports are highly disturbing considering the broad purpose of NCLB, the NIEA published its report to increase awareness among lawmakers, voters, and educators of the many issues facing schools in Native American communities. All U.S. citizens have a right to discuss and make adjustments to federal policy. Although the Native American viewpoint has consistently been overlooked in the past, they are looking for an equal voice now and in the future.

To learn more about this issue and others facing Native American education and to read the NIEA's report, visit www.niea.org.

European Influences on American Education

American education has been and continues to be influenced by European educational systems. Two important contributors to modern education were Friedrich Froebel and Maria Montessori.

Froebel's Kindergarten

Friedrich Froebel (1782–1852) devoted his life to developing a curriculum and methodology for educating young children and earned the distinction of "father of the kindergarten." Froebel's primary contributions to educational thought and practice are in the areas of learning, curriculum, methodology, and teacher training. He believed that the educator's role, whether parent or teacher, was to observe the natural unfolding of children's development and to provide activities that would enable them to learn what they were ready to learn when they were ready to learn it.

Froebel compared children to seeds that germinate, bring forth a new shoot, and grow from young, tender saplings to mature productive trees. He likened the role of educator to that of a gardener. In his **kindergarten**, or "garden of children," he envisioned children being educated in close harmony with their own natures

Kindergarten   A program for children before they begin formal schooling at the elementary level based on the ideas of German educator Friedrich Froebel.

and the nature of the universe. Children unfold their uniqueness in play, and it is in the area of unfolding and learning through play that Froebel makes one of his greatest contributions to early childhood curriculum.

Froebel developed a systematic, planned curriculum for the education of young children and was the first educator to encourage young, unmarried women to become teachers.

The Montessori Method

Maria Montessori (1870–1952) greatly influenced curriculum and instruction in preschool and primary education. She devoted her life to developing a system for educating children and youth, and her system has influenced all contemporary early childhood programs and many elementary programs as well. Although Montessori's first intention was to study children's diseases, she soon became interested in educational solutions for students with special needs.

Montessori believed that respect for children was the cornerstone on which all approaches to teaching should rest. She thought that because each child is unique, education should be individualized for each child. She also maintained that children are not miniature adults and should not be treated as such. Furthermore, Montessori believed that children are not educated by others but rather educate themselves. To help them achieve this self-education, she recommended a prepared environment in which children could do things for themselves. Regarding the role of the teacher, Montessori believed teachers should make children the center of learning, encourage children to learn through freedom provided in the prepared environment, and be keen observers in order to plan appropriately for children's learning.

In her first school, named the Casa di Bambini (or Children's House), she tested her ideas and gained insights into children and teaching that led to the perfection of her system. The best-known portion of Montessori's system is for children between ages 3 and 5. With contemporary interest in infant and toddler programs, applications of the Montessori method for this age group are gaining more popularity in the United States. Also, many public schools are using the Montessori method in the elementary grades. The Montessori program was first implemented in the public schools in 1968 in Philadelphia, Pennsylvania, at Benjamin Franklin Elementary School by Patricia McGrath. As of 2007, more than 5,000 classrooms in public schools offer Montessori Programs.[24]

REFLECT & WRITE

In addition to Froebel and Montessori, can you think of other European influences on early childhood education, past and present?

Education Reform in the Progressive Era

The period from 1890 to 1920 was a period of great change in American society. Industrialization and urbanization continued, with accompanying economic, political, and social problems, such as poverty, poor housing, and unsafe and unhealthy workplace conditions. Cities were undergoing rapid growth, and the mostly rural economy of the states was transforming into a modern industrial society. Additionally, immigrants from Europe, with their diversity of languages and cultures, created assimilation challenges for education and the work force.

These new waves of immigrants, combined with the migration of people from rural to urban areas, produced tremendous increases in public school enrollment, which created public concern about how to address differing needs in American education. This period was known as the Progressive Era, and educators and others attempted to address these monumental social problems through innovative ideas and practices that came to be known as progressivism.

The Progressive Era was also a time of many reform efforts for workers' rights and women's suffrage. The suffrage movement sought the right of women to vote and to have greater access to economic and occupational advancement. The women's rights movement had started a century earlier. On July 16, 1848, Elizabeth Cady Stanton assembled the Women's Rights Convention at a church in Seneca Falls, New York. She called the meeting in an effort to secure equal participation by women in the trades, professions, and commerce. The movement eventually led to the ratification of the Nineteenth Amendment in 1920, which grants women the right to vote.

Progressive education An educational philosophy emphasizing change in educational thought and political control, child-centered teaching and curriculum planning, and scientific management, with the goal of making democracy work through education.

The needs of the Progressive Era resulted in the educational reform movement known as **progressive education**, which "revolved around . . . (1) change in the political control of education, (2) change in educational thought, (3) innovations in school curriculum and other school practices, (4) justifications of schooling in terms of professionalism, and (5) the importing of scientific management into school administration."[25]

John Dewey (1859–1952) was a leading reformer of the Progressive Era. Dewey's theory of schooling emphasized students and their interests rather than subject matter. From this student-centered emphasis came the terms *child-centered curriculum* and *child-centered schools*. The progressive movement in education also maintained that schools should be concerned with preparing students for the realities of today rather than for some vague future time. As Dewey expressed in *My Pedagogical Creed*, "Education, therefore, is a process of living and not a preparation for future living."[26] Thus, out of daily life should come the activities in which students learn about life and the skills necessary for living. Dewey believed that traditional curricula and methods imposed knowledge on children; instead, children's interests should be the springboard for learning skills and subject matter.

Progressive education is about educating students for democratic living, making schools democratic environments, and educating to the fullest extent every child who comes to school. Educational practices based on progressive ideas exist in many classrooms today, from the preschool to the university level. Some progressive education-based practices include students working cooperatively in groups; discovery and inquiry-based learning; assessment of students through portfolios, performances, and projects; family or multi-age grouping; and flexible scheduling.

Committee of Ten A high school study committee of the National Education Association (NEA) that recommended reforms for secondary education.

The reform of secondary education occurred primarily as a result of the recommendations by a high school study committee of the National Education Association (NEA) known as the **Committee of Ten**. In 1893, they published their study, which recommended that:

■ High schools should consist of grades 7 through 12.
■ The curriculum should consist of four alternative curricula consisting of classical, Latin-scientific, modern languages, and English. Students would elect one of the four curricula.

- No differences in the courses of study should exist for college-bound or non-college-bound students. Any of the four curricula would be appropriate for college-bound or non-college-bound students.
- Any of the four courses of study would be appropriate preparation for college entrance.

The recommendations of the Committee of Ten, with their emphasis on the role of high schools as college preparatory, had a tremendous influence on the shaping of American secondary education that is evident to the present time.

> **? What Does This Mean for You?**
>
> **The Committee of Ten** identified four curricula that should be taught to high school students. These curricula were classical, Latin-scientific, modern languages (such as French and German), and English. Basic courses, such as other foreign languages, mathematics, science, English, and history, were included in each curriculum. What impact has this committee's suggestions had on modern classrooms? In what ways will you have to incorporate these types of curricula in your classroom?

REFLECT & WRITE

Should courses of study for college-bound students differ from those for students who do not intend to attend college immediately after graduating from high school? If so, in what ways would they differ?

_____
_____
_____
_____
_____

HOW DID AMERICAN EDUCATION CHANGE AFTER WORLD WAR II?

A number of forces have greatly influenced educational thought and practice from World War II to the present. For example, the Civil Rights Movement, the Cold War, the War on Poverty, legislation for students with disabilities, the women's liberation movement, the Vietnam War protest era, and conservative reaction to the 1960s and 1970s (see Figure 9.3 on page 322).

Two significant events occurred almost immediately after World War II that helped create a new national interest in education from preschool to the university. The first was a series of judicial decisions and social events that shaped the contemporary Civil Rights Movement. The second event was the launching of *Sputnik* by the Soviet Union on October 4, 1957, which spurred an intensification of the Cold War between the United States and Russia (see Chapter 1).

These two events changed education practice in two important ways. First, they influenced specific policies, programs, and legislation affecting what students would learn, know, and be able to do. Second, they changed the public's attitude about what is best for the nation's children and youth and how America should educate its children and youth.

■ INTASC

STANDARD 3 The teacher understands how students differ in their approaches to learning and creates instructional opportunities that are adapted to diverse learners.

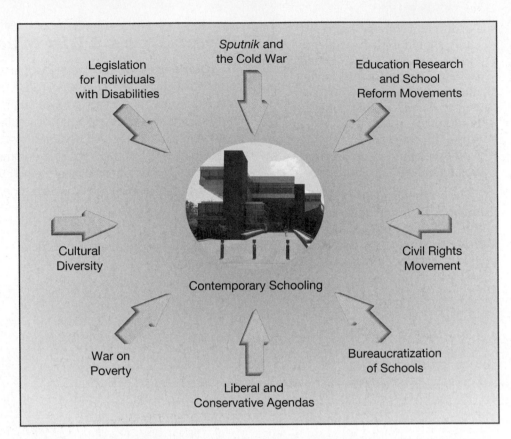

FIGURE 9.3 Postmodern Influences on Education in the United States.

Contemporary schooling will always be influenced by political and social needs and agendas.

REFLECT & WRITE

What other postmodern influences would you add to Figure 9.3? What three postmodern influences do you think have changed education the most?

_____

_____

_____

_____

_____

The Cold War

The 1960s and 1970s were periods of intense anticommunism dominated by a nuclear arms race between the United States and Russia and communist bloc countries. The Cold War rivalries intensified America's efforts to demonstrate its superior economic, political, military, and educational capabilities. Spurred by the Soviet Union's lead in space exploration, politicians and educators were determined to catch up with and surpass the Soviets.

In 1958, the U.S. government passed the **National Defense Education Act** to meet national education needs, particularly in the sciences. Universities received federal grants to develop national curricula in science and mathematics. Many teachers attended summer institutes at universities to learn how to implement

National Defense Education Act A federal law passed in 1958 to provide funds for upgrading the teaching of mathematics, science, and foreign languages and for establishing guidance services.

them. Through such programs, large numbers of teachers were retrained and received advanced degrees.

The Civil Rights Movement

The Civil Rights Movement began in the 1920s and 1930s and gained impetus during the 1950s and 1960s. The 1955 Montgomery bus boycott, which began when Rosa Parks refused to sit at the back of the bus, added momentum to a series of court cases and demonstrations for civil rights and human dignity. The fight for civil liberties spread quickly to the school arena. As a result, the rights of children and adults to public education were and are being clarified and extended.

As we saw in Chapter 8, the Supreme Court in *Brown v. Board of Education of Topeka* (1954) overturned the historic separate-but-equal practices of many school districts, especially those in the South. The Court ruled that "in the field of education the doctrine of 'separate but equal' has no place." The Court's decision raised many questions about educational opportunities for African Americans, Hispanic Americans, Asian Americans, and women. Equality in education soon came to mean equity, which involves adequately and appropriately addressing all students' needs. The outcomes of the *Brown* decision have included desegregation efforts, busing for school integration, and the creation of magnet schools.

Education for Students with Disabilities

Key federal and state legislation relating to the education of students with disabilities, which is essentially civil rights legislation, changed forever the way students with disabilities are educated. Three of the most important pieces of legislation in this regard were the Education for All Handicapped Children Act (PL 94-142), the Education of the Handicapped Act Amendments (PL 99-457), and the Individuals with Disabilities Education Act (IDEA; PL 101-476). These laws extend to children with special needs and their parents and families regarding access to educational and social services. These laws, with their tremendous educational implications, also broaden and extend civil rights. Consequently, more students than ever before have the right to a free, appropriate, individualized education, as well as to humane treatment.

Equal Rights for Women

Equal rights for women have their basis in the Fourteenth Amendment, which provides for due process and equal protection under the law. Additionally, **Title IX of the Education Amendments** of 1972 states: "No person in the United States shall, on the basis of sex, be excluded from participation in, be denied the benefits of, or be subjected to discrimination under any education program or activity receiving federal financial assistance." As we saw in Chapter 8, the provisions of Title IX took effect in 1975 and essentially said that any gender discrimination in educational programs that receive federal funds is against the law. In 1987, Congress strengthened Title IX by passing the Civil Rights Restoration Act, which states that entire institutions are subject to civil rights laws and regulations if any program within the institution receives federal aid.

In 1974, Congress passed the **Women's Education Equity Act (WEEA)**, which was designed to eliminate sex discrimination and provide gender equity in education. In 1994, Congress reauthorized and strengthened WEEA. WEEA provides for programs and materials to support training in equitable practices in classrooms, the implementation of alternative assessments designed to eliminate bias in testing instruments and assessment processes, and improved representation of women in educational administration.

Go to MyEducationLab and select the topic "History of Education" read the article "Beyond Brown: The New Way of Desegregation Litigation" then answer the questions that follow.

INTASC

STANDARD 3 The teacher understands how students differ in their approaches to learning and creates instructional opportunities that are adapted to diverse learners.

Title IX of the Education Amendments Part of the Education Amendments of 1972 that prohibits discrimination on the basis of sex or exclusion from participation in an education program or activity receiving federal financial assistance.

Women's Education Equity Act (WEEA) This 1974 act was designed to promote gender equality in education. It was strengthened by Congress in 1994 to provide programs and support materials in equitable practices in classrooms and other aspects of education.

The War on Poverty

The Educational Opportunity Act (EOA) of 1964 was designed to reduce social class divisions and to wage a War on Poverty, the slogan President Lyndon Johnson made popular in the 1960s and 1970s. One of the main purposes of EOA was to break intergenerational cycles of poverty by providing educational and social opportunities for children from low-income families. The Economic Opportunity Act created the Office of Economic Opportunity, and from this office **Project Head Start** was developed and administered. The national Head Start program has a budget of $6.7 billion and serves about 1.05 million children, less than 60 percent of those eligible.[27]

The **Elementary and Secondary Education Act (ESEA)** of 1965 was designed to continue the War on Poverty by providing funds to schools to improve the learning of disadvantaged children. Such federal involvement has been important for minority children, who are the recipients of ESEA programs. One major political effect of the ESEA is that it has enabled private schools to receive federal monies to support their programs. Provisions in the ESEA state that private institutions that receive federal funding must apply it toward programs that are secular, neutral, nonreligious, and nonideological. Additionally, the schools receiving these funds must qualify under the provisions of the ESEA as "at risk," or significantly underfunded.[28]

The NCLB Act of 2001 is an updated version of the ESEA and currently funds 50,000 schools. As well as instituting a national standardized testing system, NCLB funds disadvantaged schools through Title I. Title I funds may be used for children from preschool age to high school, but most of the students served (65 percent) are in grades 1 through 6; another 12 percent are in preschool and kindergarten programs.[29] Legislation stemming from the Civil Rights Movement and the War on Poverty led to equal opportunity and entitlement programs that have transformed American education.

Conservative Reaction to the 1960s and 1970s

In the 1980s and 1990s, the conservative movement embraced education as one of its main political platforms. Much of the conservative agenda evident in the educational community originated as a reaction against federal legislation relating to poverty and civil rights, the student protests of the 1960s, and the struggles of minorities and women to achieve equality. Many conservatives blame the public schools for social problems such as teenage pregnancy and school violence and a general decline in values and moral standards among children and youth.

The school agenda of the conservative movement in education is evident in continuing attempts to remove "objectionable" materials from school libraries and classrooms; support of home schooling as a means of providing children with an education consistent with parents' values; back-to-basics schooling, which emphasizes the basic skills; the return of school prayer to schools and classrooms; the teaching of creationism and other knowledge in keeping with biblical accounts; and the teaching of values and character traits consistent with biblical principles.

Project Head Start   A national program that promotes school readiness by enhancing the social and cognitive development of children through the provision of educational, health, nutritional, social, and other services to enrolled children and families.

Elementary and Secondary Education Act (ESEA)   A 1965 act providing funds to schools to improve the education of disadvantaged children.

■ INTASC

STANDARD 3   The teacher understands how students differ in their approaches to learning and creates instructional opportunities that are adapted to diverse learners.

REFLECT & WRITE

History is literally all around us, and society is "making" history every day. Think back over the last 5 years and identify people, events, and reforms that should be included in a contemporary history of education.

The Current Landscape of Education

Seven themes dominate the educational landscape today: standards, accountability, testing and assessment, basic skills learning, emphasis on early education, increased federal and state roles in the funding and control of education, and educational reform. Standards have played, are playing, and will continue to play a major role in determining what students should learn and be able to do. The accountability movement continues to be one of the major forces driving much of educational reform. The public wants schools to be more accountable for student learning and achievement and for the use of public funds and resources. Ongoing testing of all students in grades K through 12 is one means for measuring student achievement and for holding teachers accountable for student learning. Chapter 10 explores these topics in greater detail and shows how they influence the course of educational practice and, consequently, the history of education.

With dropout rates continuing to rise and increasing numbers of functionally illiterate young adults struggling in the job market today, there is a decided push to return to basic skills and academic-based curricula. The *Los Angeles Times* reported in 2006 that in Los Angeles alone, only 40 percent of the district's high school students pass Algebra I, forcing many of them to retake the class and causing a growing number to drop out. Some students seek alternative education, some go to technical schools, but many remain in the lowest socioeconomic class of workers who have no high school degree and who are relegated to the lowest wages and toughest jobs.[30] As dropout rates increase, lawmakers, educators, and administrators continue to seek viable means for establishing a basic education in the nation's schools. Much of the curriculum emphasis of the twenty-first century will reflect concern over how to provide a high-quality education for all students, regardless of their culture, gender, socioeconomic status, and future life goals.

President George H. W. Bush declared the 1990s as the "Decade of the Brain." At this time, the nation discovered the role of the brain in learning, how young children learn, and the importance of early learning. With these discoveries came a renewed interest in young children and early childhood education. This, in turn, affected public educational policy. This interest in brain-based learning resulted in increased funding for early childhood programs and renewed interest in developing curricula for promoting children's cognitive development. This emphasis on children's early years will likely continue for at least the next decade, and educational historians will recognize the period of 1990 to 2010 as the golden age of early childhood education.

Beginning in 1995, state governors assumed a much more powerful role in setting education policy and crafting legislation for the reform of education. Historians will identify the migration of control from local school boards to the statehouse as one of the most significant educational occurrences of the late twentieth century and early twenty-first century. Concurrent with the usurpation of local educational control by state governors, the federal government also began to

---

INTASC

STANDARD 8   The teacher understands and uses formal and informal assessment strategies to evaluate and ensure the continuous intellectual, social, and physical development of the learner.

INTASC

STANDARD 1   The teacher understands the central concepts, tools of inquiry, and structures of the subject being taught and can create learning experiences that make these aspects of subject matter meaningful for students.

? What Does This Mean for You?

Throughout this book, I have continually tried to emphasize that education is a political process. In fact, it is literally impossible for me to think of any educational topic from the teaching of reading to teaching Advanced Placement (AP) classes that does not have political issues and implications swirling around it. What does this mean for you? It means:

- You must include politics in your life as a teacher. You must consider being involved in matters that will make a difference in how education is funded and how to best teach children and youth.
- You will need to know as much as you can about the pros, cons, and political points of view regarding the subjects you teach and other aspects of schools.
- You will need to be able to explain the various educational and political points of view to parents, colleagues, and the community.
- You will need to be an articulate spokesperson for your profession.

play a larger role in education matters. President George W. Bush ran on a strong education reform platform, and Secretary of Education Margaret Spellings is committed to expanding the federal influence over education through the funding of specifically targeted educational programs such as early literacy. The NCLB Act authorized $24.4 billion for K–12 education. Some of the requirements for receiving this federal funding include:

- Annual state tests in reading and science for every child in grades 3 through 11 will be conducted by the end of the 2007–2008 school year and at least once during high school.
- Schools that are identified as needing improvement are required to provide students with the opportunity to take advantage of public school choice, and low-income students may receive funding for tutoring or transportation to another school.
- NCLB authorized a substantial increase in Title I aid to funding schools that qualify.
- The act mandates that schools must raise all students' reading and math proficiency by 2013–2014. Schools must also close gaps in scores between wealthy and poor students and white and minority students.
- For teachers, NCLB requires that within four years all are qualified to teach their subject areas. This means that they must either obtain undergraduate or graduate degrees and/or pass subject tests in their teaching area.

NCLB is significant for several reasons. First, it authorizes a huge increase in federal spending, including a 29 percent increase in total federal education funding (from $42.2 billion in 2001 to $54.4 billion in 2007) for elementary and secondary education. Second, it greatly expands the federal government's role in the American education system, which traditionally has been controlled by states and local districts.

If there is one word that describes the educational events of the last 20 years, it is *reform*. Educational reform has dominated the educational landscape and has touched the life of every student, teacher, and administrator in America. Educational reform is directed toward improving America's schools, increasing student achievement, and providing well-educated citizens and workers. Reform will continue to shape educational practice for years to come, and reform initiatives will shape your career as a teacher.

Education in the Twenty-First Century

Because education is an ongoing process, it inevitably undergoes never-ending change. Your career and your profession—like many others in our fast-moving times—will always be changing. We are a decade into the twenty-first century, but in just these few short years the educational landscape has radically altered.

Here are some of the changes that are occurring even as you are preparing to teach:

- **The growing influence of the federal government in all matters and all levels of education.** As continually discussed in this text, the federal government is playing a larger role in prescribing what is taught and how it is taught. The NCLB Act is one of the most significant pieces of federal legislation in the last 50 years. Its impact on education in the United States is comparable to that of *Brown v. Board of Education*. The role of the federal government in the process of education will become larger and more directive over the coming decade.
- **The growth of the educational industry and influence of the business community on education.** Education is big business, and a lot of money is invested in and spent on education. As a result, the education industry plays a significant

● *Your Turn*

You are a fourth-grade teacher in a politically conservative area. The president of the parents' organization has just written to you asking to spend a day in your classroom observing and to review the books on your shelves. What will you do?

role in what is taught and how it is taught. This is evident in such technological programs for young children as Leap Frog; the for-profit K–12 virtual school of former Secretary of Education William Bennett; the growth of private, online for-profit colleges in higher education; and the expanded role of companies exercising control over kinds of tests students take and how they take them.

- **The integration of technology with learning technology.** Technology promises to change how teachers teach and how education is delivered in pre-K–12. Many schools are now discussing the elimination of hard-copy textbooks and doing all textbook-based instruction online. We will discuss the technological influences on education in more detail in Chapter 12.

Although these are by no means all of the reforms that have occurred in the last decade, they are major ones and are wide ranging in their influence and effects.

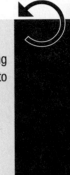

REFLECT & WRITE

Given the vast changes occurring in education, how do you hope to grow and adapt as a teacher? Which of your ideas about education do you think you will keep? What ideas will you change according to the changing standards of education?

_____

_____

_____

_____

_____

HOW IS PHILOSOPHY RELEVANT FOR CLASSROOM TEACHERS?

Just as the history of education is important to your professional practice, so too is understanding the basic philosophies of education and applying them to your own beliefs about teaching and your classroom practices. As a beginning teacher, each of your days will be filled with decisions about what to teach, how to teach it, how to best provide for the needs of all your students, and how to prepare lessons and curricula that challenge your students and enable them to learn. Your decisions about these endeavors will be guided by your beliefs about life, your students, and teaching. Professional interactions, meetings, and discussions with colleagues and administrators will be shaped by your own personal philosophy about education and learning. There is nothing that you will engage in as a teacher that will be unaffected by your own beliefs about education. Therefore, it is important to take a close look at the basic philosophies of education, examine your own philosophy of education, and then explore how the two meld.

Philosophy Is Based on Core Values

What you believe in your heart and mind about education and teaching is based on core values that dictate how you live. Your philosophy of education is based on your philosophy of life. What you believe about yourself, about others, and about life infuses and determines your philosophy of education. Knowing what others believe is important and useful, because it can help you clarify what you believe; but when it is all said and done, you have to decide what you believe. What you believe moment by moment, day by day, influences what you will teach and how you will teach it.

• *Your Turn*

What teachers believe about the purposes of education makes a difference in their teaching. As a teacher of 12th grade English in an inner-city school with a high minority population, what goals would you find most important?

REFLECT & WRITE

Your teaching style will be influenced by your personal philosophy. What basic philosophical beliefs will you incorporate into your classroom practice?

_____

_____

_____

_____

_____

A philosophy of life and education is more than an opinion. It factors into every decision you make, whether you are always conscious of it or not, and it is based on your core values. *Core values* are your beliefs about your purpose in life as well as the overall nature and purpose of life. They often dictate your relationships and responsibilities to others and to the greater community. These values come from a culmination of experiences, beliefs, and value systems that are formed as you grow into adulthood. Your value systems and beliefs will influence your teaching, your relationship to your students, and your ideas about yourself as a teacher.

Educational Philosophies

Educational philosophy   General theories and ideas about the educational process, development, and achievement.

When creating an **educational philosophy**, you must consider what education really means and what it should accomplish. How do you know when a person is educated? Is it solely determined by a degree or diploma? As you have read, many thinkers have influenced educational philosophy, as well as social customs and policies. To determine your own philosophy of what education is and should accomplish, it may be helpful to reflect on the ideas of others, for example:

- "Plants are shaped by cultivation and men by education . . . We are born weak, we need strength; we are born totally unprovided, we need aid; we are born stupid, we need judgment. Everything we do not have at our birth and which we need when we are grown is given us by education."—Jean Jacques Rousseau, *On Philosophy of Education*[31]
- "An exaggerated competitive attitude is inculcated into the student, who is trained to worship acquisitive success as a preparation for his future career."—Albert Einstein, physicist[32]
- "The whole art of teaching is only the art of awakening the natural curiosity of young minds for the purpose of satisfying it afterwards."—Anatole France, writer[33]
- "Prejudices, it is well known, are most difficult to eradicate from the heart whose soil has never been loosened or fertilized by education; they grow there, firm as weeds among rocks."—Charlotte Bronte, writer[34]

Do you agree with some of these thinkers? Ideas about education span centuries and all cultures. Every civilization has had some way of educating its young people. By looking at your own views and ideas about education as well as reading the ideas of others, you will begin to form your own perspective.

When applying for your first teaching job, you will often be asked to define your personal philosophy of education. This helps the administrators decide

Go to MyEducationLab and select the topic "Philosophy of Education" then read the article "Pathways to Reform: Start with Values" to learn about how a school's philosophy can foment reform.

whether you will be a good match for their school. The following prompts can help you begin thinking about these important questions:

- I believe the purposes of education are . . .
- I believe students learn best when they are taught under certain conditions, such as . . .
- The curriculum of any classroom should include certain "basics" that contribute to students' social, emotional, intellectual, and physical development. These basics are . . .
- Students learn best in an environment that promotes learning, which includes . . .
- All students have certain needs that must be met if they are to grow and learn, which include . . .
- A teacher should behave in certain ways and have qualities such as . . .

REFLECT & WRITE

Your culture, religion, family values and beliefs, education, political preferences, and personal experiences will all shape your philosophy of education. Discuss how these factors will impact your own philosophy.

HOW DO THE BRANCHES OF PHILOSOPHY RELATE TO EDUCATION?

The word *philosophy* comes from the Greek words *philo* (love) and *sophos* (wisdom). **Philosophy** is a love of wisdom and a pursuit of knowledge. William James (1842–1910) said this about philosophy:

It "bakes no bread" as has been said, but it can inspire our souls with courage. . . . No one of us can get along without the far-flashing beams of light it sends over the world's perspectives.[35]

By inspiring our souls with courage and by shedding far-flashing beams of light on such questions as "What is good?" "What is true?" "What is beauty?" and "What is knowledge?" philosophy influences life's decisions and course. In answering these questions, people develop their world outlook and the values they hold dear. Educational philosophy, the general theories of education, serves the practical and important purpose of influencing the daily educational decisions of parents, community members, and teachers.

Philosophy has three main branches: metaphysics, epistemology, and axiology (see Figure 9.4). Each of these branches asks questions whose answers shape core beliefs.

Philosophy   From the Greek *philos* (love) and *sophy* (wisdom); literally, the "love of wisdom" and the pursuit of wisdom.

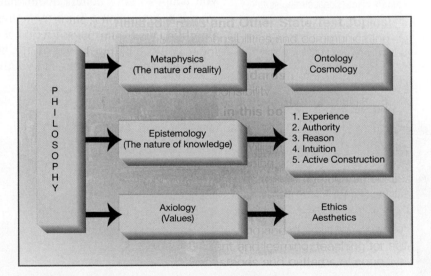

FIGURE 9.4   The Three Classical Branches of Philosophy

Philosophy is divided into several areas—metaphysics, epistemology, and axiology—that directly influence teaching theory and practice.

Metaphysics   The field of philosophy concerned with the nature of reality; addresses such questions as "What is the self?" "What is the nature of existence?" and "What is real?"

Cosmology   The part of philosophy that deals with the nature and origin of the universe.

Ontology   An area of philosophy concerned with questions of being and existence.

Metaphysics—What Is Real?

Metaphysics is the field of philosophy concerned with the nature of reality. William James wrote that "metaphysics inquires in the cause, the substance, the meaning, and the outcome of all things."[36] Metaphysics asks such questions as "What is real?" "What is the nature of existence?" "What is the meaning of life?" and "What should I do?" Metaphysics has two branches: cosmology and ontology.

Cosmology deals with the nature and origin of the universe. Cosmological questions are a part of everyday life and events. Scientists, with the use of the Hubble telescope, search for the beginnings of the universe. They want to know more about quasars, black holes, and expanding galaxies. **Ontology** examines questions and issues about existence and being. For example, people wrestle with issues about when life begins, abortion, capital punishment, the "right to die," cloning, and recent experiments on making human cells "immortal."

Metaphysical issues have particular meaning for teachers. For example, what teachers believe about human nature affects how they view and interact with students. When students are viewed as basically good, teachers will see students' behavior as motivated by good rather than bad intentions. Conversely, a negative view of human nature will influence a teacher's perspective. If students are viewed as basically bad, the teacher will see the students' behavior as motivated by bad intentions. This can have an enormous influence on classroom atmosphere and teaching techniques, because attitudes and beliefs toward situations can have a lasting impact on their outcome.

The metaphysical question "What should I do?" shapes teacher practice. For example, when teachers see subject matter as the most important factor in education, they are likely to stress it more than other teaching areas. However, if students are considered most important, teachers will base their curriculum on student needs and interests.

Consider the following situation: A student comes to you with a complaint that she's being bullied. How will you react? Will your first impulse be to sympathize with her, or will it be to criticize her for not standing up for herself? If a student accuses another student of doing something harmful, how will you treat it? Is it your job to be a bit of a counselor and friend to your students, or merely an instructor? What is the role of the teacher all about, and how will you adapt to your beliefs about that role?

How you answer these metaphysical questions will determine how you live your life. Your decision to become a teacher most likely involved questions about the meaning and importance of life, how to spend your life most meaningfully, and the importance of children and youth to society.

REFLECT & WRITE

As a teacher you will help children answer the metaphysical question "What is the meaning of life?" What do you believe life is all about? How might this belief influence your teaching?

_____

_____

_____

_____

_____

Epistemology—How Do We Know?

Epistemology is concerned with the nature of knowledge and how knowledge is acquired. Basic questions of epistemology include "How does knowing take place?" "How do we define knowledge?" "How is knowledge acquired?" and "How do we decide what knowledge should be taught?" Epistemology is of great importance because all teachers have beliefs about how students acquire knowledge and how they learn best. Other questions that affect teaching are "Is what I am teaching my students true?" and "What philosophy is guiding my teaching?" It is natural that teachers and others stress the knowledge and beliefs that support their own experiences and backgrounds. Nonetheless, it is important to consider and include knowledge that stems from other backgrounds. This is the essence of multiculturally aware teaching (see Chapter 4).

There are many ways of knowing about life and its meaning. People can come to know about the world through experience, through authority, through reason, through intuition, and by active construction.

> **Epistemology** The field of philosophy concerned with the nature of knowledge. Epistemology asks such questions as "What is the nature of knowledge?" "How do we learn?" "What is worth knowing?"

Knowing through Experience

One way we learn and gain knowledge about the world is through experience. Acquiring knowledge through experience and the senses is known as **empiricism**. You use the empirical approach when you base your actions on your own experiences.

> **Empiricism** Knowledge acquired through the senses.

Knowing through Authority

Authoritative sources of knowledge are teachers, clergy, politicians, and scientists. Documents such as textbooks and religious publications are examples of written authority stating what is right and wrong and what constitutes the truth. For example, teachers often tell students that "the right answer is in the book." Thus, students come to accept textbooks as authoritative sources. However, some teachers believe it is in students' best interests to learn to challenge what is in textbooks. It is the teacher's job to teach students how to identify reliable sources of information and how to use them for research.

> **Deductive reasoning** Inferring specifics from a general principle or drawing a logical conclusion from a premise.
>
> **Inductive reasoning** Thinking from the particular to the general or drawing a logical conclusion from instances of a case.

Knowing through Reason

Logic is a subfield of epistemology that deals with reasoning and the rules that govern our reasoning. There are basically two kinds of logical reasoning: deductive and inductive. In **deductive reasoning**, students use a general rule and identify examples and applications of the rule. An example of deductive reasoning is taking two statements and coming to a logical conclusion based on those statements. For example, the statement "Sharks have vertical tail fins" is true, and the statement "Fish have vertical tail fins" also is true. Therefore, using deductive reasoning, the statement "Sharks are fish" is a logical conclusion. In **inductive reasoning**, the opposite of deductive reasoning, students are taught to reason from the particular to the general, examine particular instances of a phenomenon, and arrive at a general conclusion based on their observations.

Nature offers many learning opportunities that cannot be duplicated in a classroom. What could these students be learning?

The following statements demonstrate inductive reasoning: "Ice is cold. Therefore all ice is cold" and "Spiders have eight legs. Other insects have six. Therefore, spiders must not be insects." Leading students to learn through inductive reasoning using a process of inquiry is a skill all teachers need to possess. Inquiry frequently is used to teach reasoning, problem-solving, and critical-thinking skills.

Knowing through Intuition

Basing behavior on intuitive knowledge is necessary for creativity and invention and includes "the educated guess." Such behavior is based on accumulated learning acquired from experiences, reading and study, the advice of others (for example, parents and teachers), and the process of schooling. Teachers often use a particular teaching strategy because their educated guesses lead them to believe it will work.

For example, as a beginning teacher, you will have days where you have planned a lesson that seems perfect and fills up every second of your class time with what you believe is valuable and applicable instruction. First period comes in, and you begin your lesson. Halfway through, you notice several kids nodding off and several others fidgeting. You blame it on being the morning class, which is usually more tired than your afternoon class. The lesson is completed, but you get the feeling that your students did not retain the information you taught. Then second period comes in. Your students are more rowdy, and you do not complete the entire lesson because you spent 15 minutes quieting them down. The same thing happens in third period, only this time you get even less accomplished. Exhausted by the time your lunch break rolls around, you reflect on the morning. What could you do to make the lesson more interesting and approachable? You make an educated guess based on your professional intuition. You decide to try an exercise requiring individual reflection at the beginning of class to help your students focus. You try it out on your next class, and, sure enough, the day goes more smoothly. You've adapted your lesson and have created a more stimulating environment where students really learn.

Knowing through Active Construction

Learning and knowing occur through mental and physical activity. As children and adults engage in activities and have new experiences, they come to know about, make sense of, and develop an understanding about the world. They literally construct their knowledge of reality. By engaging in stimulating activities, individuals learn to organize, structure, and restructure experiences in accordance with their thoughts, ideas, and previous knowledge. In this way, we are all active participants in the development of knowledge.

As children grow and develop, they become increasingly able to act on the environment and learn from it. Acting on the environment enables them to explore, test, observe, and organize information, which they then use in their thinking processes and social interactions. Actively interacting with others also contributes to and promotes learning. Because we learn from others, it is not necessary to reinvent all of the knowledge and information already accumulated by our culture.

REFLECT & WRITE

Give an example from your own experience of knowing through active construction—"learning by doing."

_____

_____

_____

_____

_____

Epistemological Questions and Teaching

There are a number of implications for classroom teachers concerning epistemo-logical questions, or ways of knowing. First, teachers should acknowledge that there are different ways of knowing and provide opportunities for students to learn in a variety of ways. Second, teachers must respect the beliefs of students and parents about how knowledge is acquired, regardless of their own values and beliefs. Figure 9.5 illustrates teaching methods based on epistemology.

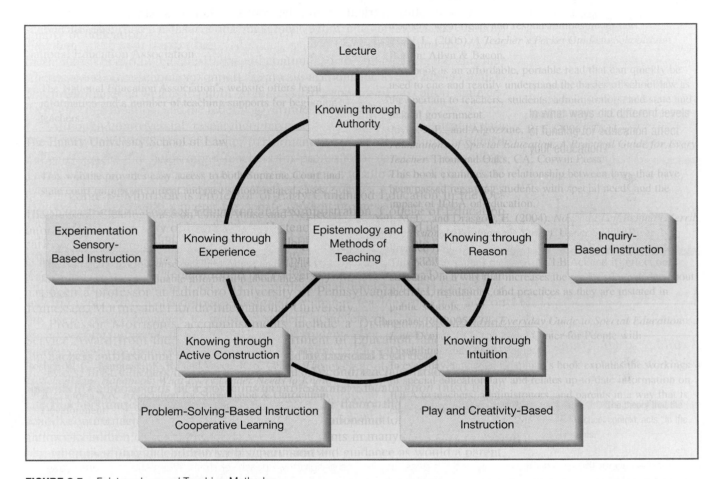

FIGURE 9.5 Epistemology and Teaching Methods

This figure illustrates how the branches of epistemology relate to different type of teaching.

REFLECT & WRITE

Teaching students about democracy and preparing them for democratic living are two of the perennial goals of American education. Which of the above teaching method(s) would you select for these essential goals?

Axiology A branch of philosophy that addresses human conduct (ethics) and beauty (aesthetics).

Ethics A branch of philosophy focusing on questions of right and wrong, good and bad, and the basis for moral judgments.

■ **INTASC**

STANDARD 2 The teacher understands how children learn and develop, and can provide learning opportunities that support their intellectual, social, and personal development.

■ **INTASC**

STANDARD 4 The teacher uses various instructional strategies to encourage students' development of critical thinking, problem solving, and performance skills.

Axiology—What Is Right?

Axiology is the branch of philosophy that addresses human conduct (ethics) and beauty (aesthetics). These two areas involve questions of values, right behavior, and the quality of individuals' lives as well as the quality of human life in general. Axiological questions include those such as "What values are of most importance?" "Whose values are of most importance?" "How should we relate to and get along with others?" and "What constitutes beauty?" (See *In the Classroom with Nina Fue*.)

The education curriculum and the books included as part of the curriculum promote certain values and convey messages about what is good, true, and beautiful. What students read and discuss can enrich and expand their ideas and conceptions about the nature of beauty and the arts. Teachers who want students to exhibit certain values need to provide opportunities for students to discuss and internalize value decisions. Any presentation of values needs to be examined in the context of culture and family beliefs.

Ethics

Questions of right and wrong and good and evil are the focus of **ethics**. These questions relate not only to how teachers conduct their own classes but also to teachers' relationships with students, colleagues, and parents. Ethics is integral to how teachers practice their profession. Teachers are governed by their own per-

In the Classroom
with **Nina Fue**
Axiological Questions and Teaching

Teachers like Nina Fue, New Jersey Teacher of the Year, are concerned about the values they convey and the ones they encourage and promote in their students' behaviors.

As always, Nina Fue starts the day in her fourth-grade classroom by checking parental signatures. Anyone who forgot to show his homework to Mom or Dad risks a sweetly stern reminder and a demerit mark in Mrs. Fue's book.

"I'll bet you didn't forget to eat dinner last night," Mrs. Fue tells a sheepish Korey Sickler. "Well, this should be like that. Happens all the time."

Because it's Monday, Mrs. Fue chooses her student of the week. Then as every day, she asks how her fourth-graders are feeling on a scale of 1 to 10. Jillian has an earache. Stephanie feels bad but doesn't want to say why. ("That's okay. Some things are private.")

In 30 short minutes, before the academic day has even begun, Nina Fue teaches responsibility, perseverance, and the art of compassion. . . .

Values are as clearly a part of what Mrs. Fue teaches as geography, English, or math. When she mentions growing up and getting a job during a grammar lesson, she teaches the work ethic. When she explains, during reading, how the mountain changed with the help of the bird, she teaches cooperation.

Nina Fue teaches values as part of the curriculum and daily classroom activities. When teachers stress the importance of doing something for the good of all—such as meeting the goals the class has set for good behavior—they are teaching a lesson about the effects of one person's behavior on others. Teachers also teach values and character traits by how they act. Linda Bates, a New Mexico Teacher of the Year, thinks that "it is unrealistic to expect students to be better than their role models. I read somewhere that values are caught as well as taught."

Source: K. McLarin (1995). "Curriculum or not, Teachers Teach Values," *The New York Times*, p. A13. Copyright 1995 by the New York Times Company. Reprinted by permission.

sonal ethics as well as the ethics of their profession. Ethical questions repeatedly guide personal choices and classroom discussions, particularly around such current concerns as violence, substance abuse, teenage pregnancy, and other social issues. In addition, state boards of education and professional organizations have codes of ethics for teachers to guide their professional practice (see the NEA Code of Ethics in Chapter 2).

When parents say they want schools to teach their children to be "good" citizens, they are talking about the ethical aspect of axiology. Society considers schools and teachers to be the guardians of acceptable behavior and conduct and wants them to impart such values as honesty, respect for others, and fair play.

Aesthetics

The term **aesthetics** refers to beauty associated with art, music, dance, drama, and literature. Questions relating to aesthetics include "What is a work of art?" "What is beauty?" and "What makes something beautiful?"

Aesthetics A branch of philosophy that addresses questions about the nature of beauty and values in human endeavor.

Many school districts emphasize aesthetics in their curricula. In fact, some have established arts magnet schools that enroll students throughout a district or region. One such example is the New World School of the Arts, a unique institution operated by three agencies—the Dade County (Florida) Public Schools (which considers the arts as a basic skill), Miami Dade Community College, and Florida State University. The New World School enrolls talented students from south Florida and enables them to explore and develop their artistic talents. Topics of values as they relate to daily living are embedded in the school day and curriculum. These values influence what is taught about beauty and the arts. Involving students in discussions of aesthetic issues enables them to have a deeper understanding of beauty and its nature.

REFLECT & WRITE

What values do you think are the most important for teachers to convey to students?

_____
_____
_____
_____
_____

The Impact of Culture on Philosophical Questions

The cultural background of groups and individuals, including cultural values, family styles, and religion, helps determine knowledge and behaviors that affect daily living and educational practices. For example, "Muslims in the United States feel strongly about teaching the Qur'an [Koran, Holy Book], the Arabic language, and basic Islamic beliefs to members of their communities, especially their children. Therefore, wherever there is a large concentration of Muslims, Arabic-Islamic schools have been developed."[37] These schools are designed to augment public school education.

■ INTASC

STANDARD 3 The teacher understands how students differ in their approaches to learning and creates instructional opportunities that are adapted to diverse learners.

Cultural beliefs and practices have many implications for how teachers teach children. Teaching practices and activities need to be multiculturally appropriate. For example, skill expectations of children born into low-income immigrant families might differ from families of the same ethnic backgrounds who have lived in the United States for more than a generation. Similarly, attitudes toward teachers

In what ways does culture impact the core values and philosophical questions relating to teaching and learning?

and what is considered to be appropriate behavior differs in many cultures. In some Asian countries, it is considered rude to look a teacher directly in the eye when speaking. This is very different from the standard American cultural concept of appropriate behavior. Teachers who do not make themselves aware of their students' customs and cultures might experience difficulties relating information to them and might alienate or discourage them inadvertently.

Being culturally sensitive requires teachers to incorporate their students' cultural backgrounds and the needs of students and their families into their teaching and into their educational philosophy. For example, questions about what is beauty and what constitutes "good" art and music need to be answered in the context of culture. Thus, teachers and students have to incorporate the ideas of beauty and the criteria for judging art and music as well as the cultural contributions of other cultures.

Go to MyEducationLab and select the topic "Diversity and Multiculturalism" and click on the student artifact, "Your Eyes Are Bigger than Your Stomach." Answer the questions that follow.

OBSERVE & LEARN

As a beginning teacher, you will have students of many different backgrounds, cultures, and ethnicities in your classroom. Many of these cultures might present behaviors that are very different from what you are used to. You must prepare yourself with the necessary skills to teach all of your students and adhere to their varying needs. Observe students from different cultures and backgrounds at a local school. How do they interact with the teacher? Which teaching methods seem to work best with the students? Use your observations to modify your lesson plans and teaching style in order to connect with all of the students you teach.

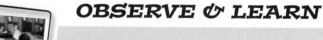

Events throughout our history serve as stark reminders of the importance of and need for cultural awareness and sensitivity, particularly considering the ever-changing face of American society. The American education system, and teachers in particular, play a critical role in promoting cultural sensitivity and inclusion. We need look no further than the events of September 11, 2001, and their aftermath when there seemed certain to be an extended backlash of anger and outrage against Muslims and people of Middle Eastern descent and even those mistakenly perceived to be of Middle Eastern descent. Educational and religious leaders alike addressed the public sense of outrage immediately with educational training oriented toward understanding differences in beliefs and cultures. Many of these efforts were aimed at young people, with the intent of promoting tolerance of differences and transforming hatred. Teachers seized the opportunity to help students discuss the events in the light of known facts, separate facts from rumor, and understand that judgments about people and cultures should be based on accurate knowledge and understanding. Many teachers and schools initiated service projects designed specifically to help people from other cultures and racial backgrounds. Former U.S. Secretary of Education Rod Paige urged educators to take a leading role in preventing harassment and violence directed at students of particular cultures or perceived to be of particular ethnic backgrounds. Paige said, "We are all committed to making sure [all] children across America can attend school in a safe, secure environment, free from harassment and threats."[38]

_____

_____

_____

_____

_____

• *Your Turn*

Many Americans with European backgrounds tend to place great value on the individual. Many other Americans, such as those with Asian backgrounds, tend to place greater value on the family or society or to value the group and the individual equally. You are teaching a tenth-grade English class. One-third of your class is composed of students from an Asian-American background. How will the difference in values between you and your students affect your teaching and your relationships with your students and their parents?

REFLECT & WRITE

Think about the culture in which you grew up. How has your culture affected your desire to teach? How will it impact your teaching style? What can you do to understand other cultures better so that you may become a better teacher?

WHAT ARE THE MAJOR PHILOSOPHIES OF EDUCATION?

Six educational philosophies have a major influence on educational practice today: perennialism, essentialism, progressivism, social reconstructionism, humanism, and existentialism. Table 9.1 presents their characteristics. Figure 9.6 presents the corresponding curriculum and instruction focus.

Perennialism

Perennialism, which grows out of idealism, the belief that ideas are the only true reality, was developed by Robert Maynard Hutchins (1899–1977). As president of the University of Chicago, he developed an undergraduate curriculum based on the Great Books Curriculum. The Great Books Curriculum consists of 100 selections of literature, including Homer's *Iliad* and *Odyssey*, Melville's *Moby Dick*,

■ **INTASC**

STANDARD 1 The teacher understands the central concepts, tools of inquiry, and structures of the subjects being taught and can create learning experiences that make these aspects of subject matter meaningful for students.

Perennialism An educational philosophy that emphasizes constancy and unchanging truth.

TABLE 9.1   Six Contemporary Educational Philosophies

Goal of Education	Role of Students	Role of Teachers	Teaching Methods	Curriculum Emphasis
PERENNIALISM				
Develop timeless virtues, such as justice, temperance, fortitude, and prudence; instill knowledge for the sake of learning.	Develop and use virtues in life's decisions; acquire knowledge.	Instill virtues; know subject matter; teach subject matter to all students.	Teacher-centered; lecture	Subject matter and common core curriculum; emphasis on arts and sciences
ESSENTIALISM				
Promote and instill cultural literacy in all students; provide a common core of cultural knowledge.	Acquire and use cultural knowledge; learn and use thinking skills.	Provide a common core cultural literacy curriculum integrated with basic school subjects.	Primarily subject- and teacher-centered methods	A uniform curriculum for all students emphasizing subject matter and cultural knowledge
PROGRESSIVISM				
Use student interests as a basis for understanding and ordering students' experience.	Participate in formulating the purposes that are the basis for the student-centered curriculum.	Act as a facilitator for student learning; determine student interests for developing curriculum.	Learning centers; cooperative learning; student-led and -initiated discussion	Student interests and needs; democracy; morality; social development
SOCIAL RECONSTRUCTIONISM				
Use education to help solve significant social problems and, as a result, make democracy more efficient and effective.	Identify social problems and use thinking skills and knowledge to solve problems.	Facilitate process of students identifying and solving community-based problems.	Facilitate cooperative learning and group problem solving; encourage students to use problem-solving skills	Integrated knowledge of and solution of social problems in the regular curriculum
HUMANISM				
Emphasize self-actualization, help students become self-actualized, and blend the cognitive and the affective; help students assimilate knowledge into their daily lives; stress human values.	Develop healthy attitudes toward self, others, and learning experience; become self-actualized.	Help students to become self-actualized and make sense of learning; connect individuals to their learning and help them apply curriculum to themselves, the community, the nation, and the world.	Group processes; one-on-one teacher-student interaction	Physical and emotional needs of students and development of learning experience so that students can fulfill their needs and resolve developmental crises
EXISTENTIALISM				
Create climate of freedom and choice where individuals can choose and be responsible for their decisions.	Accept responsibility for choices and actions; learn to set personal goals and achieve them by developing independence, making decisions, and problem solving.	Create an environment for independent action and enable students to make choices and accept responsibility for behavior.	Analysis and discussion regarding students' choices	Social studies; humanities

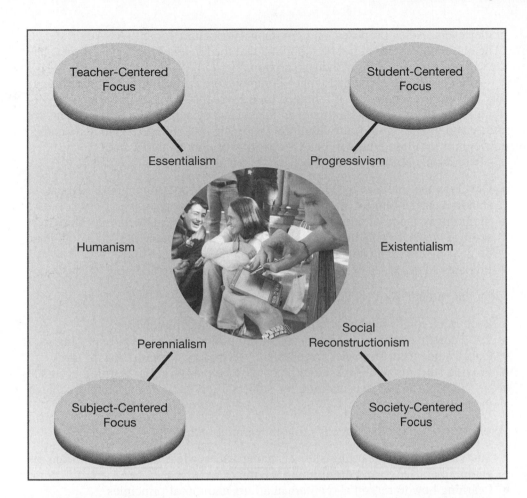

FIGURE 9.6 Six Educational Philosophies: Curriculum and Instruction Focus

Use these six types of philosophies to develop your own philosophical approach to teaching.

Darwin's *The Origin of Species*, and other masterpieces of Western civilization. Hutchins believed:

> Education implies teaching. Teaching implies knowledge. Knowledge is truth. Truth is everywhere the same. Hence education should be everywhere the same. I do not overlook the possibility of differences in organization, in administration, in local habits and customs. These are details. I suggest that the heart of any course of study designed for the whole pupil will be, if education is rightly understood, the same at any time, in any place, under any political, social, or economic conditions.[39]

Those in the perennialist camp believe that truth is perennial—that is, enduring. They believe it is the role of education and the job of educators to focus on the search for and the dissemination of the unchanging truths that are to be found in the experiences of humans over the centuries, as reflected in their culture and literature. Perennialists are concerned that society, schools, and teachers will focus exclusively on the new and faddish and will abandon the enduring truths of the ages. They believe enduring truths develop the intellect and form the basis for reason and rationality and that it is this process that helps separate humans from animals. For the perennialist, the goal of teachers and schools is to develop rational students grounded in and strengthened by the truths of the ages.

Mortimer Adler (1902–2001) continued Hutchins's work. Adler is often referred to as a neoperennialist, because in his Paideia Proposal he gave new life and meaning to the perennialist position. Among other issues, such as bringing philosophy to the masses by introducing thought-provoking literature and ideas at all

■ INTASC

STANDARD 2 The teacher understands how children learn and develop, and can provide learning opportunities that support their intellectual, social, and personal development.

■ INTASC

STANDARD 4 The teacher uses various instructional strategies to encourage students' development of critical thinking, problem solving, and performance skills.

grade levels, Adler proposed one common curriculum for all. As Adler stated, "The one-track system of public schooling that the Paideia Proposal advocates has the same objective for all without exception."[40]

Adler's supporters maintain that a common core curriculum is nondiscriminatory and promotes equity. It is intended for all students. They believe that one curriculum for all is more egalitarian than the current system of tracking students by ability and providing one curriculum for those who are college bound and another curriculum for those who will enter the work world after high school.

Perennialist philosophy emphasizes a curriculum that:

- Develops the intellect of all learners. In this regard, perennialists advocate a standard curriculum for all that is challenging and rigorous.
- Supports the study of mathematics (because it trains the mind and develops reasoning), science, and the humanities (literature—through the study of great books—history, philosophy, and art).
- Prepares students for life rather than merely for the here and now.

From the perennialist perspective, the teacher's role is to:

- Lecture on topics relating to truth, values, and critical knowledge
- Use Socratic questioning as a means of promoting thinking and reasoning
- Coach students in strategies for problem solving and learning how to think
- Provide students with supervised practice to help ensure that learning occurs
- Set high goals and expectations for students and encourage them to achieve the goals

Perennialists believe the student's role in learning includes:

- Studying hard and learning subject matter and academic skills as a means of gaining knowledge and disciplining the mind
- Learning how to reason about human affairs and moral principles
- Learning to value the past and masterpieces of literature and art

Perennialism is a philosophy that continues to generate thought and discussion in the education community. Most teachers make use of the parts of a philosophy that agree with their own beliefs about education and investigate others, such as those presented in the following pages, for additional support in their teaching styles.

REFLECT & WRITE

Which aspects of perennialism do you agree with? How will you apply them in your classroom?

_____

_____

_____

_____

_____

_____

INTASC

STANDARD 1   The teacher understands the central concepts, tools of inquiry, and structures of the subjects being taught and can create learning experiences that make these aspects of subject matter meaningful for students.

Essentialism   The educational philosophy that there is an indispensable, common core of culture that should be taught to all.

Essentialism

Essentialism as an educational philosophy maintains that there is a common body of knowledge all students need to learn as a prerequisite for functioning effectively in society. Essentialism began as a reaction against the decline of intellectual and moral standards in the schools. In 1938, a group of professional educators met to outline the essentialist position. In part, they stated:

> Should not our public schools prepare boys and girls for adult responsibility through systematic training in such subjects as reading, writing, arithmetic, history, and English, requiring mastery of such subjects, and, when necessary, stressing discipline and obedience?[41]

William C. Bagley (1874–1946), professor of education at Columbia Teachers College and educational critic, founded the Essentialistic Education Society to promote essentialist ideas. Bagley felt the school curriculum was too diluted by nonessentials and should consist of essential facts and a common culture. Bagley advocated an intellectual curriculum rather than a curriculum focused on growth and development. He believed that education requires hard work and respect for authority.

Like many school critics of today, the essentialists believe schools have suffered a decline in academic rigor. They recommend that all students learn an academic-based core of knowledge that will enable them to be productive members of society. Essentialists would include vocational education in the curriculum on the condition that it is practical, useful, and capable of helping students be productive members of society.

E. D. Hirsch, Jr. (1928–), former professor of English at the University of Virginia, is the contemporary articulator and proponent of the essentialist position. In 1987, Hirsch outlined his essentialist position in *Cultural Literacy: What Every American Needs to Know*. He has established the Core Knowledge Foundation as a means of promoting a core-essentialist curriculum. Others who support cultural literacy include William Bennett, former Secretary of Education, author of the popular *Book of Virtues*, and founder of K–12 Inc., an online school. (See Chapter 12.)

Essentialists support a curriculum that:

- Develops cultural literacy—those things that constitute the "common core" of a literate citizenry and that form the basis of American civilization
- Teaches students, beginning in kindergarten (and even before, in the home), the names, dates, and events that constitute the foundation of our national cultural heritage
- Is practical and oriented toward citizenship and vocational training
- Views learning as a goal in itself, enabling students to function as members of society
- Teaches the basic skills—reading, writing, and mathematics—at the elementary level as well as the arts and sciences

For essentialists, the teacher's role includes:

- Imparting knowledge to students, whose job it is to learn—whether they feel like it or like what they are learning
- Initiating and promoting learning, motivating students to learn, and maintaining the appropriate discipline for learning. Emphasis is placed on having students learn the basics they need for success in life.
- Engaging in teacher-directed activities characterized by discipline and teacher authority

For essentialists, the student's role includes:

- Acquiring and using Western cultural knowledge
- Learning and using thinking skills
- Expending effort and being devoted to the learning process

Essentialists and perennialists share many ideas, but they differ in the following ways:

- Perennialists base their beliefs on realist ideas, such as that the purpose of education is to develop rational thinking. Essentialists do not.
- Essentialists believe in practical curriculum and subjects that will help students be useful citizens, such as vocational training. Perennialists do not.
- Essentialists view learning as its own goal—learning for learning's sake—whereas perennialists believe that education can be used to solve societal problems.
- Essentialists do not universally agree on what constitutes the "essentials," but look to the Western tradition for content.

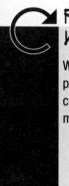

REFLECT & WRITE

What are some implications of perennialism and essentialism for culturally diverse students and multicultural curricula?

_____

_____

_____

_____

_____

Progressivism

Progressivism   An educational philosophy maintaining that since life is ever changing, students should acquire problem-solving skills; emphasizes child-centered teaching and curriculum planning.

Progressivism begins with the child rather than the subject matter. The progressive education movement developed in great measure primarily through the efforts and influence of John Dewey. Since its beginnings in the 1920s, progressivism has had a major effect on educational thought and practice.

Dewey (1859–1952) was an educational pragmatist who maintained that experience is the teacher. Thus, the instructor implementing Dewey's ideas is not a teller of facts and knowledge but rather a facilitator of problem-solving skills. Progressivism emphasizes the importance of students' interests and experiences in education. Dewey believed that to promote an interest in the intellectual—solving problems, discovering new things, and figuring out how things work—students should be given opportunities for inquiry and discovery. Dewey also believed that social interest, referring to interactions with people, should be encouraged in a democratically run classroom.

Those who embrace progressive ideas are focused on change. They believe knowledge is only tentative and not necessarily true forever. There are no lasting truths, and yesterday's values are not necessarily the ones students use today to guide their behavior. Therefore, major purposes of schooling are to educate students who can adapt to change and who can solve problems and discover new knowledge and values for themselves. Progressivists believe that students are basically good and naturally inclined to explore and inquire, that they are capable of deciding what is best for them. This helps justify why students, in a progressive curriculum, are given considerable freedom and are allowed to choose what they will learn. Progressivists believe that what students select is best for them as learners and as people.

Many educational practices used in today's classrooms are based on Deweyan progressive ideas. These include cooperative learning, multi-age grouping, arranging rooms into interest and activity centers that enable children to choose what they will learn and where they will learn it, the establishment of supportive relationships with students, curricula that emphasize students' self-esteem, and the teaching of conflict resolution skills and techniques for getting along with others.

Basic education principles of progressivism are:

- Education is child centered, and schooling should take into consideration the whole child; that is, students' needs and interests in all areas—cognitive, physical, social, and emotional.
- Students should have direct experience with their environments. Learning is active, not passive, and students learn best through a process of doing.
- The curriculum should be based on and built around students' interests.
- Thinking and problem solving are important parts of the curriculum, because students' knowledge and values today may not be the same tomorrow.
- Problem solving, the ability to define and solve human problems, is more important than knowledge of or about human problems. Society constantly changes, so preparation for productive living includes learning how to live productively in a world of change.
- Schools should not be isolated from the community. Progressivism considers the community a rich field for both learning experiences and resources. The move to require community service as a condition for high school graduation is the result of progressive beliefs that education should have a socially useful value.

> **■ INTASC**
>
> **STANDARD 4** The teacher uses various instructional strategies to encourage students' development of critical thinking, problem solving, and performance skills.

The teacher's role in the progressive classroom includes:

- Taking into account the whole child, that is, the intellectual, social, emotional, and physical aspects of the child, when planning and teaching
- Acting as a resource person and guiding and facilitating students' learning. For progressives, the teacher is envisioned more as a "guide on the side" rather than as a "sage on the stage."
- Asking appropriate questions to help students discover knowledge and truth for themselves
- Preparing the learning environment to enable students to experiment and engage in learning on their own
- Involving students in democratic living. For progressives, the learning environment—classroom and school—is considered a microcosm of a democratic society. Accordingly, students, teachers, and staff interact and live and learn as they would in a democratic society. Group activities, which foster cooperative and collaborative learning, enable children to participate democratically and prepare for democratic living.
- Emphasizing methods—learning how to learn—more than knowledge or subject matter. Teachers see their role as helping children learn how to learn in any situation, time, and place. Some of the methods are reading, experimenting, interviewing, observing, and writing.
- Developing a curriculum based, in part, on the interests of children rather than solely on subject matter

The student's role in a progressive classroom includes:

- Learning to be an independent and self-directed learner
- Participating cooperatively with others in group work and processes
- Learning skills related to getting along with others
- Developing responsibility for helping to care for and maintain the learning environment

- Engaging in planning for what to learn and how to learn it
- Participating actively in learning-by-doing activities
- Learning problem-solving strategies and applying them to real-world problems

REFLECT & WRITE

With an emphasis on a learner-centered environment, progressivism influences modern educational thought in a variety of ways. How will you incorporate progressivism into your classroom?

_____

_____

_____

_____

_____

Social Reconstructionism

Social reconstructionism A philosophy based on the belief that people are responsible for social conditions and can improve the quality of life by changing the social order.

Social reconstructionism has its roots in pragmatism, the belief that the truth of ideas is tested by their practical consequences, and the progressive education movement. Social reconstructionism and progressivism are closely aligned in their beliefs. Many of the leaders of the social reconstruction movement were progressives.

As the name implies, social reconstructionists believe that teachers, students, and the schools can play a key role in reconstructing society and building a new social order resulting in more effective democratic living. Thus, they are concerned about the relationship of school curricula and activities to social, economic, and political developments. Social reconstructionists look to current social issues as a guide in determining what the schools should teach. Because schooling is a social process, sanctioned and supported by society, it is only natural that society should look to the public schools to help solve its problems and make society better. Thus, social reconstructionist agendas often have public support, which has implications for contemporary school curricula. For example, in many states students are required to take a government class to graduate from high school. Such classes teach students about the structure and functions of the government in an effort to encourage students' understanding and future participation in the democratic process.

Marxism Social and political philosophy derived from the works of Karl Marx and Friedrich Engels. It is characterized by many ideas, but chiefly includes the idea that social consciousness and political reform can bridge the material gap between the classes.

Social reconstructionists whose thinking is influenced by **Marxism** believe that the schools often serve the interests of the dominant socioeconomic group of the state and tend to perpetuate the capitalistic system. Neo-Marxists often are critical of education, pointing out the social injustices that result from schooling. For example, neo-Marxists may feel that the schools are creating a generation of illiterates by not providing technological opportunities to low-income schools and children.

The social reconstructionist philosophy:

- Holds that social reform should be the goal of education. Schools can do this by participating in this reconstruction or reform by preparing students to be capable of promoting social reform.
- Advocates a curriculum that helps students develop their full potential in this and other areas.
- Believes in confronting students with the problems facing society and developing curricula that stress responsibility to self, others, and society.

- Supports student awareness of and involvement in addressing solutions to major social problems, such as violence, crime, homelessness, gender and socioeconomic inequities, substance abuse, and global warming. Students engage in firsthand efforts to address these problems. For example, students might educate their peers about the effects of global warming on planet Earth and mount a campaign to have the school district implement green practices, such as recycling, solar energy use, and alternative fuels for its fleet of buses.
- Agrees with efforts to involve students in community service as a requirement for school graduation.

The teacher's role in social reconstructionism includes:

- Confronting students with contemporary social problems
- Having students learn about social issues and guiding students in addressing these issues
- Drawing heavily on the behavioral sciences as a source for the curriculum
- Conducting classrooms based on equity and social justice and in keeping with democratic principles
- Encouraging and promoting cooperation and collaboration with community leaders and agencies
- Integrating the curriculum, directing the study of all subjects toward solving community problems

The student's role in a social reconstructionist program includes:

- Using personal interests to help find solutions to social problems
- Learning problem-solving skills as a means of addressing community-based and global problems
- Learning to value social activism

Both the teacher and the student learn to confront social issues and problem-solve through social reconstructionist thought. These ideas can create a very stimulating environment for learning through social consciousness.

■ INTASC

STANDARD 3 The teacher understands how students differ in their approaches to learning and creates instructional opportunities that are adapted to diverse learners.

REFLECT & WRITE

What are two ways that you could implement social reconstructionist ideas in your classroom?

_____

_____

_____

_____

_____

Humanism

Humanism is a philosophy concerned with human nature and the human condition. Humanism emphasizes the basic goodness of humans and our capacity for free will and self-fulfillment. Jean-Jacques Rousseau (1712–1778), a humanist philosopher during the Enlightenment, clarified humanistic beliefs when he argued for a naturalistic education that is free of artifice and that does not restrict or interfere with the child's natural growth and development. Rousseau believed the true nature of children—what they are to be—unfolds as a result of natural processes of maturation.

Humanism A branch of philosophy concerned with human nature and the human condition.

Self-actualization The state in which the basic needs Maslow postulates are met so that individuals can fully use their talents and abilities.

Abraham Maslow (1908–1970) had a profound influence on humanistic philosophy. Maslow theorized that all human beings have certain basic needs, that these basic needs are interrelated, and that all of them must be met in order for individuals to become self-actualized, whereby they fully use their talents, capacities, and abilities. Maslow's *Hierarchy of Needs* identifies basic human needs in the order in which they motivate an individual to **self-actualization**. These basic human needs include physiological needs (air, food, water, clothing, shelter), safety (security, freedom from threat or physical/psychological harm), belongingness (love and affection), esteem (respect, recognition, self-esteem), and self-actualization. Maslow's hierarchy of needs has played and continues to play an important role in education today. For example, school lunch programs help meet physiological needs. Safe schools and classrooms help promote safety. Empathetic, considerate, and supportive teachers help meet the need to be loved and feel a sense of belonging. Teachers who provide for individual needs and abilities and ensure achievement contribute to self-esteem needs. High expectations of teachers and administrators motivate students to do their best, thereby working toward self-actualization. Maslow's **humanistic theory** has been particularly influential in the self-esteem movement, which aims to provide students with a greater sense of worth and address their needs for recognition, attention, and self-confidence.

Humanistic theory A school of psychological thought that emphasizes the human context and development of psychological theory.

The humanistic educational philosophy:

- Encourages the development of students as persons, including their self-concepts, personal growth, and self-esteem
- Emphasizes the affective side of development; that is, how students feel about learning and learning experiences and the connections they make between learning and their lives
- Puts students at the center of learning and emphasizes "self-actualization" and "the teaching of the whole person"

Based on humanistic philosophy, the teacher's role includes:

- Developing meaningful relations between teacher and students
- Emphasizing the affective side of education, including aesthetics, ethics, and morality
- Helping students cope with their psychological needs
- Facilitating self-understanding of each individual student and promoting self-understanding among students

According to humanist philosophy, a student's role includes:

- Seeking independence and self-direction
- Developing greater acceptance of others
- Using talents and abilities to become fully actualized

To understand humanist philosophy and psychological theory, it is important to know its origins. Several thinkers of the existentialist movement played key roles in developing humanism, as you will see in the following section.

REFLECT & WRITE

Many conservative educational critics oppose humanistic approaches in education, feeling they interfere with the promotion of academic achievement. Discuss their argument. Which side of this argument are you on? Why?

Existentialism

Existentialism is a philosophy that focuses on the subjectivity of human experience and the importance of the individual. Meaning is determined by individuals, not by external criteria. Existentialism grew from the ideas of Søren Kierkegaard, a Danish theologian (1813–1855), and the writings of the French philosopher Jean-Paul Sartre (1905–1980). Kierkegaard believed that through education humans come to understand themselves and their destinies. He further maintained that people must recognize their responsibility for making choices and the consequences of their choices. Sartre was the leading twentieth-century articulator of existential thought and is famous for his dictums "Existence [being] precedes essence [meaning]" and "We are condemned to be free."[42] Accordingly, an individual's existence is the result of each person working out his or her own destiny and meaning of life through individual choices.

Maxine Greene, Professor Emeritus at the Teacher's College of Columbia University, is a well-known contemporary supporter of existential philosophy. As part of the humanistic educational process, Greene advocates a "new pluralism" in which "stereotypes and labels are scorned and students are allowed to develop their true identities in environments of diversity and equal regard for all cultures."[43] In order to achieve this goal, "a student must be regarded as a constantly evolving individual who is the sum of many parts."[44] An example of existentialist teaching might be to raise moral questions regarding the U.S. invasion of Iraq; if, how, and when to pull troops out; and how individual decisions resulted in particular moral and ethical courses of action.

Existentialists believe that we cannot escape the responsibility of choosing. Individuals always have a choice and therefore should always make the most of any situation. The choices people make determine their lives, and in this sense, choices determine the future.

Existentialism as applied to education:

- Involves a quest for personal meaning. Students are encouraged to make their own decisions rather than having others make or dictate their choices.
- Encourages students to search for their own meaning in life and to identify their own values rather than to have them imposed by others.
- Views education as a process of helping students become autonomous, free thinking, self-actualized individuals engaged in a search for self.
- Holds that education begins with the individual. Education should help students become what they want to become, not what others or society think they should become.

Based on existential philosophy, the teacher's role includes:

- Providing for, supporting, and maximizing student freedom of choice
- Providing students with experiences that will enable them to determine the meaning of their lives
- Engaging students in journal writing and appropriate literature and film to foster their abilities to engage in self-examination
- Providing students with individual freedom
- Engaging students in a dialogue of questions designed to promote self-reflection
- Encouraging and helping students examine institutional and societal forces that limit freedom
- Challenging the "taken for granted," the "given," the "bound," and the "restricted"[45]

According to existentialist philosophy, a student's role includes:

- Asking questions about the purpose and the meaning of life
- Being involved in inquiries and problem solving that lead to conclusions about and insight into their lives

Existentialism A philosophy emphasizing the necessity for individuals to determine the course and nature of their own lives.

■ **INTASC**

STANDARD 1 The teacher understands the central concepts, tools of inquiry, and structures of the subjects being taught and can create learning experiences that make these aspects of subject matter meaningful for students.

■ Being aware of and responsible for their own education and self-determination
■ Being aware that their choices are theirs to make

Knowing and applying the ideas and philosophies discussed in this section may help you grow on your path to becoming a better teacher. As many thinkers have stated, knowledge is the greatest liberator and truly, you can be a liberating force in your students' lives by creating an environment of questioning and critical thinking. Today's society is highly influenced by the accessibility and availability of information, information that your students will bring to your attention and that you will bring to their attention. Knowing your own personal philosophies and ideas will help guide you in the best way to present your students with thought-provoking content while still adhering to academic requirements.

REFLECT & WRITE

After reviewing the educational philosophies discussed in this section, which ones are closest to your own beliefs? How will you incorporate these philosophies into your own classroom?

_____

_____

_____

_____

_____

WHAT ARE THE IMPLICATIONS OF PHILOSOPHIES OF EDUCATION FOR YOU AND YOUR STUDENTS?

What teachers believe makes important differences in their lives and the lives of the students they teach. There is a constant tension between philosophies of education and the educational practices that support them in the public schools. Beginning in the 1980s, public schools came under heavy criticism because they had not educated youth to the extent and degree necessary to keep the nation economically competitive. As a result, reform movements seek to change the role and scope of education (see Chapter 1). The educational philosophies discussed in this chapter are outgrowths of reform efforts directed at having schools better meet societal needs and goals.

Throughout this chapter you have read about philosophies and philosophies of education and how these affect educational practice. I now invite you to reflect on and rewrite your philosophy of education. Perhaps you are in agreement with the beliefs of one of the philosophies discussed. Or you may take a more eclectic approach, drawing your ideas from several philosophies. Whatever your approach, your personal beliefs and philosophy of education will influence all your activities in the classroom—what you think should be taught; how to teach it; how to interact with students, parents, and colleagues; and how you conduct your professional life.

Developing your personal educational philosophy takes time, work, commitment, and a willingness to think, study, and share ideas with others. Your philosophy of education will develop from your philosophy of life and who you are. This means that as you grow and develop as a person and as a professional, your philosophy of life as well as your educational philosophy may change or be refined.

■ INTASC

STANDARD 1   The teacher understands the central concepts, tools of inquiry, and structures of the subjects being taught and can create learning experiences that make these aspects of subject matter meaningful for students.

Taken together, history and philosophy provide a foundation on which you can build your teaching career. The history of education informs us of where we have been, enlightens us as to how and why we conduct current practice, and provides road maps for us to use in navigating the future of educational practice. Your philosophy of education, based on the six educational philosophies we have discussed, will enable you to confidently and proactively engage in the art and craft of teaching.

REFLECT & WRITE

Do you believe the U.S. educational system trains Americans to be conformists? Was that your experience in attending school?

_____

_____

_____

_____

_____

ETHICAL DILEMMA

Dress Code for Teachers

OVER THE CENTURIES, the public view of teachers has changed. Although today's teachers have much more freedom and fewer restrictions than those of yesteryear, the public still thinks that teachers should be like Caesar's wife: "Above reproach." It is this dilemma of shifting values in which first-year chemistry teacher Leslie Lawrence finds herself embroiled in. Principal Marc Adams thinks that many of the high school's teachers, especially the 21 new staff, dress too much like the students. "I'm tired of the 'anything goes' policy we have around here for teacher attire. I thought teachers would be responsible and dress with decorum. But it isn't working. I want to change this." Principal Adams has asked Leslie to represent the new teachers on a committee he is forming to develop a policy on teacher attire. Leslie is opposed to teacher attire guidelines and does not want to serve on the committee. However, she does not want to risk getting on the principal's "bad side" and risk her career.

What should Leslie do?

SUMMARY

- Schooling during the time of the American colonies was strongly influenced by religion and varied greatly from colony to colony.

- Nationhood changed American education with the development of common schools, the spread of education for women, the expansion of high school education, the increased demand for textbooks, and the spread of higher education.

- American education changed drastically after the Civil War with education for African Americans, the development of Indian schools, and education reform.

- American education changed after World War II due to the Civil Rights Movement, education for students with disabilities, equal rights for women, the War on Poverty, the conservative reaction to the 1960s and 1970s, and the No Child Left Behind Act.

- Philosophy based on core values, as well as learning education philosophies of the past, is relevant for classroom teachers.

- The branches of philosophy—metaphysics, epistemology, and axiology—relate to education, as does the impact of culture on philosophical questions.

- The major philosophies affecting education are perennialism, essentialism, progressivism, social reconstructionism, humanism, and existentialism.

- Philosophies of education have a great impact on both teachers and students.

KEY TERMS

Academies   307
Aesthetics   335
Axiology   334
Bureau of Indian Affairs (BIA)   317
Committee of Ten   320
Common schools   310
Cosmology   330
Dame schools   306
Deductive reasoning   331
Educational philosophy   328
Elementary and Secondary Education
   Act (ESEA)   324
Empiricism   331
Epistemology   331
Essentialism   340
Ethics   334

Existentialism   347
Hornbook   306
Humanism   345
Humanistic theory   346
Inductive reasoning   331
Kalamazoo case   309
Kindergarten   318
Land grant colleges   313
Latin grammar schools   306
Marxism   344
McGuffey readers   312
Metaphysics   330
Morrill Land Grant University
   Act   313
National Defense Education Act   322
Normal schools   313

Northwest Ordinance Acts of 1785
   and 1787   309
Old Deluder Satan Act   305
Ontology   330
Perennialism   337
Philosophy   329
Primer   306
Progressive education   320
Progressivism   342
Project Head Start   324
Self-actualization   346
Social reconstructionism   344
Title IX of the Education
   Amendments   323
Women's Education Equity Act
   (WEEA)   323

APPLICATIONS FOR ACTIVE LEARNING

Connections

1. Think back to the chapter-opening vignette on the two-room schoolhouse in Vermont. Some people think that to lose the one- and two-room schoolhouse is to lose an important part of American education. Do you agree? What has American education lost, if anything, with the passing of such schoolhouses?

2. Think about the concepts in this chapter. Create a picture, graphic, or figure that shows connections among this chapter's key ideas and information that are meaningful to you.

Field Experiences

1. It is very interesting to hear about the educational experiences of previous generations. Interview your grandparents or others of their generation and have them share with you their most rewarding educational experiences. You could organize your interviews by topic, for example, by teachers, subjects, extracurricular experiences, and so on. Write about your interviewees' remembrances and how they relate to American education today.

2. Interview five veteran teachers and ask them how their roles have changed over the years. What historical events and trends have affected their careers as teachers and their classroom practice? How do they evaluate those changes?

Personal Research

1. Online news sources and online educational publications such as www.educationnews.org/ frequently feature news stories that reflect changes in educational philosophy. Perform a Web search for articles that demonstrate this and write a paragraph about a story you find interesting. What philosophy is influencing these events? If applicable, explain which historical perspective could help or hinder the situation.

2. Many historical events have influenced the process of education in the United States. Identify five events you think have been the most influential. Provide a rationale for each of your selections.

PREPARING TO TEACH

For Your Portfolio

1. Set aside some time in your daily schedule over the next several days to write, revise, and complete the "final" version of your philosophy of education. Analyze the ways in which your final version differs from your original draft. How did you change your thinking? Why did you change your thinking?

2. Consider your own experience as a learner. Who and what have been the defining influences that are responsible for who you are today? Consider those influences that have helped to shape you as a student engaged in field experiences and write a reflective essay on your own growth as a teacher.

LEARNING AND KNOWING MORE

Websites Worth Visiting

The history of education is extremely interesting and informative. We can see where we have been and hopefully learn where we are going as a profession. You may want to begin your research into the history of education with the History of American Education Web Project, located at ww.nd.edu/~rbarger/www7/. It lists Web resources, from simple to complex and from all over the world, on the history of education, and also provides texts and sources.

For a more current perspective on education, the staff of *Education Week*, with contributions from leading scholars, have written "Lessons of a Century," which examines all aspects of the educational landscape of twentieth-century America. You can access "Lessons of a Century" at www.edweek.org.

Daily life provides us opportunities to reflect on what we believe and why and how our beliefs influence our lives and the lives of others. One way you can do this is through the American Philosophical Association website www.apa.udel.edu/apa/index.html. The American Philosophical Association is the main professional organization for philosophers in the United States. You will find much useful information including newsletters, electronic text, and links to other sources and philosophers discussed in this chapter.

Society for Philosophical Inquiry
www.philosopher.org

The Society for Philosophical Inquiry (SPI) is a nonprofit organization composed of philosophical inquirers of all ages and walks of life. SPI is dedicated to helping individuals articulate and explore their philosophies of life and in the process, hopefully, cultivate a more acute social and intellectual conscience.

John Locke
http//plato.stanford.edu/entries/locke

This website offers background material on and selected essays by the English philosopher John Locke. Additionally, there are links provided to other resources on Locke and other philosophers.

Philosophy of Education materials
http://commhum.mccneb.edu/PHILOS/phileduc.htm

This site contains a rich collection of further readings, including original sources on the major philosophies of education.

The Blackwell History of Education Museum
www.cedu.niu.edu/blackwell

The Blackwell History of Education Museum and Research Collection is one of the largest collections of its kind in the world. Much of the collection can be found on their website. The Blackwell Museum has developed a variety of instructional materials (also listed on its site) designed to help you learn more about the antecedents of American education.

Books Worth Reading

Fullinwinder, R. K. (1996). *Public Education in a Multicultural Society: Policy, Theory, Critique.* New York: Cambridge Press. This important collection of essays offers a sustained philosophical examination of fundamental questions raised by multicultural education in primary and secondary schools.

Kozol, J. (1999). *Amazing Grace: The Lives of Children and the Conscience of a Nation.* Minneapolis: Econo-Clad Books. Kozol draws a vivid picture of an urban ghetto, with its hunger, poverty, drugs, disease, and violence, using a series of interviews with the people of the Mott Haven section of the South Bronx, the poorest congressional district in the country.

Noddings, N. (2006). *Philosophy of Education* (2d ed.). Boulder CO: Westview Press. Acclaimed as the "best overview in the field" and predicted "to become the standard textbook in philosophy of education" by *Educational Theory*, this second edition includes a new chapter on the problems of school reform, which examines issues of equality, accountability, standards, and testing.

Palmer, J. A., Bresler, L., & Cooper, D. E. (2001). *Fifty Major Thinkers on Education: From Piaget to the Present Day.* New York: Routledge.

Palmer J. A., Bresler, L., & Cooper, D. E. (2001). *Fifty Modern Thinkers on Education.* London: Routledge.
    Picks up the intellectual history of educational thought where *Fifty Major Thinkers on Education* leaves off, examining 50 of the twentieth century's most significant contributors to the debate on education.

Penrice, R. R. (2007). *African American History for Dummies.* Hoboken, NJ: John Wiley & Sons.

Everything you need to know about important achievements and historical contributions by African Americans in education, philosophy, politics, science, art, and culture.

Peters, M. A. (2006). *Education, Globalization, and the State in the Age of Terrorism.* Boulder, CO: Paradigm Publishers.
    This book focuses on the theme of education in an age of terrorism, exploring the conflicts of globalization and global citizenship, feminism post–9/11, youth identities, democracy in a culture of permanent war, and the relation between education and war, with a focus on the war in Iraq.

IV Teaching and Learning

As a teacher, you will play an important role in teaching and helping students meet state and local standards and in preparing them for their futures. Models for teaching and learning offer a variety of approaches for integrating standards and activities into your teaching to meet the needs of today's diverse learners. These approaches help develop the problem-solving and critical-thinking skills students need to become productive and contributing members of society. In addition, the contemporary curriculum, what teachers teach and students learn, is focused on meeting local and state standards.

Teachers in the twenty-first century face the exciting challenge of educating increasingly diverse students in an increasingly accountable and technological culture. Accountability is one of the most important—and high-profile—issues in education today. You will be accountable for teaching all your students so they achieve at high levels and pass state tests. Technology is changing not only how we teach, but also what we think of as literacy and learning. Instructional technologies are among the most important tools for teaching and learning today. Integrating technology into the curriculum and classroom practices will continue to be of crucial importance. Students need technological literacy for employment and participation in today's and tomorrow's work world.

Technological and instructional advances, higher academic standards, greater accountability, and a rising demand for teachers are leading to creative ways of becoming qualified to teach. The chapters in Part Four will help you in your quest to become an outstanding teacher in this age of accountability and technology.

10 Standards and Assessment: Their Impact on Teaching and Learning

COURTNEY FOX A strong, coherent educational program aligns a standards-based curriculum with daily instruction and assessment. Standards and assessment are tools every teacher uses to improve student learning. Standards must be looked at not in isolation, but instead as a way for teachers to organize goals and help plan instruction. Assessment must go beyond being seen as a measure for report cards, grade books, and placement in instructional groups; it must be presented as descriptive feedback that clearly identifies learning targets and creates opportunities for learning and growth.

As you read this chapter . . .

Think about:

■ How standards are changing teaching and learning

■ The impact of standards-based education on teaching and learning

■ How testing is changing teaching and learning

■ How standards and assessment are changing how teachers and schools report student achievement

As teachers, we should be constantly assessing our students. Using assessment tools, formal and informal, we can truly come to understand our children's skills. We do not want to waste any of the precious time we are given teaching children something they are not ready for or something that they already know; we want to give each child exactly what he/she needs to move forward on the continuum of learning. We must take advantage of every moment we can teach all of our students, one-on-one, so we can gauge their understanding and discover what we can do to best meet each of their needs. This type of ongoing assessment, in combination with familiarity with the standards, should be used to help all children achieve.

In my classroom, learning targets are always posted. Each week, I think about the big idea that I want students to learn and we write them together on a large chart that is visible from everywhere in my classroom. These learning targets are basically the standards I am teaching written in kid-friendly language. This way, students know exactly what we are working on, and according to them, "Having targets helps you remember what we are learning," and "It helps us so we don't forget what we are working on."

> **Standards and assessment are tools every teacher uses to improve student learning.**

Teaching children to self-assess their work, reflect, and refine also helps them grow as individuals and creates an environment where students understand the expectations. To help my first-graders self-assess, I teach them to use checklists. Once children understand how to use these, they can work on something and then go back and revise their work so they can meet the learning targets. For example, after mastering a learning target on writing, we add it to a checklist. Then, when students finish a writing piece, they get out a checklist and review their piece to see if they are using all of the skills taught. When I asked students how they felt about using checklists, they said, "It tells us how to make our work better," and "[it tells us] if what we are doing is right or wrong."

Standards serve as a guide that helps teachers set goals for their students across grade levels. As teachers, we must know the patterns of development and curriculum so that we can understand what our children know and what knowledge they have yet to acquire. While standards mandate *what* content we need to teach, it is our responsibility to remember *who* we are teaching.

In classrooms where great gains are being made, teachers are going beyond teaching the grade level standards or assigned curriculum. These teachers are

Courtney Fox teaches first grade at Mount Pleasant Elementary School in Delaware. She was recognized as Delaware's Teacher of the Year in 2008.

▶▶ Go to MyEducationLab and select the topic "Assessment" then watch the video "Forms of Assessment."

looking at children as individuals and are assessing each child's needs, and planning instruction to meet all of those needs. In successful classrooms, teachers use assessment and standards to improve instruction and increase student learning. It is critical that we continue to move in a direction that uses every resource—standards and assessment included—to make our education system stronger and enhance the education that every student receives.

HOW ARE STANDARDS CHANGING TEACHING AND LEARNING?

In school districts all across the country—from Bangor to Miami and New York to Los Angeles—standards, tests, and accountability are topics on the front burner of the educational agenda. The headlines say it all: "Student Test Scores: Some Up, Some Down," "Illinois Looking into Record-Low Test Scores," "Washington Test Scores Stagnant on 'Nation's Report Card.'" As a beginning teacher, you will be involved in many ways with standards, tests, and accountability. Standards and tests will also influence what and how your students learn and their success in school and life. They will shape and determine how you teach, what you teach, your success as a teacher . . . and your pay.

Standards and Standards-based Education

The No Child Left Behind Act includes a state accountability system that is based on the development of state content and academic achievement standards. State assessments are used to measure these standards. The results are then compared to the adequate yearly progress (AYP) expectations. Each state is allowed to develop its own standards, assessments, and AYP expectations, which are reviewed by the U.S. Department of Education.

Every state receiving NCLB funding must develop both content and academic achievement standards in reading/language arts, mathematics, and science; these must be aligned with assessments in the same subject areas for grades 3–8 and high school.[1]

Standards Statements of what all students, pre-K through 12, should know and be able to do.

Standards are statements of what all students, pre-K through 12, should know and be able to do. They are goals that identify what students should learn at various grade levels. The classic example of this grade-level expectation is when President George W. Bush said that the federal government's expectation is that all children will read on grade level by grade 3. In addition, standards serve other functions and roles:

- **Standards serve as expectations for what teachers should teach.** When teachers make decisions about what to teach, they look to the state standards. Although the standards are not, and should not be, the only curriculum teachers teach, they are the beginning points.
- **Standards serve as a foundation for reform and accountability.** Simply put, politicians and educators use standards to reform education. By mandating standards that specify what children will know and be able to do, states play a major role in reforming education. Standards focus on essential concepts, knowledge, skills, and behaviors for children in the twenty-first century. As such, they are designed to increase achievement, one of the major reform goals of the current educational scene.

- **Standards are used in efforts to increase accountability for teaching and learning.** Standards become the basis for teaching and testing. Teachers and schools are evaluated and rewarded on how well children perform on local and state tests. The Texas Essential Knowledge and Skills (TEKS) specifies what Texas children K through 12 should know and be able to do. The Texas Assessment of Knowledge and Skills (TAKS) measures how well children have learned. Many other states have similar assessment systems, such as the Pennsylvania System of School Assessment (PSSA).

- **Standards exert greater state and federal control of local education.** Constitutionally, education is a state responsibility. Historically and traditionally, states have delegated responsibility for education to the local school districts. However, one of the educational trends of the past decade is that state legislatures and governors now play much more prominent roles in educational affairs.

- **Standards provide a way of addressing the educational needs of low-achieving students.** Although standards represent the minimum benchmarks for grade-level achievement, they nonetheless make it clear what all students should learn and each school's responsibility in that effort. In this way, standards can be used as a means of preventing school failure and dropout.

To take some specific examples, the Florida Sunshine Standards require that all third-grade students be able to use a variety of strategies to prepare for writing. Colorado's Model Content Standards state that all middle school students should be able to identify and analyze ways in which advances in science and technology have affected one another and society. The Michigan Curriculum Framework maintains that all high school students must be able to analyze and generalize mathematical patterns including sequences, series, and recursive patterns.

A **standards-based education** is the process of basing teaching, learning, and assessment on national, state, and local educational standards. Although on the surface this may seem to be a straightforward and uncomplicated process that would draw little controversy, standards have created and are creating a great deal of controversy, turmoil, and conflict within and outside the educational arena. In fact, standards are one of the main topics of educational and political rhetoric and debate in this decade. Consider, for example, the 2007 results of the National Assessment of Educational Progress (NAEP)—"the Nation's Report Card"—which show that 33 percent of fourth-graders are reading below level.[2] Figure 10.1 shows 2007 NAEP scores for fourth and eighth graders in reading and math. These graphs reveal very little improvement over the last decade. In addition, the NAEP assessment reveals that the achievement gaps between white students and African American and Latino students remain.

• *Your Turn*

Investigate the standards and assessment issues in your state. What are the expectations of schools in your state with regard to standards, assessment, and accountability of schools and teachers?

Standards-based education The process of basing teaching, learning, and assessment on national, state, and local educational standards.

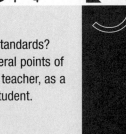

REFLECT & WRITE

Why do we need standards? Respond from several points of view—as a future teacher, as a parent, and as a student.

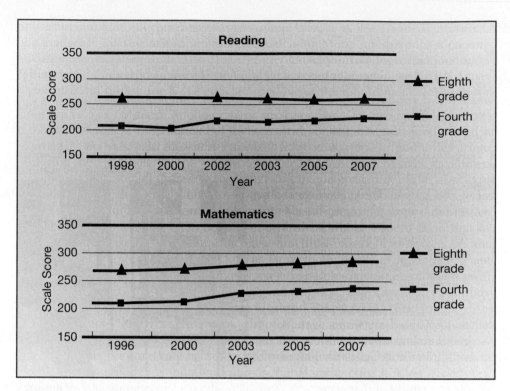

FIGURE 10.1 Average NAEP Scores in Reading and Mathematics, Grades 4 and 8

Students in the United States are not achieving at the levels expected by society. Test scores from the 2007 National Assessment of Education Progress (NAEP)—the "Nation's Report Card"—show that reading and mathematics scores have not improved much over the last decade.

Source: National Assessment of Education Progress website. (Online). Available at http://nces.ed.gov/nationsreportcard/pdf/main2007/2007494.pdf.

Accountability for Teaching All Students

A major topic of debate about standards is that it is almost impossible to separate standards from assessment of student progress and teacher and school accountability. Standards specify what students will learn; assessment measures if and what students have learned. Results of assessment often have **accountability provisions** tied to them, such as performance-based pay, school ratings and rankings, and administrator, teacher, and staff bonuses. Supporters of standards say these accountability provisions help make schools responsible for ensuring that all students achieve at high levels. Critics claim that standards narrow the curriculum, discriminate against minorities, and erode local control of education.

The popularity of standards has grown out of decades of political and public demand for increased accountability of teachers and schools to ensure that the nation's students learn and achieve at a high level. The standards-based reform movement began in 1983 largely in response to *A Nation at Risk: Imperatives for Educational Reform*, a report on the state of American education. This document painted a grim picture of American public education and set the tone for school reform, which still reverberates through America today. The report threw down the gauntlet of educational reform:

> If an unfriendly power had attempted to impose on America the mediocre educational performance that exists today, we might well have viewed it as an act of war. As it stands, we have allowed this to happen to ourselves. We have even squandered the gains in achievement made in the wake of the *Sputnik* challenge.

Accountability provisions
Performance-based pay, school ratings and rankings, and administrator, teacher, and staff bonuses.

Moreover, we have dismantled essential support systems, which helped make those gains possible. We have, in effect, been committing an act of unthinking, unilateral educational disarmament.[3]

(See Chapter 1 to review other reasons for current school reform movements.)

Recent national test scores underscore that the nation's students still do not achieve as well as society wants or thinks they can. This kind of data fuels the critics of public schools and drives efforts to reform schools through standards, tests, and incentives for improvement.

Supporters of standards also maintain that standards are necessary to enhance what advocates see as a stagnant curriculum that fails to challenge students or provide them with the knowledge and skills they need for living and working in the twenty-first century. The phrase **high and rigorous standards** is often used to convey that the curriculum can and should be more challenging for all students.

Additionally, those who favor standards say they are a way to increase expectations for students, teachers, and schools. As discussed in Chapter 1, one of the characteristics of good teachers and schools is that they have high expectations for all students. Although many schools do have high expectations for all their students, many do not. Critics of the schools maintain that although expectations may be too low for all students, they are particularly too low for minority students. A poll by the Metropolitan Life Foundation and the Committee for Economic Development reported that 56 percent of secondary school principals believed strongly that teachers have high expectations for students. However, when researchers asked students if they believed their teachers had high expectations for them, only 25 percent agreed. The poll also showed that teachers in high minority schools had lower expectations for their students than do most teachers in schools that do not have large numbers of minorities.[4] This "soft bigotry of low expectations" is one reason students do not achieve as well as they could and should. In other words, they and others believe high standards will help ensure that all students will learn at their highest levels and will learn what they need to know for college and careers.

Opinion is beginning to coalesce around the usefulness of standards. According to Reality Check 2006, the standards movement continues to attract widespread support among teachers and parents, and public school students nationwide appear to be adjusting comfortably to the new status quo.[5] Here are Reality Check's findings:

- The vast majority of parents and students continue to voice strong support for raising academic standards. Most say updating classes to match the skills employers want would improve American high schools. Eight in 10 students say that requiring students to meet higher standards for graduation and promotion is a good idea. Eighty-six percent of parents say their own district has been "careful and reasonable" in its efforts to raise standards, and only about 1 percent believe schools would be better if districts returned to the policies of the past.[6]
- Standards advocates have long worried about a backlash to testing among parents and students as districts increase testing and put more tangible consequences into place. Although teachers are quite concerned about current levels of testing, Reality Check shows very little evidence of a broad backlash from parents and students. Fewer than 1 in 5 parents complain that their child has to take too many tests. Seventy-one percent of students say that the number of tests they take is about right, and that about 79 percent of the questions are fair. Most students endorse the idea of a high school exit exam, and relatively few say they get so nervous about tests that they cannot do their best. Many parents still do not know enough about NCLB to have an opinion about it.[7]
- Among all the groups surveyed, teachers have historically had more concerns about the standards movement than parents, students, or administrators. Even

• *Your Turn*

You are a fourth-grade teacher. The NAEP suggests that although many students are improving in math and reading, there is still a long way to go. What ideas do you have for how to increase your students' reading and math scores?

High and rigorous standards The idea that curriculum can and should be more challenging for *all* students.

■ **INTASC**

STANDARD 2 The teacher understands how children learn and develop, and can provide learning opportunities that support their intellectual, social and personal development.

so, most teachers do not question the intrinsic value of standards and testing. More than 8 in 10 teachers support a high school exit exam covering either basics (62%) or more advanced skills (24%). Nineteen percent of teachers say standardized tests do more harm than good, and most give their local district good marks for being careful and reasonable in putting higher academic standards in place; however, 7 in 10 teachers say their students have to take too many tests, and 70 percent of teachers also say that NCLB is causing problems in local schools.[8]

Standards and Accountability for Students with Disabilities

Under NCLB, each state must have a state assessment system that serves as the primary means for determining whether schools and districts receiving federal funds are making adequate yearly progress (AYP) toward enabling all students to reach high standards. For accountability purposes, state assessment systems must assign a score to every student who has attended school within the school district for a full academic year. In addition, states must explain how scores from alternate assessments are integrated into their accountability systems.

All students with disabilities are included in the state assessment system. This means that all of these students' scores must be included in the assessment system. For some students with more severe cognitive impairments, alternative assessments are administered. The following *You Decide* feature captures some of the

---

I am a special education teacher in Montgomery County, Maryland, and am disturbed that students with severe special needs are being deprived of their desperately needed education to meet their most basic and pressing needs.

In compliance with the federal No Child Left Behind Act, Maryland mandates that all special education students take some form of the Maryland State Assessment test, which is used to measure student success and is ultimately responsible for determining if a school has made adequate yearly progress (AYP). Schools that do not make AYP may eventually be taken over by the state.

For students with considerable cognitive impairment, an alternative assessment, the Alternate Maryland State Assessment (AltMSA), has been created to satisfy the No Child Left Behind Act. The purpose of the alternate test is to measure the progress of students like mine.

And herein lies the problem. The federal government is requiring the state of Maryland—and, in turn, this county and special-education teachers such as myself—to spend inordinate amounts of time (guesstimate—2 to 3 months last year, more this year) teaching multihandicapped students material which is totally irrelevant and in no way aligns with the yearly goals and objectives on their individual education programs (IEPs) but does align with AltMSA. AltMSA in no way takes into account the students' true, critical, and most basic needs for survival as civil participants in society.

To add insult to injury, my school is in danger of being taken over by the state of Maryland because, among other reasons, these neediest of students have not passed that state assessment. The parents of my students are, as am I, outraged by the gross loss of learning time for their children because of the requirements of this mandatory assessment.

Marcy Myers
Potomac, MD

What do you think about students with disabilities having to take state assessment tests? Do you agree with Marcy Myers? If you disagree with her, why?

Source: Mathews, J. (2006, November 23). Using the wrong standards for students with disabilities. *The Washington Post,* p. G206. (Online). Available at www.washingtonpost.com/wp-dyn/content/article/2006/11/22/AR2006112201193_pf.html.

YOU DECIDE

Should Students with Disabilities Take State Assessment Tests?

controversy surrounding the assessment of students with disabilities. This feature presents a letter by special education teacher, Marcy Myers, who vents her frustration and anger about state assessment and her students.

REFLECT & WRITE

How do the Reality Check 2006 findings square with your opinions and views regarding standards? Which of the findings do you agree/disagree with the most? Why?

_____

_____

_____

_____

_____

HOW IS STANDARDS-BASED EDUCATION AFFECTING TEACHING AND LEARNING?

A close look at standards-based education in America today reveals a multifaceted system that involves agencies at every level of decision making and affects everyone involved in determining the educational future of America's children.

Standards for Students

Recall from Chapter 3 that responsibility for education is a state function. Consequently, if the federal government wants to implement a particular educational program or objective, it does so through federal grants and other means of funding.

National Standards

Examples of national standards that relate to the curriculum include having all children read on grade level by grade 3, making the Head Start program more "academic," and the eLearning initiative, which ensures that all students have access to and knowledge of the proper use of technology. IDEA, which was discussed in Chapter 5, mandates an individualized education plan (IEP) for every student with a special need. All these federal funding programs contain explicit required provisions that, in effect, become national standards. Consider the 2008 $62.6 billion federal education budget. As a condition for receiving this money, states and school districts must meet certain requirements. Some of these requirements, in effect, become the equivalent of standards. In essence the federal government is using the stick-and-carrot approach to reforming education. You want the money, then meet the standards. If standards are not met, student performance is low. If states and districts do not meet provisions of federal legislative rules and guidelines, then funding may be withheld.

As technology has advanced and computers have become an integral part of our daily lives, students' knowledge and skill levels in computers and technology need to be higher as well. In response, most state and local standards now call for technology training as a part of the educational curriculum.

National professional organizations, such as the National Council of Teachers of Mathematics and the National Science Teachers Association, have played, and will continue to play, a prominent role in developing and promoting national standards. Top scholars and respected members in each of the fields have collaborated to identify basic levels of knowledge and skills for the disciplines they consider to be appropriate and achievable by all students. In turn, developers of state and local standards are influenced by these professional standards and incorporate them into their own. For example, the National Council of Teachers of Mathematics (NCTM) has described curriculum "focal points," which outline important mathematical topics for each grade level. The following is one focal point for eighth-graders:

Data analysis and number and operations and algebra: Analyzing and summarizing data sets

Students use descriptive statistics, including mean, median, and range, to summarize and compare data sets, and they organize and display data to pose and answer questions. They compare the information provided by the mean and the median and investigate the different effects that changes in data values have on these measures of center. They understand that a measure of center alone does not thoroughly describe a data set because very different data sets can share the same measure of center. Students select the mean or the median as the appropriate measure of center for a given purpose.[9]

State Standards

Go to the Resources section of MyEducationLab to learn more about your state standards.

All 50 states have academic standards that define the knowledge, concepts, and skills students should know for each grade level. In addition, all states have tests to measure how well students are learning and, in many cases, how well students and schools are meeting the set standards. In addition, many states have systems in place to hold teachers and schools accountable for test results.

Teachers use state standards to plan for teaching, and they incorporate them into their lessons. For example, Krista Winn, Northwest Washington National Elementary School Teacher of the Year, has created and developed an elementary health and fitness curriculum that is aligned with the National Association for Sport and Physical Education (NASPE) and Washington state standards. The curriculum is referred to as the "Body Shop." Within the Body Shop, students compare their bodies to cars and learn how to take care of the most important machine they will ever own with the help of "Head Mechanics," the physical education specialists. Krista says her classroom management system rewards successful classes with "Body Bucks." Classes earn Body Bucks based on a 4-point scale by reflecting on their listening skills, following directions, and engaging in teamwork, cooperation, and positive sportsmanship. Body Bucks are collected and later used to purchase bones, muscles, or guts to build a complete classroom skeleton of Krista.[10]

Local Standards

Local standards are in addition to, supplement, and enrich national and state standards. They express the will and desires of the local community. For example, the San Mateo Foster City School District in California has developed local standards that enrich state standards. In Washington, D.C., a committee is completing a draft of academic standards for world languages, physical education, and health that includes teaching same-sex education topics. The school system also has developed new standards in English, math, science, and social studies. The proposal for world languages, health, and physical education represents the next phase of setting standards in academic subjects.[11]

Standards for Teachers

Just as there are standards stating what students should know and be able to do, there also are national, state, and local standards for initial teacher certification, recertification, and advanced certification. These standards state what teachers should know and be able to do in order to engage in initial teaching, hold an ongoing license to teach, and gain recognition as a highly skilled and advanced teacher.

Initial Teacher Certification

Initial teacher certification is tied to state standards. Examples of these standards were shown in Chapter 1 (Figures 1.1 and 1.2, pp. 6 and 7) for the states of Texas and Kentucky. Review these again and reflect how they influence what teachers should know and be able to do and the basis on which teachers are tested for initial recertification.

Recertification

Teacher recertification is also tied to state standards. School districts and states will often formulate their own, independent recertification standards. For example, the Chicago Public Schools have initiatives in place for the following functions:

- Develop an informational brochure to educate and inform all Chicago teachers and administrators (private and public) of the tenets of NCLB.
- Disseminate information to teachers and host meetings throughout the city.
- Design a template for the 5-year plan that teachers can use as a model while developing their certificate renewal plans.
- Assist teachers in the development of exemplary plans.
- Establish a procedure to monitor and support teachers during the entire 5-year implementation period of their professional development plans.
- Network with area colleges and universities to establish multiple, rigorous programs teachers may access to meet the state requirements for professional growth and development.
- Coordinate the efforts of the Chicago Public Schools Office with the Teachers' Academy, the Departments of Curriculum and Instruction, Accountability, Specialized Services, and other units to offer joint training programs.
- Establish regional review teams and provide ongoing training to the teams to ensure consistency and rigor in the certificate renewal process.[12]

■ INTASC

STANDARD 7   The teacher plans instruction based upon knowledge of subject matter, students, the community, and curriculum goals.

Standards Alignments

As we have learned by now, education is a topic full of issues, contradictions, and concerns. Standards are no different. As educators implement standards, administer tests, and apply accountability provisions, controversies and conflicts arise. A number of issues exist and need to be considered within the context of broader-based educational issues.

Standards and Curriculum Alignment

Curriculum issues that are as old as teaching itself involve frequently asked questions such as "What should I teach?" and "What's worth knowing?" As usual, the answer is "It depends." It depends on what teachers think is important and what local districts, states, and the federal government think is important. In the context of this chapter, it depends on what national, state, and local standards say are important. Therein lies the issue of how to develop curriculum that is aligned with standards.

Increasing student achievement and how to accomplish this goal are at the center of the standards movement. Policymakers believe that given appropriate standards, teaching, and rewards, student achievement will increase. Policymakers and educators view standards, tests, and teaching alignment as a viable and practical way to help ensure student achievement. **Alignment** is the arrangement of standards, curriculum, and tests so that they complement one another. The curriculum should be based on what the standards say students should know and be able to do. Tests should measure knowledge that standards require.

Florida has aligned its standards (Florida Sunshine Standards), its assessment system (Florida Comprehensive Assessment Test [FCAT]), and the Governors A+ Program, which grades schools based on how well they measure on the FCAT. This alignment of state standards with curriculum, tests, and school ranking represents a comprehensive approach to educational reform.

Curriculum alignment is the process of making sure that what is taught—the content of the curriculum—matches what the standards say students should know and be able to do. One way educators achieve alignment is through the use of **curriculum frameworks**, which specify the curriculum teachers will teach. In addition to aligning the standards and curriculum, some school districts also specify or suggest instructional activities and strategies for teachers to use so that the curriculum is implemented in ways to meet the standards. A related issue is how to teach the curriculum so that students learn what teachers teach. A deeper philosophical and pedagogical issue involves whether what standards specify is really worth knowing.

Alignment   The arrangement of standards, curriculum, and tests so they are in agreement.

Curriculum alignment   The process of making sure that what is taught matches the standards.

Curriculum frameworks   Specify the curriculum that teachers will teach.

Professional Staff Alignment

Aligning professional staff development with the state standards is one way to help ensure that teaching aligns with standards. Professional staff development in some school districts used to be fairly casual. Traditionally, many districts and schools have left decisions about staff development to teachers' preferences. Staff development is serious business and plays a major role in district efforts to increase student achievement. Staff development often includes specific training on the state and local standards, the state test, how to prepare students to achieve the standards, and how to take tests. For example, California has professional development institutes that align teacher training to the state standards.

Should teachers be told how to teach to standards? Or, should teachers be told that they are to produce the results specified by the standards?

Standards and Textbook Alignment

Publishing companies, by their very nature as for-profit companies, are always engaged in keeping up with what politicians demand and what educators need. Consequently, they are continuously engaged in the task of aligning their textbooks with state standards and accompanying curriculum frameworks that specify curriculum content appropriate for teaching the standards. Frequently, curriculum frameworks include suggested and, in some cases, mandatory teaching activities. Many publishers align their textbook content to the standards of states such as Texas and California, large states that "adopt" textbooks for the entire state. In these "whole-state" textbook adoption states, school districts can use state funding to purchase only those books that are on the state textbook adoption lists. In order for a publisher to have its textbooks on the state list, it must include content that teaches to the state standards. Because Texas and California represent large revenue potential, many educators fear textbook content may be unduly influenced by the requirements of these large adoption states. Publishers, however, must appeal to a national audience and therefore work to provide a balance. In addition, for some disciplines, publishers now develop state-specific texts meant to be marketed only in these large states. When selecting texts to use in the classroom, the materials available to you for meeting your state and local standards may depend on the state in which you teach.

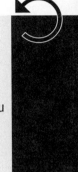

■ **INTASC**

STANDARD 9   The teacher is a reflective practitioner who continually evaluates the effects of his/her choices and actions on others (students, parents, and other professionals in the learning community) and who actively seeks out opportunities to grow professionally.

**REFLECT &
WRITE**

What if you teach in a school or district in which the textbooks you have do not align with the state standards? What would you do?

_____

_____

_____

_____

_____

Ranking Schools

Many states rank and rate their schools on how well students achieve. Florida grades its schools much like teachers grade their students (on a letter scale from A to F),[13] whereas Texas rates its schools with a hierarchy of titles (Exemplary, Recognized, Academically Acceptable/Acceptable, and Academically Unacceptable/Low-Performing).[14] Ranking of schools is spreading across the country. Indiana ranks its schools in five categories based on how a school's students perform on the Indiana State Testing for Educational Progress–Plus exam (ISTEP+). The five categories are Exemplary Progress, Commendable Progress, Academic Progress, Academic Watch/Priority, and Academic Probation/High Priority.[15] As a teacher, you will be teaching in a school that is labeled and known by its rating. When you interview for a job, one of the things you will want to find out is "What is the rating of the school where I will be teaching?" In your interview you will want to ask why the school is ranked as it is and what plans administrators and teachers have for improvement. This is important information that will help you make a career decision about teaching in a particular school.

Must Teachers Teach to the Test?

Standards have changed the art and craft of teaching. Standards and curriculum alignment have a profound impact on teachers and their teaching. Teachers have always developed their own curricula and will continue to do so, but standards have transformed teaching from an input model to an output model. As a result of standards, teachers are no longer able to say, "I taught Mario algebraic equations."

Now the questions are "Is Mario able to use and apply algebraic equations?" and "Will Mario do well on algebraic equations on the state test?" Good teachers have good ideas about what and how to teach and they always will. However, the time and opportunity to do this are reduced by increasing requirements that teachers teach to the standards and teach so that students will master the standards. Consider the case of Elizabeth Walker. Minutes before her eighth-grade class shows up, she clicks on a website that shows her which writing lesson she needs to teach. She's supposed to go over three ways to persuade: *logos* (facts), *ethos* (ethics), and *pathos* (feelings). Like the other eighth-grade teachers in her school district, she is using the novel *Animal Farm* to help illustrate these writing techniques. Elizabeth does not have the option of choosing a different novel for her students to read. Nor does she have the option of teaching poetry before persuasive writing. Elizabeth's experience is not exclusive to Washington State. In the name of student achievement, more teachers, from Los Angeles to New York, are following scripts that mandate what and how they teach. On a local level, the Bellevue School District in Washington appears to be doing a good job of adhering to its standards-based curriculum. In some subjects it has a long list of required lessons, one for nearly every school day.[16]

Many educators admit that standards must not become the only curriculum. Teachers must have the time and freedom to supplement the content specified by the standards with material they think is important and to be able to teach to the teachable moment. Standards-based education should not hurt or interfere with teacher creativity. Figure 10.2 identifies some strategies for integrating standards and improving student achievement.

Paul George, a professor at the University of Florida, visited fifty schools to determine what they are doing to raise student achievement. Here are ten strategies that work:

1. **Set urgent goals.** Focus on making a quick breakthrough in student achievement.
2. **Engage school personnel.** Develop cohesiveness and commitment among a small group of school and teacher leaders.
3. **Use school achievement data.** Skilled analysis of student achievement data has become a crucial step in breaking through the barriers of low achievement.
4. **Strengthen professional development.** Student achievement data point to the need for professional development in specific subject areas and grade levels.
5. **Align the curriculum.** The role played by standards-focused curriculum alignment stands out clearly.
6. **Increase time for academics.** Decrease the amount of time usually available for subjects that are not currently tested to increase the amount of time devoted to tested subjects.
7. **Choose instructional materials to support standards.** Use a mix of state-produced, commercial, and local curriculum materials targeted to improve achievement, focusing on those designed for new state standards.
8. **Build interdisciplinary teams.** Encourage collaboration among teachers and a more careful focus on small groups of students.
9. **Promote the test.** Target public relations efforts at students, teachers, and parents to persuade them of the importance of the standards and the state test.
10. **Redefine school leadership.** Principals now see themselves as instructional leaders, as mandated for professional survival by standards-based reform.

FIGURE 10.2 Strategies for Integrating Standards and Improving Student Achievement

There are many ways educators can improve student achievement. Use these strategies as a guide to help you improve student achievement in your own classroom.

Source: P. George (2001 Spring). *Principals under pressure: School leaders and standards-based accountability programs,* Association for Supervision and Curriculum Development. (Online). Available at www.coe.ufl.edu/faculty/george/A+.htm.

Local autonomy is another casualty of alignment. Traditionally and historically, local districts have had a great deal of autonomy over the goals of education and how to best teach to these goals.

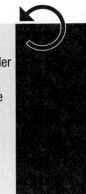

REFLECT & WRITE

Pause for a moment and consider what is worth knowing for the students you will teach. List five things you think are "non-negotiable" for what your students should know and be able to do.

_____

_____

_____

_____

_____

HOW IS TESTING CHANGING TEACHING AND LEARNING?

Testing has always been a part of teaching and the process of schooling. Over the last 25 years in particular, testing has assumed a major role in helping reform public education. Although testing is designed to measure student achievement, it also can be used to demonstrate or document what students know and do not know and to hold teachers and schools accountable.

The National Test

The National Assessment of Educational Progress (NAEP), also known as "the Nation's Report Card," has been conducting assessments since 1969 and is the only national test that assesses what "America's students know and can do" in various subject areas. These assessments are administered between late January and early March of each year. NAEP does not report scores for individual students or schools; instead, it bases its results on a sample of students and provides data at the state and national level. As a requirement of NCLB, states and districts receiving federal funds must participate in state-level NAEP tests in reading and mathematics at grades 4 and 8 every 2 years. State participation in other state NAEP subjects (science and writing) remains voluntary.[17] The National Assessment Governing Board, appointed by the U.S. Secretary of Education but independent of the U.S. Department of Education, governs the program.

One of the strategic and political purposes of standards and testing is to hold teachers and schools accountable for students' achievement. Accountability for high achievement for all students is a major theme of educational practice today.

NAEP assessments also are conducted on the state level. States that choose to participate receive assessment results that report on the performance of students in that state. When national education officials refer to student achievement, it is usually NAEP test scores they use when making comparisons and advocating for reform. These also are the tests that state officials refer to when looking at their state scores in comparison to national test results. For example, consider the following response to the 2007 NAEP report by Jack

O'Connell, the State Superintendent of Public Instruction for California Public Schools:

> California's scores on the National Assessment of Educational Progress reflect the trends we see on our state standards-based tests, and also the challenges faced in educating California's diverse population. Once again, these results point out stark and persistent racial and socioeconomic achievement gaps in our schools that must be addressed if our students and our state are to thrive in the demanding global economy.
>
> I am pleased that achievement in reading has improved and that we've not lost ground in other areas since 2005. While there are valid reasons to question the fairness of state-to-state comparisons, it is also clear that California schools have much work to do to raise the achievement levels of all groups of students.
>
> There has been a steady increase in the average scale scores of black and Hispanic students since 1998 in fourth grade reading and since 2000 in fourth grade and eighth grade mathematics. However, the achievement gap remains between white or Asian students and their African American or Hispanic peers. We know all children can learn to the same high levels, so we must confront and change those things that are holding groups of students back.
>
> When considering the NAEP scores, it is important to remember some significant differences between NAEP and our state assessments, and also to take a close look at California's demographics and the performance of specific student groups.
>
> Even so, California's Hispanic students showed a significant 5 percentage point increase since 2005 in the proportion of students performing at basic or above in fourth grade reading, and Hispanic students who were not classified as English learners increased overall by nearly 5 points.[18]

You can learn more about the 2007 NAEP at http://nces.ed.gov/nationsreportcard/.

REFLECT & WRITE

Given a diverse classroom where all children are capable of learning at high levels, what can teachers do on a day-to-day basis to lessen the achievement gap?

■ INTASC

STANDARD 3 The teacher understands how students differ in their approaches to learning and creates instructional opportunities that are adapted to diverse learners.

Testing All Students

A number of issues accompany the heavy emphasis on testing. Many of these issues involve questions of equity, equality, fairness, and preparedness. (See *In the Classroom with Richard Middleton*.)

Equity

Should one test fit all? Generally, one state test is given to all students regardless of their backgrounds or disability. Critics of the one-test-fits-all approach maintain that such a procedure does not take into account students' developmental levels, cultures, socioeconomic status, past education and experiences, and present circumstances. They further claim that until states provide a system of differentiated testing, policies of using one test will remain inherently unequal and discriminatory.

In the Classroom
with **Richard Middleton**
Testing and Accountability

Richard Middleton is Superintendent of Northeast Independent School District, San Antonio, Texas.

Testing has always been an essential part of the educational process. In recent years, however, the tendency to use testing data as the most significant indicator of learning achievement has increased. Promotion and retention policies, graduation requirements, whole-school rankings, and even the entire standards movement rely heavily on test data to define their validity. However, educators must urge caution about policy-making based on a single measure of performance. In a volatile stock market, wise investors measure success over the long term. Educators must do the same; our goal must be to increase test scores over time.

In education, true accountability is derived from raising student performance on increasingly higher standards. Rather than indicators for abandoning public schools, test scores present school districts with maps for programmatic change. Student performance data can provide both direction and impetus for educators to make systemic changes that will afford our diverse student population equal opportunities for learning. The education of children is vital to our democracy, and it is imperative that we now accept this challenge on behalf of our students.

Overtesting

Overtesting is one of the outcomes of the increase in the number of states requiring more standardized tests. State tests compete with district tests tied to local curriculum and standards. Many school districts are reducing or eliminating their district tests in an effort to scale back the number of tests their students have to take.

High-Stakes Testing

Social promotion is another casualty of standards-based education, although critics of social promotion do not decry its demise. The theory behind social promotion has always been that it is better for students to progress through the grades in the company of their social peers rather than be held back or retained. Many school districts have routinely practiced social promotion and have promoted students to the next-highest grade regardless of how well they did or did not do in course work and tests. However, with the implementation of standards and tests, fewer teachers and school districts use social promotion.[19] In fact, New York City mayor Michael Bloomberg and New York Public Schools' Chancellor Joel Klein announced a new initiative to end "social promotion" in public schools. Mayor Bloomberg stated, "This year, for third graders, we're putting an end to the discredited practice of social promotion. . . . We're not just saying it this time. This time, we're going to do it."[20] In Chicago, social promotion has been prohibited, and **gateway grades** have been established. Under this system, students must pass standardized tests to be promoted to the next grade. This practice is part of what is known as **high-stakes testing**, where tests act as a gate or barrier to promotion, graduation, or participation in an activity or program. In recent years, many states have adopted policies mandating that students pass an achievement test as a requirement for graduation. For example, according to the Texas Education Agency,

■ INTASC

STANDARD 8   The teacher understands and uses formal and informal assessment strategies to evaluate and ensure the continuous intellectual, social, and physical development of the learner.

Social promotion   Promoting students to the next-highest grade regardless of how well they do or do not do in course work and tests.

Gateway grades   Students must pass standardized tests to be promoted to the next grade.

High-stakes testing   A gate or barrier to promotion, graduation, or participation in an activity or program.

nearly one of every six high school seniors—a record 40,182 students in the Class of 2007—did not receive a diploma after failing to pass all sections óf the state's high school graduation test. Minority students were hit hardest by the test requirement; approximately one in four black and Latino seniors were unable to make the grade and did not receive diplomas during graduation ceremonies.[21]

For example, Wisconsin requires its juniors and seniors to take a test that determines whether they can graduate from high school. Giving graduation or **exit exams** to students in tenth and eleventh grade is one way for educators to determine the areas in which students have not done well and provides an opportunity to develop programs to give students needed help in order to successfully pass the examination and graduate.

For students, the consequences of not passing end-of-year and exit exams are high, and perhaps life changing. In Cleveland, Ohio, more than 1,300 high school seniors who failed the state graduation exam did not receive their diplomas.[22]

For the most part, teachers and parents alike back the use of high-stakes standardized tests as a means to motivate students and identify those who are struggling. In Broward County, Florida, 4,200 third-grade students failed the Florida Comprehensive Assessment Test and had to repeat third grade.[23] The use of high-stakes testing to determine graduation has met resistance on many fronts. In Massachusetts, the adjustment to high-stakes testing has been rocky since the introduction of the Massachusetts Comprehensive Assessment System (MCAS).

Some states and school districts have no-pass, no-play policies whereby students cannot play in athletic events if they do not pass a grade. High-stakes tests also serve as a basis for compulsory participation in a program such as summer school as a requirement for promotion to the next grade.

Test Preparation

With so much riding on the outcomes of testing, critics argue that the focus of the curriculum now is more on preparation than on content. One of the most common complaints about mandatory testing is that in order to ensure that all students pass the tests, some teachers "teach the test," or as James Popham, noted test expert, says, "item teach."

> In item teaching, teachers organize their instruction either around the actual items found on a test or around a set of look-alike items. For instance, imagine that a high-stakes test includes the multiple-choice subtraction item "Gloria has 14 pears but ate 3." The test-taker must choose from four choices the number of pears that Gloria now has. Suppose the teacher revised this item slightly: "Joe has 14 bananas but ate 3." The test-taker chooses from the same four answers, ordered slightly differently. Only the kind of fruit and the gender of the fruit-eater have been altered in this clone item; the cognitive demand is unchanged.
>
> Curriculum teaching, however, requires teachers to direct their instruction toward a specific body of content knowledge or a specific set of cognitive skills represented by a given test. In curriculum teaching, a teacher targets instruction at test-represented content rather than at test items.[24]

Test besting, also known as test prep, occurs when schools and districts teach students how to take and pass tests. The purpose of test besting is to teach specific test-taking skills such as managing time, how to bubble, and how to identify distractions so that students will have an "edge" on test taking. Commercial programs are available to accomplish this goal, and districts and schools also develop their own programs. For years, for-profit companies have been helping students prepare for examinations. Perhaps you used a test prep company such as Kaplan or Princeton Review to help you with the SAT, ACT, or some other test as a prerequisite for college entrance. Now the students you teach are doing the same thing to prepare for state exams, many of them in their own classrooms. For example, at Point Pleasant (New Jersey) Middle School students use computer-based programs developed by SkillsTutor that seek to improve students' basic skills and prepare them

Exit exams Achievement tests used as a requirement for graduation.

You can review the MCAS initiative at www.doe.mass.edu/mcas/.

Go to MyEducationLab and select the topic "Assessment" then watch the video "Standardized Tests." Complete the activities that follow.

Test besting When schools and districts teach students how to take tests.

You can learn about the SkillsTutor program at www.skillstutor.com.

for state examinations. The entry of test prep companies into the state testing picture only underscores that education is big business and that there is money to be made from standards and testing. (See *What's New in Education?*)

Test besting also occurs when teachers use specific content and instructional activities to teach course content. Some districts have teachers allocate a set amount of time, for instance, 30 minutes a day, to reviewing algebraic equations or teaching first-graders decoding (phonics) skills. Critics maintain that such practices take away from teaching time that could be spent on other knowledge and skills not on the test. Some parents, teachers, and administrators claim that state and national tests "hijack" time from teaching and learning.

Testing has also taken time away from social and recreational activities such as recess. For many kids today, the recess bell tolls for too little time, or even not at all. Pressure to raise test scores and adhere to state-mandated academic requirements is squeezing recess out of the school day. At Flint Hill Elementary School in Vienna, Virginia, recess is 15 minutes a day. In the District of Columbia, officials say schools "aim for" 20 minutes. At Rosemary Hills Primary School in Sliver Spring, Maryland, the kids get half an hour. But at most middle schools, recess has been eliminated.[25] In justifying such decisions, the Bozrah, CT, School Superintendent and Principal Maureen McLaughlin Scott presents a strong argument for eliminating recess for fifth- through eighth-graders at Field Memorial School and implementing a new schedule.

The state requires a minimum of 900 hours of classroom instruction a year. Students in Bozrah were receiving only 808 hours per year. The new schedule now provides 987 hours of classroom learning. It also provides teachers with common planning time allowing them to make better use of the time in the classroom.

Bozrah's Connecticut Mastery Test scores for Bozrah students suggest there needs to be more emphasis on teaching the skills students need to succeed. With

What's *New* in Education?

Prepping Students for College

When the state of Maine replaced its state assessment test with the SAT because it believed this requirement would open new opportunities to those students who never considered going to college previously, Karan Goel, CEO of PrepMe, a test preparation company, wanted to help. As a result, he has offered free online test preparation courses to all high school juniors who will be taking the SAT. This adds up to a $4.5 million contribution.

In the Boston Public School district, other opportunities are being offered to students in order to help prepare them for their upcoming tests. October has been designated "College Month," featuring activities and resources to help city students pursue higher education. In partnership with area colleges and universities, as well as community organizations, the district offers college access programs and services throughout the year. The month of October is a particularly active and important time for students of all ages to learn more about continuing their education after high school.

According to Boston Superintendent, Carol Johnson, "For our students to be competitive in today's workforce, a college degree is essential . . . That's why Boston high schools are preparing students not only to earn a high school diploma but to gain the knowledge and skills needed to succeed in higher education and beyond."

Sources: "Company offers free online SAT preparation to Maine juniors," *Boston Globe,* February 1, 2007. (Online). Available at www.boston.com/news/local/maine/articles/2007/02/01/company_offers_free_online_sat_preparation_to_maine_juniors/; Boston Public Schools. "Boston Public Schools declares October 'College Month.'" September 27, 2007. (Online). Available at http://boston.k12.ma.us/bps/news/news-9-27-07.asp.

OBSERVE & LEARN

As a beginning teacher, you will have many opportunities to participate in testing students. Observing how school districts prepare students for tests and administer them can be a very worthwhile activity. It can provide you with useful information that you can apply to your own teaching and that will help your students as they prepare for tests throughout the school year. Make arrangements to observe in a local district as it prepares its students for state tests. As you observe, make a list of useful tips and information that you will apply to your teaching.

■ **INTASC**

STANDARD 2 The teacher understands how children learn and develop, and can provide learning opportunities that support their intellectual, social, and personal development.

■ **INTASC**

STANDARD 3 The teacher understands how students differ in their approaches to learning and creates instructional opportunities that are adapted to diverse learners.

the exception of seventh grade reading and writing, and fourth grade reading, Bozrah's scores are near or at the bottom. Scott believes her plan will put the emphasis back on teaching those skills, and result in higher scores.[26]

Tests and Discrimination

Many argue that tests discriminate against minorities and immigrants and that they perpetuate social and educational inequalities. For example, African American students have made some promising gains on Missouri's state exams, yet they still lag far behind their white and Asian peers. At every subject and grade tested, African American students had the lowest scores of any racial or ethnic group, illustrating the "achievement gap," a problem that confronts educators nationally.[27] Evidence for the racial test achievement divide is an issue in most states.

"The gap exists at the state level, the district level, and at the classroom level," says Ohio State Superintendent of Public Instruction Susan Tave Zelman. Dr. Zelman is committed to closing achievement gaps between Ohio's lowest- and highest-performing students, especially low-income and minority students. To do this, she inspired the creation of the State Board of Education's Closing Achievement Gaps Task Force. Schools that are high-poverty and high-performing are sharing their best practices through her Schools of Promise program. A task force to redesign Ohio's high schools has made recommendations to ensure that all students graduate and are prepared for college and the workforce.[28]

Kati Haycock, director of the Education Trust and the Advocacy Agency for Minority Students, believes that schools that have had success closing the achievement gap share the following six characteristics:

1. *They focus on what they can do.* Educators know they cannot change things such as poverty and where their students live, so they instead focus on what they can do to get students on track academically.

2. *They don't leave anything about teaching to chance.* They give teachers a very clear sense of what should be taught, what kind of work students should be given, and what constitutes "good enough." This keeps teachers from lowering expectations simply because students are behind.

3. *They set high goals.* These schools don't just focus on achieving proficiency, but on getting their students to advanced levels.

4. *They are obsessive about instructional time.* Research shows that, by the time some schools account for holidays, conference days, school trips, and other events, the amount of instructional time each year is reduced drastically. Schools that have had success narrowing the achievement gap remove distractions and try to maximize instructional hours.

5. *They are driven by students' needs.* For example, schools that are closing the gap provide extra instruction in areas where students need improvement.

6. *They know how much teachers matter and act on that knowledge.* Studies show that poor students and students of color are often far more likely to have inexperienced teachers. Top-performing schools, by contrast, match experienced teachers with students who most need their help.[29]

Help should be provided for all students who have difficulty mastering the standards. This help can come in the form of summer school, weekend and after-school programs, and tutoring and mentoring. (See *What's New in Education?*)

Consider, for example, what one Denver Public School ninth-grade math teacher, Taylor Betz, did to motivate two students. At an inner-city public school, where she was running an after-school program for failing ninth graders, Betz was teaching a session one February day, when she looked out her classroom window and saw two boys, who were two of her lowest-performing students, sitting idly on a park bench. She stopped the session and marched outside, "You two! Get upstairs right now!" she told the boys, sternly. They grumbled, but complied—and, at her insistence—kept coming back. Her initiative—and their hard work—paid off. Last spring both boys passed their end-of-the-year math test.[30]

Anna Rios, a student at Roger L. Putnam Vocational Technical High School in Springfield, Massachusetts, dislikes the idea that she has to pass a statewide test to earn a high school diploma. Nonetheless, the slight 15-year-old in jeans and a baseball cap stays after school to bone up on the algebra on the Massachusetts Assessment of Comprehensive Skills, which sophomores must pass to graduate. "I know I need help," she explained, "so I decided to come for the after-school program."

Besides the after-school sessions for some 64 students, the school offers a breakfast club that provides academic enrichment. And there is also a support group in which upperclassmen who have already passed the exam help tenth-graders planning to take the test. For those ninth-graders who start high school more than 2 years behind in reading or math, the school has created a separate academy to bring them up to speed as quickly as possible. Summer school also awaits students who are struggling academically.[31]

> Learn how you can help struggling students in your classroom at www.glencoe.com/sec/teachingtoday/subject/high_stakes.phtml.

> **■ INTASC**
>
> **STANDARD 8** The teacher understands and uses formal and informal assessment strategies to evaluate and ensure the continuous intellectual, social, and physical development of the learner.

What's *New* in Education?

Lower Income, Lower Scores Linked, State Tests Shows

Students from Colorado's poorest families scored significantly lower on this year's state proficiency exams than their better-off peers, a review of state Department of Education data shows.

In most cases, the gaps between high-performing low-income students and all other students on the Colorado Student Assessment Program exams were more than 30 percentage points.

While the state scores are far from surprising in an era when achievement among poor and minority students is at the forefront of education policy, they underscore the situation many Colorado students face in their classrooms every day.

"We know we have a problem in the state," said Jefferson County schools Superintendent Cindy Stevenson, who has studied poverty and education in Colorado. "Districts are working on it, but it's not rapid progress; it's very slow progress."

Figures from the recently released CSAP exams indicate performance gaps are prevalent at every grade level and subject, from reading to writing to math and to science.

Results also reveal other sobering trends. An achievement gap of about 30 percentage points persists between the scores of white and Asian students and their black and Latino peers. In the fifth-grade science test, for example, 14 percent of Latino students were proficient in science, compared with 50 percent of white students.

"Closing the achievement gap is a top priority for the state," said Jared Polis, a member of the state Board of Education. It's a matter of "raising the bar for everyone's achievement."

Sources: Created by the author from data from R. Sanchez, "CSAP Tests Expose Gap," *Rocky Mountain News*, August 7, 2004. (Online). Available at www.susanohanian.org/atrocity_fetch.php?id=2878; K. Rouse, "CSAPs: Kids Score, State Wins," *The Denver Post*, August 3, 2006. (Online). Available at www.denverpost.com/news/ci_4128348.

REFLECT & WRITE

Regardless of how you feel about testing, it is here to stay. As a beginning teacher, what are some things you can do now to prepare yourself for the brave new world of testing?

HOW DO TEACHERS AND SCHOOLS ASSESS AND REPORT STUDENT ACHIEVEMENT?

Many schools are finding that traditional ways of reporting student progress are not sufficient given emphasis on standards and tests. One approach to grading is based on norm-referenced comparisons. In this approach, often called "grading on the curve," each student's achievement is compared to every other student's achievement in the class. This comparison can result in a ranking of students. Based on the **normal curve**, the teacher assigns so many As, Bs, and so forth. Grading on the curve is seen more frequently at the college level than at the K–12 level. Its critics feel this approach is inherently unfair and that there are better ways to assess student performance and achievement.

In contrast, with criterion-referenced grading, each student's performance is compared to his or her performance on the standards, regardless of how well other students perform. An issue here is how the teacher judges that achievement and how a teacher measures the level of student achievement.

Normal curve The bell-shaped curve used for grading based on the assumption that any group of students represents a range of achievement or ability.

Teachers play a powerful role in teaching and assessment. They set high expectations. They assess students' learning throughout the school day and year and adjust their teaching to what students have learned and what they need to know.

Types of Assessment

Designing and implementing assessment strategies is one of the most important roles of a teacher. Assessment is a component of teaching that is necessary if learning is to occur. As discussed, testing often occurs only at the end of a course or grade, is used to compare and rank students in schools, is used to make high-stakes decisions about grade failure program exit and entry, and so forth. Teacher assessment, on the other hand, is used to guide instruction, improve student learning, improve teaching, provide ongoing feedback to students about their performance, identify students' strengths and weaknesses, and enable teachers to provide students with more enriched learning experiences.

Teachers assess students' learning throughout the school day and year and adjust their teaching in accordance with what students have learned and what they need to know. The goal is for students to feel confident in taking end of semester and end of year tests.

The following are a number of different types of assessments that teachers use in their classrooms. Each assessment type allows teachers to learn something different about what their students know, what they still need to learn, and how they learn.

- **Paper-pencil closed tasks.** Using this type of assessment, students do not express their opinion. They demonstrate their knowledge of facts and concepts. The format includes multiple-choice items, true-false items, fill-in-the-blank statements, and problem-solving responses.
- **Paper-pencil open tasks.** Students answer questions using different formats and approaches. This type of assessment tool might include essays, extended writing activities, or open-ended questions. It is an excellent way for gaining insightful data.
- **Informal assessments.** This method of obtaining information can be used to learn about characteristics of children or programs by using assessment tools other than standardized instruments. For example, a teacher might select an observation goal and then observe students in order to discover answers to the following types of questions:
  - How does Emily understand, define, or explain the task?
  - How does Bryce approach the task?
  - Which organizational patterns, tools, or resources does Rita utilize?
  - Does the student plan ahead or look back?
  - Does Olivia monitor and adapt her processes, actions, and progress in response to success or difficulty?
  - Is Samantha able to identify and describe the strategies she is using?
  - Does Jacob make connections or see relationships? Does he relate the task to previous knowledge or skills?
  - Can Alex provide evidence for an answer?
  - Can Emma generalize results?
  - How does Michael interact with others or engage in cooperative group work?

Teachers also use teacher checklists as a type of informal assessment (see Figure 10.3).

Go to MyEducationLab and select the topic "Assessment" and choose the artifact, "Assessment Methods (3–8)." Answer the questions that follow.

FIGURE 10.3 Skills/Abilities Checklist

Can you think of any skills/abilities you would add to this checklist?

Source: Missouri Department of Elementary & Secondary Education. (2006). Student selection overview and examples. (Online). Available at www.dese.mo.gov/divimprove/fedprog/grantmgmnt/PDFFiles/Student Selection Multiple Criteria 1006.pdf on December 19, 2007.

SKILLS/ABILITIES CHECKLIST

Grade 4 Reading

STUDENT NAME_____ DATE_____ GRADE_____

SCHOOL_____ TEACHER'S NAME_____

RATING SCALE—INSTRUCTIONS: Read each item carefully. Please indicate in the parentheses which most closely reflects your judgment of the frequency of the described behavior.

	1 almost always	2	3	4	5 almost never
1. Uses pictures, titles, contexts, structures of texts, patterns of language, and personal experiences to make predictions and comprehend texts.	( )	( )	( )	( )	( )
2. Gathers information from firsthand experiences and secondhand sources.	( )	( )	( )	( )	( )
3. Recognizes similarities and differences in words, stories, and ideas.	( )	( )	( )	( )	( )
4. Uses story elements (characters, setting, problem, events, and ending) to predict and recall events.	( )	( )	( )	( )	( )
5. Asks questions to clarify understanding.	( )	( )	( )	( )	( )

- **Performance-based assessment tasks.** Teachers use performance-based assessment tasks to monitor students' progress in relationship to identified learner outcomes. This method of assessment requires students to create extended projects that demonstrate their knowledge or skills and/or to put together a portfolio in which students collect all of their work over time. Required portfolio items are closely tied to standards and learning outcomes. This type of assessment differs from traditional testing methods that require a student to select a single correct answer or to fill in the blank.

- **Self-assessment or reflection.** Self-assessment encourages students to reflect on their learning and results in their improving how they learn. Teachers can implement strategies to support the development of students' abilities to assess their own work. Effective tools for learning how students learn include student journals and reflection logs. For example, students start a personal journal that they write in at the end of each week. They can write about what they have done in class, new information they have learned, terminology, and so on. Students can include any poetry they have written or extracts from texts or quotes they appreciate. They could add photographs, illustrations, and images of things they are interested in. These types of entries give teachers insight into how their students think, what interests them, and how they best process information.

REFLECT & WRITE

Which types of assessment do you feel would be most useful in helping you learn about your students? Which would be least helpful? Why?

_____

_____

_____

_____

_____

■ INTASC

STANDARD 3 The teacher understands how students differ in their approaches to learning and creates instructional opportunities that are adapted to diverse learners.

■ INTASC

STANDARD 8 The teacher understands and uses formal and informal assessment strategies to evaluate and ensure the continuous intellectual, social, and physical development of the learner.

The Role of Technology in Testing and Learning

Although we think that a No. 2 pencil is the standard piece of equipment for taking a standardized test, this procedure is quickly changing in the fast-paced world of educational reform. Now, with a new model of taking required state and district tests, students stare intently at computer screens, their hands grasping the mouse. This testing model is known as the Technology Enhanced Student Assessment System, and the click of a mouse has replaced filling in a bubble with a pencil. The Texas Education Agency (TEA) is transitioning its assessment programs to an online testing environment. Texas Assessment of Knowledge and Skills (TAKS) tests will be made available in an online format in all grades and subjects, including Spanish versions. In addition, new end-of-course examinations will be implemented exclusively online.[32] Likewise, Oregon has partnered with American Institutes for Research to create a new online testing system that will assess student's mastery of Oregon content standards. The Technology Enhanced Student Assessment system is available in mathematics, reading/literature, and science.[33]

The use of computers versus pencils and answer sheets raises a number of issues. First, if students are used to and comfortable working with computers, then they are more likely to be comfortable with taking tests online. But for students whose primary mode of learning is paper and pencil, then taking a test with paper and pencil is the mode with which they will be most comfortable. As Randy Bennett of Educational Testing Services says, "It's very clear that as kids become used to and routinely do writing on computers, paper and pencil tests don't do a fair job of determining their skills. Tests that are delivered in a mode that's different from one [in which students are learning] will eventually become indefensible."[34]

Perhaps the greatest obstacle to computer testing will be access to computers. A serious digital divide exists between poor schools and affluent schools, which are more likely to have more computers and use them in the learning process. In addition, students from minority groups are less likely to have computers in their homes. *In the Classroom with Terry B. Grier* on page 378 illustrates how one school district has been able to bridge the digital divide.

? *What Does This Mean for You?*

Accountability is one of the most visible topics in education today. You and your colleagues will be held accountable for student classroom performance and achievement, test scores, and how well your school does in relation to other schools in your district and state. As part of the accountability movement, policymakers are rewarding achievement and forcing low-performing schools and districts to redesign themselves so that all students pass state exams. This emphasis on accountability means:

- Performance is the name of the game in the schoolhouse today. You and your colleagues, faculty, and administrators will be called on to ensure that the curriculum, the instructional process, and the administrative frameworks are in place to enable all students to pass state exams.
- You will be in the public spotlight. The spotlight is the district and state report cards provided to parents and the public detailing performance. Reports of school and district performance will trigger public discussions regarding how well you, your colleagues, and your district are doing to ensure that all children learn.
- Your students will also be held accountable. An increasing number of states—currently 20—require students to pass a test to graduate from high school. Nine states tie student promotion to test scores.

You must be prepared to help all students achieve at high levels and pass state tests. You must take your place as a member of school-based teams charged with redesigning curriculum, instructional processes, and the administrative procedures necessary to help ensure that all students learn. You will need to become an articulate spokesperson about your school's and district's performance.

REFLECT & WRITE

Think back to standardized tests that you took, using No. 2 pencils. Do you believe that using computerized assessments will be more effective? Why or why not?

In the Classroom

with Terry B. Grier

Using Technology to Drive Assessment

Terry Grier is the superintendent of Guilford County Schools in North Carolina. During his tenure with the Guilford County Schools, which began in 2000, great progress has been made in the name of academic achievement. With a growing student body, a diverse ethnic mix among students, and 50 percent of students receiving free or reduced price meals, the district has overcome a number of potential obstacles. In fact, 13 of its 14 high schools were recognized among *Newsweek*'s Top Performing American High Schools. What accounts for Guilford County's success?

Among the many initiatives and programs that have contributed to the schools' success, Grier discusses the role that technology has played:

> We have computer labs in all of our schools that are used for remedial and accelerated learning. In addition, all high schools have new PLATO labs that use a software program designed to help them recover credit for courses previously failed. One of our key strategies has been to use technology as the platform to drive our assessment program. Regular assessments have provided teachers with on-time measures of student performance and have helped them to determine what students have mastered and what skills need to be retaught. We are also experimenting with wireless school environments and interactive mobile projector/white boards that allow the classroom teacher greater flexibility in tailoring teaching methods to meet a variety of student needs.

> Technology plays an integral role in our success. Below is a snapshot that captures the wraparound role technology has in providing tools that enhance learning, deliver services, and monitor the outcomes:

1. **Dropouts.** We have one of the lowest dropout rates in the nation for a large metropolitan school district. We use the No-Show Database to find students who have dropped out of school. It allows staff at schools to quickly locate students who have enrolled in other schools within the district who failed to notify their "base" school.

2. **Data warehouse.** Several years ago, we established a district data warehouse to collect, store, and disseminate district data. We use the data to make professionally informed decisions.

3. **Benchmarking.** The district has established a system of administering locally developed assessments on a quarterly basis. This online process allows teachers to reteach, based on where students are scoring on test items that measure how much curriculum is being taught. Teachers can see results of their class benchmarks online very quickly. District level staff can also view the results by teacher, subject, school, and district.

4. **Instructional practices.** Technology is used for teachers to provide instructional strategies via interactive white boards. Mission Possible schools have laptop computers for all math teachers. This is part of a wireless solution that enables the teachers to access math content and lesson material online. We will be entering into another laptop teacher initiative with Cisco in the near future. We have a district license for United Streaming, which provides searchable access to video clips on hundreds of curriculum-related subjects.

5. **Network/infrastructure.** All schools have broadband Internet access. All secondary schools will have building-wide wireless coverage by the end of the school year.

6. **New technology/Bond schools.** Audio enhancement systems are provided for all classrooms. The teacher wears a small microphone and speaks at his or her normal voice level. The sound uses a "spread" technology that distributes the sound evenly to all students. Classrooms are also being equipped with interactive solutions. In most situations, an audiovisual cart includes a projector, a document camera, and Interwrite SchoolPads. The SchoolPad is a handheld device that provides the same functionality as a SmartBoard. It gives the teacher freedom to move around the room. They can also allow the student to use the device. New schools are also receiving VoIP systems.

7. **Computers.** Guilford County owns more than 23,500 computers. We replace those computers on a 5-year plan. We typically replace computers on a school-by-school basis, which totals more than 4,700 computers each year.

Grier believes that the role of assessment has been a key factor in the success of the school district. The role of technology has helped pave the way.

Learn more about what Terry Grier has done to improve his school district at www.ednews.org/articles/18429/1/An-Interview-with-Terry-B-Grier-On-Academic-Success/Page1.html.

Source: M. F. Shaughnessy, "An interview with Terry B. Grier: On academic success," *Education News*, October 14, 2007. (Online). Available at www.ednews.org/articles/18429/1/An-Interview-with-Terry-B-Grier-On-Academic-Success/Page1.html.

WHO SHOULD BE ACCOUNTABLE FOR TEST SCORES?

Tests are the primary tools schools and districts use in measuring adequate yearly progress. Under the No Child Left Behind Act of 2001, every state must establish a definition of **adequate yearly progress (AYP)** and a plan to determine how to measure the AYP of each school district and school.

Adequate yearly progress (AYP) The definition established by each state to determine the progress of each school district and school.

The federal government approves each state's definition of and plan for measuring AYP. In defining AYP, each state sets the minimum levels of improvement. Schools and school districts must achieve these levels of improvement according to time frames specified in the law. According to the Department of Education (DOE), to meet federal requirements established under NCLB,

- Each state begins by setting a "starting point" that is based on the performance of its lowest-achieving demographic group or of the lowest-achieving schools in the state, whichever is higher.
- The state then determines the level of student achievement that a school must accomplish after 2 years in order to continue to show adequate yearly progress.
- Subsequent thresholds must be raised at least once every 3 years, until, at the end of 12 years, all students in the state are achieving at the proficient level on state assessments in reading/language arts and math.[35]

Holding States Accountable

To hold states accountable for student achievement, NCLB requires states to submit annual report cards. According to DOE, these report cards must include:

Go to MyEducationLab and select the topic "Assessment" then read the article "The Lessons of High-Stakes Testing." Answer the questions that follow.

- State assessment results by performance level (basic, proficient, and advanced), including (1) 2-year trend data for each subject and grade tested; and (2) a comparison between annual objectives and actual performance for each student group.
- Percentage of each group of students not tested.
- Graduation rates for secondary school students and any other student achievement indicators that the state chooses.
- Performance of school districts on adequate yearly progress measures, including the number and names of schools identified as needing improvement.
- Professional qualifications of teachers in the state, including the percentage of teachers in the classroom with only emergency or provisional credentials and the percentage of classes in the state that are not taught by highly qualified teachers, including a comparison between high- and low-income schools.[36]

Holding School Districts and Schools Accountable

To hold schools and school districts accountable, NCLB requires that they issue to the public local report cards. These reports cards provide stakeholders information about student performance. By issuing their report cards, districts demonstrate accountability on three levels—basic, proficient, and advanced. According to the DOE:

> Achievement data must be disaggregated, or broken out, by student subgroups according to: race, ethnicity, gender, English language proficiency, migrant status, disability status, and low-income status. The report cards must also tell which schools have been identified as needing improvement, corrective action, or restructuring.[37]

Schools in Need of Improvement

A school or school district that doesn't meet the state's definition of "adequate yearly progress" (AYP) for two straight years (schoolwide or in any major subgroup) is considered to be "in need of improvement."[38]

■ INTASC

STANDARD 8   The teacher understands and uses formal and informal assessment strategies to evaluate and ensure the continuous intellectual, social, and physical development of the learner.

FIGURE 10.4 Accountability and NCLB: Schools Needing Improvement

NCLB has implemented drastic changes to improve the academic achievement of schools nationwide. The five-year improvement plan is designed to help states meet the requirements of NCLB and maintain high standards.

Source: U.S. Department of Education, "Key Policy Letters Signed by the Education Secretary or Deputy Secretary" (July 24, 2002). (Online). Available at www.ed.gov/policy/elsec/guid/secletter/020724.html.

Annual Yearly Progress (AYP)

Schools identified for improvement must receive technical assistance from the school district that enables them to specifically address the academic achievement problem that caused the school to be identified for improvement. In addition, the following must take place:

Year 1

- All students are offered public school choice.
- Each school identified for improvement must develop or revise a two-year school improvement plan, in consultation with parents, school staff, the local educational agency, and other experts, for approval by the school district. The plan must incorporate research-based strategies, a 10 percent set-aside of Title I funds for professional development, extended learning time as appropriate (including school day or year), strategies to promote effective parental involvement, and mentoring for new teachers.

Year 2

- Make available supplemental educational services to students from low-income families.

Year 3

- Replace school staff responsible for the continued failure to make AYP.
- Implement a new curriculum based on scientifically based research (including professional development).
- Significantly decrease management authority at the school level.
- Extend the school day or school year.
- Appoint an outside expert to advise the school on its progress toward making AYP in accordance with its school plan; or
- Reorganize the school internally.

Year 4

- Reopen school as a charter school.
- Replace principal and staff.
- Contract for private management company of demonstrated effectiveness.
- State takeover.
- Any other major restructuring of school governance.

Year 5

Implement alternative governance plan no later than first day of school year following year 4 described above.

Figure 10.4 shows the corrective actions and consequences for districts that fail to make adequate yearly progress.

Holding Teachers Accountable

As we have discussed, teachers are accountable for student achievement. Traditionally, teacher raises were tied to years of service, advanced degrees, and completion of certification and re-certification requirements. All of this is changing, however. Increasingly, teachers are being rewarded on the basis of how well their students achieve. For example, the Guilford North Carolina School District implemented "Mission Possible"—a comprehensive differentiated/merit pay plan, whereby teachers are offered annual incentives and can earn up to $4,000 in merit pay for producing positive academic outcomes.[39]

OBSERVE & LEARN

As a beginning teacher, you, too, will be held accountable for ensuring that your students learn. Observing in classrooms and seeing how teachers take their accountability responsibilities seriously is a good way to learn what it means to be accountable in the classroom. Observe your school district's Teachers of the Year with the specific intent of identifying the many ways in which they demonstrate accountability for student learning in their daily practice.

REFLECT & WRITE

Do you think that the consequences of failure to make annual yearly progress are appropriate? What would you change or add to the list?

_____

_____

_____

_____

_____

ETHICAL DILEMMA

They Were Passed—One Way or Another

GRACE is a strong advocate for her group of 10 seventh- and eighth-graders with mixed disabilities. Grace is not a supporter, however, of the school district's policy that all children with disabilities should achieve to the state standards, and that they should take year-end district tests. Grace confides to her col-league, Amy, that if it comes right down to it, she will help her children pass the tests one way or another. Amy is a fourth-grade teacher with a class of students of mixed abilities. Although she does not entirely agree with the school district's policy, she believes that it is her responsibility to adhere to it.

What should Amy do?

SUMMARY

- The No Child left Behind Act, standards-based education, and accountability requirements are changing teaching and learning. Standards also are changing teaching and learning by implementing standards for students with disabilities.

- Standards-based education in America today implements standards for students and teachers. Whereas in the past teachers created their own curricula, they must now adhere to a model based on standards.

- Tests and assessment have always been a part of schooling. However, how tests are used, the purposes for which they are used, and how they are administered is changing teaching and learning. Many issues accompany the topic of testing, such as whether testing is fair for all students.

■ Teachers and schools must assess and report student achievement through many types of assessment. Technology plays a large role in the testing process, but many schools do not have access to the required technology, such as computers. Through the results of testing, the government is able to hold states and teachers accountable for student success.

KEY TERMS

Accountability provisions 358
Adequate yearly progress (AYP) 378
Alignment 364
Curriculum alignment 364
Curriculum frameworks 364

Exit exams 370
Gateway grades 369
High and rigorous standards 359
High-stakes testing 369
Normal curve 374

Social promotion 369
Standards 356
Standards-based education 357
Test besting 370

APPLICATIONS FOR ACTIVE LEARNING

Connections

1. The values and beliefs you bring to the teaching profession help determine your views on the topics of standards, testing, and accountability. For each of these topics, state some of your core basic beliefs and explain how they influence your views. For example, if you believe that all students have a basic right to learning essential knowledge and skills, then you might support high and rigorous standards for all students.

2. Go online and find your state's definition of adequate yearly progress (AYP). Compare this definition with that of three other states and the state in which you plan to teach. What are the similarities and differences? Next, review the AYP for the school district and schools you attended. For each one, tell what you feel they should do, or what you could do in your classroom, to improve their ranking.

Field Experiences

1. Interview elementary, middle, and high school teachers about their views and experiences with standards-based education. Use the following questions to guide your interviews. Do you think standards are helping or hurting education? Has your teaching been affected for better or for worse by standards? Do you think it is fair to hold teachers accountable for student learning? Compare how teachers' views differ across grade levels.

Personal Research

1. Given the fact that more and more teacher raises are being tied to student achievement and schoolwide performance, do you think that all teachers should be compensated in this way? Interview teachers at the elementary, middle, and high school levels to determine their opinions about whether or not raises and merit pay should be tied to increases in student achievement.

2. Go online and locate the state standards for Texas, Florida, California, and Oregon. How do they compare? If there are significant differences, describe them. What might account for these differences?

PREPARING TO TEACH

For Your Portfolio

1. If you have not already done so, put your state standards in your teaching portfolio.

2. As a beginning teacher of the grade of your choice, what will be your teaching goals for your first year? How will you integrate the state standards into your teaching?

Idea File

Select your state standards for a particular subject area and grade you plan to teach. Develop a lesson plan for that standard at the beginning level. Include instructional strategies and activities that would provide for rich knowledge and understanding on the part of your students.

LEARNING AND KNOWING MORE

Websites Worth Visiting

As you begin your teaching career and begin incorporating standards into your teaching practices, you may feel somewhat overwhelmed. Remember that you are not alone. Many novice and veteran teachers are doing their best to keep up with how standards and tests are changing teaching. The following websites will help you integrate national, state, and local standards into your curriculum and instructional practices.

The National Endowment for the Humanities
http://edsitement.neh.gov

This site lists hundreds of lessons that align with both standards and student interests. Lesson plans cover literature and language, foreign language, art and culture, and history and social studies.

Science NetLinks
www.sciencenetlinks.org

The American Association of Science provides lessons organized by Project 2061 benchmarks, which outline what all students should know in science and mathematics by the end of grades 2, 5, 8, and 12.

PBS Teachers
www.pbs.org/teachers

You can search more than 2,000 lessons by grade, subject, and keyword and then see how the lessons match many U.S. national, state, and district standards.

Achieve
www.achieve.org

Media coverage of standards and a searchable data base of state, national, and international standards are provided in four main content areas.

Mid-continent Research for Education and Learning
www.mcrel.org/topics/products/141

Mid-continent Research for Education and Learning (MCREL) draws upon the best of more than 30 years of education research to create practical, user-friendly products that help educators create classrooms that provide all students with opportunities for success.

The National Center for Research on Evaluation, Standards, and Student Testing
http://www.cse.ucla.edu

This website is the place to find reports, policy briefs, and a newsletter on K–12 assessments, accountability, and standards.

Books Worth Reading

Ainsworth, L. B. (2006). *Common Formative Assessments: How to Connect Standards-Based Instruction and Assessment.* Thousand Oaks, CA: Corwin Press.
This text offers a powerful means to closely align curriculum, instruction, and assessment to the standards essential for student success. You will learn how teams of teachers in the same content area or grade level can collaboratively develop, test, and refine common formative assessments in order to gain reliable and timely feedback on student progress.

Burke, K. (2006). *From Standards to Rubrics in Six Steps: Tools for Assessing Student Learning, K–8.* Thousand Oaks, CA: Corwin Press.
This book offers a practical, comprehensive six-step walk-through of how to create tasks that promote learning for all students and write rubrics linked straight to the requirements of state standards and the No Child Left Behind Act.

Gallagher, C. W. (2007). *Reclaiming Assessment: A Better Alternative to the Accountability Agenda.* Portsmouth, NH: Heinemann.
This book describes teacher-designed assessments through a local-control assessment system that a Nebraska school district utilized as opposed to national and state test-based accountability policies. It presents vital conceptual details and practical information for alternative methods of assessment.

Perna, D. M. (2006). *Aligning Standards and Curriculum for Classroom Success.* Thousand Oaks, CA: Corwin Press.
This guide provides teachers with the tools and strategies they need to plan instruction that meets state and national standards by including the latest research about standards and curriculum design, expanded coverage of the development of criterion standards, increased attention to assessment, and sample instructional plans.

11 Teaching the Curriculum

DRU TOMLIN When farmers plant seeds, they can determine fairly accurately when the seeds will germinate and when crops will rise. It takes a great deal of planning, tenderness, time, and nurturing to make crops grow—and though children are far more complex, the same kind of care and attention must be afforded them.

The day-to-day reality of teaching is not always filled with glorious teachable moments, glowing realizations, and eager faces with congenial smiles. Rather, it can feel like an endless mountain of paperwork, assessment, and policies. It is very easy to get bogged down in the tedium of the day. But if you remember why you are really there—for the kids—then all the paperwork and minutia gradually dissolve into the background. That is definitely one way to coach students toward academic success—to make their education your paramount concern every day. In other words, remember to drop all your other baggage at the door.

It's also vital to learn about all of your students and the baggage that they might be carrying. To coach students toward academic success, acknowledge them first. I try to connect everything I do with their lives. Before I read anything in a language arts class, I look for the broad, universal themes so I can make the story or novel applicable to their lives. We talk about those themes and create a community of learning in which everyone has something valuable to say.

When I plan a unit, I keep in mind the various learning styles in my classroom and create lessons and assessments that meet them all. When you take that step, when you try at every turn to experience your students' lives, you will speak to them more genuinely, create assignments that better meet their individual needs, and build an educational experience for them that is authentic and responsive—not distant and prescriptive.

One of my favorite stories is about a student named J. D. J. D. arrived from his previous middle school preceded by stories of his obstinacy, his surliness, and his disobedience. When he sauntered in during third period, I decided to put away everything that I had heard about him. He was wearing a tan sweatshirt that screamed "NO FEAR" across the chest, and I took that as my motto: I refused to be afraid of J. D. or how he might behave. I felt in my heart that this kid deserved a chance. That morning, my students and I were conducting interviews with each other to get our minds going about writing topics. I grabbed my legal pad and motioned J. D. to sit next to me. I explained the activity, and he turned his head slowly to look at the other students, unconvinced. But as I asked him questions, he began to open up. He talked about his summer job tending baby chickens on a farm in Virginia. He described watching a chick hatch from its tiny egg, holding the soft, infant bird in his hands, and placing it gently back on the dusty ground. It was the start of a new J. D.—and all I did was ask him questions about his life. Our relationship wasn't all smooth sailing, but he trusted me.

> ## When you see it happen, it's worth every minute.

Dru Tomlin, an eighth-grade teacher at River Trail Middle School, is 2003–2004 Fulton County (Georgia) Teacher of the Year. In addition to teaching, he coaches River Trail's Academic Bowl Team, which recently won first place in the state tournament.

As you read this chapter . . .

Think about:

- The role of curriculum in education
- What the contemporary curriculum is like
- How teachers plan and deliver instruction
- How teachers use models of direct instruction in the classroom
- How teachers use models of nondirect instruction in the classroom
- The curriculum influences for the twenty-first century
- What works in the classroom

▶▶ Go to MyEducationLab and select the topic "Curriculum and Instruction" then watch the video, "Leading a Student-Centered Curriculum"

That's the miracle of the teaching profession. Teachers have the power to make people grow. It takes vast amounts of time, patience, understanding, and empathy, but when you see it happen, it's worth every minute.

WHAT IS THE ROLE OF CURRICULUM IN EDUCATION?

Curriculum All the experiences students have while engaged in the process of schooling.

Explicit curriculum The behavior, attitudes, and knowledge schools intend to teach students.

Students come to school to learn. What should they learn? Why should they learn it? What is it that they learn? These questions and others like them are at the heart of teaching and learning. Think for a moment about what you learned in school. You learned how to read, write, and compute. You also learned about such subject areas as history, geography, and English. More than likely you acquired other knowledge, such as how to get along with others, how to participate in athletic activities, or how to help edit a school newspaper.

There is more to a curriculum than academic subjects and programs. What about debate, dance, and detention? Are these part of the school's curriculum as well? What about values, vaccinations, and views of other peoples and cultures? These, too, are part of the curriculum. Consequently, **curriculum** is all the experiences students have while engaged in the process of schooling. This means that the curriculum consists of experiences while on the school bus, on the playing fields, in the classroom, in the school halls, in the cafeteria, and anywhere else students are in the school setting. As a beginning teacher, you will want to provide your students with curriculum experiences that will promote their full growth and development.

Kinds of Curricula

Schools and teachers seldom provide one kind of curriculum experience for students, although some educators recommend a one-curriculum-fits-all approach. As shown in Figure 11.1, the four basic kinds of curricula are *explicit*, *hidden*, *null*, and *extra*. Each of these are examined in the following subsections to give you information for developing your own educational programs to meet the needs of your students.

The Explicit Curriculum

The **explicit curriculum**, sometimes called the *official* or *formal* curriculum, consists of all the experiences relating to content and the instructional procedures and materials for teaching that content. Whatever a district, school, or

FIGURE 11.1 Four Basic Kinds of Curricula

There are basically four kinds of curricula. Each one plays an important role in what is taught and not taught in the classroom. Which of these four curricula do you think plays the largest role in the process of schooling? Why?

teacher regards as a subject, lesson, class, or course of study is included in the formal curriculum. The explicit curriculum also includes goals, aims, policies, and guidelines issued by a state board of education or local education agency regarding what should be taught in the schools. Today, state outcome standards, which are expectations of what students should know and be able to do, play a central role in helping determine the explicit curriculum. As you will see, there is much more to the curriculum than state standards.

In addition to stating the knowledge and skills that should be taught, the explicit curriculum identifies the attitudes and values to be taught, such as those regarding careers, social interaction, cultural diversity, and helping others. For example, students in Barbara Vogel's fifth-grade classroom at Highline Community School in Aurora, Colorado, formed their own antislavery organization called STOP—Slavery That Oppresses People. They raised more than $50,000 to help free more than one thousand slaves in the Sudan. According to Ms. Vogel, "The kind of people we are determines what kind of country we have. It is the school's responsibility to teach and model humanitarianism—to help children learn how to be good citizens."[1]

The explicit curriculum also is expressed in the textbooks that are chosen or adopted at the state and local level. It is also evident in a school's philosophy and in learning materials, such as computer software, course descriptions, curriculum guides, and teacher lesson plans.

The Hidden Curriculum

The **hidden curriculum** is what schools do not intend to teach but nonetheless do. For example, teacher-student relationships and the climate of expectations created by these relationships influence, both positively and negatively, how and what students learn. All these are part of the hidden curriculum. When students sign up to be on the staff of the school newspaper and the teacher tells them, "You better be prepared to work hard in here because we are going to print the best newspaper this school ever had," the teacher is influencing how students perceive their roles and individual efforts. In this case, students are learning that by working hard they can achieve a quality result. All the things teachers do to gain and achieve success are part of the hidden curriculum.

The Null Curriculum

Have you ever thought that schools should teach something that they do not? The **null curriculum** is what is left out or not included, for whatever reasons. Elliot Eisner describes the null curriculum as "the options students are not offered, the perspectives they may never know about, much less be able to use, the concepts and skills that are not a part of their intellectual repertoire."[2] For example, students may not have an opportunity to learn how to think critically, to appreciate or participate in fine arts, or to learn career skills because these areas were intentionally or unintentionally left out of the curriculum. Additionally, when students do not have an opportunity to address or consider contemporary issues, such as those relating to gender, social class, and poverty, they may have a different perspective on these issues than do students who encounter these issues in their school curriculum.

Making the Null Curriculum Explicit

A number of recent incidents involving school violence is one such contemporary issue. For example, the 2007 shooting of students at Virginia Tech raises serious concerns about student safety, social and academic pressures, and the roles of educators in reporting antisocial tendencies. Violence is not confined to college campuses. In Cleveland, a 14-year-old boy, Asa H. Coon, who had been suspended the previous week for threatening violence the week before, shot four people in his

■ INTASC

STANDARD 1   The teacher understands the central concepts, tools of inquiry, and structures of the subjects being taught and can create learning experiences that make these aspects of subject matter meaningful for students.

■ INTASC

STANDARD 2   The teacher understands how children learn and develop, and can provide learning opportunities that support their intellectual, social, and personal development.

Hidden curriculum   The behaviors, attitudes, and knowledge the school culture unintentionally teaches students.

Null curriculum   The intellectual processes and subject content that schools do not teach.

downtown high school before he killed himself. One of his classmates, Doneisha LeVert, explained, "He's crazy. He threatened to blow up our school. He threatened to stab everybody . . . We didn't think nothing of it."[3] Two weeks later, in Memphis, police charged a 15-year-old with aggravated assault following the shooting of a Manassas High School student.[4]

This surge in school violence might be attributable to copy-cat behavior; the outcome of the shooters being bullied or being bullies themselves; or poor mental health. What can schools and teachers do to help prevent shootings and to make students feel safe? First, schools can increase their efforts to increase safety measures and make schools safe havens for students. Many schools still do not have metal detectors, school safety personnel, or programs designed to spot and help troubled youth. Second, schools can implement student mental health and antibullying programs. One innovative educator, Keith Schadt, created an antibullying program that he has brought to Jefferson County Public Schools in Louisville, Kentucky. At one school, where he worked with fifth- and sixth-graders, he showed students the first-hand effects of bullying. Playing the role of "Big Keith," he made fun of one student's basketball skills in front of his classmates. When the other students laughed he stopped them. "See, stop!" Schadt said to them all. "You've become part of the problem. It's your fault too that Big Keith will continue to pick on people. When you laugh, you're a third party to the bullying." Schadt then had students watch a video, role-play, and discuss times they've been bullied. Schadt listened and gave advice based on district conduct codes and on his experiences being bullied.[5]

As a new teacher, you can encourage discussions to address possible solutions to these problems. Often, teachers use news-related stories as teaching tools to encourage students to talk as a means of easing fears. You can also:

■ Encourage students to talk about their concerns and to express their feelings.
■ Talk honestly about your own feelings regarding school violence.
■ Validate the child's feelings.
■ Empower students to take action regarding school safety.
■ Discuss the safety procedures that are in place at your school.[6]

The National Institute on Drug Abuse (NIDA), a component of the National Institutes of Health (NIH), has a website to educate adolescents ages 11 through 15 (as well as their parents and teachers) on the science behind drug abuse. NIDA enlisted the help of teens in developing the site to ensure that the content addresses the appropriate questions and timely concerns.[7] If your middle school students do not know about or use this website, then they are missing a valuable antidrug resource.

As a beginning teacher, you will have opportunities to examine the null curriculum in your school and to include or not include certain subjects or topics in your teaching. Also, you will want to work with your colleagues to plan for and make decisions about what should or should not be included in the curriculum and to explain the reasons for your decisions. Whatever you and your colleagues decide, you are influencing learning. Your decisions do matter.

You can access NIDA for teens at www.teens.drugabuse.gov.

You can also log on to NIDA's main website at www.drugabuse.gov.

REFLECT & WRITE

What might you include in your high school curriculum that is not part of the explicit curriculum?

_____

_____

_____

_____

The Extracurriculum

Many schools have a well-developed program of **extracurriculum**, or the cocurricular activities designed to supplement, extend, and enrich the explicit curriculum. As the name implies, extracurriculum activities are seen as an addition to the academic curriculum. However, many extracurriculum activities—such as clubs, sports, study groups, school plays, cheerleading, and band—have important educational goals and are regarded as key parts of the school curriculum.

High school activities support the educational mission of schools, are educational, and contribute to success throughout life. Some of the clubs at West High School in Madison, Wisconsin, include the Anime (Japanese animation) Club, Chess Club, Crimestoppers, Debate Club/Forensics, Drama Club, Gay/Straight Alliance, Green Earth Organization, Math Club, National Honor Society, Pep Band, Photography Club, Science Olympiad, Students for Women's Issues, and Yearbook Staff.

Extracurriculum Noncredit activities that are over and above the required curriculum.

REFLECT & WRITE

Think back to your own high school experience. What extracurricular activities did you find to be the most enriching?

Influences on Curriculum Planning and Design

From colonial times to the present, school curricula have been, and continue to be, influenced greatly by religious, political, social, and economic forces and events. Forces that influence the curriculum include sociopolitical views and values concerning education—what people think is important for schools to teach and what elected officials and reformers advocate for curriculum priorities. Legislators and governors have greatly influenced what schools should teach and how they teach it, as we have seen through the provisions of the No Child Left Behind Act. This political influence on the curriculum will continue unabated over the next decade.

In addition, as discussed in Chapter 8, laws and court decisions influence the curriculum. Economic and demographic factors, such as the composition of student populations, also affect what is taught. For example, many affluent school districts emphasize curricula that are college preparatory, and many rural districts have curricula that emphasize vocational and technical skills relating to agriculture. Figure 11.2 summarizes influences on curriculum planning and design.

Social values are reflected in the curriculum in numerous ways, such as global warming education, character education, programs to reduce violence in the schools, and education about genocide in Darfur, Sudan. Schools play a significant role in developing students' social values by encouraging an awareness of world events. Many states require curricula relating to particular issues and concerns, such as studies on environmental preservation and conservation, substance abuse, and health issues. It is important for you to make your students aware of these topics and to promote thinking about them. You should seek to guide your students to

■ INTASC

STANDARD 3 The teacher understands how students differ in their approaches to learning and creates instructional opportunities that are adapted to diverse learners.

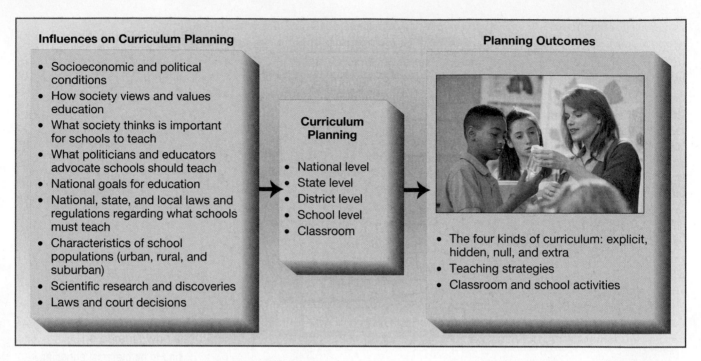

Influences on Curriculum Planning

- Socioeconomic and political conditions
- How society views and values education
- What society thinks is important for schools to teach
- What politicians and educators advocate schools should teach
- National goals for education
- National, state, and local laws and regulations regarding what schools must teach
- Characteristics of school populations (urban, rural, and suburban)
- Scientific research and discoveries
- Laws and court decisions

Curriculum Planning

- National level
- State level
- District level
- School level
- Classroom

Planning Outcomes

- The four kinds of curriculum: explicit, hidden, null, and extra
- Teaching strategies
- Classroom and school activities

FIGURE 11.2 Influences on Curriculum Planning and Design

This figure includes many of the factors that influence the curriculum in American schools. Ultimately, schools teach what society believes students should learn and what local communities think is important.

think critically on their own within the parameters of the school curriculum. As a beginning teacher you will be involved in debates over who decides what should be taught. However, remember schools are accountable to local school boards, state departments of education, and federal agencies for what gets taught.

? *What Does This Mean for You?*

As a beginning teacher and as a member of a grade school or district curriculum committee, you will be called on to make scientifically-based research (SBR) decisions. Here is one example of how decisions about scientifically based curricula will involve you.

You are teaching in an elementary school serving 500 students in grades 1 through 3. Seventy percent of the students are bilingual and are not achieving to grade-level standards. You and your colleagues are considering adopting a literacy model that claims to benefit all students, including bilingual students. Before adopting the new program, you should ask some questions about the research: Was this program tested under controlled circumstances in which some schools used the program and some did not? Was the sample size reasonable and relevant to the service provided?

Log on now to www.ncrel.org/csri/tools/gkey7/science.htm to review all seven keys involving criteria about scientifically based curricula and for other examples about how you will be involved in curriculum decision making.

REFLECT &
WRITE

Which of the influences in Figure 11.2 do you think plays the most important role in determining what should be taught at the local school level?

The Curriculum and Scientifically Based Research

In curriculum planning meetings across America, one of the most often used and heard phrases is **scientifically based research (SBR)**. The reason for this is that all schools receiving Title I funds under NCLB must spend their curriculum dollars on programs that are scientifically based. In fact, NCLB mentions SBR at least 110 times! NCLB uses seven key criteria as guidelines in determining if curricula and other reform strategies are scientifically based. Essentially, this means, Does the curriculum work? Does it increase student achievement? For example, if a publisher or program developer makes claims of effectiveness, then these should be one of the "keys" for determining if the program is based on scientifically based research. See *In the Classroom with Gary Baird* on page 392.

For example, educators, parents, and administrators have been concerned about students' math achievement. One way SBR has been used to direct curriculum change is by conducting studies to ascertain what helps students who have trouble in math. Based on the results of some of these studies that revealed that students learn effectively with peer tutors, there has been an increased push for peer tutoring in the classroom.

Scientifically based research (SBR) Research that involves applying rigorous, systematic, and objective procedures to obtain reliable and valid knowledge relevant to education activities and programs.

Curriculum and Standards-Based Education

Since the 1980s, education reform has been a very important part of curriculum development in public schools. **Standards-based education** refers to curricula that promotes rigorous academic assessment and sets higher expectations for both students and teachers.

Statewide standardized testing is a common form of standards-based assessment. This methodology seeks to reward academic success while highlighting areas in need of improvement. The goal of standards-based education is to clearly delineate expectations of students and teachers so that there is little confusion about what should be taught and when. Those who believe in this methodology think that setting definite standards for all levels of education ensures that all students receive an education that meets these standards. Although this is the stated goal of standards-based education, the use of standardized testing to determine student and teacher achievement has been controversial. Because students in low-income schools and school districts do not have the benefit of the same enriching environment, students who speak English as their second language do not have the same frames of reference as native English speakers, and not all students have the benefit of high-quality teachers, many educators question the fairness of using standards-based education to assess student achievement.

Standards-based education Curricula that promotes rigorous academic assessment and sets higher expectations for both students and teachers.

In the Classroom

with **Gary Baird**

*How to Use
Data-Driven Instruction*

Gary W. Baird is the principal at Lead Mine Elementary School in Raleigh, North Carolina.

You don't have to go back to *Little House on the Prairie* to find a teaching style that is predicated on "getting through" the curriculum. Curriculum coverage is not the same as student learning. Recent accountability initiatives, including No Child Left Behind, have brought about a shift in focus from covering subject matter, to meeting the needs of each student. There is only one way to determine whether or not the needs of the student are being met, and that is through an ongoing analysis of assessment data.

We ask a lot of our teachers, so we should ask what we can do to help make their lives easier. Technology is used at Lead Mine Elementary School to provide a big assist. We use Success Maker software by Pearson Digital Learning to provide the teachers with data, instructional support, and an important means of differentiation. All of our kindergarten, first-, and second-grade students come to the lab twice a week to take part in the program. Each child receives instruction at his or her own level, as determined by the computer placement assessment. This is a unique opportunity for students to receive completely individualized instruction. The lab manager prints out reports for the teachers, which become a part of the body of data used to make instructional decisions about students. The lessons on the computer are aligned with the North Carolina Standard Course of Study. The program also provides enrichment opportunities and lessons in Spanish.

Lead Mine Elementary School reflects the changing demographics taking place in America today. Over 43 percent of our students are eligible for free or reduced lunches, and for many students, English is not their primary language. Yet despite these challenges, our test scores have shown steady growth over the years. Our teachers had to learn to teach smarter and to use technological resources as their ally. They use the following six-step process:

1. Start the school year by analyzing existing data. Before your students arrive, examine their cumulative record files to get a general profile of each student. At Lead Mine, we conduct a formal initial assessment process for incoming kindergarteners before creating our kindergarten class lists.

2. Align assessments to objectives. Plan collaboratively with your grade-level colleagues to determine when you will be teaching district and state standards and how you will assess each standard.

3. Begin the data collection process. There are a number of ways to collect classroom data. You may use formal assessments such as written assignments, quizzes, and tests. You may use informal assessments such as observation and discussions. You may also use technology to help you collect data. A variety of instructional learning systems on the market allow you to track student progress with instructional software.

4. Analyze data. At the completion of the data-collection process for a unit of study, you should sit down with your grade-level colleagues and look at the data for trends. Did the majority of the students reach the standard? Does the data reveal needs that have to be addressed?

5. Use data analysis to make decisions on the next course of study. After examining the data, use it to guide your next steps in the instructional process. Which students are ready to move on? Which students need remediation? Which students need enrichment? In creating your plan to meet the needs of all students, you might consult with resource teachers, such as the academically gifted teacher, the ESL teacher, the computer lab manager, or any other specialists in the school who could help meet a student's specific needs. Students might also be assigned to appropriate software.

6. Repeat the process. Making data-based decisions to guide instruction is an ongoing process. Throughout the school year, you are constantly assessing your students, analyzing their data, and readjusting the plans you have made to best meet their educational needs.

You can learn more about data-driven instruction at www2.edc.org/asap/data_subtheme.asp?pkTheme=38.

WHAT IS THE CONTEMPORARY CURRICULUM LIKE?

The curriculum of most public schools includes the content areas of language arts, English, mathematics, science, social studies, physical education and health, foreign languages, vocational education, and the arts. Each of these areas has an identifiable body of knowledge and skills that teachers use as the basis for selecting curriculum and planning instruction. Furthermore, professional organizations such as the National Council of Teachers of Mathematics (NCTM) and the National Science Teachers Association (NSTA) develop standards and issue guidelines and recommendations about the curriculum content of their specific areas.

Reading and Language Arts

Today, improving literacy is a major goal in all content areas and across all grade levels, pre-K through 12. In the last decade, the emphasis has been on literacy and reading in grades pre-K through 8. All states have adopted an educational agenda with a strong literacy focus and have set the goal of having all children read at grade level. During the 1990s, educators waged spirited battles known as the "reading wars" about how best to teach reading. Based on linguistic theories, many educational programs advocated a **whole language** approach. Whole language is a philosophy of language instruction emphasizing the integration of all language skills (reading, writing, speaking, and listening), as well as reading for meaning and contextualized language learning. Another group advocated for the use of **phonics** instruction, which involves teaching letter-sound correspondence and decoding, or a "bottom-up" approach to language learning. Some whole-language instructors altogether avoided reading and writing instruction based on phonics, although others included some phonics for individual students as needed.

A Balanced Approach

With the advent of the new century, the reading wars have more or less come to an end. Instead, professional efforts focus on how to achieve a **balanced** (or comprehensive) **approach to reading**, one that includes all available strategies to help children learn to read, based on their own learning styles and developmental needs.

Also, educators have supported the following changes in the reading and literacy curriculum and accompanying instructional practices:

- Giving students a more active role in the reading process. This can be done, for example, through self-directed learning. Self-directed learning involves a three-step process: modeling desired behavior, guiding students' practice in the desired behavior, and organizing the classroom environment and instructional process so that students can work independently or in cooperative learning groups.
- Emphasizing reading comprehension and activities to promote comprehension.
- Integrating reading with all content areas. This is known as "reading across the curriculum."
- Placing less emphasis on teaching reading as an isolated skill.
- Making reading more practical and tied to daily life and events.
- Using reciprocal teaching to improve students' reading comprehension. To do so, teachers employ four comprehension strategies: predicting, questioning, clarifying, and summarizing. Teachers scaffold these four strategies by modeling, guiding, and applying the strategies while reading; guide students to become metacognitive and reflective in their strategy use; and help students monitor their reading comprehension using the four strategies. Teachers use the social nature of learning to improve and scaffold reading comprehension and to strengthen instruction in a variety of classroom settings—whole class sessions, guided reading groups, and literature circles.[8]
- Integrating thinking skills into the reading and language arts curriculum.

■ **INTASC**

STANDARD 1 The teacher understands the central concepts, tools of inquiry, and structures of the subjects being taught and can create learning experiences that make these aspects of subject matter meaningful for students.

■ **INTASC**

STANDARD 2 The teacher understands how children learn and develop, and can provide learning opportunities that support their intellectual, social, and personal development.

Whole language An approach based on the idea that language development, reading, writing, speaking, and listening are interrelated processes and should be taught concurrently rather than sequentially.

Phonics Teaching reading by letter-sound correspondence.

Balanced approach to reading A reading program that includes all of the essential components of reading instruction.

Go to MyEducationLab and select the topic "Curriculum and Instruction" then watch the video "Poetry Project." Complete the activities that follow.

REFLECT & WRITE

How did you learn to read? What do you consider the advantages and disadvantages of that method?

_____

_____

_____

_____

_____

● *Your Turn*

Research the science and math requirements in high schools in your area. Are students receiving comparable educations in science and math? Do you think all schools in a district should provide comparable education in these areas?

■ INTASC

STANDARD 4 The teacher uses various instructional strategies to encourage students' development of critical thinking, problem solving, and performance skills.

Science

Science and the teaching of science are fast-changing enterprises. To see these changes in the role of science and in science teaching, read *In the Classroom with Joel M. Kuper* on the Wyoming Ethnobotany Project. The Wyoming Project provides an example of the ways teaching science in grades pre-K through 12 has changed and is changing. These changes will affect you and influence how you teach.

In addition to changing the way science is taught, the sequence of teaching the sciences is changing. For decades, the sequence of science has been ninth-grade biology, tenth-grade chemistry, and eleventh-grade physics. Now some schools are making physics the first course in the sequence and the basis for other science learning.

A leading science education reformer, Marge Bardeen, manager of the Fermi National Accelerator Laboratory Education Office, notes that what we learn in science courses could relate more to everyday life.

> Generally, I think people do not understand that science is a way of approaching problems rather than a body of knowledge. As a result, they are often unable to assess claims and counterclaims as they make choices on critical issues that face them as citizens. This is what we need to be concerned about—as we call it, scientific literacy for citizenship.[9]

Mathematics

Mathematics, like science, is being reformed. What is taught, how math is taught, and the sequence in which math skills and concepts are taught are changing. The current mathematics reform is often referred to as the "new new math" to distinguish it from the "new math" reforms of the 1960s and 1970s. The current reforms in mathematics are spurred by standards developed by the NCTM and state standards-based education. The mathematics reform movement focuses on the following initiatives:

- Emphasis on providing all students with meaningful mathematics experiences
- Hands-on math at all grade levels
- Less emphasis on rote learning and memorization. This deemphasis on calculation and basic arithmetic skills is a hallmark of mathematics reform. It is also one of the bones of contention with critics of contemporary math reform.
- Student-centered learning and involving students in independent and group investigations of real mathematics problems
- High mathematical expectations for all students. This equity emphasis includes students with disabilities, females, minorities, and low-income students.

In the Classroom

with Joel M. Kuper

The Wyoming Ethnobotany Project

Joel M. Kuper teaches science at Greybull High School in Greybull, Wyoming, and is a recipient of the 2003 Subaru National Science Teaching Awards.

Wyoming has a rich cultural heritage that extends back to Native American influences. However, many students have little appreciation of the applications of that heritage in our current society. In looking for a way to improve the teaching of science at Greybull High School, I developed the Wyoming Ethnobotany Project. This integrated program investigates indigenous plants in northwestern Wyoming that were used by Native Americans for their medicinal properties. These plants are used to produce extracts that are tested using twenty-first-century tissue culture and biochemical analyses to evaluate their potential as medicines and supplements in today's society.

The program has been incorporated into a number of classes. The botany course does background research into plants used by the Shoshone, Arapaho, and Crow tribes from this area. Students learn to identify the plants and develop a data base on historic uses through consultation with tribal contacts and the Plains Indian Museum at the Buffalo Bill Historical Center in Cody, Wyoming. They do field work in mapping locations and collecting samples for lab evaluation. Our chemistry classes are involved with making extracts of the plant materials. Extractions are made with water, ethanol, and acetone in order to evaluate polar and nonpolar substances. The collected extracts are turned over to students enrolled in the school's research seminar course. These students select a topic for in-depth experimental research. In the Ethnobotany Project, many of these students elect to work with the native plant extracts to evaluate their effectiveness in a variety of situations. The in-depth projects are the basis of the student's research work that competes at the regional, state, and ISEF levels.

Today, there are literally no boundaries between science and other academic disciplines. The Wyoming Ethnobiology Project illustrates critical ways in which contemporary science teaching is changing:

- How science teaching is integrated across grades and subject areas
- How science teaching is interdisciplinary
- How science is applied to everyday life
- How science can reform cultural understanding and perspectives
- How science is applied to environmental issues
- How students are involved in projects and learn science by acting as scientists act
- How students use science to think and develop thinking skills

Source: Subaru of America, Inc. Reprinted by permission.

More about this project can be found at www.science.subaru .com/teaching_ideas/ b_joelkuper.shtml.

- Gender equity. The emphasis here is to dismantle the stereotype that math is for males only.
- The use of differentiated instruction to achieve equity goals
- Integration of technology applications—computers, calculators, and personal hand held devices—to "do math"
- Implementation of standards-based teaching

Within the math discipline, attention is being focused on algebra, which math educators see as the foundation for mathematical problem solving. Since the 1990s, schools nationwide have quietly begun requiring algebra for more and more students, hoping they'll develop skills for college and a changing workplace—not to mention everyday life, with its computer spreadsheets and cell phone applications. Twenty-one states now require students to pass algebra to graduate, and teachers (and textbook publishers) are being prodded to stress real-world situations while

> **■ INTASC**
>
> **STANDARD 1** The teacher understands the central concepts, tools of inquiry, and structures of the subjects being taught and can create learning experiences that make these aspects of subject matter meaningful for students.

Go to MyEducationLab and select the topic "Curriculum and Instruction" then watch the video "Debate." Complete the activities that follow.

minimizing calculation and theoretical concepts that dogged students a generation ago. Algebra is increasingly being taught more and more as part of elementary and middle school curricula.

"Thirty years ago, we only taught algebra to a select group," says Linda Antinone, a 19-year veteran math and physics teacher at Paschal High School in Fort Worth, Texas. "If you weren't college bound, you didn't get algebra."[10] Now algebra is for everyone. When we say algebra is for everyone, this is exactly the point. Algebraic concepts are being integrated throughout the K–12 curriculum.

Social Studies

Go to www.ncss.org for more information about the association.

The National Council for the Social Studies (NCSS) defines social studies as "the integrated study of the social sciences and humanities to promote civic competence." Within the school program, social studies courses provide coordinated, systematic study drawing on a wide variety of disciplines, including anthropology, archaeology, economics, geography, history, law, philosophy, political science, psychology, religion, and sociology as well as appropriate content from the humanities, mathematics, and natural sciences. In essence, social studies promote knowledge of and involvement in civic affairs.

The NCSS framework consists of ten themes incorporating fields of study that correspond with one or more relevant disciplines. The organization believes that effective social studies programs include the following categories in the curriculum:

1. Culture
2. People, places, and environments
3. Individuals, groups, and institutions
4. Production, distribution, and consumption
5. Global connections
6. Time, continuity, and change
7. Individual development and identity
8. Power, authority, and governance
9. Science, technology, and society
10. Civic ideals and practices

Social studies does not always receive the attention and recognition it deserves. It is sometimes forced to take a back seat in the curriculum to science, math, English, or language arts. This is unfortunate, because civic virtue is at the core of democratic living.

History is the leading discipline of social studies across all grades, K through 12. Many states require that state history be taught, typically between grades 4 and 8; if your state is one of these, you need to familiarize yourself with the content. In fact, some states require a state history course as a condition for obtaining a teaching certificate. History teachers are trying to keep history from being squeezed out by the emphasis of many assessment tests on reading, math, and science. They also are trying to move from rote teaching and memorization of facts to other approaches that make history come alive and be meaningful to students. These include:

Creative teachers help their students connect to social studies.

- Historical role-playing
- Study and use of primary sources, such as actual historical documents.

- Reading of historical narrative (e.g., journals, diaries, and letters)
- Use of the Internet to access primary sources

Character Education

Related to civic virtue, **character education** is part of the social studies curriculum. It is an example of a curricular application of developmental approaches to learning. Programs aim to help students acquire positive character traits, such as initiative, diligence, loyalty, tact, kindness, generosity, courage, and other traits believed to be good by society in general. Georgia's Quality Core Curriculum (QCC) includes core values taught in the Georgia public schools, such as citizenship, respect for others, respect for self, self-esteem, and the work ethic. Character education seeks to directly teach character traits such as those in Figure 11.3.

Service learning, or community service, is often touted as a means for promoting character education. However, at the present time, Maryland is the only state requiring such service as a condition for graduation.

Character education An approach to education that emphasizes the teaching of values, moral reasoning, and the development of "good" character.

The following is a Calendar of Character Traits created by the Duval County (Florida) Public School District. This chart shows how each month, teachers are asked to instruct students on different aspects of social responsibility, to explain how to treat each other with respect, and to show how students can benefit from practicing these character traits. The goal of this exercise is to create an atmosphere in the schools where students can safely practice those behaviors until such behaviors become the norm.

August	**Responsibility and Attentiveness.** *Responsibility*—having moral, legal, or mental accountability; being reliable and trustworthy. *Attentiveness*—being mindful of another's speech, needs, and so on.
September	**Citizenship and Cooperation.** Becoming an active member of the community; working within the community to achieve the common benefit.
October	**Fairness.** Treating others in a consistent, impartial way—free from self-interest, prejudice, or favoritism.
November	**Patriotism.** Showing love of, devotion to, and pride in one's country.
December	**Kindness and Caring.** Feeling interest or concern for others and being kind.
January	**Courage and Initiative.** Showing mental or moral strength and taking the first step to do so.
February	**Respect and Tolerance.** Showing regard for the worth of everyone and everything; also, respecting the individual differences, views, and beliefs of others.
March	**Honesty and Trustworthiness.** Practicing adherence to the facts, fairness, and straightforwardness of conduct; also being worthy of confidence.
April	**Self-control.** Exercising restraint over one's impulses, emotions, and desires.
May	**Patience and Perseverance.** The capacity, habit, or fact of bearing pains or trials calmly or without complaint; the steady persistence in adhering to a course of action and/or a belief or purpose.

FIGURE 11.3 Calendar of Character Traits

This calendar lists 10 strong character traits. What others might your add to your own calendar?

Source: Character Education. *Duval County Public Schools.* (2007–2008) (Online). Available at www.dreamsbeginhere.org/static/ourschools/studentinfo/character.asp#traits.

• *Your Turn*

Think of some ideas for integrating character education into your curriculum and instructional practices. Identify specific examples and the specific contexts for integrating character education appropriately. Begin by recording your first ideas and discussing them with classmates.

More information concerning Georgia's Quality Core Curriculum is available on their website at www.doe.k12.ga.us.

Character Education Resources, an organization based in New Hampshire, provides a wealth of information about character education on their website at www.charactereducationinfo.org.

Physical Education and Health

After years of schedule cuts and playing second fiddle to reading, math, and science, physical education finds itself in the spotlight. Physical educators have a national crisis to thank for their new-found attention—childhood obesity. Physical education is no longer just for students interested in athletics. Now it is for everyone. It is for everyone because more states and schools are requiring it. Alarmed by growing numbers of overweight children and obesity-related health risks, Texas recently passed a law requiring elementary students, K through 6, to spend 30 minutes a day in physical education classes or structured physical activity; however, the "new" physical education is not what the "old" physical education was. The new physical education focuses on the whole student and relates physical fitness to all aspects of life.

Physical Fitness

Physical fitness education is increasing in our nation's schools. Some changes have been mandated at the state level, some at the federal level. In 1956, President Eisenhower held the President's Council on Youth Fitness after a report showed that U.S. children were less fit than their European counterparts. Since that time, physical fitness has become a priority in U.S. public education. In 2002, President George W. Bush rejuvenated this council to promote health consciousness in all U.S. citizens, with an emphasis on youth health. Many states have passed legislation requiring added physical education and health funding, increasing the amount of time students are required to spend in physical education classes, and establishing standards of measuring physical fitness among students.

These changes will continue on a state and national level. In 2007, Texas Governor Rick Perry signed Senate Bill 530, which implements new standards for public school physical fitness examinations. The bill requires physical fitness evaluations of all Texas public school students in grades 3–12, which started with the 2007 school year. It also increases the physical education requirement from two semesters to four semesters for students in middle school. Such changes at the state and federal level will continue to impact physical fitness awareness programs in our public schools for years to come.

Health

Encouraging and helping children lead healthy lifestyles also is a top priority of school districts today. Many districts are serving healthier food in school cafeterias and limiting students' access to junk food. For example, Francisco Macias doesn't really like the standard fare at the Hammocks Middle School cafeteria. But the Miami sixth-grader sure likes to chow down on treats from the school's new vending machines. As part of a pilot program, Hammocks' two cafeterias boast dispensers filled with healthy versions of standard snacks and drinks. They range from low-fat chips to Nesquik-flavored milk and Gatorade. Francisco favors Frito-Lay's Ruffles baked potato chips. He knows they're healthier than the high-fat type, so he feels better about eating them, he says.[11]

Students' health and wellness knowledge and skills are guided by Health Education Standards. The standards are the same for grades K through 12; however, the benchmarks for the grade levels are different.

REFLECT & WRITE

Do you think schools should assume responsibility for providing students with health information, knowledge, and skills? Why? Why not?

_____

_____

_____

_____

_____

The Arts

Today, despite strained school budgets, treating art education as a major content area rather than as part of the extracurriculum is a trend in curriculum development. Some even suggest that art become the fourth R! Why is this trend occurring? Stephanie Perrin, the headmistress of Walnut Hill School in Natick, Massachusetts, offers the following reason:

> What is required of workers at all levels in our post-industrial society is that they be creative thinkers and problem solvers and able to work well with others or independently. Schools can no longer simply train students for specific tasks; schools must educate them in terms of broad skills, so they will be able to function in a number of capacities. Students must be active learners, they must be judicious risk takers, they must be able to push themselves toward high levels of achievement, and they must have the courage of their convictions. Arts training develops such skills.[12]

For example, in theater, students practice thinking and memory skills, problem-solving skills, and social skills. They also apply the basic skills of reading, writing, and arithmetic. Other important reasons for teaching theater include fostering student self-confidence and understanding, promoting creative thinking, developing interpersonal skills, and cultivating an understanding of human values.

As an alternative to integrating arts into the general curriculum as a content area, many school districts have established magnet arts schools that enroll students throughout a district or region. One example is the School for Creative and Performing Arts (SCPA) in Cincinnati, Ohio. SCPA is one of the older comprehensive public high schools that offers a vocational arts curriculum, and it has frequently been studied as a model by other school districts considering the establishment of a magnet arts program. It offers instruction in vocal and instrumental music, dance, acting, musical theater, creative writing, and visual arts, in addition to a core curriculum of academic subjects. Enrolling students in grades 4 through 12, SCPA was the first magnet arts school to enroll elementary students.[13]

■ INTASC

STANDARD 3   The teacher understands how students differ in their approaches to learning and creates instructional opportunities that are adapted to diverse learners.

REFLECT & WRITE

In what ways were the arts part of your schooling? How has this changed in contemporary schooling?

A growing number of school districts and teachers consider the arts to be a foundation for and a part of the education process. Yet a National Assessment of Educational Progress (NAEP) Arts Report Card indicated that many students lag behind in learning how to draw, dance, or play a musical instrument. Why do you think this is?

Comprehensive School Reform and the Curriculum

Educators have made many efforts to redesign and reform schools and curricula to improve American schools. The Obey-Porter Comprehensive School Reform Demonstration program (CSRD) legislation, reauthorized under the No Child Left Behind Act of 2001, funds research-based comprehensive models designed to help ensure the academic success of all students. Such reform models generally focus on changing all aspects of a school's operation, with an emphasis on increasing student learning, and are referred to as "whole school" and "systematic reform programs." The models are developed and implemented with federal and private funds. Many are designed to be used in low-performing schools, and their implementation is supported by Title I funds and aimed at helping low-achieving students in high-poverty schools.

These models provide teachers and administrators with a framework in which they can implement research-based instructional programs that are designed to help schools improve based on their specific needs.

REFLECT & WRITE

Use the Web to research whole school reform model programs. How can the information provided by the models be used to enhance teaching and learning? What types of teaching methods are used? Which would you implement in your classroom?

HOW DO TEACHERS PLAN AND DELIVER INSTRUCTION?

Of all of the many roles of a teacher, planning and providing instruction are the most essential. The instructional methods you use will have a major effect on the way you interpret the curriculum and address curriculum goals. Your planning will also determine to a large extent if what you teach is interesting, understandable, and integrated with what students already know. The more effective you are at planning, the more successful you will be at delivering engaging instruction.

Instructional Goals and Learning Objectives

When you plan for implementing the curriculum, one of the tasks is to identify standards and **instructional goals**—statements regarding what students will learn. As we learned in Chapter 10, national, state, and local standards are the starting place for instructional goals. In addition, you need to consider the objectives and outcomes of the instructional process.

One of the first persons to provide a model for curriculum planning was Ralph Tyler, who called the purposes of education **learning objectives**. Tyler was an educator, author, and lecturer. In 1949, he published *Education: Curriculum Planning and Evaluation*. This work examined the importance of stating clear objectives in the classroom and meeting them through qualified instruction. Tyler's influence led to an emphasis on stating learning objectives in behavioral terms that specify what students should master in each subject at each grade level. Traditionally, this kind of planning results in a **scope-and-sequence approach** to curriculum and instruction. For example, students might master the correct use of capitalization and end punctuation in grade 1 and then go on to more complex punctuation rules in grades 2 and 3. Robert Mager, an award-winning educator and the creator of a widely used system for writing instructional objectives, maintained that a well-stated learning objective has three parts: a description of what students should do, the conditions under which the student will perform, and the students' performance will be evaluated.[14]

Bloom's Taxonomy

Benjamin Bloom was an educational psychologist who developed a system of classification for the levels of learning in 1956. Bloom was frustrated by the fact that over 95 percent of test questions at the time were geared toward the lowest levels of learning, such as recall of information. His research has greatly influenced the course of curriculum instruction in the United States. Bloom classified learning objectives based on the domains they address. He identified three distinct learning domains, or areas, in which learning can be classified. The three domains identified by Bloom are the *cognitive, affective,* and *psychomotor domains.*

- *The affective domain* deals with learning related to emotions, empathy, social behavior, and conflict resolution. This domain is acquired as a result of responses to behaviors, parenting, social situations, and the environment, all of which play an important role in shaping a child's emotional state.
- *The psychomotor domain* deals with learning related to physical abilities. Eye-hand coordination, motor skills, and other basic physical aptitudes are a part of this domain.

■ **INTASC**

STANDARD 1 The teacher understands the central concepts, tools of inquiry, and structures of the subjects being taught and can create learning experiences that make these aspects of subject matter meaningful for students.

Instructional goals What students will learn; what they will know and be able to do.

Learning objectives Purposes of education stated in behavioral terms and specifying what students should master in each subject at each grade level.

Scope-and-sequence approach An approach to teaching that emphasizes stating and gradually meeting learning objectives in classroom instruction.

■ **INTASC**

STANDARD 7 The teacher plans instruction based upon knowledge of subject matter, students, the community, and curriculum goals.

Although education should encompass parts of all domains, *the cognitive domain* is the chief concern of many academic programs. This domain includes six objectives, or types of learning acquired:

▪ **Knowledge.** This primary objective refers to the most simple, factual understanding of the subject. The question, "What are the bones of the human skull?" addresses the most basic and fundamental aspects of human skull anatomy.

▪ **Comprehension.** This second objective refers to the ability to understand the purpose of what has been learned. The question, "What functions do the bones of the skull serve?" addresses the students' level of understanding about this topic.

▪ **Application.** The third objective requires more complex reasoning. For example, the question, "What can scientists learn by looking at skulls?" compels the students to go beyond simple reasoning.

▪ **Analysis.** The fourth objective moves students toward the more complex and conceptual. "How does this skull reveal human traits?" asks the student to consider not just bone type, shape, and purpose, but the effect this structure has on human characteristics, such as the ability to learn or comprehend due to a larger brain size.

▪ **Synthesis.** This objective refers to a higher-learning level and requires the most cognitive skill. "What might the owner of this skull have looked like in the flesh?" is a question that requires students to synthesize previous knowledge and use creative thinking to imagine the outcome.

▪ **Evaluation.** This objective requires students to think the most deeply about the topic question, "What are some problems in interpreting skeletal evidence scientifically?"; students must use all the other objectives in order to answer this question.

Go to MyEducationLab and select the topic "Curriculum and Instruction" then watch the video "Planning for Instruction." Complete the activities that follow.

REFLECT & WRITE

What general learning goals would you establish for your classroom? How would you incorporate the affective and psychomotor domains?

_____

_____

_____

_____

_____

Outcome-Based Education

Outcome-based education (OBE) An educational approach that focuses on developing students' ability to demonstrate mastery of certain desired outcomes or performances.

A contemporary approach based on learning objectives is called **outcome-based education (OBE)**. In OBE, broader outcomes of learning are evaluated rather than the mastery of specific behavioral objectives. For example, a student's science project might demonstrate broader outcomes such as concern with environmental stewardship, participation in local affairs, and personal accomplishment. At the same time, the project might demonstrate an array of curriculum goals, such as being able to apply the scientific method, to measure accurately, and to communicate learning. William Spady, an influential proponent of OBE, defines outcomes as "high quality, culminating demonstrations of significant learning in context."[15]

Some critics of outcome-based education favor step-by-step teaching and evaluation of basic skills. Others claim that demonstrations of student learning are often difficult or impossible to assess and report to parents and that training teachers to assess outcomes is costly and time consuming. However, advocates claim that OBE offers an opportunity for all students to succeed, because they have more time to achieve mastery before products of their learning are evaluated. Students also can demonstrate their learning in relation to real-life situations. (See *What's New in Education?*)

• *Your Turn*

The school in which you teach will have a particular approach to the curriculum and testing. What are some questions you will ask about the curriculum and your "freedom to teach"?

REFLECT & WRITE

Do you think that outcome-based education is an effective way to teach? How can incorporating Bloom's cognitive learning objectives enhance an outcome-based education curriculum?

_____

_____

_____

_____

_____

What's *New* in Education?

Ninth-Graders in Lab Jackets, Mastering Newtonian Mechanics

Maybe you have seen the television quiz show "Are You Smarter Than a Fifth-Grader?" and proudly attest that you are. But how might you stack up against the students in Faye Cascio's ninth-grade physical science class?

Consider the following problem: You fall into a swiftly moving river and are in need of a flotation device. You see a life preserver bobbing 3 meters downstream of you and another one the same distance behind. Which preserver should you swim toward?

The school year is still young, and so, too, is the Academy of Science, a sneakily rigorous high school magnet science program in Loudoun County, Virginia, of which Ms. Cascio's physics class is a part. Already her freshmen students cannot only ace exercises in Newtonian mechanics such as the sample cited here, but they can also explain the reasoning behind every answer they give.

Many people wring their hands over the state of science education and point to the appalling performance of America's students in international science and math competitions. Yet some of the direst noises about our nation's scientific prospects might be premature. Far from rejecting challenging science courses, students seem to be embracing them.

This year, for example, the American Institute of Physics said that the percentage of high school students taking physics courses was at an all-time high. With programs like Ms. Cascio's—and there are others like her course throughout the country—students will experience physics in a way that keeps them engaged and challenged. Consequently, enrollment numbers will continue to climb.

Source: N. Angier (2007, October 30), In science classrooms, a blast of fresh O_2. *New York Times*, pp. D1–D2.

Prepared Curricula

One of the oldest and most discussed curriculum issues centers around a teacher's right to use the curricula and materials they want and to teach in the ways they want. This chapter and this book stress the theme that high-quality teachers make high-quality decisions and deliver high-quality instruction resulting in student achievement. However, teachers also teach from textbooks that have a particular approach, content, and sequence. In addition, more textbooks are becoming highly scripted—that is, they come with detailed teacher guides that outline daily lessons and teaching scripts. These kinds of textbooks will become more common, and teachers will be expected to follow them.

As educational policymakers move toward increasingly evaluative assessments, textbooks will keep up with the changing market by creating material based around those standards. This is not to say that you must rely solely on the textbook as a means of instruction. However, this growing trend toward standardization, which is likely to continue in the future, will require teaching materials that meet the necessary standards.

WHAT ARE SOME MODELS OF DIRECT INSTRUCTION?

Direct instruction Highly structured, teacher-centered strategy that capitalizes on such behavioral techniques as modeling, feedback, and reinforcement to promote basic skill acquisition, primarily in reading and mathematics.

In **direct instruction**, as the name implies, teachers determine what students will learn and how they will learn it by directly transmitting information, skills training, and concepts. Direct instruction is used primarily and most often successfully to teach students basic skills and structured knowledge, such as phonics, reading vocabulary, grammar rules, math computation, and science facts. Teaching practices most associated with direct instruction are lectures, teacher-prepared lessons, and demonstrations. The following section explores two models for delivering knowledge through direct instruction: explicit instruction and master teaching.

Explicit Instruction

Explicit instruction Instruction that is directly focused on the improvement of learning through the mastery of basic skills.

Barak Rosenshine, an educational psychologist and researcher who specializes in teacher performance, has studied this subject for over thirty years and continues to lecture and write on direct instruction methods. Direct instruction refers to highly structured, teacher-centered strategies that capitalize on behavior techniques such as modeling, feedback, and reinforcement. **Explicit instruction**, one of the models of direct instruction, focuses on improving student learning by having students master basic skills. This methodology is commonly practiced, and it is important to know how it is implemented in the classroom. Rosenshine identifies the following six basic teaching functions that guide teaching practice.

1. Review and check the previous day's work.
2. Present new material.
3. Provide guided practice.
4. Give feedback and correctives.
5. Provide independent practice.
6. Review weekly and monthly.[16]

These teaching functions serve as a framework in which to teach basic skills using explicit instruction.

This teacher is using direct instruction to teach his class. Which type of direct instruction do you think this teacher is using?

Examples of curriculum that employ explicit instruction are:

- *Open Court Reading:* This is reading that uses systematic, explicit instruction of phonemic awareness, phonics and word knowledge, comprehension skills and strategies, inquiry skills and strategies, and writing and language arts skills and strategies.[17]
- *Distar Language:* Language for Learning provides practice in vocabulary, word and sentence variety, and development of precise word knowledge and in hard-to-teach concepts such as some/all/none and same/different.[18]

You can use these methods of instruction in a variety of ways. Language arts instruction, for example, would rely heavily on the principles of Open Court Reading. However, it is important to remember that using phonics and word knowledge is equally important in other content areas, such as science, math, and history, where students might be unfamiliar with some of the words in a text or instruction guide. Teaching good comprehension skills and strategies impacts every aspect of learning and should be implemented in any content area. Distar Language also emphasizes vocabulary comprehension, and should not be left solely to language arts teachers. All content area teachers can benefit from using Distar Language techniques as they pertain to their subject. These methods increase student comprehension and might notably affect student performance.

● **Your Turn**

Assume you are teaching third-grade students. Choose one of the following four situations: (1) making a watercolor painting of a bowl of apples, (2) writing a thank-you note for a birthday present, (3) playing a game of ping-pong, or (4) performing a science experiment (your choice of experiment). Break the situation down into (1) basic skills and structured knowledge that seem best suited to learning through methods of direct instruction and (2) other knowledge or skills that would not benefit from direct instruction.

REFLECT & WRITE

Some critics say that direct instruction stifles students and limits teacher creativity because it is systematic and scripted. What do you think? Support your answer with some examples.

_____

_____

_____

_____

_____

Mastery Teaching

Mastery teaching Teaching designed to help ensure that students learn particular skills and concepts.

Another model of direct instruction, called **mastery teaching**, was developed by Madeline Hunter. It includes the following five steps:

1. Anticipatory set—that is, using techniques to get students' minds ready to learn
2. Instruction or providing information, including modeling and checking for understanding
3. Guided practice
4. Closure or checking for performance
5. Independent practice[19]

Guided practice and independent practice are derived from different principles than the other three steps, but both relate to how learners retain information. **Guided practice** emphasizes the teacher's role in instruction, especially through modeling, or demonstrating the task or information to be learned. Once the learner is proficient in performing the task or understanding the information relayed, the learner may move on to **independent practice**. This way, the student becomes responsible for retaining the information and using it without the teacher's help.

Guided practice A teaching technique that emphasizes the teacher's role in instruction, especially through modeling, or demonstrating the task or information to be learned.

Independent practice A student's ability to retain new information and use it without the teacher's help.

Teachers use these techniques in the classroom daily. For example, say a science teacher wants to introduce the topic of cellular reproduction in her biology class. As an anticipatory set, she has her students watch an entertaining cartoon that shows cells splitting and becoming independent cells. Then she begins instruction. She will begin by introducing and explaining terms such as *mitosis*, *meiosis*, *cell division*, and so forth. To check for understanding, she asks questions related to her instruction. She will then guide the class in an experiment. When she sees that all students have successfully completed the exercise, she will give them instructions for independent practice. This may be homework, a lab, or individual or partnered exercises for a grade, which might determine their comprehension level.

WHAT ARE SOME MODELS OF NONDIRECT INSTRUCTION?

Nondirect instruction Any form of instruction that is not transmitted directly to the students by the teacher.

Nondirect instruction is any form of instruction that is not transmitted directly to the students by the teacher. The teacher's role is to structure opportunities for students to advance their own learning. Thus, nondirect instruction includes learning that students acquire on their own through reflection, experimentation, or discovery. It also includes learning that students acquire through interaction with other students in peer-mediated instruction, such as group investigation and cooperative learning.

Nondirect instruction is used primarily to provide opportunities for students to learn higher-level thinking and problem-solving skills and to assimilate content-area knowledge that is open-ended rather than basic. Further development and testing of teaching models based on nondirect instruction is a current trend in education.

Discovery Learning

Discovery learning Learning that occurs from students' efforts to discover knowledge for themselves rather than from being taught directly by a teacher.

A classic example of nondirect instruction is **discovery learning**. Discovery learning was developed during the 1960s by Jerome Bruner[20] and reflects Jean Piaget's and Lev Vygotsky's principles of instruction. Bruner was a psychologist whose work stressed the ability of humans to make sense of their surroundings, to categorize, and to learn by making connections about the world around them. Piaget advocated children's active involvement in learning activities as the primary means of promoting cognitive development.

In discovery learning, students are allowed to experiment with materials to gain new understandings and to discover information for themselves through active participation. For example, students provided with various classes of objects to roll down ramps can discover and state principles of friction and velocity.

Teaching and Learning through Social Interaction

Students' cognitive development and learning are facilitated and enhanced through their interactions with others. When students work collaboratively with more competent peers, teachers, and adults, they learn more than when they work on their own. Cooperative learning and scaffolding are ways to facilitate students' social interaction as a basis for promoting student learning.

Cooperative Learning

In cooperative learning, as noted in Chapter 1, students work together in small mixed-ability groups, sharing responsibility for their learning. Students are responsible for their own learning, for helping other group members, and for overall group success. There are now many different kinds of cooperative learning programs that have been formally developed and researched, such as Teams-Games-Tournaments (TGT), Jigsaw II, Learning Together, and Student Team Learning (STL).[21]

In a cooperative learning group, students are assigned certain roles and tasks. For example, in one program a group leader announces the learning task or problem, a praiser praises group members for their answers and work, and a checker assesses results. Group responsibilities and membership rotate as the group engages in different tasks. Students are also encouraged to develop and use interpersonal skills, such as addressing classmates by their first names, saying, "Thank you," and explaining to their group-mates why they are proposing an answer. Listening and communication skills also are enhanced. (See *In the Classroom with Rosa E. Lujan* on page 408.)

Research suggests that five basic elements are needed for cooperative learning to be successful:

- **Positive independence.** Students have to believe that they are in the learning process together and that they care about each other's learning.
- **Verbal, face-to-face interaction.** Students have to explain, argue, elaborate, and connect what they are learning now to what they learned previously.
- **Individual accountability.** All members of the group have to realize that they are responsible for their own learning.
- **Social skills.** Students must learn appropriate leadership, communication, trust-building, and conflict-resolution skills.
- **Group processing.** Group members have to assess how well they are working together and how they can do better.[22]

Research on cooperative learning is overwhelmingly positive, and cooperative approaches are appropriate for all curriculum areas.[23] Cooperative learning activities enable students to learn how to cooperate rather than compete and how to respect and learn from one another. Students also gain opportunities to learn the cooperative skills they will need later in life in the family and in the workplace. Also, cooperative learning groups are low-risk contexts in which lower-ability students can improve their skills. During cooperative learning, teachers can provide one-on-one instruction. As a teaching method, cooperative learning may not be appropriate for all learning tasks or all students. Cooperative learning activities usually require large blocks of time and must be carefully planned and evaluated to work well.

■ **INTASC**

STANDARD 1   The teacher understands the central concepts, tools of inquiry, and structures of the subjects being taught and can create learning experiences that make these aspects of subject matter meaningful for students.

■ **INTASC**

STANDARD 2   The teacher understands how children learn and develop, and can provide learning opportunities that support their intellectual, social, and personal development.

■ **INTASC**

STANDARD 5   The teacher uses an understanding of individual and group motivation and behavior to create a learning environment that encourages positive social interaction, active engagement in learning, and self-motivation.

Go to MyEducationLab and select the topic "Curriculum and Instruction" then watch the video "Cooperative Learning." Complete the activities that follow.

■ **INTASC**

STANDARD 3   The teacher understands how students differ in their approaches to learning and creates instructional opportunities that are adapted to diverse learners.

In the Classroom

with **Rosa E. Lujan**

The Classroom "Familia"

Texas Teacher of the Year Rosa E. Lujan participated in a long-term national research project on the effectiveness of cooperative learning with fifth- and sixth-grade Hispanic American students at Ysleta Elementary School in El Paso, Texas. The cooperative learning program used was Cooperative Integrated Reading and Composition (CIRC). The study showed that CIRC is an effective method for bilingual and second-language instruction as well as for monolingual instruction.

In CIRC, cooperative learning is used to follow up reading group instruction. Students work in teams containing two pairs of students from two different reading-level groups. The students take turns reading stories to one another; answer questions about the characters, setting, and plot of each story; practice new vocabulary together; help each other with reading comprehension skills and spelling; and write about the stories they have read. While the students are working in teams, the teacher provides one-on-one instruction and feedback as needed.

Rosa Lujan found many benefits of cooperative learning, including more effective use of her instructional time and of students' time on task. She adds:

> The greatest result, though, has been the increased self-esteem and achievement of my students. Even the most reluctant learner becomes actively involved in learning. Students know they are important, a part of the classroom familia. Academically, they are now reading and writing in two languages.

To learn more about the Cooperative Integrated Reading and Composition (CIRC) program, visit http://ies.ed.gov/ncee/wwc/reports/beginning_reading/circ/info.asp.

Scaffolding

Scaffolding　The teacher builds a structured learning environment through communication and provides opportunities for interaction that support modeling and learning.

Cross-age tutoring　When older students tutor younger students, with the idea that both learn from the experience of giving and receiving instruction.

Zone of proximal development　The area of development a child can achieve through social interaction with another, more competent person.

Scaffolding is another approach for facilitating learning through social interaction. It is based on the learning theory of Lev Vygotsky. Student learning can be scaffolded in several ways. You can choose activities that interest students and prepare students for activities before presenting them. For example, many teachers like to create a game that relates to a topic that they have introduced in class and have gone over with the students. This helps teachers who have done a formal assessment to gauge students' understanding. Such exercises also allow students to access what they have learned without direct aid from the teacher.

You can actively monitor activities in progress by providing immediate guidance and feedback. And, you can follow up activities with opportunities for review and reflection. Providing information as needed, suggesting where students can find information and resources, and giving hints and clues to help students think through their ideas are also good methods for scaffolding. For older students, lecture outlines and study guides can serve as scaffolds for their learning. Pairing more competent learners with less competent learners, as in cooperative learning, is an application of Vygotsky's theory of scaffolded learning in a social context.

In **cross-age tutoring**, for example, older students tutor younger students in their **zone of proximal development**. See *In the Classroom with Lev Vygotsky*. In elementary grades, fifth- and sixth-grade students might tutor kindergartners, first-graders, and second-graders. Studies show that cross-age tutoring improves the attitudes and academic achievement of both the tutor and the tutee.[24]

In the Classroom
with **Lev Vygotsky**
Teaching in the Zone

Lev Vygotsky (1896–1934), born the same year as Piaget, increasingly inspires the practice of educators. Vygotsky, a Russian psychologist, developed a theory of learning that is particularly useful in describing children's cognitive, language, and social development.

Vygotsky believed that children's mental, language, and social development is enhanced by learning that occurs through social interactions. "Learning awakens a variety of developmental processes that are able to operate only when the child is interacting with people in his environment and in collaboration with his peers. Once these processes are internalized, they become part of the child's independent developmental achievement." This is a "contextual" view of cognitive development in which learners are embedded in social contexts such as family, home, friends, and school.

Vygotsky is known for developing three key concepts about the way children learn. These concepts are the zone of proximal development, scaffolding, and collaborative learning:

- *Zone of proximal development (ZPD)* was defined by Vygotsky as "the difference between what the child can accomplish independently and what he or she can achieve in conjunction with another, more competent person. The zone is thus created in the course of social interaction." The more skilled adult builds on the competencies the child already has and presents activities that support a level of competence slightly beyond the child's current abilities.
- *Scaffolding* is the process of guiding the student's classroom learning within the zone of proximal development. The teacher builds a structured learning environment through communication and provides opportunities for interaction that support modeling and learning. These supports scaffold the learner, until the child reaches new heights in intellectual development.
- *Teacher–learner collaboration*, Vygotsky believed, is effective when the learner uses concepts acquired in the collaborative process to solve problems independently of the teacher.

Social interaction and collaboration are part of many current instructional practices, such as cooperative learning, joint problem solving, coaching, mentoring, peer-mediated learning, and other forms of assisted learning. According to Vygotsky, "Learning is a necessary part and universal aspect of the process of developing culturally organized, specifically human, psychological functions."

Learn more about Lev Vygotsky at www.psy.pdx.edu/PsiCafe/KeyTheorists/Vygotsky.htm.

Sources: L. Vygotsky, *Mind and society* (Cambridge, MA: Harvard University Press, 1978); J. R. H. Tudge (1992, December), Processes and consequences of peer collaboration: A Vygotskian analysis. *Child Development 63*(6), 1365; L. Vygotsky, *The collected works of L. S. Vygotsky: Problems of general psychology* (New York: Plenum, 1987), p. 216.

REFLECT & WRITE

Which models of direct and nondirect instruction appeal to you the most at this time? What are your reasons?

Individual Differences–Differentiated Instruction

You know from your own classroom experiences that all students are different. Think, for a moment, about the students that were with you in first grade, eighth grade, and twelfth grade, and the differences they demonstrated. All students are different, have particular learning needs, and learn differently. How do you provide for the individual learning needs of students? One approach is through **differentiated instruction (DI)**, a process of providing different learning experiences to meet students' learning needs. There are a number of approaches to differentiated instruction:

Differentiated instruction (DI)   Providing different learning opportunities for differing student needs.

- **Differentiate the content.** Ways to vary the content are to let students work at their own rates and have students who know the content go directly to application activities.
- **Differentiate the process/activities.** This is a process of varying learning activities.
- **Differentiate the product.** The product that students create to demonstrate mastery of the concepts can be varied according to student interest and choice.
- **Differentiate the environment and accommodate individual learning styles.** One way to differentiate is according to different students' learning styles.

In effective differentiated classrooms

- Teachers and students accept and respect one another's similarities and differences.
- Assessment is an ongoing diagnostic activity that guides instruction. Learning tasks are planned and adjusted based on assessment data.
- All students participate in respectful work that is challenging, meaningful, interesting, and engaging.
- The teacher is primarily a coordinator of time, space, and activities, rather than a provider of information. The aim is to help students become self-reliant workers.
- Students and teachers collaborate in setting class and individual goals.
- Students work in a variety of group configurations, as well as independently. Flexible grouping is evident.
- Time is used flexibly in the sense that pacing is varied based on student needs.
- Students often have choices about topics they wish to study, ways they want to work, and how they want to demonstrate their learning.
- The teacher uses a variety of instructional strategies to help target instruction to student needs.
- Students are assessed in multiple ways, and each student's progress is measured, at least in part, from where that student begins.[25]

In differentiated classrooms, teachers often are not the sole providers of instruction. This does not mean that teachers in such classrooms are less active; they moderate learning while providing activities and strategies for students to solve problems on their own.

■ INTASC

STANDARD 3   The teacher understands how students differ in their approaches to learning and creates instructional opportunities that are adapted to diverse learners.

■ INTASC

STANDARD 4   The teacher uses various instructional strategies to encourage students' development of critical thinking, problem solving, and performance skills.

REFLECT & WRITE

Perhaps you had a high school teacher who used differentiated instruction methods. What can you remember about the effectiveness of that teacher? How do you think you could implement some of these techniques in your future classroom?

Data-Driven Instruction

Standardized tests and other forms of assessment provide a great deal of data regarding student achievement and how students learn. One of the administrative and teaching challenges is how to capture and effectively use these data to focus teaching and increase student achievement. **Data-driven instruction** refers to the practice of using student outcomes on various measures to plan curriculum and instruction. Teachers can use data to plan diverse instructional strategies in response to the differences in how students think and learn. Data-driven instruction is being used to reform how teachers plan, teach, and assess. As a beginning teacher, it is highly likely that you will be involved in processes related to using student data to tailor-make plans and instructional activities designed to ensure that all children learn and meet state and national standards. Read again about data-driven instruction in *In the Classroom with Gary Baird*, page 392.

Data-driven instruction   The practice of using student outcomes on various measures to plan curriculum and instruction.

For an interesting look at how Lead Mine Elementary School in Raleigh, North Carolina, implemented a program of data-driven instruction, go to www.infotoday.com/ MMSchools/mar03/decker.shtml.

WHAT WILL INFLUENCE CURRICULUM IN THE TWENTY-FIRST CENTURY?

As a result of reading this chapter and other chapters in this book, you are aware that educational reform has created, and will continue to create, many changes, innovations, and new approaches regarding how teachers teach and students learn. As a beginning teacher, you will stand in the eye of the hurricane of educational reform. Without a doubt, politicians, educators, and society are radically reforming and changing education. The majority of these reforms and changes will find their permanent place in schoolhouse practice. Some of these reforms and their influences that will continue into the future are:

- **The rapid pace of radical school reform is here to stay.** The first decade of the twenty-first century will be known as the decade of rapid reform. Indeed, more educational change has occurred in the past 10 years than in the previous 50. Teachers' roles are rapidly changing and will continue to change. For example, teachers of the recent past were able to say "I taught Mario reading." Teachers of today and tomorrow will say "I taught Mario to read, he met district and state standards, and achieved at a high level."
- **The three Rs of reading, writing, and mathematics are the crown jewels in the curriculum crown.** They will continue to be the major benefactors of instructional time, funding, and testing for grades pre-K through 12.
- **Standardized testing at the district, state, and national levels is here to stay.** Tests will be used to assess student achievement, hold teachers and schools accountable, and drive instructional planning and decision making.
- **Accountability is and will be a way of life for teachers and school districts.** Accountability for all facets of the educational process will be a hallmark of education in the years to come. For example, in 2001 NCLB implemented a federal policy of standardized tests for every state in the United States. These changes are unlikely to diminish, and statewide testing is likely to increase.
- **The accountability movement has created competition among schools.** This competition for students, for performance-based dollars, and for recognition will continue. More "market-driven"

OBSERVE & LEARN

You will need to adjust or accommodate what and how you teach based on gender, ability, and disability. Observe some classrooms and take notes about how teachers accommodate or adjust their teaching for students with disabilities.

approaches—such as outsourcing of services, privatizing of schools, and choice—will be applied to schoolhouse practices.

■ **Inclusive classrooms are a reality for most teachers.** This reality means you will have to adapt your instruction to children of any gender, cultural background, socioeconomic status, or disability in your classroom.

All of these changes are designed to make education for all children a better and more meaningful experience. You should not be fearful or apprehensive about participating in any of these activities, as they will enhance your life as a professional and add value to your future as a teacher.

REFLECT & WRITE

How are you responding to the twenty-first century changes in American education? What "ah-ha!" moments are you having?

_____

_____

_____

_____

_____

_____

WHAT WORKS IN THE CLASSROOM?

Teachers work hard and spend a lot of time and effort developing plans, activities, and instructional resources to continue instruction in reading and writing effectively in the middle and secondary grades. They bring different styles and approaches to the classroom.

But, as you know from your school experiences, some teachers do a better job than others. Why is this? Judith Langer at the National Research Center on English Learning and Achievement studied a range of middle and high school English classrooms, and came up with an answer. In fact, she came up with six answers—six features that occur in effective middle and secondary English teaching. These features are applicable to most classrooms.

1. **Students learn skills and knowledge in multiple lesson types.** Teachers use a variety of different teaching approaches based on student need. For example, if students need to learn a particular skill, item, or rule, the teacher might choose a *separated* activity to highlight it. Students would study the information as an independent lesson, exercise, or drill without considering its larger meaning or use (e.g., they might be asked to copy definitions of literary terms into their notebooks and to memorize them). To give students practice, teachers prepare or find *simulated* activities that ask students to apply concepts and rules within a targeted unit of reading, writing, or oral language. To help students bring together their skills and knowledge within the context of a purposeful activity, teachers use *integrated* activities. These require students to use their skills or knowledge to complete a task or project that has meaning for them.

2. **Teachers integrate test preparation into instruction.** The knowledge and skills for performing well on high-stakes tests are made overt to both teachers and students. Teachers, principals, and district-level coordinators often create

working groups of professionals who collaboratively study the demands of the high-stakes tests their students will take. This reflection helps teachers understand the demands of the test, consider how these demands relate to their current practice, and plan ways to integrate the necessary skills and knowledge into the curriculum, across grades and school years. In addition, students learn to become reflective about their own reading and writing performance. Teachers provide students with ways to read, understand, and write in order to gain the abilities that are necessary for being highly literate for life, not merely for passing a test.

3. **Teachers make connections across instruction, curriculum, and life.** Teachers work consciously to weave a web of connections within lessons, across lessons, and to students' lives in and out of school. They make connections throughout each day, week, and year. And they point out these connections so that students can see how the skills and knowledge they are gaining can be used productively in a range of situations. Teachers also work together to redevelop and redesign curriculum. They share ideas and reflect on their work.

> Go to MyEducationLab and select the topic "Curriculum and Instruction" then read the article "You Can Teach for Meaning." Answer the questions that follow.

4. **Students learn strategies for doing the work**. It is important for students to learn not only subject matter content, but also how to think about, approach, and do their work in each subject. They provide strategies not only for how to do the task but also how to think about it. These strategies are discussed and modeled, and teachers develop reminder sheets for students to use. In this way, students learn the process for completing an assignment successfully.

5. **Students are expected to be generative thinkers**. All of the teachers in the higher-performing schools take a generative approach to student learning. They go beyond students' acquisition of skills or knowledge to engage students in creative and critical uses of their knowledge and skills. Teachers provide a variety of activities from which students will generate deeper understandings. For example, when studying literature, after the more obvious themes in a text are discussed, teachers and students together explore the text from many points of view, both from within the literary work and from life.

6. **Classrooms foster cognitive collaboration**. In higher-performing schools, students work in communicative groups, and teachers help students participate in thoughtful dialogue. Students engage in the kind of teamwork that is now so highly prized in business and industry. They bring their personal, cultural, and academic knowledge to these interactions, in which they play the multiple roles of learners, teachers, and inquirers and have opportunities to consider issues from multiple perspectives. Minds bump against minds as students interact as both problem generators and problem solvers.

REFLECT & WRITE

Teaching requires many new skills, along with the skills you have already learned. How might you incorporate Langer's six features of effective teaching into science or math teaching?

ETHICAL DILEMMA

"The Lost Arts"

MAYRA RODRIGUEZ teaches at Southwest Independent, a school with very little funding. Recently the school's administration made the decision to make major cuts to the school's art program, including the dance and theater arts program, in order to transfer more money to the school's math and reading programs. Many of Mayra's students, most of whom are from low socioeconomic backgrounds, participate in the school's dance and theater arts program. Mayra is worried that without these activities the students will become disinterested in their studies, score lower on standardized tests, and maybe even drop out of school. Mayra expressed her concerns to the school principal that the lack of arts in the curriculum will lead to a performance decrease in the very programs that are receiving more funding—math and reading; however, the principal told her that the school does not have enough money to keep these "extra" programs and that the math and the reading curricula are more important.

What should Mayra do?

SUMMARY

- Curriculum has several roles in education from explicit curriculum, the hidden curriculum, the extracurriculum, to the null curriculum. Aside from what is and is not taught in schools, the role of curriculum is influenced by history, politics, social values, and scientifically based research.

- The contemporary curriculum involves reading and language arts, science, mathematics, social studies and character education, physical education and health, and the arts. Although these subjects are standard in most public schools, educators and stakeholders are making constant efforts to reform curricula to improve American schools.

- Teachers plan and deliver instruction by creating instructional goals and learning objectives. Many teachers today are using outcome-based education and prepared curricula to aid them in their teaching.

- Teachers use direct instruction in their classrooms to successfully teach students basic skills and structured knowledge. Forms of direct instruction include explicit instruction and mastery teaching.

- Nondirect instruction is used to provide students opportunities to learn higher-level thinking and problem-solving skills. Students learn by nondirect instruction through discovery learning, social interaction, and from their own individual differences. Teachers can aid in the nondirect instruction of students by providing for the individual learning needs of students through differentiated instruction. Data-driven instruction can aid teachers in creating differentiated instruction.

- School reform, the accountability movement, and technology have heavily influenced curriculum in the twenty-first century.

- Curriculum instruction varies from teacher to teacher; however, a few features are present in most successful classrooms, such as using multiple lesson types, integrating test preparation into instruction, making connections to the curriculum that students can relate to, and teaching students to think about the subject matter as opposed to simply "doing the work."

KEY TERMS

Balanced approach to reading   393
Character education   397
Cross-age tutoring   408
Curriculum   386
Data-driven instruction   411
Differentiated instruction (DI)   410
Direct instruction   404
Discovery learning   406
Explicit curriculum   386
Explicit instruction   404

Extracurriculum   389
Guided practice   406
Hidden curriculum   387
Independent practice   406
Instructional goals   401
Learning objectives   401
Mastery teaching   406
Nondirect instruction   406
Null curriculum   387
Outcome-based education (OBE)   402

Phonics   393
Scaffolding   408
Scientifically based research (SBR)   391
Scope-and-sequence approach   401
Standards-based education   391
Whole language   393
Zone of proximal development   408

APPLICATIONS FOR ACTIVE LEARNING

Connections

1. Review Dru Tomlin's vignette about coaching. Consider how you could apply Dru's approaches using the curriculum content of this chapter.

2. As you have learned in this chapter, all teachers must develop lesson plans. Find a lesson plan that is used at a particular school or go to MyEducationLab (www .myeducationlab.com) to find ideas for creating lesson plans. Write a lesson plan for a content area that you would like to teach. Be sure to specify which state or district standards you will integrate into your lesson (see Chapter 10).

Field Experiences

1. Go online and locate the websites of nearby schools and identify teachers who you feel are doing interesting things in their classrooms that you would like to observe. Make a checklist of skills, techniques, and strategies you want to observe, including how technology is used as a teaching and learning tool in the classroom. Following your observations, annotate your list, noting what strategies and skills you found to be most effective. Place your observations in your teaching portfolio.

2. Ask teachers about their experiences with cooperative learning. What do they see as the benefits and drawbacks of this model?

Personal Research

1. Research the curriculum standards in your state or district for the grade level and content area you plan to teach. What instructional goals are expressed in this curriculum? How will you prepare to implement this curriculum? Are there parts of it that you might wish to augment, eliminate, or change? If so, how could you begin to go about doing so?

2. Add to your clipping file articles on curriculum controversies and curriculum reform initiatives in your state or in your content area. What spheres of influence have an impact on the curriculum? What concerns do public protests and reform efforts represent regarding the curriculum?

PREPARING TO TEACH

For Your Portfolio

1. Add to your portfolio artifacts from your personal research, such as curriculum guidelines and textbook selection criteria.

2. Revise your position statement on your teaching philosophy to reflect information you've gained through reading this book. Keep both versions in your portfolio as a record of your development as a beginning teacher.

Idea File

By now, you may have a pretty good idea of the grade and content area you want to teach. Even if you want to teach in the elementary grades, you must be knowledgeable in the content areas of reading, science, math, social studies, the arts, and so on. Go online and browse education journals (many are available online) to learn about different ideas and activities that you can use to teach your preferred grade and content area.

LEARNING AND KNOWING MORE

Websites Worth Visiting

Accountability is one of the major themes of schooling of the new millennium. Schools are making greater efforts to be accountable to the public for what they teach and the achievement of their students. How well schools do is a matter of public record. For example, many community newspapers make local school district report cards and analysis of student achievement results available on the World Wide Web. Access the following newspaper websites:

www.latimes.com/news/education
http://seattletimes.nwsource.com/html/education
Compare how the two school districts involved report to the community. Which one do you like the best and why?

National Science Teachers Association
www.nsta.org

The National Science Teachers Association (NSTA) is the largest organization in the world committed to promoting excellence and innovation in science teaching and learning for all.

Teaching K–8 IdeaSite
www.Teachingk-8.com

Teaching K–8 is a monthly professional magazine for kindergarten through eighth-grade teachers. This IdeaSite highlights articles in the current issue and provides new ideas and resources spanning the curriculum.

Teacher Connections Home Page
www.nytimes.com/learning/teachers/index.html

Contains the latest news featured in *The New York Times* as part of *The New York Times* Learning Network.

"What Works Clearinghouse" Office of Educational Research and Improvement, U.S. Department of Education.
http://ies.ed.gov/ncee/wwc

The What Works Clearinghouse was established by the U.S. Department of Education's Institute of Education Sciences to provide educators, policymakers, and the public with a central, independent, and trusted source of scientific evidence of what works in education.

ERIC Clearinghouse Digest
http://eric.uoregon.edu/publications/digests/digest167.html

This digest describes the generally accepted characteristics of scientifically based research and anticipated implications for school leaders.

Curriculum Archive
www.buildingrainbows.com/CA/ca.home.php

The Curriculum Archive is a central repository for free lessons and classroom projects. It is intended to be a forum for creating, distributing, and archiving education curricula for all grade levels and subject areas.

PBS Teacher Source
www.pbs.org/teachersource

This source aids teachers in using PBS resources to teach lessons and activities to their students.

Books Worth Reading

Benjamin, A. (2005). *Differentiated Instruction Using Technology: A Guide for Middle and High School Teachers.* Larchmont, NY: Eye on Education.
An easy to read and simple to implement guide that demonstrates how you can manage the complexities of differentiated instruction—and save time—by using technology as you teach. It showcases classroom-tested activities and strategies that are easy to apply in your own classroom.

Neuman, S., Roskos, K., Wright, T., and Lenhart, L. (2007). *Nurturing Knowledge: Building a Foundation for School Success by Linking Early Literacy to Math, Science, Art, and Social Studies.* Scranton, PA: Scholastic Teaching Resources.
In this comprehensive and practical resource, early literacy experts Susan Neuman and Kathy Roskos share five essential early literacy practices—creating a supportive learning environment; shared book reading; songs, rhymes, and word play; developmental writing; and play—and show how and why to apply these in math, science, social studies, and art so students acquire the knowledge and the skills they need to become successful readers and writers.

Pfeffinger, C. R. (2003). *Character Counts! Readers Theatre for Character Education.* Portsmouth, NH: Teacher Ideas Press.
This collection provides teachers with scripts to promote and reinforce character education. Each script presents a wide variety of dilemmas and situations, often drawn from true events, and includes suggestions for presentation and props.

Serafini, F. (2004). *Lessons in Comprehension: Explicit Instruction in the Reading Workshop.* Portsmouth, NH: Heinemann.
This text introduces and reinforces meaning-making concepts that scaffold understanding and responsibility for novice readers. Based on scientific-based research, each lesson within the text offers a complete framework to take you and your students from theory through guided practice and beyond.

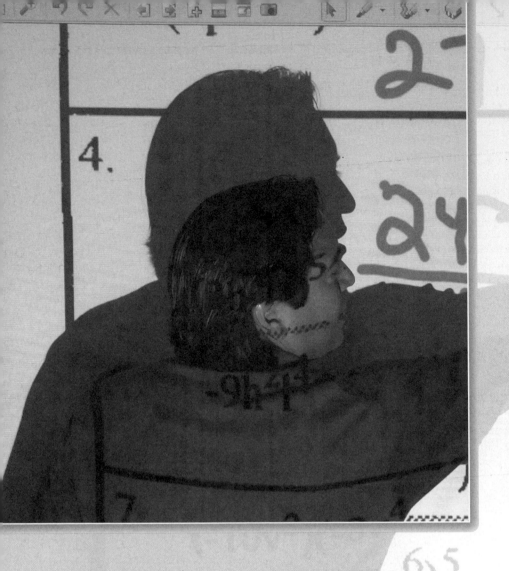

12 Technology, Teaching, and Learning

ERIC LANGHORST Think back to the class that you enjoyed the most in school. It was that one class that motivated you so much that you couldn't wait to research your assignments in the library or to tell your parents about when they asked what you did in school that day. The class periods in that subject area flew by, and you wished for more. Now think about the class that you found most difficult. No matter how hard you tried, you still needed extra help to make it through. Maybe it took you several attempts to cover the material before you really grasped it and understood the core concepts. As a teacher, it is important that you acknowledge that you have both of those students sitting in your class at any given time. It can be a challenge to try to engage the student who loves your class as you provide support to the student who is struggling. Each teacher must find a tool that will reach both ends of the spectrum—for me that tool is technology.

As you read this chapter . . .

Think about:

- How technology affects your life and our society

- How technology has changed the definition of literacy

- How advances in technology have affected teaching and learning

- The advantages and disadvantages of digital learning

- Effective teaching strategies for using technology responsibly

I started to slowly integrate technology into my eighth-grade American history classroom roughly 10 years ago; at first, I'd have a multimedia presentation once in a while and an occasional trip to the media center to check out a website. Today, I view technology as a critical tool that extends the impact of my classroom beyond the 45-minute blocks of time I have with my students. The tools and applications are readily accessible and free to teachers who are ready to expand the reach of their classroom.

Take, for example, one assignment in which we have students read the historical novel, *Guerrilla Season* by Pat Hughes, which depicts Missouri at the start of the Civil War. Over 300 students in our building read this novel at the same time and participate in a book blog—a place for discussion that is accessible 24 hours a day. We include parents, students in other states, and other participants from around the world. Most importantly, the author joins in daily from over 1,200 miles away.

> **Technology . . . allows my students to become active participants in their learning . . .**

Another way in which I have integrated technology into our curriculum is to help students prepare for upcoming tests. I record a 20-minute review of the material as an MP3 file—we call this a "StudyCast." I then post the MP3 file on the Internet and include the link on our classroom website so that students can listen directly through the computer. The StudyCast is also available as a free download from iTunes for students who want to place it on their iPods or MP3 players. I also make it available to students who do not have an Internet connection at home as an audio CD. Students have told me they find it easier to study for tests, because they can listen as they exercise, ride the bus, or mow the lawn.

Technology also allows my students to become active participants in their learning by creating a dynamic project. When we study the presidential election of 1860, for example, my students are given a mission from Abraham Lincoln himself.

Eric Langhorst is an eighth-grade American history teacher at South Valley Junior High in Liberty, Missouri, and an adjunct education professor at Park University. He produces the "Speaking of History" podcast and implements emerging technologies in his classroom. He has been awarded the 2007/2008 Missouri Teacher of the Year and the 2006 Cable Leaders in Learning Award in recognition of his use of innovative technology strategies, including blogging, podcasting, and online applications.

▶▶ Go to MyEducationLab and select the topic "Technology in the Schools," watch the video "Virtual English Course."

Students are told that Lincoln has hired them to produce a 60-second TV ad to help him win the presidency. Students use free and accessible video-editing software to create the commercial, which they produce after they have researched and developed a deep understanding of the candidates' issues.

The use of emerging technologies such as blogging, podcasting, wikis, and online simulations have the potential to make your curriculum more exciting and engaging to your students. The students in my class who love history have the opportunity to learn more through extracurricular activities, and students who struggle are provided additional support in the form of digital copies of notes and resources. Reaching both of these kinds of students is probably the most difficult challenge I have as an educator, and technology has helped me accomplish this task.

WHAT IS TECHNOLOGY?

Y ou've checked your email, which included a reminder that your antivirus software is about to expire and pictures of your parents' vacation; posted the results of your "What should I name my new puppy?" survey on MySpace.com; uploaded a video that you recorded with your cell phone of your puppy chasing birds at the park; downloaded that great new song to your MP3 player; and paid your cell phone bill. Now it is time to get to work. You log onto the campus e-learning platform and check your to-do list. There is a new thread on your biology class discussion board and a link to an article about genetic research on autism to read for the next F2F; you got an A on last week's exam—reviewing those podcast lectures really paid off. DING. You have an IM from Sam . . . *R U ther?* . . . *HOAS.* You upload your summary for chapter 3 and text back *MEt me 4 lch . . . dun b l8!* You set the DVR to record your favorite show, grab your cell phone, and text Sam, *b ther n a min.*

Today, every area of society is affected and influenced by technology. Although technology can be defined as the application of scientific, mechanical, material, and human resources to address human needs, its role goes beyond that as it expands into the social and pedagogical realm.

Computers and computer-based technology continue to have an explosive impact on the economy, health care, government, and education. In the health care arena, electronic medical records, better diagnostic tools, and the ability to access all the data necessary to make the right decision have improved the quality of care, reduced medical errors, and prevented deaths. Candidates in the 2008 presidential election participated in the first ever online-only debates. The computer and the Internet have become integral tools in U.S. classrooms, literally putting information at our fingertips. We have moved from leafing through traditional hardback encyclopedias and other resource books to logging on and "googling" a topic.

Since the World Wide Web became available in 1994, the Internet has become a source of entertainment, information, and communication. According to the 2007 Digital Future Project, more than three-quarters of Americans age 12 and older go online, and more than two-thirds use the Internet at home. Faster broadband connections and greater availability of service have contributed to the use of the Internet as a growing tool for personal engagement through social networking with online communities.[1]

Technological changes over the past several decades have been rapid, widespread, and influential in changing how schools operate, how teachers teach, and how students learn. Nearly all U.S. schools have high-speed Internet access. Federal aid for disadvantaged schools has provided billions of dollars for equipment and training to get everyone up to speed on the information highway.[2] But there is more to learn about technology than merely using it to get class assignment information off the Internet. This is where you enter the picture. Perhaps you are wondering what your role will be as a teacher in the technological future and how you will use technology to help you and your students learn. One thing is certain: Technology is playing a major role in how students learn and what they learn.

Today's teacher must be technologically literate and capable of integrating technology into the teaching-learning process. (See *In the Classroom with Dr. James Distler.*) Many of today's classrooms have laptop computers, handheld computers, smart phones, LCD projectors, digital e-books, podcasting tools, and multimedia

■ **INTASC**

STANDARD 3 The teacher understands how students differ in their approaches to learning and creates instructional opportunities that are adapted to diverse learners.

In the Classroom
with **Dr. James Distler**

Using Robots to Inspire Young Minds

Dr. James Distler is an engineering teacher at Montgomery Blair High School in Maryland.

James Distler believes students need options—options for how to spend their time and educational options to hook kids into learning. "You'll either get them into the positive stuff, or they'll get into the negative," he explained. To help open doors for students in Montgomery County, Distler started a program that teaches children about engineering by designing robots built out of Legos.

Distler brought the event to South Lake Elementary School in Montgomery Village and Monocacy Elementary School in Poolesville as a summer program.

His annual elementary robotics event for the children of the Blair community attracts a great deal of attention and is eagerly anticipated by the community.

The program uses Lego Mindstorm robotics kits, which cost about $200 each. The cost for the 2-week program is $210, which helps pay the student and adult supervisors and buys some equipment and snacks, Distler said. The robots are self-contained battery-operated computers that can be programmed to do a variety of tasks, such as going up ramps, climbing walls, and catching and throwing balls. Once the task is chosen, a nearby corresponding desktop computer sends out directions from a remote-controllike transmitter.

Students at South Lake were programming their trucklike robots to follow a path outlined on a table with masking tape. The robots used lasers to determine where the line was and then follow it.

Nivetita Ravi, a rising fourth-grader at South Lake, said the program has taught her about gears, programming, and building and has helped teach her new vocabulary words.

Janhvi Barthwal, a rising sixth-grader, said she decided to participate because she was interested in robots and how they work. She said she enjoys programming them to do what she tells them.

Despite the fact that all of the children in the program at South Lake are gifted and talented students, Distler emphasized that the program is open to everyone. The engineering program is about much more than just how to build and program robots. Distler said he makes a point of talking to the kids about school and how to treat others with respect.

The program is an offshoot of Distler's Career Exploration and Mentoring Program, which he started when he was a teacher at Takoma Park Middle School. There, Distler helped get the school's technology program off the ground and began teaching industrial arts to students after school. The group learned how to use tools and build birdhouses, among other skills; the program grew from 5 or 6 students to 180.

Distler left Takoma Park Middle School to begin teaching at Blair in 2000, and it was then he decided to train high school students in both robotics and mentoring skills and let them teach younger students. This way, Distler said, younger children will get an enrichment option and older kids can earn a little money.

"I want to spread the joy—I want to spread the enthusiasm," Distler said. Learn more about Lego Mindstorm robotics at http://mindstorms.lego.com/default.aspx?domainredir=www.legomindstorms.com.

Source: Stanley, B. W. (2004). Robot-building program helps to inspire young minds. *Gazette.net*. Online. Available at www.gazette.net/gazette_archive/2004/200431/montgomery/news/228111-1.html. Accessed December 6, 2007.

applications. Like you, today's "plugged in" students use computers for journaling, instant messaging, sharing photos, and playing games. Are you ready to develop and implement technology-rich activities and projects that meet current curriculum and technology standards? Assess your technology skills using Figure 12.1.

STANDARD 1—TECHNOLOGY OPERATIONS AND CONCEPTS

Teachers demonstrate a sound understanding of technology operations and concepts.

STANDARD 2—PLANNING AND DESIGNING LEARNING ENVIRONMENTS AND EXPERIENCES

Teachers plan and design effective learning environments and experiences supported by technology.

STANDARD 3—TEACHING, LEARNING, AND THE CURRICULUM

Teachers implement curriculum plans that include methods and strategies for applying technology to maximize student learning.

STANDARD 4—ASSESSMENT AND EVALUATION

Teachers apply technology to facilitate a variety of effective assessment and evaluation strategies.

STANDARD 5—PRODUCTIVITY AND PROFESSIONAL PRACTICE

Teachers use technology to enhance their productivity and professional practice.

STANDARD 6—SOCIAL, ETHICAL, LEGAL, AND HUMAN ISSUES

Teachers understand the social, ethical, legal, and human issues surrounding the use of technology in pre-K–12 schools and apply that understanding in practice.

FIGURE 12.1 Technology Standards for Teachers

While the technological tools we have available to us may change, these six standards will remain.

Source: International Society for Technology in Education, *National Education Technology Standards for Teachers—Preparing Teachers to Use Technology* (Washington, D.C.: International Society for Technology in Education, 2002). Reprinted by permission.

 REFLECT & WRITE

Compare your skills with those listed in Figure 12.1. How do you stack up? What technology skills will you have to work on to be prepared to integrate technology into your classroom?

WHAT IS TECHNOLOGICAL LITERACY?

Technology is changing society, and in the process it is changing the goals of education, what it means to be educated, and the meaning of literacy. Literacy is considered to be the foundation of American democracy and fundamental to success in work and life. In the digital age, individuals not only have to be able to read, write, listen, and speak, they also need to learn to use technology to be truly literate.

The federal government and advocates of **technological literacy** agree that all students must have experience with and become proficient with a wide range of

Technological literacy The ability to understand and apply technology to meet personal goals.

available resources. According to the North Central Regional Education Laboratory, students who are technologically literate:

- Demonstrate a sound conceptual understanding of the nature of technology systems and view themselves as proficient users of these systems
- Understand and model positive, ethical use of technology in both social and personal contexts
- Use a variety of technology tools in effective ways to increase creative productivity
- Use communication tools to reach out to the world beyond the classroom and communicate ideas in powerful ways
- Use technology effectively to access, evaluate, process, and synthesize information from a variety of sources
- Use technology to identify and solve complex problems in real-world contexts[3]

To access and use the Internet and other communication technologies, both teachers and students must be technologically literate. Although many of today's students are technologically savvy in many ways, they must be carefully guided toward reputable and respected resources. Teachers must motivate and guide students as they encounter vast amounts of information from a variety of sources.

The challenge for today's teachers and students is to keep up with the rapid changes in order to stay technologically literate. Technology is moving toward being fully integrated throughout the curriculum, just as technology is being integrated into all facets of society. Just as teachers have been teaching students to find and use reliable information when conducting research, the same standards should be required when using the Internet as a resource. Just as teachers of the past have insisted on ethical behavior and the responsible use of information, the same is expected of students today. Today, however, responsible use and ethical behavior might be more of a challenge, because it is more difficult for students to identify which information is reliable and which is not. Teachers and students must use critical thinking and analytical skills to sort fact from error, truth from fiction, and clarity from distortion. Almost anyone can publish information on the Internet, but that does not mean that it is valid or true. Students must understand how technology influences what and how they learn now and in the future. Once armed with this information, teachers then work with students to evaluate and arrange information using print, video, audio, and graphic formats in visually appealing ways.[4]

Go to MyEducationLab and select the topic "Technology in the Schools" then read the article "Making Sense of Online Text." Answer the questions that follow.

REFLECT & WRITE

How do you measure up to the standards for technological literacy? Could you stay ahead of your students in this area? If your answer is no, what could you do to improve?

Technological Divides

Discussions continue about the "great divide" that exists between the technological haves and the technological have-nots. The metaphor that comes to mind is a gulf we must bridge by laying optic cables to connect one side to the other.

Today's world is fast-paced and technology-dependent, making technical fluency necessary. How technologically fluent do you consider yourself? Do you think most schools are prepared to address today's technology needs?

■ **INTASC**

STANDARD 3 The teacher understands how students differ in their approaches to learning and creates instructional opportunities that are adapted to diverse learners.

For more information about TIP, see www.txtip.info/.

Peer networking Using the Internet to enable and enhance professional communication and collaboration.

Videoconferencing Using audio and video telecommunications to bring people at different sites together for a meeting.

This conception of the "great divide" is incomplete; there is not one digital divide, but rather many technological divides that separate students from teachers, teachers from students, schools from schools, and communities from communities. A more appropriate metaphor to explain the technological disparities and inequalities that exist is a split computer cable with many different wires representing different technological divides. The goal is to connect the breaks in this metaphoric cable by providing high-quality equipment, software, Internet access, and appropriate use for all students.

A decade ago, the major focus of education policy was on equipping all schools to access to the information superhighway. To ensure that no child was left behind, the federal government created the E-rate program, which provided aid to disadvantaged schools for the purchase of equipment and services to help them get up to speed. When the program began in 1997, less than two-thirds of U.S. public schools had Internet access and only 14 percent of those had connections on classroom computers. Today, virtually all schools have high-speed Internet access.[5]

Although students of all levels of family income have the opportunity to use computers at school, a substantial gap exists in computer use at home. In a 2006 statistical report of student computer use, students in the lowest income bracket (under $20,000) used computers at home less than half that of students in the highest income bracket ($75,000 or more). Although policymakers and school districts work to provide computer and Internet access for all students in the classroom, it is increasingly difficult to level the playing field when students in the highest income bracket use computers at home as well as in school.[6] In an effort to close the school-home computer gap, the federal government has initiated the Technology Immersion Pilot project, or TIP, which provides laptop computers to students and teachers in select districts. This program, which uses a concept of immersion to immerse students and faculty in the use of technology, has shown encouraging results, including improved school–home communication, reduced discipline referrals, and increased academic progress.[7]

Technology can also help to improve teacher education in rural areas, which often have difficulty attracting and keeping talented math and science teachers. Through a federal grant, the Western Governors University (WGU) offers Web-based courses to assist teachers working toward advanced degrees in remote locations, such as the San Juan School District in Utah.[8]

The State Educational Technology Directors Association (SETDA) released findings from nine states—West Virginia, Texas, Iowa, Arkansas, Maine, North Carolina, Pennsylvania, Tennessee, and Wisconsin—that received a total of $15 million from the federal government to study the impact of educational technology on student achievement. These states reported that professional development in technology is a major spending priority. The pace of change requires teachers to continually "hit the refresh key" in order to keep up with available equipment and applications. For example, a statewide professional development program in Iowa provided training in **peer networking** and **videoconferencing** to improve teacher practice. As a result, fourth-grade math and reading scores have increased by an average of 13 to 14 percent.[9]

Technology and Standards of Learning

In a unique partnership with educators, industry leaders, and policymakers, the International Society for Technology in Education (ISTE) has created National Educational Technology Standards (NETS) for students, teachers, and administrators. The standards for students are listed in Figure 12.2. These standards are foundational, representing both the essential and the minimum that students need to be technologically literate.

Almost all states have implemented technology education as a distinct subject or have embedded it into other curriculum areas. Michigan was the first to require that every student take part in some type of online learning experience as a high school diploma requirement. Moreover, states are increasingly requiring annual testing to ensure that students know how to learn effectively and live productively in our increasingly digital world.[10]

• Your Turn

In an interview for your first teaching job, you are asked to give three examples of how you will integrate technology into your teaching. How will you respond?

---

1. CREATIVITY AND INNOVATION

Students demonstrate creative thinking, construct knowledge, and develop innovative products and processes using technology. Students:

- Apply existing knowledge to generate new ideas, products, or processes.
- Create original works as a means of personal or group expression.
- Use models and simulations to explore complex systems and issues.
- Identify trends and forecast possibilities.

2. COMMUNICATION AND COLLABORATION

Students use digital media and environments to communicate and work collaboratively, including at a distance, to support individual learning and contribute to the learning of others. Students:

- Interact, collaborate, and publish with peers, experts, or others employing a variety of digital environments and media.
- Communicate information and ideas effectively to multiple audiences using a variety of media and formats.
- Develop cultural understanding and global awareness by engaging with learners of other cultures.
- Contribute to project teams to produce original works or solve problems.

3. RESEARCH AND INFORMATION FLUENCY

Students apply digital tools to gather, evaluate, and use information. Students:

- Plan strategies to guide inquiry.
- Locate, organize, analyze, evaluate, synthesize, and ethically use information from a variety of sources and media.
- Evaluate and select information sources and digital tools based on the appropriateness for specific tasks.
- Process data and report results.

4. CRITICAL THINKING, PROBLEM-SOLVING, & DECISION MAKING

Students use critical thinking skills to plan and conduct research, manage projects, solve problems and make informed decisions using appropriate digital tools and resources. Students:

- Identify and define authentic problems and significant questions for investigation.
- Plan and manage activities to develop a solution or complete a project.
- Collect and analyze data to identify solutions and/or make informed decisions.
- Use multiple processes and diverse perspectives to explore alternative solutions.

5. DIGITAL CITIZENSHIP

Students understand human, cultural, and societal issues related to technology and practice legal and ethical behavior. Students:

- Advocate and practice safe, legal, and responsible use of information and technology.
- Exhibit a positive attitude toward using technology that supports collaboration, learning, and productivity.
- Demonstrate personal responsibility for lifelong learning.
- Exhibit leadership for digital citizenship.

6. TECHNOLOGY OPERATIONS AND CONCEPTS

Students demonstrate a sound understanding of technology concepts, systems, and operations. Students:

- Understand and use technology systems.
- Select and use applications effectively and productively.
- Troubleshoot systems and applications.
- Transfer current knowledge to learning of new technologies.

FIGURE 12.2   National Educational Technology Standards for Students: The Next Generation

After reviewing the list, ask yourself if your school or classroom curriculum meets these standards.

Source: International Society for Technology in Education, *National Educational Technology Standards for Students* (June 2007). (Online). Available at: www.iste.org.

REFLECT & WRITE

Do you think it is realistic for students to meet the ISTE standards? Should students be required to participate in online learning before they complete high school?

_____

_____

_____

_____

_____

HOW HAS TECHNOLOGY CHANGED TEACHING AND LEARNING?

Throughout history, technology has changed how people communicate and interact with language. From the first human writing to the first printing press, which allowed books and other texts to be produced more cheaply and more widely than ever before, the written and printed word has transformed how humans teach and learn. With the advent of the computer, which allowed more information to be processed ever more quickly, the evolution continued and then exploded as the Internet and other information and communication technologies surfaced. This communication transformation continues to change the landscape of schooling at an exceedingly rapid pace.

REFLECT & WRITE

Think back to when you started high school. How has the role of technology changed the way you learn? How do you anticipate it will change for your future students?

_____

_____

_____

_____

_____

Innovations in Instructional Devices

Web log, or blog An online diary or journal providing commentary or news on a particular subject, such as a period in history or a favorite author; or a personal space for posting observations, thoughts, and reflections.

The instructional equipment found in most U.S. classrooms has changed dramatically over the past decade. Keyboards are replacing pencil and paper, newly constructed schools have interactive whiteboards instead of chalkboards, and teachers no longer rely on film for video and audio presentations. High-tech tools might be changing the way classrooms look, but experts fear that the majority of educators still rely on the traditional tools they are most familiar with. Tim Wilson, author of "The Savvy Technologist," a **web log**, or **blog,** for educators who are integrating technology into their instruction, believes that many teachers use technology only when absolutely necessary.[11] He and other technology specialists work hard to train and support classroom teachers in integrating technology into their lesson plans.

This student is using the Internet to communicate with other students in his home town, state, across the nation, and around the world.

The following are some of the latest technologies available for use in the classroom:

- Handheld computers, such as personal digital assistants (PDA) or **smartphones**, can be used for instruction, assessment, and administrative tasks. Eighth-grade algebra teacher Mark Pukys knows in an instant if his students understand a math concept. Every student has a TI-Navigator personal response calculator, which electronically collects and transmits answers so Mr. Pukys knows how many students got the right one. He can then assess students' academic progress and adjust instruction accordingly.[12]

- **Interactive whiteboards** are digital wall panels connected to computers that respond to the touch of a wireless pointer or pen. Students in the University Liggett School in Grosse Point Woods, Michigan, answer Jeopardy-like questions to test their knowledge of science concepts, such as magnetism, and use individual wireless devices to record their choices. Before wireless interactive systems became available, teachers had to stay close to the computer to tap keys or click the mouse.[13]

- Multimedia presentations in the classroom are not new, but now teachers can access digital videos on classroom computers from websites. Many districts, such as the nation's twenty-fifth largest district, Maryland's Baltimore County Public Schools, have done away with media libraries of DVDs and CDs and have installed **video-on-demand servers** that allow teachers to choose from more than a thousand program segments that can be integrated into classroom lessons.[14] Students are producing their own segments, too. High school students in Miami's Broward Schools can participate in a student-produced news program shown on the district's television station, BECON-TV. With guidance from teachers, they plan, write, film, and edit the stories.[15]

- Students can use portable MP3 players to listen to audio books, foreign language lessons, and teacher-created **podcasts** while on the go. Ipsos, a Market research firm, reports that more than half of all teens own a portable MP3 player. Though few use the device for educational purposes, many teens listen to music to help them concentrate while they study.[16]

Many of these innovative technologies enable teachers to better meet the needs of diverse learners. See *What's New in Education?* on page 428 to learn about a program that helps teachers to bring technology into the classroom so that they can help all students, including those with disabilities, reach their potential.

Smartphone   A mobile phone with computer and Internet capabilities, such as a screen, an operating system, and Internet and e-mail connections.

Interactive whiteboards   A device that interacts with a computer to display anything that can be presented on a computer monitor.

Video-on-demand server   A system that allows connected users to select and watch videos over a network as part of an interactive television system.

Podcasts   An audio and/or video file that can be downloaded from the Internet and listened to on a computer's media player or on an MP3 player.

What's *New* in Education?

Qwest Foundation Learning Technology Grants

High-tech equipment helps students with disabilities reach their potential, but paying for assistive technology can be a challenge. Salt Lake County students in Michelle Tanner's class for the Deaf and the Blind at Gerald Wright Elementary in Utah now have the use of iPods as a result of the Qwest Foundation Learning Technology Grants. In the past, Tanner recorded herself on videotapes that were sent home so parents could help students with vocabulary lessons. The process was cumbersome and often failed, because some parents did not have a VCR at home. Podcasting gives her, and her students and their parents, greater flexibility.

Another example of how Qwest grant funds brought state-of-the-art equipment to the Salt Lake County school district can be seen in Laurel Steele's eighth-grade classroom at Bryant Middle School. Her students now have an interactive whiteboard that helps them to take a closer look at how science really works. For example, when studying the concept of momentum, they watch an image of a bouncing ball and view a corresponding chart that tracks how the energy of the ball changes as it hits the ground and bounces back.

The Qwest Teachers and Technology grant program is a unique opportunity for educators to bring technology into the classroom and help students to succeed. Each year the Qwest Foundation receives hundreds of grant applications from teachers who want to use technology in new and innovative ways to improve student performance.

Source: E. Stewart "Classrooms go high-tech," *Deseret Morning News*, March 6, 2007.

REFLECT & WRITE

What types of technology do you find most helpful to you as a student? How will you incorporate that into your own teaching?

_____

_____

_____

_____

Educational Technology Resources

User-created content tools Media content produced by end users (e.g., students and teachers) as opposed to traditional media producers (publishers), which encourages self-publishing and interactions with other people's postings.

Wiki A communal, subject-specific website where users are free to add or edit content.

Web 2.0 The second generation of applications for Internet technology where users create and share information.

Teachers and students can share responsibility for researching and developing educational resources and materials with **user-created content tools,** such as blogs, **wikis,** and multimedia software. **Web 2.0** refers to the second generation of applications for Internet technology where users create and share information rather than just retrieve it. For example, a class in Texas can get together with a class in Ohio and write a book by switching off chapters—one class writes chapter 1, the other writes chapter 2, and so on. Or, the classes could edit and revise each other's work.

More than 1 billion people are connected to the Internet, and a new blog is created almost every minute. According to Will Richardson, the author of a how-to manual to help teachers make the most of Web 2.0, students must learn how to manage the flood of available information in order to survive in the global community. Students are learning to use these tools with or without the help of educators. Richardson believes that user-created content has the power to transform the culture of teaching and learning and offers the potential to develop self-motivated, lifelong learners.[17] Read more about Will Richardson and Web 2.0 in *In the Classroom with Will Richardson.*

In the Classroom
with **Will Richardson**
Web 2.0

Will Richardson learned about the power of blogs in 2002 at Hunterdon Central Regional High School in Flemington, New Jersey. Richardson was an English teacher at the time, looking for a way to expand dialogue outside the classroom about *The Secret Life of Bees* by Sue Monk Kidd. He decided to set up a blog so students could post their thoughts about the book and set up one for parents to join the discussion, too. Then he took his idea one step further and asked Kidd to join in on the blog conversation and share her inspiration for the book. She did and posted a 2,300-word response, telling the students that their insights had taught her about her own book. From that point on, blogs became a staple of every class Richardson taught. He was sold on the power of blogs to foster dialogue at a whole new level of transparency and range.

Richardson is now an educational technology consultant and shares what he has learned about blogs, wikis, podcasts, and other Web tools in workshops around the nation. He says, "The Internet isn't about technology anymore." He encourages educators to get on board with technological literacy and to engage students as active content producers. According to Richardson, the Internet is no longer just a source of information; it is also a learning environment, capable of connecting users from around the globe, where students can share interests and express themselves.

A self-confessed "blogvangelist," Richardson has made it his mission to convert educators to his viewpoint. He believes the Internet has the power to created self-motivated learners and prepares them for the real world. Students will learn about and use these tools, with or without the help of their teachers. Learn more about using blogs to enhance your teaching at http://blogs4teachers.com.

Source: P. McCloskey, "The Blogvangelist," *Teacher Magazine*, October 1, 2007.

REFLECT & WRITE

How will you use Web 2.0 applications for self-publishing to share student projects, post lesson plans, and encourage student interaction online?

Another technological resource garnering respect among educators is computer-based video games. No longer seen as time-wasters that get in the way of learning, games are now viewed as a way to make schools more engaging for the current generation of students who cannot remember a world without cell phones, computers, and the Internet.[18] Today's video games are slick and sophisticated, with high-quality graphics and simulated scenarios, which students interact with as they seek information, problem-solve, make decisions, and

■ **INTASC**

STANDARD 10 The teacher fosters relationships with school colleagues, parents, and agencies in the larger community to support students' learning and well-being.

Edutainment   Software programs designed to educate as well as entertain.

Augmented reality   An environment that includes both virtual reality and real-world elements.

Massively multiplayer educational games   Brings many players together in activities that are sometimes collaborative and sometimes competitive, with specific educational objectives.

evaluate consequences. For example, *Restaurant Empire* by Enlight Software is a simulation-style video game that requires students to build and successfully manage a restaurant. Teachers report using this game with high school economics classes and junior high social studies classes. Students gain an understanding not only of the concepts of profit and loss, but also come to realize that business ownership depends on meeting the cultural needs of the neighborhood and attention to customer service.[19] Once called **edutainment**, video games are now thought to provide rich learning experiences that can be used in innovative and engaging ways to support learning.

Two emerging trends, which are expected to have a huge impact on educational technology over the next few years, are **augmented reality** and **massively multiplayer educational games**. These applications allow students to collaborate and compete as they work through challenging obstacles and rely on higher-order thinking, creativity, math, and literacy skills to formulate answers.

REFLECT & WRITE

Do you play any computer-based video games? Do you believe they can be effective educational tools?

_____

_____

_____

_____

Online Communication

One of the most efficient uses of the Internet is for paperless communication. Years ago, when the fax machine was first used to transmit paper documents over a telephone line, it seemed like magic. Now, many businesses can operate mostly without paper, saving money, time, and trees. Schools, such as the Dallastown Area School District in Pennsylvania, are moving toward electronic operations and saving taxpayers thousands of dollars. The Dallastown school district began going paperless slowly, converting school board documents, informational items, and reports to electronic media. Today, teachers no longer receive a paper stub if they have their paycheck deposited electronically; stubs can be seen over a secure website. This saves time and money, because stuffing envelopes and money for postage are no longer required. The district estimates a savings of more than $65,000 each year on paper alone.[20]

What does going paperless mean for school district residents, parents, and students? Newsletters, cafeteria menus, and other correspondence can be read quickly and at any time if users have the ability to access the Internet from home. However, what about families that do not have access to the Internet? Park Associates, a technology market research firm, reported that of the 29 percent of U.S. homes without Internet access, about 14 percent of parents from these homes are able to access the Internet at work. Almost half of those 31 million families said they saw little use for the Internet in the home and had no plans to get it.[21]

These statistics indicate that we are well on our way to being a paperless society. However, teachers must use a variety of communication venues to reach as many parents as possible. Although technology offers promising avenues for distributing information and quick and frequent parent-teacher contact, teachers must be aware of which families have access and which families do not. They must also offer hard-copy alternatives to their online communications.

Communication and interaction with parents is a primary goal of schools and teachers. District and school Web pages are an excellent way to inform, involve, and collaborate with parents and families. E-mail features enable parents to communicate with administrators and teachers, provide Web resources (e.g., help with homework), and publish student work. Websites also contain school "report cards," as required by No Child Left Behind.

The millions of American families who do have access to the Internet can benefit from the rich assortment of ways parents and teachers can exchange and gain information. Websites directed to parents contain resources for tutoring and extending learning activities. In addition, parents who choose to home school their children now have ready access to a wealth of curriculum sources and a way to connect with other home school families. As parents and students become more comfortable with online capability for education, teachers must do a better job of communicating with families about the positive benefits of integrating technology into everyday activities.

REFLECT & WRITE

In what ways can technology, such as the Internet, support the family-school partnership, which is critical to students' school success?

Computers and Young Children

The National Association for the Education of Young Children (NAEYC) and early childhood professionals recognize that technology has reshaped children's lives and the process of learning and development. Software designed for infants, toddlers, and preschoolers, such as those from the Learning Company and Knowledge Adventure, are engaging and can be part of a positive introduction to early math and literacy concepts. Even so, not everyone agrees that such software is developmentally appropriate.[22] The NAEYC emphasizes that a computer is a tool, just like a book or a crayon, which can be used to supplement activities known to promote child development, such as shared book reading, art, blocks, and dramatic play.[23] Parents and educators should consider the following guidelines when using computers with young children:

- Monitor what young children are doing on the computer and the Internet. Just as young children should not cross the street alone, adults must supervise children with computers.
- Establish guidelines for how long young children can use the computer or Internet. Decide what programs or websites children can access.
- As with most activities for young children, interaction with a responsive adult will enhance the educational value of experiences with technology. Keep the computer in an area where children can ask and receive help as they are learning new skills.

Research has proven that adult-child interaction improves learning.[24] Most of the software for young children includes a recommendation that parents join their child at the computer to enhance the learning experience.

REFLECT & WRITE

If software for young children is used as recommended by the manufacturer, which do you think provides the best educational experience, a computer game or adult-child interaction?

_____
_____
_____
_____
_____

Supporting the Learning of Students with Special Needs

Assistive technology   Any item, device, or piece of equipment or product system used to assist individuals with disabilities.

Assistive technology covers a wide range of products and applications from simple devices, such as adaptive spoons and switch-adapted battery-operated toys, to complex devices, such as computerized environmental control systems. You will

Today's students come from an increasingly diverse range of backgrounds and have many varied special needs. Assistive technology is particularly important for students with physical and learning disabilities. Technology not only can provide the means to expand these students' physical capabilities—such as speech, hearing, and mobility—but can play a crucial role in helping them learn and interact socially.

have opportunities to use many forms of assistive technology and modified educational software with all ages of students with special needs.

Assistive technology is particularly important for students with disabilities who depend on technology to help them communicate, learn, and be mobile. For example, closed circuit television can be used to enlarge print, a braille printer can convert words to braille, and audiotaped instructional materials can be provided for students with vision impairments. Closed captioned television and FM amplification systems can assist students who are deaf or hard of hearing. Touch-screen computers, augmentative communication boards, and voice synthesizers can assist students with limited mobility or with disabilities that make communication difficult. In addition, computer-assisted instruction provides software tools for teaching students at all ability levels, including programmed instruction for students with specific learning disabilities. (See also the discussion in Chapter 5.)

Go to MyEducationLab and select the topic "Technology in the Schools" then watch the video "An Adaptive Keyboard." Complete the activities that follow.

WHAT ARE THE ADVANTAGES AND DISADVANTAGES OF DIGITAL LEARNING?

As a beginning teacher, you will be faced with a number of issues related to the uses of technology and will be involved in many decisions regarding how to use technology. You will likely play an advocacy role in promoting access to technology for you and your students. (See *In the Classroom with Mark Piotrowski* on page 434.)

Ensuring Equitable Access to Technology

All students must have equitable access to technology that is appropriate for them. Although some might think it a worthy goal to have all students spend the same amount of time on a computer, students' needs and abilities vary. Some students might have to spend more time to master the objectives of their particular grade and subject, whereas others might not need as much time or might prefer other ways to learn.

Equity issues affect how you, as a teacher, approach your students' needs to learn how to use relevant technology to become technologically literate. If one group, socioeconomic class, or gender is more comfortable with, skillful with, and proficient in the use of technology, inequities and technological illiteracy can result. Digital equity is more than an equal distribution of equipment and services; it is ensuring that all students have equal access and opportunity to use technology in order to increase their knowledge, skills, and awareness.

As mentioned earlier, today virtually all schools have computers and access to the Internet. The U.S. Census Bureau reports that there is about one computer for every four students in our nation's classrooms.[25] This is great news, and it shows the value our society places on technology. Yet, many students only have access to technology in one place—school. The majority of these students are from families in poverty and from families where the parents do not have a high school education. Students from families with high incomes are more than twice as likely to use a computer at home than those from lower-income families. Likewise, significantly more white students than black or Latino students use computers at home. Figures 12.3 and 12.4 show the percentage of students in K–12 using computers at home by family income and race, respectively.

■ INTASC

STANDARD 3 The teacher understands how students differ in their approaches to learning and creates instructional opportunities that are adapted to diverse learners.

In the Classroom

with **Mark Piotrowski**

Using Technological Skills to Change the Culture after School

Mark Piotrowski teaches technology education at Lower Merion High School in Ardmore, Pennsylvania. He has been recognized by Who's Who Among America's Teachers and recently received the High School Teacher Excellence Award from the International Technology Education Association.

The Technology Engineering Club at Lower Merion High School (LMHS) in Ardmore, Pennsylvania, offers students the opportunity to participate in the Technology Student Association (TSA) (www.TSAweb.org) and FIRST Robotics (www.USFIRST.org); both offer students a variety of opportunities to develop their technological literacy. The main focus of the Technology Engineering Club is to help students develop and use their technological skills and knowledge to improve the school, community, and world in which they live. The club currently has over 60 student members, with five teacher-advisors certified in science, technology education, math, communications, and English.

Students become well versed in the technological problem-solving process as they design and create diverse systems to enter for competition at the regional, state, and national levels. The TSA offers over 40 different competitive events in categories such as animatronics, architecture, biotechnology, computer-aided design, and more. FIRST Robotics offers students the opportunity to design and build robots to perform specific tasks within a "coopertition" environment, which involves cooperating with student teams from different schools.

In its sixth year, the LMHS Technology Engineering Club has been recognized nationally, winning numerous awards for students' technical designs. Students of all grades, learning styles, and levels enjoy the challenge of using their skills and knowledge in creative ways. However, the greatest benefit for students has been developing their awareness of the social and environmental implications of using technology and seeing how they can use their skills and knowledge to have positive impacts. The students are required to participate in at least one community service project where they use their abilities in the school and community. The response has been so positive that students actually seek out opportunities for community service and make suggestions for additional projects.

Teacher-advisors offer intense leadership training for students to become club officers; these officers then serve to not only sustain the club, but also to affirm and maintain its vision. Many of its graduates go on to pursue degrees and careers in science, technology, engineering, and mathematics-related fields. For the teacher-advisors, it gives them the opportunity to get to know the students in a relaxed and fun after-school environment. Learn more about incorporating technology in the classroom by visiting www.techlearning.com.

REFLECT & WRITE

How will you ensure that software aimed at helping you teach a diverse population will respect and help preserve that which is unique and special about your students' ethnic heritages and cultural differences?

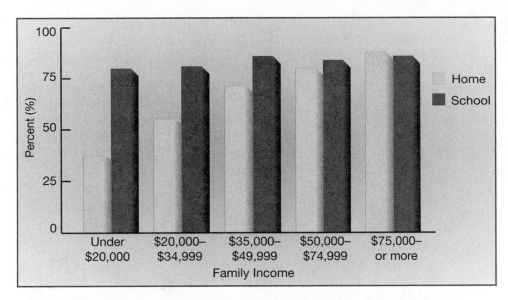

FIGURE 12.3   Percentage of Children in Nursery School and Students in Grades K–12 Using Computers at Home and at School, by Family Income: 2003

What can schools do to ensure equity and access to technology?

Source: U.S. Census Bureau, Current Population Survey (CPS), October 2003.

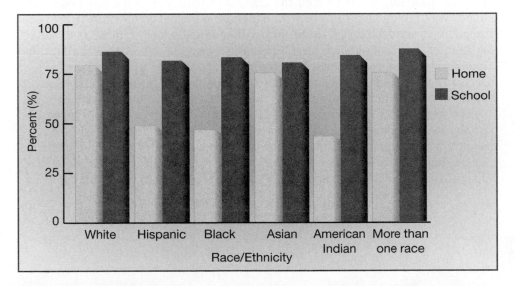

FIGURE 12.4   Percentage of Children in Nursery School and Students in Grades K–12 Using Computers at Home and at School, by Race/Ethnicity: 2003

As a teacher, what will you do to even the technological playing field?

Source: U.S. Census Bureau, Current Population Survey (CPS), October 2003.

Bridging the Gender Gap

Taylor Saxena and Allison Parker no longer worry about the boys. They are two of the 14,000 girls from 19 countries who participated in the Girl Scout's EDGE program, which is focused on empowering girls to become more comfortable with science, engineering, math, and technology.[26] Although the gender gap for computer use at home and school has closed, girls take fewer high school classes in computer science and tend to shy away from technology-oriented careers.[27] By

Equitable access to technology means that all students, regardless of gender, background, or ability, are provided equal opportunity to use technology in the schools. Many school districts have programs that ensure access for all children to computers and other technological tools, such as calculators and interactive video.

■ INTASC

STANDARD 3   The teacher understands how students differ in their approaches to learning and creates instructional opportunities that are adapted to diverse learners.

developing activities more appealing to girls, such as using computer graphics to create their own design to print and heat transfer onto a T-shirt or creating a digital scrapbook page, programs such as the EDGE introduce girls to the various applications of technology.

It has been a stereotype that boys are adept at technology and girls are not. Now that technology has entered the classroom, this stereotype has once more gained sway. Although girls have proven themselves equal competitors in the areas of academics and athletics, it seems they will once again have to prove themselves, this time in the technological arena. This gender gap is reflected in the fact that computer and technology classes are mainly attended by boys rather than girls. If girls do enroll in computer classes, they most likely will enroll in a class such as data processing, whereas boys will enroll in advanced computer science courses.

The gender gap in technology is serious, but will not be around forever. The past shows that gender gaps shrink and often become nonexistent. Women have made tremendous gains in the last century. They have become leaders in math and science, have flown on space shuttle missions, and are successful leaders in all walks of life. The same will hold true regarding the technology gender gap.

⤺ REFLECT & WRITE

Have you experienced the technological gender gap in your own education? As a beginning teacher, try to do what you can to ensure that the technological gender gap between boys and girls is eliminated.

_____

_____

_____

_____

_____

■ INTASC

STANDARD 7   The teacher plans instruction based upon knowledge of subject matter, students, the community, and curriculum goals.

Distance Learning

Not only has technology use in teaching and learning moved from wishful thinking to public policy to reality, it has also, in some cases, moved outside of the classroom.

More than 700,000 elementary and secondary school students participated in some type of online, or **distance learning**, course in 2006.[28] Distance learning courses are online courses that take place in real time or at times that are convenient to students and teachers. They often are effective in meeting the individual needs of students who need extra help or who want to take on more advanced coursework. They also provide more individualization for children by allowing them to work at their own pace, which may be faster or slower than the 25 other students in a typical classroom. For students in rural settings, online courses offer access to an infinite number of subjects not offered in their local schools.

Distance learning courses can be offered as either strictly online courses or as **blended learning**. Blended learning combines traditional face-to-face learning with an online component. Both types of distance learning courses require students to be self-motivated and to have good organizational skills. Unlike in a brick-and-mortar classroom, there is no teacher in the room to provide encouragement and support. Blended courses, however, allow for more supervision and interaction between teachers and students.

Common misconceptions about distance learning are that it is easier to pass online courses and that it is easier for students to cheat. Students often report that they are surprised to find how much work their online courses require. Teachers report that they can often spot academic dishonesty. They can also use online tools, such as the TurnItIn website, to identify the use of unoriginal material. Such sites also act as a deterrent to plagiarism. Distance learning has become an important part of education by helping to provide high-quality instruction to a greater number of students.

? What Does This Mean for You?

Virtual schools might be the hottest trend in U.S. education. Today, more than 25 state programs and more than 170 virtual schools are serving an estimated 500,000 to 1 million students. Proponents of such schools claim they are the answer to an outdated and overly rigid educational system. Julie Young, president and CEO of Florida Virtual School (FLVS) in Orlando, Florida, describes her program as "cutting edge" and believes that virtual learning has almost unlimited potential. As one of the nation's oldest and largest virtual schools, FLVS is a pioneer and a model for other programs.

Is it possible that the classroom will one day be like a scene from a science fiction movie? Will students no longer attend class in a brick-and-mortar building, instead doing all of their schooling from the comfort of their high-tech home? And what does this mean for teachers? Can a good classroom teacher automatically become a good online instructor? Educators skilled in traditional stand-and-deliver teaching methods will need to become effective in creating interactivity and thoughtful discussion while motivating students who might be in a different city or state. As more and more districts embrace online learning, virtual schools will generate dialogue about the future of education.

Distance learning   Delivering instruction to students who are not physically on site. Teachers and students can use electronic media to communicate in real time or at times of their own choosing.

Blended learning   Distance learning courses that require a physical on-site presence for any reason, such as for orientation or for taking examinations.

Visit the TurnItIn website at
www.turnitin.com/

REFLECT & WRITE

Have you participated in distance learning as a teacher or student? Do you believe it is an effective instructional delivery system?

Virtual Field Trips

Virtual field trip A guided exploration of other locations via the Internet. Trips are organized as a collection of prescreened, thematically based websites into a structured online learning experience.

A class field trip can spark student interest as well as nurture their critical-thinking skills. Whereas students in rural schools might benefit the most from distance learning, all U.S. students can benefit from **virtual field trips**. By electronically opening the doors to the world, a virtual field trip allows students to "visit" places near and far without ever leaving the classroom. Although virtual field trips have been available since 1995, enhanced multimedia technology has improved commercially produced trips, making these "getaways" more popular than ever before.

Some of the more popular virtual field trips involve the use of a guide and real-time audio and videoconferencing that allow students to ask questions as they learn about people and places in another location. As a result, more schools are purchasing videoconferencing equipment to make these trips possible. According to Ruth Blandenbaker of the Center for Interactive Learning and Collaboration in Indianapolis, "Two years ago, schools could choose among 120 virtual field trips. Today, the number is 850, and the number is changing monthly."[29]

In Stamford, Texas, students produced a segment on growing cotton. Teachers are teaming up with classes around the world to explore exciting locations, such as the Great Barrier Reef in Australia. Jody Kennedy's class in White Plains, New York, "traveled" there with a class from Mexico. Together they watched as a diver spoke to them—underwater—about sharks.[30]

Go to MyEducationLab and select the topic "Technology in the Schools" then watch the video "Virtual School Advantages." Complete the activities that follow.

However simple or complex, virtual field trips can extend and enhance students' learning by providing opportunities for new discovery in the classroom, without ever leaving their seats.

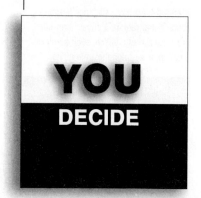

YOU DECIDE

Skipping the Classroom

At the turn of the twenty-first century, 50,000 students were enrolled in online schools, also known as *cyberschools*. Today, more than 1 million students from elementary through secondary school are taking classes online. Cyberschools are growing so quickly in popularity that many educators and politicians are concerned about their impact on traditional educational settings; they also are concerned about the quality of education that students are receiving. For students who are being taught exclusively through cyberschools, educators are concerned about students' inability to interact socially and participate in the quintessential customs of typical teenage life, such as clubs, sports, and other extracurricular activities. Parents who have chosen cyberschools for their children disagree.

Many parents and educators who support cyberschools cite benefits, such as curriculum individualization, flexible schedules, the wide selection of courses, and the ability for students to work at their own pace.

Those opposed to cyberschools believe that the quality of courses is hard to control, that students miss out by not having daily contact with their teachers, and students have little interaction with their friends and, therefore, little opportunity to develop social skills.

As parents and students become more comfortable using computers and the Internet as learning tools, cyberschools will continue to have greater appeal. However, there will always be those who feel the shortcomings outweigh the benefits.

What do you think? Do some online research and see what you can find out about two cyberschools. Given the benefits and drawbacks, state your opinion on cyberschools.

Source: A. Damast, "Be true to your cyberschool," *BusinessWeek*, April 19, 2007. (Online). Available at: www.businessweek.com/bschools/content/apr2007/bs20070419_375162.htm.

How Can Schools Pay for Technology?

Congress created the educational rate, or **E-rate**, to assist schools in attaining new technology, such as computers and Internet connections, by providing them with a technology discount. The E-rate was part of the federal Telecommunications Act passed in 1996 (PL 104-104) and is administered by the Schools and Libraries Corporation, which is part of the Federal Communications Commission (FCC).[31] The E-rate follows the 1934 tradition of universal service, which states that everyone should have access to telephone service. The E-rate extends the tradition by saying that telephone service includes "advanced" telecommunications. To apply for the E-rate, schools and libraries must develop a technology plan that should specify how they will integrate technologies into their curricula and programs. Specifically, plans should address the following five criteria:

- **Goals.** The plan must establish clear goals and a realistic strategy for using telecommunications and information technology to improve education or library services.
- **Staff.** The plan must have a professional development strategy to ensure that the staff knows how to use these new technologies to improve education or library services.
- **Needs.** The plan must include an assessment of the telecommunication services, hardware, software, and other services that will be needed to improve education or library services.
- **Budget.** The plan must provide for a sufficient budget to acquire and support the nondiscounted elements of the plan: hardware, software, professional development, and other services that will be needed to implement the strategy.
- **Evaluation.** The plan must include an evaluation process that enables the school or library to monitor progress toward the specified goals and make midcourse corrections in response to new developments and opportunities as they arise.[32]

The E-rate discount program has played a central role in bridging the digital divide by bringing new technologies and Internet access to America's schools and libraries. As a result of this program, students are able to experience innovative new learning models as they connect to the global community and become lifelong learners.

E-rate Educational rate—a technology discount given to schools to assist them in purchasing new technology such as computers and the Internet.

REFLECT & WRITE

In your opinion, what are the advantages and disadvantages of using technology in the classroom?

_____

_____

_____

_____

_____

WHAT IS CONSIDERED RESPONSIBLE USE OF TECHNOLOGY?

You probably would not walk into a job interview naked; introduce yourself with the nickname, "Hi, I'm Macho Man"; or respond with, "Well, this past week end we had an awesome tail gate party before the game," when the interviewer asks you

Fair use A concept that allows individuals to reproduce copyrighted material, with some limits, as long as it does not harm the market.

● *Your Turn*

You are teaching a high school English class, and your students have just completed their final writing assignment for the year. You want to anonymously post the best and worst examples of their writing on a new website you're designing. Do you have a legal right to post their work without their permission? Do you have an ethical right to post their work without their permission?

REFLECT & WRITE

Ask for a copy of your school district's copyright policy and review it to make sure that you and your students are in compliance. How would its provisions apply to you and your students?

to describe your last big project. However, as the Internet increasingly becomes a system of social networking to find a job, make a love connection, or just keep in touch with friends, private information becomes public and unintended readers access your personal blogs or profiles. The rapid acceleration of information available on the Internet has presented thorny issues for the general public and educators. There are no easy solutions to many of these issues, which await future determinations by the legislature and the courts.

Copyright Law and the Use of Technology

The United States has had a copyright law since 1790. The law protects eight types of works: literary works; musical works; dramatic works; pantomimes and choreographic works; pictorial, graphic, and sculptural works; movies and other audiovisual works; sound recordings; and architectural works.

A main issue in copyright law is the idea of fair use. **Fair use** is a concept that allows individuals to reproduce copyrighted material, with some limits, as long as it does not harm the market. Congress has no precise definition of fair use, but the law does cite four issues to consider in determining if fair use does exist:

- The purpose or the character of the use
- The nature of the copyrighted work
- The amount used
- The effect on the work's potential market value

Guidelines for fair use were approved in 1996 at the Conference on Fair Use (CONFU). For example, the guidelines say that teachers and students may use 10 percent or 1,000 words of a book (whichever is less). Many of the guidelines have come under criticism from educational organizations that believe the guidelines to be overly restrictive and a hindrance to interdisciplinary instruction.

With regard to the Internet, copyright law may not be specific, but it still applies. The same rules that apply to print, recordings, and videotape also apply to the Internet. Refer to Table 12.1 for specifics about copyright law for teachers.

Since the advent of the Internet and online publication, the public has often violated the copyright law. Instead of practicing the principle of fair use, many people copy documents, Web pages, and other materials from the Internet, which, in some cases, is a direct violation of copyright law. However, legally there has been no violation, because until now there was no specific copyright law for the Internet. In 1998 Congress passed the Digital Millennium Copyright Act, which imposes new safeguards for software, music, and written works on the Internet and outlaws technologies that can crack copyright protection devices. Although the act has been long overdue, it has come under criticism from academics, computer researchers, and librarians, who say that it will allow companies to build digital tollgates, thus hindering fair use rights that let educators copy and share material with certain limitations. The Library of Congress will set rules for exactly who is allowed exemptions from the new act, and with the help of the Commerce Department will determine if the new act blocks fair use access to copyrighted materials.[33]

TABLE 12.1   Relevant Copyright Law for Teachers

Medium	Specifics	What You Can Do	The Fine Print
Printed material (short)	■ Poem fewer than 250 words ■ Excerpt of 250 words from a poem greater than 250 words ■ Articles, stories, or essays fewer than 2,500 words ■ Excerpt from a longer work (10% of work or 1,000 words, whichever is less, but a minimum of 500 words) ■ One chart, picture, diagram, graph, cartoon, or picture per book or per periodical issue ■ Two pages (max) from an illustrated work fewer than 2,500 words (e.g., children's books)	■ Teachers may make multiple copies for classroom use and incorporate copies into multimedia for teaching classes. ■ Students may incorporate text into multimedia projects.	■ Copies may be made only from legally acquired originals. ■ Only one copy allowed per student. ■ Teachers may make copies in nine instances per class per term. ■ Usage must be "at the instance and inspiration of a single teacher" (i.e., not a directive from the district). ■ Don't create anthologies. ■ "Consumables," such as workbooks, may not be copied.
Printed material (archives)	■ An entire work ■ Portions of a work ■ A work in which the existing format has become obsolete (e.g., a document stored on a Wang computer)	■ A librarian may make up to three copies "solely for the purpose of replacement of a copy that is damaged, deteriorating, lost, or stolen."	■ Copies must contain copyright information. ■ Archiving rights are designed to allow libraries to share with other libraries one-of-a-kind and out-of-print books.
Computer software	■ Software (purchased) ■ Software (licensed)	■ Library may lend software to patrons. ■ Software may be installed on multiple machines and distributed to users via a network. ■ Software may be installed at home and at school. ■ Libraries may make copies for archival use or to replace lost, damaged, or stolen copies if software is unavailable at a fair price or in a viable format.	■ Only one machine at a time may use the program. ■ The number of simultaneous users must not exceed the number of licenses; and the number of machines being used must never exceed the number licensed. A network license may be required for multiple users. ■ Take aggressive action to monitor that copying is not taking place (unless for archival purposes).
Internet	■ Internet connections ■ World Wide Web	■ Images may be downloaded for student projects. ■ Sound files may be downloaded for use in projects (*see portion restrictions above*).	■ Resources from the Web may *not* be reposted onto the Internet without permission. However, links to legitimate resources can be posted. ■ Any resources you download must have been legitimately acquired by the website.

Sources: United States Copyright Office Circular 21; Sections 107, 108, and 110 of the Copyright Act (1976) and subsequent amendments, including the Digital Millennium Copyright Act; Fair Use Guidelines for Educational Multimedia; cable systems (and their associations); and Copyright Policy and Guidelines for California's School Districts, California Department of Education.

Social Networking

Social networking   Internet services that provide a variety of ways for users to interact, such as posting photos, blogs, and messages.

Social networking is tightly woven into the fabric of life in the twenty-first century. Students in middle school and high school tend to "socialize" on websites such as MySpace.com and FaceBook.com. Younger children have a variety of websites available to them as well, such as Club Penguin and Webkinz. Some school districts have blocked access to social networking sites from school computers, yet for those schools that have not, some educators are finding innovative ways   to tap into the benefits of social networking sites to make better connections with their students.

Teachers warn, however, that it is important to stay professional when sharing Web space with students. For example, Jennifer Copson, a Maryland high school English teacher, is careful about what she posts on her personal page. She asks her adult friends to not post things that could be a problem, such as photos or comments about drinking or partying. Despite the pitfalls, social networking sites may be a valuable tool for building relationships with students in a whole new way.[34]

REFLECT & WRITE

Think for a moment about how you would use social networking with students in your class. What do you think would be the major benefits of social networking for you and your students?

_____

_____

_____

_____

_____

Cyberbullying

Cyberbullying   Online bullying that harasses or threatens others.

Although most online social networking among children and teens takes place outside of school, its ramifications often infiltrate the classroom. Such is the case with **cyberbullying**, which is online bullying that intentionally causes sadness or grief to others. Students can annoy, abuse, threaten, or harass via the Internet or other electronic device, such as cell phones. In the United States, anonymous cyberbullying is a federal crime punishable by a fine and/or up to 2 years imprisonment.[35] Both MySpace.com and FaceBook.com have taken steps to reduce or eliminate cyberbullying by providing links to report abuse and instructions to notify a responsible adult or law enforcement officer.[36]

Cyberbullying can be as simple as continuing to send e-mail to someone who has said they want no further contact with the sender. Yet it can be more severe, such as when an individual assumes the identity of another person and issues threats, sexual remarks, or other harassing messages that appear to come from the victim. Cyberbullies have been known to publish personal contact information for their victims, putting them at risk for sexual predators.

John Halligan, of Essex Junction, Vermont, knows intimately the results of cyberbullying. His 13-year-old son, Ryan, was bullied online for months with instant messages issued from his tormentors that announced to his peers that he was gay. Not only did they send e-mails and instant messages, but these cyberbullies created an entire website filled with hateful accusations and comments,

Learn more about how you can take a stand against cyberbullying at www.stopcyberbullying.org.

asking others to join in.[37] Unable to handle the constant harassment, Ryan committed suicide in 2003. Mr. Halligan is now pushing for comprehensive rules to punish cyberbullies.

With more than 43 percent of teens reporting that they have been victims of cyberbullying in the last year, students, parents, and educators must all take a role in preventing cyberbullying. The National Crime Prevention Council provides strategies to take a byte out of cyberbullying. As teachers, you can help keep your students safe by passing on these strategies, which include the following:

- Never give out personal information online.
- Never give out passwords to anyone except your parents, not even your close friends.
- Do not respond to mean or threatening messages, but show it to an adult who can help you stop future messages.
- Only open messages from people you know.
- Think before you put anything online that you may not want classmates to see, even in an e-mail message.
- Do not send messages when you are angry. Before clicking "Send," ask yourself how you would feel if you received the message.[38]

REFLECT & WRITE

Have you or someone you know received unwanted online messages that caused unhappiness? How can you use this experience to teach students how to respond to cyberbullying?

ETHICAL DILEMMA

Authority Beyond the Schoolhouse Door?

ELEVENTH-GRADE ART TEACHER Chris Walker heard rumors about a MySpace Web page announcing an upcoming fight involving students at his school. Mr. Walker found the site, which confirmed the rumors and indicated that the brawl was to take place away from campus. He had recently attended a workshop developed by the National School Boards Association and had received information about policing students' online activity. Lawyers advised school leaders to limit their intervention if the bad behavior was an off-campus event. Last year, the basketball coach was almost sued when he told a parent about some inappropriate comments their child made about some of his teammates. The parent told the coach that what happened off the court and off campus was none of his business.

What would you do if you learned online of a potential problem between your students?

SUMMARY

- Technological changes in the past several decades have been rapid, widespread, and influential in changing how schools operate, how teachers teach, and how students learn.

- Technological literacy means that individuals must be able to find, evaluate, and arrange information using print, video, audio, and graphic formats in visually appealing ways.

- Technology education standards as a distinct subject or embedded into other curriculum areas have affected teaching and learning.

- While there have been both advantages and disadvantages to digital learning, there have been new options available to students and teachers including distance learning and virtual classrooms.

- An increase in Internet use has ushered in some negative issues, such as plagiarism, cyberbullying, and concerns over responsible use.

KEY TERMS

Assistive technology 432
Augmented reality 430
Blended learning 437
Blog 426
Cyberbullying 442
Distance learning 437
Edutainment 430
E-rate 439

Fair use 440
Interactive whiteboards 427
Massively multiplayer educational
   games 430
Peer networking 424
Podcasts 427
Smartphone 427
Social networking 442

Technological literacy 422
User-created content tools 428
Videoconferencing 424
Video-on-demand server 427
Virtual field trip 438
Web log 426
Web 2.0 428
Wiki 428

APPLICATIONS FOR ACTIVE LEARNING

Connections

1. After reading about teaching and learning using technology in this chapter, reflect on how you can teach technological literacy to your students. Make a list of five ideas sparked by your reading.

2. The need for computer literacy has become an essential part of education. Does this mean that components of the traditional educational curriculum are no longer needed? In other words, to make room for technological literacy should some subjects be eliminated from the curriculum?

Field Experiences

1. Visit classroom programs that provide services to students with disabilities. Cite five ways in which technology is used to implement curriculum, help teachers teach, and promote learning.

2. Interview K–12 teachers in a local school district. What barriers must they contend with in their efforts to include technology in the curriculum? What implications do these barriers have for what you may be able to accomplish as a teacher?

Personal Research

1. This chapter presented many Internet resources and links about technology and its application to teaching and learning. Select five of these and, as you explore them, make notes of ideas for use in your teaching.

2. Choose a particular theme and write a lesson plan to show how you would integrate technology relating to that theme into a subject you plan to teach.

PREPARING TO TEACH

For Your Portfolio

In the first section review, you made a list of some things you thought you could do to make yourself more technologically literate. Review this list now and develop plans for how you can accomplish your goals.

Idea File

In Chapter 10, you wrote a paragraph on each of your three most important educational goals. Write another paragraph describing how your mastery of technology could help you achieve those goals.

LEARNING AND KNOWING MORE

Websites Worth Visiting

The website of the International Society for Technology in Education (ISTE) provides information about the society's mission and projects as well as technology standards for students and teachers. The site provides effective methods for enhancing student learning through the use of new classroom technologies. You can reach the ISTE at www.iste.org/.

First published in March of 1998, *eSchool News* is a monthly print newspaper providing the news and information necessary to help K–20 decision makers successfully use technology and the Internet to transform North America's schools and colleges and achieve educational goals. The print newspaper is read by more than 311,000 school leaders, and a companion website—*eSchool News Online* (www .eschoolnews.com)—is visited by more than 349,000 visitors each month.

A WebQuest is an inquiry-oriented lesson format in which most or all the information that learners work with comes from the Web. Student centered and inquiry based, a WebQuest challenges students to explore the Web for information about a specific topic. WebQuest provides topics that are appropriate for students to research as well as suggestions for further research. Visit WebQuest at www.webquest.org.

Teaching, Learning, and Technology (TLT) is a nonprofit group that helps educational institutions, associations, and corporations around the world improve teaching and learning by making more appropriate and cost-effective use of information technology without sacrificing what matters most. You can access the TLT website at http://www.tltgroup.org/.

Coaster Quest is an excellent example of the use of amusement rides to promote a deeper and more profound understanding of select scientific and mathematical principles. Coaster Quest is an educational activity designed for high school and middle school physics and mathematics students. You can access Coaster Quest at www.dorneypark.com/public/news/coasterquest/.

The National Council of Teachers of English and the International Reading Association provide educators and students with access to the highest-quality practices and resources in reading and language arts instruction through free, Internet-based content by offering a wide array of standards-based lesson plans that meaningfully integrate Internet content into the teaching and/or learning experience. Check out www.readwritethink.org/ for more information.

Discovery Education offers solutions that meet the needs of the educational community. DiscoveryEducation.com is an educational gateway that combines the power of digital media with ongoing assessment. Today, educators can access content from Discovery Education™, Discovery Education Science, and more from www.discoveryeducation.com.

Another excellent resource to extend technology learning for you and your students is the Global SchoolNet Foundation (GSN). GSN is a nonprofit corporation and is a major contributor to the philosophy, design, culture, and content of Internet-based learning. Their mission is to "harness the power of the Internet" to provide ongoing opportunities to support learners both inside and outside of the school environment. You can find more information about the GSN at www.gsn.org.

Hands-On Universe™ (HOU) is an educational program that enables students to investigate the Hands-On Universe while applying tools and concepts from science, math, and technology. HOU is currently developing activities and tools for middle school students, designing informal education centers, and implementing HOU in regional high school networks across the world, including Department of Defense dependent schools. Access their website at www.handsonuniverse.org and determine if you could use these activities in courses and subjects you plan to teach.

The following Websites also offer a wealth of information and activities.

Logo Foundation
http://el.media.mit.edu/logo-foundation

The Logo Foundation supports a "constructivist" approach to teaching math skills and other subjects through the use of "Logo programming environments," which educators have used since the late 1970s. Includes current information and tips.

KidzOnline
www.kidzonline.org

Kidz Online is an educational organization dedicated to reducing the widening gap between the "information haves and have-nots." The members feel this can best be accomplished by having kids teach kids. The organization brings kids together electronically to share ideas, exchange viewpoints, and learn from each other.

Assistive Technology, Inc.
www.assistivetech.com

Assistive Technology, Inc., was founded in 1995 to develop innovative hardware and software solutions to increase the opportunity and enhance the quality of life of people with disabilities. This corporation provides innovative solutions to help people with learning, communication, and access difficulties lead more independent and productive lives.

Stanford University Libraries
http://fairuse.stanford.edu

This site contains a searchable data base for up-to-date information relating to copyright law and fair use.

Eisenhower National Clearinghouse
www.enc.org

This site offers links to outstanding math and science sites and free publications on topics related to teaching math and science. It provides information on assessment, conferences, grants, online courses, and school reform.

SuperKids Educational Software Review
www.superkids.com

This site offers teachers and parents objective reviews of educational software. Also has online activities for children.

The Global Schoolhouse
www.globalschoolhouse.com

The site is for the well-connected educator. It contains articles and features on educational technology. Also, teachers are welcome to submit their favorite websites.

Blue Web'N
www.kn.pacbell.com/wired/bluewebn/

An online library of Blue Ribbon learning sites.

Classroom Connect
http://corporate.classroom.com

Classroom Connect is a dynamic Internet site that provides many "connections" to the classroom. Check out the searchable GRADES Internet links.

Federal Resources for Educational Excellence (FREE)
www.ed.gov/free

This site offers quick access to learning and teaching resources from the federal government.

Books Worth Reading

Prensky, M. (2007). *Digital Game-based Learning.* St. Paul, MN: Paragon House Publishers.
Written by former vice president of human resources at Bankers Trust and present founder, CEO, and creative director of the groundbreaking games2train.com website, this timely and innovative book defines digital game-based learning, explains its advantages and benefits far into the future, and identifies where it can be used and how.

Richardson, W. (2006). *Blogs, Wikis, Podcasts, and Other Powerful Web Tools for Classrooms.* Thousands Oaks, CA: Corwin Press.
This guide demonstrates how Web tools can generate exciting new learning formats and explains how to apply these tools in the classroom to engage all students in a new world of

synchronous information feeds and interactive learning. With detailed, simple explanations, definitions and how-tos, critical information on Internet safety, and helpful links, this exciting book opens an immense toolbox, with specific teaching applications for:

- Web logs, the most widely adopted tool of the read/write Web
- Wikis, a collaborative Webspace for sharing published content
- Rich Site Summary (RSS), feeding specific content into the classroom
- Aggregators, collecting content generated via the RSS feed
- Social bookmarking, archiving specific Web addresses
- Online photo galleries

Solomon, G., and Schrum, L. (2007). *Web 2.0: New Tools, New Schools.* Washington, DC: International Society for Technology. This book provides a comprehensive overview of the emerging Web 2.0 technologies and their use in the classroom and in professional development. Topics include blogging as a natural tool for writing instruction, wikis and their role in project collaboration, podcasting as a useful means of presenting information and ideas, and how to use Web 2.0 tools for professional development.

Williams, B. (2007). *Educator's Podcast Guide.* Washington, DC: International Society for Technology in Education.
Author Bard Williams begins with a complete introduction to podcasting, including hardware and software needs, integrating podcasts into your curriculum, and managing podcasts in the classroom. Williams then introduces a smorgasbord of education-related podcasts sorted by curriculum area. Part user manual, part curriculum planning tool, and part implementation survival guide, *The Educator's Podcast Guide* is an essential resource for any educator who would like to integrate this exciting new tool into the classroom.

13 Your Teaching Career

ELIZABETH MENENDEZ I am a kindergarten teacher. There's a saying that goes something like: "Everything you ever needed to learn, you learned in kindergarten." This is, of course, just a little pressure for all of us who are teaching kindergarten! I do know that attending kindergarten taught me a lot of important lessons, but I think that teaching kindergarten has provided me with even more significant lifelong lessons.

I remember my first day of kindergarten—and no, I'm not referring to when I was 5! I'm actually thinking of when I was 22 years old and teaching my first day of kindergarten in the South Bronx in New York City. I was, of course, incredibly prepared, and I had everything ready. The tables were set, the pencils were sharpened, the crayons were multicultural, and the door said, "Welcome, Bienvenidos." Then, the children walked in. Eric walked in screaming, "I don't want to go! Help, Help!" Anna walked in—well actually Anna didn't walk in she sashayed in— and confidently declared "Ms. Menendez, I already know how to write my name." Luis walked in with his head low and very shyly said, "Good morning Ms. Menendez" in a voice that sounded shockingly like Barry White. These three children definitely surprised me . . . in fact, everything about that day surprised me! But the more interesting surprises began about 5 minutes after we said good-bye to all the mommies and daddies. A lot of children started crying, except for Anna of course, who just rolled her eyes in frustration at the "immaturity" of her fellow kindergarteners. And then there was Eric, who decided that that particular moment would be the perfect time to wet his pants. So at that particular moment, I thought to myself, "How did I get here?"

In my first few moments as a kindergarten teacher I started singing all the nursery songs I knew as I led the class down the hall to the bathroom. We got Eric cleaned up from his "accident," and I convinced Anna to become a class leader and soothe the crying children. I survived that day. And to be honest, I owe a lot of thanks to Anna!

> **My first year: An amazing and magical experience!**

But to be perfectly honest, that first day frightened me! In fact, I think new teachers spend a lot of their first year frazzled—as they try to juggle all of these new experiences and challenges. I literally spent most evenings in my classroom from 3:00 to 7:00 planning and preparing for the next day.

So how did my first school year with Teach for America go? Well, I can definitely say that we were kindergarten at its best. We learned to read. We learned to write stories (Eric discovered that he especially loved writing stories about the beach!). We learned addition and subtraction. We learned in two languages, English and Spanish. We sang songs. We went to the zoo. We had caterpillars in the classroom and watched them turn into butterflies to learn about life cycles (Luis with the "Barry White voice" was especially interested in the butterflies!). Through developing strong parent relationships I was able to visit my children after school and take them to trips outside of the Bronx (trips to the Natural History Museum were definitely among Anna's favorites!). I still remember our graduation party on the last day of school when, after having sung the theme song to the

Elizabeth Menendez joined Teach for America in 1996 and continues to teach kindergarten in New York City Public Schools.

As you read this chapter . . .

Think about:

- What you can do to prepare for teaching
- How you can find your first teaching position
- How you can benefit from beginning teacher programs
- How you can survive and grow in your first year

▸▸ Go to MyEducationLab and select the topic "Professional Development" then watch the video "Peer Observation and Feedback."

"Laverne and Shirley" television show ("We're gonna make our dreams come true!")—no one wanted to leave the classroom!

I, in particular, really didn't want to leave the classroom. So I haven't. It has definitely been an amazing and magical experience.

Source: Adapted from White House Conference on Preparing Tomorrow's Teachers presentation by Elizabeth Menendez. (Online). Available at www.ed.gov/print/admins/tchrqual/learn/preparingteachersconference/menendez.html.

WHAT CAN YOU DO TO PREPARE FOR TEACHING?

■ INTASC

STANDARD 10 The teacher fosters relationships with school colleagues, parents, and agencies in the larger community to support students' learning and well-being.

Like all beginning teachers, you are engaged in the challenging process of becoming a professional. You have read a lot about teaching and are looking forward to your first year of teaching. Chapters 1 and 2 covered many of the factors involved in becoming a good teacher. This chapter continues the discussion of the themes of becoming a professional teacher in the context of looking forward to and getting ready for your first year of teaching.

As you prepare for your first year of teaching, you will want to reflect on and make decisions based on experiences and advice of teachers like Elizabeth and others you've read about in this and other chapters. Your course work, field experiences, and other involvements are helping you prepare for teaching as you think about the many routes to getting your teaching license and becoming a teacher. This chapter provides additional ideas for what you can do now to ensure that you are successful in becoming a highly qualified teacher.

REFLECT & WRITE

Make a list of some things you need to do now to prepare for your first year of teaching. Add to your list as you read this chapter.

_____

_____

_____

_____

_____

Learn by Observing

Throughout this course, you have learned a lot about teaching. You have read about teachers' experiences in the classroom. You have learned the importance of understanding what each student in a diverse classroom needs. You have also learned how standards and assessments have changed teaching and learning. However, you can't learn everything you need to know about teaching simply by reading. You need to see, hear, and experience diverse classrooms. For example, Jody Powell wants to teach children with disabilities. She wants to know how teachers provide for the particular needs of children with Down syndrome. Mat Portz wants to know what strategies teachers use to enhance student learning in biology. Erica Hernandez wants to learn more about how to arrange a third-grade classroom to minimize behavior problems. Ana Chou wants to observe the local school district Teacher of the Year teach an honors creative writing class. All these future teachers want to learn as much about teaching as they can. Observation is one way for them to do this. **Observation** is intentional, systematic looking at the behavior of a student or students in a particular setting, program, or situation. Observation is sometimes referred to as "kid watching," "student watching" or "teacher watching." Now it's a good time for you to go into Laura Fridley's classroom and "teacher watch." (See *In the Classroom with Laura Fridley* on page 452.) How can you take the knowledge and skills that Laura learned in her first year teaching and apply them to your professional practice?

Purposes of Observation

Observation enables you to gather information on which to base decisions, make recommendations, develop curriculum, plan activities and learning strategies, and assess your students' growth, development, and learning. For example, sometimes teachers and parents are more concerned with whether students are safe and orderly than with what students are doing or why they are engaged in a particular behavior or activity. Through observation, you are able to

- **Determine the cognitive, linguistic, social, emotional, and physical development of students.** A good way to learn about students in general is to observe a particular student. One method you can use is to develop a "portrait" of a student. Through your observation, you can assess and record your student's cognitive, linguistic, social, emotional, and physical development.
- **Identify students' interests and learning styles.** Today, teachers are interested in developing learning activities, materials, and classroom centers based on students' interests, preferences, and learning styles. Students' interests provide a channel for motivation and learning.
- **Facilitate intentional planning.** The professional practice of teaching requires planning on a daily, ongoing basis. Observation provides useful, authentic, and solid information on which you can base your intentional planning for activities.
- **Meet students' individual needs.** Meeting the needs of individual students is an important part of teaching and learning. Observation provides information about these individual needs. For example, a student may be advanced cognitively but be overly aggressive and lack the social skills necessary to interact cooperatively with others. Through observation, you can gather information to develop a plan for helping the student gain these skills.
- **Determine students' progress.** Systematic observation, over time, provides a rich, valuable source of information about how individual students and groups of students are progressing in their learning and behavior.
- **Provide information to parents.** As a teacher, you will report to and conference with parents on an ongoing basis. Observational information adds to other sources of data, such as test results and student work samples. Observation will provide you a fuller and more complete picture of individual students' learning and abilities.
- **Gather behavioral information.** A great deal of the consequences, causes, and reactions to students' behaviors can only be assessed through observation. Observation enables you to gather data that cannot be assessed by formal, standardized tests, questioning, or parent and student interviews.
- **Learn about students' prosocial behavior and peer interactions.** Observation can help you plan for appropriate and inclusive activities to promote the social growth of students. Additionally, your observations can serve as the basis for developing multicultural learning activities.
- **Provide a basis for assessing developmental stages.** Many learning skills are developed sequentially. Through observation, you can determine whether students' abilities are within a normal range of growth and development.

Observation   The intentional, systematic looking at student behavior in a setting, program, or situation.

■ **INTASC**

STANDARD 2   The teacher understands how children learn and develop, and can provide learning opportunities that support their intellectual, social, and personal development.

▪ **Assess performance over time.** Documentation of daily, weekly, and monthly observations of students' behaviors and learning provides a data base for the cumulative evaluation of each student's achievement and development.

In the Classroom

with **Laura Fridley**

"What I Learned My First Year Teaching"

Laura Fridley is a seventh-grade teacher at Rocky Run Middle School in Chantilly, Virginia.

The empty classroom surrounding me as I type serves as inspiration for today's final blog entry. It hasn't been this quiet in here since that very first day when I, bewildered and wide eyed, opened the door to room 118 and gawked at the 30 desks pushed against the wall beside the stacks of plastic chairs, feeling the knot in my stomach grow while wondering, "Now what do I do?" After spending all of yesterday cleaning and packing (with the help of about a dozen students who were willing to spend their first day of summer vacation hauling textbooks and cleaning desks so long as they were promised free pizza, National Junior Honor Society credit, and the chance to hang on to seventh grade for just a few more hours), my room looks remarkably like it did on that first day. The floors are not as pristine, and the chalkboards are covered in farewell wishes from the students, but otherwise this classroom is just as I found it.

I, on the other hand, am much changed.

Just as my once-bare file cabinets are now brimming with materials, I can now say that I am brimming with teaching experience. I know so much more than when I started:

▪ I know what it's like to teach a lesson that really excites the students, and also what to do when a lesson takes a nose-dive and an impromptu backup plan becomes necessary.

▪ I know now how to communicate with upset parents, and also how uplifting it feels to receive a parent's compliment.

▪ I know now that you should keep half of your art supplies (markers, glue, and colored pencils) hidden for the first part of the school year, so you can pull it out for the second half when the children have somehow lost/destroyed the first batch of supplies.

▪ I know that asking for help is not admitting defeat, but honoring the experience of your coworkers.

▪ I know that e-mails should always be responded to promptly.

▪ I know that games are the best way to review content with students, and that every teacher should keep a ball, a bag of candy, a pack of flashcards, a timer or stopwatch, and a set of white boards with markers in their classroom.

▪ I know that all students enjoy being read aloud to.

▪ I know that students are more likely to follow your rules when they see you following your rules.

▪ I now know that you should always keep band-aids, tissues, and hand sanitizer close by.

▪ I know that when a student comes to your class, he or she is not always searching for education, but is always seeking respect and acceptance, and will eventually gain the former so long as you ensure the latter.

Last Friday, I gave each of my 130 students a simple gift: a plastic baggie filled with candy and cookies and a tiny card that read, "You made my first year of teaching so sweet! Thank you! From: Ms. Fridley." My ever-supportive fiancé, Greg, and I spent 2 hours putting the bags together the night before (my coworkers laughed, "That's what happens when you marry a teacher!"), but it was worth it to see the delight and surprise on my students' faces. "This was your first year of teaching, Ms. Fridley?" the children asked incredulously. I admitted to them that I didn't want to tell them my little secret at the beginning of the year for fear that they'd question my ability to teach them. The best compliment came from one of my honors students, "But you teach like you've been doing it for a long time! You don't seem like you're new."

Read more blogs and articles from Virginia teachers at www.veaweteach.org.

Source: L. Fridley, What I learned my first year of teaching, Virginia Education Association. (Online). Available at www.veaweteach.org/search_results_detail.asp?ContentID=2250.

In summary, intentional observation is a useful, informative, and powerful means for informing and guiding teaching and helping you prepare for teaching and to ensure that all students will learn. The steps involved in the process of systematic, purposeful observation are shown in Figure 13.1. You can use these steps to help prepare yourself for teaching.

Talk to and Observe Teachers

Talking to teachers and observing them in action is a great way for you to learn firsthand from the professionals what teaching is really like. Seasoned teachers can give you tips about:

- How to prepare for your first day
- Classroom management
- Managing stress
- Classroom organization
- Handling and staying on top of paperwork
- Planning and time management

> ■ **INTASC**
>
> **STANDARD 9**   The teacher is a reflective practitioner who continually evaluates the effects of his/her choices and actions on others (students, parents, and other professionals in the learning community) and who actively seeks out opportunities to grow professionally.

Observe in Schools

Observing in a variety of different schools can be a real advantage for you as you prepare to teach. I recommend to my students that they observe in at least six schools in addition to their field placement schools and the school where they will student teach. These six schools should be two elementary, two middle, and two high schools. Students planning to teach in the elementary grades often question why they should observe in middle and high schools. My reply is always the same: "Education is about students, pre-K–12. In order to do a good job in your grade, you need to be familiar with all grades."

OBSERVE & LEARN

Observe in a grade level or subject area you would like to teach. Notice some of the students' characteristics, pay attention to how learning occurs, and note specific methods used by teachers. Explain how your observation will be helpful to you in your first year of teaching.

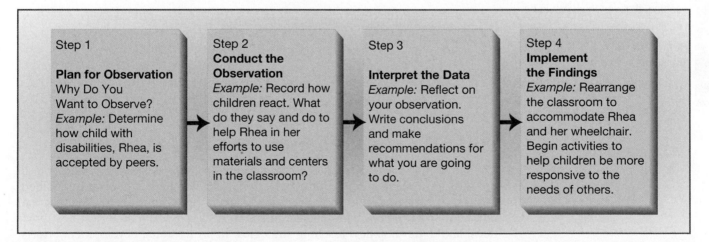

Step 1

Plan for Observation
Why Do You Want to Observe?
Example: Determine how child with disabilities, Rhea, is accepted by peers.

Step 2
Conduct the Observation
Example: Record how children react. What do they say and do to help Rhea in her efforts to use materials and centers in the classroom?

Step 3
Interpret the Data
Example: Reflect on your observation. Write conclusions and make recommendations for what you are going to do.

Step 4
Implement the Findings
Example: Rearrange the classroom to accommodate Rhea and her wheelchair. Begin activities to help children be more responsive to the needs of others.

FIGURE 13.1   Four Steps for Effective Observation

Intentional observation is a useful, informative, and powerful means of gathering data and informing and guiding your teaching.

REFLECT & WRITE

Observation helps ensure that you can provide for the learning needs of all your students. How might intentional observation help you during your first year as a teacher?

_____
_____
_____
_____
_____

Make the Most of Your Field Experiences

School classrooms are only one setting in which you can gain field experiences. Other sites that provide experience and knowledge of students and families include private schools, homes, public agencies (for example, the March of Dimes), child-care centers, and social service agencies serving children, youth, and families. Although some teacher preparation programs provide only student teaching as a field experience, more and more programs are finding ways to involve their students in schools and classrooms from the very beginning.

Field experiences help you gain knowledge, skills, and insights not usually available in the college classroom. These experiences help you bridge the gap between theory and practice and give you firsthand experience with students and teachers. As Figure 13.2 suggests, participating in field experiences brings you, early in your career, into contact with the reality of teaching and allows you to test your ideas, reconsider your beliefs, and clarify your values about teaching and the professional role.

> ■ **INTASC**
>
> **STANDARD 7**   The teacher plans instruction based upon knowledge of subject matter, students, the community, and curriculum goals.

REFLECT & WRITE

What are some kinds of field experience, in addition to student teaching, that you think would be useful? Can you think of experiences that you can arrange yourself to fit your needs?

_____
_____
_____
_____
_____

Participate in a PDS Program

Chapter 2 introduced professional development schools (PDSs) and their role in the reform of teacher education. Professional development schools are intended, in part, to give preservice and inservice teachers opportunities to reflect on and talk about their practices, to engage in action research designed to test best practices, and to develop new teaching strategies. In professional development efforts, PDSs have four critical functions:

■ Preparing teachers and other educators
■ Providing continuing education for professionals

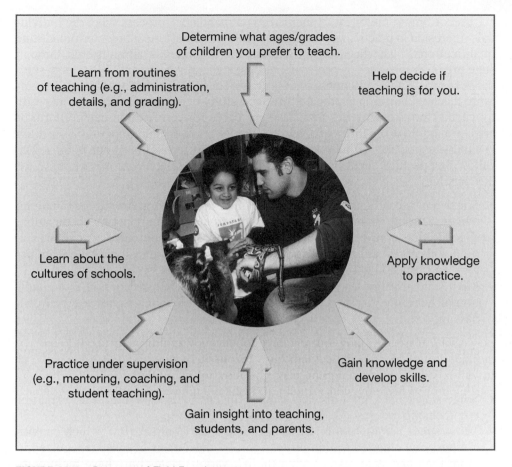

FIGURE 13.2 Purposes of Field Experiences

Field experiences help you gain knowledge and skills for teaching. Although some teacher preparation programs provide only student teaching as a field experience, more and more programs are finding ways to involve their students in schools and classrooms from the beginning.

- Conducting inquiry
- Providing an exemplary education for all pre-K–12 students enrolled[1]

You might do part or all of your preservice training in professional development schools. Not all university teacher preparation programs have developed a PDS relationship with local districts. Some states, such as Texas, mandate by law that all teacher education programs establish and conduct preservice teacher education activities in professional development schools.

Pathways to Teaching

One of the ways to prepare for your first year of teaching is by completing requirements for certification. *Certification* and *licensure* are two terms people use synonymously and interchangeably. Simply put, **certification** is a voluntary process through which the profession recognizes individuals meeting high qualifications. The National Board of Professional Teaching Standards (NBPTS) is responsible for the advanced certification of teachers. A teaching certificate specifies that you have met certain requirements and completed a program of skills training preparing you to teach.

Certification A voluntary process whereby the profession recognizes individuals meeting high qualifications. The NBPTS is responsible for advanced teacher certification.

Licensure The mandatory process whereby individuals interested in practicing the teaching profession must meet predetermined state qualifications.

According to the NEA, "**Licensure** is a mandatory process whereby individuals interested in practicing the teaching profession must meet predetermined state qualifications."[2] The licensing process in the 50 states is administered through state organizations such as professional state standards boards (PSSBs), state standards boards, and departments of education. These agencies set standards that require teacher education candidates to successfully demonstrate that they are ready to teach. Thirty-seven states now have standards for certification that conform or are comparable to the Interstate New Teacher Assessment and Support Consortium (INTASC) standards (which appear in the margins throughout your book!). The following specifics about licensure will assist you in planning for your first year of teaching:

- States have specific academic and education course requirements for obtaining a license. Some common course requirements include foundations of education, special education, bilingual/multicultural education, computer education, and drug abuse prevention. In addition, courses such as state history, American history, and psychology may be required.

Go to the Resources section of MyEducationLab to learn more about the licensure process.

- Most states require teacher candidates to pass a state examination as a condition of licensure. On the Praxis (see Chapter 2), individual states set their own passing scores.
- Some states provide a provisional teaching license that requires further study and/or the successful completion of a beginning teacher program before issuing a "permanent" license to teach. Most states issue a license with certain provisions such as further study and testing.
- Some states and school districts require fingerprinting and drug tests as part of the licensing process.
- Many states belong to the NASDTEC Interstate Contract (IC), which enables teachers and other education professionals to have their licenses recognized in more than one state. Even within the IC, various states only have reciprocity with certain other states. For instance, Pennsylvania has reciprocity agreements with all 50 states, whereas Connecticut has reciprocity agreements with only 36 other states. In Pennsylvania, all candidates for certification must pass the Praxis test. Figure 13.3 lists certification requirements that states have in com-

- B.A. or B.S. degree
- Completion of an approved program of teacher preparation
- Criminal background check
- Fingerprinting
- Recommendations from the college or previous employer
- Passing score on a basic skills and/or pedagogical knowledge and/or content knowledge test, such as Praxis or a state exam
- Minimum age (usually 18)
- Application fee (ranging from $125.00 in Alaska to $12.00 in Ohio)
- Ten states have a loyalty oath
- Course work in special education
- Disclosure of prior license invalidation, dismissal, prior arrest, and prior conviction
- Recertification after the initial teaching certificate

FIGURE 13.3 Typical Features of States' Requirements for Certification

For you to receive a teaching certificate, you need to complete all of the requirements in the state in which you plan to teach. Although specific requirements vary from state to state, most states share the 12 shown here.

Source: Certification Requirements for 50 States. (Online). Available at www.uky.edu/Education/TEP/usacert.html.

mon. Reciprocity agreements are arrangements among states to honor one another's teacher certifications.

To receive a teaching certificate, you need to complete all of the requirements in the state in which you plan to teach. Although specific requirements vary from state to state, most states share the 12 requirements shown in Figure 13.3.

Performance-Based Licensure

Many states are implementing a system of performance-based licensure (PBL), a process that requires beginning teachers to demonstrate their knowledge and ability to teach. The following is part of the PBL process in North Carolina:

1. A first-year teacher in North Carolina is an initially licensed teacher (ILT) and has 3 years to earn PBL. In essence, these 3 years are an apprenticeship period, a common practice in other trades and professions.

2. Each beginning teacher is assigned a mentor teacher, who acts as a coach, consultant, and mentor.

3. Over the 3 years, beginning teachers convert their initial licensure into a performance-based licensure through the completion of a performance-based product.

4. The performance-based product is based on INTASC standards. Material relating to the INTASC standards are identified in the margins throughout this text.

5. The performance-based product is developed in the second year of teaching and is designed to demonstrate the ability to teach. Examples of evidence and artifacts that constitute the performance-based product are:

   - Unit and daily lesson plans
   - Teacher-made assessment materials
   - Classroom management plan
   - Parent communications log
   - Samples of student work
   - Photographs of student activities, classroom, etc.
   - Student, parent, and colleague surveys
   - Record of professional activities
   - Awards, recognitions, etc.
   - Publications

6. Salary increases are tied to the completion of the performance-based licensure and the earning of tenure in the fourth year. This process is in keeping with the national trend of tying pay to performance.

REFLECT & WRITE

What does your state require for teacher certification? How prepared are you to meet these requirements?

_____

_____

_____

_____

_____

Quality assurance programs (or warranty programs)   Colleges and universities ensure the success of their teachers by providing mentoring and specialized assistance to those who do not meet school district standards.

Alternative certification   The process whereby those with a bachelor's degree in a field other than education become licensed to teach.

Quality Assurance Programs

Some colleges of education are instituting **quality assurance programs**—guarantees or warranties for their new teachers in order to provide for quality assurance. The public wants colleges of education and teacher preparation programs to improve the quality of their graduates. As a result, more schools will institute quality assurance programs.

Alternative Certification

Traditionally, the only route to teacher certification has been the completion of a bachelor's degree, including specified education courses in a college or university teacher education program approved by a state department of education. However, now another means is through **alternative certification**, the process whereby those with a bachelor's degree in any field can become licensed to teach. Alternative certification (AC) is a growing trend, and a number of factors contribute to its popularity:

- An overall teacher shortage, especially in certain fields such as mathematics, science, and exceptional student education. Many school districts recruit mathematicians and scientists from business and industry to fill the need for teachers in these areas.
- Teacher shortages in inner-city and rural areas.
- The number of people seeking to enter teaching as a second career. For example, many unemployed turn to teaching as a second career. Alternative certification is one way to help the unemployed enter the teaching profession.
- Dissatisfaction with the ways colleges of education have trained teachers. As discussed in Chapter 2, criticism of teacher training has led to new ways of educating and licensing teachers. One of the outcomes of teacher education reform is the desire of school districts, especially big-city school districts, to play a greater role in teacher education and certification. State departments of education are taking a more active role in helping design and implement alternative routes to certification. For example, the New Jersey Provisional Teaching Program provides training for candidates with bachelor's degrees before and during teaching as part of its certification process.

Across the nation, alternative certification programs are growing by leaps and bounds. For example, in Texas, over 50 percent of first-year teachers come from nontraditional sources. In the coming decades, the primary source of new teachers will be from alternative certification programs.[3]

REFLECT & WRITE

In 2007, about 1 in 5 new teachers were certified through alternative certification programs. While proponents see benefits, opponents don't feel this route produces high quality teachers. What do you think?

_____

_____

_____

_____

_____

What's New in Education?

Troops in the Classroom

Each year, thousands of students are taught by military veterans. Hundreds of teachers have served first in the military and then in the schools through Troops to Teachers, a government program that trains veterans to become teachers.

Former Army Captain Antonio Magwood began his teaching career as a social studies teacher to 36 seventh-graders. Although he found his students to be his most intimidating audience, he said, "My goal—just like the soldiers—is to let them know that I care for them."

Retired Sgt. 1st Class Ritchie Holliman spent 20 years in the military. As a social studies teacher in Atlanta, he manages 80 sixth-graders. "I feel more pressure here than in the army,

because I'm responsible for each individual's future," he said. Holliman is one of hundreds of Georgia servicemen and -women who have gone from the armed services to the classroom through Troops to Teachers.

Sources: The Miami Herald. (2006, August 17). Extroops on frontline as teachers. (Online). Available at www.districtadministration.com/newssummary.aspx?news=yes&postid=16749; C. Reinolds. (2006, September 18). Georgia program turns military men, women into teachers. (Online). Available at www.districtadministration.com/newssummary.aspx?news=yes&postid=17073 on November 23, 2007.

Emergency Certification

In addition to alternative certification, many states and school districts provide **emergency certification** in areas of teacher shortage. Emergency certification is given to someone who lacks the skills and knowledge necessary for teacher certification. Emergency certification is usually valid for a period of 2 to 3 years. School districts may have particularly hard-to-fill areas owing to special circumstances; for example, higher rates of immigration may create a need for more bilingual teachers. As the demand for teachers continues to rise and as colleges of education fail to fully meet demand, alternative certification and emergency certification programs will increase. Other alternative routes, such as Teach for America and Troops to Teachers, provide an inviting way to enter the teaching profession. (See *What's New in Education?*)

Emergency certification   Temporary certification to teach granted to individuals without formal credentials, typically in hard-to-fill specialties.

Bilingual teachers are in great demand. Many school districts actively recruit both beginning and experienced teachers with bilingual abilities. Additionally, some districts pay higher salaries for bilingual teachers or offer signing bonuses to those teachers in short supply, such as special education teachers. The demand for special education teachers and for teachers to work with minority students will continue to increase.

REFLECT & WRITE

As the movement for accountability grows, universities that train teachers are responding to the pressure for "quality control." Do you think such warranties of new teacher quality are worthwhile?

_____

_____

_____

_____

_____

Prepare for Teacher Examinations

The majority of states require the completion of the Praxis series of professional assessment for beginning teachers (see Chapter 2). Other states require their own state initial certification tests. Praxis I (Academic Skills Assessment) covers the areas of reading, writing, and mathematics, often referred to as "basic skills" and "enabling skills." Praxis II (Subject Assessments) tests students' knowledge of the subjects they will teach. Praxis III (Classroom Performance Assessments) is a performance-based assessment system for first-year or beginning teachers.

The Praxis website—www.ets.org/praxis—has a comprehensive list of each state's required exams. Sample items from the Praxis are available on the Praxis website.

More than likely, you will participate in and successfully complete a beginning teacher program (BTP) that involves Praxis III–type assessment. The requirements of a BTP vary according to state and school district, but generally include the help of a **mentor teacher**—an experienced teacher judged highly effective and professional by colleagues and administration—the development of a portfolio, and evaluations by principals or other district personnel. Completion of the beginning teacher program can also include a performance-based assessment system such as Praxis III that covers planning and implementing instruction, classroom management, and evaluating student progress and instructional effectiveness.

Mentor teacher   An experienced teacher—leader, guide, role model, supporter, and sponsor—who mentors beginning teachers.

You should check with the state agency responsible for teacher licensure to be certain you are taking the proper tests required for your beginning teacher's license.

REFLECT & WRITE

Identify three specific actions you can take to begin preparing yourself for your certification exam.

_____

_____

_____

_____

_____

HOW CAN YOU FIND YOUR FIRST TEACHING POSITION?

As you progress through your teacher education program, you can engage in a continuous process of searching for the job you want. Too often, students wait until the end of their program or after graduation to start the job hunt. There are a number of things you can and should do now.

Know Yourself

Your job search begins with you—who you are, your hopes and dreams, your strengths and weaknesses, the subjects you want to teach, and the students you want to teach. Ask yourself, "Am I a flexible person who is willing to try new things?" You should honestly analyze each of these areas. Review the self-assessment you completed in Chapter 2 in answer to the question, "Is teaching for you?" Now that you have finished this course, what items in the self-assessment might you answer differently, and why? Also, review the self-assessment you completed in Chapter 9 on your philosophy of education and reflect on your responses. You might be surprised to find how your capacity for professional reflection and self-knowledge has grown. This capacity will help you be a better teacher and be clear about your priorities and goals as you look for your first teaching job. (See *In the Classroom with Christopher Wiler*.)

> ■ **INTASC**
>
> **STANDARD 9** The teacher is a reflective practitioner who continually evaluates the effects of his/her choices and actions on others (students, parents, and other professionals in the learning community) and who actively seeks out opportunities to grow professionally.

In the Classroom

with **Christopher Wiler**

Apple Pi for the Teacher

Christopher Wiler would love for his students at Chester A. Arthur School in Philadelphia to be stars in math and reading, but the thing he wants most is for the boys and girls he has guided for 6 years to be ready for the real world.

"Mother Nature help the soul if I ever walk up to them on the street and see them doing what?" Wiler asked his eighth-grade class on a recent morning, pausing from a language arts lesson. Xavia Witherspoon's hand shot up.

"If you ever see us on the corner with a 40 in a paper bag," Xavia said seriously, referring to a common size of bottle used to package malt liquor or beer.

Wiler first taught the South Philadelphia students in third grade, when they had superhero backpacks and baby faces. But a combination of circumstances—Arthur adding new grades every year and a strong bond with the class—kept him in the rare spot of moving up with his students every year.

"We're not playing with a hat factory. We're playing with minds. We have got to figure this out," he said, referring to getting students ready for the larger world. Academics are peppered with practical lessons. During one recent language arts period, members of the class wrote and discussed their life goals. "What's the grand prize of high school, the prize for doing the right thing?" asked Wiler. It was Paul Cordona-Johnson's turn to answer. "Holding high standards. Not doing what everybody else is doing. You do the right thing," Paul said.

Academics are clearly at the center of Wiler's classroom. He is a math specialist, and his classes have scored multiple wins in the Philadelphia School District's pi contest, which celebrates the ratio of a circle's circumference to its diameter.

The class's graduation was a bittersweet thing for Wiler—sending his pupils off into the wider world, hoping his years with them had made an indelible impression on their lives. "I think of them as my own kids, and every kid has to feel good about themselves," he said. "I've been so blessed, so impressed by their love of learning. Some of their lives aren't the best, and yet they have such resilience."

Source: K. Graham. (2007, June 20). A teacher worthy of apple and pi, *The Philadelphia Inquirer.* (Online). Available at www .philly.com/philly/columnists/kristen_graham/20070620_Kristen_ Graham_Phila_teacher_worthy_of_apple_and_pi_too.html.

REFLECT & WRITE

From your knowledge about yourself, what are the three most important factors that will guide your job search?

_____

_____

_____

_____

_____

Teacher portfolio A selected collection of data that describe a person's expertise and proficiency in areas associated with effective teaching.

Go to the Resources section of MyEducationLab to learn more about preparing your portfolio.

Prepare a Portfolio

Developing and compiling a portfolio is both a process and a product that will help you be a better teacher and also will help you get your first job. A **teacher portfolio** is a selected collection of data that describe your expertise and proficiency in areas associated with effective teaching. Your portfolio can be used as a record of authentic assessment and as an overall evaluation of your performance. As a portrait of you, it is an invaluable tool for interviews and other situations in which you need to provide evidence of your abilities.

A portfolio serves many other useful purposes as well. It helps you reflect on and evaluate your performance over time and provides a record of your past accomplishments as a benchmark against which to constantly improve your performance. You can also continually add to your portfolio as you progress toward certification. Many colleges and universities use portfolios in their teacher preparation programs as one measure of assessment to augment standardized tests and classroom observations. Many teachers continue to develop their professional portfolios throughout their careers.

What you include in your portfolio depends on the specific purposes for which you will use it. You can add to and delete from your portfolio according to circumstances. A portfolio is not a collection of all your work, only the best and most relevant. Some artifacts to consider for inclusion are:

- DVDs of yourself during student teaching presenting lessons with different students in a variety of situations
- An up-to-date resume
- A statement of your philosophy of teaching
- Photographs documenting and illustrating your performance, student products, and so forth (for example, show you with students, your classroom, classroom activity outcomes, and bulletin boards you arranged)
- Your teaching journal or samples from it demonstrating how you have reflected on and improved your teaching. (Your responses to many of the reflection write-ins in this textbook would be suitable for inclusion in your portfolio.)
- Examples of lesson plans
- Observations and recommendations by supervising teachers, college instructors, and colleagues
- Examples of students' work and specific examples of how you have evaluated students' work and made suggestions for improvement
- Letters and notes from parents and others commenting on your performance and efforts during your field experiences and student teaching
- Summaries and commentaries of professional development activities in which you have participated

The "For Your Portfolio" feature at the end of each chapter of this textbook gives you more ideas for what to include in your portfolio. You will find that your portfolio can be an invaluable tool to help you grow as a professional. In addition, it can help you get the job you desire. You can include all the information and artifacts described above in your electronic portfolio, which is easily copied and transmitted.

Analyze Job Opportunities

Knowing yourself as a teacher helps you establish your personal and professional criteria for evaluating job opportunities. Finding a match between what you want and what is available is the central task of any job search, and this includes knowing where the jobs are.

Review the information in Chapter 2 about teacher supply and demand nationwide. Part of your analysis of job opportunities would include finding areas where demand is high or where there are teacher shortages. Demand is greatest, for example, in urban and rural areas and in areas of greatest population growth, such as in the southeastern and southwestern United States.

Matching your qualifications with areas of critical shortage is another consideration in analyzing job opportunities. If you have training in special education, bilingual education, or science, for example, you can expect to find a greater number of job opportunities to investigate. In addition, teaching jobs are more plentiful at certain times of the year, such as the beginning of the school year when many school districts have last-minute vacancies. Teachers seeking local positions take advantage of last-minute vacancies that appear in the Help Wanted sections of newspapers and on school district websites near the end of every summer and at the beginning of school breaks. For example, in the summer of 2007 the Prince George's County (Maryland) public school system spent $300,000 on an advertising campaign in which it enlisted appeals from its students in hopes of attracting the country's best teachers for the nearly 800 jobs that remained vacant 3 weeks before school started. The campaign used a dozen students who appeared in what the district called "America's Classroom" ads, which ran in local and national newspapers, in teacher trade magazines, and on job websites for educators.[4]

You can find information about teaching opportunities through a variety of sources and agencies.

Recruiters and Job Fairs

Your first job in teaching and your teaching career might begin with the visit of school district recruiters to your campus. Many large school districts actively recruit teachers all across the United States. For example, administrators and representatives of the Duncanville, Texas, ISD district participate in regional, state, and national job fairs throughout the year to recruit highly qualified and experienced professional educators. Toward the end of the recruitment season, the Duncanville High School hosts a job fair to attract applicants. All district administrators, as well as selected teachers, are available throughout the day for interviewing the over 500 potential candidates who attend the fair.[5]

Job fairs provide an excellent opportunity to learn where the teaching jobs are. Many job fairs are an employment smorgasbord: Districts showcase a wide range of job opportunities—some you might not even have thought about! In addition, you have an opportunity to talk with school and district administrators who can explain what their districts and schools are looking for.

College Placement Services

Many colleges have a placement service that helps college graduates find jobs. Placement services provide help with resume writing and developing interview skills and act as clearinghouses for prospective employers by assisting them in

Go to MyEducationLab and select the topic "Teaching Profession" then watch the video "Why Work with Children with Special Needs." Complete the activities that follow.

Visit the following sites for information about teaching opportunities: http://k12jobs.com and www.educationamerica.net.

At a job fair, you have an opportunity to "sell" yourself. Many job seekers walk away from a job fair with interviews scheduled—or even their first teaching job!

■ **INTASC**

STANDARD 9 The teacher is a reflective practitioner who continually evaluates the effects of his/her choices and actions on others (students, parents, and other professionals in the learning community) and who actively seeks out opportunities to grow professionally.

Visit the Dallas ISD website at www.dallasisd.org. Search for teaching jobs at Career Builder at www.careerpath.com and the Monster Board at www.monster.com.

setting up and conducting on-campus interviews. Placement services also have lists of vacancy notices from school districts across the country. Check with your placement agency to see if these vacancy announcements are available online.

Letters of recommendation are part of your file. When asking people to write letters of recommendation for you, select people who are very familiar with your abilities and performance. These are usually professors, a supervising teacher, and a former employer. Be sure to tell whoever is writing your recommendation the kind of positions you are applying for and share with them significant facts about you that they can include in their letter. You want your letters of recommendation to set you apart from other candidates. Letters of recommendation state your significant achievements and describe your personality and character traits. It is important that a letter of recommendation emphasizes your ability to work with many kinds of students and parents, and states your ability to work well with others.

State Departments of Education

State departments of education continually update website lists of teacher vacancies throughout their state. Contact the state where you are interested in teaching and request a list of job openings.

Networking

There is probably no better way to find a teaching job than through personal networking. Often it is who you know that counts. As a prospective teacher, you will want to network with the people who can tell you about job openings and school district needs and/or who can connect you with those who know where jobs are or who have the authority and responsibility for hiring. Make your availability and preferences known, and do not hesitate to ask others to help you find a job. The more others know about your job search, the more likely that someone will help you make the right connection.

School District Contacts

Is there a particular school district that interests you? If so, you will want to learn of current and potential vacancies. A letter of inquiry asking for a list of position vacancies or a visit to the district's website will provide current information that you can get directly from the source. Also, job announcements published by a district usually have much information that is good to know, including starting salary, where to send letters of application, and a job description. Most school districts have websites that you can access to find out about employment opportunities. For example, when you visit the Dallas Independent School District's website, you can click on an "employment" button to access the district's current job openings. In addition, numerous job search engines are on the Web, including Career Builder and the Monster Board, both of which allow you to post your resume and search job listings geographically. (See *What's New in Education?*)

Teacher Salaries

Part of analyzing job opportunities is to evaluate the salary being offered. When teachers identify their reasons for teaching, love of money is not one of them. Nonetheless, you need to be realistic about what you can expect as a new teacher and

What's *New* in Education?

Talent Search for New Teachers

What's quick, easy, and sorts applicants for teaching jobs by how much promise they show?

Until recently, that riddle was perplexing. Putting prospective teachers though standardized interviews about their approach to the job might fulfill a sorting function, but it was time consuming on both sides. Online applications, though they can be relatively quick and easy, tend to give a school district too little information about the real-world potential of candidates.

But with the latest in technology, some district hiring experts and their partners in the private sector say

they've got the answer. By giving candidates a short online talent assessment that returns results to the district almost immediately, a school system has a better chance of snagging the best people at a cost it can afford—a practice that is gaining ground.

Kenexa Technologies, Inc., offers online hiring and retention services to help school districts hire great teachers. The company uses a process called Positive Psychology as a basis for understanding what it takes to be a great teacher. Based on this process, the company creates a validated assessment tool that deter-

mines how closely a candidate is aligned to the profile of a successful teacher. Districts can then use this information during the hiring process. The information provided enables the district to understand the strengths and limitations of a candidate. The information can also be used to generate a development report that will help the candidate to grow and develop once hired. This process enables school district recruiters to spend more time on the best candidates, which increases recruitment efficiencies in the district. The Boston Public School District in Massachusetts and the Sioux Falls School District in South Dakota are just two of many school districts' using Kenexa Technologies' services.

Source: Dr. Richard Harding, personal communication 2007.

what you will need to be able to meet your expenses. Look back at Figure 2.5, and then look at Figure 13.4 for a better idea of what you can expect. Does it pay to have more education as a teacher? As you can see in Figure 13.4 the answer is "yes." However, some school districts do not compensate for additional education. Therefore, you need to determine if the school district you plan to teach in does provide such compensation and decide how important additional money tied into additional education is to you.

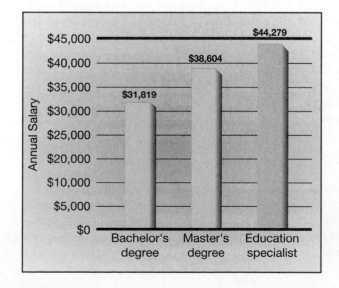

FIGURE 13.4 Average Teacher Salary by Degree for First-Year Teachers

Does it pay to have more education as a teacher? As you can see from the graph, the answer is yes. However, some school districts do not compensate for additional education. Therefore, you need to determine if the school district you plan to teach in does and how important additional money tied into additional education is to you.

Source: U.S. Department of Education, National Center for Education Statistics, Schools and Staffing Survey (SASS). (2006). (Online). Available at http://nces.ed.gov/programs/digest/d06/tables/dt06_071.asp.

REFLECT & WRITE

In analyzing job opportunities, what information about a school or school district would be most important for you to know? What salary range would you consider?

_____

_____

_____

_____

_____

Go to the Resources section of MyEducationLab to learn more about preparing an effective résumé.

Apply for a Teaching Position

Applying for a job is one of your most important responsibilities as you finish your program of teacher preparation. It is also one of the most rewarding experiences of your life, for you will always remember your first job and how you got it. As you embark on your job hunt, you will need to prepare a résumé, which is a clear and succinct summary of your education, experiences, and accomplishments. When writing your résumé, use the KISS principle—keep it short and sweet—one page is usually enough and is about all a prospective employer wants to read. Have one of your professors review your résumé and advise you on content and format. Your goal is to have an error-free résumé that will persuade an employer to hire you. The following list suggests what you should include in your résumé:

- Educational background
- Honors, recognitions, and awards
- Teaching and other experiences (Make sure you include all that might be of interest to a future employer. The fact that you volunteered in an inner-city literacy program may make the difference between getting and not getting an interview.)
- Professional memberships
- Activities, interests, and involvements in organizations related to teaching

The list of items to include in a résumé can also serve as a guide for what you should be doing now to ensure that you have qualifications and experiences to include in your résumé when applying for your first teaching job. The figures on the next several pages provide examples of some of the documents you will need to prepare when seeking a teaching job and other information that can help you prepare for potential interviews. The better prepared you are, the greater your chance of finding the right job. The process begins with the résumé. Figure 13.5 is the résumé of Maria del Carmen Lopez, which you can use as a model. Be sure to personalize your résumé so that you are "putting your best foot forward." As you read Maria's résumé, think about what information you will include in your résumé.

When applying for a job, you will be writing three kinds of letters: a letter of inquiry, a letter of application, and a follow-up thank-you letter:

- Your letter of inquiry introduces you, states the positions you are seeking, inquires about the procedure for applying, and requests an application. Maria del Carmen's letter of inquiry is shown in Figure 13.6. Note the kinds of information that Maria provides to her potential employer. You might think of other information to include in your own letter.

Maria del Carmen Lopez
1234 South 56th Avenue
Miami, Florida 33133
(305) 555-7890

OBJECTIVE

Employment as an elementary school teacher in Dade County

COLLEGE EDUCATION

Bachelor of Arts in Elementary Education, 2009
Minor in Psychology   GPA: 3.7
Florida International University
—Phi Delta Kappa
—Alpha Phi Omega Service Fraternity

PROFESSIONAL AFFILIATIONS

Member of National Association for the Education of Young Children
Member of Florida Association for the Education of Young Children

TEACHING EXPERIENCE

Spring 2007	Coral Reef Elementary School, Miami, Florida	
	Third-Grade Student Teacher	
	Banyan Elementary School, Miami, Florida	
	Kindergarten Student Teacher	
Fall 2006	South Miami Heights Elementary School, Miami, Florida	
	Practicum Student in Fifth-Grade Classroom	
2002–2006	Upward Bound, Miami, Florida	
	Volunteer Reading Tutor	

OTHER EXPERIENCE

Volunteer Work: Big Brothers and Big Sisters Program
Special Olympics Coach
Pee-Wee Soccer Coach

References Available upon Request

FIGURE 13.5 Sample Résumé

This sample résumé provides you with a general outline of information to use as a guideline for writing your résumé. As you read Maria's résumé, think about what additional information you will include in your résumé.

- With your letter of application, you apply for a particular position. Your letter states your specific qualifications for the position and why you are an excellent candidate. This letter is, in essence, your sales pitch that determines whether you will get an interview. In the letter, you must indicate if you are having your credentials sent by the placement office. Your resume should accompany this letter. Figure 13.7 shows Maria del Carmen's letter of application. Note how Maria stresses her previous teaching experiences. She also mentions her field experiences and her enthusiasm for teaching. You will want to include the same things in your own letter of application.
- Your thank-you letter is a follow-up letter to either your letter of application or an interview. In it, you should thank your interviewer for considering you for the position and, once again, use the opportunity to explain why you are the best candidate for the position.

Maria del Carmen Lopez
1234 South 56th Avenue
Miami, Florida 33133
(305) 555-7890

March 15, 2009

Ms. Barbara García
Dade County Public Schools
2800 Thames Drive
Miami, Florida 33000

Dear Ms. García:

In two months I will be graduating with a Bachelor of Arts degree in elementary education from Florida International University.

My formal education program included a fifth-grade teaching practicum at South Miami Heights Elementary School and a kindergarten student teaching position at Banyan Elementary School. I am currently involved in a third-grade student teaching position at Coral Reef Elementary school. As you can see I have worked in a variety of schools and a wide range of grade levels.

My primary objective is to start working in my field as soon as I graduate, so I am available to accept whatever position may be available for either the summer or fall of 2008.

I believe my extensive field experiences and my enthusiasm for teaching make me an excellent addition to any elementary school staff.

Please send any application material I may need to the address above.

Sincerely,

Maria del Carmen Lopez

Maria del Carmen Lopez

FIGURE 13.6 Sample Letter of Inquiry

In this letter of inquiry pay particular attention to the kinds of information that Maria provides to her potential employer. You may think of other information you want to include in your letter.

REFLECT & WRITE

If the school district you teach in does not provide monetary rewards for advanced degrees, would this persuade you, one way or the other, to pursue or not pursue one?

Maria del Carmen Lopez
1234 South 56th Avenue
Miami, Florida 33133
(305) 555-7890

May 9, 2009

Ms. Barbara García
Dade County Public Schools
2800 Thames Drive
Miami, Florida

Dear Ms. García:

Enclosed please find a completed application, along with references and résumé, for employment as an elementary teacher in the Dade County Public Schools.

I graduated from Florida International University (FIU) in April with a Bachelor of Arts degree in Elementary Education. My training at FIU included a fifth-grade teaching practicum at South Miami Heights Elementary School. As a student teacher, I was placed at Banyan Elementary School in kindergarten and Coral Reef Elementary School as a third-grade teacher. I have worked in a variety of school settings and a range of grade levels.

I believe my extensive field experiences and my enthusiasm for teaching make me an excellent addition to an elementary school staff.

I am available for an interview on Mondays and Wednesdays and can be reached at home after 3:00 p.m. at (305) 555-7890.

I look forward to meeting you soon.

Sincerely,

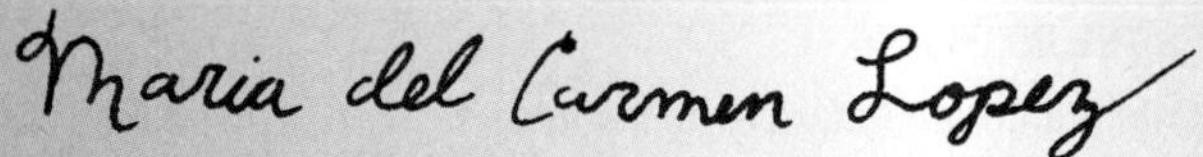

Maria del Carmen Lopez

Maria del Carmen Lopez

FIGURE 13.7 Sample Letter of Application

Notice in her letter of application how Maria stresses her previous teaching experiences. She also mentions her field experiences and her enthusiasm for teaching. You will want to include the same things in your letter of application.

Have a Successful Interview

Your interview is one of the most important parts of getting your first job. In many respects, it is the make-or-break part of job hunting. It is important that you be well prepared for the interview by anticipating what will be asked and how you will answer specific questions. Figure 13.8 gives guidelines for preparing for your interview. The purpose of the interview is twofold: to enable the school district to decide if they want to hire you and for you to convince the school district they should hire you. Consider the questions that might be asked of Maria del Carmen Lopez, such as those shown in Figure 13.9. You should be prepared for interview questions such as these. Review the questions in Figure 13.9 and prepare answers for each one. In addition to these interview questions, research online resources to find information on what to expect in your first interview.

• *Your Turn*

As you begin to line up interviews, ask administrators and experienced teachers for tips about how to approach an interview. What do they look for in candidates that they interview? Use their responses to guide your answers during your interviews.

BEFORE THE INTERVIEW

Your successful interview starts long before the interview itself. Here is what you can do to prepare for the interview.

- **Anticipate what questions will be asked.** You will be asked questions about classroom discipline, a typical day in your classroom, why you chose teaching as a career, and your philosophy of education.
- **Write out your answers to potential interview questions.**
- **Practice interviewing with a colleague.** You can use your prepared answers from simulated interviews to help answer the real questions in an interview.
- **Complete all the paperwork that accompanies an application and the interview.** Many districts have an application process that includes many forms. All paperwork needs to be completed thoroughly and neatly. Your application is you. If the application requests all official transcripts, make sure you have requested them, and that they are with the application.
- **Develop a short list of questions you want to ask the interviewer.** It is important for you to ask questions so that you have the information you need to make an informed decision and to demonstrate that you are genuinely interested in the position. Some questions you may want to ask are:
  1. What are some important characteristics of the school district and the student population?
  2. What is the philosophy of the district or school? (Ask for a copy of the district's mission statement.)
  3. What is the curriculum in the grades and subject areas I will be teaching?
  4. What does the district do to support professional development? Does the district reimburse for graduate study?
  5. Will I be assigned to a school and grade level, or will I get to choose the school and grade level I want? (A question such as this depends on the local school district. In smaller school districts, you are generally interviewing for a particular job. In large districts, after a general interview, you may be sent to local schools to interview with principals.)

6. What other assignments are included in the job?
7. What is the starting salary? What are the benefits?
8. How does the beginning teacher program work?

DURING THE INTERVIEW

- **Dress professionally.** Although the law does not allow for discrimination on the basis of dress or hair, appearance does matter to professionals, students, and parents.
- **Speak clearly and forthrightly and answer the questions asked.** Avoid answering just "yes" or "no" to a question. Expand on the questions you are asked.
- **Be positive and enthusiastic.**
- **Don't limit yourself to a particular age group, grade level, or subject area.** You may be able to teach things you never thought you could before. Many principals want teachers who are willing to try different things and get involved. If in the interview you say you are willing to consider teaching more than one grade level and to be involved in after-school activities, you will make yourself more desirable as a candidate and more valuable to the school and district. Principals and hiring committees are looking for teachers who can help get the job done.
- **Be prepared to respond to a number of people during the interview.** In addition to the principal, you may also be interviewed by teachers, parents, and community members.
- **Talk about the satisfaction you have gained from teaching.** Hearing your feelings and thoughts gives interviewers insight into your attitudes and goals.
- **Describe how you and others assess your effectiveness as a teacher.**

AFTER THE INTERVIEW

- **Write thank-you letters to all involved.**
- **Reflect on the interview process.** Analyze what went well and how you can improve.
- **Make necessary changes.** Revise your responses, and plan how you will approach your next interview.

FIGURE 13.8 A Successful Interview

There is a lot to do to prepare for a successful interview. Use the guidelines listed here to help you prepare for your interviews with potential employers.

REFLECT & WRITE

Which of the interview questions in Figure 13.9 would you have the most difficulty answering? Which of these interview questions will you have to prepare for the most?

■ **Your Education and Background:**	Briefly describe your education background and explain how it has prepared you to teach.
■ **Work Experiences:**	What work and volunteer experiences have you had, and how have they helped prepare you for teaching?
■ **Strengths and Weaknesses:**	What do you consider to be your particular strengths as a beginning teacher? What are your weaknesses, and how do you plan to strengthen them?
■ **Teaching:**	Why did you select teaching as a profession?
■ **Meeting Diverse Needs:**	How do you plan to meet the diverse needs of students in your classroom? Give an example of how you would plan to meet the special needs of a student in your classroom with a disability.
■ **Curriculum:**	What kind of curriculum do you think is appropriate for the students you will teach? What was your most successful lesson?
■ **Preparation and Planning:**	What are things you will do to prepare and plan for instruction? What kind of planning have you done?
■ **Instruction:**	What instructional strategies do you think are most effective? How will you meet the individual needs of your students?
■ **Evaluation:**	What techniques will you use to evaluate student learning?
■ **Classroom Management:**	What kind of classroom management techniques do you plan to use?
■ **Parent/Family/Community Involvement:**	Describe how you plan to involve and communicate with parents.
■ **Philosophy/Beliefs:**	What are your core values and beliefs about education? About students? What is your philosophy of education?
■ **Collaboration:**	Do you get along well with others? What are some people skills that you use when collaborating with others?
■ **Extracurricular Activities:**	What extracurricular and community activities have you participated in? What extracurricular activities would you be able to supervise?

For more guidance on how to prepare for an interview, go to the Resources section of MyEducationLab.

FIGURE 13.9 Typical Interview Questions

Review the typical interview questions listed above and prepare answers for each one. In addition to these interview questions, research online resources to help you know what to expect in your first interview.

HOW CAN YOU BENEFIT FROM BEGINNING TEACHER PROGRAMS?

The first year of teaching is a formative time in a teacher's life and career. First-year teachers are under close scrutiny and must prove they are good teachers and are able to help students learn. Also, as a beginning teacher you will be entering a social system with a particular culture and climate. You will need to get along and fit in with students, faculty, staff, parents, and the community. Proving one's worth, fitting in, and getting along are important tasks associated with the first year of teaching. Helping beginning teachers successfully accomplish these tasks is the primary purpose of beginning teacher programs.

Participate in an Induction Program

As a novice or beginning teacher, you will probably participate in a program of induction and mentoring. **Induction** is a planned program that focuses on providing teacher training, assistance, support, and retention for 2 or 3 years. Two important processes of induction programs that are supported by research are mentor teachers and ongoing opportunities for learning.

■ **INTASC**

STANDARD 10 The teacher fosters relationships with school colleagues, parents, and agencies in the larger community to support students' learning and well-being.

Induction A planned program intended to provide some systematic and sustained assistance, especially to beginning teachers, for at least one school year.

Professional development is ongoing throughout your entire career. You will want to make sure to partake in activities and programs that will help you learn, grow, and become a better teacher.

Induction programs help bridge the gap between theory and practice and enable novice teachers to reflect about and develop new insights into the teacher's role. In this regard, the beginning teacher program is very much an ongoing professional development process.

Learn through Professional Development Programs

Many teachers, including the teachers who have shared their experiences with you in this text, all agree that they benefited from or would benefit from having a skilled professional teacher provide them with help and assistance. You will want to establish a mentoring relationship with such a professional as you begin teaching. A mentor teacher can help you "learn the ropes" and support you as you develop your own distinctive teaching style and approach. Mentors also provide moral support, guidance, and feedback as you progress toward your goal of becoming a good teacher.

Although professional development is a lifelong process, becoming a professional involves participating in programs and activities that will provide you opportunities to continually grow, learn, and become more expert in your work. As staff development opportunities become available, use them as a means of collaborating with your colleagues and of taking risks—trying new things, experimenting with new ideas. Many school districts list staff development opportunities on their websites. You can access the websites in local districts near you and evaluate the nature and quality of their staff development programs.

OBSERVE & LEARN

Mentor teachers are special people, because they have been given the responsibility to guide the next generation of teachers. Observe two mentor teachers at a local school. Before you observe, develop a checklist of what you think you might see. Following your observation, make a list of things you can apply to your own teaching.

Mentors

As a novice teacher you will probably be assigned to a mentor teacher—a teacher, leader, guide, role model, supporter, and sponsor. Although not a new concept, mentoring is a growing trend and represents a major professional responsibility. Mentors are usually chosen by administrators, colleagues, and in some cases, teacher unions.

Qualifications for mentor teachers and their responsibilities vary by state and school district. For example, Texas has the following requirements for being a mentor teacher:

■ Have a minimum of 3 years of teaching experience with a superior record of assisting students in achieving improvement in student performance.
■ Complete a research-based mentor-and-induction training program approved by the commissioners.
■ Complete a mentor-training program provided by the district.

The following are the duties of a mentor teacher in Texas:

1. Participate in beginning teacher orientation.
2. Meet weekly with the beginning teacher.

What qualities would you prize in a mentor? How might you use a partnership with a master teacher to develop professionally? How would you be contributing to your mentor's professional development?

3. Maintain documentation of mentor/beginning teacher activities.

4. Attend regularly scheduled campus mentor-support meetings and training.

5. Provide support to new teachers in collecting and analyzing student data, classroom management, curriculum planning, and other activities related to pedagogy and improved student achievement.

6. Conduct observations and assessments of the beginning teacher.

7. Complete all requirements of the school district's beginning teacher induction and mentoring program.[6]

Mentors act as coaches. In their role of coaching, they promote interactions that support reflection and develop professional capacity. Mentors also are consultants, sharing their experiences and providing technical assistance. In all their roles, mentors collaborate through shared planning and problem solving.

The mentoring function is designed to support novice teachers, facilitate their induction into the profession, and promote collaboration and leadership as part of a teacher's career development. Working with a mentor can improve the quality of your beginning teacher experience and be a positive process for all involved.

Staff Development Programs

Staff development is an important part of reforming educational practices, making schools function well, and establishing teaching as a professional occupation. Staff development includes considerations of curriculum content, instructional strategies, and the ways in which the staff interact with each other and with students. Staff development is ongoing education, training, and study designed to help you and your colleagues improve skills, attitude, knowledge, and performance. The ultimate goals of staff development are to have high-quality teachers who achieve the school's mission, implement its programs, and help students achieve at high levels. As a novice teacher you will participate in ongoing staff development throughout your career. School districts invest a great deal of money in staff development.

● ***Your Turn***

Interview some experienced teachers who are teaching at a grade level you would like to teach. Ask them if they went through an induction program during their first year of teaching. Do they now serve as teacher mentors for new teachers? What did they learn from their induction program? What is the most valuable advice they have passed on to those whom they have mentored?

_____

_____

_____

_____

_____

Become a Part of Your Learning Community

Your success during your first year of teaching and beyond will depend, in part, on people who make up your learning community. Everyone who can be a source of help to you is part of your learning community; however, a number of significant groups play a particularly important role. These include members of the administration and staff, peers, specialists and service providers, students, parents and families, and community leaders.

You will want to establish friendly, cooperative, collaborative working relationships with everyone you work with in your learning community. In addition, you will want to convey the feeling that you are a team player, a member of the learning community who is willing to seek help and give help to others. Guidelines for achieving these goals are:

- **Ask for help.** Administrators are interested in your success. Your being a successful teacher means the school is successful. Make sure you establish a good working relationship with the administration. Usually, the principal, assistant principal, and your mentor will evaluate your work, so seek their advice and guidance. You can also request assistance from colleagues. You will be surprised how helpful your colleagues can be when they recognize that you are willing to ask for help. Many of the ideas mentioned above for administration and staff apply equally to peers.

- **Be a teachable person.** You will want to give the impression that you are open to new and different ways of planning and teaching and that you can learn from your more experienced colleagues. It is important to avoid giving the impression that you have all the answers because you have recently graduated from college.

- **Be willing to take on responsibilities.** Being positive and professional about your job, career, and the people you work with is a lifelong habit you will want to develop. Let others know that you are a "can do" person willing to help with activities, sponsor clubs, and serve on committees.

- **Participate in school governance and professional activities.** Get involved in professional activities and special events, such as American Education Week, open-house activities, and other events that help advance the profession and the school.

- **Work toward making the school a success.** If your colleagues have decided to implement a new initiative, such as block-scheduling or a special reading curriculum, be part of the team to work toward making these programs successful.

- **Be friendly with everyone.** You will develop friendships with many people in the school and others whom you are particularly close to, but be friendly to all the school staff, including custodians, front office staff, and support staff.

- **Be collegial and sociable with teachers and other professionals and staff members.** Colleagues can validate your feelings about what you are experiencing. The social dimension of the teaching world—and your friendly relations with those in it—can contribute to your success and happiness. Collegiality is the process of identifying with and interacting with colleagues as esteemed peers.
- **Develop trusting relationships.** As we discussed in Chapter 7, trust is a cornerstone of successful teaching. You will want to develop a trusting relationship with your students, colleagues, administration, and parents. Remember that at the heart of trust is the belief that people can depend on you.

Some colleagues will have more enthusiasm for teaching than others. Those who are positive and dedicated to doing their best for students and the profession are good models for you to follow. Through observing, listening, and questioning, you will soon learn who are the leaders of your school. These are the colleagues with whom you want to associate.

Other colleagues include specialists and service providers, such as itinerant teachers, guidance counselors, speech pathologists, special educators, psychologists, social workers, home visitors, and parent-involvement specialists. Support staff might also include librarians; technology resource staff; and specialists in music, art, and physical education. Make a point of finding out who all your colleagues are, how their work fits in with yours, and how, together, you can best meet the needs of students and their families. *In the Classroom with Constance Slaughter-Jordan* on page 476 offers advice on how you can become part of the learning community.

■ **INTASC**

STANDARD 9 The teacher is a reflective practitioner who continually evaluates the effects of his/her choices and actions on others (students, parents, and other professionals in the learning community) and who actively seeks out opportunities to grow professionally.

Establish Relationships with Students and Parents

The relationships you establish with students are among the most important in your teaching career. As discussed in Chapter 4, you will establish relationships with a variety of students from all cultural and socioeconomic backgrounds and ability levels. Students are your allies in the teaching-learning process and also can be a valuable resource in the classroom. For example, they can help identify and clarify rules, routines, and procedures and provide insight into school culture and the expectations they have for themselves and the school.

Parents hold one of the keys to the academic and social success of their children. You hold another. For these reasons and others, as discussed at length in Chapter 6, you will want to involve parents in your program. Most parents and other family members want the best for their children. They look to you and the schools to assist in achieving this goal. Many parents will assist you in making your first year and all your years of teaching successful if you provide them with the opportunity. Parents and other family members differ in the time they have to be involved. Although it is unrealistic to think that all parents will be involved, it is not unrealistic to try to encourage the involvement of all parents.

Others from the community have a wealth of talent and abilities to share. Many are waiting for you to contact them for help and assistance. For example, an engineer from a local industry might be an ideal person to assist you with your math project and to mentor students for participation in the local science fair.

As discussed in Chapter 1, one of the major changes in education over the past decade has been the increased direct involvement of the community in education. As you embark on your career, keep in mind that there are many untapped resources at your disposal that can help make you a successful teacher. Learn about your community, get to know your students' families, and think about how you can enhance your students' experience in your classroom.

In the Classroom
with
Constance Slaughter-Jordan
Advice to New Teachers about Getting a Good Start

Constance Slaughter-Jordan is a Kentucky Middle School Teacher of the Year. She and her team at Winburn Middle School in Lexington provide the following suggestions:

- **Don't worry about being popular and well liked by students.** Classroom management and discipline come first. Develop a plan of fair discipline, stick with it, and students will respect you. Follow through with reasonable and attainable consequences. If you say you are going to do something, do it. Don't take students' behavior personally. Stay objective and consistent, and deal with the actual behavior. Remember, you are a professional and must always act as one.

- **Save everything before you begin teaching and everything you do the first year of teaching.** Begin now and develop a file system of ideas, concepts, and materials relating to topics and activities that you can use in your classroom. Sometimes you don't have all the materials you want or need when you need them. Your materials file gives you a resource to draw from that is immediately accessible.

- **Get in touch with the interests of your students and make assignments around their interests.** For example, if some students are particularly interested in baseball, make math assignments and projects that involve baseball statistics and so forth.

- **Be a multicultural teacher in knowledge, attitude, and practices.** For example, we have had an influx of Japanese into our community because of the Toyota plant, and we needed to provide for their culture. We held Saturday classes for the Japanese students be-cause their parents expected classes 6 days a week. Today's classrooms are very diverse, and you have to enable students to express their feelings and ideas from their cultural point of view while at the same time incorporating cultural ideas into your lessons.

- **Make initial, positive contact with parents.** For example, at the end of July, we make visits to the homes of our incoming sixth-graders. Last year, we made 121 visits to homes. As teachers we have to get in touch with families. Our team of six teachers visits homes in groups of three. We go to the homes, meet, and talk with the students and parents. We leave information about the initial school orientation, the curriculum, and what we expect of sixth-graders and their parents. When we visit, some parents invite us in, some talk to us outside, and others talk to us through the screen door. The important thing is that we visit them. The ones we can't visit in person, we call. (See Chapter 6 for more information on involving parents and families.)

- **Develop friendships with everyone: teachers, staff, and parents.** You need to be a friend and make friends; you can't be antisocial in the teaching profession.

- **Have a plan for dealing with stress.** Stress comes with the job. You need a way to relax and relieve stress, such as aerobics, walking, or whatever method you want to work out for yourself.

- **Have a motto for yourself and, if appropriate, others whom you teach with.** Our team motto is "Look past the mess and see the mind—look past the hassle and see the heart."

REFLECT & WRITE

Of all of the guidelines listed in *In the Classroom with Constance Slaughter-Jordan* for becoming part of your learning community, which do you find the most daunting? Which will come the most naturally to you? How might you strike a comfortable balance?

_____

_____

_____

_____

_____

HOW CAN YOU SURVIVE AND GROW IN YOUR FIRST YEAR?

One of the primary things you can do to help ensure your success as a first-year teacher is to begin now to do those things that lead to success. In this section, you will consider how to plan for your first year and prepare for your first day of teaching. You will also develop a leadership plan for how you will become a successful teacher.

Preparing for Your First Year

Just as preparation for a successful teaching career begins now, so, too, does preparation for a successful start to the school year. Read about the Developing Teachers Fellowship Program in the *What's New in Education?* feature. Also keep in mind the advice of the teachers in the *In the Classroom* features in this chapter about how to make your first year successful.

Preparing for Your First Day

Preparing for your first day is an important part of being successful in your first year. The following guidelines will contribute to that success and will ease some of the anxiety that comes with starting a new year as a new teacher.

- **Know your school.** If possible, visit the school ahead of time and find out about the layout and facilities—where the library, gym, cafeteria, and other rooms are located. If you are slated to teach students who are new to the building—for example, kindergartners or an entering class of middle or high school students—you will want to orient them to their new surroundings, so it is important to be familiar with the building. Ask someone to give you a tour of the school.
- **Get to know your students, families, and community.** A good way to do this is to spend some time in the community, walking or driving, to learn what is in the community and where things are. Knowing the community is also beneficial to your students because you can relate classroom activities to community places and events.
- **Organize your classroom before school begins.** Consider decorating bulletin boards, arranging desks, chairs, and tables, and setting up learning centers.
- **Ask other teachers for advice.** Find out what you can plan for before the opening of school. This is where your mentor teacher can help. If you don't have a mentor teacher, ask the principal for the names of teachers you can call on for guidance.

Go to MyEducationLab and select the topic "Teaching Profession" then read the article "Responding to New Teacher's Concerns." Answer the questions that follow.

What's *New* in Education?

The Developing Teachers Fellowship Program

The Developing Teachers Fellowship Program is designed to enhance the group-building skills of New York City teachers. A select group of public and charter school teachers will be chosen for this innovative program that develops teachers' capacities to create more collaborative, creative, playful, and participatory learning environments for themselves and their students. Fellows will receive a $2,500 stipend for the year. The program includes:

- Biweekly Saturday workshops
- Monthly on-site supervision
- Participation in an online supervisory group

- A final classroom or school demonstration project

Whether working with a small group or a class of 40, teaching workshop style, or engaging in creative play, teachers are always working with groups. Teachers of all grade levels and content areas can benefit greatly from learning the latest innovations in group process. Many teachers feel unprepared for the complex challenges of today's classrooms: mixed learning styles and grade levels; cultural diversity; lack of motivation—all with the pressure to raise standards. In order to meet these demands, teachers need

new tools for developing a rigorous and inclusive community in the classroom. The program:

- Introduces teachers to innovative ways of organizing groups to work more supportively.
- Gives teachers a new understanding of what groups are and how they work.
- Provides teachers with practical ways for creating classroom environments in which students discover their capacity to create with others.
- Helps teachers attend to individual learning styles while working with the whole class.

Source: Adapted from East Side Institute, The Developing Teachers Fellowship Program. (Online). Available at www.eastsideinstitute.org/DevelopingTeachersAnnouncement.htm.

REFLECT & WRITE

What are the most important things you can do to prepare for your first year? What are your major concerns as you look forward to beginning teaching? What can you do now to address these concerns?

_____

_____

_____

_____

_____

Developing a Leadership and Management Plan

Chapter 1 identified and analyzed metaphors for teachers and teaching. "Teacher as manager" is a metaphor often used to describe teachers' approaches to classroom management. This metaphor implies that teachers focus on exercising authority and control over students. The teacher is strong and assertive, and students are expected to be loyal and obedient. Although the manager view of the teacher's role is widely held, there is currently a shift toward more student-centered approaches in which power is shared and students are involved in decision making. Teachers act as guides to help students be responsible for their own behavior.

The following guidelines can help you develop a plan for leading your students and maintaining a learning-oriented classroom:

- **Develop a philosophical basis for classroom management and how you will implement it.**
- **Make a list of "best practices."** Base this list on your observations of how successful, experienced teachers manage their classrooms and encourage students to be responsible for their own behavior.
- **Observe how classroom environment influences behavior and learning.** Environment includes such conditions as seating arrangement, placement of workstations, and traffic patterns, among others.
- **Consider how your beliefs affect your teaching approach.** Your ideas about how students learn and your role as a teacher influence the way you manage the learning environment.
- **Understand that leadership, classroom management, and instruction are interrelated and integrated.** For example, when teachers plan for instruction and make decisions about how time and resources will be used and how the classroom will be arranged, they are making decisions about classroom management.
- **Take as many opportunities as you can to work directly with children.** During your field experiences, and in as many settings as possible, gain experience managing children's learning and behavior. The problem many beginning teachers encounter is a lack of experience in applying the theories and ideas they have about classroom management.
- **Anticipate potential management problems and develop preventive approaches.** For example, developing routines and making smooth transitions from one learning activity to the next can help prevent misbehavior. Times that need special attention and planning include when students enter the classroom, the beginning of class, transitions from one topic or activity to another, changing from whole-group to small-group activities, and getting, distributing, or collecting materials.
- **Think about how students' behaviors are influenced by their prior experiences and home background.** Students come to school with many needs—for example, the need for acceptance—and home environments. Developing classrooms where students are accepted, valued, and respected affects how they behave in school.
- **Consider ways students can be encouraged to control and manage their own behavior.** A primary goal of classroom management is to have students manage their own behavior and learning activities.

Today's teachers are instructional leaders. How you teach, manage the classroom, and interact with students helps to determine students' achievement and, in the long run, helps to determine your success as a teacher.

• *Your Turn*

Imagine you are a sixth-grade social studies teacher. With groups of students, develop rules and procedures to be used in the classroom. *Rules* specify what students can and cannot do. *Procedures* specify how things are done. Add these ideas to your developing model of classroom management.

REFLECT & WRITE

How will your values and the views you hold about your role and your students' role in the classroom influence how you manage your classroom?

_____

_____

_____

_____

_____

Develop a Teaching Identity

In your journey from a novice to a veteran teacher, you will be involved in creating your image, your reputation, and your outlook on teaching. You will want to make sure that your teaching identity will stamp you as highly qualified and one of the best teachers. Your teaching identity includes the following:

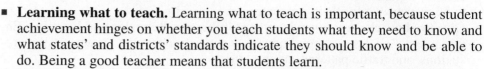

Go to MyEducationLab and select the topic "Teaching Profession" then read the article "Examining the Teaching Life." Complete the activities that follow.

- **Learning what to teach.** Learning what to teach is important, because student achievement hinges on whether you teach students what they need to know and what states' and districts' standards indicate they should know and be able to do. Being a good teacher means that students learn.
- **Learning how to teach.** Knowing yourself as a teacher is important. Part of your self-knowledge as a teacher includes knowing what methods and activities to use; knowing what teacher roles to assume to reach the goal of being an effective teacher; and a constructive and personal teaching style.
- **Knowing the school and community.** Knowing the environment in which you teach is important. Part of your teaching identity involves learning what the school and the community expect of you as a teacher. Schools and communities shape teaching identity. Some schools and communities give teachers much more freedom than others do to be instructional leaders and play significant roles in the school and community organizations. For your personal and professional happiness, you will want to select a school and community that give you the freedom to construct an identity that will characterize you as a high-quality and high-worth teacher.

Looking beyond the First Year

As you progress through the early stages of your teaching career, a legitimate question to ask is: What does the future hold? In the teaching profession, the future appears to be challenging and exciting. A number of themes will dominate the teaching profession in the coming years. Some of these are:

- **High-quality teachers.** The term *high-quality teacher* is one that resonates with the profession, parents, and the community. There is no doubt that all parents want high-quality teachers to teach their children. So, throughout your career, there will be an ongoing emphasis on how to be sure that all teachers are of high quality. You will want to make sure that you are.
- **New kinds of teachers.** Today's teacher and tomorrow's teacher are vastly different from Miriam Tupper, my first-grade teacher. Ms. Tupper was a "spinster," a lifelong teacher who devoted her whole life to the process of teaching. Today's and tomorrow's teachers represent a new breed. Many come to the teaching profession after having successful careers in other fields. Many teachers have had two or three careers by the time they come to teaching. Other teachers will use teaching as one of their two or three careers over a lifetime. As teachers enter teaching from other careers, they bring different viewpoints to the educational environment and decision making and help create a different culture for schools and classrooms. (See *In the Classroom with Barb Vogel.*)

In this chapter, you have learned about preparing for and being successful in your first year of teaching. Getting your first job, getting ready for the first day and the school year, and teaching students to the fullest extent of your abilities offer significant professional challenges. The checklists and guidelines presented here can be of real assistance in helping you become the best teacher you can be. Preparation and forethought can help you achieve success. Good luck and all the best for a successful teaching career.

In the Classroom
with **Barb Vogel**
I Am a Life Sentence!

Barb Vogel and her fifth-graders are the founders of Slavery That Oppresses People (STOP). (See Chapter 11 for more information.)

"I am a life sentence! You don't get Barb Vogel for a year, you get her for life!" That has been the trademark of my 26 years teaching elementary school children. For me, teaching is a chance to make a friend for life. My motto is "Today a teacher, tomorrow a friend." I have stayed in contact with more than 85 percent of my former students and their parents over the years. I have been matron of honor in their weddings, sat by their side in the delivery room because their own parents were in jail, held them in my arms after they lost a parent, and brought them to my home to spend the weekend when times were tough in their homes. I have clothed them, car pooled them, and fed them—and what a joy it has been!

I also try in all that I do with children to recognize the importance of balancing their hearts and minds. I have found that once you touch the heart of a child, the mind easily and willingly follows. While teaching a diverse, mobile, and too often troubled group of children, it has become clear to me that given challenging, consistent, and loving expectations, all children will thrive. Children want to succeed, and I feel blessed to be able to show them the way to success.

One way that I help children reach their highest potential is by providing a loving environment. I expect my students to respond to each other in a caring and respectful manner. Once children feel safe and loved, they will more easily take risks in their thinking and learning. We call ourselves a "school family," and we meet each other morning and afternoon in a family group. Here we sit together on the floor to discuss our plans, feelings, and goals for our day. I meet individually with all the children as they arrive and before they leave at the end of the day. I know this extra time spent meeting their personal needs pays off. I see it reflected in their test scores year after year. We continually receive the highest scores in our school. Last year, our class average was in the eightieth percentile, and all these children's test scores greatly increased.

Another method I use to help balance the minds and hearts of my students is to place before them guidelines that I feel are unique to our classroom. For example, our guidelines include:

- Do small things with great love.
- Do unto others as you would have them do unto you.
- Never doubt that a small group of thoughtful, committed people can change the world: Indeed it is the only thing that ever has!
- The pen is mightier than the sword.
- Be a part of the caring majority.
- The greatest sin of our times is not the few that have destroyed but the vast majority who have sat idly by.

Many of these precepts are drawn from famous humanitarians like Martin Luther King, Jr., Mother Teresa, and Margaret Mead. Over the years, we have put into practice the beliefs that run our classroom through community projects. We work monthly with the elderly, collect food and clothing for the needy, and we volunteer to help the homeless in our city.

ETHICAL DILEMMA

Who Will Ever Know?

STEPHANIE BOSWELL and her friend Corina Wright are preparing their resumes to send to some of the local school districts. Stephanie gives Corina her resume to read. Corina is surprised when she sees all of the things Stephanie has listed. "Stephanie, I didn't know that you were involved in so many activities and that you have so much experience working with young children." "I don't, but who will ever know? They don't check on these kinds of things. All I'm interested in is getting a good job."

What should Corina do?

SUMMARY

- As a beginning teacher, you will want to prepare for teaching by learning from other teachers and observing them in classrooms. You can do this by making the most of your field experiences and participating in a PDS program. You will also want to make sure that you have completed your requirements for certification as well as prepared for your teacher examinations.

- To find your first teaching position you should first and foremost know yourself. Creating a portfolio will deepen your knowledge of yourself and your teaching abilities. Analyze the job opportunities available to you through options such as job fairs and college placement services. When you apply for a position be sure to include a letter of inquiry, a letter of application, and a follow-up thank-you letter. Re-

searching basic interview questions will help you to have a successful interview.

- You can benefit from beginning teacher programs by participating in an induction program, attending development programs, learning from a mentor teacher, getting involved with your learning community, and establishing relationships with students and parents.

- Though your first year of teaching can be intimidating, one thing you can do to survive and even grow in your first year is to start the school year prepared. Prepare for your first year by creating a leadership and management plan and developing a teaching identity. Remember to keep looking beyond your first year.

KEY TERMS

Alternative certification   458
Certification   455
Emergency certification   459

Induction   471
Licensure   456
Mentor teacher   460

Observation   451
Quality assurance programs   458
Teacher portfolio   462

APPLICATIONS FOR ACTIVE LEARNING

Connections

1. Reread the opening vignette of Elizabeth Menendez's discussion of her first year. Identify five reasons why Elizabeth's first year was "amazing and magical."

2. Think about the concepts in this chapter. Create a picture, graphic, or figure that shows connections that are meaningful to you among this chapter's key ideas.

Field Experiences

1. You can learn a lot from talking with first-year teachers. Arrange to informally interview two teachers. From your interviews, develop a list of 10 tips that will be helpful to you in your first year of teaching.

2. Teachers who have recently completed their first year of teaching can give you helpful ideas and insights for your first year. Ask second-year teachers the following questions and use their answers to develop a personal action plan for your first year of teaching:

   - What did you do to plan for your first year?

   - What went well for you in your first year?

   - What did not go as well as you expected?

   - What would you do differently if you were starting now?

   - What were your major challenges?

   - How have your beliefs about teaching changed since your first year?

   - What areas of teaching do you plan to strengthen now?

   - On what committees and sponsorships do you serve?

   - In what professional development activities have you participated?

Personal Research

Certification information from all 50 states is available in the NASDTEC Manual on Certification 2004. Certification information and information about reciprocity agreements among states are available on the Internet and through the U.S. Department of Education. Explore electronic sources of information to find out more and to talk online to other preservice teachers who are seeking certification.

PREPARING TO TEACH

For Your Portfolio

Write your philosophy of classroom leadership and develop a model for managing students' learning and behavior. Incorporate ideas from the profiles in this chapter, tips you gath-

ered from experienced teachers, the rules and procedures you developed with students, and the thoughts you wrote down from other exercises in this book.

Idea File

The first days and weeks of a new school year can be a stressful time, especially for a new teacher. Gather information using a variety of resources, including websites, observation, interviews, and books, and then record ideas you can use to help you prepare for the opening of the school year. Remember that veteran teachers can provide you with wonderful information based on their experiences.

LEARNING AND KNOWING MORE

Websites Worth Visiting

As stressed throughout this text, technology can play a powerful role in your professional development. As a beginning teacher and throughout your teaching career, you can use the Internet as a source of knowledge and information regarding your journey toward licensure, tenure, advanced certification, and advanced degrees. You can begin that journey now by accessing the wealth of information on the following websites.

National Council for Accreditation of Teacher Education
www.ncate.org

NCATE is a coalition of 33 specialty professional associations of teachers, teacher educators, content specialists, and local and state policymakers. This website includes detailed descriptions of the organization and its standards, history, and role in the quality assurance continuum.

Beginning Teacher's Tool Box
www.inspiringteachers.com

This site offers an "Ask Our Mentor a Question" section, where you can e-mail questions or concerns to a veteran teacher, and a "Tips for New Teachers" section, which includes inspirational and humorous quotes and a top-10 "to do" list before school starts.

Teachers Helping Teachers
www.pacificnet.net/~mandel/index.html

Educators provide basic teaching tips to beginning teachers at this site. Teachers can immediately implement these ideas in the classroom and can download lesson plans and such features as "Poem of the Week" and "This Week's Stress Reduction Moment."

Teachers.net
www.teachers.net

Teachers.net brings together educators in category-specific chats, including a chatboard specifically for beginning teachers. Also available are lesson plans, live meetings, a resource list, and a newsletter.

What to Expect Your First Year Teaching
www.ed.gov/pubs/FirstYear/index.html

The U.S. Department of Education offers this free online book (in PDF format, requiring Acrobat Reader) that is a compilation of award-winning first-year teachers' experiences, challenges, and successes.

The National Center for Education Information
http://ncei.com

The National Center for Education Information (NCEI) is a private, nonpartisan research organization in Washington, D.C., specializing in survey research and data analysis. NCEI is the authoritative source of information about alternative teacher preparation and certification.

Teachnet
http://teachnet.org

Teachnet is a nationwide, educational, nonprofit organization that supports innovative teachers who exemplify professionalism, independence, and creativity in public school systems.

Books Worth Reading

Burke, J., and Krajicek, J. (2006). *Letters to a New Teacher: A Month-by-Month Guide to the Year Ahead.* Portsmouth, NH: Heinemann.
This book is an opportunity to read the letters and e-mails author Jim Burke exchanged with novice teacher Joy Krajicek—letters in which Jim opens his practice, his mind, and his heart to guide Joy through her first year in the classroom.

Feirsen, R., and Weitzman, S. (2004). *How to Get the Teaching Job You Want: The Complete Guide for College Graduates, Returning Teachers, and Career Changers.* Sterling, VA: Stylus Publishing.
Specifically written by school administrators, this book offers insights and experiences from two authors who do the hiring. A detailed, step-by-step program for taking charge of your teaching career is offered.

Johnson, S. M. (2007). *Finders and Keepers: Helping New Teachers Survive and Thrive in Our Schools.* San Francisco, CA: Jossey-Bass.
This book highlights the cases of ten teachers whose stories vividly illustrate the joys and disappointments of new teachers in today's schools. It documents why they entered teaching, what they encountered in their schools, and how they decided whether to stay or move on to other schools or other lines of work.

Thompson, J. G. (2007). *First Year Teacher's Survival Guide: Ready-To-Use Strategies, Tools, and Activities for Meeting the Challenges of Each School Day.* Hoboken, NJ: John Wiley & Sons, Inc.
Gives new teachers a wide variety of tested strategies, activities, and tools for creating a positive and dynamic learning environment while meeting the challenges of each school day. Packed with valuable tips; this book helps new teachers with everything from becoming effective team players and connecting with students to handling behavior problems and working within diverse classrooms.

Wyatt, R. L., and White, J. E. (2007). *Making Your First Year a Success: A Classroom Survival Guide for Middle and High School Teachers.* Thousand Oaks, CA: Corwin Press.
Provides specific and practical advice, from how to create lessons to dealing with difficult parents, all geared to the needs of middle school and high school teachers.

Endnotes

CHAPTER 1

1. Quam, J., and Campbell, C. (2007, January 17). *2007 National Teacher of the Year finalists chosen.* The Council of Chief State School Officers. (Online). Available at www.acei.org/2007NTYFinalists.pdf. Accessed April 12, 2007.

2. Ibid.

3. Good, T. L., & Brophy, J. E. (2003). *Looking in classrooms* (9th ed.). Boston: Allyn & Bacon.

4. Smith, K. (2005). *Positive classroom environment and student–teacher rapport: Preventing challenging behavior in the classroom.* (Online). University of Minnesota, Minneapolis Institute on Community Integration: Minneapolis, Minnesota. Available at www.education.umn.edu/ceed/projects/preschoolbehavior/tipsheets/posclass.pdf. Accessed July 8, 2007.

5. 2000 Teacher of the Year Finalists Announced by *Technology & Learning Magazine.* (2000, October 27). PR Newswire. (Online). Available at www.prnewswire.com/cgi-bin/stories.pl?ACCT=104&STORY=/www/story/10-27-2000/0001351387&EDATE=. Accessed October 1, 2007.

6. Zehm, S. J., & Kottler, J. A. (2000). *On being a teacher: The human dimension.* Newbury Park, CA: Corwin Press, pp. 5–15.

7. Chesterfield County Public Schools. (2007, July 19). *Chesterfield names 2008 Teacher of the Year.* (Online). Available at www.midlothianexchange.com/npps/story.cfm?ID=1153. Accessed March 3, 2007.

8. Jampol, R. (2007, July 31). *Assessment, assessment, assessment.* (Online). Available at www.townonline.com/newton/opinion/x809747993. Accessed September 8, 2007.

9. Eiselein, M. (2007, July 20). Academy turns fun, games into learning tools. *The Press Enterprise.* (Online). Available at www.pe.com/localnews/inland/stories/PE_News_Local_R_racademy21.4159055.html. Accessed March 5, 2007.

10. The de Paul School. (2007). *Teaching methods, the art and science of teaching at de Paul.* (Online). Available at www.depaulschool.org/teaching.html. Accessed May 9, 2007.

11. Knobloch, N. A., & Whittington, M. S. (2003). Novice teachers' perceptions of support, teacher preparation quality, and student teaching experience related to teacher efficacy. *Journal of Vocational Education Research 27*(3), 331–341.

12. Hoy, A. W. (2002). *The influence of resources and support on teachers' efficacy beliefs.* Paper presented at the annual meeting of the American Educational Research Association, session 13:82, April 2, New Orleans, Louisiana.

13. Soodak, L. C., & Podell, D. M. (1993). Teacher efficacy and student problems as factors in special education. *Journal of Special Education 27*(1), 66–81.

14. Judge, T. A., & Bono, J. E. (2001). Relationship of core self-evaluations traits (self-esteem, generalized self-efficacy, locus of control, and emotional stability) with job satisfaction and job performance. *Journal of Applied Psychology 86*(1), 80–92.

15. Ross, J. A. (2003, April). Prior student achievement, collaborative school processes, and collective teacher efficacy. *Ontario Institute for Studies in Education.* Presented at the annual meeting of the American Educational Research Association, Chicago. (Online). Available at www.oise.utoronto.ca/field-centres/ross/abstract.htm. Accessed June 10, 2007.

16. Goddard, R. D., Hoy, W. K. & Hoy, A. W. (2000). Collective teacher efficacy: its meaning, measure, and impact on student achievement. *American Educational Research Journal 37*(2), 482–486.

17. Lieberman, J., Landrieu, M., & Coleman, N. (2007). All Students Can Achieve Act. (Online). Available at http://lieberman.senate.gov/documents/asca.pdf. Accessed July 24, 2007.

18. Desimone, L. M., Porter, A. C., Garet, M. S., Yoon, K. S., & Birman, B. F. (2002). *Effects of professional development on teachers' instruction: Results from a 3-year longitudinal study.* American Institute for Research. (Online). Available at http://epa.sagepub.com/cgi/content/abstract/24/2/81. Accessed July 17, 2007.

19. CSUN *Collaborative for Quality Teaching.* (Online). Available at http://www.csun.edu/~collabqt/anne_marie_wotkyns.html. Accessed on November 29, 2007.

20. Hirsch, E., Koppich, J., & Knapp, M. (2007). *Revisiting what states are doing to improve the quality of teaching: An update on patterns and trends.* (Online). Available at www.ncsl.org/programs/educ/TPrep.htm. Accessed May 29, 2007.

21. Denver ProComp. (2007, September 4). *Denver Public Schools.* (Online). Available at http://denverprocomp.org. Accessed April 16, 2007.

22. Hobbs, E. (2007, September 9). Merit pay for teachers reveals sway of affluence. *Orlando Sentinel.* (Online). Available at www.orlandosentinel.com/news/local/orange/orl-star0907sep09,0,1890540,print.story. Accessed September 6, 2007.

23. *Issue Brief: Supporting high quality teachers.* (2006, June). House Committee on Education and the Workforce. (Online). Available at http://republicans.edlabor.house.gov/archive/

issues/109th/education/teachers/summary.htm. Accessed March 23, 2007.

24. U.S. Department of Education, Office of Post Secondary Education. (2006). *The Secretary's Fifth Annual Report on Teacher Quality: A highly qualified teacher in every classroom.* Jessup, MD: ED Pubs, Education Publication Center, U.S. Department of Education. (Online). Available at www.title2.org/Title_II_06 .pdf. Accessed August 5, 2007.

25. Cooper, J. M. (2003). The teacher as decision maker. In J. M. Cooper (Ed.), *Classroom teaching skills* (7th ed.). Lexington, MA: Houghton Mifflin.

26. Center for American Progress. (2006, April). *Can we improve teacher effectiveness?* (Online). Available at www .americanprogress.org/events/2006/4/b593305ct2152565.html. Accessed August 27, 2007.

27. Bullough, R. V., & Stokes, D. K. (1994). Analyzing personal teaching metaphors in preservice teacher education as a means for encouraging professional development. *Teaching, Learning, and Human Development 31*(1), 197–224.

28. Stapler, T. (2004). Personal communication.

29. Manning, A. (2002, November 12). Sister's hard work, belief pay off. *USA Today.* Available at www.usatoday.com/news/ education/2002-11-11-hess_x.htm. Accessed on November 30, 2007.

30. Anderson, E. (2007, July 19). Love of teaching motivates associate superintendent. *The Georgia Bulletin, the Newspaper of the Catholic Archdiocese of Atlanta.* Available at http://www .georgiabulletin.org/local/2007/07/19/teaching/?s=any%20 good%20administrator%20has%20to%20have%20a%20love %20for%20teaching%20%20first%20and%20 foremost%20%20I%20think%20having%20as%20your%20 objective%20what%20is%20best%20for%20the%20 students%20%20whether%20you%20stand. Accessed on November 30, 2007.

31. National Center for Education Information. (2005). *Profile of teacher in the U.S. 2005: Results of a national survey of K–12 public school teachers conducted by the National Center for Educational Information.* (Online). Available at www.ncei.com/ POT05PRESSREL3.htm. Accessed May 15, 2007.

32. Bemis, A. E., & Palmer, E. A. (1999). *Year-round education.* (Online). Available at http://cehd.umn.edu/CAREI/Reports/ docs/Year-round.pdf. Accessed September 9, 2007.

33. Martin, A. The school cafeteria, on a diet. (2007, September 5). *New York Times*, p. C1.

34. Briggs, T. W. (2007, September 4). *Book's not closed on texting. USA Today*, p. 9D.

35. National Commission on Excellence in Education. (2000). *A nation at risk: The imperatives for educational reform.* (ERIC ED 279603). Washington, DC: US Government Printing Office, p.1.

36. Department of Labor, DC. Secretary's Commission on Achieving Necessary Skills. (1991). What work requires of schools: A SCANS report for America 2000. (ERIC# ED332054). Available at www.eric.ed.gov/ERICDocs/data/ericdocs2sql/content_ storage_01/0000019b/80/22/ee/16.pdf. Accessed on November 30, 2007.

37. National Center for Education Statistics. (2007, September). *Status and trends in the education of racial and ethnic minorities.* (Online). Available at http://nces.ed.gov/pubs2007/ minoritytrends/tables/table_7_3.asp?referrer=report. Accessed October 1, 2007.

38. U.S. Census Bureau. (2007, May 17). *Minority population tops 100 million.* (Online). Available at www.census.gov/Press-Release/www/releases/archives/population/010048.html. Accessed June 11, 2007.

39. Morris, J. (2007, August 30). Junior high teacher in Liberty is Missouri Teacher of the Year for 2007–08. *Missouri Department of Elementary and Secondary Education 41*(57). (Online). Available at http://dese.mo.gov/news/2007/toy.htm. Accessed June 24, 2007.

40. Louis Harris and Associates. (2003). *Metropolitan life survey of the American teachers*, p. 10, New York: MetLife.

CHAPTER 2

1. Wise, A. E. (2005). Establishing as a profession: The essential role of professional accreditation. *Journal of Teacher Education 56*(4), 319.

2. U.S. Census Bureau. (2004). *Facts for features.* April 22. (Online). Available at www.census.gov/Press-Release/www/ releases/archives/facts_for_features_special_editions/001737. Accessed April 16, 2007.

3. Praxis Series. (2007). *State requirements.* (Online). Available at www.ets.org/praxis/prxstate.html. Accessed March 12, 2007.

4. National Council for the Accreditation of Teacher Education. (2008, Fall). *NCATE unit standards.* (Online). Available at www.ncate.org/documents/standards/UnitStandardsMay07 .pdf. p. 4. Accessed August 8, 2007.

5. Colorado Association for Health, Physical Education, Recreation and Dance. (2006). *2006 award winners.* (Online). Available at www.coahperd.org/convention/awardwinners06/winners06 .html. Accessed September 30, 2007.

6. National Council for the Accreditation of Teacher Education. (2008, Fall). *NCATE unit standards.* (Online). Available at www .ncate.org/documents/standards/UnitStandardsMay07.pdf. p. 5. Accessed August 8, 2007.

7. Ibid., p. 6. www.ncate.org/documents/standards/ UnitStandardsMay07.pdf. p. 6. Accessed September 18, 2007.

8. Ibid., p. 11.

9. Colorado Association for Health, Physical Education, Recreation and Dance. (2006). *2006 award winners.* (Online). Available at www.coahperd.org/convention/awardwinners06/winners06 .html. Accessed April 8, 2007.

10. National Council for the Accreditation of Teacher Education. (2008, Fall). *NCATE unit standards.* (Online). Available at www .ncate.org/documents/standards/UnitStandardsMay07.pdf. p. 7. Accessed May 5, 2007.

11. Wong-Briggs, T. (2007, May 17). For the 2006 All-USA Teacher Team, it's all about the students. *USA Today.* (Online). Available at www.usatoday.com/news/education/2006-10-17-allstar-teachers_x.htm. Accessed May 27, 2007.

12. Bredekamp S., and C. Copple, eds. (1997). *Developmentally appropriate practice in early childhood programs.* Washington, DC: National Association for the Education of Young Children, p. 9.

13. Quinones, E. (2007, May 31). Princeton honors outstanding secondary school teachers. Princeton University. (Online). Available at www.princeton.edu/main/news/archive/S18/06/27Q02/. Accessed July 21, 2007.

14. Perlman, H. B. (2006, June 29). *Two teachers honored for outstanding accomplishments.* Massachusetts Department of Education. (Online). Available at www.doe.mass.edu/news/news.asp?id=2963. Accessed July 18, 2007.

15. Commonwealth of Massachusetts Department of Education. (2007). *Meet the 2007 Massachusetts Teacher of the Year: Jessie L. Auger.* (Online). Available at www.doe.mass.edu/eq/recognition/toy/07broch.pdf. Accessed April 13, 2007.

16. Auger, J. L. (2001, Fall). Who do we hear? *Rethinking Schools 16*(1). (Online). Available at www.rethinkingschools.org/archive/16_01/Who161.shtml. Accessed May 22, 2007.

17. National Council for the Accreditation of Teacher Education. (2008, Fall). *NCATE unit standards.* (Online). Available at www.ncate.org/documents/standards/UnitStandardsMay07.pdf. p. 9. Accessed September 29, 2007.

18. California State University San Marcos College of Education. CSUSM College of Education Professional Dispositions. (N.D.) (Online). Available at http://lynx.csusm.edu/coe/about/Dispositions.htm. Accessed September 3, 2007.

19. East Chapel Hill High School. (2003). *Student Handbook 2003–04*: Section One. (Online). Available at www.chccs.k12.nc.us/echhs/studenthandbooksec1.htm. Accessed July 15, 2007.

20. Brophy, J. (1998). The uses and abuses of educational research. *Educational Research Network 2*(1), 12–15.

21. American Association of Colleges for Teacher Education. (2006). *Professional development schools.* [Online]. Available at www.aacte.org/Programs/PDS/faqpds.aspx. Accessed March 22, 2007.

22. University of South Carolina College of Education. (2000). *Dean's message: Professional development schools.* [Online]. Available at www.ed.sc.edu/pds/dmessage.htm. Accessed May 11, 2007.

23. Zeichner, K. (2006). Professional development school partnerships: A place for teacher learning. *New Horizons for Learning.* [Online]. Available at www.newhorizons.org/spneeds/inclusion/staff/zeichner.htm. Accessed March 22, 2007.

24. U.S. Department of Education. (2006, October 5). Improving teacher quality state grants ESEA Title II part a non-regulatory guidance. [Online]. Available at www.ed.gov/programs/teacherqual/guidance.pdf. Accessed March 22, 2007.

25. National Education Association. (2006). *NEA factsheet.* (Online). Available at www.nea.org/presscenter/neafact.html. Accessed March 22, 2007.

26. American Federation of Teachers. *Mission statement.* (2000). [Online]. Available at www.aft.org/about/index.htm. Accessed March 22, 2007.

27. National Education Association. (2006). *NEAFT partnership.* (Online). Available at www.nea.org/aboutnea/NEAFTPartnership.html. Accessed March 22, 2007.

28. United Federation of Teachers. Available at www.uft.org/. Accessed November 30, 2007.

29. Kochuk, N. (2005, February). Clearing a path for teacher diversity. *NEA Today.* (Online). Available at http://findarticles.com/p/articles/mi_qa3617/is_200502/ai_n9478186. Accessed October 4, 2007.

30. Ravitch, D. (2006–2007, Winter). Why teacher unions are good for teachers and the public. *American Federation of Teachers.* (Online). Available at www.aft.org/pubs-reports/american_educator/issues/winter06–07/includes/ravitch.htm. Accessed April 24, 2007.

31. Carnegie Forum on Education and the Economy. (1986). *A nation prepared: Teachers for the 21st century.* Report of the Carnegie Task Force on Teaching as a Profession. Washington, DC: Author.

32. Londergan, J. M. (2001, December). Preparing urban teachers to use technology for instruction. *ERIC Clearinghouse.* (Online). Available at www.ericdigests.org/2002–3/urban.htm. Accessed April 24, 2007.

33. Holmes Partnership homepage. (Online). Available at www.holmespartnership.org/. Accessed April 24, 2007.

34. Chief Council of State School Officers homepage. (Online). Available at www.ccsso.org/. Accessed April 24, 2007.

35. American Council on Education. (1999). *To touch the future: Transforming the way teachers are taught.* (Online). Available at www.acenet.edu/bookstore/pdf/teacher-ed-rpt.pdf. Accessed April 24, 2007.

36. National Education Association. (2007, 12 April). Statement of Steve Burroughs—Education and Labor Subcommittee U.S. House of Representatives. (Online). Available at www.nea.org/lac/esea/041207testi.html. Accessed April 23, 2007.

37. *Education Roundtable.* (2007). *A petition calling for the dismantling of the No Child Left Behind Act.* (Online). Available at: http://educatorroundtable.org/er_petition.pdf. Accessed April 23, 2007.

38. Grant, C. A. (1994, Fall). Best practices in teacher preparation from urban schools: Lessons from the multicultural teacher education literature. *Action in Teacher Education 16*(3), 13. (Reprinted with permission of the American Teacher Association.)

39. National Center for Education Information. (2005). *Profile of teachers in the U.S. 2005.* (Online). Available at www.ncei.com/POT05PRESSREL3.htm. Accessed April 24, 2007.

40. National Center for Education Statistics. *Characteristics of schools, districts, teachers, principals, and school libraries in the United States 2003–04, Schools and Staffing Survey,* 2006, tables 18–19, 2. (Online). Available at http://nces.ed.gov/pubs2006/2006313.pdf. Accessed April 24, 2007.

41. Miami-Dade County Public Schools. (2003, October). *Statistical highlights, 2002–2003.* (Online). Available at http://drs.dadeschools.net/Highlights/Highlights%2002–03.pdf. Accessed April 24, 2007.

42. Knich, D. (2007, March 12). 'Call Me Mister' looks for more misters. *The Post and Courier.* (Online). Available at www.ciclt .net/clemson/main.asp?PT=n_detail&Client=clemson&N_ID= 200085. Accessed April 18, 2007.

43. Johnson, J. (2005, May). State financial incentive policies for recruiting and retaining effective new teachers in hard-to-staff schools. *Education Commission of the States.* (Online). Available at www.ecs.org/clearinghouse/61/61/6161.htm. Accessed April 23, 2007.

44. Dotinga, R. (2005, June 14). Calls to commend teachers—with cash. *The Christian Science Monitor.* (Online). Available at www.csmonitor.com/2005/0614/p13s02-legn.htm. Accessed April 23, 2007.

45. Johnson, J. (2005, May). State financial incentive policies for recruiting and retaining effective new teachers in hard-to-staff schools. *Education Commission of the States.* (Online). Available at www.ecs.org/clearinghouse/61/61/6161.htm. Accessed April 23, 2007.

46. Podgursky, M. (2002, August 14). The single salary schedule for teachers in K-12 public schools. Discussion paper prepared for the Center for Reform of School Systems. (Online). Available at http://web.missouri.edu/~podgurskym/papers_ presentations/reports/teacher_salary_schedules.pdf. Accessed April 25, 2007.

47. Carroll, T. G., Fulton, K., Abercrombie, K., and Yoon, I. (2004). *Fifty years after Brown v. board of education: A two-tiered education system.* (Online). Available at www.nctaf.org/ documents/Brown_Full_Report_Final.pdf. Accessed April 25, 2007.

48. McCollum, S. (2001, February). Educational leadership: How merit pay improves education. *Association for Supervision and Curriculum Development 58*(5), 21–24.

49. The Associated Press. (2001, June 22). Lottery offers California teachers cheap housing. CNN. Available at http://cnnstudentnews.cnn.com/2001/fyi/teachers.ednews/06/ 22/teacher.lottery.ap/index.html. Accessed November 30, 2007. (2001, June 23). Helping teachers feel at home. *Dallas Morning News*, p. 16A.

50. Sandham, J. L. (2000, July 12). California sweetens pot to ease teacher shortage. *Education Week*, p. 24.

51. National Center for Education Statistics. (2002). *Digest of education statistics, 2002.* Washington, DC: U.S. Government Printing Office, table 68.

52. National Association of Independent Schools. (2003). *ISAC Salaries and Tuition: 2002–2003.* (Online). Available at www .isacs.org/ftpimages/72/download/download_group374_id3056 .pdf. Accessed April 25, 2007.

53. National Center for Education Statistics. (2005). *Digest of Education Statistics: 2005, Introduction.* (Online). Available at http://nces.ed.gov/programs/digest/d05/. Accessed April 25, 2007.

CHAPTER 3

1. Robelen, E. W. (2005, April 13). 40 years after ESEA, federal role in schools is broader than ever. *Education Week.* (Online). Available at www.edweek.org/ew/articles/2005/04/13/31esea .h24.html. Accessed July 6, 2007.

2. Peters Township School District website. (Online). Available at www.ptsd.k12.pa.us. Accessed July 7, 2007.

3. Klein Oak High School Mission Statement. (Online). Available at http://kleinoak.kleinisd.net/default.aspx?name=about .mission. Accessed July 11, 2007.

4. Commission on the Reorganization of Secondary Education. (1918). *Cardinal principles of secondary education.* (Bulletin 1918). Washington, DC: Bureau of Education, U.S. Department of the Interior, pp. 12–13.

5. Rothstein, R., & Jacobsen, R. (2006, December). *The goals of education.* Economic Policy Institute. (Online). Available at www.epinet.org/content.cfm?id=2568. Accessed July 11, 2007.

6. House Committee on Science and Technology. (2006, March 30). *Testimony of Margaret Spellings Secretary U.S. Department of Education on the role of education in global competitiveness before the United States House Committee on Science.* (Online). Available at http://gop.science.house.gov/ hearings/full06/March%2030/spellings.pdf. Accessed May 30, 2007.

7. National Center for Education Statistics. (2005). *National digest of education statistics, table 85.* (Online). Available at http://nces.ed.gov/programs/digest/d05/tables/dt05_085.asp. Accessed May 29, 2007.

8. Great Schools. (2007). *Belmont Senior High School.* (Online). Available at www.greatschools.net/modperl/browse_school/ca/ 1930. Accessed May 29, 2007.

9. National Center for Education Statistics. (2005). *National digest of education statistics, table 5.* (Online). Available at http://nces.ed.gov/programs/digest/d05/tables/dt05_005.asp. Accessed May 29, 2007.

10. Gross, L. Kentucky Department of Education. (2007, May 29). Personal communication.

11. Gardner, M. (2007, January 3). An after-school struggle to juggle kids and work. *The Christian Science Monitor.* (Online). Available at www.csmonitor.com/2007/0103/p14s01-legn .htm. Accessed July 6, 2007.

12. National Institute of Out-of-School Time. (2003). *Wellesley centers for women.* (Online). Available at www.niost.org. Accessed July 6, 2007.

13. Learning Point Associates. (2006, July). *21st Century Community Learning Centers (21st CCLC) analytic support for evaluation and program monitoring: An overview of the 21st CCLC program: 2004–2005.* (Online). Available at www.ed.gov/ programs/21stcclc/2006report.doc. Accessed May 29, 2007.

14. Sharing Success Technical Assistance Center. (Spring 2004). *Research brief: Summary of new research on topics of interest to New York state educators.* (Online). Available at www .sharingsuccess.org/code/bv/summerschool.pdf. Accessed July 6, 2007.

15. Kenning, C. (2006, July 17). Teachers see benefits in year-round schools. *The (Louisville) Courier Journal.* (Online). Available at www.nayre.org/Louisville%20CJ%20July% 2017.pdf. Accessed May 30, 2007.

16. National Association for Year-Round Education. (2006). *Statistical summaries of year-round education programs: 2005–2006.* (Online). Available at www.nayre.org/2005–06%20STATISTICAL%20SUMMARIES%20OF%20YRE.pdf. Accessed May 30, 2007.

17. Florida Department of Education. (2007). *Florida's guide to public high school graduation—it's a major opportunity!* (Online). Available at www.fldoe.org/APlusPlus/pdf/MAJORSGuideHSGraduation2007.pdf. Accessed May 30, 2007.

18. The Carnegie Foundation for the Advancement of Teaching. (2006). *The Carnegie unit: What is it?* (Online). Available at www.carnegiefoundation.org/about/sub.asp?key=17&subkey=1874. Accessed July 11, 2007.

19. Cromwell, S. (2005). Block scheduling: A solution or a problem? *Education World.* (Online). Available at www.educationworld.com/a_admin/admin/admin029.shtml. Accessed July 11, 2007.

20. National Center for Education Statistics. (2005). *National digest of education statistics, table 91.* (Online). Available at http://nces.ed.gov/programs/digest/d05/tables/dt05_091.asp. Accessed May 31, 2007.

21. National Center for Education Statistics. (2005). *National digest of education statistics, table 92.* (Online). Available at http://nces.ed.gov/programs/digest/d05/tables/dt05_092.asp. Accessed May 31, 2007.

22. Stevenson, K. (2006). *Education trends shaping school planning and design: 2007.* National Clearinghouse for Education Facilities. (Online). Available at www.edfacilities.org/pubs/trends2007.pdf. Accessed July 9, 2007.

23. National Center for Education Statistics. (2005). *National digest of education statistics, table 92.* (Online). Available at http://nces.ed.gov/programs/digest/d05/tables/dt05_092.asp. Accessed June 1, 2007.

24. Jimerson, L. (2006, August). *The hobbit effect: Why small works in public schools.* Randolph, VT: The Rural School and Community Trust. p. 7.

25. Kent Lawrence, B., et al. (2005). *Dollars & sense II: Lessons from good, cost-effective small schools.* Cincinnati, OH: Knowledge Works Foundation, Concordia, and Architects of Achievement. p. 18.

26. Bosman, J. (2007, June 30). Small schools are ahead in graduation. *New York Times.* (Online). Available at http://select.nytimes.com/gst/abstract.html?res=F30C10F93C5A0C738FDDAF0894DF404482. Accessed July 9, 2007.

27. Howley, C. B., & Bickel, R. (2000, February). *When it comes to schooling . . . small works: School size, poverty, and student achievement.* Randolph, VT: Rural School and Community Trust. ERIC Clearinghouse (Online). Available at www.eric.ed.gov/ERICWebPortal/custom/portlets/recordDetails/detailmini.jsp?_nfpb=true&_&ERICExtSearch_SearchValue_0=ED447973&ERICExtSearch_SearchType_0=eric_accno&accno=ED447973. Accessed July 11, 2007.

28. Johns, E. (2007, February 27). "Growing districts try to build big with small feel." Farmington, Minnesota *Star Tribune.* (Online). Available at http://nl.newsbank.com/nl-search/we/Archives?p_product=MN&p_theme=mn&p_action=search&p_maxdocs=200&p_field_label-0=Section&s_dispstring=allfields(Growing%20districts%20try%20to%20build%20big%20with%20small%20)%20AND%20date(2/25/2007%20to%202/28/2007)&p_field_date0=YMD_date&p_params_date-0=date:B,E&p_text_date-0=2/25/2007%20to%202/28/2007)&p_field_advanced-0=&p_text_advanced-0=("Growing%20districts%20try%20to%20build%20big%20with%20small%20")&p_perpage=10&p_sort=YMD_date:D&xcal_useweights=no. Accessed July 11, 2007.

29. Lear, R. J., and Wasley, P. A. (2001, March). Small schools, real gains. *Educational Leadership*, pp. 23–24.

30. Barnett, W. S., Hustedt, J. T., Hawkinson, L. E., & Robin, K. B. (2006). *The state of preschool 2006.* National Institute for Early Education Research. (Online). Available at http://nieer.org/yearbook/. Accessed July 9, 2007.

31. Head Start Bureau. (2007, February). *Head start program fact sheet fiscal year 2007.* (Online). Available at www.acf.hhs.gov/programs/hsb/research/2007factsheet.pdf. Accessed June 1, 2007.

32. Education Commission of the States. (2005, April). *State statutes regarding kindergarten.* (Online). Available at www.mespa.net/files/1838Kindergarten_Statutes.pdf. Accessed July 11, 2007.

33. National Institute for Early Education Research (2006). *New study shows full-day pre-kindergarten helps kids do better in literacy and math; closes gap between rich and poor.* (Online). Available at http://nieer.org/mediacenter/index.php?PressID=53. Accessed July 11, 2007.

34. National Education Association (2006). Early childhood education. *NEA on pre-kindergarten and kindergarten.* (Online). Available at www.nea.org/earlychildhood/images/prekkinder.pdf. Accessed July 11, 2007.

35. Garcia, D. R., & Molnar, A. (2005, May 1). At last, we find out what parents want. *The Arizona Republic.* (Online). Available at www.azcentral.com/arizonarepublic/viewpoints/articles/0501molnar0501.html. Accessed June 17, 2007.

36. Indiana University Bloomington School of Education. (2007, January 16). *Survey by CEEP finds full-day kindergarten has support.* (Online). Available at www.indiana.edu/~soenews/news/news1168466303.html. Accessed June 17, 2007.

37. Manzo, K. K. (2001). Missed opportunities. *Education Week.* (Online). Available at www.edweek.org/ew/ewstory.cfm?slug=05mscurric.h20. Accessed July 11, 2007.

38. Office of Program Policy Analysis & Government Accountability. (2005, January). *K–8 schools may help school districts improve student performance.* Report No. 05-02. Washington DC: Author, p. 1.

39. Education Week Research Center. (2007). *High school reform.* (Online). Available at www2.edweek.org/rc/issues/high-school-reform. Accessed July 11, 2007.

40. Shafer, R. (2001, September). Personal communication.

41. U.S. Department of Education. *Elementary & secondary education: Part C—Magnet schools assistance.* (Online). Available at www.ed.gov/policy/elsec/leg/esea02/pg65.html. Accessed July 11, 2007.

42. U.S. Department of Education. (2006, August 8). *Innovations in education: Creating successful magnet school programs.* (Online). Available at www.ed.gov/admins/comm/choice/magnet/report_pg14.html#houston. Accessed July 11, 2007.

43. Rossell, C. (2003). The desegregation efficiency of magnet schools. *Urban Affairs Review 38*(5), 697–725.

44. Christenson, B. (2003). *Evaluation of the magnet schools assistance program, 1998 grantees.* Washington DC: American Institutes of Research, p. vi.

45. National Center for Education Statistics. (2006). *Indicators of school crime and safety: 2006.* (Online). Available at http://nces.ed.gov/programs/crimeindicators/. Accessed July 11, 2007.

46. Los Angeles Unified School District. (Online). Available at www.lausd.net. Accessed July 11, 2007.

47. Reading School District. (Online). Available at www.readingsd.org/. Accessed July 11, 2007.

48. Richardson, L. (1994, October 26). Little country school copes with change. *New York Times*, p. A12.

49. Johnson, J. (2005). *Why rural matters 2005.* The Rural School and Community Trust. (Online). Available at http://files.ruraledu.org/whyruralmatters/WRM2005.pdf. pp. 85, 86. Accessed April 8, 2007.

50. Lindsay, D. (1994, August 3). E.D. report hails rural schools as a "model of strength." *Education Week*, p. 3.

51. Williams, T., & Kirst, M. (2006, March/April). School practices that matter. *Leadership*, p. 9.

52. Association for More Effective Schools. (1996). *Correlates of effective schools.* (Online). Available at www.mes.org/correlates.html. Accessed July 11, 2007.

CHAPTER 4

1. U.S. Bureau of the Census. (2007). *Minority population tops 100 million.* (Online). Available at www.census.gov/Press-Release/www/releases/archives/population/010048.html.

2. Figlio, D. N. (2004). *Names, expectations, and the black–white test score gap.* Education Commission of the States. University of Florida. (Online). Available at www.ecs.org/html/offsite.asp?document=http%3A%2F%2Fbear%2Ecba%2Eufl%2Eedu%2Ffiglio%2Fblacknames1%2Epdf+.

3. National Center for Education Statistics. (2007). *Racial/ethnic distribution of public school students.* (Online). Available at http://nces.ed.gov/programs/coe/2007/section1/indicator05.asp.

4. Abedi, J., & Dietel, R. (2004, June). Challenges in the No Child Left Behind Act for English-language learners. *Phi Delta Kappan 85*(10), 782.

5. Mishel, L., and Roy, J. (2006). Rethinking high school graduation rates and trends. *Economic Policy Institute.* (Online). Available at www.epi.org/books/rethinking_hs_grad_rates/rethinking_hs_grad_rates-FULL_TEXT.pdf.

6. National Center for Education Statistics. (2007). *The condition of education 2007.* (Online). Available at http://nces.ed.gov/programs/coe/2007/pdf/24_2007.pdf. Accessed October 1, 2007.

7. Ibid.

8. Puyallup School District. (2006, September 13). *Jackson encourages community to embrace diversity.* (Online). Available at www.puyallup.k12.wa.us/ourdistrict/diversity/details/tjackson.cfm. Accessed June 8, 2007.

9. Reid, T. R. (2005, December 9). Spanish at school translates to suspension. *Washington Post*, p. A3.

10. Fox, T. G. (2007, March 12). Behind burqa, Student gets an education in bigotry. *The Hartford Courant.* (Online). Available www.campus-watch.org/article/id/3118. Accessed July 17, 2007.

11. Montgomery, D. (2006, June 15). Muslim students get help juggling school and faith. 2006 June 15. *Seattle Times.* (Online). Available at http://seattletimes.nwsource.com/html/education/2003062394_prayer15m.html. Accessed March 11, 2007.

12. Banks, J. A. (1993). *Multiethnic education: Theory and practice* (3rd ed.). Boston: Allyn & Bacon, p. 147.

13. National Council for Accreditation of Teacher Education. (2006). *Professional standards for the accreditation of schools, colleges, and departments of education.* (Online). Available at www.ncate.org/documents/standards/unit_stnds_2006.pdf.

14. National Center for Education Statistics. (2007). *The condition of education 2007.* U.S. Department of Education. (Online). Available at http://nces.ed.gov/pubs2007/2007064.pdf.

15. Florida Department of Education. (2005). *Breakdown of school district K–12.* The Beacon Council. (Online). Available at www.beaconcouncil.com/Web/Content.aspx?Page=breakDownK_12.

16. Los Angeles Board of Education. (2006, April). *Los Angeles Unified School District R30 language census report 2005–2006.* (Online). Available at http://search.lausd.k12.ca.us/cgi-bin/fccgi.exe.

17. NCLB Act, Sec. 3101a and c.

18. Northwest Regional Educational Laboratory. (2003, May). *The implications of No Child Left Behind for the mainstream teacher.* (Online). Available at www.nwrel.org/request/2003may/implications.html.

19. Peterson, B., and Dawson-Salas, K. (Fall 2004). *Working effectively with English-language-learners.* (Online). Available at www.rethinkingschools.org/publication/newteacher/NTBilingual.shtml. Accessed August 23, 2007.

20. Federal Interagency Forum on Child and Family Statistics. (2007). *America's Children: Key National Indicators of Well-Being, 2007.* Available at http://childstats.gov/americaschildren/famsoc5.asp. Accessed December 1, 2007.

21. National Center for Education Statistics. (2007). *The condition of education 2007.* U.S. Department of Education. (Online). Available at http://nces.ed.gov/pubs2007/2007064.pdf. Accessed November 1, 2007.

22. Capps, R., Fix, M. E., Murray, J., Ost, J., Passel, J. S., and Herwantoro, S. (2005). *The new demography of America's schools: Immigration and the No Child Left Behind Act.* (Online). Available at http://www.urban.org/UploadedPDF/311230_new_demography.pdf. p. 18. Accessed March 5, 2007.

23. Cosentino de Cohen, C., and Chu Clewell, B. (2007, May). *Putting English Language Learners on the Educational Map.* (Online). Available at www.urban.org/UploadedPDF/311468_ell.pdf.

24. Ibid.

25. Ibid.

26. Ibid.

27. Ibid.

28. U.S. Department of Education. (2005). Trends in educational equity of girls & women: 2004. Available at http://nces.ed.gov/pubs2005/equity/. Accessed December 1, 2007.

29. Thomas, D. (2004, November 19). *Study shows educational achievement gender gap shrinking.* U.S. Department of Education. (Online). Available at www.ed.gov/news/pressreleases/2004/11/11192004b.html. Accessed August 15, 2007.

30. The Education Alliance. (2007, Winter). Gender differences in reading achievement: policy implications and best practices. *The Education Alliance*, p. 3.

31. Ibid., p. 6.

32. Kleinfield, J. S., & Yerian, S. (Eds.). (1995). *Gender tales: Tensions in the schools.* New York: St. Martin's Press, p. 4.

33. National Coalition for Women and Girls in Education. (2002, June). *Title IX at 30: Report card on gender equity, report of the National Coalition for Women and Girls in Education.* (Online). Available at www.ncwge.org/PDF/title9at30-6-11.pdf. Accessed May 14, 2007.

34. Single Sex Schools. (n.d.). *New regulations released March 2004.* (n.d.). (Online). Available at www.singlesexschools.org. Accessed July 27, 2007.

35. Schemo, D. J. (2006, October 25). Federal rules back single-sex public education. *New York Times.* (Online). Available at www.nytimes.com/2006/10/25/education/25gender.html?pagewanted=1&ei=5088&en=70f2ee029e27c6c3&ex=1319428800&partner=rssnyt&emc=rss.

36. Vu, P. (2006, September 19). "Single-gender schools on the rise." *Stateline.* (Online). Available at www.stateline.org/live/details/story?contentId=142575.

37. Schemo, D. J. (2006, October 25). Federal rules back single-sex public education. *New York Times.* (Online). Available at www.nytimes.com/2006/10/25/education/25gender.html?pagewanted=1&ei=5088&en=70f2ee029e27c6c3&ex=1319428800&partner=rssnyt&emc=rss.

38. Ibid.

39. American Association of University Women. (2007, March 3). *Separated by sex: Title IX and single-sex education.* (Online). Available at www.aauw.org/issue_advocacy/actionpages/positionpapers/singlesex.cfm.

40. U.S. Department of Education Office of Planning, Evaluation and Policy Development. (2005). Single-sex versus coeducational schooling: A systematic Review. *Policy and Programs Studies Service*, pp. 83–86. (Online). Available at www.ed.gov/rschstat/eval/other/single-sex/single-sex.pdf.

CHAPTER 5

1. Public Law 108-446, 2004.

2. National Research Center on Learning Disabilities (2005). *Twenty-five years of progress in educating children with disabilities through IDEA.* Available at www.nrcld.org/resources/osep/historyidea.shtml. Accessed March 11, 2007.

3. Hechinger, J. (2007, June 25). Mainstreaming trend tests classroom goals. *Wall Street Journal.* (Online).

4. U.S. Department of Education. (2005). *Building legacies.* Washington, D.C.: Author. (Online). Available at http://idea.ed.gov/. Accessed April 12, 2007.

5. Public Law 108-446, 2004.

6. Mayes, S. D., Calhoun, S. L., & Crowell, E. W. (2000, September/October). Learning disabilities and ADHD: Overlapping spectrum disorders. *Journal of Learning Disabilities, 33,* 417–424.

7. American Psychiatric Association. (2000). *Diagnostic and statistical manual of mental disorders,* 4th ed., text revision. Washington, D.C.: APA.

8. National Center on Birth Defects and Developmental Disabilities. (2007, February 8). *Prevalence of the autism spectrum disorders in multiple areas of the United States, surveillance years 2000 and 2002: A report from the Autism and Developmental Disabilities Monitoring (ADDM) Network.* Washington, D.C.: Centers for Disease Control. Available at www.cdc.gov/od/oc/media/pressrel/2007/r070208.htm. Accessed April 14, 2007.

9. American Psychiatric Association. (2000). *Diagnostic and statistical manual of mental disorders,* 4th ed., text revision. Washington, D.C.: APA.

10. Adams, C. (2007, March). Girls & ADHD: Are you missing the signs? *Instructor Magazine.* Available at http://content.scholastic.com/browse/article.jsp?id=11532. Accessed June 18, 2007.

11. Meek, C. (2006, December). From the inside out: A look at testing in special education students. *Phi Delta Kappan*, pp. 293–298.

12. Cassidy, M. (2006, December). For kids, whatever it takes. *Mercury News.* Available at www.mercurynews.com/search/ci_4886690?nclick_check=1. Accessed September 7, 2007.

13. Weiner, H. M. (2003). Effective inclusion: Professional development in the context of the classroom. *Teaching Exceptional Children 35*(6), 12–18. (Online). Available at http://journals.sped.org.

14. Council for Exceptional Children. (1995). *Creating schools for all our students.* Reston, VA: Author, p. 58.

15. Raskind, M. H. (2000). Assistive technology for children with learning disabilities. In Kristin Stanberry (Ed.). *Bridges to reading.* (2nd ed.). San Mateo, CA: Schwab Foundation for Learning.

16. Ross, P. O. (1993). *National excellence: A case for developing America's talent.* Washington, D.C.: Office of Educational Research and Improvement, U.S. Department of Education.

17. Samuels, C. S. (2007, April). States seen renewing focus on education of gifted. *Education Week, 26*(32), 20–23.

18. Bintrim, L. (2001). Mentoring taps talent. *Education Update 43*(6), 2.

19. Ibid.

20. Hess, M. (1999). Teaching in mixed-ability classrooms. Wisconsin Education Association. (Online). Available at www.weac.org/kids/1998–99/march99/differ.htm.

21. Wehrmann, K. (2000, September). Baby steps: A beginner's guide. *Education Leadership*, pp. 21–22.

22. Fass, S., & Cauthen, N. K. (December 2006). *Who are American's poor children: The official story.* The National Center for Children in Poverty. (Online). Available at http://nccp.org/pub_cpt06a.html. Accessed May 17, 2007.

23. Douglas-Hall, A., Koball, H., & Chau, M. (2006). *Basic facts about low-income children: Birth to age 18.* National Center for Children in Poverty. (Online). Available at www.nccp.org/pub_lic06b.html. Accessed July 17, 2007.

24. Ibid.

25. Johnston, L. D., O'Malley, P. M., Bachman, J. G., & Schulenberg, J. E. (2007). *Monitoring the future national results on adolescent drug use: Overview of key findings, 2006.* Bethesda, MD: National Institute on Drug Abuse.

26. Partnership for a Drug-Free America. (2007, July 6). *Prescription medicine abuse: A Growing Problem.* (Online). Available at www.drugfree.org. Accessed _____.

27. Johnston, et al. (2007). Accessed June 25, 2007.

28. Wills, T., McNamara, G., Vaccaro, D., & Hirky, A. (1996). Escalated substance use: A longitudinal grouping analysis from early to middle adolescence. *Journal of Abnormal Psychology 105,* 166–180.

29. Hoffman, S. (2006). *By the numbers: The public cost of teen childbearing.* Washington, D.C.: the National Campaign to Prevent Teen Pregnancy.

30. Ibid.

31. Center on Adolescent Sexuality, Pregnancy, and Parenting. (Online). Available at http://outreach.missouri.edu/hes/impact/impact99/centeraspp.htm.

32. U.S. Dept. of Health and Human Services. The Child Abuse Prevention and Treatment Act of 1974. Washington, DC. (Online). Available at www.utk.edu/~orme00/PowerPoint/cw/tsld001.htm.

33. U.S. Department of Health and Human Services, Administration on Children, Youth and Families. (2007). *Child maltreatment 2005.* Washington, D.C.: U.S. Government Printing Office.

34. Dinkes, R., Cataldi, E. F., Kena, G., & Baum, K. (2006). *Indicators of school crime and safety.* Washington, D.C.: Bureau of Justice Statistics.

35. DeVoe, J. F., and Kaffenberger, S. (2005). *Student reports of bullying: Results from the 2001 school crime supplement to the National Crime Victimization Survey* (NCES 2005–310). U.S. Department of Education, National Center for Education Statistics. Washington, D.C.: U.S. Government Printing Office.

36. Snyder H. N., & Sickmund, M. (2006). *Juvenile offenders and victims: 2006 National Report.* Washington, D.C.: U.S. Department of Justice.

37. Alliance for Excellent Education. (2006). *Saving futures, saving crime reduction and earnings.* Washington, D.C.: Author.

38. Carnegie Council on Adolescent Development. Great transitions. (Online). Available at www.carnegie.org/reports/great.transitions/gr_intro.

39. Schweinhart, L. J. (1994). Lasting benefits of preschool programs. (Online). Available at ericps.ed.uiuc.edu/eece/pubs/digests/1994/schwei94.html.

CHAPTER 6

1. After-School-for-All (1999). *Afterschool alliance.* (Online). Available at www.afterschoolalliance.org/funding. Accessed June 24, 2007.

2. Donors Choose. (2000). Teachers ask. You choose. Students learn. (Online). Available at www.donorschoose.org/homepage/main.html. Accessed December 3, 2007.

3. American Youth Policy Forum. (2003, May 9). *A new wave of evidence: The impact of school, family, and community connections on student achievement.* (Online). Available at www.aypf.org/forumbriefs/2003/fb050903.htm. Accessed May 3, 2007.

4. Lopez, M. E., Kreider, H., and Caspe, M. (2004–2005). *Co-constructing family involvement.* (Online). Available at www.gse.harvard.edu/hfrp/projects. Accessed March 11, 2007.

5. U.S. Census Bureau. (2005). *American fact finder.* (Online). Available at http://factfinder.census.gov/servlet/STSelectServlet?_lang=en&_ts=205938198218. Accessed May 18, 2007.

6. U.S. Department of Education. (2002). No Child Left Behind Act of 2001. (PL 101-110). Washington, DC: Author, Sec. 1118.

7. Wisconsin Department of Public Instruction. (2005, February 22). ESEA Information Update Bulletin No. 03. 04. (Online). Available at www.dpi.state.wi.us/esea/pdf/bul_0304.pdf. Accessed April 3, 2007.

8. U.S. Department of Health and Human Services, Administration of Children and Families. (2007). *Head Start program fact sheet, fiscal year 2007.* (Online). Available at www.acf.hhs.gov/programs/hsb/research/2007factsheet.pdf. Accessed August 12, 2007.

9. U.S. Department of Labor, Bureau of Labor Statistics. (2007, May 9). *Employment characteristics of families in 2006.* (Online). Available at www.bls.gov/news.release/pdf/famee.pdf. Accessed September 15, 2007.

10. The Boston Public Schools and Communication Office and Office of Family & Community Engagement. (2006). *2006–2007 Guide to Boston Public Schools for families and students.* (Online). Available at http://boston.k12.ma.us/info/GuideSY06.pdf. Accessed October 23, 2007.

11. Connected Mathematics. (2007). *Helping parents help their children.* (Online). Available at www.phschool.com/math/cmp/parent_help_children.html. Accessed July 8, 2007.

12. Schumm, J. (2005). *How to help your child with homework: The complete guide to encouraging good study habits and ending the homework wars.* New York: Free Spirit Publishing.

13. U.S. Department of Education. (2005). *Helping your child with homework.* (Online). Available at www.ed.gov/parents/academic/help/homework/homework.pdf. Accessed June 26, 2007.

14. Generations United. (n.d.). *Linking youth and old through inter-generational programs.* Washington, DC: Author.

15. U.S. Department of Education (2002). No Child Left Behind Act of 2001: Parental involvement—Title I, Part A, Nonregulatory guidance, p. 3.

16. Shartrand, A. M., Weiss, H. B., Krieder, H. M., and Lopez, M. E. (1997). *New skills for new schools: Preparing teachers in family involvement.* Cambridge, MA: Harvard Family Research Project.

17. Vincent, C. (1996). Parent empowerment? Collective action and inaction in education. *Oxford Review of Education,* 22(4), 465–482.

18. Julian, T., McKenry, P., and McKelvey, M. (1994). Cultural variations in parenting: Perceptions of Caucasian, African-America, Hispanic, and Asian American Parents. *Family Relations 43*(1), 30–37.

19. Coleman, James S. (1998). Social capital in the creation of human capital. *American Journal of Sociology, 94*(S): S95–S120.

20. Epstein, J. L., Sanders, J. G., Simon, B. S., Salinas, K. C., Jansorn, N. R., and Voorhis, F. L. (2002). *School, family, and community partnerships: Your handbook for action.* Thousand Oaks, CA: Corwin Press.

21. National Network of Partnership Schools. (1999). Promising Partnership Practices 1999: Providing immunizations for advancing middle school students. Available at www.csos.jhu.edu/p2000/PPP/1999/pdf/35.pdf. Accessed December 3, 2007.

22. National Network of Partnership Schools. (2000). Promising Partnership Practices 2000: New notes in 99. Available at www.csos.jhu.edu/p2000/PPP/2000/pdf/08.pdf. Accessed December 3, 2007.

23. Epstein, J. (2005). Volunteerism. *The Parent Educator.* Available at www.parenting-ed.org/parent_educator/Feb%202005.pdf. Accessed December 3, 2007.

24. National Network of Partnership Schools. (2004). Promising Partnership Practices 2004: Family reading and literacy night. Available at www.csos.jhu.edu/p2000/PPP/2004/pdf/16.pdf. Accessed December 3, 2007.

25. National Network of Partnership Schools. (2000). Promising Partnership Practices 2000: Potluck PTO meetings. Available at www.csos.jhu.edu/p2000/PPP/2000/pdf/37.pdf. Accessed December 3, 2007.

26. Epstein, J., & Salinas, K. (2004). Partnering with families and communities. *Educational Leadership, 61*(8), 12–18. Available at http://pdonline.ascd.org/pd_online/success_di/el200405_epstein.html. Accessed December 3, 2007.

27. Van Voorhis, F. L. (2004). Reflecting on the homework ritual: Assignments and designs. *Theory into Practice, 43*(3), 205–211.

28. National PTA. (2000). *Building successful partnerships: A guide for developing parent and family involvement programs.* Chicago: Author.

29. Rose, L. C., & Gallup, A. M. (2006). The 38th annual Phi Delta Kappa/Gallup Poll of the public's attitudes toward the public schools. Available at www.pdkmembers.org/e-GALLUP/kpoll_pdfs/pdkpoll38_2006.pdf. Accessed December 3, 2007.

30. *Zelman, Superintendent of Public Instruction of Ohio, et al. v. Simmons-Harris et al.* (Online). Available at http://supct.law.cornell.edu/supct/html/00-1751.ZS.html.

31. U.S. General Accounting Office. (1995). *Charter schools: New model for public schools provides opportunities and challenges.* Washington, DC: Author, p. 4.

32. National Charter School Data. (2007). *School year 2006–2007.* (Online). Available at www.edreform.com/_upload/ncsw-numbers.pdf. Accessed June 27, 2007.

33. "Kids Love a Mystery Night," www.education-world.com/a_admin/admin323.html. Accessed December 5, 2007.

34. Organization of Black Airline Pilots. (2007). OBAP pilots in schools program. (Online). Available at www.obapseast.com/pilots.htm. Accessed April 1, 2007.

35. Coalition for Community Schools. (2007). *Community schools in the news.* (Online). Available at www.communityschools.org/. Accessed April 18, 2007.

CHAPTER 7

1. CBS News. (2007, October 18). *Birth control for Maine middle schoolers.* (Online). Available at www.cbsnews.com/stories/2007/10/18/national/main3379737.shtml. Accessed October 25, 2007.

2. Oleck, J. (2007, August 1). San Jose Unified School District implements solar power at four high schools. *School Library Journal.* (Online). Available at www.schoollibraryjournal.com/article/CA6464645.html. Accessed October 25, 2007.

3. McLaughlin, T. (2007, October 10). Local students learn career skills. *The Bakersfield Californian.* (Online). Available at www.bakersfield.com/hourly_news/story/257295.html. Accessed October 16, 2007.

4. Kilgannon, C. (2007, October 24). A high school under the hood. *New York Times.* (Online). Available at www.nytimes.com/2007/10/24/automobiles/autospecial/24school.html?ex=1350964800&en=3e9afd51cd95df00&ei=5088&partner=rssnyt&emc=rss. Accessed October 25, 2007.

5. Associated Press. (2007, July 30). Kids' letter campaign spells end for green beans. (Online). Available at www.msnbc.msn.com/id/20043068/from/ET. Accessed October 25, 2007.

6. U.S. Department of Education. The federal role in education. (Online). Available at www.ed.gov/about/overview/fed/role.html. Accessed November 2, 2007.

7. Office of Governor Janet Napolitano. (2006). (Online). Available at www.azgovernor.gov/BioJN.asp. Accessed November 2, 2007.

8. National Association of State Boards of Education. (2007). (Online). Available at www.nasbe.org. Accessed November 2, 2007.

9. Texas Education Agency. (n.d.). (Online). Available at www.tea.state.tx.us/. Accessed November 5, 2007.

10. Vermont Department of Education. (2007, November 5). Programs and services: Professional standards. (Online). Available at http://education.vermont.gov/new/html/pgm_prostandards.html. Accessed November 5, 2007.

11. Cashman, C. (2007, September 14). States to convene summits on expanded learning opportunities. National Governors Association. (Online). Available at www.nga.org/portal/site/nga/

menuitem.6c9a8a9ebc6ae07eee28aca9501010a0/?vgnextoid=
7a8db474e4405110VgnVCM1000001a01010aRCRD.   Accessed November 2, 2007.

12. Monroe #1 BOCES. (2007). About BOCES. (Online). Available
at www.monroe.edu/aboutboces.htm. Accessed November 5,
2007.

13. National Center for Education Statistics. (2006). *Digest of
Education Statistics, 2006 Table 83.* (Online). Available at
http://nces.ed.gov/programs/digest/d06/tables/dt06_083.asp?
referrer=list. Accessed November 5, 2007.

14. Mendels, P. (2005, November). Trench fighting: Former business leaders are trying to fix our troubled schools. *The Chief
Executive.* (Online). Available at http://findarticles.com/p/
articles/mi_m4070/is_213/ai_n15876030. Accessed November
5, 2007.

15. Stump, J. (2006, November 6). Public school accountability
under the No Child Left Behind Act. *Public School Accountability LSC Members Only Brief.* Vol. 126, Issue 13.

16. School Accountability Report Card. (Spring 2007). Chavez Elementary School. San Diego Unified School District. Available at
http://studata.sandi.net/research/sarcs/2006–07/SARCoboshort
.pdf.

17. Florida Department of Education. (2007). Florida School
Grades. (Online). Available at http://schoolgrades.fldoe.org/
xls/0607/districtgrades20062007.xls. Accessed November 7,
2007.

18. National Education Association. (2008). Accountability—A
Shared Responsibility. Available at www.nea.org/accountability/
index.html. Accessed February 25, 2008.

19. Sergiovanni, T. J. (1996). *Moral leadership: Getting to the
heart of school improvement.* San Francisco: Jossey-Bass.

20. Jefferson County Public Schools. (2007). School-based decision making. (Online). Available at http://jeffcoweb.jeffco
.k12.co.us/cdm/. Accessed November 7, 2007.

21. Pinellas County Schools. (2004). *The school advisory council.*
(Online). Available at www.pinellas.k12.fl.us/CI/SAC/. Accessed November 7, 2007.

22. Lakeville Area Public Schools. (2007, August 4). Chemical
Health Advisory Committee. (Online). Available at www
.isd194.k12.mn.us/curr_chemadv.shtml. Accessed November 7,
2007.

23. National Center for Education Statistics. (2006). Fast Facts.
(Online). Available at http://nces.ed.gov/fastfacts/display
.asp?id=372. Accessed November 7, 2007.

24. Ibid.

25. National Center for Education Statistics. (2006). Digest of
Education Statistics 2006. (Online). Available at
http://nces.ed.gov/programs/digest/d06. Accessed November 7,
2007.

26. Ibid.

27. Administration for Children and Families. (2007). *Head Start
Program Fact Sheet.* (Online). Available at www.acf.hhs.gov/
programs/ohs/about/fy2007.html. Accessed November 7, 2007.

28. National Center for Education Statistics. (2006). *Digest of Education Statistics 2006.* (Online). Available at http://nces.ed

.gov/programs/digest/d06/tables/dt06_158.asp. Accessed November 7, 2007.

29. Wiehle, A. (2006, September 5). Garnati reminds parents about
strict truancy laws. *Southern Illinoisan.* (Online). Available
at www.southernillinoisan.com/articles/2006/09/05/afternoon
_evening/doc44fdd36e9464a141554641.txt. Accessed Novem-
ber 7, 2007.

30. National Center for Education Statistics. (2006). *Digest of Education Statistics 2006.* (Online). Available at http://nces.ed
.gov/programs/digest/d06. Accessed November 7, 2007.

31. Labb, T. (2007, March 22). Gates Foundation to give D.C. students push to college. *Washington Post.* Available at www
.washingtonpost.com/wp-dyn/content/article/2007/03/21/
AR2007032102168.html. Accessed November 7, 2007.

32. Gootman, E. (2006, April 28). Annenberg grant to help smaller
schools. *New York Times.* (Online). Available at www.nytimes
.com/2006/04/28/nyregion/28grant.html. Accessed November
7, 2007.

33. Rose, L. C., and Gallup, A. M. (2007, September). The 39th annual Phi Delta Kappa/Gallup Poll of the public's attitudes toward
the public schools. *Phi Delta Kappan.* (Online). Available at
www.pdkmembers.org/e-GALLUP/kpoll_pdfs/pdkpoll39
_2007.pdf. Accessed November 8, 2007.

34. Gill, B. (Spring 2007). Takeover overtaken. RAND Review.
Available at www.rand.org/publications/randreview/issues/
spring2007/takeover.html. Accessed December 6, 2007.

35. National Center for Education Statistics. (2007, June). *Revenues
and Expenditures for Public Elementary and Secondary School
Districts: School Year 2004–05 (Fiscal Year 2005).* (Online). Available at http://nces.ed.gov/pubs2007/revexpdist05/
tables/table_2.asp?referrer=list. Accessed November 8, 2007.

36. Rose, L. C., & Gallup, A. M. (2003, September). The 36th annual attitude toward the public schools. *Phi Delta Kappan.* (Online). Available at www.pdkintl.org/kappan/k0409pol.htm
#assess. Accessed November 8, 2007.

37. PBS. (2007). School reform in Philadelphia. (Online).
Available at www.pbs.org/newshour/bb/education/reform/
companies.html. Accessed November 8, 2007.

38. Hoover's North America. (2007). *Imagine Schools, Inc.* (Online). Available at http://premium.hoovers.com/subscribe/co/
factsheet.xhtml?ID=103537. Accessed November 8, 2007.

CHAPTER 8

1. Alderman, J. H. (2007, March 6). Mass stabbing victim
chosen randomly. *Washington Post.* Available at www
.washingtonpost.com/wp-dyn/content/article/2007/03/06/
AR2007030601946.html. Accessed December 5, 2007.

2. Forrest, B. (2005, October 5). Expert witness in Kitzmiller v.
Dover says intelligent design is disguised creationism. *American
Civil Liberties Union.* Available at www.aclu.org/religion/
schools/20301prs20051005.html. Accessed December 5, 2007.

3. *Deskbook encyclopedia of American school law.* (1994). Eagan,
MN: Data Research, Inc., p. 480.

4. ACLU School Board. (2006, March 10). ACLU of Virginia
sets stage for student privacy victory. *American Civil Liberties*

Union. Available at www.aclu.org/drugpolicy/testing/24706prs20060310.html. Accessed December 5, 2007.

5. Jacobson, L. (1997, May 14). Appeals court allows moment of silence in Georgia schools. *Education Week.* (Online). Available at www.edweek.org/we/vol-16/33ga.h16.

6. *Steven I. Engle et al., Petitioners v. William J. Vitale, Jr. et al.* 370 U.S. 421 (1962).

7. *School District of Abbington Township, Pennsylvania v. Edward Lewis Schempp et al.* 374 U.S. 203 (1963).

8. Ibid.

9. Biema, D. V. (2007, March 22). The case for teaching the Bible. *Time.* Available at www.time.com/time/magazine/article/0,9171,1601845,00.html. Accessed December 5, 2007.

10. *Deskbook encyclopedia of American school law*, p. 51.

11. Celis, W. III. (1994, May 18). Aftermath of '54 ruling disheartens the Browns. *New York Times*, p. B8. (Copyright © 1994/95 by the New York Times Company. Reprinted by permission.)

12. Frazier L. (1995, October 30). Busing is hurting Black children, some in P.G. say; parents point to vacant slots in gifted, magnet programs. *Washington Post.* Available at www.washingtonpost.com/wp-srv/local/longterm/library/pg/schools/pgbuses.htm. Accessed December 5, 2007.

13. Ibid.

14. Hutton, T. (2003, May). Boston School Committee's student assignment policy does not discriminate against white students. *National School Boards Association.* Available at www.nsba.org/site/doc_cosa.asp?TRACKID=&DID=11722&CID=164. Accessed December 5, 2007.

15. Hispanics boost enrollment in high school. (2004, January 29). *USA Today.* (Online). Available at www.usatoday.com/news/education/2004-01-29-hispanics_x.htm.

16. Wells, A. S., & Crain, R. L. (1994, Winter). Perpetuation theory and the long-term effects of school desegregation. *Review of Educational Research*, pp. 531–555.

17. Manzo, K. K. (1998, October 7). Curtain falls on desegregation era in Nashville. *Education Week*, p. 3.

18. The White House. No Child Left Behind act of 2001. Available at www.whitehouse.gov/news/reports/no-child-left-behind.html. Accessed December 5, 2007.

19. *Edgewood Independent School District v. Kirby.* 777 S.W. 2nd 391 (1989).

20. Imber, M. (2004). Equity in school funding. *American School Board Journal.* Available at www.asbj.com/MainMenu Category/Archive/2004/October.aspx. Accessed December 6, 2007.

21. The University of Alabama Superintendents' Academy. (2005). Financial and education law training program. Available at http://uasa.ua.edu/Education%20Law%20Modules/37%20Organizational%20Issues%20-%20Liability%20and%20Immunity.pdf. Accessed December 4, 2007.

22. Ibid.

23. Ibid.

24. *Deskbook encyclopedia of American school law*, p. 12.

25. Ibid.

26. Summary of child maltreatment, 2002. (2004). *Administration for Children and Families.* (Online). Available at www.acf.hhs.gov/programs/cb/publications/cm02/summary.htm.

27. Walsh, M. (1994, October 12). Supreme Court refuses "duty to protect" case. *Education Week*, p. 18. (Reprinted with permission from *Education Week*, Vol. 14, No. 6, October 12, 1994.)

28. Lawyers. (2007). Qualified immunity. Available at http://research.lawyers.com/glossary/qualified-immunity.html. Accessed December 4, 2007.

29. Summary of child maltreatment, 2002. (2004). *Administration for Children and Families.* (Online). Available at www.acf.hhs.gov/programs/cb/publications/cm02/figure2_1.htm.

30. U.S. Department of Education Office for Civil Rights. (2001). Revised sexual harassment guidance: Harassment of students by school employees, other students, or third parties. U.S. Department of Education. Available at www.ed.gov/offices/OCR/archives/pdf/shguide.pdf. Accessed December 6, 2007.

31. State of Connecticut. (2005). An act concerning marriage quality. Available at www.cga.ct.gov/2005/tob/s/2005SB-00963-R00-SB.htm. Accessed December 4, 2007.

32. Yared, C. (1997). Where are the civil rights for gay and lesbian teachers? *Human Rights: Journal of the Section of Individual Rights & Responsibilities.* 24(3). 22–24. Available at www.abanet.org/irr/hr/yared.html. Accessed December 6, 2007.

33. *Deskbook encyclopedia of American school law,* pp. 251–302 (1994).

34. *Epperson v. Arkansas.* 393 U.S. 97(1968).

35. Boyle, A. (2005, December 20). Judge rules against "intelligent design". *MSNBC.* Available at www.msnbc.msn.com/id/10545387/. Accessed December 6, 2007.

36. *Pickering v. Board of Education.* 391 U.S. 563 (1968).

37. Dowling-Singer, B. (1998, June). A matter of fairness. *American School Board Journal*, pp. 14–15.

38. *Tinker v. Des Moines Independent Community School District.* 393 U.S. 503 (1969).

39. Bensman, T. (1998, June 8). Censorship or caution? *Dallas Morning News*, pp. A13, A15.

40. *Hazelwood School District v. Kuhlmeier.* 86–836 S. Ct. (1988).

41. Ibid.

42. *Bethel School District v. Fraser.* 478 U.S. 675 (1986).

43. Clips, L. (2006, March 10). *Frederick v. Morse.* 439 F.3d 1114 (2007). *National School Boards Association.* Available at www.nsba.org/site/doc_cosa.asp?TRACKID=&CID=487&DID=38063. Accessed December 6, 2007.

44. *Goss v. Lopez.* 419 U.S. 565 (1975).

45. *New Jersey v. T.L.O.* 469 U.S. 325 (1985).

46. Walsh, M. (1997, November 19). Supreme Court lets stand ruling on alleged student strip search. *Education Week*, p. 18.

47. Edlaw Online Library. (1997). Jenkins v. Talladega, 115 F.3d 821, 65 USLW 2786, 118 Ed. Law Rep. 867. Available at www.faculty.piercelaw.edu/redfield/library/case-talladega.htm. Accessed December 6, 2007.

48. Dowling-Sendor, B. (1998, April). Before you search that locker. *American School Board Journal*, pp. 24–25.

49. *U.S. v. Lopez.* 64 F.3rd 1425. 9th Cir. (1995).

50. National Center for Education Statistics. (2007). Fast facts: Do you have any statistics on school safety? Available at http://nces.ed.gov/fastfacts/display.asp?id=49. Accessed December 6, 2007.

51. High schools must give student info to military. (2002, December 27). *The Rocky Mountain News*, p. 18A.

52. Hoff, D. J. (1998, November 25). Venerable national honor society catching flak from some quarters. *Education Week*, pp. 1, 12.

53. Gay Straight Alliance Network. (2002). About the network. Available at www.gsanetwork.org/about/index.html. Accessed December 6, 2007.

54. Bilingual Education Act, Pub. L. No. (93-380), 88 Stat. 503 (1974).

55. U.S. Census Bureau. (2005, August 11). Texas becomes nation's newest "majority-minority" state, Census Bureau announces. Available at www.census.gov/Press-Release/www/releases/archives/population/005514.html. Accessed December 6, 2007.

56. U.S. Census Bureau. (2003, October 8). Nearly 1-in-5 speak a foreign language at home; Most also speak English 'very well,' Census Bureau reports. Available at www.census.gov/Press-Release/www/releases/archives/census_2000/001406.html. Accessed December 6, 2007.

57. No Child Left Behind Act bill summary. (2004). *House Education and the Workforce Committee.* (Online). Available at http://edworkforce.house.gov/issues/108th/education/nclb/billsummary.htm.

58. National Center for Education Statistics. (2001). *Digest of education statistics, 2000.* (Online).

59. *Board of Education v. Rowley.* 102 S.C. 3034 (1984).

60. *Deskbook encyclopedia of American school law*, p. 123.

61. Supreme Court gives "disabled" status to HIV diagnosed people. (1998, June 26). *Christian Science Monitor.* (Online). Available at www.csmonitor.com.

62. Paton, D. (2005, May 18). Rift over recruiting at public high schools. *The Christian Science Monitor.* Available at www.csmonitor.com/2005/0518/p02s01-ussc.html on December 6, 2007.

63. *Pierce v. Society of Sisters of the Holy Names of Jesus and Mary.* 268 U.S. 510 (1925).

64. *Wisconsin v. Yoder.* 406 U.S. 219 (1972).

65. Armour A. (2007, May 16). Home education week: Many county parents opt for homeschooling. *Itawamba County Times.* A1. Available at www.djournal.com/pages/archive.asp?ID=243041. Accessed December 6, 2007.

CHAPTER 9

1. McCullough, D. C. (1984, June 4). Historian address: Wesleyan. *New York Times*, B5.

2. Good, H. G. (1962). *A history of American education* (2nd ed.). New York: Macmillan, p. 37.

3. Pulliam, J. D. (1991). *History of education in America* (5th ed.). New York: Macmillan, p. 18.

4. Cubberley, E. P. (1948). *The history of education.* Cambridge, MA: Riverside Press, p. 326. (Copyright © 1948 by Houghton Mifflin Company. Reprinted by permission.)

5. Kaestle, C. (1983). *Pillars of the Republic: Common schools and American society, 1780–1860.* New York: Hill and Wang.

6. Ford, P. L. (1962). *The New England primer: A history of its origin and development.* New York: Teachers College Press.

7. Good, *A history of American education*, p. 386.

8. Gwynne-Thomas, E. H. (1981). *A concise history of education to 1900 A.D.* Lanham, MD: University Press of America, pp. 151–152.

9. Cremin, L. A. (1980). *American education: The national experience.* New York: Harper & Row.

10. Cohen, *A history of colonial education*, pp. 188–189.

11. Ibid., p. 146.

12. Fogel, D. (1988). *Junipero Serra, the Vatican and enslavement theology.* San Francisco, CA: ISM Press, p. 53.

13. Farrell, R. V. (2001). *The conquest of minds: Lessons and strategies from Latin American education.* Florida International University. (Online). Available at www.cedu.niu.edu/blackwell/farrell01.htm.

14. Ripp, S. A. (1984). *Education in a free society.* New York: Longman, p. 43.

15. The Northwest Ordinance. (Online). Available at http://earlyamerica.com/earlyamerica/milestones/ordinance/text.html.

16. Urban, W., & Wagoner, J., Jr. (1996). *American education: A history.* New York: McGraw-Hill, p. 73.

17. Ibid., pp. 168–169.

18. *From here to there: The road to reform of American high schools.* (2004). Issue paper of the High School Leadership Conference, sponsored by the Office of the U.S. Secretary of Education. (Online). Available at http://www.ed.gov/about/offices/list/ovae/pi/hsinit/papers/history.doc.

19. U.S. Census Bureau. *African American History.* (Online). Available at www.census.gov/pubinfo/www/multimedia/AfricanAm.html. Accessed February 27, 2008.

20. Washington, B. T. (1963). *Up from slavery: An autobiography.* Garden City, NY: Doubleday, pp. 1, 2, 5, 18–20.

21. Butts, R. F. (1973). *The education of the West.* New York: McGraw-Hill, p. 464.

22. Ibid.

23. Office of Indian Education Programs. *Information brochure.* Washington, DC: Bureau of Indian Affairs, U.S. Department of the Interior.

24. Mathews, J. (2007, January 2). Montessori, now 100, goes mainstream. *Washington Post*, B1.

25. Urban & Wagoner, *American education*, p. 190.

26. Archambault, R. D. (Ed.). (1964). *John Dewey on education—selected writings.* New York: Random House, p. 430.

27. Hart, K., & Shumacher, R. (2004). *Moving forward: Head Start children, families, and programs in 2003.* Center for Law and Social Policy. (Online). Available at www.clasp.org/publications/hs_brf_5.pdf.

28. U.S. Department of Education. (2005). *Improving basic programs operated by local educational agencies.* (Online). Available at www.ed.gov/policy/elsec/leg/esea02/pg2.html#sec1120.

29. Ibid.

30. Helfand, D. (2006, January 30). A formula for failure in L.A. schools. *Los Angeles Times.* (Online). Available at www.latimes.com/news/education/la-me-dropout30jan30,0,3211437.story.

31. Rousseau, J. (1979). *Emile or On Education.* Bloom A. (translator). New York: Basic Books.

32. Einstein, A. (1949, May). Why socialism? *Monthly Review.* Available at www.monthlyreview.org/598einst.htm. Accessed December 10, 2007.

33. France, A. (2004). *The crime of Sylvestre Bonnard.* Hearn, L. (translator). MT: Kessinger Publishing Co.

34. Bronte, C. (1997). *Jane Eyre.* New York: Penguin Group.

35. James, W. (1908). *Pragmatism: A new name for some old ways of thinking.* New York: Longmans, Green, p. 6.

36. James, W. (1948). *Some problems of philosophy: A beginning of an introduction to philosophy.* New York: Longmans, Green, p. 31.

37. Al-Ani, S. H. (1995). Muslims in America and Arab Americans. In *Comprehensive multicultural education: Theory and practice* (3rd ed.). Boston: Allyn & Bacon, p. 137.

38. Murphy, R. D. (2001). School officials urged to prevent harassment of muslim and Arab-American students. United States Department of Education. (Online). Available at www.ed.gov/news/pressreleases/2001/09/09092001c.html.

39. Sartre, J. P. (1978). Existentialism. In J. M. Rich (Ed.), *Readings in the philosophy of education.* Belmont, CA: Wadsworth, pp. 98, 101.

40. Shea, C. (1993). *Reporter, 23*(6). (Online). Available at http://wings.buffalo.edu/publications/reporter/vol25/vol25n6/5a.txt.

41. Ibid.

42. Shaw, R. P. (2000). The educational theory of Maxine Greene. (Online). Available at www.newfoundations.com/GALLERY/Greene.html.

43. Hutchins, R. M. (1936). *Higher learning in America.* New Haven: Yale University Press, p. 166. (Copyright 1936 by Yale University Press. Reprinted by permission.)

44. Adler, J. M. (1982). *The Paideia proposal.* New York: Macmillan, p. 15.

45. Myer, A. E. (1949). *The development of education in the twentieth century.* Englewood Cliffs, NJ: Prentice Hall, p. 149.

CHAPTER 10

1. National Coalition for Parent Involvement in Education. (2002). NCLB Action Briefs: Standards and Assessment. (Online). Available at www.ncpie.org/nclbaction/standards_assessment.html.

2. National Center for Education Statistics. (2007). The nation's report card. (Online). Available at http://nces.ed.gov/nationsreportcard/pdf/main2007/2007496.pdf.

3. Barksdale-Ladd, M. A., & Thomas, K. F. (2000, November/December). What's at stake in high-stakes testing: Teachers and parents speak out. *Journal of Teacher Education, 51*(5), 384–397.

4. Metropolitan Life survey of the American teacher. (2001). (Online). Available at www.metlife.com/Companyinfo/Community/Found/Docs/ed.html.

5. Public Agenda Reality check 2006. Online. (2006). Is support for standards and testing fading? *Education Insights*, no. 3. (Online). Available at www.publicagenda.org/research/pdfs/rc0603.pdf.

6. Ibid.

7. Ibid.

8. Ibid.

9. National Council of Teachers of Mathematics. Curriculum focal points for prekindergarten through grade 8: Mathematics. (Online). Available at www.nctm.org/standards/focalpoints.aspx?id=340&ekmensel=c580fa7b_10_52_340_10.

10. National Association for Sport and Physical Education (2006). Northwest National Elementary School Teacher of the Year. (Online). Available at www.aahperd.org/naspe/pdf_files/TOY_Winn.pdf.

11. Labb, T. (2007, November 2). Some academic standards drafted. *Washington Post*, p. B4.

12. Chicago Public Schools, Office of Teacher Recertification and Professional Standards. (1999). Available at www.cps.k12.il.us/AboutCPS/Departments/OTRPS/otrps.html.

13. Florida Department of Education. (2007). Available at http://schoolgrades.fldoe.org/reports/.

14. Texas Education Agency. (2007). (Online). Available at www.tea.state.tx.us/perfreport/account/2007/manual/.

15. Indiana School Rankings 2006. (2006, August). (Online). Available at www.indystar.com/data/education/indiana_rankings_2006.shtml.

16. Shaw, L. (2007, June 24). Set lesson plans stir controversy. *Seattle Times.* (Online). Available at http://seattletimes.nwsource.com/html/localnews/2003760509_curriculum24m.html.

17. Kentucky Department of Education. (2007, September 29). NAEP (National Assessment of Educational Progress). (Online). Available at http://education.ky.gov/KDE/Administrative+Resources/Testing+and+Reporting+/Reports/NAEP+-+National+Assessment+of+Educational+Progress/.

18. Slater, P. (2007, September 25). State schools Chief Jack O'Connell comments on release of 2007 National Assessment of Education Progress, California Department of Education. (Online). Available at www.cde.ca.gov/nr/ne/yr07/yr07rel122.asp.

19. Public Agenda Online. (2001). Reality check 2001. (Online). Available at www.publicagenda.org/specials/rc2001/reality.htm.

20. Herszenhorn, D. M., Gootman, E., & Moynihan, C. (2004, March 16). Bloomberg wins on school tests after firing foes. *New York Times.* (Online). Available at http://query.nytimes.com/gst/fullpage.html?res=9F03E2DB1731F935A25750C0A9629C8B63.

21. Stutz, T. (2007, May 12). 16% fail TAKS graduation test. *Dallas Morning News.* (Online). Available at www.dallasnews.com/

sharedcontent/dws/dn/education/stories/051207dntextaksfails
.5c9ba6b1.html.

22. Stephens, S. (2007, June 7). More crises on schools' last day. *Plain Dealer.* (Online). Available at www.cleveland.com/clevelandschools/plaindealer/index.ssf?/base/news/1181205257158771.xml&coll=2.

23. Shah, N. (2007, May 3). Nearly one in five third-graders may be held back in Broward. *Miami Herald*, p. 1A.

24. Popham, J. (2001, March). Teaching to the test? *Educational Leadership*, pp. 16–17.

25. Pressler, M. W. (2006, June 1). Schools, pressed to achieve, put the squeeze on recess. *Washington Post*, p. A1.

26. Norwich Bulletin. (2007, September, 12). Our view: Decision to cut recess needed, but poor. GateHouse Media. Available at www.wickedlocal.com/norwich/opinions/x1212851475. Accessed January 22, 2008.

27. Hacker, H. K. (2001, October). Racial gap persists in standardized testing. *STL Today*, p. B4.

28. Ohio Department of Education. (2007, June 26). Susan Tave Zelman. (Online). Available at www.ode.state./Templates/Pages/ODE/ODEDetail.aspx?Page=3&TopicRelationID=690&Content=31913.

29. NYSUT News Wire. (2007, October 26). Education expert Haycock: With change, achievement is possible. (Online). Available at www.nysut.org/cps/rde/xchg/nysut/hs.xsl/endingthegap_8761.htm.

30. Phillips, M., & Tyre, P. (2007, September 18). A bonus, sir, with love. *Newsweek.* (Online). Available at www.newsweek.com/id/40987/output/print.

31. Olson, L. (2001, April). A quiet crisis: Unprepared for high stakes. *Education Week, 20*(31), 1.

32. Texas Education Agency. (2006 October 4). Briefing on online testing. p. 1.

33. Oregon Assessments of Knowledge and Skills. (Online). Available at www.oaks.k12.or.us/index.asp.

34. Testing computerized exams. (2001, May). *Education Week*, pp. 1–17.

35. U.S. Department of Education. (2003, September 7). Questions and answers on No Child Left Behind. (Online). Available at www.ed.gov/nclb/accountability/schools/accountability.html.

36. Ibid.

37. Ibid.

38. CBIA Education Foundation. (2003). Connecticut's adequate yearly progress (AYP) and how it is applied. (Online). Available at www.cbia.com/ed/NCLB/ayp.htm.

39. Shaughnessy, M. F. (2007, October 14). An interview with Terry B. Grier: On academic success. *Education News.* (Online). Available at http://www.ednews.org/articles/18429/1/An-Interview-with-Terry-B-Grier-On-Academic-Success/Page1.html.

CHAPTER 11

1. For more information, visit www.iabolish.com.

2. Eisner, E. W. (1985). *The educational imagination: On the design and evaluation of school programs* (2nd ed.). New York: Macmillan, p. 107.

3. MSNBC. (2007, October 10). Four shot at Cleveland school. (Online). Available at www.msnbc.msn.com/id/21224357/.

4. Phillips, A. (2007, October 24). Teen charged in Manassas High School shooting. Eye Witness News. (Online). Available at www.myeyewitnessnews.com/mostpopular/story.aspx?content_id=789c7ac1-8bcd-405f-9740-3005e6ed92cb.

5. Cunningham, S. (2007, September 3). Kids learn to make bullies back off. *The Courier-Journal.* (Online). Available at www.districtadministration.com/newssu.aspx?news=yes&postid=48187.

6. MSNBC. (2007). Talking to kids about school shootings. (Online). Available at www.msnbc.msn.com/id/15109195/.

7. National Institute on Drug Abuse. About NIDA. (Online). Available at http://teens.drugabuse.gov/about.asp.

8. Reciprocal teaching focuses on four strategies: predicting, questioning, clarifying, and summarizing. (2003, August/September). *Reading Today*, p. 12.

9. Pattanayak, V. (2003, February). Physics first in science education reform. *Journal of Young Investigators.* (Online). Available at www.jyi.org/volumes/volume6/issue7/features/pattanayak.html.

10. Toppo, G. (2004, August 12). Algebra's for everyone now—Expectations are rising; 21 states require it for a high school diploma. *USA Today*, p. 1A. (Online). Available at www.usatoday.com/news/education/2004-08-11-algebra_x.htm.

11. Much, M. (2004, May 24). A lesson in selling healthy snacks. *Investor's Business Daily*, p. A12.

12. S. Perrin, Walnut Hill School, Natick, Massachusetts. (1996). Personal communication.

13. Corathers, D. A. (1989, November). The fame factory. *Journal of Basic Education*, pp. 9–10.

14. Mager, R. F. (1975). *Preparing instructional objectives* (2nd ed.). Belmont, CA: Fearon.

15. Spady, W. G. (1994). Choosing outcomes of significance. *Educational Leadership 51*, 18.

16. Rosenshine, B. (1988). Explicit teaching. In D. Berliner & B. Rosenshine (Eds.), *Talks to teachers*. New York: Random House, pp. 75–92.

17. Science Research Associates. Open Court Reading. (Online). Available at www.sraonline.com/oc_discover.html?PHPSESSID=d02f1289afe9d4f1da45b30c6f596207&open=.

18. Science Research Associates. Direct instruction. (Online). Available at www.sraonline.com/di_family.html?PHPSESSID=f3e9be6e6948e26f529c44d2f359f7c7&section=3&family=3258.

19. Hunter, M. C. (1982). *Mastery teaching*. El Segundo, CA: TIP Publications.

20. Bruner, J. S. (1960). *The process of education*. Cambridge, MA: Harvard University Press.

21. Slavin, R. E. (1994). *Educational psychology: Theory into practice* (4th ed.). Boston: Allyn & Bacon.

22. Madden, N. A., Slavin, R. E., & Stevens, R. J. (1986). *Cooperative integrated reading and composition: Teacher's manual.* Baltimore, MD: Center for Research on Elementary and Middle Schools, Johns Hopkins University.

23. Brandt, R. (1987). On cooperation in schools: A conversation with David and Roger Johnson. *Educational Leadership, 45,* 14–19.

24. Good, T. L., & Brophy, J. E. *Looking in classrooms* (6th ed.). New York: HarperCollins, p. 304.

25. NCATE. (2000). Program standards. (Online). Available at www.ncate.org/public/programStandards.asp?ch=4; INTASC. (1995). INTASC core standards. (Online). Available at www.ccsso.org/content/pdfs/corestrd.pdf.

CHAPTER 12

1. Digital Future Project. (December 2006). *2007 Digital Future Report.* Los Angeles, CA: Center for the Digital Future/USC Annenberg School for Communication.

2. Trotter, A. (2007, March 29). Getting up to speed. Technology counts 2007: A digital decade. *Education Week, 26*(30), 10–16.

3. 21st Century Skills. *North Central Regional Educational Laboratory.* (2004). Available at www.ncrel.org/engauge/skills/techlit.htm. Accessed December 6, 2007.

4. Bailey, G. D., & Lumley, D. (1999). Fishing the net. *Electronic School.* (Online). Available at www.electronic-school.com/199901/0199f4.html.

5. Technology counts 2007: A digital decade. (2007). *Education Week, 26*(30), 8.

6. Trotter, A. (2007, March 29). Getting up to speed. Technology counts 2007: A digital decade. *Education Week, 26*(30), 10–16.

7. Givens, A. (2007, April). Laptops boost responsibility, aid learning in Texas. *eSchool News.* (Online). Available at www.eschoolnews.com/news/showstory.cfm?ArticleID=6988.

8. $3 million grant to aid online teacher education (2007, April). *eSchool News.* (Online). Available at www.eschoolnews.com/news/showstory.cfm?ArticleID=6979.

9. Pierce, D. (2007, June) States: Ed tech is raising student achievement. *eSchool News.* (Online). Available at www.eschoolnews.org/news/pfshowStory.cfm?ArticleID=7166.

10. Michigan first to mandate online learning. (2006, April). *eSchool News.* (Online). Available at www.eschoolnews.com/news/PFshowstory.cfm?ArticleID=6233.

11. Wilson, T. (n.d.) The savvy technologist: Great teaching and learning with technology. Available at http://technosavvy.org/.

12. Cavahagh, S. (2006, November). Technology helps teachers home in on student needs. *Education Week, 26*(12), 10–11.

13. Woods, G. P. (2007, March). Throw out the chalk, teaching goes high-tech. *Detroit News Online.* Available at www.detnews.com/apps/pbcs.dll/article?AID=/20070302/SCHOOLS.

14. Devaney, L. (2007, April). Video helps overhaul district's curriculum. *eSchool News* (Online). Available at www.eschoolnews.org/news/PFshowStory.cfm?ArticleID=7015.

15. Sampson, H. (2007, April 29). Teen news real, not reality, TV. *The Miami Herald.*

16. Black, L. (2007, May). High school changes tune, lets students use iPods. *Chicago Tribune.* (Online). Available at www.chicagotribune.com/news/local/chi-0705130026.

17. McCloskey, P. (2006). The blogvangelist. *Teacher Magazine, 18*(2), 22–29.

18. Tyre, P. (2007, April 16). Gaming the system. *Newsweek,* p. 17.

19. Clem, F., & Simpson, E. (2007, February). Meeting students where they learn can have a profound effect on education. *eSchool News,* p. 27. Available at www.eschoolnews.com/news/top-news/index.cfm?i=5668&CFID=1084637&CFTOKEN=71428447. Accessed December 6, 2007.

20. Kauffman, C. (2007, July 25). Dallastown school district looks to go paperless. *The York Dispatch.* Available at http://yorkdispatch.inyork.com/.

21. Many Americans see little point to Web. (2007, March 23). *Reuters.* (Online). Available at www.reuters.com.

22. Kaiser Family Foundation. (December 2005). *A Teacher in the Living Room: Educational Media for Babies, Toddlers, and Preschoolers.* Menlo Park, CA: Kaiser Family Foundation.

23. National Association for the Education of Young Children. (1998). Position statement: Technology and young children, ages 3 through 8. *Young Children,* pp. 11–16.

24. American Academy of Pediatrics. (August 2, 1999). Media Education Policy Statement. *Pediatrics, 104*(2), 341–343.

25. U.S. Census Bureau. (2006). *Facts for features: Back to school 2006–2007.* Washington DC: U.S. Department of Commerce.

26. Garza, K. (2007, February 1). Not your mother's Girl Scouts. *The Daily Texan.* (Online.) Available at http://media.www.dailytexanonline.com/media/storage/paper410/news/2007/02/01/LifeArts/Not-Your.Mothers.Girl.Scouts-2691229.shtml. Accessed December 6, 2007.

27. National Center for Educational Statistics. (2004). *Trends in Educational Equity of Girls & Women.* Washington, DC: U.S. Government Printing Office.

28. Online learning surging in popularity. (2007, April). *eSchool News.* (Online). Available at www.eschoolnews.com/news/showStory.cfm?ArticleID=6966.

29. Fuson, K. (2007, January 30). No permission slips needed. *USA Today.* (Online). Available at: http://www.usatoday.com/printedition/life/20070130/virtual_field_trips.art.htm.

30. Ibid., p. 7D.

31. P.L. 104-104. The Telecommunications Act of 1996.

32. E-Rate application tips (n.d.) Available at www.e-ratecentral.com.

33. Schools police home Web sites. (1998, June.) (Online). Available at www.electronic-school.com

34. Kepner, A. (2007, May 10). Students and teachers share Web space. *The Delaware News Journal.* Available at www.delawareonline.com/apps/pbcs.dll/frontpage. Accessed December 6, 2007.

35. Chaker, A. M. (2007, January 24). Schools act to short-circuit spread of 'cyberbullying.' *The Wall Street Journal.* Available at http://online.wsj.com/public/article/SB116960763498685883-dqgulnMDweJcpi9mqbO48rsKWjY_20080124.hmtl?mod=tff_main_tff_top. Accessed December 6, 2007.

36. Ibid.

37. States seek laws to curb eBullying. (2007, April). *eSchools News,* p. 13. Available at www.eschoolnews.com/news/top-news/index.cfm?i=45498&CFID=944759&CFTOKEN =81608424. Accessed December 6, 2007.

38. National Crime Prevention Council. (2006). *Harris Interactive Cyberbullying Research Report.* (Online). Available at www .NCPC.org.

CHAPTER 13

1. National Education Association, Center for Teaching and Learning. (n.d.). Professional development. In *The profession builder.* Washington, DC: Author, p. 4.

2. National Education Association. (n.d.). Professional state standards boards. In *The profession builder*, p. 1.

3. Dahlkemper, L. (2001). Are alternative certification programs a solution to the teacher shortage? *SED Letter 13*(2). Southwest Educational Development Laboratory (Online). Available at www.sedl.org/pubs/sedletter/vl3n02/2.html.

4. Carter, D. (2007, July 26). Students enlisted in ads to recruit teachers. *Washington Post.* (Online). Available at www .washingtonpost.com/wp-dyn/content/article/2007/07/25/ AR2007072501235_pf.html.

5. Duncanville ISD. (2007, December 5). District job fair. (Online). Available at www3.duncanvilleisd.org/index.php?option= com_content&task=view&id=172&Itemid=293.

6. Texas Education Agency (2007). Chapter 153: School District Personnel. (Online). Available at www.tea.state.tx.us/rules/ commissioner/adopted/0507/153-1011-two.pdf.

Index

James, William, 330
Jefferson, Thomas, 309
Jimerson, Dr. Lorna, 89
Job fairs, for teachers, 464
Job security, for teachers, 27
Johnson, Diana M., 64
Jones, Crishanna, 90
Junior high schools, 95
"Junk food," school food choices, 27, 28

K

K-8 schools, 95, 96
Kalamazoo case, 309
Kamras, Jason, 20
Kansas
   charter schools, 205
   dealing with cultural diversity, 122-123
   teacher salaries, 65
   teacher standards, 58
   teaching in, 3, 34
Keeping Children and Families Safe Act (2003), 272
Kelly, Michael, 45
Kennedy, Jody, 438
Kentucky
   antibullying program in, 388
   discrimination due to pregnancy and marital status, 290
   school districts, 229
   school funding, 268
   school organization, 84-85
   "Schools-to-Watch" program, 97
   state standards, 7
   teacher salaries, 65
   teaching in, 10, 475
   year-round education, 87
Keyes v. School District No. 1, 260
KidzOnline (website), 446
Kindergarten, 93-94
   defined, 318
   Froebel's kindergarten, 318-319
Klein, Joel, 231, 369
Knowledge base, for teachers, 5-6
Kraus, Susan, 52
Kuper, Joel, 395

L

Lab School for Creative Learning (Colorado), 99
Labor issues
   bargaining and right to strike, 278-279
   contracts and tenure, 276-277
Labor organizations, 53, 54
Lamb's Chapel et al. v. Center Moriches Union Free School District et al., 260
Lampol, Robert, 9
Land grant colleges, 313

Langer, Judith, 412
Langhorst, Eric, 33, 34, 419-420
Language
   bilingual education, 130, 282, 291-292
   bilingual teachers, 459
   demographic statistics, 292
   developmental ELL programs, 131
   dual-language education programs, 131
   English as a second language (ESL), 130, 131
   English language learners (ELL), 120, 129-130, 130-132, 138, 268, 291-292
   home language, 291
   language-minority parents and families, 199-200
   limited English proficiency (LEP), 291, 292
   multicultural approach to, 125
   teaching and learning and, 129-132
   transitional ELL programs, 131
Language arts curriculum, 393, 405
Language for Learning, 405
Language impairment, 145
   See also Students with disabilities
Language-minority parents and families, 199-200
Lankford v. Doe, 272, 282
Late exit ELL education, 131
Latin grammar schools, 306-307
Lau v. Nichols, 130, 282
Lavlinskaia, Nina, 46
Law
   sources of in U.S., 252
   See also Legislation; School law
Leaders, teachers as, 24
Leadership, 234
Learning
   active learning, 33
   alternative learning programs, 99-101
   cooperative learning, 33
   cooperative learning, 33, 407-408
   digital learning, 434-439
   discovery learning, 406-407
   distance learning, 436-437
   positive learning environment, 19-22
   service learning, 397
   through social interaction, 407-409
Learning communities, 88, 90, 474-475
Learning disabilities, 145, 153-155
   defined, 153
   See also Students with disabilities
Learning environment
   cultural factors, 21
   economic factors, 21
   organizational structures, 20
   physical components, 19
   political factors, 21
   sociological factors, 20-21

performance pay for teachers, 233
prayer in the schools, 261
school size, 90
single-sex education, 137
teacher certification, 260
teacher salaries, 65
The Young Women's Leadership School (TYWLS), 113
NGA. *See* National Governors' Association
NHSP. *See* National Head Start Program
NICHCY. *See* National Dissemination Center for Children with Disabilities
Nickleson, Rev. Michael, 101
NIDA. *See* National Institute on Drug Abuse
NIEA. *See* National Indian Education Association
No Child Left Behind Act of 2001 (NCLB), 16, 29, 30, 324, 326
    accountability, 50, 246, 380, 381
    bilingual programs, 292
    core components of, 31
    English Language Acquisition, Language Enhancement, and Academic Achievement Act, 130
    English language learners (ELL), 120, 138, 292
    federal funding, 326
    merit pay for teachers, 14
    NAEP participation, 94
    Native American culture, 318
    parental involvement and, 185-186, 191
    professional development, 53
    reauthorization of, 222
    school choice, 203
    standardized testing, 268, 324, 381
    teacher education reform and, 56, 58-59
    21st CCLC, 87
Noddings, Nel, 23
Nondirect instruction, 406-411, 414
Nondiscrimination
    AIDS, 294
    English language learners, 291-292
    gender and sexual identity, 290-291
    special education, 292-294
    students' right to, 290-294
    teachers' right to, 275-276
    See also Discrimination
Normal curve, 374
Normal schools, 59, 313
    See also Teacher education
North Carolina
    advocacy by teachers, 48
    data-driven instruction, 391
    English language learners in, 129
    merit pay for teachers, 379
    teacher licensure, 457
    teacher organizations, 54
    teacher salaries, 65
    technology in education, 424

testing, 377
North Dakota, teacher salaries, 65
North Haven Board of Education v. Bell, 260, 275
Northwest Ordinance Acts of 1785 and 1787, 309
Null curriculum, 387-389
Nurturers, teachers as, 23, 24
Nutrition, school food programs, 27

O

OBE. *See* Outcome-based education
Oberti v. Board of Education of the Borough of Clementon School District, 150
Obesity, and school food choices, 27, 28
Obey-Porter Comprehensive School Reform Demonstration program (CSRD), 400
Observation, 451-453, 482
O'Connell, Jack, 227, 368
Office of Indian Education Programs (OIEP), 317
Office of Special Education and Rehabilitative Services (OSERS), 180
Official curriculum, 386
Ohio
    charter schools, 101
    discrimination in testing, 372
    family/community involvement, 194
    gender equality in athletic programs, 291
    high school graduation, 370
    junior high schools, 95
    school funding, 268
    school vouchers, 260
    single-sex education, 137
    socioeconomic status of students, 112
    teacher salaries, 65
OIEP. *See* Office of Indian Education Programs
Oklahoma
    random drug testing, 254, 283
    teacher salaries, 65
Old Deluder Satan Act, 305
Old Order Amish, compulsory attendance, 297
One-teacher schools, 88
Online learning, 437
Online resources, 37, 73, 101, 111, 140, 180, 212, 300, 351, 383, 416, 445-446, 483
Online testing, 376
Ontology, 330
Open Court Reading, 405
Open education, 28
Opportunities to learn, 8
Oregon
    compulsory attendance, 297
    English language learners, 129
    public school attendance, 282
    teacher salaries, 65
    testing in, 376

Organizational structure, 20
Orthopedic impairments, 145
　　See also Students with disabilities
OSERS. *See* Office of Special Education and Rehabilitative Services
Out-of-school time, 86
Outcome-based education (OBE), 402-403
Overtesting, 369
Owasso Independent School District v. Falvo, 283

P

Paddling, court case, 282, 287
Paige, Rod, 337
Palmetto State Teachers Association, 54
Paper-pencil closed tasks, 375
Paper-pencil open tasks, 375
Pappas Schools, 167, 168
Paraeducators, 156
Paraprofessionals, 156
Parent empowerment, 202-205, 211
Parent empowerment approach, 192
Parent/family conferences, 195-197
Parent involvement. *See* Parental involvement
Parent-teacher conferences, 186
Parental choice, alternative schools, 99
Parental information and consent, 296
Parental involvement, 157, 185-206, 211
　　culturally appropriate family involvement, 200-201
　　defined, 191
　　family-centered programs, 188-191, 211
　　home visits, 197, 198
　　IDEA, 144-146, 147, 152
　　language-minority parents and families, 199-200
　　legislation and laws, 187
　　major approaches to, 192
　　MAPPS program, 190
　　No Child Left Behind Act of 2001 (NCLB), 185-186, 191
　　parent/family conferences, 195-197
　　parent-teacher conferences, 186
　　school choice, 30, 124, 203-204
　　school-parent compact, 186
　　single-parent families, 197, 199
　　tips for, 210
　　types of, 193-202
　　volunteering, 194
Parents, 476
　　choice of school, 124
　　grandparents as, 184-185
　　language-minority parents and families, 199-200
　　parent empowerment, 202-205, 211
　　rights and responsibilities of, 295-298
　　school choice, 30, 124, 203-204
　　single-parent families, 197, 199
　　as stakeholders in education, 219
　　See also Parental involvement
Parker, Allison, 434

Parks, Rosa, 323
Parochial schools
　　government aid to, 260
　　teaching in, 69
Partial inclusion, 150
Partnerships, 75
Pay-for-play fees, 222
PBL. *See* Performance-based licensure
PBS Teacher Source (website), 416
PBS Teachers, 383
PDAs. *See* Personal digital assistants
PDS. *See* Professional development schools
Peer acceptance, diversity and, 123
Peer mediation, 172
Peer networking, 424
Pennsylvania
　　accommodation, 159
　　charter schools, 101
　　intelligent design, 280
　　minority students, 119
　　prayer in the schools, 260, 261
　　rural schools, 106
　　school districts, 229
　　school goals, 79
　　school uniforms, 285
　　single-sex education, 137
　　state control of schools, 242
　　teacher certification, 456
　　teacher salaries, 65
　　teachers' right to strike, 279
　　teaching in, 461
　　technology in education, 424, 430, 433
　　urban schools, 103
Perennialism, 337-340, 342
Performance-based assessment tasks, 370
Performance-based licensure (PBL), 457
Performance-based teaching, 13-14
Performance pay, 67, 233
Perrin, Stephanie, 399
Perry, Rick, 398
Personal digital assistants (PDAs), 427
Personal metaphors of teaching, 22, 24
Peterson, Andrea, 4
Phi Delta Kappa, 62
Philosophy
　　axiology, 329, 334-335
　　branches of, 329, 350
　　core values, 49, 327-328, 350
　　cultural beliefs and practices and, 335-337
　　defined, 329
　　epistemology, 329, 331-333
　　metaphysics, 329, 330
　　See also Educational philosophy
Philosophy of education, 49
Phonics, 393
Physical abuse, 272

Photo Credits

Chapter 1

p. 2 and 1a: ERproductions Ltd/Blend Images/Getty Images; p. 5 and 1c: Michael Newman/PhotoEdit, Inc.; p. 8: Jim Cummins/Corbis; p. 12: Gabe Palmer/Corbis; p. 18, T: Tom Lindfors Photography; p. 18, B: Yellow Dog Productions/Digital Vision/Getty Images Royalty Free; p. 21 and 1d: Jupiterimages/Creatas/Alamy Royalty Free; p. 25: Kablonk!/Golden Pixels LLC/Alamy Royalty Free; p. 35: Frank Siteman;

Chapter 2

p. 38, and 1b,: Andreanna Seymore/Stone/Getty Images; p. 42: B2M Productions/Photographer's Choice/Getty Images Rights Ready; p. 46: Ellen B. Senisi; p. 51: David Bacon/The Image Works; p. 54: Bob Daemmrich/PhotoEdit, Inc.; p. 60: Tom Lindfors Photography; p. 62: Elizabeth Crews Photography;

Chapter 3

p. 76 and 75a: Ellen B. Senisi; p. 83, T: John Neubauer/PhotoEdit, Inc.; p. 83, B: Felicia Martinez/PhotoEdit, Inc.; p. 93: Creative Eye/MIRA.com; p. 96: AP Photo/The Press Tribune, Joe Rowley; p. 98: Kathy McLaughlin/The Image Works; p. 103, T: Tony Freeman/PhotoEdit, Inc.; p. 103, BL: David Frazier/PhotoEdit, Inc.; p. 103, BR: David Frazier/PhotoEdit, Inc.; p. 104: Boston Globe/Bill Greene /Landov; p. 106: Jim Craigmyle/Corbis;

Chapter 4

p. 112 and 75b: JLP/Jose L. Pelaez/Corbis; p. 119: John Berry/Syracuse Newspapers/The Image Works; p. 126: Ron Chapple Stock/Corbis; p. 127: Michael J. Doolittle/The Image Works; p. 130: Robert Finken/Photo Researchers, Inc.; p. 134: Peter Hvizdak/The Image Works;

Chapter 5

p. 142 and 75c: Jim West/PhotoEdit, Inc.; p. 156: Bob Daemmrich; p. 163: Jim Cummins/Corbis; p. 169: Will Faller; p. 171: Bob Daemmrich/The Image Works;

Chapter 6

p. 182 and 75d: Jeff Greenberg/Alamy; p. 185: Ariel Skelley/Blend Images/Getty Images; p. 188: Floresco Productions/Corbis; p. 193: Michael Newman/PhotoEdit, Inc.; p. 196: Cindy Charles/PhotoEdit, Inc.; p. 203: Bob Daemmrich/The Image Works; p. 207: Courtesy of Organization of Black Pilots.

Chapter 7

p. 214 and 213a: AP Photo/Charles Krupa; p. 219: AP Photo/J. Pat Carter; p. 230: Jeff Greenberg/PhotoEdit, Inc.; p. 235: Max Whittaker/Corbis; p. 239: David Hunsinger/The New York Times/Redux; p. 241: Dennis MacDonald/PhotoEdit Inc.;

Chapter 8

p. 250 and 213b: Bob Rowan/Progressive Image/Corbis; p. 252: Cultura/Cultura/Corbis; p. 261: Gideon Mendel/Corbis; p. 265 and 213d: Library of Congress; p. 270: Elizabeth Crews/The Image Works; p. 278: Bill Pugliano/Getty Images; p. 288: David Young-Wolff/PhotoEdit, Inc.; p. 294: Jeff Greenberg/The Image Works;

Chapter 9

p. 302 and 213c: Courtesy of Amy Braun; p. 308: North Wind Picture Archives; p. 315, T: Library of Congress; p. 315, B: North Wind Picture Archives; p. 317, L: Minnesota Historical Society/Corbis; p. 317, R: Ed Kashi/Corbis; p. 322: Dennis

MacDonald/PhotoEdit, Inc.; p. 331: Robert Harbison; p. 336: PhotoDisc/Getty Images Royalty Free; p. 339: AP Photo/Marcio Jose Sanchez;

Chapter 10

p. 354 and 353a: Charles Gupton/Corbis; p. 361: David Young-Wolff/PhotoEdit, Inc.; p. 367: Barbara Rios/Photo Researchers, Inc.; p. 374: Frank Siteman;

Chapter 11

p. 384 and 353b: Ellen Senisi/The Image Works; p. 386: David Young-Wolff/PhotoEdit, Inc.; p. 390: Comstock Royalty Free; p. 396: Bob Daemmrich/The Image Works; p. 400: Ellen Senisi, The Image Works; p. 405: Digital Vision/Getty Images Royalty Free;

Chapter 12

p. 418 and 353c: Bob Daemmrich/PhotoEdit, Inc.; p. 424: GTD/Getty Images; p. 427: Corbis Royalty

Free; p. 431: Courtesy of Tim Farmer, Principal and Pat Tarrant, Computer Teacher & Website Administrator/Remington Middle School, Franklin, MA; p. 432: John Birdsall/ The Image Works; p. 436: Carl Walsh/Aurora/Getty Images;

Chapter 13

p. 448 and 353d: Robert Harbison; p. 455: Nancy Sheehan; p. 459: Bob Daemmrich/The Image Works; p. 464: Spencer Platt/Getty mages; p. 472: Anthony Magnacca/Merrill Education; p. 473: Tom Lindfors Photography;

Features

In the Classroom: Scott Cunningham/Merrill Education; Observe & Learn: Michael Newman/ PhotoEdit, Inc.; Chapter Opener Design Circles (clockwise from top left): Comstock Royalty Free Division; Ann Summa/ Pearson Learning Photo Studio; Anthony Magnacca/Merrill Education.